CW00504158

1 MONTH OF
FREE
READING

at
www.ForgottenBooks.com

By purchasing this book you are eligible for one month membership to ForgottenBooks.com, giving you unlimited access to our entire collection of over 700,000 titles via our web site and mobile apps.

To claim your free month visit:
www.forgottenbooks.com/free77406

ISBN 978-0-265-61831-8
PIBN 10077406

THE

HISTORY OF SUDBURY,

MASSACHUSETTS.

1638-1889.

BY

ALFRED SERENO HUDSON.

There is no past so long as books shall live. — *Bulwer.*

PUBLISHED BY

THE TOWN OF SUDBURY.

1889.

Copyright, 1889,

BY

ALFRED S. HUDSON.

PRINTED BY R. H. BLODGETT,

30 Bromfield St., Boston.

Alfred S. Hudson

TO MY FAMILY,

AND THE

FAMILIES PAST AND PRESENT OF SUDBURY,

𝕿𝖍𝖎𝖘 𝕳𝖎𝖘𝖙𝖔𝖗𝖞

IS AFFECTIONATELY AND RESPECTFULLY INSCRIBED

BY THE AUTHOR.

TO MY FAMILY,

AND THE

FAMILIES PAST AND PRESENT OF SUDBURY,

This History

IS AFFECTIONATELY AND RESPECTFULLY INSCRIBED

BY THE AUTHOR.

PREFACE.

In submitting this volume to the public, we do not expect to be so fortunate as to have avoided all mistakes. We hope, however, that it contains as few as could be expected in a work relating to so broad a field of facts and so long a period of time. The following statements concerning the general plan of the work may assist the reader to a fairer estimate of its merits.

The primary object of the writer has been to present the annals or general history of Sudbury. The age of the town, its importance and prominence in the past, and the fullness of its records have left no room for complete genealogies, and partial sketches of families or individuals have been given only so far as pertains to the general design of the work.

The second object has been to make the book readable. If a local history is to be read it must be more than a collection of statistics, or quotations from records, or a compilation of facts given apart from their relation to each other or to events in the country at large. To accomplish the second object, whenever local events have been connected with general history, we have taken the space for the latter which we considered essential to show this connection, and thus to broaden the view of the reader and add interest to the subject. As, for example, the statement that some French Neutrals were for a time cared for by the inhabitants of Sudbury might be invested with no interest to the general reader, and soon be forgotten, unless somewhat of the history of those unfortunates was also given.   Secondly, we have intended, while we have not neglected minor things, to give greater prominence to events in which the general public is most interested.   Thirdly, in some instances when we have quoted records verbatim, we have also taken space to give the same in our own language that, by enlarging upon the events recorded, we might add prominence and interest.

In gathering historic material we have relied upon original sources of information, except in such instances as the reputation of an author has warranted us in accepting of his statements.   The original sources from which we have drawn are the voluminous mass of town records, the loose, fragmentary papers of the Stearns Collection, the State Archives, the traditions of old inhabitants, and histories whose authors were contemporaneous with the events they recorded.   The first source referred to consists of several large record books, the first of which dates from the beginning of the settlement, and is followed by a series of well-kept books containing a detailed and unbroken record of the transactions of the old historic town.   These books cover a space of two hundred and fifty years, and in instances the paper is worn and the writing illegible.   The Stearns Collection is made up of manuscripts which were gathered by Dr. Thomas Stearns of Sudbury.   Some of these bear an early date, and consist of deeds, wills, journals or diaries, and fragmentary bits of information.   The State Archives contain valuable information not found in the town books. This is especially so as regards the early wars.   The town books contain but little about the war with King Philip, and the conflicts that occurred during the last of the seventeenth and the first of the eighteenth century, and also but little about the French and Indian wars.

The old inhabitants referred to are some who are now living and some who have passed away since this work was commenced. Among the former are Mr. John Maynard, Capt. James Moore and Mr. James S. Draper of Wayland. Among the latter are C. G. Cutler, Esq., Mr. Josiah Haynes, Mrs. Samuel Jones, Mrs. J. P. Allen, Mr. Reuben Rice of Concord and Mr. Abel Heard of Wayland, formerly East Sudbury. We have also obtained valuable information from local histories of modern date.

In our system of arrangement, we have combined the chronological with the topical; that is, we have, since 1650, considered the history of the town in successive periods of a quarter century each, taking topically, in the main, the events which each contained. We consider the advantage of this system to be that, after a careful perusal of this work, the reader will be able to take a general view of the town in all its relations — civil, social, and religious — *at any period of its history.*

In the selection of material we have been guided by the main object of the history, namely, to give a correct and vivid impression of times, characters, and events.

We have endeavored not to pass lightly by any event that had an especially formative or far-reaching influence; but, in the history of two hundred and fifty years of a town once the largest in the county, it may be expected that much will be left out which would otherwise be gathered up.

In making reference to the town books the page has been generally omitted, partly to save space, partly because some of the books are not paged, and partly because the date sufficiently indicates the place where the record may be found.

In seeking information we have been kindly received, and we extend our thanks to all those who have rendered assistance, and to all who, by the confidence they have reposed in us and their interest in the work and appreciation of its magnitude, have made the difficult task more pleasant. The author would acknowledge his indebtedness to the members of his own family for substantial aid; and especially to Mrs. L. R. Hudson, who has shared with him in the arduous work, and without whose sympathy, encouragement, and assistance, this history would have been longer in completion and of less value.

Thanks are also especially due to Mr. Jonas S. Hunt, Sudbury's efficient and courteous town clerk, whose hearty co-operation as well as substantial assistance demand the gratitude of both the town and the author.

Thanks are due to Mr. John Ward Dean, Librarian of the New England Historic-Genealogical Society, for kindly giving access to the books of the Society, Mr. James S. Draper of Wayland, for his assistance in locating and drawing a map of the early homesteads of the settlers, Mr. Asahel Balcom of Maynard, for facts about the north-west district, Mr. George H. Barton of the Institute of Technology, Boston, for preparing a paper on the geology of Sudbury, Miss G. A. Goodnow, for facts concerning the Methodist church, and others who have furnished valuable information.

We would also acknowledge the valuable assistance received from Temple's History of Framingham, Shattuck's History of Concord, Saunderson's History of Charlestown, N. H., Reed's History of Rutland, and Drake's History of Middlesex County. We would also take this occasion to express our thanks to the town of Sudbury for the liberal appropriation which has enabled us to complete the work.

ALFRED S. HUDSON.

AYER, June 1st, 1889.

CONTENTS.

CHAPTER I.

CHAPTER II.

CHAPTER III.

CHAPTER IV.

CHAPTER V.

CHAPTER VI.

CHAPTER VII.

CHAPTER VIII.

CHAPTER IX.

CHAPTER X.

CHAPTER XI.

1675–1700.

CHAPTER XII.

1675–1700.

CHAPTER XVI.

1700-1725.

CHAPTER XVII.

1725-1750.

CHAPTER XVIII.

1725-1750.

CHAPTER XIX.

1750-1775.

CHAPTER XX.

1775-1800.

CHAPTER XXI.

1775-1800.

CHAPTER XXII.

1775-1800.

CHAPTER XXIII.

1775-1800.

CHAPTER XXVI.

1825-1850.

CHAPTER XXVII.

1850-1875.

CHAPTER XXVIII.

1850-1875.

CHAPTER XXIX.

1850–1875.

CHAPTER XXX.

1850–1875.

CHAPTER XXXI.

CEMETERIES.

CHAPTER XXXII.

TAVERNS.

CHAPTER XXXIII.

PHYSICIANS.

CHAPTER XXXIV.

TEMPERANCE.

CHAPTER XXXV.

COLLEGE GRADUATES AND PROFESSIONAL MEN.

CHAPTER XXXVI.

NATURAL FEATURES.

CHAPTER XXXVII.

THE RIVER MEADOWS.

CHAPTER XXXVIII.

CHAPTER XXXIX.

CHAPTER XL.

LIST OF ILLUSTRATIONS.

HISTORY OF SUDBURY.

CHAPTER I.

> 'Tis like a dream when one awakes, —
> This vision of the scenes of old ;
> 'Tis like the moon when morning breaks,
> 'Tis like a tale round watch-fires told.
>
> PIERPONT.

THE town of Sudbury was settled in 1638, and received its name in 1639. It was the nineteenth town in the Massachusetts Bay Colony, and the second situated beyond the flow of the tide. Originally it was bounded on the east by that part of Watertown which is now Weston, on the north by Concord, and southerly and westerly by the wilderness, or the unclaimed lands of the Colony. Up to the year 1637 there was no white man's trail through the length or breadth of ·this land tract. The smoke of no settler's cabin curled upward through the tree-tops of its far-stretching forests, and it was only the home of the Indian and the haunt of wild beasts and birds.

The Indian name of the river and country adjacent on the north was Musketaquid, or Musketahquid, and it is presuma-

ble that the same name was applied to this region. Musketahquid is supposed to be made up of two Indian
words, *muskeht*, meaning "grass," and *ahkeit*, which signifies
"ground," the whole signifying "grassy ground;" and if
applied to the river, "grassy brook," or "meadow brook."
The name formed by these words, it is stated, as nearly
resembles Musketahquid as the Indian dialect will allow.
(Shattuck.)   As the same stream runs through Concord and
Sudbury, and the meadows in these places are equally green
and broad, it is not by any means unlikely that the same
term was applied to each place and the river as it runs
through them both.   This is rendered still more probable by
the fact that Karte, the Indian owner of the land first granted
at Sudbury, was also an owner, with others, of the territory
at Concord; as the Colony records inform us that Karte, with
Tahattawan, the sachem of that place, with some others,
consented to the sale of territory to the English in 1637.
(See Chapter II.)   As Karte lived in the territory that is
now Sudbury, and his wigwam was not far from the river, it
is presumable that he would call the stream as it flowed near
his home by the same name that it was known by as it flowed
through his domains a few miles farther north.   Moreover, it
is not to be supposed that the Sudbury Indians had no name
for their river.

Probably the first Englishman who made a record of this
word was William Wood, in a work entitled "New England
Prospects." Mr. Wood, it is supposed, came to this country
about 1633; that he then visited the Musketahquid region,
and was so charmed with its resources and scenery that, by
representations of it on his return to England, plans were
formed for a settlement at Concord.   However this may be,
he first made a record of this Indian name of the river and
the adjacent country, and that before any town boundaries
could have limited its application or made local the name of
this old natural landmark.

The country about Sudbury at the time of its settlement
was largely covered with heavy timber.   That tar making
was, to an extent, an early occupation indicates that these
trees were, many of them, pines.   But probably not one of

them now remains; the rapid growth and early decay of these trees, and their fitness for building purposes, causing them to disappear long since. A solitary pasture oak, left here and there for a landmark or serviceable shade, is about all that remains of those old monarchs of the wood.

But, notwithstanding there was formerly so much timber land, we are not to suppose the country was one unbroken forest; on the contrary, it was interspersed with clearings; and the fact that in those first years the town was choice of its timber, and passed stringent laws concerning it, indicates that these clearings were considerable. The following are some of the laws. In 1645 Edmund Goodnow was appointed to look after the timber on the common, and liberty was given him to designate what timber should be taken; and " it was ordered, that, if any one took any without his leave, they were to forfeit nineteen pence a tree."

In 1646, "Ordered, that no oak timber shall be fallen without leave from those that are appointed by the town to give leave to fell timber, that shall hew above eighteen inches at the butt end."

Also, " That no man that hath timber of his own to supply his want shall have any timber granted upon the common."

In 1647, " It was ordered that the people should have timber for that year to supply their wants, for every two shillings that they paid the ministry, one tree."

On different occasions persons were permitted to take the town's timber as an encouragement to business, as when a blacksmith was allowed so much as was necessary to build a shop, on condition he would set up his trade in town.

In 1664 "timber was granted to Elias Reives for his building, and also timber and hoop poles for carrying on his cooper's trade, in case he would live in Sudbury six years, and honestly and carefully do the town of Sudbury's cooper work the said six years, both for making and trimming casks at such honest rates as they are made and trimmed for at the bay of Boston."

The cleared spaces were occasioned by both natural and artificial causes. The Indians, by setting fires, cleared places for their planting grounds and sunny spots for their homes.

The natural openings were the broad, beautiful meadows on the river and brooks.

A remarkable feature of these forests was their freedom from underbrush. The early settlers could traverse large portions of them on horseback and meet with few obstacles, except the streams and swamps. In places the forests were kept clear by means of the annual fires which the Indians set to facilitate transit and the capture of game. These fires were set in the autumn, after the equinoctial storm, that they might burn with less intensity and be more easily controlled. Afterwards the Colonial Court enacted laws regarding forest fires. It was ordered that " whoever kindles fires in the woods before March 10 or after April 2, or on the last day of the week or Lord's day, shall pay any damages that any person shall lose thereby, and half so much to the common treasury."

The country afforded fine ranges for wild animals, and was well stocked with game, which made it an attractive hunting ground for the Indians. (See Chapter II.) Deer reeves were annually chosen by the town for years after the settlement, and wolves were considered such a pest that a bounty was set upon them. Prior to 1646 ten shillings were offered apiece for them ; and repeatedly were laws enacted for the destruction of these forest marauders. Bears found favorite resorts among the highlands of Nobscot and Goodman's Hill, and tradition informs us that within about a century one has been killed at Green Hill. Beaver pelts were an article of merchandise through a large part of the Musketahquid country. Wild fowl were abundant. Turkeys strutted with stately tread in the lowlands by the meadow margins, and large flocks of water fowl frequented the streams and made their nests on their sedgy borders. Pigeons were plentiful, and grouse enlivened the shrubbery of the numerous swamps. The supply of fish was ample, including salmon, alewives, shad and dace.

The following is a description of the place as given by Johnson, a writer of 1654, in a book entitled " Wonder-Working Providence : " " This town is very well watered, and hath store of plow-land ; but by reason of the oaken roots they have little broke up, considering the many Acres the place affords; but this kinde of land requires great strength to break up, yet brings very good crops, and lasts long without mending. . . . The place is furnished with great plenty of fresh marsh, but, it lying very low, is much indamaged with land floods, insomuch that when the summer proves wet they lose part of their hay; yet they are so sufficiently provided that they take in cattel of other towns to winter."

In those early times meadow land had a meaning a little unlike that which it now has. The term, at least in places, was used to designate mowing land of whatever description, after the manner of its significance in England. This distinction may have been made here by the early writer just quoted. The marsh he refers to is doubtless the meadow on the so-called Great River, and the meadows those tracts by the higher banks of the brooks and those found in natural forest openings, or wherever the grass land abounded.

Before the Plantation of Sudbury was commenced, there passed through the southeasterly corner of its territory a memorable trail. This was a part of the "Old Connecticut Path." This highway extended from the sea-board settlements far into the interior. From Watertown it passed through what is now Waltham and Weston to that section of Sudbury now Wayland; from thence southwesterly to the north side of Cochituate Pond, and on through the wilderness towards Connecticut. It is, we believe, the road now traveled from Weston Corner, by the "Five Paths," Wayland, to Framingham. Mention is made of this way in the town records as early as 1643, and again in 1648. Where it passed through the town it was called "the road from Watertown to the Dunster Farm," a tract of six hundred acres granted in 1640 to President Dunster of Harvard College, bounded on the west by Cochituate Pond, and early leased by Edmund Rice of Sudbury. This trail was first made known to the English by some Nipnet Indians, who came to Boston bringing corn at a time when there was a scarcity of it in the colony. From this time for years it was the way travelled by the English in their journeyings to the Connecticut valley. In 1633 John Oldham and several others journeyed by it to

the westward, in search of a settlement. In 1635 some
inhabitants of Watertown took this way as they travelled to
Wethersfield, Conn., where a large part of them settled. A
year later the ministers Hooker and Stone, with about a hundred others and their families, took this path in their emigration to Hartford.

Thus through a portion of Sudbury passed an old and
historic road, which is interesting because of the things now
mentioned. But other associations also may cluster about
it. Because of this path, perhaps, the plantation at Sudbury
was started. This supposition is favored by various circumstances. The Watertown people, as they journeyed to Connecticut, may have been pleased with the country along this
part of the way, and as some of them returned to Watertown, at which place a plantation at Sudbury was afterwards
planned, favorable reports may have been rendered concerning it.

It was easy to obtain a view of it from the top of Reeves's
Hill, along which their path led, and it is not at all improbable that more than one traveler ascended that sightly eminence, and from it obtained a broad view of the Musketahquid
and its adjacent meadows. The slow-winding stream, as it
flashed afar in the sunlight, and the wood-covered hills that
extended beyond, together with the proximity of such a
desirable spot to their Watertown home and the sea-board
towns, may have led to the plan of its early settlement.
Favorable to this conjecture is the fact that the Watertown
people petitioned for the land soon after the return of the
emigrants. But whether or not emigration through the place
by this path suggested or originated the settlement, it must
have aided it when once begun, and promoted exploration in
that locality.

A trail so near what was to be the first street of Sudbury
would be quite helpful in the conveyance of the various commodities that were essential in starting a settlement. The
planters journeying from Watertown could follow this well-
worn way almost to the spot assigned for their house-lots
where they erected their cabin homes.

Besides this path from the sea-coast to the Nipnet country,

other trails doubtless led through the place, which were used by the Indians, and which afterwards may have become traveled roads. As the town afforded favorite fishing resorts, there were doubtless paths from various quarters leading to them. There were doubtless such to the fishing weir and fording place in the town's northerly part, and to the rocky falls of the Sudbury River at the south. Karte probably had a path from his hill-top home to the lodge of Tahattawan at Concord. The old pasture path at Nobscot, which still winds along the northern hill-slope by the spring and the Nixon farm, was perhaps the well-known way of Tantamous as he visited the wigwam of Karte at Goodman's hill, or attended the preaching of John Eliot at Natick, or with a pack of candle or light-wood upon his back, went with spear or net to the Musketahquid to fish. Thus the country of Sudbury at the time of its settlement was, perhaps, more than ordinarily broken by paths; and its timber lands, rich pasturage, and facilities for the capture of game and fish, made it attractive to both the Indians and the English.

CHAPTER II.

> Chief, sachem, sage, bards, heroes, seers,
>   That live in story and in song,
> Time, for the last two hundred years,
>   Has raised, and shown, and swept along.
>   PIERPONT.

THERE is no evidence that many Indians lived in Sudbury
at the time of its settlement by the English. But few of their
names have been found on the town records, and comparatively little is there mentioned of business transactions between the natives and whites. About the beginning of the
seventeenth century, a great pestilence prevailed among the
Indians in the vicinity of Massachusetts Bay, and it is not
improbable that it affected the population of Sudbury. This
pestilence or plague was in places severe. It is stated that
the New England Indians, before its outbreak, could muster
about eighteen thousand warriors, but were reduced by it to
about eighteen hundred. Thousands of Indians died in the
country along the south shore. The Pilgrim fathers were
informed of the sad ravages of this dreadful disease by
Squanto, an early visitor among them. It is stated that
Obbatinawat, a sachem living at Shawmut, now Boston,
treated the English very kindly, and was glad to submit himself to King James, that he might find protection from his
enemies, as his once powerful tribe was reduced by the pestilence of 1616.

Beside this sickness, there was another that raged a little later. This was the small-pox scourge, which prevailed during the winter of 1633. Drake says of the fatality of it, that "The Indians died by scores and hundreds; so fast, indeed, that the services of the white men were called into requisition to give them burial." He says the pestilence was not confined to a single locality, but swept with destructive effect through all the sea-board nations. The Narragansetts were reported to have lost seven hundred men, and the warlike Pequots an unknown number. If such was the fatality of these diseases along the Massachusetts Bay shores, it is not unlikely that it extended as far inland as Sudbury, and if so, that it thinned out the inhabitants. The supposition that this was the case is strengthened by the absence, in the records, of many Indian names of places. Few of these names suggest that there were few people to speak them, or to pass them along to the race that next possessed the land. There are but few places in Sudbury whose names are suggestive of the murmuring woods or the rippling streams. They are more of English than of Indian origin. The name of Nobscot is still the reminder of a race that has passed away. Cochituate Lake and the highlands about it, places once near the town's southeasterly limits, have a name unmistakably Indian. Assabet or Assabeth, the name of a stream running through Maynard, a place once a part of the town, savors in sound of the Indian dialect; yet the origin of this term has been a matter of doubt, as it has been spelled Assabeth, Elizbeth, Elzebet and Elizebeth. Even the name of Karte, who once owned a large part of the town's territory, has been spelled and pronounced Cato, and the place of his abode called Goodman's Hill, with all its prosaic simplicity. The "Great River," as the town's principal stream was once called, now bears no name suggestive of its natural features; of meadows green with their grassy covering, outstretching to forest and flowery bank, or winding along its swampy outskirts, where the vine and berry bush produce their rich, plentiful fruit; but it is now known as plain "Sudbury River."

But although no distinct tribe is known to have existed in

the territory when it was settled, and the evidence is that the town was not largely occupied by Indians, it is nevertheless probable that at some period they were considerably numerous. That this may be so is indicated by various circumstances. First, the natural features were such as would invite them to it, and induce them to remain. There was the hill, valley and plain, just suited for corn lands or fine ranges for game, while the streams and ponds had supplies of fish. It is doubtful if there is a town about it where more advantages meet to make the Indian life easy than here. The natives depended largely for subsistence upon maize, game and fish; hence good land, easily worked and in close proximity to places where they could take game and fish, were the conditions of Indian comfort. That these natural advantages were once improved by the Indians is evident from the number of relics which have been found in various localities. These consist of arrow and spear heads; stone plummets; chisels and gouges; mortars and pestles, implements for pounding and crushing corn; stone tomahawks or hatchets; and what may have been the stone kettle. Beside these, there have been unearthed by the plowshare small stones, that show the probable action of heat, and which may have been used for their hearthstones, or to form rude ovens for the purpose of cooking. Where these stones are found under circumstances favorable to the supposition, they indicate the former existence of a wigwam or cluster of wigwams. The favorable circumstances are the neighborhood of a fishing or fording place, or the common conveniences of a life in the woods. These wigwams were more or less on dry, sandy spots, such as are in the present wind-swept, and sparsely covered with grass. Such places were probably selected as natural forest openings, where, because of the light, sandy soil, the wood growth would likely be small, and where the rays of the winter sun would more easily penetrate, to give light and heat. When in such places various relics are found, it is highly probable that there may have been situated an Indian dwelling-place.

In several such spots in Sudbury, various relics have been found, notable among which is one by the river meadow, just east of the Jonathan Wheeler place. It is between the meadow margin and the Water Row road, and has an area of one or two acres. It is a light, sandy upland, in places, almost or quite without sod. Arrow-heads and plummets have been found there in abundance, and of a kind of stone unlike any native to the neighborhood. These relics have not only been unearthed there by the plow or spade, but some have been uncovered by the wind. Another place where relics have been found in abundance is on the Coolidge estate, by the Lanham Meadows, a little south of the East Sudbury depot. This spot is also of a light, sandy soil, and has a sand pit within it. A little farther north in this district, on the Frank Walker estate, arrow-heads and parts of a mortar or stone kettle were found; while southerly of Lanham Brook, on the Albert Larkin estate, on an upland some rods west of the house, arrow-heads have been quite numerous.

Another place worthy of mention is at South Sudbury, on the east side of Mill Brook, on what was lately the farm of Israel How Brown. The spot is a little southeasterly of a rock by the brook called "Great Rock," and midway between that and the Goodnow Library. On this place, which is a light, loamy upland, within the space of a few rods have been plowed up quite a quantity of loose, discolored stones, that look as if they had been subjected to the action of fire, and also coal and charred pieces of wood. The nature of the place at South Sudbury is such as would be favorable to Indian occupation. Before the mill was erected there was probably quite a fall to Hop Brook, and for some distance the shoal, sparkling stream might form a fine fishing place in the season of the alewives or shad.

In the west part of the town, at a sandy spot between the Solomon Dutton and Otis Parmenter places, Indian relics have also been extensively found.

At North Sudbury there were likewise indications of the presence of these former inhabitants. Says Mr. John Maynard, "I have found on my land, east of Cedar Swamp, a stone axe, part of a tomahawk, a gouge, chisel, flaying knife, and other strange things; also about four hundred arrow-heads, one-half of them broken. I have plowed over seven or eight collections of paving stones that were discolored by fire, that I suppose were the hearthstones of Indian wigwams."

There are some parts of the town which we will especially notice as being places that were perhaps occupied by the Indians in considerable companies. These are the neighborhood of Nobscot, the River, Weir Hill, and Cochituate Pond. In the vicinity of Nobscot there is little doubt but that Indians once made their homes; as tradition, record and relics give evidence of it. As we shall notice further on, a noted Indian by the name of Jethro had a wigwam near there, and it is supposed the Indians had a lookout there. At the base of the hill, along the plain land, on the estate of Hubbard Brown, by the brook, and also on the land south of the Framingham road, more or less stone relics have been discovered. The old "Indian wash-bowl," so called, is pointed out in a field about east of the hill. This is an excavation shaped like a wash-bowl, formed in a large rock, and may have been made by nature or art. Probably it was never used as a washing place by the Indians, but, if made or used by them at all, it may have been for grinding corn.

That the Indians largely frequented the neighborhood of the river is quite evident. They probably lived along almost its whole course, as relics of them have been found here and there from one bound of the town to the other. On the east side of the river was an Indian burial place. (See chapter on cemeteries.) An Indian skeleton has been exhumed by the roadside at Sand Hill. This was discovered when the road was built, by a person who was passing by. He drew it from the bank, together with several Indian relics. The "old Indian bridge" was supposed to be southerly of Sand Hill, over West Brook, and formed a crossing in the direction of Heard's Pond. The home of Karte was not far from the river. From his wigwam home on the hill, he could easily reach the mooring place of his birch canoe, or look down upon the expanse of broad meadow lands, green with their covering in Summer, or brown with the frosts of Fall. He could watch the early flight of wild water fowl, or per-

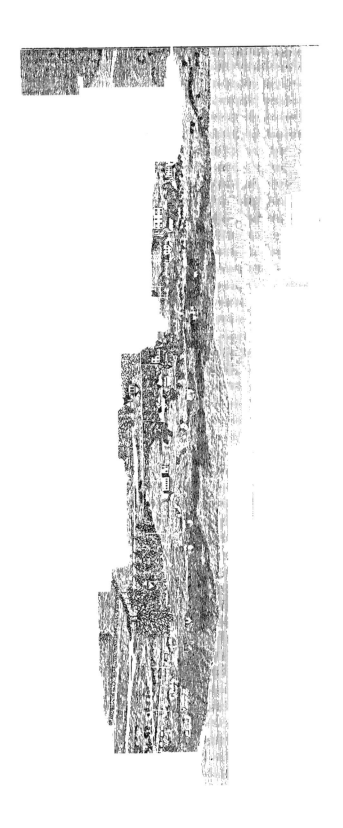

VIEW OF HOP BROOK VALLEY AND NOBSCOT.

Taken from Rogers' Hill

haps catch a glimpse of the canoe of Tahatawan as it glided up the Musketahquid.

But the places where it is supposed the Indians were more numerous than at any other point along the river were toward the town's northeast bound. Near this point were fording and fishing places. One of these was at Weir Hill, below Sherman's Bridge. The very locality of this place is favorable for Indian occupancy. It is situated at a point of the river where, as we have been informed, at low water the river can be forded. On its opposite bank a hill extends almost to the stream, and on either side the meadow bank is hard, which is a circumstance rare on the river course. At this place tradition says there was an Indian fishing weir, which old inhabitants state was about northeast of Weir Hill; and from this the hill has derived its name. The fishing weir was an important thing for the Indians, as by means of it large quantities of fish could be taken. The principle of construction was the placing across the river of an obstruction, as perhaps some kind of a fence, which, running diagonally from either bank to the centre of the stream, left a small aperture at the apex, where the fish could be taken in a wicket work or net. Such an apparatus, at a favorable place on the river, would supply fish for a considerable village. These fish served not only a present purpose, but were dried and preserved for future use. Another inducement for Indians to locate in this part of the town was a good fording place just below Weir Hill, which is at or near a small hill called Mount Headley, and is between the river and the county road. That this locality was improved by the Indians is evident from the quantities of relics that have been found there. Both about here and at Weir Hill more or less of these have been picked up; and, at the latter place, their hearthstones have been unearthed by the plowshare, with the coals still upon them.

As has been stated, there are indications that the Indians once dwelt in considerable numbers about Cochituate Pond. The region about there was favorable to Indian occupation, not only on account of the lake itself, but because of its nearness to the falls of Sudbury River (Saxonville). The name of the locality has been spelled Wachittuate, Cochituet, Chochichawicke, Coijchawicke, Catchchauitt, Charchittawick, Katchetuit, Cochichawauke, Cochichowicke. The word as now spelled is found in a record dated 1644, in connection with laying out the Glover farm. "The southwest bounds are the little river that issueth out of the Great Pond at *Cochituate*." This record, as well as others, also shows that originally the term was applied, not to the pond, but to the region near the outlet. Temple states that the word signifies, "place of the rushing torrent," or, "wild dashing brook." On the westerly side of the pond was an Indian fort, and, near by, a permanent settlement.

Not very much is known, at most, of the Indians who lived in Sudbury at the time of its settlement; but a few facts are on record concerning some of them.

Karte was owner of the first land tract which was sold to the Sudbury settlers. His home at one time was at Goodman's Hill, — sometimes called Wigwam Hill, — but where he lived in his last years is unknown. That he was a man of some prominence in and about the town is probable, not only from the amount of his landed possessions there, but from his association with certain rulers or sagamores at the sale of a weir and planting grounds at Concord. Of this transaction the following account is found in the Colony Records: —

"5th, 6mo., 1637. — Wibbacowett; Squaw Sachem; Natanquatick, alias Old Man; Carte, alias Goodmand; did express their consent to the sale of the Weirs at Concord, over against the town: and all the planting ground which hath been formerly planted by the Indians, to the inhabitants of Concord; of which there was a writing, with their marks subscribed, given into court expressing the price."

It is said that he was an attendant upon the ministry of Rev. Edmund Brown, first minister of Sudbury; and that by his preaching he was converted to the Christian religion.

Another Indian of some notoriety was Tantamous, who was also called Jethro. He had a son called Peter Jethro. On an old survey is "Peter Jethro's field," near Nobscot Hill, where Jethro lived. This field was upon a farm once in the possession of Mr. Ezekiel How. According to Drake,

Tantamous lived at Nobscot Hill at the beginning of King Philip's war, and there were about twelve persons in his family. He was present with Waban of Natick, and some other natives, at the sale of the territory which is now the town of Concord. When about seventy years old, he made a deposition about the transaction, and in connection with that deposition is spoken of as a Christian Indian of Natick. In 1674, Tantamous was appointed missionary to the Indians at Weshakim (Sterling), but remained there for a short time only. Mr. Gookin speaks of him as a "grave and pious Indian," and says he was sent to be a teacher at a place near Lancaster. In 1675, while Tantamous was living at Nobscot with his family, he was ordered by the Colony to Deer Island, Boston Harbor, for security. Resenting the ill usage that was received from those conducting them there, Jethro and his family escaped in the darkness of night. He was betrayed, however, by his son, Peter Jethro, into the hands of the English, by whom, according to Hubbard, he was executed, Sept. 26, 1676.

Peter Jethro, or Jethro the Younger, who was perhaps also called Ammatohu (as this term was applied to one of the Jethros), was connected with several real estate matters. He was among the Indians who conveyed to John Haynes and others thirty-two hundred acres of land east of "Quinsigamoge Pond," in Worcester. In 1684, he was among the Indian grantors of the two-mile tract which was granted to the Sudbury settlers, and laid out on the town's westerly side. In 1683, Peter Jethro lived at Dunstable, with Mr. Jonathan Ting; and in consideration of this man's kindness, as shown to himself and his uncle, Jethro gave Mr. Ting a tract of land six miles square at Machapoag, north of Wachusett Mountain and west of Groton, which he had obtained from his uncle Jeffy.

Still another Indian of some prominence was Nataous. He was also called William of Sudbury. "Indian William's Meadow" is mentioned in the Colony Records as early as 1658. Rev. Edward Brown was to have "one small parcell of three acres formerly called 'Indian William's Meadow,' lying toward the falls of Cochittuat River." It is stated that

in 1662, he lived at Nipnax Hill, a place about three miles
north of the plantation at Natick, perhaps Reeves' Hill.
Hubbard speaks of him as being "very familiar with the
whites." Gookin states that he was among the "good men
and prudent" who were rulers at Natick. He was designated also as the Nipmuck Captain, and was called, in the
Colony Records, Netus; and by this name he was known in
some of the sad scenes of his subsequent life. This Indian,
whose beginning as a Christian was so bright, and who left
on record a religious confession, did sad work in Framingham,
by leading, near the outset of Philip's war, a party who
destroyed the house of Mr. Thomas Eames, a former resident
of Sudbury.

In 1668, Mr. Thomas Eames leased the "Pelham Farm"
(in Wayland), and it was ordered, that during his lease of
the place he should "pay to the minister fore pound (for) a
man and 20sh. to every £20 rate." Mr. Eames subsequently
moved to Framingham, and made his home near Mt. Waite,
in the southerly part of that town. When absent on a journey to Boston for a stock of ammunition, a party of Indians,
Feb. 1, 1676, burned his dwelling-house and barn, and killed
or carried away captive his family. We may not know all
the circumstances that led to this act, but it is supposed that
some of them were of an aggravating character.

English distrust had doubtless led to Indian suspicion.
The removal of certain parties from their homes to Deer
Island might not have been understood. Besides this, it is
said these Indians had been to Maguncook, an Indian station
near by, and, on finding that corn had been removed from
their granaries, they started out, partly for food and partly
for revenge, toward the nearest English settlement. Netus,
or Nataous, from this time probably joined the hostile tribes,
and made common cause with King Philip. We hear of
him afterwards near Sudbury, with a war party which was
attacked in the night, March 27, 1676, by a party of English
from Sudbury and from the garrison at Marlboro. (See
chapter on Philip's War.) In that night encounter Netus
was slain, with several others of the enemy, while they were
asleep about their camp-fire. Thus sad were the closing

scenes in the history of Tantamous and Netus, these illustrious sons of the forest.

The following are Indian names that have been preserved in documents concerning real estate transactions in Sudbury: Jehojakim, Magos, Muskqua, Musquamog, Wenneto, Nepamun.

That no more Indian names are found in the records is no evidence that other Indians did not inhabit the town at the time of its settlement. Those whose names are recorded were landed proprietors, and so connected with real estate transactions; but others of humble condition, and possessed of nothing but a few utensils for the wigwam and chase, may have ranged through the valley and over the hills.

Beside the Indians whose abode was in Sudbury, it is also probable that Indians from neighboring hamlets or clans made use of the town's hunting grounds, and were more or less residents of them. On the north, east, and west were Indian villages of considerable importance. At Natick they were gathered in Christian relations by John Eliot, the apostle of the Indians. At Concord were Tahattawan's subjects, and at Nashoba, now Littleton, there was a praying band of Indians. On the west, at Whipsuffrage, now Marlboro, other Indians were gathered in friendly relations; while at Magunkaquog, or Maguncook, a place in Ashland, there was also another station which had been established by Mr. Eliot.

It is hardly supposable that, when so many Indians lived in the surrounding localities, they did not from time to time traverse the town, and resort to it for fishing and hunting, so that, if the native inhabitants were few, the place might yet be considerably occupied. It should furthermore be considered that one Indian householder might have a numerous family. An Indian wigwam, as will be farther observed, sometimes had capacity for several residents. It is said that a dozen Indians lived at Jethro's house at Nobscot. Karte's wigwam, at Goodman's Hill, may not have been the home of a single inhabitant, but a numerous family may have been about him. His wigwam may have sheltered several families. About the hill may have resounded many a merry voice at

the coming of the early green corn, or the gathering in of
berries or nuts, or when the alewife or shad returned in the
spring; or at the fall migration of birds, when the whistle of
the wild water fowl's wing was heard, and the pigeons made
their way over the plains.

Thus merry may have been the places where even a single
wigwam stood ; and in those silent, now far-away times, there
may have been more of liveliness connected with aboriginal
life than we are wont to suppose. The inmates of wigwams
or villages may have had more or less intercourse in a neighbor-like way, — Nataous visiting the residence of Karte, and
Karte calling on Tantamous. Tahattawan or his people may
have often passed through Sudbury from Concord to visit
John Eliot at Natick, and more than one may have been the
rough wilderness paths they trod on errands of toil or friendly
intercourse. So that the town, if not very populous, may
have been far from a desolate or lonely place.

The character and habits of the Indians about Sudbury
were naturally in common with those of others in the near
vicinity. Probably no authority on this subject is more reliable than that of Mr. Gookin. He was associated with Mr.
Eliot in his labors, and was conversant with the mission stations in the vicinity of the town. From him we learn the
following about the customs, houses and food of the aborigines in this part of the country. The houses were called
" wigwams," and were made by placing poles in the ground,
and fastening them together at the top by the bark of trees.
The best of these structures were covered neatly, and made
quite warm by strips of bark placed upon them. The bark
used for this purpose was stripped from the trees when the
sap was up, and made into great flakes by the pressure of
weighty timbers. By thus securing and using them when
green, the flakes when dry retained the form to which they
were fitted. The more meanly made wigwams were covered
over with mats made of bulrushes. The Indian houses varied
considerably in size ; some were twenty, some forty feet long.
Says Gookin, " I have seen one fifty or a hundred feet long,
and thirty feet broad."

We are informed by Mrs. Rowlandson (see chapter on Philip's War) that, after the Wadsworth fight, the Indians made a wigwam sufficiently large to contain an hundred men as a place in which to celebrate their victory. These wigwams were kept warm by a fire or fires made within. In the smaller dwelling one fire was made in the centre; in the larger, two, three or four were sometimes made. A door was formed by a mat hung at the entrance, to be raised as the person entered, and dropped when he was within. Thus there may have been more of warmth and comfort in these rude forest homes than some are wont to suppose. Says Gookin, "I have often lodged in these wigwams, and found them as warm as the best English houses." In the wigwam was a sort of mattress or couch, raised about a foot high. This was covered with boards split from trees, upon which were placed mats or skins of the bear or deer. These couches were large enough for three or four persons to sleep on. They were six or eight feet broad, and could be drawn nearer to or farther from the fire, as one chose.

The food of the Indian, to an extent, consisted of game, — the streams furnishing an abundance of fish, and the forests a supply of game. Such a diet would be most easily obtained, and the methods of obtaining it most in accord with the Indian's wild nature and life. But this food was by no means all. Says Gookin, it consisted chiefly of Indian corn boiled. Sometimes they mixed beans with their corn, and frequently they boiled in their pottage fish and flesh of all sorts, either fresh or dry. Bones also were cut in pieces and used; but, says our authority, "they are so dextrous in separating the bones from the fish when eating that they are never in danger of being choked." They also mixed with their pottage various kinds of roots, ground nuts, pompions (pumpkins), squashes, acorns, walnuts and chestnuts, dried and powdered. Sometimes they beat their maize into meal, and sifted it through a basket made for that purpose. With this meal they made bread, which they baked in the ashes, after covering it with leaves. They also made of this maize meal what was called "Nokake," which it was said was sweet, toothsome and hearty, — so much so that when the Indian was going on a journey, he would often take with him no food but a bag or basket of this.

The corn was planted in places perhaps first cleared by fire. It was planted when the oak-leaf was about the size of a mouse's ear, and fertilized by a fish placed in the hill. Gookin states that the Indian was given much to hospitality, and that strangers were given their best lodging and diet. Their religion consisted in the belief in a Good Spirit called Kiton, and a Bad Spirit called Hobbammoc, and in a happy hunting ground beyond the grave. They had their pow-wows and medicine men who served the place of a rude priesthood among them, and they conformed to various cus-toms which corresponded to their wild ways of life. Some of these customs, as well as some of the coarse phases of Indian character, are indicated by the following orders drawn up and agreed upon at Concord, and as set forth by Rev. Thomas Shepherd, an early minister at Cambridge.

These "conclusions and orders made and agreed upon by divers sachems and other principal men amongst the Indians at Concord in the end of the eleventh month (called Janu-ary), An. 1646."

"2. That there shall be no more Powwowing amongst the Indians. And if any shall hereafter powwow, both he that shall powwow, and he that shall procure them to powwow, shall pay twenty shillings apiece."

"6. That they may be brought to the sight of the sinne of lying."

"8. They desire that no Indian hereafter shall have any more but one wife."

"16. They intend to reform themselves in their former greasing."

"20. Whosoever shall play at their former games shall pay ten shillings."

"23. They shall not disguise themselves at their mourn-ing as formerly, nor shall they keep a great noyse by howl-ing." (Shattuck's History of Concord.)

Johnson speaks of them as "being in very great subjection to the Divel," and the powwows as being "more conversant with him than any others." But to the great glory of the religion of Christ, it is said these notions were corrected wherever civilization and Christianity were introduced. The money or medium of exchange was wampumpage.

In the capture of game the methods were various. Fish was taken both with the hook and spear. In the migrations of the alewife and shad, the birch-bark canoes, torch and spear, were probably effective means in the catch. The canoes were sometimes forty feet long, says Gookin, and would carry twenty men. The larger animals were perhaps sometimes caught by the pitfall, a place dug in the ground, and covered lightly with sticks and leaves, through which the game when passing would fall; sometimes by a forest drive, by which means a portion of country was traversed by a company of men deployed at short distances, who moved towards a given point, where was a partial enclosure, through which the animals were forced to pass; at the place of exit, hunters were stationed to dispatch the game as it strove to make its way through.

Part of the Indians living in Sudbury, when its territory was transferred to the English, belonged, as it is supposed, to the Massachusetts Indians who lived about Massachusetts Bay, and the remainder to the Nipmucks or Nipnets, who lived in the interior of the State. Those who belonged to the former were probably of the Mystic Indians, the chief of which tribe was in the early part of the seventeenth century Nana-pashemit. The home of this chieftain was at Medford, situated on a prominent place which overlooked the Mystic River. He was killed by the Tarrentines, a tribe of eastern Indians. After his death, his wife reigned under the name of the squaw sachem. She married Wibbacowett, the chief powwow or priest (Shattuck). She also lived near the Mystic. The subjects of this sachem or squaw probably extended nearly or quite to the Nipmuck country, as it embraced Tahattawan and his tribe at Concord.

Tribal relations so extended would probably include some of Sudbury's Indians. Such is supposed to be the case.

It is stated in the Colony Records, that, in 1637, Karte was associated with the squaw sachem at Medford in the sale of a fishing weir at Concord, "and all the planting grounds which hath been planted by the Indians there." Nataous, it is supposed, was of Nipnet origin. If these prominent natives of Sudbury had different tribal relations, so may it have been with others less prominent; but whether they belonged to the Nipnet or Massachusetts Indians, they all alike belonged to the great family of Algonquins. The Algonquin Indians included the class of American aborigines who inhabited that part of the country extending for hundreds of miles between the Atlantic Ocean and the Mississippi River. They included Canada on the north, and their southern limits extended as far as North Carolina. Among these Indians were various and powerful tribes, inhabiting various parts of this extended territory. "The New England Indians inhabited the country from Connecticut to the Saco River. The principal tribes were the Narragansetts in Rhode Island and the western shores of the Narragansett Bay, the Pokanokets and Wampanoags on the eastern shore of the same bay and in a portion of Massachusetts, the Nipmucks in the centre of Massachusetts, the Narragansetts in the vicinity of Boston and the shores southward, and the Patuckets in the northeastern part of Massachusetts, embracing the Pennacooks of New Hampshire." (Lossing.)

In the early years of the town's history, the Indians in and about the place were on friendly terms with their pale-faced brethren. As has been noticed, on several sides of the town were Indian mission stations, from which wilderness outposts went forth the voice of prayer and praise. Influences so salutary not far from the borders of Sudbury might be expected to reach into the town itself, and tend to bring its people to a right way of life. These stations were, to an extent, made up of people gathered from various parts. It was so at Natick. Mr. Eliot gathered the natives from different directions, and fostered with fatherly care those who sought at his hands the truth, until be.fell, as has been stated by another, "like a great tree in the stillness of the woods." Truly it might be expected that such influences, radiating like light through the dark shadows of the unenlightened land, would bring peace to the people, and that a loving, neighbor-like spirit would pervade the life of both the Indian and his white benefactors. Such natural results did prevail prior to Philip's war. But that war and the death of Mr. Eliot were sad blows to the poor aborigines: by the latter they lost a friend, and by the former they were called to turn their backs on the graves of their fathers, knowing not what the end was to be. Allured, perhaps, by designing men of their race to join Philip, and ordered from their homes to another locality, it is not strange if some were demoralized, and that the Indians should become a weak and broken band. It is said that at one time about three hundred Indians gathered at Natick on a training occasion. But, as years passed on, they grew rapidly less, even at this their old mission home. The last family hereabouts has long since disappeared, their name is unspoken, and their very graves are unknown. They have been gathered to their fathers, with little to tell the stranger where once they dwelt. The streams still sparkle, but not for them; the hills are crowned with our corn; in the valley our gardens smile; our grain makes yellow the plain. The town's natural outlook, in a measure, remains unchanged, · but a race has vanished, and the customs, language, and life of another race is here.

> " Like leaves on trees the race of man is found,
> Now green in youth, now withering on the ground;
> Another spring another race supplies,
> These fall successive, and successive rise.
> So generations in their course decay,
> So flourish these when those have passed away."

It is true the Indian is still in the land, but how neglected and lone! As another has said : —:

> " His eye rests on the earth, as if the grave
> Were his sole hope, his last and only home.
> . . . .
> His pride is dead; his courage is no more ;
> His name is but a by-word. All the tribes
> Who called this mighty continent their own
> Are homeless, friendless wanderers on earth."

But while this race is passing, let us cherish what is good

in their history, and in charity excuse what we reasonably can of their faults. Above all, let us present to them the truths that their great apostle, Mr. Eliot, so long and so successfully used.

CHAPTER III.

Origin of the Sudbury Settlement. — Why it was formed. — Names of Early Settlers: Residents of Watertown, Emigrants from England. — Passenger List of the Ship "Confidence." — Tradition about John Rutter. — Character of the Settlers. — Biographical Sketches.

> And that pale pilgrim band is gone,
>   That on this shore with trembling trod;
> Ready to faint, yet bearing on
>   The ark of freedom and of God.
>   PIERPONT.

IN passing from the early condition of the territory of Sudbury, and its aboriginal inhabitants, we will next notice who they were, who became possessed of this territory as settlers, and so changed its condition; whence they came, their names, and their character.

The town was settled by Englishmen. The plan of settlement originated at Watertown, which was settled a few years previous by Sir Richard Saltonstall and Company, who came to America in the ship "Arbella." Mr. Saltonstall's party landed at Salem, went from there to Charlestown, and thence about four miles up Charles River, where they founded Watertown. Few, if any, colonial places were better prospered than this. It rapidly grew in strength and importance, and soon parties went out from it to form new settlements. Some went to the places now Dedham and Concord, and some as far off as Wethersfield, Conn. In fact, emigration from Watertown helped form some of the best towns of the period.

In 1637, it was proposed that a company proceed westerly, and settle at what is now Sudbury. The reason for starting this settlement was, as the petitioners state in their paper, " straitness of accommodation, and want of more meadow." Going westerly, they could obtain both these objects; for, bordering on the mother town was a territory through which ran a large stream, with abundance of fresh water marsh. But though the plan of settlement originated in Watertown, not all of those who carried it into effect were inhabitants of that place. To a large extent, the settlers came direct from England. Bond, the historian of that town, says, " Only a small proportion of the names of the early grantees of Sudbury are on the Watertown records; and some who went there returned. Some, whose names are on the records of both places, were either residents of Sudbury but a very short time, or, it may be, never lived there at all." The explanation of this may be, first, that the plantation was not proposed because *all* the petitioners designed to make it their permanent home, but that it might be an outlet to an over-populous place. Watertown, it was considered, had too many inhabitants. The emigrants of ship after ship, as they arrived at these shores, went to the older places; and this led to what was called "straitness of accommodation." New land would present greater allurements to the new comers, and the earlier settlers would thus be left undisturbed in their original estates. Secondly, speculative purposes may have led some to engage in the scheme for the Sudbury settlement. More or less doubtless enlisted in the enterprise designing to transfer their titles to others, as fresh emigrants came to the country. Sharing with the residents of the settlement the expense of the undertaking, they had a right to convey the lands that were allotted them, and receive such compensation therefor as their increased value might bring. Thus, while the plan of the settlement of Sudbury originated at Watertown, and some of the settlers came from there, yet largely, as we have said, it was settled by emigration direct from England. Most or all of the names of the earlier settlers have been preserved, and are repeatedly given in connection with land divisions prior to the close of 1640.

From the town records we have compiled the following list of the early grantees or settlers, who went to the Sudbury Plantation about 1638 or 1639 : —

Mr. William Pelham,	John Parmenter, Senior,
Mr. Edmund Browne,	Edmond Rice,
Mr. Peter Noyse,	Henry Rice,
Bryan Pendleton,	Wyddow Buffumthyte,
Walter Haine,	Henry Curtis,
John Haine,	John Stone,
John Blandford,	John Parmenter, Jun.,
Hugh Griffyn,	John Rutter,
Edmond Goodnowe,	John Toll,
Robert Beast,	Henry Loker,
Thomas Noyse,	John Wood,
Thomas Browne,	John Loker,
Robert Darnill,	Widow Wright,
William Browne,	John Bent,
Thomas Goodnow,	Nathaniel Treadaway,
John Freeman,	Robert Hunt,
Solomon Johnson,	Widow Hunt,
William Ward,	John Maynard,
Richard Newton,	Joseph Taintor,
John Howe,	Robert Fordum, or Fordham,
George Munnings,	Thomas Joslyn, or Jslen,
Anthony Whyte,	Richard Sanger,
Andrew Belcher,	Richard Bildcome,
John Goodnowe,	Robert Davis,
John Reddock,	Henry Prentiss,
Thomas Whyte,	Wm. Kerly,
John Knight,	Thomas Hoyte,
William Parker,	Thomas Flyn.

The following are names of persons who were at the settlement soon after it began : —

Thomas Axdell,	John Moore,
Thomas Read,	Thomas Bisbig.

Thomas Plympton,	John Waterman,
Hugh Drury,	Goodman Witherell,
Philemon Whale,	John George,
Wm. How,	Thomas King,
John Smith,	Peter King,
Thomas Buckmaster,	Jonas or James Pendleton,
John Grout,	John Woodward,
Thomas Cakebread,	Shadrach Hapgood,
John Redit,	Edward Wright.

Of the Sudbury settlers who once lived in Watertown, we have the following names: Robert Betts (Beast), Thomas Cakebread, Henry Curtis, Robert Daniel (Darnell), John Grout, Solomon Johnson, John Knight, George Munnings, William Parker, Bryan Pendleton, Richard Sanger, Joseph Tainter, Anthony White, Goodman (John) Wetherell, Nathaniel Treadaway, John Stone.

Some of these men were prominent and valuable citizens of Watertown. Bryan Pendleton was one of its early Selectmen. Nathaniel Treadaway and John Stone were sons-in-law of Elder Edward How. Robert Betts had a share in the Great Dividend Allotment, and the Beaver Brook "plow lands." Of those who came direct from England, we have on a single ship's list of passengers the names of some of the most prominent persons in the Sudbury Plantation, namely:

" The list of the names of the Passeng[rs] Intended for New England in the good shipp the Confidence of London of C C. tonnes John Jobson Mr And thus by vertue of the Lord Treas[rs] warr[t] of the xjth of April, 1638. Southampton, 24° Aprill 1638.

" Walter Hayne of Sutton Mandifield in the
    County of Wilts Lennen Weaver   55
Eliz: Hayne his wife
Thomas Hayné ⎫ their sonnes
John Hayne ⎬ under 16
Josias Hayne ⎭ yeares of age.
Sufferance Hayne ⎫ their
Mary Hayne   ⎬ daughters

John Blanford) their 27
John Riddett } 26
Rich Bildcombe) servants 16

Peter Noyce of Penton in the
County of South[n] (Southampton) yeoman 47
Thomas Noyce his sonne 15
Eliz: Noyce his daughter
Robert Davis) his 30
John Rutter } 22
Margarett Davis) servants 26

Nicholas Guy { Upton Gray, Co. of { carpenter 50
{ Southampton {
Jane his wife
Mary Guy his daughter
Joseph Taynter) servants
Robert Bayley)

John Bent of Penton in the
County of South[n] Husband-
man 35
Martha Bent his wife
Robert Bent)
William Bent, | their children
Peter Bent, } all under y[e] age
John Bent | of 12 years
Ann Bent)

John Goodenowe of Semley
of Welsheir Husbandman 42
Jane Goodenowe his wife
Lydia Goodenowe) their
Jane Goodenowe) daughters

Edmund Goodenowe of Dun-
head in Wilsheire Husbandman 27
Ann Goodenowe his wife

John Goodenowe) their sonnes
Thomas Goodenowe } 4 years and
) under
Richard Sanger his servant

Thomas Goodenowe of Shasbury.§   30
Jane Goodenow his wife
Thomas Goodenowe his sonne
Ursula Goodenowe his sister
Edmond Kerley) of Ashmore   22
William Kerley (Husbandmen "

It is not certain that the young men mentioned in this ship's list as " servants," or " hired men," ever came in that capacity. John Rutter was by trade a carpenter; Richard Sanger was a blacksmith ; one had a family when he came ; two others were afterward sons-in-law of the persons in whose employ they ostensibly came ; and all of them took their place among the substantial men of the settlement.

It was a tradition among the descendants of John Rutter, without their having a knowledge that this ship's list was in existence, that their ancestor came to this country disguised as a servant.

The state of the times and the strictness of English laws at that period, with regard to ships and emigrants coming to America, might be a reason why some might come in disguise. If this was so in the case of one, it might have been so with regard to the rest.

In connection with the names of the settlers, it is appropriate to state something of their character. In attempting this, perhaps we can do no better than to say that they fitly represented the noble element that came to the New England shores at that period. They were Puritans both in theory and practice ; and afar from the conveniences and luxuries of their native land, sought in a new country a home remote from ecclesiastical and political strife. They embarked for America at a time when England was in an unsettled condition, and when ship after ship was bringing to these shores some of her purest and stanchest citizens. As we pass along, we shall see that they were a practical people, and possessed of energy equal to the emergencies incident to pioneer life ; and that they began the settlement as men who could forecast what a substantial and prosperous community would require. The whole trend of their conduct is indicative of self-reliance, though recognizing all proper authority. What the common weal required they took hold of with zest; and in their adherence to what they thought suitable, they showed a perseverance truly commendable. Their proceedings in town-meeting, and the manner in which the records were kept, indicate that the education of a part of them at least was good for the times ; and the measures enacted for the common convenience and welfare show common sense and sagacity.

As a religious people, they in no way lacked what we ascribe to the historic Puritan. Although compelled by circumstances to economize all their resources, and to make the most of time, talents and strength to meet the demands of every day life, yet they found time to serve their Creator, and praise and adore Him in their forest home. Their Christianity manifested itself in their steadfast adherence to the Christian faith, in their reliance on God, and their love for His holy law.

Industry was a prominent characteristic. From the minister down to the humblest citizen, each had a share in the manual work of the settlement. Though the minister's salary was in part paid in produce, yet he was assigned lands and attended to husbandry. Another characteristic trait of the settlers seems to have been their desire for territorial enlargement and possession, and for the pioneering of new places. To such an extent did this spirit prevail in Sudbury and its neighboring town, Concord, that the following law was passed by the Court in 1645 : —

" In regard of the great danger that Concord, Sudbury and Dedham will be exposed unto, being inland Townes and but thinly peopled, it is ordered that no man now inhabiting and settled in any of the s'd Townes (whether married or single) shall remove to any other Town without the allowance of the magistrates or the selectmen of the towns, until they shall obtain leave to settle again."

The settlers of Sudbury were young men, or in the prime of stirring manhood : they were not patriarchs near the close of their pilgrimage. Even those with whom, because of their prominence, we most associate dignity and gravity were comparatively young men when the settlement began. By the passenger-list of the "Confidence" it will be noticed that only Walter Haine had reached the age of 55, and John Rutter was only 22; Robert Davis, 30; John Blandford, 27; John Reddet, 26; Peter Noyes, 47; John Bent, 35; John Goodenow, 42; Edmund Goodenow, 27; Thomas Goodenow, 30. These ages are doubtless correct, as we have in 1666 a deposition made by one of them, Edmund Goodenow, in which he alleges that he is about fifty-five years old. Rev. Edmund Browne was in about the prime of life when he came to the plantation; and Edmund Rice was about thirty-four. In fact, we find in an old petition presented at the close of Philip's war in 1676, from a dozen to a score or more of names that may have belonged to the early grantees. Probably from a quarter to a half century passed before there was a generation of old men in Sudbury. Having noticed thus much of the character of the Sudbury settlers collectively, we will give a few facts concerning them individually. These facts will serve the purpose not so much of genealogy, as an introduction of these ancient worthies, with whom the history of our town is so closely connected.

WILLIAM PELHAM came to this country in the fleet with Winthrop, and may have been a brother of Herbert and John Pelham. Savage states that he lost the passage with the "Govenor's son Henry, by going ashore at Cowes from the 'Arhella,' and trusting fortune for another ship." It is recorded in the Colonial Records, 1645, that "Mr. William Pelham being recommended to this Court by ye town of Sudbury for the Captaine, and Edmund Goodnow as the Ensign, were both accepted and confirmed in their places by this Court." In 1645-6 he was selectman, and representative in 1647. He returned to England, and was there in 1652.

EDMUND BROWNE. (See chapter on First Minister, Meeting-House, etc., and period 1675-1700.)

PETER NOYES came from England in the ship "Confidence," 1638. He is called "yeoman" in the ship's passenger list, but is repeatedly mentioned in the records of this

country as "gentleman;" and the term "Mr." is often
applied. After a short stay in America, he returned to
England, but came back the next year in the ship "Jonathan," with, it is supposed, other children, viz., Nicholas,
Dorothy, Abigail and Peter; also the servants John Waterman, Richard Barnes and William Street. Mr. Noyes was a
freeman May 13, 1640, a selectman eighteen years, and represented the town at the General Court in 1640, '41 and '50·
He died Sept. 23, 1657. Three years before his death he
gave his estate in England to his son Thomas. The day
before his death he made a will in which he made his son
Thomas his executor, and named the following other children: Peter, Joseph, Elizabeth (wife of Josiah Haynes),
Dorothy (wife of John Haynes), Abigail (wife of Thomas
Plympton), his daughter-in-law Mary (wife of his son
Thomas), and his kinsman Shadrach Hapgood. The Noyeses
have lived in various parts of the town. The mill on the
west side was built by them. (See period 1650–75.) Prominent members of the family are buried in the Old Burying-
ground, Wayland.

BRYAN (or Brian) PENDLETON came from England in
1634, and became a freeman Sept. 3, 1634. He went to
Sudbury from Watertown, where he was a grantee of ten lots
of land, which he sold when he left the place. He was one
of the prominent petitioners for a plantation at Sudbury, and
his name is on the town records as one of the foremost business men of the place. He was early appointed to lead the
"train band," and was one of the early selectmen. A hill
in the centre of the town still bears the name of "Pendleton
Hill." (See chapter on Cemeteries.) Mr. Pendleton did not
live long in Sudbury, but returned to Watertown, which
place he represented in the Colonial Court for several years.
About 1642 he moved to Portsmouth, of which he was representative some years, and from thence went to Saco. At the
close of the Indian war of 1676, he returned to Portsmouth,
where he died in 1681, leaving a will which was made Aug.
9, 1677, and probated Aug. 5, 1681.

WALTER HAYNES (Hayne or Haine) came to America
from England on the ship "Confidence," in 1638. (See

ship's passenger-list.) He was a freeman May 13, 1641. He represented the town in the General Court in the years 1641, '44, '48 and '51, and was a selectman ten years. Mr. Haynes was probably one of the first grantees to erect a house on the west side of the river, which house was probably the "Haynes Garrison." He died Feb. 14, 1665. In his will, Thomas is mentioned as being away from home, and Sufferance as being the wife of Josiah Treadway, and Mary as the wife of Thomas Noyes. One piece of property disposed of in his will was a tenement in Shaston, Dorsetshire, Eng. The Haynes family has been well known and quite numerous in Sudbury. Members of it have lived in various parts of the town, and held prominent offices, both civil and military. Capt. Aaron Haynes commanded a Sudbury company that marched to Concord on the memorable 19th of April, 1775, and participated in the stirring events of that day. Dea. Josiah Haynes was slain in that contest at the age of eighty, and Joshua Haynes was killed at the battle of Bunker Hill. (See Revolutionary period.) One of the descendants was Capt. Israel Haynes, who represented the town in the Legislature at the session when Charles Sumner was first elected United States Senator. (See chapter on Pantry District.) A descendant now living in town is Hon. C. F. Gerry, who has served both in the House of Represenatives and the Senate of Massachusetts, and whose wife, a great-granddaughter of Judge Foster, the first representative in Congress from New Hampshire, was a well-known authoress.

JOHN HAYNES, son of Walter, came with his father, in 1638, in the "Confidence," at the age of sixteen. We hear of him about 1658, with other Sudbury parties, in possession of lands in the territory of Worcester. (See chapter on Colonists from Sudbury.)

JOHN BLANDFORD came from England in the ship "Confidence," in 1638, at the age of twenty-seven. He came in the employ of Walter Haynes, and, it is supposed, brought with him Mary, his first wife, who died Dec. 4, 1641. He married for his second wife Dorothy Wright. He had at least four children, all born in this country, Sarah, Hannah, John and Steven. He made a will, dated Oct. 21, 1687, probated Nov. 23 following before Sir Edmund Andros. His widow received all of the estate for her life.

HUGH GRIFFIN (or Griffing) was a freeman in 1645, and held the office of the first town clerk in Sudbury. The Colony Records state that, in 1645, Hugh Griffin was "appointed clerk of the writs in place of Walter Haynes." He married Elizabeth Upson, a widow, who had one daughter by a former marriage. He died 1656, and left a will in which are mentioned as his children, Jonathan, Abigail (born Nov. 16, 1640), Sarah (born Nov. 20, 1642), Shemuel (born Jan. 9, 1643, O.S.), and also Hannah, daughter of his wife by her former marriage. Among his descendants was Rev. Edward Dorr Griffin, D. D., who was a professor of Sacred Rhetoric at Andover, a pastor of Park-Street Church, Boston, and third president of Williams College. Dr. Griffin was born at East Haddam, Conn., in 1670, and graduated at Yale College in 1790.

EDMUND GOODNOWE (Goodnow, Goodinow, Goodenow or Goodenough) came in the "Confidence," in 1638. The house-lot assigned to him was on the north street, the third east of the meeting-house, and adjacent to that of John Haynes. He was an early inhabitant on the west side, and probably built the "Goodnow Garrison." (See chapter on Philip's War.) He was a freeman May 13, 1640. He repeatedly represented the town at the General Court, was appointed to lay out land, and was a captain of the town militia. He died April 6, 1688, aged seventy-seven. His wife, Ann, died March 9, 1675, at the age of sixty-seven. Edmund Goodnow and wife were buried in the Old Burying-ground, Wayland. Mr. Haynes brought with him to America his children John and Thomas. Hannah and Sarah were born afterwards. Thomas, it is supposed, died young. Hannah married James Pendleton, April 29, 1656. Sarah married John Kettle. The Goodnow family has had a prominent position in town from an early date. It has largely dwelt on the west side of the river, and to quite an extent in the south part of the town. One of the descendants was John Goodnow, the donor of the Goodnow Library, who was for many years a well-known merchant of Boston; as was also George Goodnow, who gave a fund for the aid of the poor in Sudbury. Their father, John Goodnow, lived to be over a hundred years old, and was the last survivor in Sudbury of those who did service in the Revolutionary War. He was born on the Noah Clapp farm, about half way between Sudbury Centre and South Sudbury, from which he went in early life to lands in Lanham, formerly owned and occupied by Thomas Read and his descendants.

ROBERT BETTS (Best or Beast) came from Watertown, where he owned lands. He died at Sudbury in 1655, bequeathing his estate to his brother-in-law, William Hunt, and other relatives.

THOMAS NOYES. (See sketch of Peter Noyes.)

THOMAS BROWNE was at Concord in 1638, and was perhaps a brother of Rev. Edmund and William Browne. He was a freeman March 14, 1639. His wife's name was Bridget, who died Jan. 5, 1681, and he had several children. It is supposed he removed to Cambridge. He died Nov. 3, 1688.

ROBERT DARNEL (Darniel or Darvell) came to Watertown, where he was a grantee of five house-lots. He died in 1655.

WILLIAM BROWN, Bond says in his history of Watertown, has been thought to be of the lineage of Christopher Brown of Hawkedon, of the Parish of Bury St. Edmunds, County of Suffolk, Eng.; but no evidence of it has been discovered. Probably William, Thomas and Edmund Brown were relatives, if not brothers, and all perhaps arrived at Sudbury at or about the same time. William Brown was assigned a house-lot on the south street of the settlement, the fourth east of the first meeting-house, adjoining that of Edmund Goodnow. He eventually settled near Nobscot, on a tract of land of two hundred acres, which was granted him by the General Court in answer to a petition presented by him in 1649. (Colonial Records, Vol. III., p. 155.) He was a freeman June 2, 1641, and became a prominent man at the plantation, and at one time captain of the militia. He was the first deacon of the church at Sudbury, and a representative under the new charter in 1692. About 1643 he "was chosen and sworne surveyor of the armes of Sudbury." He was married Nov. 15, 1641, to Mary, daughter of Thomas Berbeck or Bisby. (See sketch of Thomas Bisby.) He had seven children, Mary, Thomas, William, Edmund, Hopestill, Susanna and Elizabeth. His son Thomas, born May 22, 1645, known as Maj. Thomas Brown, was a man of considerable prominence, because of his public position and services. He married, in 1667, Patience Foster, who died August, 1706, aged fifty-two. He married for his second wife Mary Phipps of Cambridge, widow of Solomon Phipps, Jr., and daughter of Dep.-Gov. Thomas Danforth. His daughter Mary married, Jan. 8, 1691, Jonathan Willard of Roxbury. Major Brown was a man much engaged in town business, a representative for successive years, and commanded a company of horse in the Indian war. In 1701 he was allowed by the General Court compensation for a horse lost in pursuit of the Indians in 1697. He died May 7, 1709, and the following note is found concerning him in the diary of Judge Sewall: " Maj. Thomas Brown, Esq., of Sudbury, was buried in the Old Burying-place." We consider it quite probable that the " Old Brown Garrison " in Sudbury was built by Major Brown. (See chapter on Philip's War.) Hopestill, another son, married for his first wife Abigail Haynes, and for his second wife Dorothy, the widow of Rev. Samuel Paris of Salem witchcraft notoriety. (See period 1675–1700.) The original William Brown homestead at Sudbury was probably at, or not far from, the spot where the house now occupied by Hubbard Brown formerly stood, which was by a large buttonwood tree on the hillside, a short distance to the westward of its present location. A short distance southerly, at or near the edge of the plain, is still visible the site of another building. Either of these may be the spot where William Brown erected the first house on his grant of two hundred acres at Nobscot. The Brown family has been numerous in Sudbury, living for the most part on the west side of the river. Members of the family have never ceased to dwell, and occupy land, in the neighborhood of Nobscot. In the old homestead located there the three brothers, John, Israel How and Edward, were born; and on the ancestral estate Everett and Hubbard, two sons of Edward, still live. A third son is Dr. Frank Brown of Reading, a graduate of Amherst College, and surgeon in the Union army in the civil war.

THOMAS GOODNOW was a brother of John and Edmund, and became a freeman in 1643. He was twice married, and had seven children by his first wife, Jane. In his will, bearing date 1664, he mentions his brother Edmund and John Ruddocke. He was petitioner for the Marlboro Plantation, and moved there at its settlement. In 1661, '62 and '64, he was one of its selectmen. At least two of his children were born in Sudbury, Thomas, and Mary, who was born Aug. 25, 1640. The house of his son Samuel, who was born in 1646, was one of the Marlboro garrison houses. Mary was killed and scalped by the Indians in 1707.

JOHN FREEMAN. We have received but few facts relating to this early grantee of Sudbury. His wife's name was Elizabeth, and he had one child, Joseph, who was born March 29, 1645, and who was a freeman in 1678.

SOLOMON JOHNSON became a freeman in 1651. He was twice married, his first wife, Hannah, dying in 1651. By this marriage he had three children, Joseph or Joshua and Nathaniel, who were twins (born Feb. 3, 1640), and Mary (born Jan. 23, 1644). He married for his second wife Elinor Crafts, by whom he had four children, Caleb, who died young, Samuel (born March 5, 1654), Hannah (born April 27, 1656), and Caleb, again (born Oct. 1, 1658). He assisted in the formation of the Marlboro Plantatation, and was assigned a house-lot of twenty-three acres there. He was selectman from 1651 to 1666. His son Caleb purchased, with Thomas Brown and Thomas Drury, the Glover farm near Cochituate Pond, of John Appleton, Jr. Upon this land Caleb erected a house near Dudley Pond, Wayland, and died there in 1777. In the inventory of his real estate one piece of land was " Beaver-hole meadow."

WILLIAM WARD came to this country about the time of the settlement of Sudbury, bringing with him, it is supposed, five children, John (born 1626), Joanna (born 1628), Obadiah (born 1632), Richard (born 1635), and Deborah (born 1637). He became a freeman in 1643. By his second wife,

Elizabeth, he had eight children born in America, Hannah (born 1639), William (born Jan. 22, 1640). Samuel (born Sept. 24, 1641), Elizabeth (born April 14, 1643), Increase (born Feb. 22 1645), Hopestill (born Feb. 24, 1646), Eleazer (born 1649), and Bethia (born 1658). In 1643 Mr. Ward represented the town as deputy to the General Court He was prominent in helping to establish a plantation at Marlboro, and moved there in 1660. He was made deacon of the church at its organization, and was sent as representative of the town in 1666. He died there Aug. 10, 1687, leaving a will made April 6, 1686. His wife died Dec. 9, 1700, at the age of eighty-six.

RICHARD NEWTON came from England, and was a freeman of the colony in 1645. He was a petitioner for the Marlboro Plantation, and settled in that part of the place now Southboro. It is supposed he was twice married, and that Hannah, his last wife, died Dec. 5, 1697. He died Aug. 24, 1701, at the age of about one hundred years. He had six children, the first of whom, John, was born in 1641. The second son was Moses, who, when the Indians attacked Marlboro, in 1676, causing the inhabitants who were at church to suddenly disperse, nobly remained to assist in the escape of an aged woman. He received a ball in his arm, but succeeded in removing the woman to a place of safety.

JOHN HOW (or Howe) was a son of John How, whom it is supposed came from Warwickshire, Eng., and was descended from John How, the son of John of Hodinhull, who was connected with the family of Sir Charles How of Lancaster, Eng. John How was admitted a freeman in 1641, and two years later was one of the town's selectmen. In 1655 he was appointed to see that the youth were well behaved on the Sabbath. He was said to be the first white settler on the new grant land. He was petitioner for the Marlboro Plantation in 1657, and moved to that place about the same year. He was located east of the Indian "planting field," and was the first tavern-keeper in Marlboro, having kept a public house there as early, at least, as 1670. At this ordinary his grandson, who afterwards kept the Sudbury

"Red Horse Tavern," may have been favorably struck with the occupation of an innholder, and thus led to establish the business at Sudbury. Mr. How was a man of kindly feeling and uprightness of character, and both Sudbury and Marlboro were favored with the presence of successive generations of the family. John How died at Marlboro in 1687, at which place and about which time his wife also died. (See chapter on Wayside Inn.)

GEORGE MUNNINGS (or Mullings), aged thirty-seven, came from Ipswich, County of Suffolk, Eng., in the ship "Elizabeth," in 1634. He was accompanied by his wife, Elizabeth, aged forty-one, and two children, Elizabeth and Abigail, aged respectively twelve and seven, and perhaps a daughter Rebecca. He was for a time at Watertown, and became a freeman March 4, 1635. He was an active man, and prominent in public affairs, both of church and state. He was in the Pequot war, and lost an eye in the service. In 1845 he resided at Boston, at which place he died Aug. 24, 1658. By a will, made the day before his death, he gave his estate to his wife.

ANTHONY WHYTE (or White), aged twenty-seven, came from Ipswich, County of Suffolk, Eng., in 1634. He came to this country in the "Francis," went to Watertown, and subsequently engaged in the enterprise of a settlement at Sudbury. Afterwards he returned to Watertown. He married Grace Hall, Sept. 8, 1645, and had three children, all born in Watertown, Abigail, John and Mary. He died March 8, 1686, leaving a will, of which Rebecca, widow of his son John, was named executrix.

ANDREW BELCHER married Elizabeth, daughter of Nicholas Danforth of Cambridge, Oct. 1, 1639. His occupation at one time was that of taverner. He had six children, Elizabeth (born Aug. 17, 1640), Jemina (born April 5, 1642), Martha (born July 26, 1644), Mary (born ———), Andrew (born Jan. 1, 1647), and Ann (born Jan. 1, 1649). He died June 26, 1680, leaving a widow.

JOHN GOODNOWE was a brother of Edmund, and came with him in the ship "Confidence," at the age of forty-two. He was a freeman June 2, 1641, and a selectman of Sudbury

in 1644. His daughters Lydia and Jane came with him.
He died March 28, 1554.

JOHN REDDOCKE (Ruddocke or Reddick) became a freeman of the colony in 1640. He was actively engaged in
forming the plantation at Marlboro, and in the assignment
of house-lots he received fifty acres of land. His homestead was northwesterly of the Marlboro meeting-house. He
was three times married, his second wife, Jane, being sister
of Rev. Mr. Brimsmead, pastor of the Marlboro church. He
built one of the first frame houses in Marlboro, was one of
its first selectmen, first town clerk, and deacon of the church.

THOMAS WHITE was a freeman May 13, 1640. He was a
selectman in 1642, and shared in the first three divisions of
land.

JOHN KNIGHT came from Watertown, where he lived in
1636. He was a freeman in 1642, and was by trade a
maulster.

WILLIAM PARKER came from Watertown. He became a
freeman June 2, 1641. The name of his wife was Elizabeth,
and he had two children, Ephraim (who died in 1640, aged
five months) and Ruhamah (born Sept. 19, 1641). He had
land assigned him in the first and second division of meadow
lands, which amounted to five and one-half acres. The
house-lot assigned him was on Bridle Point Road, adjacent
to Peter Noyes. None of the Parker family bearing the
name now live in Sudbury.

JOHN PARMENTER, SR., (Parmeter or Permenter) came
from England to Watertown, and from there to Sudbury,
and was made a freeman May 13, 1640. He was accompanied to America by his wife Bridget and his son John,
who became a freeman May, 1642. Other children may have
come from England with them. His wife died April 6, 1660,
after which he removed to Roxbury, Mass., where he married Aug. 9, 1660, Annie Dane, widow of John Dane. He
died May 1, 1671, aged eighty-three. Mr. Parmenter was
one of the early selectmen, and second deacon of the
church, to which office he was chosen in 1658. Sept. 4,
1639, he was appointed one of the commission to lay out
the land.

EDMUND RICE was born in 1594, and came to this country from Barkhamstead, Hertfordshire, Eng. He was twice married. His first wife, Tamazine, died at Sudbury, where she was buried June 18, 1654. His second wife, whom he married March 1, 1655, was Mercie (Hurd) Brigham, widow of Thomas Brigham of Cambridge. He had twelve children, nine of whom were born in England, and the others in Sudbury: Henry (born 1616), Edward (born 1618), Edmund, Thomas, Mary, Lydia (born 1627), Matthew (born 1629), Daniel (born 1632), Samuel (born 1634), Joseph (born 1637), Benjamin (born 1640), Ruth (born 1659), and Ann (born 1661). Mr. Rice died May 3, 1663, at Marlboro, aged about sixty-nine, and was buried in Sudbury. His widow married William Hunt of Marlboro. Mr. Rice was a prominent man in the settlement. He early owned lands in and out of the town, some of which came by grant of the General Court. His first dwelling-place at Sudbury was on the old north street. Sept. 1, 1642, he sold this place to John Moore, and Sept. 13 of the same year leased, for six years, the Dunster Farm, which lay just east of Cochituate Pond. He bought of the widow Mary Axdell six acres of land and her dwelling-house, which were in the south part of the town, and some years afterwards he bought of Philemon Whale his house and nine acres of land near "the spring" and adjacent to the Axdell place ; and these taken together, in part at least, formed the old Rice homestead, not far from the "Five Paths" (Wayland). This old homestead remained in the Rice family for generations. Edmund sold it to Edmund, his son, who passed it to his sons John and Edmund, and afterwards John transferred his share of it to his brother Edmund, by whom it passed to others of the family, who occupied it till within the last half century. On Sept. 26, 1647, Mr. Rice leased the "Glover Farm" for ten years, and April 8, 1657, he purchased the "Jennison Farm," which comprised two hundred acres, situated by the town's southerly boundary, and between the "Dunster Farm" and what is now Weston ; and June 24, 1659, the "Dunster Farm" was purchased by Mr. Rice and his son. Mr. Rice was one of the substantial men of the Sudbury plantation. He was a freeman May 13, 1640, and was one of the committee appointed by the Colonial Court, Sept. 4, 1639, to apportion land to the inhabitants. He served as selectman from 1639 to 1644, and was deputy to the General Court several successive years. He was prominent in the settlement of Marlboro, for which he was a petitioner in 1656. The Rice family in Sudbury have been numerous, and the name has been frequently mentioned on the town books.

HENRY RICE was the son of Edmund (see sketch of Edmund Rice), and was born in England, 1616. He was assigned a house-lot on the south street of the settlement, adjacent to that of John Maynard on the east, and his father, Edmund, on the west.

WIDOW BUFFUMTHYTE (or Buffumthrope). We have received no facts concerning this early grantee, except that she received early allotments of land.

HENRY CURTIS (or Curtice) had his homestead on the north street of the settlement, probably about where, until within nearly a half century, an old house called the Curtis House stood. His descendants have been conspicuous, not only in town history, but also in that of the county and colony. Ephraim, his son, was a famous Indian scout. (See chapter on Philip's War.) Major Curtis, whose grave is in the west part of the "Old Burying-ground," Wayland, was a distinguished citizen. (See chapter on Cemeteries.)

JOHN STONE came to Sudbury from Cambridge, and was son of Dea. Gregory Stone of that place. He was born in England, and accompanied his father to America. He married Ann, daughter of Elder Edward Howe of Watertown, and had ten children, most of whom were born in Sudbury. He was at one time an elder in the church, and in 1655 was town clerk. He was an early settler on land now in Framingham, and at one time owned the land that is now included in Saxonville. It is supposed when the Indian war began he removed to Cambridge. He was representative of that town in 1682–83. He died May 5, 1683, aged sixty-four.

JOHN PARMENTER, JR., was also an early proprietor, and kept a tavern or ordinary, at which the committee of the

Colonial Court and Ecclesiastical Council for the settlement of difficulties in Sudbury, in 1655, were entertained. The old ordinary was situated on the south street of the settlement (Wayland), on the house-lot assigned at the general allotment of 1639. And until near the beginning of the present century the "Old Parmenter Tavern" was continued at the same spot, a little westerly of the house occupied by the late Dana Parmenter. John Parmenter, Jr., had six children, among whom was one named John. His wife, Amy, died 1681. The Parmenter family has been numerous in Sudbury; they have lived in various parts of the town, and been a people of industry and thrift.

RUTTER.

Armes. — GULES, THREE GARBS AND CHIEF, A LION PASSANT ARGENT, OR MULLET FOR DIFFERENCE.

Nicholas Rutter descended from Kinsley Hall in Com. Chester, who came first and lived at Hilcot in Com. Glouc.

JOHN RUTTER came to America in the ship "Confidence," in 1638, at the age of twenty-two. He married Elizabeth Plympton, who came to this country in the ship "Jonathan," in 1639, having as fellow-passengers Peter Noyes, who was

on his second voyage to America, and also the mother and
sister of John Bent, both of whom were named Agnes.
(See sketch of John Bent.)   John Rutter had a house-lot
assigned him on the north street, a little westerly of Clay-pit
Hill.   He was by trade a carpenter, and engaged with the
town to build the first meeting-house. (See chapter on First
Meeting-house.)   He had three children, Elizabeth, John
and Joseph.   About the time of the settlement several acres
of land were given him by the town, in acknowledgment
of some public service.   He was selectman in 1675.   His
descendants for many years lived on the south street, Wayland ; and the old homestead of Joseph Rutter, which name
has been in the family almost from the very first, still stands,
being occupied at present by Mr. James A. Draper.   At this
spot Gen. Micah Maynard Rutter, son of Joseph, was born
in 1779.   Gen. Rutter was a prominent man in Middlesex
County.   For years he held the position of sheriff, and received the commission of General from Gov. Lincoln.   He
was energetic and public spirited, and interested in all that
pertained to the well being of the community.   He died in
1837.   Another descendant was Dr. Joseph Rutter Draper.
He was a graduate of Williams College, principal of the high
schools in Saxonville and Milford, surgeon in the Union
army in the Civil War, and a practising physician in South
Boston, where he died in 1885.   His mother's name was
Eunice, daughter of the last Joseph Rutter.   Until her marriage with Mr. Ira Draper she lived at the old homestead.
Dr. Draper well represented the John Rutter family, which
as a race was noted for purity and uprightness of character.
He was buried in the Old Burying-ground, in Wayland,
where generation after generation of this ancient family
were laid.   Another grandchild of Joseph Rutter is Mrs. A.
S. Hudson (L. R. Draper), formerly principal of Wadsworth
Academy, South Sudbury, and of the high schools of Lincoln, Wayland, and Marlboro.   The accompanying *fac simile*
of the Coat of Arms was that of Nicholas Rutter, from whom
John Rutter is supposed to have descended.

JOHN TOLL.   We have received but little information
relative to this early grantee.   His wife was named Cath-

erine, and they had three children, John (born Nov. 20, 1641, died Jan. 31, 1643), Mary (born Dec. 31, 1643), and John who died Jan. 8, 1657. As the male issue all died, the family name was not continued in Sudbury. There is still a place by the river meadows, between the old causeway and Sherman's Bridge, called "Toll's Island."

JOHN WOOD (or Woods) was one of the petitioners for the township of Marlboro, and a prominent man of that place, being one of its selectmen in 1663–5, and one of the early members of the church. He had several children; and his wife, who it is supposed was Mary Parmenter, died Aug. 17, 1690, aged eighty years.

JOHN LOKER was assigned a house-lot just west of the meeting-house, where he lived in a house with his mother as late as 1678. The town purchased of him at that date, for a parsonage, the east end of his house, together with an orchard and four acres of land, and the reversion due to him of the western end of the house, which his mother then occupied. (See period 1675–1700.) It is said that before 1652 he married Mary Draper. Families by the name of Loker have lived within the ancient limits of Sudbury since the days of its settlement, dwelling for the most part in the territory now Wayland, and more especially in the southerly portion. Isaac Loker was captain of a troop of Sudbury men on the memorable 19th of April, members of his company coming from both sides of the river. (See Revolutionary Period.)

HENRY LOKER was perhaps brother of John.

WIDOW WRIGHT (or Mrs. Dorothy Wright) early had land at Sudbury. She was assigned a house-lot on the south street, east of the meeting-house, between that of John Toll and John Bent. She married John Blandford, whose wife Mary died December, 1641. She was perhaps the mother of Edward Wright.

JOHN BENT came to America from Penton, Eng., in the ship "Confidence," in 1638, at the age of thirty-five. He was by occupation a husbandman. He was accompanied by his wife Martha, and by five children, all of whom were under twelve years of age, whose names are as follows: Rob-

ert, William, Peter, John, Ann (or Agnes) who married
Edward Rice, Joseph, and Martha who married Samuel How
in 1668.   The same year of his arrival in this country he
returned to England for others of his family, and came back
in the ship "Jonathan" the next year.   His sister Agnes
Blanchard and her infant child died on the voyage; and
his mother Agnes also died on the voyage or soon after the
ship reached our shores.   He was a freeman May 13, 1640.
He was one of the proprietors of the Marlboro Plantation,
but died Sept. 27, 1672, at Sudbury.   His wife died May 15,
1679.   His son Joseph was born at Sudbury, May 16, 1641.
The Bent family has from the first been quite numerous in
Sudbury.   Some of them have long been residents of Cochituate, formerly a part of the town.   John, Jr., purchased
land of Henry Rice near Cochituate Brook, where he built
a house; and it is said that he was the fourth person to erect
a dwelling in the territory of Framingham.   The Bents have
lived on both sides of the river, and the name is still familiar
within the present limits of the town.

NATHANIEL TREADWAY (Tredway or Treadaway) was a
weaver by trade.   He married Suffrance, daughter of Elder
Edward How, and was brother-in-law of John Stone, eldest
son of Dea. Gregory Stone of Cambridge.   He had seven
children, three of whom were born in Sudbury: Jonathan
(born Nov. 11, 1640), Mary (born Aug. 1, 1642), and perhaps James (born about 1644).   On the death of his father-
in-law he removed to Watertown.   There he was appointed
selectman.   He inherited property from Dea. Stone's estate.
His wife died July 22, 1682.

ROBERT HUNT came from Charlestown, where he was in
1638, and shared in the meadow divisions of Sudbury.

The WIDOW HUNT, one of the original proprietors, might
have been the mother or the sister-in-law of Robert.   She
had a house-lot assigned on the south street, between those
of John Wood and John Goodnow; but it is supposed she
sold this, and took one at "Pine Plain." (See map of house-
lots.)   The name of Hunt has long been familiar in Sudbury,
but more or less of this name probably descended from the
Concord Hunts.   The first of the name in Concord was

Yours Truly
Jonas S. Hunt.

William, who was there as early as 1640, became a freeman in
1641, and died in Marlboro, October, 1667, leaving an estate
of £596, and the children Nehemiah, Isaac, William, Elizabeth, Hannah and Samuel. William Hunt was born in 1605,
and married Elizabeth Best, who died in 1661. He afterwards married, while at Marlboro, Mercie [Hurd] Rice,
widow of Edmund Rice, in 1664. The descendants of
William Hunt have, for more than fifty consecutive years,
kept a store at South Sudbury. One of the descendants was
Mr. Sewall Hunt, who died in 1888, at which time he was
the oldest inhabitant of the town, and the last of a family of
ten children. " Mr. Hunt was for more than fifty years a
member of the Congregational Church of Sudbury. In political matters he was always in advance of the times, being an
'Abolitionist' when to be such required strong convictions
and great moral courage. He was the first, and for two
years the only, voter in Sudbury of the old 'Liberty party,'
and for two years a candidate of the 'Free Soilers' for representative to the General Court." His farm was called
the "Hunt place," situated a short distance from " Hunt's
bridge," which crosses Lowance Brook not far from the
southerly limit of the town. He had five children, Sereno
D., Jonas S., Samuel M., Edwin and Clara J. The eldest,
Sereno D., has been principal of the high schools at Concord, Brockton and Milton. Edwin, a graduate of Amherst
College, was assistant principal of the high school in Utica,
N. Y. Jonas S., the second son, has for many years occupied official positions in Sudbury, having been representative
to the General Court in 1876, one of its selectmen and assessors for successive years, and its postmaster and town clerk
for more than a quarter of a century, which positions he still
holds. Clara, the only daughter, married Rev. John White-
hill, a Congregational clergyman. Samuel for a time lived
on the old homestead, and died some years since.

JOHN MAYNARD was a freeman in 1644. It is supposed
he was married when he came to this country, and that he
brought with him his son John, who was then about eight
years old. Perhaps there were other children. He married
for his second wife Mary Axdell, in 1646. He had by this

marriage Zachery (born June 7, 1647), Elizabeth, Lydia, Hannah, and Mary who married Daniel Hudson. Mr. Maynard was one of the petitioners for Marlboro, and died at Sudbury, Dec. 10, 1672. The Maynard family has been prominent in the town, and honorably connected with its annals. Nathaniel Maynard was captain of a company in the Revolutionary War.

JOSEPH TAINTER (or Tayntor) was born in England in 1613. He sailed for America in 1638. He was at Sudbury for a short time, where he married Mary Guy (or Gray) about 1640, and where for a time he was a selectman. He died in 1690, aged eighty-six; and his wife in 1705, also aged eighty-six. He had nine children, four of whom were sons.

ROBERT FORDUM (or Fordham) was from Southampton, L. I., and may have come to this country about 1640. He was for a short time at Cambridge. His wife's name was Elizabeth, and he had two children. He died September, 1674.

THOMAS JOSLIN (Joslyn or Jslyn) came from London, in 1635, on the ship "Increase." He was aged forty-three, and by occupation a husbandman. His wife's name was Rebecca, and her age was forty-three. He had five children, Rebecca, Dorothy, Nathaniel, Elizabeth and Mary. He was for a time at Hingham, and in 1654 at Lancaster.

RICHARD SANGER came to America in the "Confidence." He was by occupation a blacksmith. In 1649 he went to Watertown. He married Mary, daughter of Robert Reynold of Boston. He was twice married, and had several children.

RICHARD BILDCOME came in the "Confidence," in 1638. He was sixteen years of age, and, according to the ship's passenger-list, came in the employ of Walter Haynes.

ROBERT DAVIS (or Davies) came to America in the ship "Confidence," with Margaret Davis, who was perhaps his sister. His wife's name was Bridget. He had two daughters, Sarah (born April 10, 1646) and Rebecca.

HENRY PRENTICE came from Cambridge. He was a freeman in 1650, and died June 9, 1654. His wife Elizabeth died May 13, 1643; and by his second wife, Joanna, he had six children.

WILLIAM KERLEY (Carsley or Carlsly) came in the ship "Confidence," in 1638, and was a freeman in 1666. He was a man of some prominence in the colony, having land assigned him at Pedock's Island, Nantasket, in 1642. He was a proprietor of Marlboro in 1657, and a selectman for years. At one time, also, he was sent as representative. In 1667 he was appointed by the General Court to lay out land between Concord, Lancaster, and Groton. His wife's name, as mentioned in his will, was Anna, daughter of Thomas King. He had three children, Mary, Sarah and Hannah. By his will he gave his brother Henry "his sword, belt and other arms; and also his military books."

THOMAS FLYN. This name is found among the early proprietors, on the town books, but we conjecture it may have been written by mistake for Thomas Joslyn, or Jslyn.

THOMAS AXTELL (or Axdell) came to this country about 1642. He was born at Burkhamstead, Eng., in 1619. A brother was Col. Daniel Axtell, a soldier and officer under Oliver Cromwell. He commanded the guard at the trial of Charles I.; for which he was put to death as a regicide, when Charles II. was restored. Thomas Axtell settled in Sudbury, and died there in 1646, at the age of twenty-seven. His son had land in Marlboro in 1660, married in 1665, and had several children. He was killed by the Indians, April 21, 1676. His descendants were early settlers of Grafton.

THOMAS READ (or Reed) was in Sudbury as early as 1654. He was the son of Thomas Reed of Colchester, Essex Co., Eng., a carpenter; a memorandum of whose will, dated July, 1665, and probated 1666, was published in the "New England Historical and Genealogical Register," Vol. XXL, p. 369, August, 1867, by Mr. William S. Appleton of Boston, who copied it in London. By the will of Rev. Edmund Brown, and depositions taken in court, Thomas Read was his nephew; the term cousin being used for nephew (Waters). In the will of Thomas Read of Colchester, his son Thomas in America is mentioned; also there is mention of his son-in-law, Daniel Bacon, who married his daughter Mary, who

were also living in America. Other relations are also mentioned, but not as being in this country. Thomas Read settled at Sudbury, in the Lanham district, on land which he
purchased of his uncle, Rev. Edmund Brown, while he (Mr.
Read) was in England. This locality was probably called Lanham by Rev. Edmund Brown, from a little place in England
spelled Lavenham, but pronounced Lannam, near Sudbury,
or between Sudbury and Bury St. Edmunds, about which
locality Mr. Brown and Mr. Read are supposed to have
come from, and from which place Mary Goodrich, the wife
of Thomas Read, the son of Thomas Read of Lanham, came.
Thomas Read, the older in this country, married for his first
wife Catherine, and for his second wife Arrabella. He had
one son, whose name was Thomas; and in the two following
generations there were but two children, both sons, and both
also named Thomas, the last being born in 1678. Thomas
of this latter date had five children, Nathaniel (born 1762),
Thomas (born ———), Isaac (born 1704), Daniel (born
1714), and Joseph (born 1722). Nathaniel settled in Warren; Thomas and Daniel settled in Rutland, Mass.; Isaac
and Joseph remained in Sudbury. Joseph had one son
named Joseph (born 1773), who married Olive Mossman of
Sudbury, who died there March 9, 1877, at the age of ninety-
seven, being at the time of her death the oldest person in
town. By the death of Joseph Read the last of the descendants bearing the family name ceased to be residents of Sudbury; but descendants bearing other names have long lived
there, among whom were his daughters Sybel, wife of J. P.
Allen; Almira, wife of George Heard; Sarah, wife of D. L.
Willis; and Maria, wife of Martin N. Hudson. Mr. Joseph
Read and wife are buried in Wadsworth Cemetery, in the
family lot of A. S. Hudson, a grandson. Thomas Read was
a prominent citizen of Sudbury. He was early appointed
one of the tything-men, and in 1677 he was one of the persons to whom the town gave leave to build a saw-mill upon
Hop Brook. (See period 1675–1700.) His place at Lanham was for many years in the family, and his descendants
have been widely scattered and useful citizens. (See chapter
on Lanham District.) Says the historian of Rutland of the

descendants of the Sudbury Reads, who settled there: "This family of Reads have been useful and industrious inhabitants of Rutland for one hundred and twenty years." Asahel Read was one of the two Sudbury soldiers who were killed at the battle of Concord and Lexington. (See Revolutionary Period.) For the space of about two centuries the name of Read is connected with the annals of Sudbury. One of the descendants of Nathaniel Read who settled at Warren is Alanson Read, Jr., a well-known citizen of Chicago, and one of the proprietors of Read's "Temple of Music." He has been lately engaged in preparing a history of the Read family.

JOHN MOORE was at Sudbury by 1643, and may have come to America from London in the "Planter," in 1635, at the age of twenty-four, or he may have arrived in 1638. He was twice married, his first wife's name being Elizabeth, and he had several children. His second wife was Ann, daughter of John Smith. His daughter Mary married Richard Ward, and Lydia (born June 24, 1643) married, in 1664, Samuel Wright. In 1642 he bought the house-lot of Edmund Rice. In 1645 he bought of John Stone "his house-lot, with all other land belonging to the said John Stone that shall hereafter be due to the said John Stone by virtue of his first right in the beginning of the plantation of Sudbury; and also all the fences that is now standing about any part of the said land, and also all the board and shelves that are now about the house, whether fast or loose, and now belonging to the said house." (Town Records, Vol.I., p. 54.) The Moore family have long been numerous in Sudbury, members of it living on both sides of the river, and at times taking prominent part in the affairs of the town. Ephraim Moore, who lived in the west part, was major of the Second Battalion of Rifles, M. V. M.

THOMAS BISBIG Besbedge (or Bessbeck) came to America in the ship "Hercules, in 1635, with six children and three servants. He embarked at Sandwich, County of Kent. He went to Sudbury, joined the church there, and afterwards went to Duxbury. He subsequently came back to Sudbury, where he died March 9, 1674. He left a will, which was dated Nov. 25, 1672, and probated April 1, 1674. In this will he directed that his body be buried " at the east end of the church ; " and he gives to his grandson, Thomas Brown, the eldest son of his daughter Mary, wife of William Brown, all the houses and lands in the parishes of Hedcorn and Frittenden, County of Kent, Eng.; and he mentions his great-grandchildren, Mary, Patience and Thankful, daughters of the said Thomas Brown, also other children of this daughter Mary, of whom there were seven.

THOMAS PLYMPTON (or Plimpton) was at Sudbury by 1643. He may have come to America in the ship "Jonathan," which sailed from London, for Boston, April 12, 1639, bringing among its passengers Elizabeth Plympton and Peter Noyes. Sometime before 1649 he was in the employ of Mr. Noyes, as is shown by the following record: "Peter Noyes, Sr., did give unto Thomas Plympton, once his servant, the sum of six acres of meadow, of his third addition of meadow lying on the meadow called Gulf Meadow, with the commonage unto the same belonging. Sept. 26, 1649." (Town Records, p. 89.) He married Abigail, daughter of Peter Noyes, and had seven children, Abigail. Jane, Mary, Elizabeth, Thomas, Dorothy and Peter. Thomas Plympton and Elizabeth, who married John Rutter, were probably brother and sister, as both were legatees of Agnes Bent, a grandmother of Elizabeth. He was killed by the Indians, April 20, 1676, the day before the Wadsworth fight, while he was engaged, tradition says, in endeavoring to bring a Mr. Boone and son to a garrison house. The Plympton family has been numerous, and members of it have been prominent in the annals of Sudbury. Thomas Plympton was a tower of strength to the town in the Revolutionary War, being a member of the Provincial Congress, and the one to whom the news of the approach of the British to Concord was first brought. He was at Concord the 19th of April, and had a bullet put through his clothing. (See Revolutionary period.) The old Plympton house, a large unpainted structure, was about a mile from Sudbury centre, and was demolished a few years since.

HUGH DRURY was in Sudbury as early as 1641, and was by trade a carpenter. He married Lydia, daughter of Edmund

Rice, for his first wife, who died April 5, 1675; and for his second wife, Mary, the widow of Rev. Edward Fletcher. He had two children, John and Hugh. After dwelling in Sudbury for a time, where he bought a house and land of William Swift, he removed to Boston, and died July 6, 1689, and was buried in the Chapel Burying-ground with his wife, Lydia.

PHILEMON WHALE was in Sudbury in 1646. He was a freeman May 10, 1688, and Nov. 7, 1649, married Sarah, the daughter of Thomas Cakebread. His wife died Dec. 28, 1656; and Nov. 9, 1657, he married Elizabeth Griffin. He owned land in various parts of the town, but his early home is supposed to have been not far from the head of the mill-pond (Wayland), perhaps by the present Concord road. He afterwards built a house in the neighborhood of the "Rice Spring." A culvert or bridge at the head of the mill-pond is still called Whale's Bridge; but the name, except as it is thus perpetuated, is now seldom heard within the limits of the town.

JOHN SMITH was at Sudbury in 1647. He may have been John Smith, an early settler of Watertown, or a relative of his. His wife's name was Sarah. He had assigned him lot No. 29 in the second squadron of the two-mile grant. The name Smith has been a common one in town. Capt. Joseph Smith commanded a company from Sudbury on the 19th of April, 1775. The Smiths have lived in various parts of the town, and were early settlers of what is now Maynard, the names of Amos and Thomas Smith being prominent among the pioneers of that part of Sudbury territory. A descendant of the Smiths on the east side of the river is Mr. Elbridge Smith, formerly principal of the Norwich Free Academy and present master of the Dorchester High School.

THOMAS BUCKMASTER (or Buckminster) it is supposed was of the family of John of Peterborough, Northampton-shire, Eng. He was a freeman in 1646, and was at one time at Scituate and afterwards at Boston. His wife's name was Joanna, and he had several children. He died Sept. 28, 1656. Descendants of the family early went to Framing-ham, and have been numerous and prominent. One was

Col. Joseph, an officer in the French and Indian War period. Another was Major Lawson, who was in the Revolutionary War. A third, and one well known, was Thomas, a tavern-keeper, deacon and selectman; and another was William, who was publisher and editor of "The Boston Cultivator" in 1839–41, and who established "The Massachusetts Plough-man."

JOHN GROUT came from Watertown to Sudbury about 1643, and about the same time came into possession of the Cakebread mill, and was allowed by the town "to pen water for the use of the mill" on land adjacent to the stream above. The name of his first wife was Mary, and for his second wife he married the widow of Thomas Cakebread. He had ten children, two of them by his first marriage, John (born Aug. 8, 1641) and Mary (born Dec. 11, 1643). His children by his second marriage were John, Sarah (who married John Loker, Jr.), Joseph, Abigail (who married, in 1678, Joseph Curtis), Jonathan, Elizabeth (who married Samuel Allen), Mary (who married Thomas Knapp), and Susanna (who married John Woodward).

THOMAS CAKEBREAD was from Watertown, and became a freeman May 14, 1634. In 1637 he married Sarah, daughter of Nicholas Busby. He was for a while at Dedham, and subsequently at Sudbury, where he died Jan. 4, 1643. He erected the first mill at Sudbury, for which the town granted him lands. (See chapter on First Church, Meeting-house, Mill, etc.) The Colony Records state that, in 1642, "Ensign Cakebread was to lead the Sudbury company." His widow married Capt. John Grout, and his daughter Mary married Philemon Whale, at Sudbury, Nov. 1, 1649.

JOHN REDIAT lived at Sudbury for a time. He became an original proprietor at Marlboro, and at the assignment of house-lots he received twenty-two and one-half acres. He had one child born in Sudbury, in 1652. He died April 7, 1687.

JOHN WATERMAN came to this country in the ship "Jona-than," and landed at Boston, 1639. His passage was paid by Mr. Peter Noyes, and hence it is supposed he was in his employ. No descendants of this name live in Sudbury, and we have found nothing to designate the former dwelling-place of this early inhabitant.

GOODMAN WITHERELL early received land in the town. His name is mentioned in the list of those who received land in one of the divisions of meadow.

JOHN GEORGE. We have found no facts relative to the genealogy of this early grantee, and the name is not familiar in Sudbury. He was in the town as early as 1644.

THOMAS KING was at Sudbury near 1650. In 1655 he married Bridget Davis. He owned land in the fourth squadron of the two-mile grant, his lot being No. 50, and adjoining the cow-pen in the southwest part of Sudbury. (See chapter on periods 1650–75.) He was one of the petitioners for the plantation of Marlboro, in 1656, and was on the first board of selectmen of that town.

PETER KING was at Sudbury not far from 1650. He was a man of some prominence in the town, being a deacon of the church, and a representative to the Colonial Court in 1689–90. He was one of the contracting parties for the erection of the second meeting-house. Peter King's homestead was probably not far from the town bridge, on the east side of the river, a place on the river not far from this point being still called " King's Pond." The name King was often spoken in earlier times in the town ; but perhaps not in the memory of any now living have any descendants of these early inhabitants, of this name, lived there.

JAMES PENDLETON was a son of Brian, and came from Watertown. His wife, whose name was Mary, died Nov. 7, 1655, and he married for a second wife Hannah, daughter of Edmund Goodnow, at Sudbury, April 29, 1656. By his first marriage he had one son, James (born Nov. 1, 1650), and by his second marriage he had Brian, Joseph, Edmund, Ann, Caleb and James. He was one of the founders of the first church at Portsmouth, in 1671. He lived at Stonington in 1674–8, and at Westerly in 1586–1700. He acquired the title of captain, and served in Philip's war.

JOHN WOODWARD, at the age of thirteen, came to this country in the ship " Elizabeth," in 1634. He was accompanied by his father, and was for a time at Watertown. His wife's name was Mary, and they had a son, born March 20, 1650, who it is supposed died young. He went to Sudbury, where his wife died July 8, 1654. He afterwards moved to Charlestown, and there married Abigail, daughter of John Benjamin, widow of Joshua Stubbs. He returned to Sudbury, and by his second marriage he had three children, Rose (born Aug. 18, 1659), John (born Dec. 12, 1661), and Abigail. He was a freeman 1690, and died at Watertown, Feb. 17, 1696. John Woodward received in the division of the two-mile grant lot No. 41, adjoining that of John Moore, in the fourth squadron. The name appeared from time to time in the earlier annals of Sudbury, but has for many years ceased to be as familiar to the town's people as formerly. Daniel Woodward, who died in 1760, built a mill on Hop or Wash Brook in 1740, and about one hundred and fifty years ago he also erected the house occupied by Capt. James Moore, who is one of his descendants.

SHADRACH (or Sydrach) HAPGOOD, at the age of fourteen, embarked at Gravesend, Eng., for America, May 30, 1656, on the ship "Speedwell," Robert Locke, master. He settled in Sudbury, and married Elizabeth Treadway, Oct. 21, 1664. He was killed in the Nipnet country, near Brookfield, in an expedition against the Indians under the command of Capt. Hutchinson. (See chapter on Philip's War.) He left three or more children, one of whom, Thomas, was born in Sudbury, Oct. 1, 1669. He settled in the northeast part of Marlboro, at which place he died Oct. 4, 1765, aged ninety-five. He left nine children, ninety-two grandchildren, two hundred and eight great-grandchildren, and four great-great-grandchildren.

EDWARD WRIGHT was perhaps a son of the Widow Dorothy Wright, and may have come to Sudbury with her. He married Hannah Axtell (or Adell), June 18, 1659, who died May 18, 1708. He had eight children, one of whom was Capt. Samuel Wright, one of the prominent settlers of Rutland, and conspicuous in one of the Indian wars, having charge of a company of rangers, and doing good service on the frontier. Edward Wright died at Sudbury, Aug. 7, 1703.

CHAPTER IV.

Method of Acquiring Territory. — Character and Jurisdiction of the Massachusetts Bay Colony. — Colonial Court. — Response to the Petition for a Plantation at Sudbury. — Successive Land Grants. — Purchase of Territory. — Indian Deeds. — Incorporation of the Town. — Name — Sketch of Sudbury, Eng. — Town Boundaries.

> We have no title-deeds to house or lands;
> Owners and occupants of earlier dates
> From graves forgotten stretch their dusty hands,
> And hold in mortmain still their old estates.
> LONGFELLOW.

BEFORE considering the successive steps in the settlement of the town, we will notice the methods by which the settlers became possessed of the territory. There were two parties with which contracts were to be made, namely, the Colonial Court and the Indian owners of the land. To ignore either would invalidate their claim. From the former it was essential to obtain a permit to make a settlement, to sell out and remove from Watertown, to secure the appointment of a committee to measure and lay out the land; and from the Indians they were to purchase the territory.

In order to obtain a right knowledge of the matter before us, it is important to consider, first, the authority and nature of the Colony of the Massachusetts Bay. King James of England claimed by right of discovery all the continent of North America. In the eighteenth year of his reign, he transferred a portion of this to a company called " The Colony of Plymouth in the County of Devon, for the planting, ruling, ordering and governing of New England in America." " The territory conveyed was all that part of America lying and being in breadth from forty degrees to forty-eight degrees of north latitude, and in length of and

within all the breadth aforesaid through the mainland from
sea to sea." And a condition upon which the conveyance
was made was, that "the grantees should yield and pay
therefor the fifth part of the ore of gold and silver which
should happen to be found in any of the said lands." From
this "Council of Plymouth in the County of Devon" a company, in 1628, purchased a tract of territory defined as being
"three miles north of any and every part of the Merrimac
River," and "three miles north of any and every part of
the Charles River," and extending westward to the Pacific
Ocean. Some of the chief men of this company were John
Humphry, John Endicott, Sir Henry Roswell, Sir George
Young, Thomas Southcoote, Simon Whitcomb, John Win-
thrope, Thomas Dudley and Sir Richard Saltonstall.

The proprietors received a charter from the King, March
14, 1629, and were incorporated by the name of "the Governor and Company of the Massachusetts Bay in New England." The government of this company was vested in a
governor, deputy governor and eighteen assistants, who were
to be elected annually by the stockholders of the corporation.
A general assembly of the freemen of the colony (see chapter on Town-meetings) was to be held once in four years at
the least, for purposes of legislation. The king claimed no
jurisdiction, since he regarded the affair, not as the founding
of a nation or state, but as the incorporation of a trading
establishment. But, although the common rights of British
subjects were conferred upon these Massachusetts Bay colonists, a broader and better basis was soon to be adopted.
In September, 1629, the members of the new company, at a
meeting in Cambridge, Eng., signed an agreement to transfer the charter and government to the colonists. Upon this
desirable change, enterprising men set sail for this country,
and soon that portion of it now Salem and Boston was
smiling with settlements that were founded by persons of
marked character and intelligence. In May, 1631, it was
decided, at an assembly of the people, that all the officers of
the government should thereafter be chosen by the freemen
of the colony; and in 1634 the government was changed to
a representative government, the second of the kind in

America. This government had its court, to which delegates were sent by the people, called "The Great and General Court of the Massachusetts Colony."

By the authority of a Court thus established, land grants were allowed the New England colonists. Some of these grants were to companies who designed to establish towns, and some to individuals, for considerations that the court saw fit to recognize. In the former case, certain conditions were imposed, namely, that the place sought should be settled within a specified time, that a certain number of settlers should go there, and that a church should be established and the gospel ministry maintained. These land grants were usually preceded by a petition, stating the object for which the land tract was sought, and perhaps reasons why the court should allow it. The territory of Sudbury was in part granted to the people collectively who formed the plantation and established the town, and in part to individuals. The grants to the former were allowed at three different times, and were preceded by three different petitions. The first petition met with a response Nov. 20, 1637, of which the following is a copy: —

"Whereas a great part of the chief inhabitants of Watertown have petitioned this Court, that in regard to their straitness of accommodation, and want of meadow, they might have leave to remove and settle a plantation upon the river, which runs to Concord, this Court, having respect to their necessity, doth grant their petition, and it is hereby *ordered*, that Lieut. (Simon) Willard, Mr. (William) Spencer, Mr. Joseph Weld and Mr. (Richard) Jackson shall take view of the places upon said river, and shall set out a place. for them by marks and bounds sufficient for fifty or sixty families, taking care that it be so set out as it may not hinder the settling of some other plantation upon the same river, if there be meadow, and other accommodations sufficient for the same. And it is *ordered*, further, that if the said inhabitants of Watertown, or any of them, shall not have removed their dwellings to their said new plantation, before one year after the plantation shall be sot out, that then the interest of

all such persons, not so removed to the said plantation, shall
be void and cease, and it shall be lawful for such as are
removed and settled there, or the greater part of them, being
freemen, to receive other persons to inhabit in their rooms,
in the said plantation; *provided*, that if there shall not be
thirty families at least there settled before the said time limited, that then this Court, or the Court of Assistants, or two
of the Council, shall dispose of the said plantation to any
other. And it is further *ordered*, that after the place of the
said plantation shall be set out, the said petitioners, or any
such other freemen as shall join them, shall have power to
order the situation of their town, and the proportioning of
lots, and all other liberties as other towns have under the
proviso aforesaid. And it is lastly *ordered*, that such of the
said inhabitants of Watertown, as shall be accommodated in
their new plantation, may sell their houses and improved
grounds in Watertown; but all the rest of the land in Watertown, not improved, shall remain freely to the inhabitants,
which shall remain behind, and such others as shall come to
them.

"And the said persons appointed to set out the said plantation, are directed so to set out the same, as there may be
1500 acres of meadow allowed to it, if it be there to be had,
with any convenience, for the use of the town." (Colony
Records, Vol. I., p. 210.)

A further record of Court action, dated March 12, 1637–8,
is as follows: —

"The Court thinketh meet that they (of Watertown)
should have liberty to sell their allotments in Watertown,
and they are to give their full answer the next Court,
whether they will remove to the new plantation and John
Oliver put in the room of Richard Jackson, for to lay out
the said plantation, which they are to do before the next
Court."

The Court having granted the request for a plantation at
Sudbury, allowed the petitioners to go on with their work,

and appointed a committee to establish the bounds and make an allotment of land, as set forth by the following record : —

"At Gennall Court held at Boston the 6th Day of the 7th Month, a 1638. [Sept. 6, 1638].

"The petitioners Mr Pendleton, Mr Noyse, Mr Brown, and Compa, are allowed to go on in their plantation, & such as are associated to them and Lift. Willard, Thomas Bro [Brown] and Mr John Oliver are to set out the bounds of the said plantation & they are alowed 4s a day, each of them & Mr John Oliver 5 shs a day, to bee borne by the new plantation. And the petitioners are to take care that in their alotments of land they have respect as well to men's estates & abilities to improve their lands, as to their number of persons; and if any difference fall out the Court or the counsell shall order it." (Colony Records, Vol. I., p. 238.)

The land first appropriated was supposed to comprise a tract about five miles square. It had for boundaries Concord on the north, Watertown (now Weston) on the east, and on the south a line running from a point a little east of Nobscot Hill along the present Framingham and Sudbury boundary direct to the Weston town bound, and on the west a line two miles east of the present western boundary.

The second grant was of an additional mile. This was allowed, to make up a deficiency in the first grant, which deficiency was discovered on making a survey a few years after the settlement began, and it was petitioned for May 13, 1640. The petition was for a mile in length on the southeast and southwest sides of the town; and it was allowed on condition that it would not prevent the formation of another plantation, "or hinder Mrs. Glover's farm of six hundred acres formerly granted." (Colony Records, Vol. I., p. 289.)

The third tract was granted in 1649. It contained an area two miles wide, extending along the entire length of the western boundary. The Colony Record concerning this grant is: "That Sudberry is granted two miles westward next adjoining to them for their furthr inlargement, provided it [prejudice] not Wm Browne in his 200 acres already granted." (Vol. II., p. 273).

Besides these three grants, there were others made to individuals. One of these was to William Browne, of which the record is as follows: "In answer to the petition of Wm Browne ffor two hundred ac^{rs} dew for twenty five pounds putt into the joynet stocke by Mrs Ann Harvey his Aunt, from whom he made it appear to the Court he had sufficyent deputacōn to require it, his request was grannted; viz., 200 ac^{rs} of land to be layed out to him wthout the west lyne of Sudbury by Capt. Simon Willard & Seargeant Wheeler." This land was easterly of Nobscot Hill, and about the locality where the Browns have since lived.

Another grant was the Glover Farm, situated on the town's southerly border. This tract was largely in the territory of Framingham. It consisted of six hundred acres, granted to Elizabeth, the widow of Rev. Josse Glover. Mr. Glover, rector of Sutton, Eng., in the June of 1638 made a contract with Steven Day, a printer, to come over at his expense, designing to set up a printing-press in Cambridge, the seat of the university. Shortly afterward he embarked for this country, but died on the passage, and was buried at sea. Mr. Glover had aided the colonists in various ways, and by his death they lost a valuable friend. This land tract may have been given to his widow in recognition of service received. It lay westerly and northerly of Cochituate Pond, extending to the northeast corner of Dudley Pond, thence to the Sudbury old town bound; being bounded on the west by the river, and on the south by Cochituate Brook.

Another grant was that of the "Dunster Farm," sometimes called the "Pond Farm." This was a tract of six hundred acres, granted, in 1640, to Henry Dunster, first president of Harvard College, who in 1641 married Mrs. Elizabeth Glover. This farm was situated southeasterly of the "Glover Farm," and had Cochituate Lake for its western boundary.

Beyond this farm easterly was a tract of two hundred acres, extending towards the Weston town line, and called the "Jennison Farm." This was granted, in 1638, to Capt. William Jennison of Watertown, for service that he rendered in the Pequot war. It was laid out in 1646.

Another grant was to Mr. Herbert Pelham, Sept. 4, 1639. This land grant was situated in the present territory of Wayland, and was what is called " The Island." For many years it was mostly owned and occupied by the Heards. Mr. Pelham came to America in 1638, and for a time lived at Cambridge. Savage states that he was a gentleman from the county of Lincoln, and when in London, where he may have been a lawyer, was a friend of the colony. Governor Hutchinson says, " He was of that family which attained the highest rank in the peerage, one hundred years ago, as Duke of Newcastle." He was much engaged in public service, and put into the common stock of the colony £100. He became a freeman in 1645, at which time he was chosen an assistant. He was the first treasurer of Harvard College in 1743. In 1645 Herbert Pelham, Thomas Flynt, Lieutenant Willard and Peter Noyes were appointed commissioners of sewers " for bettering and improving of ye ground upon ye river running by Concord and Sudbury" (Colony Records, Vol. III., p. 13). He returned to England in 1649, and resided at Buers Hamlet, County of Essex. He died in England, and was buried at Bury St. Mary's, in Suffolk County, July 1, 1673. By his will, dated Jan. 1, 1672, he gave his lands in Sudbury to his son Edward. His daughter Penelope married, in 1657, Gov. Josiah Winslow. "Pelham's Island" was sold in 1711 by the Pelhams, who were then in Newport, R. I., to Isaac Hunt and Samuel Stone, Jr., who in November of that year sold a part of it to Jonathan and George Read.

Land was also granted to Mr. Walgrave, who was father-in-law of Herbert Pelham. The Records state concerning both of these men that " they are granted their lots at Sudbury absolutely wth condition of dwelling there only Mr. Pelham p mised to build a house there, settle a family there and to be there as much as he could in the summer time." (Colony Records, Vol. I., p. 292).

The Colonial Court as a rule did not interfere with the disposition of the lands granted. It held in reserve the power to adjust any difficulties, and to see that the conditions on which a township was allowed were kept.

As has been already observed, the Court was not the only party with which the settlers had to deal if they would obtain indisputable titles to their estates. While the English claimed the country by right of discovery, there were those who held it by right of ancient hereditary possession, and the English were in justice called upon to recognize this right, and purchase the territory of the native proprietors.

This was done by the Sudbury settlers. The first tract for the plantation was purchased in 1638 of Karte, the Indian proprietor (see Chapter II.), and it has been supposed that a deed was given; but this is not essential as evidence of the purchase, since in the deed given by Karte for land subsequently bought he acknowledged the sale of the first tract, in the statement that it was sold to " George Munnings and to the rest of the planters of Sudbury." In this first bargain of real estate it is supposed that Mr. Munnings acted as agent for the settlers, and that he, together with Brian Pendleton, advanced the money for payment.

The second tract was also purchased of Karte, who gave a deed, of which the following is a true copy : —

INDIAN DEED.

Bee it known vnto all men by these presents that I Cato otherwise Goodman for & in consideration of fyve pounds wch I have received in commodities & wompumpeage of Walter Hayne & Hugh Griffin of Sudbury in behalf of themselves & the rest of the planters of Sudbury; doe this my write in giue & grant bargain & sell vnto the said Walter Hayne — (Haine) — & Hugh Griffin & the said planters of the town of Sudbury so much land southward & so much land westward next adjoining to a tract of land wch I said Cato formerly souled vnto George Munnings & the rest of the planters of Sudbury as may make the bounds of the said town to be full fyve miles square wth all meadows, brooks, liberties priviledges & appertenances thereto belonging wth all the said tract of land granted. And I grant vnto them for me & mine heirs & brethren that I & they shall & will at any tyme make any further assurance in writing for the more p'fct assuring of the s'd land & all the premises wth the

appertenances vnto the s'd Walter Haine & Hugh Griffin & the s^d planters & their succssors forever as they shall require.

In witness whereof I herevnto put my hand & seal the twentieth day
of the fourth month one thousand six hundred forty eight.

Signed sealed and delivered in the presence of

EMMANUEL DOWNING
EPHRAIM CHILD
CUTCHAMCKIN [mark] ⎫
JOJENNY [mark] ⎭ brothers of Cato

This deed was sealed & acknowledged by the s^d Cato (who truly understood the contents of it the day & year above written) Before mee.

JOHN WINTHROP, Governor.
Registry of Deeds
Suffolk Co. Mass.

The deed for the land last granted, or the two-mile tract
to the westward, is on record at the Middlesex Registry of
Deeds, Cambridge, of which the following is a true copy:

For as much as the Genl Court of the Massachusetts Colony in New
England hath formerly granted to the Towne of Sudbury in the County
of Middlesex in the same Colony, an addition of land of two miles westward of their former grant of five miles, which is also layd out & joyneth
to it: and whereas the English occupiers, proprietors and possessors
thereof have chosen Capt. Edmond Goodenow, Leif^t Josiah Haynes,
John Goodenow, John Brigham & Joseph Freeman to be a comittee for
themselvs & for all the rest of the English proprietors thereof, giving
them their full power to treat with & to purchase the same of the Indian
proprietors of the s^d tract of land & to satisfy & pay them for their
native, ancient & hereditary right title & intrest thereunto.

Know all People by these presents —That wee, Jehojakim, John
Magus, John Muskqua & his two daughters Esther & Rachel, Benjamen
Bohue, John Speen & Sarah his wife, James Speen, Dorothy Wennetoo, &
Humphry Bohue her son, Mary Neppamun, Abigail the daughter of Josiah
Harding, Peter Jethro, Peter Muskquamogh, John Boman, David Man-
noan & Betty who are the ancient native & hereditary Indian proprietors
of the afores^d two miles of land (for & in consideration of the just & full
sum of twelve pounds of current mony of New England to them in hand
well & truly paid at or before the ensealing & delivery hereof by the said
Capt Edmond Goodenow, Leift. Josiah Haines, John Goodenow, John
Brigham & Joseph Freeman in behalfe of themselvs & of the rest of the
English possessors, occupiers, proprietors & fellow-purchasers) the receipt
whereof they do hereby acknowledge & therwith to be fully satisfied,
contented & paid & thereof and of every part & parcell thereof they do

hereby for themselvs & their heyrs Executors Administrators & assigns
clearly fully & absolutely release, acquitt exonerate & discharge them &
all the English possessors, occupiers, proprietors & fellow-purchasers of
the same & all & every one of their heyrs Executors, Administrators,
Assigns & successors forever) Have given, granted, bargained, sold,
aliened, enseossed, made over & confirmed, & by these presents, do give,
grant, bargain, sell, alien, enseosse, make over, confirme & deliver all that
their s^d tract & parcells of lands of two miles (bee it more or less scituate lying & being) altogether in one entire parcell in the s^d Town of Sudbury in the County of Middlesex afores^d & lyeth al along throughout on
the westerne side of the old five miles of the s^d Towne & adjoyneth
thereunto (together with the farme lands of the heyrs of William Browne
that lyeth within the same tract, unto the s^d Capt. Edmond Goodenow,
Leif^t Josiah Haines, John Goodenow, John Brigham & Joseph Freeman
& unto all & every one of the rest of the English possessors, occupiers,
proprietors & fellow-purchasers thereof as the same is limited, butted &
bounded on the East by the old part of the s^d Towne of Sudbury (which
was the five miles at first granted to the s^d Towne) & is butted & bounded
northerly by the line or bounds of the Towne of Concord, Westerly by
the line or bounds of the Towne of Stow & is bounded southerly & partly
westerly by the lands of Mr Thomas Danforth. All the lands within
said bounds of hills, vallies planes, intervalls, meadows, swamps, with
all the timber, trees, woods, underwoods, grass & herbage, rocks, stones,
mines, mineralls, with all rivers, rivoletts brooks, streams, springs, ponds
& all manner of watercourses & whatsoever is therein & thereupon, above
ground & underground, with all rights members, titles, royaltyes, liber-
tyes priviledges. proprietyes, uses, proffitts & commoditjes thereof &
every part & parcell thereof & that is every way & in any wise thereunto
belonging and appertaining.   To Have, Hold, use, occupie, possess enjoy to the only absolute propper use benefitt, behoofe and dispose of them the s^d English possessors, occupiers proprietors & fellow-
purchasers of the Towne of Sudbury & their heyrs executors, administrators assigns & successors in a free full & perfect estate of inheritance
from the day of the date hereof & so for ever. And the above named
indian Grantors do also hereby covenant promise & grant to & with the
above named Edmond Goodenow, Josiah Haynes, John Goodnow John
Brigham & Joseph Freeman & with all the rest of the English possessors,
occupiers, proprietors & fellow-purchasers of the said two miles of land
(bee it more or less) as above bounded that at the ensealing & delivery
hereof, they are the only & absolute Indian proprietors of the premises
& that they (& none else) have just and full power in themselvs the same
thus to sell, convey confirme make over & deliver & they do hereby
engage & bind themselvs & their heyrs executors administrators &
assigns from time to time & at all times hereafter fully & sufficiently to
secure save harmless & forever defend the hereby granted & bargained
two miles of land (as is above bounded bee it more or less) with all the
rights, members & appurtenances there unto belonging, against all man-

ner & singular other titles troubles charges demands & incumbrances
that may be made or raysed by any person or persons (especially Indian
or Indians) else whatsoever lawfully having or claiming any right, title or
intrest in or to the premises or to any part or parcell thereof to the trouble vexation charges interruption or ejection of the above[sd] English possessors, occupiers, proprietors or fellow-purchasers of the same or any
one of them, they or any one of their heyrs executors administrators or
assigns in his or their quiet and peaceable possession free & full use
enjoyment or dispose thereof or any part or parcell thereof forever.
Furthermore wee the above named Indian Grantors do hereby
oblige & engage ourselvs all and every one of our heyrs executors
Adm[rs] assigns & successors unto the s[d] English possessors occupiers &
proprietors & fellow-purchasers & to all and every one of their heyrs
executors administraters and assigns that wee and every one of us &
ours as afores[d] shall & will from time to time & at all times readily &
effectually do (at our own propper costs & charges) or cause to be so
done any other or further act or acts thing or things that the law doth
or may require for more sure making & full confirming of all & singular the hereby granted premises unto the s[d] Edmond Goodenow, Josiah
Haines, John Goodenow, John Brigham & Joseph Freeman & unto all
& every one of the rest of the English possessors, occupiers proprietors
and fellow-purchasers of the premises & unto all & every one of their
heyrs executors administrators and assigns for ever. In Witness
whereof the above named Indian Grantors have hereunto each for themselvs & altogether sett their hands and seals, dated the 11th day of July
in the year of our Lord God one thousand six hundred eighty & four.
Annoqe Regni Regis Caroli Secundi XXXVI.

JEHOJAKIM his mark ✕ for himselfe & by order of & for John
Boman & seale. ◯
JOHN MAGOS for himselfe & by order of & for Jacob Magos his
father & seale. ◯
MUSKQUA JOHN & for his two daughters Rachel & Esther
& seale. ◯
JOHN SPEEN his marke I & for & by order of Sarah his wife
& seale. ◯
ABIGAIL Daughter of Josiah Harding and his sole heyr (⊨ her
marke & seale. ◯
SARAH C her marke who is the widdow of Josiah Harding &
mother of s[d] Abigail & her Guardian.
PETER MUSKQUAMOG + his mark & seale. ◯
BENJAMEN BOHEW his R marke & seale. ◯
DORITHY WENNETO her O marke & seale. ◯
MARY NEPAMUN he Q marke & seale. ◯
BETTY her) marke & seale
PETER JETHRO & a seale
JOHN ✕ BOMAN his marke & seale
JAMES SPEEN & seale

Cambe 15 Octo[b] 1684   All the persons that have signed & sealed this
instrument appeared before me this day & year above written & freely
acknowledged this writing to be their act & deed

DANIEL GOOKIN Sen[r] Assist.

Endorsement — All the Grantors of the instrument within written
beginning with Jehojakım & ending with Peter Muskquamog did sign
seale & deliver s[d] instrument in presence of us.

JOHN GREENE —   JAMES BERNARD —

Moreover wee underwritten did see Benjamen Bohew Dorothy Wan-
neto & Mary & Betty Nepamun signe seale & deliver this instrument
the 15th day of Octo[b] 1684.   ANDRFW PITTAMEE ¶ his marke
JAMES RUMNY marke
SAMUEL GOFF, JAMES BARNARD
DANIEL SACOWAMBATT

Feb[r] 1, 1684   Memorandum — Wee whose names are underwritten
did see Peter Jethro signe & seale & deliver y[e] within written instrument

JAMES BARNARD —   STEPHEN ꟻ GATES his marke

Peter Jethro, Indian, appeared before me the fifth day of February —
1684 & freely acknowledged this writing within to be his act & deed &
ythe put his hand & seale thereunto.   DANIFL GOOKIN Sen[r] Affift

John Boman did signe seale & deliver the within written deed the 23 :
of February in the year our Lord one thousand six hundred eighty &
four in presence of us

JOHN BALCOM ∸   + SAMUEL FREEMAN his marke.

James Speen & John Bowman appeared before me in court at Natick
& acknowledged they have signed & sealed this instrument among others
May 13th 1684.   JAMES GOOKIN Sen[r] Affift

Roxbury April 16. 85.

Charles Josias, Sachem of the Massachusetts, having read & consid-
eɪed the within written deed with the consent of his Guardians & Coun-
cellors underwritten doth for himself & his heyrs allow of, ratify &
confirm the within written sale to the Inhabitants of Sudbury & their
heyrs for ever, the lands therein bargained & sold.   To have & to hold
to the s'd Inhabitanls of Sudbury their heyrs and assigns for ever & hath
hereunto set his hand & seale the day above written.

CHARLS ⅄ JOSIAS his marke & Seale

Allowed by us   )
· WILLIAM STOUGHTON ⎰ Guardians to ⎰
JOSEPH DUDLEY   ) y[e] Sachem   ⎰   ROBERT ৪ MONTAGUE
WILLIAM W. AHOWTON

Recorded 19. 3. 1685
by THO. DANFORTH Recorder.

A true copy of record Book 9 Pages 344 to 352 inclusive

Attest   CHA[s] B STEVENS Reg.

The above deed was not received until years after the grant was made by the Court, and the lands divided up and apportioned to the inhabitants. The records do not state what occasioned the long delay, but, as was the case elsewhere, perhaps the papers were not passed until, in process of time, the settlers questioned whether the claim to the territory was valid until purchased of the Indian proprietors. A similar instance occurred at Groton, where the deed came long after the lands were occupied. The grant was allowed by the Court as early as 1655, but no title was obtained from the natives till about 1683 or 1684.

From lands thus allowed, the Plantation of Sudbury was formed. It required, however, more than the allowance and laying out of the land and the settlement of it to make it a town. A separate act of incorporation was necessary to complete the work. This was done September 4, 1639, when the Court ordered that " the newe Plantation by Concord shall be called Sudbury." (Colony Records, Vol. I., p. 271.)

By the granting of the name, the act of incorporation is supposed to have been made complete. It was a short process for an act so great, yet such was the manner of the Court. Says Mr. Sewall, in the history of Woburn, of the incorporation of that place, " The act of Court for this purpose is contained in these five words : ' Charlestown Village is called Wooborne.' " The Court action in this matter was dated Sept. 4, 1639 ; but it does not follow that this specific day of the month was the exact date of incorporation, as sometimes the date of the beginning of the Court session was given, instead of the date of the particular day when the transaction took place. As, for example, we find the permit for a division of land to be of the same date as that on which Sudbury was named.

The name ordered by the Court is that of an old English town in the county of Suffolk, from which some of the town's settlers are supposed to have come, or with which they may have had an acquaintance. It is situated near the parish of Bury St. Edmunds, at or near which place it is supposed the Browns may have dwelt. (See chap. Biographical Sketches.) It is not improbable that the name was given by Rev. Edmund

Brown, the first minister of Sudbury, who sold lands in the district of Lanham to Thomas Read, his nephew, and it is supposed may have also named that locality from Lavenham, Eng., a place between Sudbury and Bury St. Edmunds. (See sketch of Thomas Read.) The place, though spelled Lavenham, is pronounced Lannam in England (Waters). The proximity of Sudbury and Lavenham, Eng., to what was probably the original home of Mr. Brown, together with the fact that he was an early owner of the lands at Lanham, and a prominent man at the settlement, affords at least a strong presumption that Mr. Edmund Brown named both Sudbury and Lanham. It is appropriate, then, to give a sketch of this old English town, and we present the following from Lewis's Topographical Dictionary of England:—

" Sudbury is a borough and market town, having separate jurisdiction locally in the hundred of Babergh, County of Suffolk, 22 miles (why s) from Ipswich, and 50 (N. E. by N.) from London, containing, according to the last census, 3950 inhabitants, which number has since increased to nearly 5000. This place, which was originally called South Burgh, is of great antiquity, and at the period of the compilation of Domesday-book was of considerable importance, having a market and a mint. A colony of the Flemings, who were introduced into this country by Edward III. for the purpose of establishing the manufacture of woollen cloth, settled here, and that branch of trade continued to flourish for some time, but at length fell to decay. The town is situated on the river Stour, which is crossed by a bridge leading into Essex. For some years after its loss of the woollen trade it possessed few attractions, the houses belonging principally to decayed manufacturers, and the streets being very dirty ; it has however within the last few years been greatly improved, having been paved and lighted in 1825, under an act obtained for the purpose, and some good houses built. The town hall recently erected by the corporation, in the Grecian style of architecture, is a great ornament to the town, in which is also a neat theatre. The trade principally consists in the manufacture of silk crape, and buntings used for ships' flags ; that of silk was introduced by the manufacturers from Spitalfields in consequence of disputes with their workmen, and now affords employment to a great number of persons, about one thousand five hundred being engaged in the silk and four hundred in the crape and the bunting business. The river Stour, navigable hence to the Manning tree, affords a facility for the transmission of coal, chalk, lime and agricultural produce. The statute market is on Saturday, and the corn market on Thursday. Fairs are held on the 12th of March and 10th of July, principally for earthen ware, glass and toys. The first charter of incorporation was granted by Queen Mary in 1554, and confirmed by Elizabeth in 1559. Another was given by Oliver Cromwell, but that under which the corporation derives its power was bestowed by Charles II. Sudbury comprises the parishes of All Saints, St. Gregory, and St. Peter, in the archdeaconry of Sudbury, and diocese of Norwich. The living of All Saints is a discharged vicarage, rated in the king's books at £4.11.5½ endowed, £400 royal bounty, and £1200 parliamentary grant."

> "Quaint old town of toil and traffic,
> Quaint old town of art and song,
> Memories haunt thy pointed gables,
> Like the rooks that round them throng"

From this description we learn that it is a stanch old town from which Sudbury probably received its name; a place busy and of good repute. The word has been variously spelled, as: Sudberry, Soodberie, Sudwrowe, Sudborrough, Sudborow or, as it is called in Doomsday book, Sutburge.

The boundaries of the town received early attention from the settlers, and at different dates there are records concerning it. As already stated, the southern boundary line at the first was from a point a little east of Nobscot, to the northern point of Dudley Pond; thence, direct to Weston. That part of the line outside the present territory of Wayland has never varied much in its general character. Some slight changes have been made within about fifty years, by which a few acres have been taken from Sudbury and annexed to Framingham; this was the case along the line by the Brown

farm and the northerly slope of Nobscot. Before the alteration the line was slightly irregular, and the design may have
been solely to straighten it. Concerning the boundary in the
easterly part of the town's original territory, we have the
following order of the General Court, dated June 6, 1701 : —

" Ordered that the line between Sudbury and the farms
annexed to Framingham, as set forth in the plat exhibited
under the hand of John Gore, be and continue the boundary
line between the said farms and Sudbury forever, viz : from
the northerly end of Cochittwat pond to the bent of the river,
by Daniel Stone's and so as the line goes to Framingham and
Sudbury line."

Concerning the Sudbury and Watertown boundary, the following facts are recorded : " In 1649 persons were appointed
by the town to search the records for the grant of Watertown, and to see if they can find any means to prevent
Watertown from coming so near." The Colony Records
state that a year later the Court ordered that the inhabitants
of Sudbury should have their bounds recorded, and about
the same time the town sent a petition to the General Court
for a commission to lay out the boundary between the two
towns. In 1651 a report was rendered about the boundary,
which, with slight abridgment, is as follows : —

" The committee appointed to lay out the Watertown
and Sudbury boundary report that the line drawn by John
Oliver, three years previous, called ' the old line,' shall be
the line between the two towns, and forever stand. This
line, beginning at Concord south bound, ran through a great
pine swamp, a small piece of meadow to upland, and ' then
to an angle betwixt two hills.' After the line left the aforesaid angle on its southerly course, it had ' these remarkable
places therein : one rock called Grout's head, and a stake by
the cartway leading from Sudbury to Watertown, and so to
a pine hill being short of a pond about eighty-eight rods, att
which pine hill Sudbury bounds ends.' " (Colony Records,
Vol. IV., page 53.)

Such was the territory of Sudbury, the manner in which the lands were allowed, and the parties from whom they were bought. From this plantation was formed the town; and land divisions and allotments were subsequently made, until no portion of it was held by proprietary right, nor as public domain, but all passed into private estates except the highways and commons, and here and there a small three-cornered nook.

CHAPTER V.

Place and Plan of Settlement. — Data of House-lots. — Description of Map. — Course of First Street. — Sites of Early Homesteads. — Historic Highway. — Time of Settlement. — Dimensions of First Dwelling-house. — Early Experiences of the Settlers.

> Ay, call it holy ground,
>   The spot where first they trod!
> They have left unstained what there they found —
>   Freedom to worship God.
>
> MRS. HEMANS.

THE settlement of the town began on the east side of the river. The first road or street, beginning at Watertown (now Weston), extended along a course of about two miles, and by this the house-lots of the settlers were laid out and their humble dwellings stood. The plan of the settlement can, to an extent, be made out by tradition and the data of house-lots which are preserved on the Sudbury records, and

which we here give in abbreviated form, the figures in paren-
theses denoting the acres allowed : —

DATA OF HOUSE-LOTS.

Edmond Brown (80), on Timber Neck (east of Mill
Brook, Wayland).

John Blanford (3), north by highway to river, south by
Joseph Taynter.

Jos. Taynter (4), between John Blanford and Tho. Whyte.

Tho. Whyte (4), between Hugh Griffin and Jos. Taynter.

Hugh Griffin (4), north by Tho. Whyte, south by John
Howe.

John Howe (4), north by Hugh Griffin, south by Edmund
Rice; (also one acre parted from his house-lot by highway
between Edmund Rice and Hugh Griffin; also four on Pine
Plain, on road from Sudbury to Watertown, west by Mrs.
Hunt).

Edmund Rice (4), between John Howe and Henry Rice.

Henry Rice (4), between Edmund Rice and John Maynard.

John Maynard (4), between Henry Rice and highway.

Robert Daniel (8), northwest by John Maynard and Robert
Boardman (or Fordum).

Robert Boardman (4), between Robert Daniel and Robert
Best.

Robert Best (4), north by Mr. Boardman, south by John
Loker.

John Loker (4), between Robert Best and Tho. Flinn
(or Joslyn), [also (one acre) parted from his house-lot by
the highway.]

Tho. Flinn (4), between John Loker and John Haynes.

John Haynes (4), north by Tho. Flinn, south by Edmund
Goodnow.

Edmund Goodnow (4), north by John Haynes, west by
River Meadows.

Wm. Brown (4), north by Edmund Goodnow, south by
John Toll.

John Toll (4), between Edmund Goodnow and Widow
Wright.

Widow Wright (6), between John Toll and John Bent.

John Bent (6), between Widow Wright and John Wood.

John Wood (4), between John Bent and Widow Hunt.

Widow Hunt (4), between John Wood and John Goodnow.

John Goodnow (5), north by Widow Hunt, south by Henry Loker, east end on highway going to mill, and west by the great River Meadows.

Henry Loker (4), between John Goodnow and John Parmenter, Sr.

John Parmenter, Sr. (4), between Henry Loker and the highway to Bridle Point.

ON NORTHWEST ROW.

John Freeman (4), on northwest corner of highway leading to River Meadows.

Solomon Johnson (6), east by Wm. Ward.

Wm. Ward (20), on northeast side of Northwest Row.

Solomon Johnson (7), between Wm. Ward and Wm. Pelham.

Wm. Pelham (50), northeast part, near Wm. Ward.

ON THE NORTH STREET OR EAST STREET.

John Rutter (4), (near clay pits).

John Ruddick (4).

Henry Curtis (—).

John Stone (9), between Henry Curtis and Nathl. Treadway.

Nathl. Treadway (—), on East Street, between John Stone and John Knight.

John Knight (12).

ON EAST STREET.

Bryan Pendleton (5), north by Tho. Noyes south by Pond Brook that runs to the river.

Tho. Noyes (4), south by Bryan Pendleton, north by Geo. Munning.

Geo. Munning (4), between Tho. Noyes and Walter Hayne.

Walter Hayne (6), south by Geo. Munning, north by highway to Common Swamp. ·

ON BRIDLE POINT HIGHWAY.

Tho. Brown (4), north by highway leading to Bridle Point, east by the Common, south end running to Mill Brook, west by Anthony White.

Anthony Whyte (4), north by Bridle Point Road, south by Mill Brook. Between Tho. Brown and Wm. Parker.

Wm. Parker (—).

Peter Noyes (8), north by Bridle Point Road, south by Mill Brook. Between Wm. Parker and Thomas Goodnow.

Tho. Goodnow (5), north by Bridle Point Road, south by Mill Brook. Between A. Belcher and P. Noyes. He sold to P. Noyes, making Noyes' lot thirteen acres.

Andrew Belcher (4), north by Bridle Point Road, south by Mill Brook. Between Tho. Goodnow and Richd. Newton.

Richard Newton (4), north by Bridle Point Road, south by Mill Brook. Between A. Belcher and John Parmenter, Jr.

John Parmenter, Jr. (4). Between Richd. Newton and Henry Prentiss.

Henry Prentiss (4). Between John Parmenter, Jr., and Herbert Pelham.

ON MILL ROAD FROM PINE PLAIN.

William Kerley (4), on southwest side of " Pine Swamp," on highway leading to mill, northwest of Richd. Sanger.

Richd. Sanger (4), northwest by Wm. Kerley.

ON ROAD TO COTCHITUATT.

Tho. Goodnow [also on Cotchituatt Road]. Probably the present Pousland lot.

ON PINE PLAIN.

John Howe. Also four acres on Pine Plain, north side of road from Sudbury to Watertown, west by land of Mrs. Hunt.

Mrs. Hunt, or Widow Hunt. She probably sold her lot on " The Street," and took a lot here.

John How. Probably sold his lot on " The Street " to either Griffin or Rice, and took a lot on The Plain.

Henry Loker (4). Between John Goodnow and J. Parmenter, Sr.

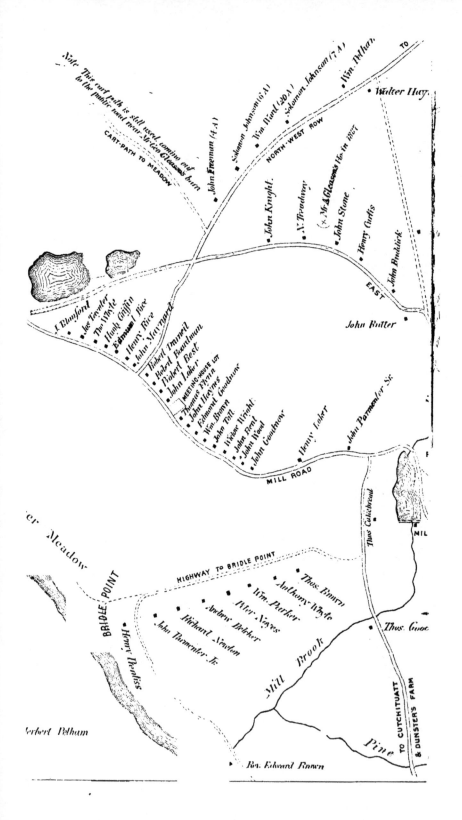

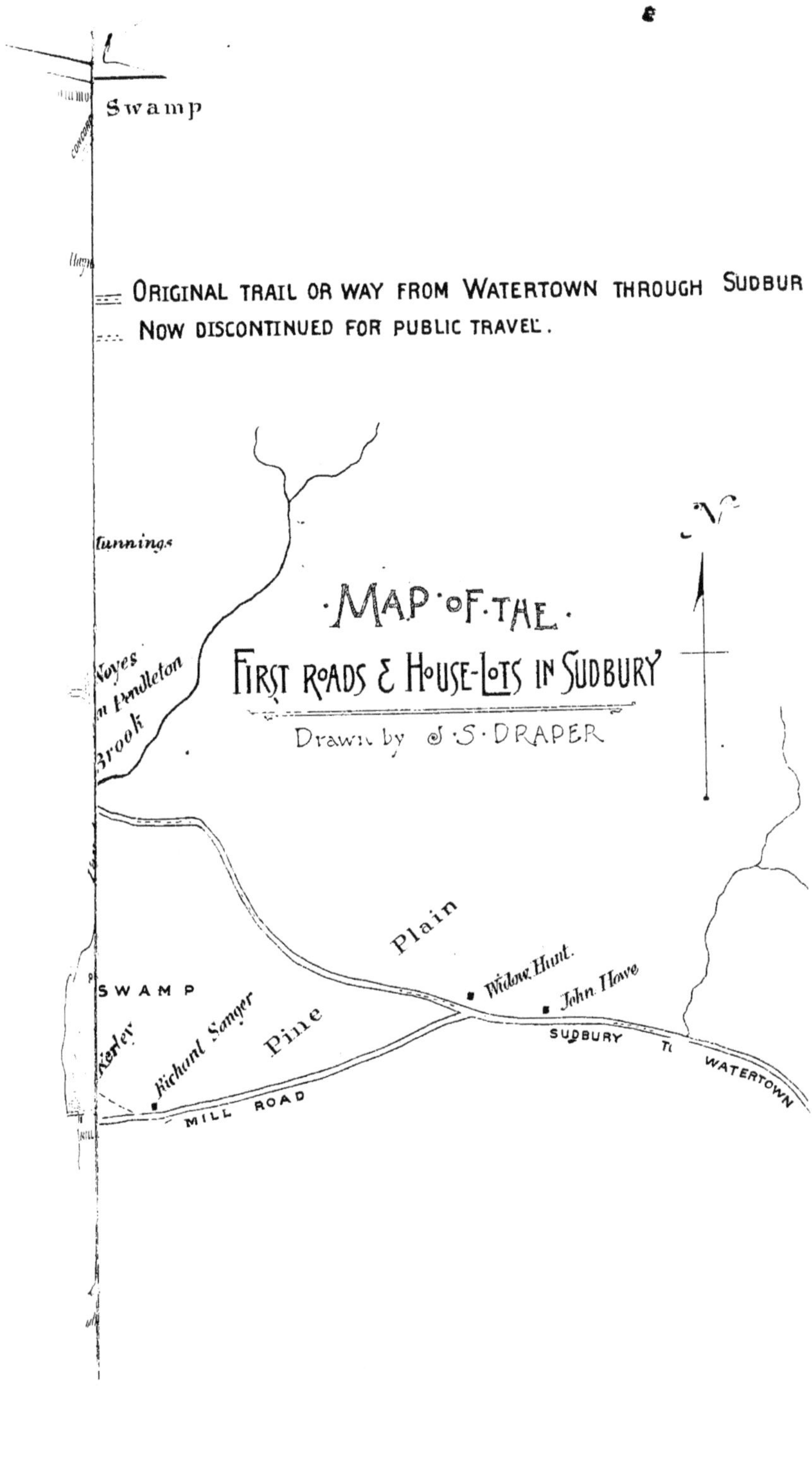

Swamp

ORIGINAL TRAIL OR WAY FROM WATERTOWN THROUGH SUDBUR

NOW DISCONTINUED FOR PUBLIC TRAVEL.

Gunnings

Noyes
n Pendleton

Brook

·MAP·OF·THE·

FIRST ROADS & HOUSE-LOTS IN SUDBURY

Drawn by J·S·DRAPER

·N·

Plain

Widow. Hunt.

John Howe

SWAMP

Korley

Richard Sanger

Pine

SUDBURY Ti

WATERTOWN

MILL ROAD

John Parmenter, Sr. (4). Between Henry Loker and Bridle Point Road.

John Goodnow (5). North by Widow Hunt and south by Henry Loker. The east end on the mill road, and the west end on the great river meadows.

Thomas Hoyt. His house-lot containing four acres, having the house-lot of Brian Pendleton on the south side, and the house-lot of George Munnings on the north side.

The map that accompanies the data of house-lots was made by James Sumner Draper of Wayland, as the result of the united investigation of himself and the writer. Mr. Draper has a life-long familiarity with the locality, is a practical surveyor, and acquainted with the traditions and old roads of this ancient part of Sudbury. It is not absolutely certain that every one to whom a lot was assigned ever became a householder in the settlement; furthermore, it may be that an exchange was, in some cases, made before the settlers began to build. With, however, a suitable allowance for possible or probable changes, and making such slight departures in certain cases from the data as was thought warranted by the circumstances, the locality, and tradition, we believe this map to be a fair representation of the locations of most, if not all, of the first homesteads in Sudbury.

We will now consider the plan of the settlement, and trace the course of the street. The settlement lay along three roads, which afterwards became the common highway. The principal one of these roads, called "the North" or "East Street," and also the "Old Watertown Trail," started at what is now "Weston and Wayland Corner," and probably followed the course of the present road over "The Plain" and Clay-pit Hill to a point near the Abel Gleason estate; from this place it is supposed to have made its way a little northerly of Mr. Gleason's house, and winding southwesterly passed just south of Baldwin's Pond, and thence to the river at the bridge. The road originally called "Northwest Row" ran from this street to what is still called "Common Swamp," and by the spot designated as the house-lot of Walter Haynes. This spot still bears the traces of having, long years ago, been

the site of a house.   The cart-path which ran from it to the
meadow is still used.

· Along this road traces and traditions of homesteads are
unmistakable: old building material has been unearthed,
and depressions in the ground are still to be seen.   Mr.
Draper, a little east of his house, by the brook, unearthed
the stones of a fire-place, with fragments of coals still upon
them.   Between this and Clay-pit Bridge (the second bridge
or culvert from the mill-pond, or the first above " Whale's
Bridge ") there are, north of the road, several depressions
indicating the sites of old houses.   Just beyond Clay-pit
Bridge, the writer, with Mr. Draper, went to look for traces
of houses on the lots assigned to Bryan Pendleton and
Thomas Noyes ; and there, in the exact locality, were distinct depressions, just where they were looked for.   The
Curtis homestead, until within a very few years, was standing in about the place assigned for the house-lot.   Thus
strong is the probability that the lots on this street were
largely built upon.

Another of the principal streets was that which, starting
from a point on the north street near the town bridge, ran
easterly along what is now the common highway, to the
head of the mill-pond, and then to the mill.   Upon this
street was the first meeting-house, at a spot in the old
burying-ground (see chapter on First Meeting-house, &c.),
and the Parmenter Tavern.   The house-lots were mainly at
the west end of this street, and the road was probably
extended northeasterly to give access to the mill.   Here,
again, tradition confirms the record of house-lots, and shows
that the lots were more or less built upon.   The John Maynard and John Loker estates were kept for years in their
families, and the Parmenter estate is still retained in the
family.   In later years the descendants of John Rutter built
on that street.

The third road was called the "Bridle Point Road."   This
started near the Parmenter Tavern, crossed the knoll at the
Harry Reeves place, and ran along the ridge of "Braman's
Hill" for about two-thirds of its length, when it turned
southerly, and, crossing Mill Brook, ran towards the town's

southern limits. While tradition positively locates this road, it points to but one homestead upon it, and that the residence of Rev. Edmund Brown, which it undoubtedly declares was at the spot designated by the house-lot data. Along this street are no visible marks of ancient dwelling-places north of Mill Brook; but beyond, various depressions in the ground, and remnants of building material, indicate that at one time this street had houses upon it. With the exception of those on the south street, the dwellings were about equally distant from the meeting - house, and all within easy access to the River Meadows and the mill. Probably they settled largely in groups, that they might more easily defend themselves in case of danger. They were in a new country, and as yet had had little experience with the Indians; hence we should not expect they would scatter very widely. In the early times so essential was it considered by the Colonial Court that the people should not widely scatter, that, three years before Sudbury was settled, it ordered, that, for the greater safety of towns, " hereafter no dwelling-house should be built above half a mile from the meeting-house in any new plantation." (Colony Records, Vol I.)

It will be noticed that the positions selected for these streets were, to an extent, where the shelter of upland could be obtained for the house. The sandy slope of Bridle Point Hill would afford a protection from the rough winds of winter; so of the uplands just north of South Street. It was also best to settle in groups, to lessen the amount of road-breaking in winter. It will also be noticed that these groups of house-lots were near, not only meadow land, but light upland, which would be easy of cultivation. Various things indicate that the most serviceable spots were selected for homesteads, that roads were constructed to connect them as best they could, and that afterwards the roads were extended to the mill. Probably the people on North Street made the short way to South Street, that now comes out at Mr. Jude Damon's, in order to shorten the way to church. Those midway of that street, for a short cut to the mill, the church and the tavern, would naturally open a path from the

turn of the road by the clay-pits to the mill. To accommodate the people on " The Plain," a road was opened to the
mill in a southwesterly course, which is in part the present
highway, but has in part been abandoned, — the latter part
being that which formerly came out directly east of the
mill.

These several sections of road probably formed what was
called the " Highway." A large share of it is in use at the
present time, and is very suggestive of historic reminiscences.
By it the settlers went to the Cakebread Mill, to the little
hillside meeting-house, and to the John Parmenter Ordinary.
By these ways came the messenger with fresh news from the
seaboard settlements, or with tidings from the tribes of the
woods. In short, these formed the one great road of the
settlement; the one forest pathway along which every one
more or less trod.

The erection of dwelling-places along these first streets
probably began in 1638; but we have no tradition or record
of the week or month when the inhabitants arrived at the
spot, nor as to how many went at any one time. They may
have gone in small companies at different dates; and the
entire removal from Watertown may have occurred in the
process of months. It is quite probable, however, that they
went mainly together, or in considerable companies, both for
the sake of convenience and safety; and that they were
largely there by the autumn of 1638. On the arrival of the
" Confidence," the emigrants would naturally be eager to
settle somewhere at once. They would hardly wait long in
Watertown, if their design was to make their homes farther
west. The cold winter being just ahead, they would presumably hasten to the proposed place of settlement, to prepare things for their comfort before cold weather fairly
set in.

We have found no record of the dimensions of any of the
first dwelling-places, but we may judge something of their
size by that of the first house of worship, and by the specifications in a lease of a house to be built by Edmund Rice
prior to the year 1655. This house was to be very small, —
" 30 foot long, 10 foot high, 1 foot sill from the ground,

16 foot wide, with two rooms, both below or one above the other, all the doors, walls and staires with convenient fixtures, and well planked under foot and boored sufficiently to lay corn in the story above head." But it is doubtful if this small, low structure fitly represents the settlers' first forest home ; very likely that was a still more simple building, that would serve as a mere shelter for a few months or years, till a more serviceable one could be built. Houses of ordinary capacity would hardly be necessary when the settlement commenced. The furniture of the dwelling would for a time, probably, be simple and scant, and consist mainly of a few household utensils, their firearms, and tools.

The way from Watertown being at first only a forest trail, it was a difficult task to transport many goods, even if they were brought to this country. That carts were made use of the first year for transportation to Watertown is doubtful, although they were used a few years later. In 1641 it was ordered, " That every cart with four sufficient oxen and a man shall have for a day's work five shillings ; " and that " none shall take above six pence a bushel for the bringing up of corn from Watertown to Sudbury and twenty shillings a day for any other goods." (Town Records, p. 17.) The transportation of corn may have been on horseback.

What the settlers experienced in the rough cabins of logs, the first years, we can only conjecture. The deep snow-fall of winter, as it covered their lonely forest path, presented a strong contrast to the mild climate from which they came. But they had enough to employ their time. There were cattle to care for, and lands to clear and make ready for the coming spring; and it was no small task to keep the household supplied with wood. The wide-mouthed fireplace, with hearth broadening to almost midway of the cabin itself, with its huge andirons, beyond which was the stout back-log, had the capacity of a dozen stoves ; and to supply this was a matter of work. But the routine of work was broken by experiences both sad and glad. In the first year or two there were the birth, bridal, and burial. On the 1st of October, 1639, " Andrew Belcher and his wife were married." " On ye first day of ye first month (March

1), 1640, Edward the servant of Robert Darnill was buried."
A year after, Joseph Rice was born. "On the third day of
the twelvth month, 1639, Joseph and Nathaniel the sons of
Solomon Johnson were born." In November, 1644, John
Rutter married Elizabeth Plimpton. The first body buried
was probably borne to the northerly side of the old meeting-
house hill, where tradition says the Indians had a burying-
ground. Here, doubtless, was buried the servant of Robert
Darnill, who was the first, or one of the first, in that long
procession which, for nearly two centuries and a half, has
been borne to the ancient burying-place upon or about that
hill. Beside these experiences, there were others that would
tend to break up the monotony of the settlers' experience,
such as "log-rollings," when the neighbors collected together
and helped clear the land of logs and brush; "house-rais-
ings," where many joined hands to help raise the heavy
frames; "road-breaking," when, with ox-teams, they cleared
the snow from the path; corn-planting in the common fields.
or "huskings," when the corn was gathered, — these, with
town-meetings, and an occasional drill of the train-band,
when Bryan Pendleton exercised his little host, would serve
to break up the monotony and enliven the scene at the settlement. Thus, —

> Toiling, rejoicing, sorrowing,
>   Onward through life he goes;
> Each morning sees some task begun,
>   Each evening sees it close;
> Something attempted, something done,
>   Has earned a night's repose.
>   LONGFELLOW.

CHAPTER VI.

> But the good deed, through the ages
> Living in historic pages,
> Brighter grows and gleams immortal,
> Unconsumed by moth or rust.
>
> LONGFELLOW.

THE first steps in the settlement of the town having been considered, — namely, the acquisition of the territory, the assignment of house-lots, and laying out of the principal highways, — we will now notice further projects for the general good. The people acted first in town-meeting; hence it may here be appropriate to consider the origin and character of these occasions, and the manner in which they were conducted. The New England town-meeting is an institution that originated in the exigencies of New England colonial life, and sprang into existence at the call of men who opposed the concentration of political power, and who would confer it on no person or persons, only as it was conferred on them by the people's choice. Situated far remote from the home government in Europe, too much time was consumed in the transmission of laws, and too little acquaintance was had by the English government with the needs of American life, to make it practicable to rely on such a source of authority.

Something was needed to meet an independent and extemporized order of things; and the result was a New England town-meeting, which is unlike any other political assembly. In the principle of its operation it is similar and modelled after the New England Congregational Church meeting. The same general freeness and equality to an extent prevailed, and by these meetings each town became like a little republic. Whatever offices were needed were made, and the men selected to fill them had a fitness based on personal merit. There were no credentials for position that came from a titled authority, or from ancient hereditary right based on manorial acquisition or influence. Before plantations became incorporated towns, and while undivided lands still remained which were held by proprietary or collective right, there were certain privileges possessed by these proprietors or land companies, which related to their real estate, such as the right to dispose of and improve their lands, or to enjoy exclusive privileges that were based upon them. But when all the lands were divided and sold, the proprietary dissolved, and left the community purely republican, in which each public meeting was an open town-meeting, whether it pertained to matters of church or state. Thus the New England town-meeting was original, and its principles of operation were in harmony with the character and purposes of the men who had fled from ecclesiastical and civil restraint.

As might be expected, the General Court, which was more or less dependent on the action of town-meetings, was in general harmony with them; and, in its definition of the power of towns, gave them the elements of democratic government. In 1635 it was "Ordered, that the freemen of any town, or the major part of them, shall only have power to dispose of their own lands and woods, with all the privileges and appurtenances of said towns, to grant lots and make such orders as may concern the well ordering of their own towns, not repugnant to the orders of the General Court." They were authorized to impose fines, not exceeding twenty shillings, and "to choose their own particular officers, as constables, surveyors for highways and the like." (Colony Records, Vol. I., p. 72.)

There were some restrictions that related to citizenship in those days that have since been removed. At one period only "freemen" could participate in the shaping of public affairs. A "freeman" was a person who, by act of the General Court, was admitted to the rights and privileges that correspond to those now pertaining to American citizenship. In early times people did not attain to political privileges, as now, by passing from minority and paying a town tax; but to attain to full citizenship. with eligibility to office, as late as 1631, it was necessary to be a member of a church within the jurisdiction of the Massachusetts Bay Colony. Later, in . 1662, the law was so changed that an Englishman, on presenting a certificate of good character, and upon giving evidence of orthodox belief, together with a certificate from a town selectman that the party was a freeholder and ratable to the county on a single rate to the amount of ten shillings, might apply to the General Court for admission as freeman. If accepted by the Court, it was on condition that the applicant take what was termed the "freeman's oath," which is as follows : —

"I, A. B., being by God's providence an inhabitant and freeman within the jurisdiction of this commonwealth, do freely acknowledge myself to be subject to the government thereof, and therefore do swear, by the great and dreadful name of the everlasting God, that I will be true and faithful to the same, and will accordingly yield assistance and support thereunto with my person and estate, as in equity I am bound, and also truly endeavor to maintain and preserve all the liberties and privileges thereof, submitting myself to the wholesome laws and orders made and established by the same ; and, further, that I will not plot nor practise any evil against it, nor consent to any that shall do so, but will timely discover and reveal the same to lawful authority now here established, for the speedy prevention thereof; moreover, I do solemnly bind myself, in the sight of God, that when I shall be called to give my voice touching any such matter of this state wherein freemen are to deal, I will give my vote and suffrage, as I shall judge in my conscience, may best conduce and tend to the public weal of the body, without respect of persons, or favor of any man. *So help me God, in the Lord Jesus Christ.*"

After being thus qualified by the vote of the Court, and by taking the above oath, the freeman was allowed to vote in the elections in the following manner and under the following penalty: "It is ordered by this Court, and by the authority thereof, that for the yearly choosing of assistants, the freemen shall use Indian corn and beans — the Indian corn to manifest election, the beans the contrary; and if any freeman shall put in more than one Indian corn or bean, for the choice or refusal of any public officer, he shall forfeit for every such offence ten pounds; and that any man that is not a freeman, or hath not liberty of voting, putting in any vote, shall forfeit the like sum of ten pounds."

But, though corn and beans were sufficient to elect an assistant, for governor, deputy - governor, major - general, treasurer, secretary, and commissioners of the united colonies, it was required that the freemen should make use of written ballots.

The freemen at first were all required to appear before the General Court to give their votes for assistants; but it was found inconvenient, and even dangerous, for all of them to assemble in one place, leaving their homes unprotected, and hence it was ordered, "That it shall be free and lawful for all freemen to send their votes for elections by proxy, in the next General Court in May, and so for hereafter, which shall be done in this manner: The deputy which shall be chosen shall cause the freemen of the town to be established, and then take such freemen's votes, as please to send them by proxy, for any magistrate, and seal them up severally, subscribing the magistrates name ou the back side, and to bring them to the Court, sealed, with an open roll of the names of the freemen that so send them."

Until as late as the nineteenth century, the town-meetings were held in the meeting-house. After the meeting-house was built sometimes they were held in a private house or at the "ordinary." As for example, Jan. 10, 1685, and again Feb. 18, 1686, there was an adjournment of town-meeting to the house of Mr. Walker, " by reason of the extremity of the cold." In 1764 the town adjourned one of its meetings to the house of "William Rice, innholder." In 1782, "adjourned town-meeting to the house of Mr. Aaron Johnson, innholder in s^d town." After the division of the town into the east and west precincts, the town-meetings alternated from the east to the west side.

In 1682-3 the time of meeting was changed from February to October, the day of the week to be Monday. The reason of this change may be found in the fact that it was difficult at some seasons to make a journey to the east side meeting-house; the passage of the causeway was occasionally rough, and town action might be thereby delayed or obstructed. The meeting was for a period warned by the board of select-men. At the date of the change just mentioned, it "was voted and ordered, that henceforth the selectmen every year for the time being shall appoint and seasonably warn the town-meeting;" but afterwards this became the work of the constables. In the warning of town-meetings at one period, the "Old Lancaster Road" was made use of as a partial line of division. A part of the constables were to warn the people on the north side of the road, and part those who lived south of it.

The town-meeting was opened by prayer. There is a record of this about 1654, and presumably it was prac-tised from the very first. At an early date voting was sometimes done by "dividing the house," each party with-drawing to different sides of the room. An example of this is as follows: In 1654, at a public town-meeting, after "the pastor by the desire of the town had sought the Lord for his blessing in the actings of the day, this following vote was made, You that judge the act of the selectmen in sizing the Commons to be a righteous act, discover it by drawing yourselves together in the one end of the meeting-house." After that was done, "It was then desired that those who are of a contrary mind would discover it by drawing them-selves together in the other end of the meeting-house."

In what was done at these meetings, marked respect was usually had for order and law. We find records of protest or dissent when things were done in an irregular way, as for instance, in 1676, we have the following record: "We do hereby enter our Decent against the illegal proceeding of the inhabitants of the town : : : for the said proceedings have Ben Directly Contrary to law. First, That the Town Clerk did not Solemnly read the Laws against Intemperance and Immorality as the Laws Require." Mention is also made of other irregularities, and the whole is followed by a list of names of prominent persons.

The town officers were mostly similar to those elected at the present time. At a meeting of the town in 1682–3, it was ordered that the town-meeting "shall be for the electing of Selectmen, Commissioners, and Town Clerk." Names of officers not mentioned here were "Constables, Invoice Takers, Highway Surveyors, and Town Marshal." About 1648 the persons chosen to conduct the affairs of the town were first called selectmen. The number of these officers varied at different times. In 1646 there were seventeen selectmen.

The service expected of the selectmen, beside being custodians at large of the public good, and acting as the town's prudential committee, were, before the appointment of tything-men (which occurred first in Sudbury, Jan. 18, 1679), expected to look after the morals of the community. This is indicated by the following order: At a meeting of the inhabitants, Jan. 18, 1679, "It is ordered, that the selectmen shall visit the families of the town, and speedily inspect the same, but especially to examine children and servants about their improvement in reading and the catechism. Captain Goodnow and Lieutenant Haines to inspect all families at Lanham and Nobscot and all others about there and in their way, . . . and these are to return an account of that matter at the next meeting of the selectmen, appointed to be on the 30th of this instant January." We infer from certain records that the selectmen's orders were to be audibly and deliberately read, that the people might take notice and observe them.

The officials known as "highway surveyors" had charge of repairs on town roads. This term was early applied, and has continued in use until now. As early in the records as 1639, Peter Noyes and John Parmenter are mentioned as surveyors.

The business of town clerk, or "clark," first held in Sudbury by Hugh Griffin, is shown by the following extracts from the town book: "He is to take charge of the records and discharge the duties of a faithful scribe." "To attend town-meeting, to write town orders for one year, . . . for which he was to have ten shillings for his labor." In 1643 he was "to take record of all births and marriages and [deaths], and return them to the recorder." "It is also agreed that the rate of eight pound 9 shillings [be] levied upon mens estate for the payment of the town debt due at the present, and to buy a constable's staff, to mend the stocks, and to buy a marking iron for the town, and it shall be forthwith gathered by Hugh Griffin, who is appointed by the town to receive rates, and to pay the town's debt.' (Town Book, p. 75.) Feb. 19, 1650, Hugh Griffin "was released from the service of the town." The work that he had performed was "to attend town-meetings, to write town orders, to compare town rates, to gather them in, and pay them according to the towns appointment, and to sweep the meeting-house, for which he is to have fifty shillings for his wages."

Other officers were "commissioners of rates," or "invoice-takers." These corresponded perhaps to "assessors," which term we find used in the town book as early as the beginning of the eighteenth century. The office of marshal was the same as that of constable. There is the statement on page 34 "that there shall be a rate gathered of ten pounds for the finishing of the meeting-house, to be raised upon meadows and improved land, and all manner of cattle above a quarter old to be prized as they were formerly prized, the invoice to be taken by the marshall."

At an early period persons were appointed for the special purpose of hearing "small causes." In 1655 "Lietenant Goodnow, Thomas Noyes, and Sergeant Groute were chosen commissioners to hear, issue, and end small causes in Sudbury, according to law, not exceeding forty shillings." In 1648 Peter Noyes was "to see people ioyne in marriage in Sudbury." (Colonial Records, p. 97.)

In the early times towns could send deputies to the General Court according to the number of their inhabitants. Those that had ten freemen and under twenty, could send one; those having between twenty and forty, not over two. (Palfrey's History.)

We infer that if a person was elected to any town office he was expected to serve. It is stated in the records of 1730 that David Rice was chosen constable, and "being called up [by] the moderator for to declare his exception, or non-exception, upon which David Rice refused for to serve as constable, and paid down five pounds money to s^d town, and so was discharged."

Having considered the nature of the town-meeting, the place where works of a public nature were discussed and decided upon, we will now notice some of the works themselves. First, Highways, the Causeway and Bridge.

HIGHWAYS.

In providing means for easy and rapid transit, it was important for the town to make haste. Indian trails and the paths of wild animals would not long suffice for their practical needs. Hay was to be drawn from the meadows, and for this a road was to be made. Another was to be made to Concord, and paths were to be opened to the outlying lands. The first highway work was done on the principal street, which was doubtless at first but a mere wood path or trail. An early rule for this labor, as it is recorded on the Town Records, Feb. 20, 1639, is as follows: "Ordered by the commissioners of the town, that every inhabitant shall come forth to the mending of the highway upon a summons by the surveyors." In case of failure, five shillings were to be forfeited for every default. The amount of labor required was as follows: —

" 1st. The poorest man shall work one day.

" 2nd. For every six acres of meadow land a man hath he shall work one day.

" 3d. Every man who shall neglect to make all fences appertaining to his fields by the 24th of April shall forfeit five shillings (Nov. 19th, 1639)."

Highways and cart-paths were laid out on both sides of the meadows at an early date. The town records make mention of a highway "from below the upland of the meadow from the house-lot of Walter Haynes to the meadow of John Goodnow, which shall be four rods wide where it is not previously bounded already, and from the meadow of John Goodnow to the end of the town bound." Also of a highway on the west side of the river, "between the upland and the meadow six rods wide from one end of the meadow to the other." These roads, we conjecture, have not entirely disappeared. On either side the meadow margin a hay-road, or "right of way," still exists. It is probable that the town way called "Water Row" may have been a part of those early roads; also, that by the margin of Sand Hill, as it extends southwesterly towards West Brook, and that by the Baldwin place, that starts north of the bridge. An important road laid out in 1648 was that from Watertown to the Dunster Farm, or the "Old Connecticut Path." (See Chapter I.) The record states, "Edmund Rice and Edm⁴ Goodenow, John Bent and John Grout, are appointed to lay out a way from Watertown bound to the Dunster Farm." Another important road laid out in the first decade was that which went to Concord. In 1648 " Edmond Goodenow is desired to treat with Concord men, and to agree with them about the laying out of the way between Concord and Sudbury." The term " laying out," as it was employed at that period, might not always imply the opening of a new path, but perhaps the acceptance or formal recognition of an old one, which hitherto had been only a bridle-way or mere forest foot-trail, that had been used as the most available track to a town, hamlet, or homestead. Tradition informs us that at an early date a way from "The Island" to the east side settlement was by a fording-place, which was by the present " Bridle-Point Bridge; " and that there was a road from " The Island " to Lanham, which passed Heard's Pond

on the north, to the right of the present highway, or between
that and the meadow margin.   By this way hay could be
drawn from the meadow on the south of West Brook, and
the Lanham settlers could pass by it to the Cakebread Mill
and to the home of their minister on Timber Neck.

BRIDGES.

In the work of bridge building Sudbury has had fully its
share from the first.   Its original territory being divided by
a wide, circuitous stream, which was subject to spring and
fall floods, it was a matter of no small importance to the settlers to have a safe crossing.   Ford-ways, on a river like this,
were uncertain means of transit.   Without a bridge the east
and west side inhabitants might be separated sometimes for
weeks, and travelers to the frontier beyond would be much
hindered on their way.   All this the people well knew, and
they were early astir to the work.   Two bridges are mentioned in the town book as early as 1641.   The record of one
is as follows: "It was ordered from the beginning of the
plantation, that there should be two rods wide left in the
meadow from the bridge at Munning's Point to the hard
upland at the head of Edmund Rice's meadow."   The
other record is of the same date, and states that there
was to be a road "between the river meadow and the house-
lot from the bridge at John Blandford's to Bridle Point."
The bridge referred to in the former of these records may
have been the "Old Indian Bridge," which is repeatedly
mentioned in the town book.   From statements on the
records we conclude it crossed the lower part of Lanham
Brook — sometimes also called West Brook — at a point
between Sand Hill and Heard's Pond.   This bridge was
probably found there by the settlers, and may have been
nothing more than a fallen tree where but one person could
pass at a time.   It doubtless was of little use to the settlers,
and may only have served them as a landmark or to designate a fording-place where at low water a person could pass.
The bridge referred to in the latter record was probably the
first one built by the English in Sudbury.   It was doubtless
situated at the locality since occupied by successive bridges,

each of which was known as the "Old Town Bridge." The present one is called the Russell Bridge, after the name of the builder. The location is in Wayland at the east end of the old causeway, near the house of Mr. William Baldwin. The first bridge at this place was probably a simple contrivance for foot-passengers only, and one which would cause little loss if swept away by a flood. The reason why this spot was selected as a crossing, may be indicated by the lay of the land and the course of the river; at this point the stream winds so near the bank of the hard upland, that a causeway on the eastern side is unnecessary. These natural features doubtless led to the construction of the bridge at that particular spot, and the location of the bridge determined the course of the road. About the time of the erection of the first bridge a ferry is spoken of. In 1642 Thomas Noyes was "appointed to keep a ferry for one year, for which he was to have two pence for every single passenger and if there be more to take two apiece." This ferry may have been used only at times when high water rendered the bridge or meadow impassable. As in the price fixed for transportation only "passengers" are mentioned, we infer that both the bridge and ferry were for foot-passengers alone. But a mere foot-path could not long suffice for the settlement. The west side was too important to remain isolated for want of a cart-bridge. About this time it was ordered by the town, "That Mr. Noyes, Mr. Pendleton, Walter Haynes, John Parmenter, Jr., and Thomas King shall have power to view the river at Thomas King's, and to agree with workmen to build a cart-bridge over the river according as they shall see just occasion." The following contract was soon made with Ambrose Leach : —

"BRIDGE CONTRACT 1643.

" It is agreed betweene the inhabitants of the towne of sudbury and Ambrose Leech, That the towne will give unto the said Ambrose 6 acres in Mr Pendleton's 2nd Addition of meadow wch shall run on the north side of his meadow lyinge on the west side of the river & shall run from the river to the upland. Allsoe foure acres of meadowe more wch shall be wth convenient as may be.   Allsoe twenty acres of upland lyinge on the west side of the river on the north side of the lande of Walter Haynes if he approve of it else so much upland where it may be convenient.   For and in considera- tion whereof the said Ambrose doth propose to build a suffi- cient cart bridge over the river three feet above high water mark twelve foot wyde from the one side of the river to the other provided that the towne doe fell and cross cutt the tim- ber and saw all the plank and carry it all to place and when it is ready framed the towne doth promise to help him raise it so that he and one man be at the charge of the sayd Am- brose and he doth promise to acomplish the work by the last day of Aug. next. —— Allsoe the towne doth admitt of him as a townsman wth right to comonage and upland as more shall be laid out and allsoe ten acres of meadowe to be layed out which other meadowe is in first addition of meadowe.

"AMBROSE LEECH   BRIAN PENDLETON
"WALTER HAYNES."

This contract is on the original town book without date. On the preceding page is a record dated 1642, and beyond is one dated 1641, which plainly shows either that events were not recorded chronologically, or that the leaves were not placed in their original order when the book was rebound in 1840.   It may then be safe to conjecture that the date of this contract was 1642 or 1643.   That Mr. Leach carried out his agreement in good faith, is indicated by the privileges that were afterwards accorded to him.   Repeatedly, on the Pro- prietors' book, in the record of their meetings held in after years, are the names of Ambrose Leach and Thomas Cake- bread included in the list of the early grantees, upon whose original rights the Proprietors based their titles to the com- mon lands.   No other names are in the list except those of the early or original grantees; and the presumption is, that they were included on account of some service performed for the town: one perhaps for building a bridge, and the other for building a mill.   The next contract for building a bridge was with Timothy Hawkins of Watertown, and is as fol- lows: —

"The 26th day of November, 16**.

"Agreed between the Inhabitants of Sudbury on the one part, and Timothy Hawkins of Watertown on the other part that the said Timothy shall build a sufficient cart bridge over the river, beginning at the west side of the' river running across the river, five rods long and twelve feet wide, one foot above high water mark, the arches to be . . . foot wide, all but the middle arch which is to be 14 feet wide, the silts — inches square 26 feet long, the posts 16 inches square the cups — — and 16, the braces 8 inches square, the bridge must have a rail on each side, and the rails must be braced at every post, the plank must be two inches thick sawn, there must be 5 braces for the plank, — the bridge the bearers 12 inches square, the bridge is by him to be ready to raise by the last day of May next. For which work the Inhabitants do consent to pay unto the said Timothy for his work so done, the sum of 13 pounds to be paid in corn and cattle, the corn at the general price of the country, and the cattle at the price as two men shall judge them worth.

"The said Timothy is to fell all the timber and saw it, and then the town is to carry it to the place."

The town was also to help raise it. The time of this contract also is uncertain. The record of the date is so mutilated that it is uncertain whether it is 1643 or 1653. On the page preceding are the dates 1652 and 1653. If this contract was made in 1643, then that with Ambrose Leach might have been earlier than has been conjectured, and the bridge built by him may have been destroyed by a flood soon after completion, which caused the erection of another so soon.

In 1645, it was ordered "that £20 should be alowed ye town of Sudbury toward ye building of their bridge and way at ye end of it to be paid y^m when they shall have made ye way passable for loaden horses, so it be done w^thin a twelve month." (Colony Records, Vol. II., p. 102.) The town was also for this reason at one time favored by an abatement of rates, as we are informed by the following record : —

"Whereas it appears to us that Concord, Sudbury and Lancaster are at a greater charge in bridges for the publicque use of the countrye than some other of theire neighbor townes, we conceive it meete that they be abated as followeth; Concord and Lancaster all theire rates, whether payd or to be payd to those two bridges above named, and Sudbury the one half of theire rates to the sayd bridges, and theire abatement to be satisfied to the undertakers of those bridges, or repayed againe to such as have payed as followeth." (Colony Records, Vol. IV., p. 307.)

The bridge built at this spot is said to be the first framed bridge in Middlesex County. The locality is one rich in reminiscences of Sudbury's early History. Over this crossing the Indians were forced, on that memorable day when King Philip attacked the town. At the "Bridge foot" were buried the bodies of the Concord men who were slain on that dismal day. (See period 1675–1700.) It was the bridge of the old stage period. Just beyond, by the "gravel pit," was the beginning of the "Old Lancaster road." Here was the crossing, over which Washington passed when he went through the town. Thus suggestive are the associations that cluster about the spot, and chime in with the natural loveliness that sometimes adorns it. When the meadows grow green in the spring-time as the floods are passing away, and the willows, standing in hedgerows like silent sentinels, send forth their fragrant perfume, here surely is a fit place for reflection, a suitable spot in which to meditate upon things that were long ago.

CAUSEWAY.

Westerly beyond the bridge was built a raised road or causeway, which was sometimes called the "Casey" or "Carsey." This is a memorable piece of highway. Repeatedly has it been raised to place it above the floods. At one time the work was apportioned by lot; and at another the Legislature allowed the town to issue tickets for a grand lottery, the avails of which were to be expended upon this causeway.

Stakes were formerly set as safeguards to the traveler, that he might not stray from the way. In 1653, it is recorded that speedy measures were to be taken to repair the causeway and highways. Just when this causeway was built we have found no record, but we infer that it was begun as early as 1643, since at that time the cart-bridge was made, and about that time the service of Thomas Noyes as ferryman ceased. With the construction of a cart-bridge, the people would naturally construct a cart causeway, since without this a cart-bridge could be of no use for vehicles. The older causeway is that which is a few rods west of the town bridge · further east, and takes a southwesterly course at the parting of the ways.

GRIST-MILL.

Another necessary convenience to the settlers was a grist-mill, or, as they expressed it, "a mill to grind the town's corn." Such a mill was erected in the spring of 1639 by Thomas Cakebread. The following is the record concerning it : " Granted to Thomas Cakebread for and in consideration of building a mill, 40 a. of upland or thereabout now adjoining to the mill, and a little piece of meadow downwards, and a piece of meadow upward, and which may be 16 or 20 a. or thereabout. Also there is given for his accommodation for his estate 30 a. of meadow and 40 a. of upland." (Town Records.)

Mr. Cakebread did not long live to make use of his mill. His widow married Sargent John Grout, who took charge of the property. "In 1643, the cranberry swamp formerly granted to Antient Ensign Cakebread was confirmed to John Grout, and there was granted to Sargent John Grout a swamp lying by the house of Philemon Whale, to pen water for the use of the mill, and of preparing it to remain for the use of the town."

Probably the house of Philemon Whale was not far from the present Concord road, near Wayland Centre, and possibly stood on the old cellar hole at the right of the road, north of the Dana Parmenter house. The bridge at the head of the mill-pond long bore the name of Whale's Bridge. This mill stood on the spot where the present grist-mill stands, near Wayland Centre, and which has been known as Reeves's, Grout's, and, more recently, Wight's mill. Some of the original timber of the Cakebread Mill is supposed to be in the present structure. The stream by which it is run is now small, but in early times it was probably somewhat larger. The dimensions of the mill are larger than formerly, it having been lengthened toward the west.

CHURCH.

The town now being laid out, and the necessary means for securing a livelihood provided, the people turned their attention to ecclesiastical matters. The church was of paramount importance to the early new England inhabitants. For its privileges they had in part embarked for these far-off shores. To preserve its purity they became pilgrims on earth, exiles from friends and their native land. Borne hither with such noble desires, we have evidence that when they arrived they acted in accordance with them. In 1640 a church was organized, which was Congregational in government and Calvinistic in creed or faith. A copy of its covenant is still preserved. The church called to its pastorate Rev. Edmund Brown, and elected Mr. William Brown deacon. It is supposed that the installation of Rev. Edmund Brown was at the time of the formation of the church. The town in selecting Mr. Brown for its minister secured the services of an energetic and devoted man. Edward Johnson says of him, in his " Wonder-Working Providence," " The church in Sudbury called to the office of a pastor the reverend, godly and able minister of the word, Mr. Edmund Brown, whose labors in the doctrine of Christ Jesus hath hitherto abounded, wading through this wilderness work with much cheerfulness of spirit, of whom as followeth : —

" Both night and day Brown ceaseth not to watch
    Christ's little flock in pastures fresh them feed,
The worrying wolves shall not the weak lambs catch;
    Well dost thou mind in wildernesse their breed.
Edmund, thy age is not so great but thou
    Maist yet behold the Beast brought to her fall,
Earth's tottering Kingdome shew her legs gin bow,
    Thou 'mongst Christ's Saints with prayers maist her mawle.

"What signes wouldst have faith's courage for to rouse?
　　See Christ triumphant hath his armies led,
　In Wildernesse prepar'd his lovely Spouse,
　　Caused Kings and Kingdomes his high hand to dread;
Thou seest his churches daily are increasing,
　　And though thyself amongst his worthyes warring,
Hold up thy hands, the battel's now increasing,
　　Christ's Kingdom's ay, it's past all mortall's marring."

The home of Mr. Brown was in the territory of Wayland, by the south bank of Mill Brook, on what was called "Timber Neck." (See map of house-lots, Chapter V.) The house was called in his will "Brunswick," which means "mansion by the stream," and stood near the junction of Mill Brook with the river, a little southeast of Farm Bridge, and nearly opposite the Richard Heard place. Nothing now visible marks the spot, but both record and undisputed tradition give its whereabouts. (For further of Mr. Brown see period 1675–1700.) Mr. Brown's salary the first year was to be £40, one-half to be paid in money, the other half in some or all of these commodities: "Wheate, pees, butter, cheese, porke, beefe, hemp and flax, at every quarters end." In the maintenance of the pastor and church the town acted as in secular matters. The church was for the town; its records were for a time town records. Civil and ecclesiastical matters were connected. If there was no state church, there was a town church, a minister and meeting-house, that was reached by and reached the masses. "Rates" were gathered no more surely for the "king's tax" than to maintain the ministry. To show the manner of raising the money for the minister's salary shortly after his settlement, we insert the following: "The first day of the second month, 1643. It is agreed upon by the town that the Pastor shall [have] for this year, beginning the first day of the first month, thirty pound, to be gathered by rate and to be paid unto him at two several payments, the first payment to be made one month after midsummer, the other payment to be made one month after Michaelmas, for the gathering of which the town hath desired Mr. Pendleton and Walter Hayne to undertake it, and also the town hath discharged the pastor from all rates, for this year, and the rate to be levied according to the rate which was for the —— meeting-house, the invoice being taken by John Freeman." Of the prosperity of this little church, Johnson says, in his "Wonder-Working Providence," "This church hath hitherto, been blessed with blessings of the right hand, even godly peace and unity; they are not above 50 or 60 families and about 80 souls in church fellowship, their Neat head about 300."

MEETING-HOUSE.

A church formed and pastor secured, an early movement was made for a meeting-house.

> "'Mid forests unsubdued
>   The Sabbath dome rose fair,
> And in their rude unsheltered homes
>   Was heard the call — to prayer."
>   SIMES.

The spot selected was at what is now the "Old Burying-ground," in Wayland. The building stood in its westerly part, and a few rods northerly of the Sudbury Centre and Wayland highway. The site is marked by a slight embankment, and by a row of evergreens set by Mr. J. S. Draper. The house was built by John Rutter, and the contract was as follows : —

"February 17th, 1642.

"It is agreed between the townsmen of this town on the one part, and John Rutter on the other part, that the said John Rutter for his part, shall fell, saw, hew and frame a house for a meeting-house thirty foot long, twenty foot wide, eight foot between joint three foot between, stude two cross dorments in the house six clear story windows, two with four lights apiece, and four with three lights apiece, and to ententise between the stude, which frame is to be made ready to raise the first week in May next.

"JOHN RUTTER.

"And the town for their part do covenant to draw all the timber to place, and to help to raise the house being framed and also to pay to the said John Rutter for the said work

six pounds, that is to say, three pound to be paid in corn
at three shillings a bushel, or in money, in and upon this
twenty seventh day, of this present month, and the other
three pounds to be paid in money, corn and cattle to be
prized by two men of the town, one to be chosen by the
town and the other to be chosen by John Rutter, and to be
paid at the time that the frame is by the said John Rutter
finished.

" PETER NOYSE,	WALTER HAYNES,
" BRIAN PENDLETON,	JOHN HOW,
" WILLIAM WARD,	THOMAS WHYTE."

(Town Book, p. 27.)

An act relative to the raising and locating of the building is
the following, dated May, 1643: The town "agreed that the
meeting-house shall stand upon the hillside, before the house-
lot of John Loker, on the other side of the way; also that
every inhabitant that hath a house-lot shall attend [the raising of] the new meeting-house, or send a sufficient man to
help raise the meeting-house." The year after the contract
was made a rate was ordered for the finishing of the house,
to be raised on "meadow and upland and all manner of
cattle above a quarter old, to be prized as they were formerly: Shoates at 6 shillings 8 pence apiece, kids at 4 shillings apiece."

A further record of the meeting-house is as follows: —

"Nov. 5th, 1645.

"It is ordered that all those who are appointed to have
seats in the meeting-house that they shall bring in their first
payment for their seats to Hugh Griffin or agree with him
between this and the 14th day of this month, which is on
Friday next week and those that are (deficient) we do
hereby give power to the Marshall to distrain both for their
payment for their seats and also for the Marshall's own labor
according to a former order twelve pence.

" WALTER HAYNE,	WILLIAM WARDE.
" EDMUND GOODNOW,	JOHN REDDICKE,
" HUGH GRIFFIN."	

Considerable importance was attached in the early times to the seating of people in the meeting-house, and in the records of new houses of worship mention is made of this matter. Respect was had to social condition and circumstance; committees were chosen to adjust these matters in the payment of rates, and references are made in the records of town-meeting to the requests of parties about their seats in the meeting-house. A rule that was general was, that the men should sit at one end of the pew and the women at the other. In the third meeting-house erected in Sudbury it was a part of a plan that the pews should be so arranged as to seat seven men on one side and seven women on the other. In this first meeting-house of Sudbury, the people purchasing seats had a right to dispose of their purchase, in case they should leave the settlement; but the right was reserved by the town of seating the parties who purchased, as is declared by the following record, Jan. 26, 1645: It was " ordered, that all those that pay for seats in the meeting-house shall have leave to sell as many seats as they pay for, provided, they leave the seating of the persons to whom they sell, to the church officers, to seat them if they themselves go out of town." About this first meeting-house a burial place was soon started. No land purchase was made for this purpose until subsequent years (see chapter on Cemeteries), but, after the old English custom, graves were gathered about the church. The services held in the first meeting-house were probably like those held in other houses of the period. There were two sermons on Sunday, with a short intermission at noon. The sermon was usually about an hour in length, and the time of preaching was measured by an hour-glass that was placed in the pulpit. Long prayers, if not in favor, were in use; and the minister prayed for the practical needs of his little flock, detailing in his supplications the wants of the sick, the sorrowful, the sinful, and asking that all things might be sanctified to the soul's spiritual good. Strangers were sometimes asked to exhort or prophesy. Scripture reading, except reading the text, and incidental readings in the course of the sermon, was not known in the early churches. We are informed by Mr. Loring's Diary that the reading of the Scriptures, as a part of the Sabbath service, was introduced into the Sudbury church, without opposition, in 1748. When the Scriptures were read, an exposition was expected; and without this it was called " dumb reading." The church music was of a congregational character, and made use of for worship. There were no useless mummeries of meaningless tunes. Most of the churches for a time after 1640 used " The Bay Psalm Book," which was gotten up by New England ministers, and which was the second hymn book used in British America. It is stated (Palfrey) that, for three-quarters of a century, not more than ten different tunes were used in public worship, among which were " York," " Hackney," " St. Martyns," " Windsor," and " St. Marys." The people were called to meeting by the beating of a drum. In a record, bearing date 1652, is a statement as follows: " It shall be agreed with Edmund Goodenow, that his son shall beat the Drum twice every lecture day, and twice every forenoon, and twice every afternoon upon every Lord's day, to give notice what time to come to meeting; for which the town will give him twenty shillings a year — and to pay him in the town rates." This son of Edmund Goodenow was John, as the records state that, in 1654, " John Goodenow was discharged from the town's engagement for beating the drum to call persons to meeting." A sexton was soon appointed, and it is recorded that, in 1644, John Toll was to " make clean the meetinghouse for one year, and to have for his labor six shillings, eight pence."

CHAPTER VII.

> These are the records, half effaced,
> Which, with the hand of youth, he traced
> On History's page.
> LONGFELLOW.

THE settlers had little more than got fairly located at the plantation, when they began dividing their territory, and apportioning it in parcels to the inhabitants. Before these divisions were made there were no private estates, except such house-lots and few acres as were assigned at the outset for the settler's encouragement or help, or such land tracts as were obtained by special grant from the Colonial Court. But divisions soon came. Piece after piece was apportioned, and passed into private possession. Soon but little of the public domain was left, save small patches at the junction of roads, or some reservation for a school-house, meeting-house or pound, or plot for the village-green.

From common land, which the undivided territory was called, has come the word "common" as applied to a town common, park or public square. And from the division of land by lot, the term "lot" has come into use, as "meadow-lot," "wood-lot," and "house-lot." The early land divisions were made, on permission of the Colonial Court, by such commissioners as the town or court might appoint. As a specimen of these permits, we give the following : —

"A Generall Court, holden at Boston the 4ᵗʰ Day of the 7ᵗʰ month 1639.

" The order of the Court, vpon the petition of the inhabitants of Sudbury, is, that Peter Noyes, Bryan Pendleton, J [John] Parmm ˄ [Parmenter], Edmond B [Brown], Walter Hayne, George Moning, & Edmond Rise have comission to lay out lands to the p'sent inhabitants, according to their estates & persons & that Capt Jeanison, Mʳ Mayhewe, Mʳ Flint, Mʳ Samuel Sheopard, & John Bridge, or auy 3 of them, shall, in convenient time, repaire to the said towne, & set out such land and accomodations, both for house-lots & otherwise, both for Mʳ Pelham & Mʳ Walgrave, as they shall think suitable to their estates, to bee reserved for them if they shall come to inhabite them in convenient time, as the Court shall think [fit]."

But while these divisions were by the permission of the court, the principles of division were largely left to the people themselves ; and in the early New England towns various methods were adopted, in accordance with the plan or compact on which the plantation was formed. In more or less of the towns, the petitioners for a land tract of which a town was to be composed were a company of proprietors which might correspond to a corporation of to-day. They had a moderator, clerk, record book, and committee. The officials of these proprietaries, before a place was incorporated, performed functions to some extent corresponding to those of town officials afterwards. The committees corresponded to the town's selectmen, the clerk to a town clerk, and the proprietors' books to town records. The proprietors' books were not only a record of their proceedings, but served also as a registry of deeds, and were the evidence of land sales, boundaries, etc.

These companies or proprietors could, by majority vote, divide up and dispose of their land in a way subject only to

the terms of the proprietors' compact, to restrictions of the
court, and the common law.   When the plantation by incorporation became a town, the proprietors did not lose their
original territorial rights, but the principle of ownership and
control was the same as before.   If, when the place was a
plantation or proprietary, a person owned certain shares in
the territory by reason of money paid in, or as a reward or
recompense for some service performed, when it became a
town he retained his right to those shares and the rights that
appertained to them : and when the lands were divided those
rights would be allowed.   Hence. whether it were plantation
or town when the division of land was made, though the act
of division was subject to a majority vote, the mode of division was to have reference to the original right of every
grantee.

The town of Sudbury, as a plantation, was formed on
what we consider the proprietary principle.   The persons
that petitioned for the land tract, and those whom they
represented, or, in other words, the original grantees, at
first possessed the whole territory.   In their collective
capacity, they had power to divide up their lands or keep
them as common property ; but when divisions were made,
it must be done in an equitable manner, that is, in proportion
as each had paid in, or in proportion to the value of the original right; or they were to dispose of them in such a way as
was, by general consent, for the common good of the company, as the selling of land to meet public expenses, or the
granting of it as a gratuity to help on the settlement; or the
setting apart of a portion of it for a common pasture.   But
while the town had a right to do any or all of these things,
as a matter of fact it did not at first divide up all of its land,
except the meadows.   These it divided proportionably, as
we have stated, and the meadows being thus divided, became
the basis of future allowance and rights ; in other words, it
is supposed that the settlers put into the enterprise different
amounts of money, and received meadow lands in proportion
to what each put in ; and that, on the basis of the amount of
meadow received, rates were raised for public purposes, and
certain rights were possessed,— as the right of commonage, or

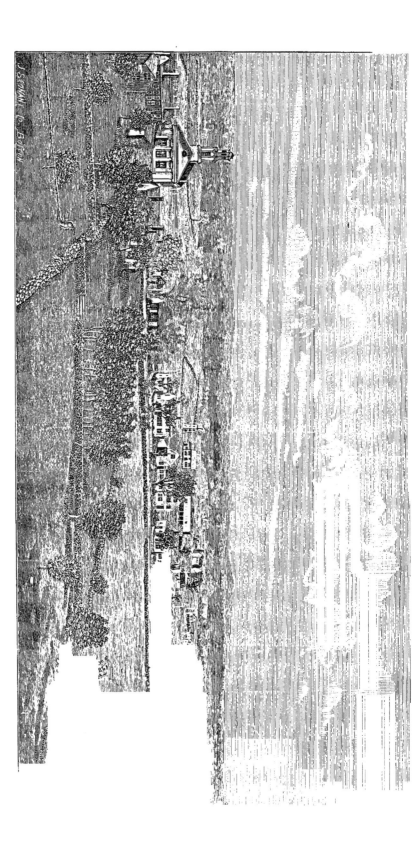

to divisions of uplands. So far as we know, no lands were sold at the outset solely and directly to construct public works, or to pay for a foot of the common territory.

Thus the division of meadow land was an important transaction. It was not only a disposal of common property of the proprietors, but it established a standard of rates, and in a certain sense of valuation. For example, money to pay for land purchased of Karto was to " be gathered according to such quantity of meadow as are granted to the inhabitants of the town." In the division of "uplands," the rule of receiving was according as a person was possessed of " meadow." In the pasturage of the extensive cow common, the people were to be limited in the number of cattle put in by their meadows, or their rates as based upon them.

In the erection of the meeting-house and pay of the minister reference was had to rates paid on the meadows. Perhaps the meadows thus assigned might properly be termed "meadow-rights." As in some places the "acre-right" would procure lands or privileges in proportion to the part paid into the common venture by the proprietor, so in Sudbury the meadow-right might do likewise ; and a person who possessed an original meadow-right might possess a right to subsequent land allotments, or the right of his cattle to commonage, so long as the town had undivided territory. Thus it might be said that the proprietors received values on their investment in the enterprise, not by monied divisions, but by land divisions. Hence, these divisions of land might be called the dividends of those early days, and the money raised by the town on the basis of these early divisions of meadow might be called assessments on the stock made to meet public expenses. We conclude that these meadow-rights or dividends were merchantable, to the extent that a person in selling them might or might not convey the right that belonged to them, as related to commonage and other allotments. The lands that were given by gratulation, for worthiness or work done for the public, might or might not have the privileges of an original meadow-right or dividend. In raising money to pay Karto for the land which the town last bought of him, it was ordered that "all meadow was to pay at one price, and that all meadow given by way of gratulation should have right of commonage."

That the original grantees, and those subsequently given the privileges of such, as a "gratulation" for services performed for the settlers, could transfer the right to subsequent divisions of the common and undivided land, is indicated by the records of the proceedings of the proprietors of these lands many years after the settlement of Sudbury. In the Proprietors' Book of Records, as will be noticed further along, are given repeated lists of the names of the early grantees, even after the most if not all of them had passed away. These lists are referred to as those possessing an original right to the town's undivided land, and may indicate that wherever or whenever one possessed that right as it had been conveyed through the years, in whatever way, that person could claim land when a division was made, or could vote on the disposal of the proprietors' undivided territory.

With this explanation, or setting forth of the principles of division, we are prepared to notice the divisions themselves, which are of two kinds: first, those made as an encouragement and help to the settlement; second, those made on the principle of meadow dividends or meadow rights. The divisions made under the first head were probably two. The first of them was that of house-lots, which, as we have said, comprised only a comparatively small area, perhaps sufficient for a garden or orchard, and a small clearing about the door, and intended as an encouragement to the owner to continue there as a citizen. It is supposed these lots were given in an equable manner, the average being about four or five acres; and when there is much variation from this, it was doubtless to make up for inequality of situation, soil, or some circumstance which called for exception. It mattered not whether married or unmarried, each received a like lot. As a rule, it was expected that those receiving lots should build upon them, as the Colony Records state (Vol I., p 222) that "Mr. Pelham and Walgrave are granted their lots at Sudbury absolutely wth out condition of dwelling there only Mr. Pelham p mised to build a house and settle a family there & to be there as much as he could in the summer time."

It was essential that the plantation should be peopled. The condition of the grant by the Colonial Court was, that there should be settled a certain number of families within a specified time; and, in case of failure, the lands were forfeited. It was an object, then, to encourage settlement by the gift of a lot for a homestead, and so much land as was essential to give the settler a start. Beside this first allotment for homes, at an early period an allotment was made of meadows, which may have also been for encouragement and help. An early rule for the apportionment of meadow, which we think may have been for this purpose, is this:—

"It was ordered and agreed that the meadows of the town of Sudbury shall be laid out and given to the present inhabitants, as much as shall be thought meet according to this rule following.

Imprimis.   To every Mr of a ffamilie 6   akers.
             To every wiffe $6\frac{1}{2}$ akers.
             To every child $1\frac{1}{2}$ akers.
To every mare, cow, ox, or any other cattle that may amount to 20 £ or so much money 3 akers."

We conjecture that lands given by this rule were for encouragement, from the fact that a house-lot of itself would not suffice to give a support, or afford food for the cattle. It was also essential that some meadow should at first be allowed on other than a property basis, as was the case in other divisions. The larger the household and the cattle herd, the more need of much meadow. We have no record to inform us how much meadow was assigned by this rule. By other rules, about a thousand acres, more or less, were divided; and if there were fifteen hundred acres of meadow in the grant which the court allowed, supposing as much was found to exist there, then about five hundred may have been divided in this way. By this rule, the settlers who came on the ship "Confidence" would receive about a hundred acres, allowing a fair amount for their stock.

We come now to consider the second class of divisions referred to, viz.: those of the meadow lands which were to

be as land dividends, or as the basis of assessments for raising
money to meet public expenses, or for the allotment of other
lands. It is supposed that three such divisions of meadow
were made on different occasions, all before the close of the
year 1640. An original record of these divisions has been
given on the town books, but it is now so worn that parts of
it are entirely gone. It is placed early in the first book, and
some one has added to it the date 1638, which is incorrect,
since no divisions were made so soon. In another part of
the first town book (p. 137) is found another list, signed by
John Grout, a subsequent clerk. The list was probably
copied by him from the original, before it became so defaced,
or the lost part may have been restored by him from his personal knowledge, or from some source not now extant. Still
another list is given in the Stearns' Collection, written by
Noah Clapp; and other lists are given in the Proprietors'
Book. We give the first list found in the original town book
so far as it can be read, together with the preamble, and complete the list from the point where the part is wanting by the
list of John Grout: —

"A record of the names of the Inhabitants of Sudbury,
with their several quantity of meadow to every one granted
according to their estates or granted by gratulation for services granted by them, which meadow is ratable upon all
common charges.

Imprimis	The first division.	Second.	Third.	Gratu-lation.
Mr William Pelham	16½	33½	25	
Mr Edmund Brown	16½	33½	25	15
Mr Noyse	16	32	24	
Bryan Pendleton	13½	30½	22	16
Walter Haine	13½	29½	22½	10
John Hayne	2½	5½	4	
John Blandford	1½	4	2¾	
hugh Griffyn	2	3	5½	
Edmond Goodnowe	5	11	8	
Bobert Beast	3½	7½	5½	
Thomas Noyse	4½	10	7¼	
Thomas Browne	7	16	11½	

	The first division.	Second[d].	Third.	Gratulation.
William Browne	$2\frac{1}{2}$	3	$2\frac{3}{4}$	
Robert Darnill	8	17	$12\frac{1}{2}$	5
Thomas Goodnow	2	4	3	
John Freeman	4	8	6	
Solomon Johnson				
william ward	$4\frac{1}{2}$	11	$7\frac{3}{4}$	
Richard Newton	2	4	3	
John Howe	2	4	3	
George Munnings	$3\frac{1}{2}$	7	$5\frac{1}{4}$	10
Anthony whyte	3	$6\frac{1}{2}$	$4\frac{3}{4}$	
Andrew Belcher	4	8	$6\frac{1}{4}$	
John Goodnowe	$2\frac{3}{4}$	9	$5\frac{3}{4}$	
John Reddock	$2\frac{1}{2}$	5	$3\frac{3}{4}$	
Thomas Whyte	5	10	$7\frac{1}{2}$	
John Parmenter Senior	$5\frac{1}{4}$	12	$8\frac{3}{4}$	
Edmond Rice	$9\frac{1}{2}$	19	$14\frac{1}{4}$	
Henry Rice	8		4	
wyddow Buffumthwyte	7	$3\frac{1}{2}$		
Henry Curtis	1	3	2	
John Stone	2	$4\frac{1}{2}$	$4\frac{3}{4}$	
John Parmenter Jun	2	$5\frac{1}{2}$	$3\frac{3}{4}$	
John Rutter				3

The following names are from
the list of John Grout : —

John Toll	5		4	
John Wood	$3\frac{1}{2}$	7	$5\frac{1}{4}$	
Henry Loker	1	$3\frac{1}{2}$	$2\frac{1}{4}$	
John Loker	1	3	2	
Widow Wright	2	4	3	
John Bent	1	14	$10\frac{1}{2}$	4
Nathaniell Treadway	5	10	$7\frac{1}{2}$	
Widow Hunt	1	3	2	10
John Maynard	$1\frac{1}{2}$		$4\frac{1}{4}$	3
Joseph Taintor	$1\frac{1}{2}$	5	$3\frac{3}{4}$	
Richard Fordom				30
Thomas Cakbread				30
Mr. Herbert Pelham				

	The first division	Second.	Third.	Gratulation
Mr. Glover				
Richard Bitlcom (Bildcome)				
Robert Davis				
Henry Prentis	1½	4	2¾	3
Wm Kerly				

Beside the list in this tabulated form, we have a record on the town book of the first two divisions of meadow, together with the reason assigned for the record and for the divisions of land, and also, in some cases, the locations of the lands. This record, which is as follows, we give in the order that is found in the book : —

" It is ordered that all the inhabitants of this town shall have ⅔ of their total meadows laid out this present year, viz.: the first divided according to discretion, and the second by lot, and the quantity of every man's particular sum amounts to the sum following.

" Here followeth a record of the particular quantity of the acres of meadows, which were laid out in the first division unto the inhabitants, as they lie successively upon the great River, with the allowance of such acres which were added to supply for the badness to be a proportionate rule to the inhabitants."

" The 22nd day of February 1639.

" It is ordered and agreed that whereas now the commissioners of Sudbury have a levy to gather some money to pay for the purchase of our plantation, and also other rates for divers occasions, do order that all our rates shall now be gathered according to such quantity of meadows as are granted to the inhabitants of the town according to the rate or fixed propotion, as in pages following, which we have annexed for future reference.

" Impr   To Henry Prentise was laid out 1½ acres being his just quantity is to be rated for, and lieith on the north side of Bridle Point, so called now, and on the other side of the river, and adjoineth to the brook, the end bounded by marked stakes.

	Acres.		Acres.
John Parmenter Junior	2½	John How	2½
Richard Newton	2	and an acre for allowance	
Andrew Belcher	4	Hugh Griffyn	2
Peter Noyse	16	and 1½ acres for allowance	
William Parker	1½	Thomas Whyte	5
Thomas Browne	7	and 3 for allowance	
John Parmenter Senior	5½	Joseph Tayntor	2½
and 2 acres for allowance		1 acre for allowance	
Henry Loker	1½	John Blandford	1½
John Goodnow	4½	¼ acre for allowance	
John Wood	3½	Bryan Pendleton	12½
Robert Hunt	1	1 acre for allowance	
Richard Whyte	2	Edmond Browne	16½
Thomas Goodnow	2	2½ for allowance	
Anthony White	3	George Munnings	3½
John Bent	7	3½ for allowance	
Widow Noyes	2	Walter Haynes	13½
William Browne	1	James Buckmaster	3
The Minister's Meadow		John Freeman	4
Thomas Joslyn	1	Goodman Witherill	2
Edmond Goodnow	5½	Solomon Johnson	3
Thomas Hayne	2½	John Knight	• 16½
John Loker	1	Nathaniell Treadaway	5
Robert Beast	3½	Henry Curtise	1
Robert Darnell	8½	John Stone	2
Thomas Noyse	4½	John Reddicke	2½
John Maynard	1½	William Pellam	16½
and one acre for allowance.			

"Here followeth a record of the particular quantity of the acres of meadow which now laid out in the second division of them unto the inhabitants, as they fall to them by lot.

	Acres.		Acres.
Impr. John How	4	Goodman Witherill	4
Bryan Pendleton	30½	Hugh Griffin	5
The Ministers Meadow		Robert Hunt	3
Nathaniel Treadway	10	Richard Newton	4
James Buckmaster	7	Thomas Flyn	3

	Acres.		Acres.
John Parmenter Senior	12	Robert Darnell	17
John Ruddicke	5	Henry Curtys	3
John Blandford	4	Robert Beast	7½
John Wood	7	John Goodnow	9½
Thomas Haynes	5½	Edmond Goodnow	11½
William Brown	3	8 for allowance	
Richard Whyte		George Munnings	7
Thomas Goodnow	4	4 for allowance	
Andrew Belcher	8½	Anthony Whyte	6½
Widow Noyse	4	Henry Prentise	4
William Pellam	33½	John Parmenter Junior	5½
Thomas Browne	16	William Parker	4
John Stone	4½	Edmund Rice	18½
Henry Loker	3½	Solomon Johnson	7

"Peter Noyse had the moiety of his second addition of meadows, his 16 acres, laid out below next Concord bounds and he has laid out 6 acres more next adjoining unto 20 acres laid out unto Edmond Browne, about and against the Bridle Point. Now in case the said Peter shall be inhibited from the enjoying of the said 16 acres last specified, it shall be lawful for the said Peter to have it laid out upon or in any meadow not laid out to any.

"Edmond Browne is to have 15 acres for his second addition, in part lying about the timber neck on the south side, if he accepteth it, and 20 acres laid out next over bridle point, which 2 acres if he shall not enjoy, or if Mr. Pellam cometh not up he is then to choose where he will have it laid out and upon any meadow that shall be assigned by and of Mr Herbert Pellam

"20th 2 m :

> "EDMOND BROWN,   PETER NOYSE,
> "BRYAN PENDLETON, WALTER HAYNES,
> "EDMUND RICE,   GEORGE MUNNINGS."

Beside the foregoing record of the first two divisions, there is a record, which directly follows, of an "addition" made Nov. 18, 1640, which is this : —

" We whose names are under written being chosen by the town of Sudbury, and part in commission for to assign to the inhabitants of such land as by order was given them which was called the third additions, have affixed unto them as followeth, the eighteenth day of November 1640.

" Granted unto

	Acres.		Acres.
John Knight	55	Joseph Tayntor	7½
Hugh Griffin	20		

These lands lie at gravel pitte.

	Acres.		Acres.
To John Stone	9	John Wood	4
Nathaniel Treadaway	16½	William Ward	8
Henry Curtys	4	John Freeman	13
John Reddicke	9½	Solomon Johnson	11
Edmond Rice	9	John Knight	6
Edmond Goodenough	7½		

Upon the south side of the land last above written.

	Acres.		Acres.
Brian Pendleton	38	Widow Hunt	4½
Walter Haynes and John Haynes	67	John Bent	23
		John Maynard	9
Edmond Goodenough	11	Thomas Jslyn	4½
John Goodenough	9	Andrew Belcher	14
William Kerly	10	Thomas Goodnough	8½
Robert Beast	8	Mr. Noyse	53
Thomas Noyse	17½	William Brown	18
John Waterman	12	Thomas Brown	29
Walter Haynes	22	Anthony Whyte	10½
Bryan Pendleton	18	Thomas Cakbread	44
John Blandford	17	John Parmenter Sr	19½
Edmond Rice	25	Henry Loker	8
John Howe	8	John Goodnough	8
Robert Darnill	18	John Wood	11½
Henry Prentiss	9	Widow Rite	8½
John Parmenter Jn	9	John Loker	6½
Richard Newton	6½		

" Peter Noyse, Bryan Pendleton, Edmond Rice, Walter Haynes, Edmund Goodnough."

Such are some of the larger land divisions recorded in the earlier days of the town, and before the division of the new grant on the west side. Other divisions took place as the years went by. Not only the meadows but the uplands were parcelled out and apportioned, some for public use, some to the early grantees, and some to individuals in return for value or service.

In 1642 an addition of upland was made "in acres according to the 1st and 2ond divisions of meadows granted unto them by the rule of their estate; and Peter Noyes, Bryan Pendleton, George Munnings, Edmund Rice and Edmund Goodenow were to have power to lay out the 3d division at their discretion."

In 1678 John Loker was to have for a house and some land which the town desired of him for the minister, and which was situated just west of the meeting-house, " twenty pounds of money of New England, and also forty acres of land on the west side of the great river of Sudbury, in some place of the common land, that he, the said John Loker, shall choose, near to that called the World's End. Only it is to be on the eastern side of the highway, that there leads from Pantry Bridge to Concord, and lieth also on the north side of the Pantry and Gulf meadows."

Rev. Mr. Sherman, also, about the same time, was to have "six acres of common upland, being on the back side of the town, at the end of Smith field; and also six acres of meadow ground, some where out of the common meadows of this town." He was also to pasture his cattle on the common lands, and have firewood and timber from them.

These records show that a variety and abundance of territory was at the disposal of the town as late as towards the last of the seventeenth century; but years after the town had ceased to apportion undivided lands to the inhabitants,· and the original grantees were all or nearly all dead, there existed a portion of territory owned and controlled by parties who were called in their record book " yᵉ Proprietors of yᵉ Common and undivided land in Sudbury." These proprietors based their claim to this property on the transferred ownership and right of the original grantees. These proprietors met at times far along into the eighteenth century. They kept a record of their meetings, transacted business in an orderly way, and determined matters by majority vote. By their records we learn that they sold and gave away lands, discontinued and laid out highways, and allowed territory to the town for public purposes. About the beginning of the eighteenth century the persons making up this proprietary, as given in their records, are as follows : —

Thomas Frink,	John Allen,
Wm. Jennison,	Jonas Barnard,
Peter Jennison,	Joseph Noyes,
David Haynes,	John Grout,
Peter Haynes,	Jonathan Rice,
Samuel Wright,	John Adams,
Widow Blandford,	John Parmenter,
Jonas Rice,	Elisha Rice,
Caleb Jonson,	Nathaniel Rice,
Samuel Howe,	Samuel Graves,
Attorney for Mr. Ed. Pelham,	Jonathan Grout,
Thomas Reed,	Benjamin Parmenter,
John Smith,	James Reed,
Thomas Godfrey,	John Long,
Joseph Moore,	John Loker,
Benjamin Moore,	John Haynes,
Jonathan Griffin,	Hopestill Bent,
Thomas Brown,	Thomas Brown, Jr.

The names of the proprietors changed as the years passed by. They held their meetings at a private residence, and one house is designated on their records as the place where they convened for years. Their lands were widely scattered throughout the town, and were divided sometimes by lot. When a difference existed that was not settled among themselves, they referred the matter to others. In 1705 a committee, consisting of Edward Goffe, Joseph Noyes and Joseph Sherman, were chosen by the proprietors for the adjustment of matters relating to their division, and the following is the report, Sudbury, March 15, 1705 : —

" We whose names are underwritten being chosen as a committee by the Proprietors of the Common Land in Sudbury to adjust and settle the difference between persons drawing their rights in the division of common land either by rate or by meadow we the subscribers do agree that he that hath right in the common land by his meadow and chooses to draw by his rate our opinion is that every person who hath a right in ye common by virtue of his meadow and chooses to draw by his rate made in the year 1655 that two shillings in s^d rate shall be equal in proportion with ye right of one acre of meadow provided the rate did arise upon their own proper estate.

"EDWARD NOYES, JOSEPH NOYES, JOSEPH SHERMAN."

Thus at an early date was the land tract first assigned by the Colonial Court for the settlement apportioned and set apart for private and public purposes. Little, doubtless, did those early inhabitants conceive of the changed condition that a century would bring forth. Little did they think that their meadow paths would become county roads, and their cow commons the site of thriving villages.

A few specimens of the proprietors' records may serve to show something of the character and doings of " ye Proprietors of ye Common and Undivided lands of Sudbury:" —

" Sudbury, Janary ye 15th 1705.

"Att a meeting of The Proprietors of ye Common and undivided Land In Sudbury Tho Browne was Chosen moderator To Cary on ye work of Sd Day   By a vote of ye Proprietors of The Common and undivided Land in Sudbury Thomas Frink was Chosen and Sworn, at ye above sd meeting, To Perform ye office of a Clark for ye proprietor as above sd.   By Thomas Brown Justes of ye peace.

" Att ye above s^d meeting, voted y^t ye proprietors of ye Common and undivided land In Sudbury will Lay out all or part of Their undivided Lands In Sudbury.   Att ye above sd meeting voted y^t Samuell King ** Graves William Jenison Are Chosen a Commitey to prosecute Those y^t have or Shall

Traspass In falling of wood or timber on our undivided lands."

" Sudbury, febuary 13th 1707–8.

" Upon the Consideration of the Great Strip and waste of ye wood and timber In the Comon or undivided Land In Sudbury, and in an espesiall manner In the Lands called the Cow Comous, for the prevention hereof we the Commetey hereafter named Doe notefy the Proprietors of said Common or undivided Land, to meet at the House of Susanna Blanford on tuesday the 24th of this Instant, feburary at ten of the Clock on said Day, then and there to take sum speedy Care for the prevention thereof, By Laying out said Lands Either part of it or the whole, Either In said Cow Commons or without the Cow commons: or any other Business said Proprietors shall see cause to act or Doe when meet on said Day."

" Sudbury October 24th, 1710 at a meeting of ye Proprietors Of ye Common and undivided Land in Sudbury which meeting was by adjournment from Sept 19 1710 Cap John Goodenow Petitioning to ye Proprietors to buy of Them one acre of land in sudbury on ye west side of The River being ye point of Land between ye road yt Leads to Marlborough Northerly: and to Lanham southerly And Esterly of ye Land of Thomas Brintnall without any violation to Her Majesa Highways on every side."

" Sudbury February 16 $\frac{12}{1713}$ At a meeting of ye Proprietors Of the Common and undivided Land in Sudbury which meeting was by adjorunment from January 12: 1712–13. Said Proprietors by a vote Granted to John Brooks and his wife During Their Natural Lives having a small Hous on the same And is Fenced in : : Shall be and Remaine for Ever for the use of the poor To be ordered and Disposed of by the selectmen of Sudbury for ye use and Benefit of the poor. Likewise said Proprietors Granted yt There should be so much Land Added to this Land as to make ye same seven acres of the Land near or adjoining to ye same —— —— Likewise ye Proprietors Granted that There should be Two Acres of Land added to the Donation of Ensign Peter Noyes to the Town of Sudbury for the use of the poor. The said Two Acres to be Laid out as said David Hayns shall Judge most conveniant Joyning to said Donation. Likewise said Proprietors Granted that There shall be a further Addition to ye above said Donation of Ensign Noyes and Impowered sarj David Hayns to lay out so much Land as he shall think needful for flowing and in larging the mill pond."

"Sudbury May 25th 1713. At a Meeting of ye Proprietors of the Common and undivided Land in Sudbury which Meeting was by Adjournment from March The 23: 1713 The Proprietors Chosen and Impowered The Comitte hereafter Named To view and lay out Two Conveniant Training places or Fields in said Sudbury and on each side ye River where it may Be most Conveniant and the Comitte are to agree with any p^rson or p^rsons y^t owneth ye Land y^t is most Convenient for said Training places if Land may not Conveniently be found for said uses in ye said undivided Land in said Sudbury: the Comitte are Capt Brown Capt Hayns Leiut Frink Leiut Hayns Ens Noyes Ens John Balcom Quart^r Brintnal Quart^r Carter ye Major part of said Comitte are Impowered to act in said affair and to make Return of Their Doings in it to ye Proprietors at their next meeting: Likewise the Proprietors Adjourned their meeting to the 14 Day Septemb 1713 to be at ye hous of Mrs Susanah Blanford in said Sudbury at Twelve of ye clock Noon on said Day."

At a meeting "of ye Proprietors of The Common and undivided Land in Sudbury on June ye 14: 1714 = said Proprietors by a vote Granted y^t the Land Layd out on ye East side of ye River in said Sudbury for a Training Field shall Lye for ye use aforesaid for ever according to ye Plott and return of ye Comitte : : Said Proprietors at said meeting by a vote Adjourned their meeting untill Monday the 28 of this Instant June at Twelve of ye Clock noon of said Day: to be at ye Hous of Mrs Susan^ah Blanford in said Sudbury."

The proprietors, at a meeting on April 5, 1715, "granted by a vote to Ens John Noyes a Liberty To fence in the old burying place but yet ye said Noyes his heirs and assigns are for ever prohibited and hindered from breaking up said burying Place or seting up any building on the same it being kept and reserved for burying ground.

"PETER HAYNS, Moderator."

"Sudbury July 1715: Upon The Desire of John Rice Jun yt he might have a high way from his hous into the Country road To pass to meeting Market & Mill &c: we the Sub-scribers being Apointed by the Proprietors &c for The Squadron have Layd out an Open high way of Two rods wide Beginning at the said Rice Land near his Barn on the south Side To ye road that leads To Framingham, and marked Trees runing from where we began The Cow Comon Land To Ensig^n Jonathan Rices Lot, so runing through that to The South east Corner of Mathew Gibbs his field, and so along by his fence to the road upon Lanham Plain, and the said Jonathan Rice being present Did Agree, Provided the Proprietors would make him Allowance And he would have his Allowances Upon the Gravel Hill by his hous.

"BENJ^MIN MOOR, ⎱ Comitte."
"SAM^LL WRIGHT, ⎰

"Sudbury February 26: 1716: 17: at a meeting of ye Pro-prietors of the Comon and undivided Land in Sudbury by adjournment from December 18: 1716 voted by the Proprie-tors that they will have another Addition as big as their Division first Layd out in the Comon and undivided Land in Sudbury. And that they will draw lots who shall be ye first and so successively till all the Lots are Drawn Pitched and Layd out and if any Proprietor after notice given him by the Surveyor or Chain . . . By ye Comittes order or ye Committe To pitch their Lots Doe neglect or refuse to Doe the same, and not pitch Their Lot or Lots in the space of Twenty four hours after notice given: That then the Comitte shall pitch It and the surveyors shall proceed to the next Lot or Lots every man paying the charge before any Record be made of it."

"The proprietors voted that there shall be a Burying place Layd out on the west side of The River of one acre and a half in ye most Convenient Place: Capt Hayns Mr Peter Hayns Sarj Benj Moors Lt Hayns Corp^l Nathan^el Rice are the Comitte Chosen by the Proprietors to Doe this work.''

"At a meeting of the proprietors held 1717 At the house of Mrs. Susannah Blanford there is the following record of roads granted to be laid out. Highway laid out in the south squadron on yᵉ West Side of The River in Sudbury Aprill 1715 by us the Subscribers A highway from yᵉ Country road To Blandford's pond of four rods wide beginning Between Samˡˡ wrights and Joseph Goodnows and so by Lt Thomas Brintnalls hous and so by Brooksˢ and over green hill and over Pinners wash to yᵉ Said Pond marked as the path now runs and So to be Lye and continue. The said highway to run up to the Thirty rod highway at the new grants This Said highway to be held four rod wide and at Benj wrights land bounded by said Land and by wrights land where it toucheth : : Also a highway out of said Highway into Lancaster Road beginning on yᵉ North end of Green hill so running Down to Noah Claps Land on the nor west corner as the path now goes by the Land of Benj Moor as the path goes to Long meadow brook Between yᵉ land of said Moor from thence as the path goes to the lower end of south meadow into Lancaster road holding four rods wide through ; and marked trees all along : Also a highway from Brooksˢ Hous into the mill path and so over Goodmans Hill as the path goes the Said road to be a bridle road through Lt Thomˢ Brintnells Land by Brooks s for People to pas and repass with horse and team without molestation or interruption with opening and shutting gates after Them : not being allowed to Cutt any wood within said Brintalls Land or fences : and to be an open road then to the end running as the path goes By the Land of Benj Moor unto the Mill Path and to the corner of Thomas Plympton Land and so over Goodmans Hill."

Such are some of "yᵉ Proprietors'" records that have date after 1700. But a few specimens have been selected from the scores of pages contained in their book. As the proprietors held their meetings several times in a year, and met occasionally more than once a month, their records considerably accumulated as time passed by. In the present, we hear little or nothing of "ye Proprietors'" acts; tradition is silent concerning them; but old bridle-ways and cart-paths, that may be marked by fallen or moss-covered walls, were first traced, it may be, by "ye Proprietors'" committee, as they laid out a right-of-way to some ancient meadow lot, or to some wood-land just divided up. Though the farm boy knows little of the lane to the pasture bars, except that the herd pass along it, and the farmer little of the history of his familiar home, yet "ye Proprietors" may have determined the locality of both homestead and lane at a meeting held at Susannah Blanford's, where they were accustomed to meet. The old oak left alone on the hillside, or that midway stands on the plain, may have been "blazed" by strokes of the proprietors' axe, and served as a boundary of some new allotment. Thus, though no chronicler may trace out their ways, nor map off their ancient domain, various farms in the town contain more or less of the many broad acres of "ye Proprietors' Common and undivided lands."

After the divisions of the town land, care was taken to have them duly recorded. This is indicated by the following record from the Town Book: —

"In a public town meeting, warned for the examination of the record of land according to the town grant, which thing was duly performed, all the record both first and last, respecting the town grant to the inhabitants, were published read and approved; and hereupon the town ordered, that any Inhabitant should have liberty to repair to Hugh Griffin our town clerk, who upon their desire, shall within three days space, give them a true copy of the record of such land as they have record of in the town book under his hand which shall be a correct title, they paying the clerk for his service."

It was not only a privilege to have a record of lands preserved, but at an early date it was made compulsory. In 1641 it was ordered that all who had land laid out should bring in a copy of it, that it might be recorded by the twentieth day of September; and, for neglecting to do this, twenty shillings were to be forfeited.

We do not propose to engage in the work of locating each allotment of land; this could not be done in many instances, and, if undertaken, would be liable to mistakes, so often did property change hands in those days. Moreover, the boundary marks that were made use of oftentimes were of a transient or changeable character, which, though familiar to the people of that generation, are now wholly obliterated. For example : —

"Here followeth the line of the new grants with the mark. 1 a black oak 2 a white oak, 3 a black oak 4 a black oak dead 5 a walnut tree, 6 a white oak near Jethro's field, 7 a lone red oak, [8] in a swamp a dead [red] oak, 9 a white ash tree in a run of water, 10 a naked pine tree on rocky hill, 11 a chestnut, 12 a white oak, 13 a white oak, 14 a white oak, 15 is a dead black oak stands at the westerly corner with a heap of stones at the root of the tree.

"JOHN GOODNOW in the name of the rest who went
       last on parambulation."
(Date 1640.)

While the early land divisions were being made, reservations were also made of lands for pasturage, which it was understood were to remain undivided. These lands were called "Cow Commons," and the record of them explains their use. The first was laid out or set apart the 26th of November, 1643, and was on the east side of the river. The record concerning the location is as follows : —

"It is concluded by the town that all the lands southward that lie from the southeast corner of the house-lot of Robert Darnill, unto the common cartbridge going to Edmund Goodnow's meadow, and so upon a strait line to Watertown bound, which lands so granted, for a cow common, shall never be reserved or laid down without the consent of every Inhabitant that hath right in commonage. All the lands we say that are contained within these terms, that is between the houselot of Robert Darnill and the cartbridge before specified, southward within the five miles bound first granted, down to the great river, and bounded on the side

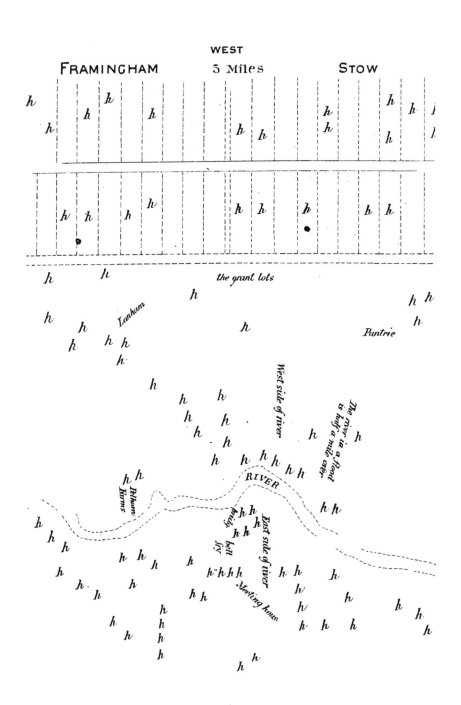

which the extremity of our line bounding Watertown and Sudbury, all our land contained within these terms except all such land as have been granted out in particular, that is to say a neck of upland lying between mill brook and Pine brook, also another neck of land with the flat belonging to it lying between the aforesaid neck and the great river on the other side, also another plat of land that lieth westward from them, containing some 3 or 4 score acres and granted out to particular men.

" The Inhabitants of the town are to be limited and sized, in the putting in of cattle upon the said common in proportion according to the quantity of meadow the said inhabitants are stated in upon the division of the meadow, or shall be instated in by purchase hereafter, provided they buy with the meadow the liberty of commonage alloted to such a quantity of acres as shall be purchased.

" BRYAN PENDLETON,   WALTER HAYNE,

" PETER NOYES,   WILLIAM WARD,

" JOHN WOOD,   THOMAS JSLYN,

" EDMUND GOODNOW,   THOMAS GOODNOW,

" JOHN REDDICKE."

It is somewhat difficult to define the bounds of this cow common exactly from the description given in the records, but the following may be considered its general outline: From Weston bound direct to Wayland centre, thence west of south to the river, and thence again direct to Weston bound.

The cow common on the west side was reserved in 1647, and is thus described in the Town Book: —

" It is ordered by the town that there shall be a cow common laid out on the west side of the river to remain in perpetuity, with all the upland within these bounds, that is to say, all the upland that lies within the bound that goes from Bridle point through Hopp meadow, and so to the west line, in the meadow of Walter Hayne, and all the upland within the gulf and the pantre brook to the uper end of the meadow of Robert Darnill, and from thence to the west line, as it shall be bounded by some men appointed by the town, except it be such lands as are due to men already, and shall be laid out according to the time appointed by the town. Walter Hayne and John Groute are appointed to bound the common, from Goodman Darnill's meadow to the west line."

The territory which was comprised in this common may be outlined, very nearly, by the Massachusetts Central Railroad on the south, the Old Colony Railroad on the west, Pantry Brook on the north, and the river on the east. It will be noticed that these two commons included most of the hilly portions of the town, on both sides of the river; and it was doubtless the design of the settlers to reserve for common pasturage these lands, because less adapted to easy cultivation. But in process of time they ceased to be held in reserve. More or less controversy subsequently arose about what was known as " sizing the commons," and by the early part of the next century they were all divided up and apportioned to the inhabitants ; and now over the broad acres of those ancient public domains are scattered pleasant homesteads and fertile farms, and a large portion of three considerable villages, namely, Sudbury, South Sudbury, and Wayland Centre.

Beside the reservation of territory for common pasturage, lands were laid out "for the use of the ministry." Two such tracts were laid out on each side of the river, consisting of both meadow and upland, which were let out to individuals, the income derived therefrom going towards the minister's salary. The lands that were situated on the west side have passed from public to private possession, being sold in 1817 for $3,200.98.

Various other portions of land were reserved for public use. In 1647 fifty acres of upland about Hop Brook Meadow (South Sudbury), "near the cart-path that goes over the brook," was "to be reserved for the use of the town when they shall set a mill upon it." (See period 1650-75.) Lands situated in various places were assigned for general planting fields. (See Chapter VIII.) A training field was laid out in 1640, consisting of about nine acres, near the present Abel Gleason estate, a portion of it lying southerly of Mr. Gleason's house. And the same year there was reserved in the space enclosed by the first streets, and lying in the direction of Mill Brook or the present Concord and Wayland highway a common pasture "for working oxen."

Besides the reservations thus made, there were small tracts set apart for timber lands or other public purposes. In 1642 three swamps were reserved; "one back of the house [lot] of Walter Haynes, and by a fresh pond;" "another lying under the north side of a hill called Long Hill lying towards Concord;" and "another swamp that butteth against Concord line; also these swamps are reserved in common for the use of the inhabitants."

April 5, 1662, it was "ordered that the town of Sudbury will keep the said one hundred and thirty acres of land which the said Thomas Noyes did lay down at Doescine Hill [Doeskin Hill, Nobscot District] to be a peculiar store of timber for the use of the town. Also voted that no inhabitant of Sudbury whatsoever shall fell any tree or trees whatsoever growing upon the said one hundred and thirty acres at Doescine Hill upon the forfeiture of 19s. a tree." In 1685 the town ordered that there should be "a piece of ten or a dozen acres of the best timber land at or about Goodman's Hill for a reserve for timber for the town's only use."

CHAPTER VIII.

Miscellaneous. — Laws Concerning Domestic Animals, Birds, Wolves, Ammunition and Fire-arms. — Common Planting Fields — Fence Viewers and Fences — Staple Crops. — Meadow Grass; Abundance, Time and Price of Cutting, Measures for Improving. — Mode of Travel. — Staking the Causeway — Climate. — Rain and Snow Fall. — Occasion of Floods. — Breaking Out Roads. — Care of the Poor — Laws for the Prevention of Poverty Enacted by the Town; by the Province. — Town Action for the Encouragement of Industry — Education. — Morality. — Instruction in the Use of Fire-arms. — Tything-men — Stocks — Lecture Day — Fasts — Baptism of Infants. — Laws Relating to Labor. — Payments Often Made in Produce. — Negroes Bought and Sold. — Copy of Bill of Sale. — Schedule of Inhabitants a Century and a Half Ago — Respect Shown by the Use of Titles; by Gratulation; by Seating in the Meeting-House — Careful of Dues. — Precaution Against Fire. — Borrowing Canoes. — Board of the Representatives. — Peculiar Names of Places.

> For the structure that we raise,
> Time is with materials filled:
> Our to-days and yesterdays
> Are the blocks with which we build.
>   LONGFELLOW.

IN early colonial days, and also later in the provincial period, laws were enacted and customs existed that now look curious and quaint. These laws and customs were the result, not only of the characteristic ways of the people, but also of the condition and circumstances of the country and the times. These changed, new rules and practices came into use ; and, as we become accustomed to them, the old look far distant, as if belonging to another race. It is our purpose in the present chapter to relate some of these customs, usages and laws, and also to give an account of some incidental matters that belong not only to this but to subsequent periods. To do this by grouping them in a single chapter will make less of a break in the narrative than to mention them in chronological order as we proceed with this work.

LAWS RELATING TO DOMESTIC ANIMALS.

In 1641 it was ordered that "every one that keeps any hogs more than his own within one fortnight after this day shall rid them out of this town only that for every hog that shall be taken in to be kept by any won more than his own for every week shall pay five shillings." In 1643 it was ordered " that every inhabitant should drive out his hog every morning into the wood, and when they come home at night to see them shut up safe or else if they be about the street to ring and yoke them." In 1648 it was voted in town meeting, " that every swine that shall be found of any man out of his own properity without a sufficient yoke and ring, after the first of March next, the owner thereof shall forfeit for every swine so taken one shilling, and if the swine be yoked and not ringed or ringed and not yoked, then six pence for any swine so taken, beside all the damage done by any such swine." It was also " agreed that all yokes should be under the throat of the swine, and so long as the swine was high and a rope go up on each side to be fastened above, and that swine should not be accounted sufficiently ringed if they could root."

In 1643 it was " ordered by the freemen of the town that all the cattle within this town shall this summer not be turned abroad without a keeper, and the keeper shall not keep any of the herd in any of the great river meadows from Bridle Point downwards towards Concord, the intent of the order to preserve the river meadows." In 1655 it was orderd that " all young new weaned calves shall be herded all the summer time."

It was ordered that "every goat that is taken in any man's garden, orchard or green corn shall be impounded and the owner shall pay for any such goat so taken 3 pence."

In 1754 it was voted " that a fine of two shillings be laid upon the owner of any dog or dogs that should cause and make any disturbance at either of the meeting-houses on the Lord's day, or Sabbath day, one half of the fine was to go to complainant and the other half to the use of the town."

There is a record of a contract made with William Brown and Edmund Goodnow for making a pound. It was to be six feet or six and a half from the ground to the top of the upper rail, the posts a foot square, with seven rails, the upper rail pinned at each end. In 1664 Joseph Noyes was to keep the pound, and to have "four pence for every particular man's cattle every time they are impounded." The only pound, so far as we know, that within a few years belonged to the town of Sudbury, was situated at the northeast corner of the Sudbury Centre old burying-ground.

In 1647 the town mark ordered by "yᵉ General Co'te for Horses to be set upoⁿ one of yᵉ nere yʳtʳˢ" was "**S**udberry." (Colony Records, Vol. II., p. 225.)

LAWS CONCERNING BIRDS.

In 1651 it was ordered by the town "that whoso shall take pains by nets, guns, line or otherwise, to destroy common offensive blackbirds, whether old or young, that for encouragement therein, they shall be paid for every dozen of heads of those birds that are brought to any public town meeting, six pence in the next town rate." The order was to continue five years, and the birds were to be killed in town and by the people of the town. The law for destroying blackbirds as late as 1700 stood thus: " Voted that what Persons of or belonging to Sudbury shall kill any old blackbirds from the 29ᵗʰ March 1700, to the last of May 1700, shall have a penny per hed." In 1654 a person who killed a woodpecker or jay might receive one penny. The same year an inhabitant killing a fox within the town precincts was allowed one shilling six pence.

LAWS CONCERNING WOLVES.

That an order was passed relating to wolves we learn from the following notice of its repeal in 1646: " The order for wolves, that was formerly made by the town was ten shillings for any wolf killed within this town, is repealed."

Whether the bounty was too great, or the wolves had become thinned out, we know not. But, though this order was repealed, an order relating to these animals was passed afterwards. In 1679 "the town granted in addition to the ten shillings which the law gave ten shillings more, upon the presentation of the wolf's head to the town constable." The wolf was to be killed in town, but it was ordered that "all borderers that paid town rates, that killed any wolf upon their own lands tho' not within the town lands, should have the reward." As this order was after King Philip's war, it may be that during its continuance the wolves increased. If some of the more exposed estates were during that period abandoned, the wild animals of the woods might have been left to a freer range than was allowed them for a season before the war. A wolf bounty was granted as late as 1709, when the town allowed "any of yᵉ inhabitants of Sudbury that kills any wolf or wolves above a month old within yᵉ Bound of Sudbury shall have ten shillings allowed him or them."

LAWS CONCERNING AMMUNITION AND FIRE-ARMS.

In 1653, "The town appointed Edmund Goodnow and Hugh Griffin to divide the shot and overplus of bullets to the inhabitants, what was wanting in shot to make up out of the overplus of bullets, and the shot and bullets to be divided to each man his due by proportion according to what every man paid so near as they can."

In 1669, "Edmund Goodnow, John Parmenter, Jr., and John Stone were to see to the barrel of powder, to the trial of it, to the heading it up again, and to take some course for the safe bestowing of it."

The same year the selectmen not only ordered for the providing of a barrel of powder, but a hundred pounds and a half of musket bullets, and a quarter of a hundred of matches. When the third meeting-house was built, it was ordered that there should be in it "a conveniant place for the storing of the ammunition of the town over the window in the southwest gable." About that time the town's stock of ammunition was divided and intrusted to persons who would "engage to respond for the same" in case that it was "not spent in real service in the resistance of the enemy."

The Colonial Court at an early date ordered that "the town's men in every town shall order that ev'y house, or some two or more houses ioyne together for the breeding of salt peetr i' some out house used for poultry or the like." The duty of looking after this matter for Sudbury was assigned to Ensign Cakebread. The saltpetre thus obtained was for the manufacture of gunpowder. In 1645, Sudbury was "freed from yᵉ taking further care about salt peeter houses : : : in answer to their petition."

In 1642 the Court made more stringent the laws previously existing against selling fire-arms to the Indians, exacting a forfeiture of £10 for the sale to them of a gun, and £5 for a pound of powder.

In 1643 the Court ordered "that the military officers in every town shall appoint what arms shall be brought to the meeting-house on the Lord's days, and other times of meeting, and to take orders at farms and houses remote that ammunition bee safely disposed of that an enemy may not possess himself of them."

COMMON PLANTING FIELDS.

In the town's earlier years it was the practice to plant fields in common; and repeatedly in the records are these common fields referred to. These planting places were situated in different parts of the town; between the old North and South street in the neighborhood of the Gleasons, also between Mill Brook and Pine Brook along "the Plain" in the vicinity of the Drapers, and towards the south bound of the town, near the new bridge. In 1642, five general planting fields are spoken of. Various reasons suggest themselves for this planting in common. The "plow lands" that were easily worked were comparatively few as late as 1654, as Johnson states in his "Wonder Working Providence." (See Chap. I.) When there was a large open space of easy cultivation, it was better to make of it one field, that several might share in its benefits. Moreover, these fields required vigilant watching to protect them from marauding beasts and birds;

the several owners of the crops could stand guard by turns, and so many hands make light work ; sometimes, also, it would be necessary to join teams. Besides these general fields, there were also " men's particular fields."

FENCE VIEWERS AND FENCES.

A good degree of attention was early bestowed by the town on its fences. Several surveyors were appointed each year to look after them ; and although the office of " fence viewer " has now gone into disuse, it was once one of considerable responsibility. As early as 1655, " Surveyors were appointed to judge of the sufficiency of the fences about men's particular properties in cases of damage and difference." We read in the records that John Maynard and John Blanford were, a certain year, to attend to the fences " of the field and the cornfield on the other side of the way from the pond to the training place." " Edmund Rice and Thomas Goodenow for all the fences of cornfields from new bridge southward within the town bound."

In 1674, " The work of fence viewing on the west side of the river was assigned to Serjeant : : Haynes, Thomas Reed and Edward Wright. These were appointed surveyors of all the field fences on the west side of the great river of the town and Lanham Penobscott new mill." The persons appointed to view the fences, likewise, had power to enforce their orders. In 1641, " It was ordered that those men who were deputed to look after the fences shall have power to distrain for every rod of fence not lawful, half a bushel of corn, the one-half to him that looks to the fence the other half to the town."

In 1666 the records state that " Persons were appointed surveyors for this year over the fields where Henry Loker dwells, and the field fences, where Solomon Johnson dwelleth." Field fences are mentioned as being on the south side of Pine Brook, also as being between Mill Brook and Pine Brook ; also, " upon the hill from the little pond by the dwelling house of John Blanford unto Mill brook." Several kinds of fences were used. One kind was made by ditching. It was ordered, in 1671, " That all the great river meadows shall be fenced, that is to say that all the proprietors of the great river meadows shall fence the heads or both ends of the meadows, and where it may be necessary, to have a ditch made from the upland to the river at the charge of the squadron that shall lie on both sides of the said ditch according to their benefit." For the upland, also, this mode of fencing was sometimes used. By the roadside, about half way between Wayland Centre and the Plain, are distinct traces of one of these ancient fences.

Hedges were sometimes made use of. Mention is made of fences that were to be made up " of good rails well set three feet and one-half high or otherwise good hedge well staked or such fences as would be an equivelant the fences to be attended to by April 1st if the frost give leave if not then ten days after." After a certain date all the field fences were to be closed, as is indicated by the following : " It is ordered, that all the fences that are in general fields, in this town of Sudbury, shall be shut up by the 10th May or else to forfeit for every rod unfenced five shillings."

STAPLE CROPS.

Some of the staple crops were Indian corn, — sometimes called by the one word " Indian," — rye, barley, wheat, peas and oats. Hemp and flax were also raised.

Hay was early a great staple article ; this, as we have noticed, the river meadows bountifully produced. To such an extent did this crop abound, that the settlers not only kept their own stock, but they received cattle from abroad. (See Chapter I.)

The time for cutting the meadow grass is indicated by such statements as these. When Sergant John Rutter hired the Ashen swamp meadow, " he was to cut the grass by the 10th of July, or else it shall be lawful for any other man to cut the said meadow." He was to pay for it that year 4s. and 6 pence. Such prices as the following are also mentioned : two bushels of wheat and one bushel of Indian corn for Long Meadow. Strawberry Meadow was let out the same year, 1667, for one bushel of wheat ; also the minister's meadow in Sedge Meadow was let out for eight shillings to be paid in

Indian corn; Ashen Swamp Meadow was let out the same year to Ensign John Grout for three shillings, to be paid one-half in wheat, the other in Indian corn. The meadow on the southeast side of the town was let out to Henry Rice for a peck of wheat. These, we think, were probably common meadows of the town, and let out from year to year.

Measures were taken from time to time for improving the meadow lands. In 1645, a commission was granted by the colonial authorities (Colony Records, Vol. II., p. 99) "for yᵉ bttʳ & impvng of yᵉ medowe ground vpon yᵉ ryver running by Concord & Sudberry." Later, also in 1671, a levy of four pence an acre was to be made "upon all the meadow upon the great river for the clearing of the river; that is, from Concord line to the south side, and to Ensign Grout's spring."

MODE OF TRAVEL.

The travel by vehicle in those early times was, for the most part or wholly, by means of the cart, as we infer from the mention of this term in connection with bridges and ways; as where the Court orders that Sudbury should make cartways, and as in a contract for a cart-bridge over the river, and a cart-bridge at Lanham. This was probably a clumsy conveyance, and used for farm work and freight, rather than for passenger travel.

Travelers probably went on horseback or on foot; in early times the pillion was used, by which two could ride on one beast. To keep people from danger in passing over the causeway, stakes were arranged along the roadside, and we read about 1742 of staking the long causeway for a guide. In 1730, the following article is found in a warrant: "To see if the town will take care and order that the fences on the north side of the Long causeway be taken or struck down so as to prevent the snow from drifting thereon."

CLIMATE.

The following records will serve to indicate the character of the climate at that period compared with the present. It was at one time ordered by the town that the fences should be set by the 1st or the 10th of April. In 1642, "it was ordered that no cattle were to be found on the planting fields and all the fences were to be up by March 1st."

Tradition says the snow-fall was formerly greater than at present. If this is so, the fact may be due to the removal of a great quantity of timber. The same cause might also lessen the fall of rain. Greater rain-falls and the retention of moisture in the vast forest tracts may have enlarged the small streams, and rendered them more efficient for mill-power than they are now. The same cause may have made extensive river floods. This may also explain the fact that formerly there were freshets, notwithstanding the absence of dams along the river course.

But if the temperature was ordinarily about the same as it is now, there were seasons of unusual severity.

"In ye year 1667 from ye middle of November until ye middle of March was the tereblest winter for continuance of frost and snow and extremety of cold that ever was remembered by any since it was planted with English; and was attended with terebell coughs and colds and fever which passed many out of time into eternity, and also through want and scarcity of fother multitudes of sheep and cattle and other creatures died. It is a duty incumbent on all those that call themselves the people of God to consider his great works and the operations of his hands.   JOHN GOODNOW *Clerk.*"

"Feb. 7, 1763. There has been no rain this Winter nor sence the snow came, and the springs is low and they grind but two bushels in a day at this mill. the snow is on a leavil 3 foot and 3 inches in open land." (Stearns' Collection.)

With great snow-falls came the necessity of "breaking out the roads." In early times this was done with ox-teams. Most of the farmers had one or more "yokes of oxen" or "steers." Perhaps a dozen of these were attached to a stout ox-sled, and thus the roads were ploughed through. Often a plow was attached to the sled's side, the more effectually to widen the path. Sometimes strips of road were abandoned entirely for the season where the way was unusually blocked.

and the fields used instead. A very merry morning it was for the men and boys when all hands were called out for this work. The train starts out with a single ox-team, but is joined by others as house after house is reached until rein-forcements make a long train.

CARE OF THE POOR.

In 1649, it was ordered that certain persons " have power to speak with Mrs. Hunt, about her person, house [or home] and estate, and to take some care for her relief." The following vote was recorded years afterwards : that " Mrs Hunt shall have fifty shillings, out of a rate to be made this present February 1665, this in respect of her poverty." In 1669 [or 7] Mrs. Hunt was to have fifty shillings pension paid out of the town rate. In 1673, " because of the poverty of her famely, it was ordered that Mr. Peter Noyes do procure and bring sergeon Avery from Dedham to the Widow Hunt of this town to inspect her condition to advise, and direct, and administer to her relief, and cure of her distemper." Ten pounds were also to be put " into the hands of Peter Noyes with all speed to assist Mrs. Hunt with."

About 1663, a contract was made with Thomas Rice to keep a person a year, " if he live as long," for which he was to have five pounds sterling; and if the person kept had any, or much sickness during the year, the town was to give Mr. Rice " satisfaction to content, for any physic, attendance or trouble." In 1663, £7 were added to the present rate, " for the use of Thomas Tfling's sickness, and to pay for intendance of him." In 1664, John White was " exempted from paying his present rate to the town, and also unto the minister." Dr. Loring, in his diary, gives repeated instances of collections taken for the afflicted in the time of his ministry; as, for example, in 1750 : " Lord's day, had a contribution for Thomas Saunders, laboring under a severe and incurable cancer; collected £16-8-0." In 1757 or '59, " had a contribution for our brother, Tristam Cheeny. £31 was gathered." About 1762, October 7th, public Thanksgiving: " A contribution was made for the wife of Asahel Knight of Worcester. £18 was collected."

LAWS FOR THE PREVENTION OF POVERTY.

But, while the people, as shown by such instances, were
generous to the deserving poor, as a town they took stringent measures for the prevention of poverty. This it did,
both by discouraging its importation, and by encouraging
what tended to thrift. In the records we find the following:
"In consideration of the increase of poor people among us,
: : : as also considering how many poor persons from other
towns come in to reside, *Ordered*, That not any one who
owned houses or lands in town should either let or lease any
of them unto any strangers that is not at present a town-
dweller, without leave or license first had and obtained of
the selectmen in a selectmen's meeting or by leave had and
obtained in a general town-meeting or otherwise shall stake-
down, depositate, and bind over a sufficient estate unto the
selectmen of Sudbury, which said estate so bound over unto
the said selectmen, that shall be in their the said selectmen's
judgment sufficient to have and secure the town of Sudbury
harmless from any charge that may so come by the said lands
so leased, and if any person notwithstanding this order shall
lease any houses or lands unto any stranger as above said
without lisence and giving good security as above said, shall
for every week's entertainment of a stranger into his houses
or lands, forfeit the sum of 19 shillings 6 pence to the town
of Sudbury; and any person bringing a stranger presuming
to come as a truant contrary to order as above said, shall for
every week's residence forfeit 19 shillings 6 pence to the
town of Sudbury."

In 1683, Mathew Rice was to be warned to come before
the town clerk, for admitting to some part of his land
Thomas Hedley, who brought his wife and child. Thomas
Hedley was also to be warned to quit the town. Another
person was censured for "taking in and harboring of Christopher Petingal, who is rendered to be a person of a vicious
nature, and evil tongue and behavior, and otherwise discouraging enough." In 1692-3 a law was enacted by the province, by which towns were allowed to warn away strangers.
If the warning was not given within three months, then the

parties so far became residents, that, if in need, they were to receive assistance from the town. If persons warned did not leave within fourteen days, the constable could remove them by law. The town repeatedly made use of this power.

ENCOURAGEMENT OF INDUSTRY.

About 1663 the town voted to grant "Mr. Stearns of Charlestown, ironmonger and blacksmith,' certain meadow lands, and "firewood for his family use, and wood for coals for to do the smithy work." He was also to take timber in the commons "to build his house and shop and fence." A little later Joseph Graves was allowed to take timber to build a house, and part of the land formerly given him to erect a smith shop upon. Also there was granted to Richard Sanger "six acres of meadow, on the west side of the river, upon the condition he stay amongst us to do our smith's work for four years, the time to begin the twenty-fourth day of August, 1646."

EDUCATION.

The following records afford some information concerning early educational advantages in Sudbury. In 1664 "the town promised to give answer at the next meeting whether or no they will accommodate Mr. Walker [with] any lands towards his encouragement to keep a free school in Sudbury." We infer that Mr. Walker was encouraged in his project by the following report on educational matters rendered in 1680 : —

"And as for schools, tho' there be no stated school in this town, for that the inhabitants are so scattered in their dwellings that it cannot well be, yet such is the case that, by having two school dames on each side of the river, that teacheth small children to spell and read, which is so managed by the parents and governors at home, and prosecuted after such sort as that the selectmen who distributed themselves did within three months last past so examine families, children, and youth, both as to good manners, orderly living, chatechizing, and reading, as that they returned from all parts a comfortable good account of all these matters, and render them growing in several families beyond expectation, rarely reprovable anywhere, encouraging in most places, and in others very commendable, so as that the end is accomplished hitherto. And for teaching to write or cypher, here is Mr. Thomas Walker, and two or three others about this town, that do teach therein, and are ready to teach all others that need, if people will come or send them."

From the report rendered the court for the county of Middlesex, in reference to education in morals, we infer that attention was early turned to that matter. In 1655 persons were "appointed for to take pains for to see into the general families in town, to see whether children and servants are employed in work, and educated in the ways of God and in the grounds of religion, according to the order of the General Court." The same year John How was "appointed by the Pastor and Selectmen to see to the restraining from the profanation of the Lord's day in time of public exercise."

The stocks were employed as a means of punishment. In 1651, "John Rutter promised to mend the stocks." They were used as late, at least, as 1722, when it was voted "by ye town to grant five shillings to bye to pad Locks for ye pound and stocks." This old-time appliance was for a period near the meeting-house, as the records state that, in 1681, "Samuel How was to build a new pair of stocks," and was "to set them up before the meeting-house." In subsequent years, tything-men were appointed, and duly sworn before the selectmen, as the law directed. All these agencies were made use of to maintain a wholesome morality. That they succeeded in accomplishing something, the following from the foregoing report of 1680 indicates: "And the selectmen having also been made acquainted that the court expects their inspection touching persons who live from under family government, or after a dissolute or disorderly manner, to the dishonor of God, or corrupting of youth, the selectmen of the town as above having personally searched and enquired into all families and quarters, in and about this town, do return this answer, that they find none such amongst us."

Not only were the youth in colonial days instructed in intellectual and moral things, but also in the use of arms.

In 1645, "it was ordered that the youth from ten to sixteen should be instructed upon ye usual dayes in ye exercise of armes, as small guns, halfe pike, bows and arrows, provided the parent did not object."

It was expected in early times that the children of believing parents would be presented in baptism. These children were usually baptized the Sabbath following their birth, and, if born on Sunday, sometimes on the day of their birth.

Besides the ordinary Sabbath exercises, religious services were held on some secular day of the week, which was called "Lecture Day." A Friday afternoon meeting was held in the Sudbury Orthodox Church until about the beginning of the last quarter century. In 1652, when a bargain was made with John Goodnow to beat the drum twice every Sabbath, he was also to beat it for service on "Lecture Day." (See Chapter VI.) "Training Days" were supposed to be opened and also closed with prayer. Fast days were more frequent than now. In some of the New England towns they were observed at the haying and planting seasons, and at the close of the harvest. Private fasts were sometimes observed. As late as July 4, 1749, there was a fast observed at the Widow Winch's, "on account of one of her daughters having a cancer. Mr. Mudge prayed and Mr. Stone preached." (Extracts from Loring's Diary.) Special seasons of prayer were also sometimes observed. "Apr. 10th, 1757, Lord's day, the church voted that they would spend a part of the last Thursday of every month in extraordinary Prayer to God, on account of the calamitous war with our enemies the French."

LAWS RELATING TO LABOR.

It was ordered "that one shall take for mowing by the acre fourteen pence for every acre, or one and thirty pence a day." It was "ordered that all Carpenters, Bricklayers and thatchers, shall have one and twenty pence for a day's work, and common laborers eighteen pence a day." It was "ordered that a yearly covenanted servant, the best of them, shall take but five pounds for a year's service, and maid servants, the best, shall take but fifty shillings the year's service." As late as 1751, the town voted that "for highway work, eight hours be accounted for a day's work, and two shillings shall be the price of a day's work, one shilling for a yoke of oxen, three pence for a good cart."

Commercial relations were not always carried on by payments in money, but sometimes wholly or in part in produce. Edmund Rice, in 1654, "for service as deputy," was to have "six pounds to be paid in wheat at John Parmenters senior, and so much more as shall pay seven pence a bushell for the carraige of it, to be paid within one week after next Michelmas." For work on the meeting-house, about the year 1688, "he was to have country pay, at country price." The country pay was to be "in good sound merchantable Indian corn, or rye, or wheat, or barley, or malt, or peas, or beef, or pork, or work." At a meeting of the selectmen, Oct. 25, 1678, it was ordered that "Mr. Peter Noyes, Peter Kinge and Thomas Stevens or any of them are appointed to collect of the Inhabitants of this town what may be wanted of the sum granted by any person or persons towards the new college at Cambridge in building according to an order by the Gen C***." This being attended to, the town received its discharge, of which the following is a copy: —

"Discharge. Received then of several persons of the town of Sudbury several parcels of corn amounting to (with the transportation from S. to Cam.) the full sum of what was there subscribed to contribute to the new building for the college.

"I say received by me,   WILLIAM MANNING."

Sometimes payments were promised either in produce or money, as, in 1696, Benjamin Parmenter was to sweep the meeting-house, from April 1 of that year to April 1 of the next year, "for ten bushells of Indian corn, or twenty shillings in money." Whether Mr. Parmenter was to take which he chose, or the party engaging him was to give which they chose, is not stated. Sometimes the produce was rated, or paid for town rates, in accordance with what the produce was rated or paid for in county rates; as, in 1673, it was ordered that "all corn or grain, paid into the towns rate for this year, shall be paid in at such prices as the county rate is paid in at for the year." We conclude that the town had the liberty to establish the value of produce that was to pay the town rates; as, for the year 1686, wheat was rated at five shillings per bushel, peas at four shillings, oats at two shillings, Indian corn at two shillings nine pence.

SERVANTS.

Jan, 9, 1653, "it was determined that the land last granted to the town by the court shall be divided to the inhabitants, according to their several estates and families, counting the family to be husband, wife, children and servants as men have, that they have either bought or brought up." In Mr. Loring's Diary is the following, dated 1758, March 1: "Died Toby, negro servant of Col. Brown."

In Vol. LXXIX., p. 247, State Archives, is a petition from Richard Heard, to the effect that he had a negro man in His Majesty's service; that he was in Captain Nixon's company, and was taken sick in Deerfield on his way home, and remained there sick for a long time; and that he had to take his two horses and go after him. He asks that the court will take his case into consideration; and the committee reported "twenty-five shillings in full to be paid to Col. John Noyes for the use of the Petitioner."

It is stated (Temple's History of Framingham) that in 1733 Thomas Frost of Framingham bought of Jonathan Smith of Sudbury, for sixty pounds current money, a negro man named Gloster, aged about thirty years. Rev. Mr. Swift of Framingham disposed of five slaves by his will, one of whom, named Nero, he gave to his son-in-law, Ebenezer Roby of Sudbury. In 1764, Josiah Richardson of Sudbury sold a negro girl named Phebe to Elizabeth Balch of Framingham, and the following is the bill of sale: —

Know All Men by these Presents, that I, Josiah Richardson Jun. of Sudbury in the county of Middlesex, Gentleman, for and in consideration of the sum of 1 Pound 6 shillings and 8 pence, lawful money, to me in hand well and truly paid at the ensealing hereof by Elizabeth Balch of Framingham Widow, the Receipt whereof I do hereby acknowledge,

and for the consideration thereof, Do Sell to the said Elizabeth Balch
and to her heirs and assigns forever, A Negro female Child named
Phebe, of about two years old, with her wearing apparel she now hath.
And I the said Josiah covenants to and with the said Elisabeth Balch
and her heirs and assigns that the said Negro Child is my slave For
Life, and that I have good right to sell and convey her in manner aforesaid for the term of her natural life; and that by force and virtue hereof
the said Elisabeth Balch shall hold her the said Phebe for a slave for
the term of her natural life. In Witness whereof, I the said Josiah
Richardson Jun., have hereunto set my hand and seal this 13th day of
August 1764.   JOSIAH RICHARDSON, JUN. [Seal.]
     In presence of SAMUEL JONES.

Colored people were sometimes held in high esteem by the
town's people, as is indicated by an entry made in the diary
of Rev. Israel Loring, April 30, 1755, where he speaks thus
of Simeon, a negro who was born and bred in his household,
and a short time before had arrived at the age of freedom:
"April 30th, 1755. This morning Simeon was taken ill of
colic, but soon recovered. May 10th, Simeon died aged 21.
Altho' he partly recovered he grew worse again. He was
greatly beloved by the family and has drowned us in tears.
In the evening we committed the remains of Simeon to the
grave. A great number of the congregation attended the
funeral." Mr. Loring preached a sermon on his death the
Sabbath following, from Psa. lxxxix. 48.

A century and a half ago but few negroes were living in
Sudbury, as is shown by the following statement: —

Number of white people in town, on both
  sides of the river   1,745
Number of negroes, males   .   . 15
Number of negroes, females .   . 12
                                       —
     Total number of blacks   27
(Memoirs of Sudbury.) ·

In early times titles were quite commonly used; and terms
designating military positions, such as "corporal," "captain," "ensign," "sergeant" or "sargeant," are not infre-
quently met with on the town records. The terms "Mr."

and " Mrs." are seldom found, except when applied to the minister and his wife. The term " esquire " is almost unknown. The term "goodman" was in quite common use. It was employed to designate a person of excellent character, rather than one of exceptional gentility. The following is its use in a record of the Town Book dated 1640: " It is ordered by the town that Goodman Hayne shall have the remainder of the meadow which Mr. Brown the Pastor divided up, except one acre that is to be divided between Goodman Knight and Goodman Hayne, if it be there."

But not alone by the application of titles was there a recognition of merit and respect shown where it was due. In 1666, the Town Book states, " We have chosen, constituted and appointed our trusty friends Mr. Joseph Noyes, Sargeant John Grout and Corporal John Rutter to read, issue and determine all matters of difference ensuing about sufficiency of fence." It was customary to "gratulate" sometimes for service done for the public. In a single list in the Town Book are the following persons, who were "gratulated" for some service done by them, and the quantity of land given : —

Brian Pendleton,	14 acres meadow.	
George Munning,	10 " "	10 of upland.
Walter Haynes,	10 " "	10 "
John Parmenter, Sr.,	10 " "	
Edmund Brown,	15 " "	20 of upland.
Peter Noyes,		20 "
John Bent,	4 acres meadow,	6 "
Edmund Goodnow,	6 " "	
William Ward,	12 " "	

Another way of showing respect was in the appointment of seats in the meeting-house. The following rule was made in 1687–8: " The most considerable rule for seating of persons in the meeting-house (the new one) shall be by what they pay to the building thereof, excepting in respect to some considerable persons as to age and other considerable qualifications."

The following records show that the town was not careless in collecting its dues: " November, 1670, " Ordered that Jon. Stanhope do see that the minister's rate be duly paid, and in case any neglect or refuse to pay their proportions to said rates when due, he is appointed and impowered by the town to summons such persons before a magistrate, there to answer for their neglect." In 1683–4 it was voted, " That whereas certain proprietors and inhabitants of the town have neglected to pay their proportions to the minister's rate, and added to the evil by not paying the proportion due upon the two six months' rates made since, to the dishonor of God, contempt of his worship, unrighteousness to their neighbors, as if they : : : slyly intended they should pay their rates for them again, and to the disturbance in and damage of this town, after so much patience used, and to the end this town may not longer be baffled : : : In his majesties name you are therefore now required forthwith to [collect] by distress upon the monies, neat cattle sheep or other beasts, corn, grain, hay, goods or any other estate movable (not disallowed by law) you can find so much of each person herein named so greatly transgressing, the several sum or sums set off against each man's name."

In the early times there were people living on the town's border, who were designated " farmers," and their estates were called "farms." It was probably with reference to these that the following order was passed in 1677–8 : " All persons bordering upon this town and who live and dwell near unto the precinct thereof shall pay (not only to the ministry but also) to all town rates, for that they belong to us, they shall be assessed their due proportions, as all other inhabitants of this town are, and in case of any of them refusing to pay, the same shall be levied by distress."

PRECAUTIONS AGAINST FIRE.

An order was issued whereby every householder was to have a ladder sufficiently long to reach the top of the house. For non-compliance with this act a person was subject to a fine of ten shillings.

BORROWING CANOES.

It was, in 1643, voted by the town " that whosoever : : : shall take away any man's canoe without the leave of the owner shall forfeit for every default so made two shillings."

BOARD OF REPRESENTATIVES.

On page 157 of the records it is recorded that " the sum of three pounds shall be added to the town rate for the payment of our deputie's diet at Hugh Drurys at Boston during his attendance at the Genral Court." Years later, in 1679, Peter Noyes " openly declared at that town-meeting that he freely gave to the town his time, charge, diet, in and about his service at the fore said session of the General Court which the town thankfully accepted."

PAYMENT AND PROTECTION OF PROPERTY.

While the people were busy in the formation of the new plantation and dividing and improving their lands, they were careful to provide means for the payment and protection of them. The records state, May 26, 1648, " Walter Hayne and Hugh Griffin are appointed to go down to the Governor and Magistrate to confirm the bargain of land now bought of Goodman's, and to take course for the payment of Goodmans, and they shall be paid for their labor."

Sept. 11, 1648: " It is agreed upon by the town that the five pound that is paid to Goodemans shall be raised only by the meadows as every man is possessed of."

" It is also agreed that all meadows that are given by way of gratulation shall have right in commonage as the meadows which are first, second, and third division of meadow, and that for the raising of the rate for the payment of the last purchase of Goodman's all meadows shall pay at one price."

MISCELLANEOUS NOTES.

In 1661 the town appointed men " to agree with Robert Proctor of Concord, about his trespass of burning up our pine for making tar." They were to sue him if they could

not agree. In 1671, James Adams was to have liberty to
feed his cattle on Sudbury bounds, and "to take old and dry
wood that shall be upon the ground, the said Adams to prevent any trespass by Concord herds, or cattle, also in our
wood and timber, forth with to give notice to the town."

PECULIAR NAMES OF PLACES.

Peculiar names have been attached to many places in Sudbury, which have been preserved, some by record and some
by usage.

One of these is "Lanham." It is mentioned in connection
with a deed as early as 1666. (See Liber III., pp. 233 and
234, Registry of Deeds, Cambridge.) The deed mentioned a
piece of land "lying and being on the west side of the Ham-
lett called Lanham." (See Chapter III., sketch of Thomas
Read ; also Chapter VI.)

"Lowance" is the name of a stream which enters Mill
Brook between South Sudbury and Lanham bridge. Probably it was first applied to the meadows along its banks. It is
found as early as 1666 (Liber III., p. 233, Registry of Deeds,
Cambridge). It is doubtless a contraction of "allowance,"
which term was used to designate lands that were allowed
the settlers in the territorial divisions. Sometimes an allowance of land was given in one place to make up for deficiency
of quality or quantity in another.

The term "Pantry," applied to one of the school districts,
is found in connection with a land sale in 1657. (Liber III.,
p. 7, Middlesex Registry of Deeds.) In the document referred
to it is used in connection with both the brook and meadow.
This term may have been derived from the words "pine"
and "tree;" and this theory receives favor from the fact
that in the Town Book, page 98, it is spelled "Pantree."

"Finers Wash," or "Pinners Wash," was a term formerly
applied to the brook above South Sudbury, commonly called
"Wash Brook." It occurs repeatedly, both on the Town
Book and the Proprietors' Book. The following record is
taken from the former, dated 1779: "To see if the town will
discontinue a town road laid out through the enclosures of
Ensign Josiah Richardson over the 'Mill Brook' or 'Piners

THE GOODNOW LIBRARY, SO SUDBURY.

See page 28

Wash' from being an open way and leave it a bridle way as formerly." This motion "passed in the negative." The road here referred to is that over Hayden's Bridge. We have found nothing definite by which to determine the origin of this name. We conjecture that this brook passed through a pine district, and that by some connection of the brook with the trees, or with those who may have lived or worked among them, who were perhaps called "Piners," the name may have come into use. "Wash Brook" doubtless came from this term.

"Indian Bridge." This is supposed to have crossed West Brook, as the lower part of Lanham Brook is called, between Sand Hill and Heard's Pond. (See Chapter VI.) The term is repeatedly found in the town records. On page 52 is the statement that Mr. Herbert Pelham was to have " all the land lotts of meadow and upland joining to his farm which lies between the Indian Bridge and the utmost bound of the great pond joining upon a short line from the Indian Bridge to the extremity of the pond, also twenty acres of upland joining to the Indian Bridge to the land granted to Mr. Herbert Pelham, and going thence downward to the hill on the west side the great pond, and west ward joineth to the land of Wm Pelham, and is parted from the west meadow by land reserved for a highway." Jan. 13, 1667, the town appointed a committee "to set a substantial mark where the old Indian Bridge was in West Meadow."

The word "sponge" was in early use as applied to localities. In 1646, "John Rutter was to have a sponge of meadow;" and the following is also a record of early date in which the word is used: "To Brian Pendleton 14 acres of meadow lying in a sponge upon the west side of the great meadow over against Munning's point." This word was formerly used in connection with real estate in New England, but long since ceased to be so used. Says Dr. Green, "It was a local word in England, used in Suffolk, and meant an irregular, narrow projecting part of a field, whether planted or in grass."

The term "Honey Pot Brook" is found. In 1778, Mr. Jonathan Puffer of Stow was released from rates on condi-

tion "that he keep the causeway and bridge over Honey Pot
brook from Stow line to the eastward of said causeway in
good repair for ten years."

The term "Cedar Croft" is spoken of in papers from 1700
to 1725 in connection with the homestead of Thomas Bryant
(Wayland). (State Archives, Vol. XVII., p. 520.) The
same term is found in Liber III., p. 233, date 1666, Middlesex Registry of Deeds, spelled "Cedar Crought."

Another term long and frequently used is " Bridle Point,"
spelled " Bridell Poynt " in a deed dated 1666. (Liber III.,
pp. 232 and 272.) This is a point of land at the southwest
end of Braman's Hill, near the wooden bridge on the new
road from Wayland to Sudbury.

The term " Gulf " is used as early as 1647. " Granted to
the Pastor to lay down his third division in the Gulf." This
term is applied to the meadows that lie along the banks of
the easterly part of Pantry Brook.

" Doeseine Hill " is mentioned in 1661. It probably means
Doeskin Hill. Thomas Noyes had one hundred and thirty
acres of land, the second lot in the new grant near this hill.

The term " Goodman's Wigwam Hill " is found in Book II.,
Town Records ; also the term " Wigwam Hill " is found in
the first part of Book I.

Other terms are "Rocky Plain" (Sudbury Centre) ; "Pine
Plain " (in the Draper neighborhood, east part of Wayland) ;
" World's End " (in the Gulf neighborhood, northeast part
of Sudbury) ; " Haynes' Island " (northeast side of Gulf
Brook) ; " Castle Hills " (north part of Wayland) ; " Spruce
Swamp " or " Cranberry Swamp " (north of the highway, by
Whale's Bridge, Wayland).

The following names are on the Proprietors' Book, and the
places they designate are on the west side : " Lake's End
Hill," " Log Slough," " Lake's End Bridge," " Pine Island,"
" Long Meadow," " Strawberry Meadow," " Mine Way,"
" Mill Field," " Hop Meadow," " Cedar Swamp Plane,"
" Ridge Meadow Brook," " Dunsdale," " Haynes' Slough,"
" Log Hole."

The following are also on the Proprietors' Book : " Hog
House Hill," " Windmill Hill," " Bow Leg Meadow," " Penny

Meadow Brook," "Swath Meadow," "Porringer Hill," "Common Swamp Bridge," "Prospect Hill," "Long Meadow," "Highway from Lake's End to Log Slough," "Path from Log Slew to Pine Island," "Common Meadow Bridge," "Ashen Swamp," "Widow Rice's Plain, "Lake End" or "Lake's End," "Gulf Neck," "Iron Works Meadow," "Walnut Tree Hill," "Bare Hill."

CHAPTER IX.

Sudbury in the Colonization of Other Towns: Framingham, Marlboro, Worcester, Grafton, Rutland.

> His echoing axe the settler swung
>   Amid the sea-like solitude,
> And, rushing, thundering, down were flung
>   The Titans of the wood;
> Loud shrieked the eagle, as he dashed
> From out his mossy nest, which crashed
>   With its supporting bough,
> And the first sunlight, leaping, flashed
>   On the wolf's haunt below.
>   ALFRED B. STREET.

THE settlement of Sudbury in its earlist stages having now been noticed, let us, before considering farther what occurred within the town limits, give our attention to the work of its people in the settlement of other towns. The sons of Sudbury wrought nobly, not only within but without their own borders. A pioneer spirit very early prevailed, and as the town's citizens reached out for new acquisitions of land, they helped establish some of the best towns in the State. In this work of colonization were both hard-

ship and hazard.   Few but such as were of an adventurous
nature would so speedily have removed from newly constructed homesteads to erect other abodes in the farther
forest.   But a brave band of frontiersmen pushed boldly forward and out into the dark outstretching wood ; and, amid
perils of climate, wild beasts, and uncivilized men, they
opened new paths and prepared the way for new settlements.   In narrating the work thus performed, we will to
an extent present an outline of facts as they are afforded by
the histories of the towns in which the work here mentioned
was done.   On the south and west of Sudbury, at the time
of its settlement, was a wilderness.   On the west was what
is now Marlboro, on the south what is Framingham and
Natick, and beyond this border territory was a far outstretching forest awaiting the approach of the English to
give it the light of civilized life.

FRAMINGHAM.

First there was an occupation of the lands on the south.
This territory — so much of it as is now Framingham, and
which was called a plantation by 1675, and was incorporated
as a town in 1700 — was, at the earliest occupation by the
English, unclaimed land of the colony.   It never was granted
to a company of petitioners, as was the case with Sudbury,
but was allowed to individuals at different dates, whose
names became associated with the lands granted.   The following is a list of the prominent grants, and the quantity
of land comprised in some of them : The Stone Grants ; the
Glover Farm, 600 acres ; the Rice Grants ; the Eames Grant,
200 acres ; the Corlett Grant, 200 acres ; the Gookin and
How Purchase ; the Mayhew Farm, 300 acres ; the Danforth
Farms ; Crowne's Grant, 500 acres ; Russell's Grant, 500
acres ; Wayte's Grant, 300 acres ; the Natick Plantation
Grants.   Several of these tracts were either granted, assigned or conveyed to, or in part settled by people from Sudbury.

THE STONE GRANTS. — Mr. Temple, in his "History of
Framingham," says : " The first man to build upon our soil
was John Stone, who removed from Sudbury (now Way-

land), and put up a house at Otter Neck, on the west side of Sudbury River, in 1646 or 1647." The lands owned by Mr. Stone were in several parcels, and granted at different times. In 1643 he had a grant of six acres in "Natick bounds;" and in 1656 he purchased lands of the Indians at the Falls of Sudbury River (Saxonville). This land was situated northwesterly of the falls, and on the southeasterly and easterly slope of the hill. It was confirmed to Mr. Stone by the Court, May, 1656, with fifty acres in addition. The land last granted was laid out May 26, 1658, by Edmund Rice and Thomas Noyes, and is described as "joining to Sudbury river at the falls of the said river, twenty acres of the said fifty being southward joining to the lands of John Stone, which said lands were purchased of the Indians, and after confirmed by the honoured Court; also the other thirty acres of the said fifty lying northward of the aforesaid purchased land and joining to it." Other land tracts were obtained by Mr. Stone in the territory of Framingham, till he possessed several hundred acres. Two of his sons, Daniel and David, settled near their father in 1667.

THE GLOVER FARM. — This was the next grant to be occupied by a Sudbury citizen. (For description, see Chapter IV.) This farm was leased Sept. 29, 1647, by President Dunster, guardian for the Glover heirs, to Edmund Rice for the term of ten years. By agreement in the lease, he was to erect a house on the place. (For dimensions of this house, see Chapter V.) He was also to build a barn, with dimensions as follows: "Fifty long, eleven foote high in the stud, one foote above ground, the sell twenty foote if no leantes or eighteen foote wide with leantes on the one side, and a convenient threshing-floare between the doares." (Barry.) These buildings, it is supposed, were located near Dudley Pond, and on that part of the Glover Farm which, by an adjustment of the town bounds in 1700, came into the town of Wayland. When the Glover estate was settled, the farm became the property of John Glover and Priscilla Appleton, his sister. Subsequently John transferred his part to his sister, and the place became known as the Appleton Farm. In 1697, John Appleton and wife sold the estate, then esti-

mated at about nine hundred and sixty acres, to three Sudbury parties, — namely, Thomas Brown, Thomas Drury, and
Caleb Johnson, — for four hundred and forty pounds. The
land was divided among these purchasers, and with the result
that, after some exchange of the property among themselves,
Mr. Brown had as his part of the upland two hundred acres
on the northerly side, and situated westerly in Framingham
territory; Mr. Drury, two hundred acres on the southerly
side, also in Framingham, and one hundred acres in the
northeasterly part in Wayland; and the land possessed by
Mr. Johnson was the middle portion, and consisted of two
hundred acres of upland, upon which he erected a dwelling,
where the Mars house now stands. Thus, not only was the
Glover Farm first occupied by a Sudbury citizen, but in its
subsequent divisions it became the property of three others.

THE RICE GRANTS. — Not only did Edmund Rice lease
the large land tract just mentioned, but, by petitioning the
General Court, he became owner of the several pieces of land
that are called the " Rice Grants." In 1652 he was allowed
three pieces of meadow, comprising about twenty acres, and
thirty acres of upland, which was situated about a mile from
Cochituate Brook, and in a part of Framingham called Rice's
End. In 1665 he again petitioned the Court, and received
about eighty acres more, which was also in the southeast
part of the town. In 1659, Mr. Rice gave a deed of the
land at Rice's End to his son Henry, who built upon it, and
who, it is supposed, was the second person to build on Framingham soil.

THE EAMES GRANTS. — These grants were of lands obtained from the General Court and the Indian owners by
Thomas Eames, who was a former inhabitant of Sudbury.
In 1669, Mr. Eames built a house and barn on the southerly
slope of Mt. Wayte, South Framingham. The land was of
the Wayte grant, and was owned by Thomas Danforth, who
purchased it of Mr. Richard Wayte. On Feb. 1, 1676, the
Indians burned the buildings of Mr. Eames, and killed or
took captive his family. (See Chapter II. and period 1675–
1700.) As a return for the loss of property then incurred,
which amounted to about three hundred and thirty pounds,

the General Court, in 1677, granted him two hundred acres of land; and by consent of the Court he obtained, in 1676–7, a tract of two hundred acres of the Indians, which was situated near where his former dwelling stood. "The Eames Farm" was situated in the southerly part of Framingham, south of Sudbury River, and ran westerly as far as Farm Pond. The grant of two hundred acres allowed by the Court in 1677 was laid out by John Brigham of Sudbury, in 1686, and is said to have been "land in the wilderness adjoining to Lancaster line."

THE CORLETT GRANT. — This land tract was laid out May 28, 1661, to Mr. Elijah Corlett, a schoolmaster of Cambridge. It was situated "about a mile distant from the southwest angle of the lands formerly granted to Sudbury; also having a parcel of meadow granted to Mr. Edmond Browne, teacher to the church in Sudbury, on the south, also being about half a mile distant northerly from the river which runneth to Sudbury, also being about a mile and a quarter distant west northwesterly of the now dwelling-house of John Stone." In 1661, Mr. Thomas Danforth purchased the land of Mr. Corlett, and the same year transferred it to Mr. John Stone.

THE GOOKIN AND HOW PURCHASE. — This was a land tract that came into possession of Samuel Gookin of Cambridge, a son of Maj.-Gen. Daniel Gookin, who was colonial commissioner to the Indians, and a co-worker with Rev. John Elliot and Samuel How of Sudbury. The tract was obtained of the Indians, who gave a deed of it dated May 19, 1682. A specification in the deed was that it contain, "by estimate, two hundred acres more or less."

THE MAYHEW FARM. — This was a land tract of three hundred acres granted to Thomas Mayhew, Oct. 17, 1643. It is described as "lying between Marlboro, Magunkook and Framingham," and was assigned by will of Thomas Mayhew, bearing date Sept. 15, 1666, to John Stone and Nathaniel Treadaway, both grantees of Sudbury. In 1708 it was laid out to their heirs.

THE DANFORTH FARM. — These lands consisted of several parcels that came to Thomas Danforth by grant or purchase.

One of these was granted in 1660, and contained two hundred and fifty acres, which were laid out adjacent to the south boundary of Sudbury, west of the river, and joining the land occupied by John Stone. Another tract was granted in 1662, and consisted of two hundred acres adjoining the "same land he hath between Conecticot path and Marlborough." The Court appointed to lay out this land "Ensign Noyes of Sudbury with old Goodman Rice and John How," and "the act of any two of these was to be valid both for quantity and quality." This tract was adjacent to and west of the two hundred and fifty acres just mentioned, and extended along the south line of the Lanham District. Other lands were allowed to Mr. Danforth until, by grant or purchase, he owned about two-thirds of the Framingham Plantation. These Danforth lands were from time to time, more or less of them, leased to individuals, and among those leasing them were Samuel Winch and Thomas Frost, who were formerly inhabitants of Sudbury, and both of whom lived at Lanham, — the former as early as 1670, when he purchased land there of Samuel How, and the latter about 1685. The lease to Messrs. Winch and Frost is dated March 25, 1693, and was of land that had been occupied by Mr. Winch on parole lease for several years. The time of the lease was nine hundred and ninety-nine years, and a payment was to be made of four pounds ten shillings per annum. The farm was bounded northerly by "Sudbury line," easterly by the river and Dea. John Stones' land, and southeasterly by "Mr. Danforth's own land," southerly by the "Lynde Farm," westerly by the six hundred acres of reserved land (at Nobscot). The tract comprised three hundred acres, more or less, and contained "all those mesuages and tenements wherein they, the said Samuel Winch and Thomas Frost, do now dwell, containing two dwelling-houses, outhouses, and lands adjoining." This estate was situated in the northerly part of Framingham, and with the Stone Farm probably comprised largely the midway border territory in the northerly part of that town.

Another Sudbury settler who was one of the early occupants of Framingham territory was John Bent, son of Peter

Bent. In 1662 he purchased of Henry Rice a piece of land westerly of Cochituate Brook, and built a house there " near the fordway over that brook on the west side of the ' Old Connecticut Path.' " (Temple.)

Other parties from Sudbury connected with the colonization of Framingham were Josiah Bradish, who it is supposed settled northerly of Nobscot Hill; John Adams, who bought two hundred acres of Gookin and How at Saxonville, and erected a dwelling not far from the location of the present railroad station; Thomas Walker, who bought eighty acres of Gookin and How, and built a house at Rice's End; Samuel King, John Loker, Mathew, David and Benjamin Rice.

Such are some of the facts which set forth the service of Sudbury in the settlement of Framingham. From Nobscot to Cochituate, and from there scattered along southerly into " Natick bounds," the frontier was pioneered by them as they marked out new trails or opened rude forest paths. It is supposed that at the time of Philip's war, the Stones, Rices, Bents, Eameses, and Bradishes were the only English occupants on the Framingham Plantation. John Stone, at the falls of Sudbury River, was one of the nearest neighbors of Thomas Eames at Mt. Wayte; and at his home in the hollow, near the locality of the present railroad station, was the only English hearthstone from which a light gleamed at night, while about Dudley Pond and Cochituate the Rices had their share of solitude in their lone woodland home. Thus the loneliness of the settlers' life was a notable circumstance in the colonization experience of these bold Sudbury frontiersmen. The wild rushing of the water in the circuitous stream at the "falls," the sounds heard in the forest as the tall tree-tops were tossed by the wintry storms, and the wind swept through the dark woody dells, were in strange contrast with the noise of business that now proceeds from that active place.

The settlers who went from Sudbury to the present territory of Framingham were called " Sudbury Out-dwellers," or " Sudbury Farmers." Their ecclesiastical and social relations were for a time with the town of Sudbury, — that is, they were expected to pay rates levied for certain objects the benefit of which they shared. To such an extent were they identified with Sudbury, that it has been supposed by some they were a part of the town. This claim, it is said, was made, among others, by Dr. Stearns. Some things indicate that they were of the town, others that they were not. That they were not of the town is indicated by the following statement made about 1694–5, in a petition to the General Court, " Whereas ourselves and sundry more families, to the number of fifty or upwards, are settled upon the waste lands lying between Sudbury, Natic, Marlbury, and Sherborn, and as yet have not been orderly settled, with a township, but are forced to travell to the nearest of the meeting-houses, some to one and some to another." It is also indicated in a petition to the General Court in 1698 for the appointment of a committee to view lands of which it was desired to make the town of Framingham. The petition was sent in by John Bent and Nathaniel Stone, and the farmers about Cochituate, who set forth that they "had been for a long time united to Sudbury in civil and social rights and privileges." A further indication of no territorial relationship to Sudbury is the following from the Sudbury Records : " Oct. 26, 1686. Agreement between the town of Sudbury and certain out-dwellers, viz., Corp. Henry Rice, Corp. John Bent, Mathew Rice, Benjamin Rice, William Brown, Daniel Stone, John Loker, John Adams, Samuel King, and David Rice, who are inhabitants bordering upon, but dwelling without the line or bounds of this town — have engaged to pay all rates for building the meeting-house, and for the maintenance of the ministry of the town, and for defraying town debts and the support of the poor — provided the town do relieve the poor amongst them and free them from repairing the highways within the town's bounds."

Still another thing that may indicate that there was no territorial relation is a report made at a selectmen's meeting in Sudbury, in 1682. They represent in this report the acres of land given to those dwelling in the town, a list of lands of persons dwelling up and down the country, and a list of men's lands bordering about or near the town. The amount in the latter list is spoken of as amounting to five thousand one hundred and three acres, in which Mr. Danforth's lands (which were in the region now Framingham) and Mr. Gookin's lands are not cast, because the contents were not certain. (See period 1675–1700.) The inference is that considerable land tracts were about Sudbury, largely on the southerly side, on which the town claimed some financial rights, but which were not claimed as territory of the town.

A reason why some may have supposed that these farmers were a part of the town of Sudbury is found in the following answer to a petition sent to the General Court, Mar. 8, 1691-2: "In answer to the petition of the Selectmen of Sudbury, ordered: That the out-dwellers adjoining unto the said Town, comprehended within the line beginning at Matth. Rice's, from thence to Cornet Wᵐ Brown's Corp. Henry Riçe's, Thomas Drury's, Tho. Walker, Jr., John How, and Samuel Winch's (not belonging to any other towne), be annexed unto the Town of Sudbury, and continue to bear their part of all duties and partake of all privileges then as formerly until further order." As to how the order was interpreted by those who had petitioned, may be indicated by a petition sent to the Court July 4, 1700, to which these same farmers attach their signatures: "The said town of Sudbury have for above a year denied your Petitioners the liberty of voting and other town privileges, utterly disclaiming them as not belonging to the said town, though your Petitioners have contributed to the building the meeting-house and maintenance of the minister, and have paid several town rates and done many town duties; wherefore they pray to be annexed to the town of Framingham."

Another statement bearing upon the question is the following from a petition sent to the Court, in 1730, by the inhabitants of Framingham living on the east and south of the river. They state "that they are principally consisting of those Farmers taken from Sudbury and Sherborn and those of Sudbury Farmers with others remote from meeting before the Court had taken emm off from Sudbury and annexed them to Framingham were designing to address the General Court to have been made a separate town : : : : : :

And your petitioners would intimate, that we of Sudbury farmers and Sherborn farmers should never have yielded to be annexed to Framingham had we not expected the meeting house had been fixed in the place where it now is."

MARLBORO.

About the time that the Sudbury settlers were pioneering on the south of their plantation, their attention was turned in a westerly course also. Marlboro, which formerly included Northboro, Southboro, Westboro, and Hudson, was a wilderness country bordering in that direction. Very naturally, as the people began to feel the need of more territory, they sought it thitherward as well as towards the south.

The result was, that, in 1656, the following petition was presented to the General Court : —

"To the Hon. Governor &c assembled in Boston. The humble petition of several of the inhabitants of Sudbury whose names are here underwritten showeth, that whereas your petitioners have lived divers years in Sudbury and God hath been pleased to increase our children which are now divers of them grown to man's estate and we many of us grown into years so that we should be glad to see them settled before the Lord take us away from hence and also God having given us some considerable cattle so that we are so straightened that we cannot so comfortably subsist as could be desired and some of us having taken some pains to view the country we have found a place which lyeth westward about eight miles from Sudbury which we conceive might be comfortable for our subsistance, It is therefore the humble request of your Petitioners to this Hon'd Court that you would bee pleased to grant unto us eight miles square or so much land as may containe to eight miles square for to make a Plantation."

This petition was signed by the following parties : "Edmund Rice, Wm Ward, Thomas King, John Wood, Thomas Goodnow, John Ruddock, Henry Rice, John How, John Bent Senr, John Maynard, Richard Newton, Peter Bent, Edward Rice."

Answer was given to this petition at a General Court session held in Boston, May 14, 1656, to the effect that a tract of land six miles square be granted, provided it hinder no prior grant, and that a town be settled thereon with twenty or more families within three years time, so that an able ministry might there be sustained. A committee was appointed to lay out the bounds, and make report to the " Court of Election." Unless they did this, the grant would be void. A portion of the territory desired had previously been granted to the Indians, on petition of Rev. John Elliot, but a committee was appointed who amicably adjusted the matter, so that each party had their lands laid out and duly confirmed. The plantation of the Indians was known as Ockoocangansett, and was partly surrounded by the plantation of the English, which for a brief period was called Whipsuppenicke. A plan of the latter was made in 1667, and approved by the authorities the same year. It contained 29,419 acres, which, with the 6,000 acres which had been reserved for the Indians, made 35,419 acres.

The first proprietors' meeting was held Sept. 25, 1656, and the same year William Ward, Thomas King, John Ruddock, and John How were " chosen to put the Affairs of the said new Plantation in an orderly way." A petition for incorporation was soon sent to the General Court, and, being favorably received, in 1660 the place ceased to be merely a plantation legally connected with Sudbury, but became a town of itself, and was called " Marlborrow."

The places where some of the Sudbury settlers early had their abodes in Marlboro are still known, and some of them have been designated in the history of the town. Such places furnish food for reflection to the thoughtful mind, and not the least so, perhaps, to the people of the town from whence the early occupants of those dwellings went forth. May the sites of those primitive dwelling-places, on which the roof-tree long since decayed, continue to be pointed out, and suggest the spirit of enterprise that inspired that little company who went forth from Sudbury in search of new lands!

WORCESTER.

But Sudbury helped settle towns still farther westward. Beyond Marlboro were the lands of what is now the city of Worcester, then a wilderness across the frontier. To this spot repaired some of the people of Sudbury. Among these was Lieutenant Curtis, the sturdy backwoodsman of whose service in the war with King Philip we are yet to speak. (See period 1675–1700.) Ephraim Curtis was a son of Henry Curtis, an original grantee of Sudbury. He was of a sturdy, adventuresome nature, a frontiersman, soldier and scout. The customs of the red men, the resort of wild game, the camp-fire and the night ambuscade, were all familiar to him. A short time before the outbreak of King Philip's war Lieut. Ephraim Curtis turned his face towards the west, and made his camp at what is now Worcester. We quote the following conconcerning his subsequent experience in that locality: " It was in the fall of 1673, as near as can now be ascertained by tradition and otherwise, that Ephraim Curtis, the first actual white settler, left Sudbury, with a pack on his back, a long, light Spanish gun on his shoulder, and an axe in in his hand, and set his face towards Worcester; arriving, after two days' travel, on the very spot still owned and occupied by his descendants, on Lincoln Street, to the sixth generation. The principal reason for his selecting this locality to settle upon was the supposition of mineral wealth in the soil, from the report of a valuable lead mine having been discovered in the vicinity by the Indians, who had a sort of rendezvous on Wigwam Hill while on their fishing and hunting excursions. Here Ephraim Curtis was all alone in the wilderness for a year or more, and in subsequent times used to tell how, after working all day, he would sit down and look towards Sudbury, and shed tears in spite of himself. But he had a will that bore him through. For a time he claimed the whole town of Worcester, but had to be content with two hundred acres near the upper part of Plantation Street, and another plantation near Grafton Gore, granted by the Great and General Court as his share of the territory of Worcester. Curtis and others (who had followed him) stayed in Worcester until driven from there by the Indians in 1675. He left the spot which he attempted to settle to his descendants, with no other personal memorials, it is said, than his gun and silver-headed cane marked 'E. C.' In his later life he returned to Sudbury, where he died at the age of ninety-two. He left Worcester plantation to the care of his son John, and in 1734 he conveyed two hundred and fifty acres, on the border of Worcester, Auburn, and Millbury, to his son Ephraim Curtis, Jr." (Fall's "Reminiscences of Worcester.")

> The violet sprung at Spring's first tinge,
>   The rose of Summer spread its glow,
> The maize hung out its autumn fringe,
>   Rude Winter brought his snow;
> And still the lone one labored there,
> His shout and whistle broke the air,
>   As cheerily he plied
> His garden spade, or drove his share
>   Along the hillock's side.
>   ALFRED B. STREET.

But the pioneer work done by Sudbury in the settlement of Worcester was by no means confined to one man. In 1657 thirty-two hundred acres were granted to Increase Nowell of Charlestown. His right was purchased by Josiah and John Haynes, Thomas Noyes, and Nathaniel Treadaway; and in 1664 they became proprietors of a large tract east of Quinsigamond Pond. Haynes, Treadaway, and Noyes petitioned the General Court for a committee "to view the country." The death of Mr. Noyes, and the disturbed condition of things, prevented the commissioners whom the Court appointed from carrying out the order. But, in 1667, the Court again took measures towards a settlement of the country, and appointed a committee, who state in their report that "about five thousand acres is laid out to particular persons, and confirmed by this Court, as we are informed, which falls within this tract of land, viz., to Ensign Noyes, deceased, his brother three thousand two hundred acres, unto the church at Malden one thousand acres, and others five hundred acres bought of Ensign

Noyes; but all this notwithstanding, we conceive there may be enough meadow for a small plantation or town of about thirty families, and if these farms be annexed to it, it may supply about sixty families." The committee recommended to the Court that it "reserve it for a town;" and, for the settling of it, it advised "that there be a meet proportion of land granted and laid out for a town, in the best form the place will bear, about the contents of eight miles square." (Colonial Records, Vol. IV., p. 587.)

Another Sudbury citizen who assisted in the settlement of Worcester was Digory Sargent. So much of interest clusters about the character and experience of this adventurous man, that we will quote entire the account of him as given in Lincoln's "History of Worcester:" "Among those who attempted the settlement of Worcester, after the first unsuccesful enterprise, was Digory Sargent, who had built his home on Sagatabscot Hill, southeastward of the present town. He was a native of Sudbury, and had been a carpenter by occupation before his removal. A will made by him in 1679 is preserved on the Middlesex records. As the list of goods and effects, strangely mingled together, presents an example of the humble personal possessions of pioneer times, and the style affords specimen of quaint peculiarity, it will not be uninteresting.

"'DIGORY SARGENT'S WILL.

"'March the 17th day 1696. The last Will and Testament of Digory Sargent. I, Digory Sargent, being in my health and strength and in my perfect memory, blessed be the Lord for it; these few lines may satisfy whom it may concern, that I, Digory Sargent, do freely give unto my daughter, Martha Sargent, my house and land with all its rights and privileges there unto belonging: this house and four score acre lot of land lieth within the township of Worcester; I likewise do give unto her all my goods; one flock bed and boulster, with one rugg, and two blankets and two coverlets; six froes; one broad ax and one pulling ax and one hand saw; one frying pan; one shave; one drawing knife; one trunk and a sermon book that is at Mrs. Mary Mason's Widow, at Boston; with one pewter pint pot; one washing tub; one cow and calf; one [—]; three iron wedges; two butte rings; and if in case the Lord should see good to take away the said Digory Serjent by death, then I, the said Digory Serjent, do leave these things above written unto George Parmenter of Sudbury to be disposed of as he shall see good to bring up the said Digory Serjent's child; and if in case that this child should die likewise, then I do freely give my house and land with all the goods above mentioned unto George Parmenter forever, and to his heirs, to look after these things and to dispose of them as he shall see cause. In witness whereof I have hereunto set my hand and seal the day and year above named. There is one gun too.

"'DIGORY SERJENT.
"'Witnessed by John Keyes, John Wetherby.'

"Having afterwards been married to the sister of Parmenter, his family became more numerous, and afforded more victims to be involved in the miseries of death and captivity. Long after the other planters had fled from the perils of the conflict that raged around them, Sargent remained with his children, the solitary occupants of the town, resisting all importunity to seek safety by desertion, and resolving with fearless intrepidity to defend from the savage the fields his industry had redeemed from the waste. During the summer of 1702 his residence was unmolested. As winter approached the committee, alarmed by his situation on the frontier of danger, sent messengers to advise his removal to a place of security. As their admonitions were disregarded, they at length despatched an armed force of twelve men, under Captain Howe, to compel compliance with the order. At the close of day the party arrived at a garrison near the mills. Here they halted for the night, which grew dark with storm and snow, and, kindling their fires, laid down to rest, while one of the band watched the slumbers of his comrades. In the morning they went onwards, and reached the house of Sargent, on Sagatabscot, at the distance of nearly two miles from the post where they had halted. They found the door broken down, the owner stretched in blood on the floor, and the dwelling desolate. The prints of many moccasins lead-

ing westward, still visible through the snow, indicated that
they had been anticipated by a short time only in the object
of their mission. It was soon found that the children of
Sargent were living in Canada. On the release of the eldest
she related the particulars of the fearful catastrophe they had
witnessed. When the Indians, headed by Sagamon John,
as it is said, surrounded the house, Sargent seized his gun to
defend his life, and was fired on. As he retreated to the
stairway, a ball took effect and he fell. The savages rushed
in, with their tomahawks completed the work of death, and
tore off his scalp from his head as a token of victory. They
seized the mother and her children, John, Daniel, Thomas,
Martha, and Mary, and, having discovered the neighborhood
of the white men, commenced a rapid retreat westward.
The wife of Sargent, fainting with grief and fear, and in
feeble circumstances, faltered, and impeded their progress.
The apprehension of pursuit induced the Indian to forego
[. . . . .] torturing his victim. As they ascended the
hills of Tataesset, a chief stepped out from the file, and,
looking around among the leafless forests as if for game,
excited no alarm in the exhausted and sinking captive, and
awoke no cry of horror to betray their course. When she
had passed by, one merciful blow from the strong arm of the
sachem removed the obstruction of their flight. The children they carried away reached the northern frontier in
safety, and were a long time in Canada. Daniel and Mary,
preferring the wild freedom of their captors to the restraints
of civilized life, adopted the habits and manners of the Indians. They never again resided with their relatives, although
they once made them a visit when Miss Williams, taken at
Deerfield, was restored. In 1715, Thomas was in Boston.
John had been liberated in 1721. Martha was probably
redeemed earlier than her brothers, married Daniel Shattuck,
and returned to dwell on the spot so fatal to her family."
(Lincoln's "History of Worcester.")

Another inhabitant of Sudbury who went to Worcester, in
the third attempt to settle that town, was Nathaniel Moore.
He was one of the most prominent citizens of that place during the first half century, and was for twelve years one of its

selectmen. Mr. Moore was one of the first two deacons of the Old South Church, an ancestor of Dr. Moore, and formerly president of Williams and the first president of Amherst College. Still another who went from the town was Capt. Moses Rice. He went to Worcester about 1719, and built a tavern there. Captain Rice was commander of a cavalry company, and fought in several engagements with the Indians. He went to Rutland about 1742, where he was killed by the Indians in 1755, aged sixty. Others who went there were Thomas Brown, Benjamin Crane, John Curtis, Simon Meyling, Jonathan Grout, — all of whom received lands in that vicinity.

GRAFTON.

Another place in whose settlement Sudbury citizens had some share was Grafton, a town in Worcester County. Its Indian name was Hassanamesit, which means a place of small stones. The land, which contained seven thousand five hundred acres, was purchased of the native proprietors, upon leases obtained of the General Court, May, 1724. The petition, asking the privilege of making the purchase, was presented by a number of persons, principally from Marlboro, Sudbury, Concord, and Stow; and the petitioners sought leave "to purchase of the Hassanamisco Indians land at that place." In the Indian deed concerning the territory, among other specific declarations is the following : " To Jonathan Rice and Richard Taylor both of Sudbury in the County of Middlesex aforesaid husbandmen each one fortieth part thereof . . . to them and their respective heirs and assigns forever." After the purchase of the territory, and the establishment of the plantation, those who composed the company laying claim to the territory held proprietors' meetings, more or less of which were at the house of Jonathan Rice in Sudbury. Their records and proceedings show the prominent part taken by Sudbury citizens in the formation of the township. A few specimens of these records are as follows: "At a meeting of the Proprietors of the common and undivided lands in Hassanamisco holden at the house of

Jonathan How in Marlboro, April, 1728, Mr. Jonathan Rice was chosen clerk for the Proprietors to enter and record all votes and orders from time to time as shall be made and passed in said Proprietors meetings." "July 9, 1728. The Proprietors held a meeting at Sudbury, at the house of Jonathan Rice, and chose a committee to take charge of building a meeting house." "Jan. 6, 1730. At the house of Jonathan Rice, voted to lay out 3 acres to each Proprietor 30 acres of land for the third division; voted to raise seven pounds of money on each Proprietor for the finishing of the meeting house and school house."

In the appointment of committees for important business Sudbury was creditably represented. The committee chosen "to take a survey of the plantation of Hassanamisco, and find out and stake the centre plot of the plantation," were Captain Brigham of Marlboro, John Hunt of Concord, and Richard Taylor of Sudbury. Jan. 16, 1734, it was voted that Col. John Chandler of Concord and Jonathan Rice of Sudbury should be "a committee to make Hassanamisco a town." Thus, at Sudbury and by her citizens, were more or less of the plans laid and business transacted at the beginning of this thriving town.

RUTLAND.

Another town, in the settlement of which Sudbury was early and creditably represented, is Rutland, Mass. This town was incorporated by the General Court at a session of 1722. The territory, however, which included the portion incorporated at this time, and which was six miles square, was some years before this explored by daring pioneers, and embraced, in its full extent, a tract twelve miles square, and took in a part or the whole of the territory of what is now Hubbardston, Princeton, Holden, Oakham, Paxton, and Barre. The original territory in these latter-named limits was purchased, for twenty-three pounds, of Puagastion of Pennicook, Pompamamay of Natick, Wananapan of Wamassick, Sassawannow of Natick, and other natives, on Dec. 22, 1686. The name of the whole place was Naquag, and the deed of it, signed and acknowledged by the above-named Indians, was received April 14, 1714, and is on record at the Middlesex Registry of Deeds, page 511 of Book XVI.

The ownership of this twelve-mile land tract was confirmed by the General Court in 1713, on petition of the heirs of Maj. Simon Willard, of Indian war fame, and others whose names were in the associate deed. One condition imposed by the Court in the confirmation of ownership was, that, within seven years, there be sixty families settled there, and a reservation of land for church and school purposes. On Dec. 14, 1715, the proprietors, at a meeting in Boston, decided that a tract of six miles square of the original twelve miles should be surveyed and set apart for the settlement of sixty-two families, in order to keep the conditions by which the grant was to be allowed. It decided to grant to Capt. Benjamin Willard, for certain considerations, one of which was that he build a mill, "one-third part of a thirty-third part of said township, or nine hundred and thirty acres." A portion of this large grant to Captain Willard passed into the hands of several prominent Sudbury citizens, who were assignees to Captain Willard. Three of them were Rev. Israel Loring, Capt. Samuel Stone, and Capt. Samuel Wright. The land thus assigned went to the parties as follows: To Mr. Loring, three hundred acres; to Captain Stone, two hundred and forty acres; and to Captain Wright, one hundred and twenty acres.

So much of the land of the twelve miles square as amounted to six miles square having now been confirmed to the claimants, and surveyed, and positions assigned for settlement, on petition to the General Court, at a session beginning May 30, 1722, an act of incorporation was passed, making of this territory the town of Rutland. The place thus being in readiness for settlement, and quite a portion of it being in the hands of Sudbury citizens, and a leader in the enterprise, Captain Wright, being a Sudbury man who, for years before Rutland was incorporated, was a manager in its affairs, it is no wonder that emigration flowed from the town into this new country. It was as the great West to a place as near the seaboard settlements as Sudbury; and the romance and adventure of pioneer life very likely took hold of the inhabitants, as the same spirit led their ancestors to seek homes about the borders of Sudbury River about a century before. Accordingly, as might be expected, we find an early exodus from the town to the place; and among the names of parties who found homes in Rutland, or in the towns of the original twelve miles square, we find the following, which now are, or have been, familiar in Sudbury: Newton, Moore, Howe, Knight, Ward, Brown, Hunt, Bent, Stevens, Wright, Read, Dakin, Goodenow, Rice, Brintnal, Haynes, Stone, Parmenter, Estabrook, Clapp, Walker, Maynard.

Other towns about Sudbury that were represented in the settlement of this place were Marlboro, Concord, and Framingham, besides some from Boston, Lexington, Lancaster, and Brookfield, and some emigrants from Ireland.

But it is not simply the matter of names and numbers of parties from the town that makes it important and interesting to mention the part taken by Sudbury in the settlement of Rutland, but the prominence of several of them. More or less were leaders in the enterprise, and active and influential in shaping the young town's life. As showing their character, we will give a short sketch of some of them.

Among the most valuable men of the place was Capt. Samuel Wright, who came from the West Parish in Sudbury, and was proprietor of lot No. 1 in the first apportionment of Rutland territory. Captain Wright was the first deacon of the church there, justice of the peace, captain of the militia, and for years held various other town offices. He was clerk and one of the proprietors of the twelve-miles-square land tract. It was at a meeting at his house that land divisions of the town were confirmed, June 26, 1721. He was the first moderator, town clerk, and selectman chosen after Rutland became incorporated. Captain Wright kept a tavern for some time opposite the first meeting-house, at which place much of the business of the town was transacted. He was prominent in defending the town against the incursions of the Indians, who assailed it savagely in its early history; and in this defense he was reinforced by soldiers from Sudbury. Captain Wright was the sixth son of

Edward Wright, who is supposed to have been a son of one of Sudbury's early inhabitants or grantees. He was born April 9, 1670. He married Mary Stevens, a daughter of Cyprian Stevens, whose wife was Mary Willard, daughter of Major Simon Willard of Lancaster, and of his third wife, Mary Dunster, who was a relative of Mr. Dunster, president of Harvard College. Captain Wright was by this marriage one of the heirs to the large land tract originally assigned as the Rutland territory, which, as we have mentioned, was, in 1713, confirmed as to ownership, on petition of the sons and grandsons of Major Simon Willard; and his daughter Mary's name was among the other heirs in the associate deed. He was also by this marriage with Mary made brother-in-law of Deacon Joseph Stevens, another early and prominent citizen of Rutland, who was the father of Capt. Phineas Stevens, the settler of whom we shall next speak in this sketch. Mr. Wright had several children, one of whom married Rev. Thomas Frink, the first settled minister of the place, and of whom mention will be made further on. The Wright family years ago almost or wholly ceased to be inhabitants of Rutland.

One of the next in prominence as an historic character in the early history of Rutland, and who lived in Sudbury and had children while there, was Deacon Joseph Stevens. He was a son of Cyprian Stevens, who, as we have seen, married Mary Willard of Lancaster. He went from Sudbury to Framingham, and from there removed to Rutland about 1719. He married Prudence Rice, a daughter of John Rice of Sudbury, and while at Sudbury his son Phineas, the Indian fighter and famous captain in the French and Indian war, was born. Mr. Stevens was thus by relationship grandson of Major Simon Willard, and by heirship had an interest in the land tract. In the homestead allotment he received lots Nos. 15 and 56. He also had two hundred acres of other land. He filled various offices, military, ecclesiastical, and civil, among which were those of captain of militia and deacon of the church. He put up a small hut on some meadow land five miles from his dwelling-place, and, there being no road to the place, he went to it daily on rackets or snow-

shoes to feed his stock.   On the 14th of August, 1723, after
the daily devotional service with his family, Mr. Stevens
started with four young men to gather hay, and while engaged in the work he was assailed by the Indians, two of his
sons were killed, the eldest and youngest were taken prisoners, and he alone escaped.   The captives were taken to Canada; and, being kept there a year, were redeemed at great
expense, after the father had taken two trips to Canada.   It
is said, that, after the capture of these boys, the Indians,
thinking that Isaac, the younger, who was but four years
old, would be troublesome to them on their way to Canada,
were about putting him to death, when their design was discovered by Phineas, who made signs, that, if his brother
were spared, he would carry him along on his back.   The
request being granted, little Isaac was carried by his brother
Phineas, then about seventeen, to the Indians' far-off wilderness home.   Isaac was so young when taken captive that he
soon acquired the customs and habits of the Indians.   It is
stated that the Indian woman who had this young child in
charge was so kind in her treatment of him, that he would
have remained among the savages.   By the redemption of
Phineas Stevens from his captivity in Canada, the country
received a man whose services were invaluable in after years.
This son of Sudbury afterward became an historic character,
from his masterly military prowess in and about Fort No. 4, a
place on the Connecticut River at Charleston, N.H.   Deacon
Stevens had three daughters, Mindwell, Mary, and Kather-
ine.   He died Nov. 15, 1769, and his wife about 1776.

Capt. Edward Rice and Rachel, his wife, were from Sudbury, and were some of the most prominent people of Rutland.   He was proprietor of two lots — Nos. 34 and 60 — and
their after divisions.   One of these lots he sold to Mr. Benjamin Dudley, and settled on the other, which was located at
Muschapauge Hill, and contained one hundred and forty-
five acres; but, after building upon it, he sold it, and bought
a lot south of Pomagussett Meadow, at which place he
lived, and where he died, at the age of sixty-seven, during
a remarkable sickness which, in 1756, swept over Rutland,

destroying during the fall months nearly sixty children. Mrs. Rice, his wife, died of small pox, Jan. 7, 1760. Captain Rice was a useful citizen for his country, town, and church. He entered into the service of his country in 1724, and after his return home held both militia and town offices.

Capt. Samuel Stone was of Lexington, but previously was a citizen of Sudbury. He was proprietor of lot No. 25; but, with his sons, he eventually became owner of about nine hundred acres of land. Samuel Stone, Jr., on Oct. 20, 1732, married a daughter of Deacon Stevens, by whom he had several children. He was an ardent patriot, and died in the service of his country at the time of the Revolutionary War. His son Isaac died in the French War, Nov. 20, 1756.

Capt. Phineas Walker and his wife, Beulah Clapp, were from Sudbury, where their first two children were born. Mr. Clapp owned land at the junction of Ware and Longmeadow Brooks, to which place he moved in 1750. He was a valuable inhabitant of Rutland, and filled various important town offices, and was also a captain in the Revolutionary War. Mr. Walker and wife, soon after arriving at Rutland, united with the church, and it is stated of them, that, though living four miles from the meeting-house, "their seats were seldom empty." In the great sickness of 1756, their two sons, Abel and John, were buried in one grave. Two of their other sons were physicians; one, named Asa, practised in Barre; the other died Nov. 30, 1797. Jonas was a minute-man and officer in the Revolution.

Col. Daniel Clapp was a Sudbury man, and in 1768 bought land in Rutland, to which place he moved from the town of Princeton. He filled many important offices while at Rutland, was an officer in the Revolutionary War, and for many years registrar of deeds for Worcester County.

Lieut. Luke Moore and Lucy, his wife, were other citizens from Sudbury. Mr. Moore was an officer of militia, and a worthy citizen. He subsequently removed from Rutland to New Hampshire. It is stated that Mr. Luke Moore was a brother of all the women of the name of Moore who went from Sudbury to Rutland.

Lieut. Paul Moore, another titled citizen, was from Sudbury. He was by trade a carpenter. He filled various town offices, as town clerk, selectman, and treasurer. Mr. Moore married, May 3, 1733, Hannah Hubbard, a daughter of Capt. John Hubbard, who moved from Worcester to Rutland about 1728; and for his second wife he married Azubah Moore of Sudbury. The wife of Lieutenant Moore was a well-known maker of deer-skin clothes. A grandson of Mr. and Mrs. Moore was Rev. John Hubbard Church, formerly of Pelham, N. H.

Cornet Daniel Estabrook and Hannah, his wife, were both from Sudbury. It is stated that Mr. Estabrook, in 1723, bought land laid out to Samuel Goodnow to his right of lot No. 46, situated on Worcester Hill; and that when he began to fell trees it was perilous going to his work without his gun, not only from exposure to Indians, but also to bears and wolves.

Another Sudbury citizen who owned land in Rutland, and whose family was represented among its early settlers, was Thomas Read, proprietor of Lot 22, with its divisions. Thomas Read, the son of Thomas, moved from Sudbury to Rutland with Sarah, his wife, and located their homestead on the lot just mentioned. They were some of the first pioneers, and shared the perils incident to a settler's life. Mr. Read had five children, Jason, Thomas, Mary, Jonathan, and Micah. All Mr. Read's sons married wives from Framingham. Mr. Read was of the old Read family in Sudbury, the first of which family in the town was Thomas, who settled at Lanham as early as 1654. It is said, in the " History of Rutland," that "this family of Reads have been useful and industrious inhabitants of Rutland for one hundred and twenty years."

Jonathan Stearns, who married Abigail Moore, bought lands adjacent to what is called the East Wing.

Moses Maynard and his wife, Tabitha Moore, bought land in Rutland adjacent to the East Wing, which was once granted to Jonathan Waldo, and first division of upland to the right of lots Nos. 26 and 27. The descendants of Mr.

and Mrs. Maynard were numerous, and settled to quite an
extent in New Hampshire and Georgia. In 1836 it was said
that Mr. Maynard was the largest man that ever lived in
Rutland, and that about a year and a half before his death,
which occurred in his sixty-eighth year, he weighed four
hundred and fifty-one pounds.

Mr. Moses Baxter, a carpenter, who married Mary Moore
of Sudbury, bought a farm joining the East Wing.

Mr. Eliphalet Howe was of the old Howe family in Sudbury, and bought land on Walnut Hill, Rutland.

Among the settlers in and about Rutland are other and
familiar Sudbury names; but those which have been given
show how much the town contributed towards the settlement. In the establishment of the church, also, Sudbury
was quite prominent. The first deacon was Samuel Wright,
at whose house was held a meeting for the signing of the
church covenant, July 18, 1727. July 24, 1721, Rev. Joseph
Willard was chosen pastor, but was slain by the Indians
August 14 of the same year. At a meeting held May 17,
1727, at which Capt. Samuel Wright presided, Rev. Thomas
Frink was chosen by unanimous vote to be the settled pastor. He was a native of Sudbury, and took his degree at
Harvard College in 1722. His father came from England,
with two brothers. He was settled at Rutland, Nov. 1,
1727, and dismissed Sept. 8, 1740. Previous to the installation of Mr. Frink, letters missive were sent to six churches,
among which were those of the East and West Parishes,
Sudbury. Samuel Wright and Lieut. Simon Davis were
chosen to sign these letters for the church. In accordance
with the invitation, Revs. Loring and Cook of Sudbury were
present. Mr. Frink and Capt. Samuel Wright joined the
church by letters brought from the West Precinct Church.
Rev. Israel Loring preached the installation sermon, from
2 Cor. ii. 16: "And who is sufficient for these things."
After laying on of hands by Revs. Loring, Prentice, Parsons, and Chenery, Mr. Frink "was ordained a Presbiter
of the Church and Pastor of Rutland." Mr. Loring gave
the right hand of fellowship. After singing part of the

Eighty-ninth Psalm, the pastor "pronounced the Blessing."

After Mr. Frink was dismissed from Rutland, he was installed pastor of the Third Church, Plymouth, Nov. 7, 1743; and October, 1753, he was installed pastor at Barre, where he labored until July 17, 1766. He married Isabella, daughter of Capt. Samuel Wright, Feb. 13, 1729, and had a family of ten children. He was a man of considerable ability, and preached the election sermon at Boston in 1758. His son Samuel was also a minister; and at the time of Mr. Whitefield's visit to the country he was rector of a church in Savannah, Ga. John Frink was a physician, and practiced in Rutland.

Thus the influence of Sudbury in the settlement of Rutland was strongly marked; and it may be gratifying to the town's people to-day that such good and prominent results have accrued from the presence of her citizens abroad.

CHAPTER X.

1650-1675.

Activity on the West Side of the River. — Early Homesteads. — Laying Out of the "New Grant." — Laud Allotments. — Owners and Occupants. — "The Thirty Rod Highway." — Settlement of Marlboro. — The "Hop Brook Mill." — Highway to the New Mill. — "Old Lancaster Road." — New Meeting-House; Contract. — The "Cow Common" Controversy.

> The smoke wreaths curling o'er the dell,
> The low, the bleat, the tinkling bell,
>   All made a landscape strange,
> Which was the living chronicle
>   Of deeds that wrought the change.
>
> A. B. STREET.

HAVING noticed the leading events in the establishment of the town, we will now consider its history mainly by periods of a quarter of a century each. In doing this we shall consider events somewhat in chronological order, taking liberty, however, to deviate as much as convenience and a proper treatment of the subject may direct.

Between 1650 and 1675 the west side had rapid development. Prior to the beginning of this period the pioneer spirit of the settlers had led to a thorough exploration of this part of the town, and they had located by its hills and along its meadows and valleys, as if undaunted by distance from the meeting-house and mill, and indifferent to the perils of the wilderness. But although there was, to an extent, an occupation of the west part of the town from the very beginning of the settlement, yet the greater activity was for a time on the east side; in that part was the centralization of people, and things were more convenient and safe. Indeed, the settlers for a season may have regarded the west side as

a wilderness country, destined long to remain in an unbroken
state. The view westward from certain points along the first
street was upon woody peaks and rocky hillsides. Beyond
the valley of Lanham and Lowance, towered Nobscot; its
slope, thickly covered with forest, might look like an inhos-
pitable waste; while the nearer eminence of Goodman's Hill,
with its rough, rocky projections, may have had a broken
and desolate aspect. It is no wonder, then, that in the earlier years of the settlement we read of so many corn-fields on
the east side of the river, and find parties desirous of obtaining new farms seeking them in a southerly rather than a
westerly direction. But when absolute wants were once
met, and things essential to existence were provided; when
the settlers had acquired a better knowledge of the country
and of the character of its native inhabitants, and a substantial causeway was made, — then began a greater development
of the west part of the town.

The indications are that these things were accomplished
about the year 1650. At this time we begin to notice the
mention of homesteads on the west side, and the construction of works for public convenience. The lands first occupied, probably, were those near Lanham and Pantry, and
along the meadows by the river course; while the more
central portion, called "Rocky Plain," was not taken till
somewhat later. This is indicated, not only by the known
locations of early homesteads, but by the locality of the west
side cow common. (See Chapter VII.) These sections
may have been first taken on account of the abundance of
meadow land, and the existence of roads which had been
made for the transportation of hay.

A prominent person who early located there was Walter
Haynes. He had a house by the meadow margin, which, in
1676, was used as a garrison, and which early in town history was called "Mr. Haynes' old house." In 1646 he was
granted liberty to run a fence "from his meadow, which lies
on the west side of the river, across the highway to his
fence of his upland at his new dwelling-house, provided that
Walter Hayne do keep a gate at each side of his meadow for
the passing of carts and the herds along the highway that

his fence may not be prejudicial to the town." Both record and tradition indicate that John and Edmund Goodenow early had lands near the Gravel Pit, and also at or near the present Farr and Coolidge Farms. By 1659, Thomas Noyes and Thomas Plympton had established houses on the west side, — the former on lands at Hop Brook, and the latter at Strawberry Bank. As early at least as 1654, Thomas Read was at Lanham; and by 1659 Peter Bent was there also.

Some public acts which indicate activity on the west side, as set forth by the records, are as follows: In 1654 it was ordered that Walter Hayne and John Stone "shall see to the fences of all the corn-fields on their side the river;" and in 1659 a committee was appointed to look after the highways there. The mention of bridges by 1641, the ferry of Mr. Noyes in 1642, and the contract for a cart-bridge in 1643, are all indications of early activity in the west part of the town. But the more important matters of a public nature were in connection with the laying out of new lands, the construction of important roads, and the erection of a mill.

LAYING OUT OF NEW LANDS.

These lands consisted of the two-mile grant, allowed in 1649. (See Chapter IV.) Its eastern boundary line extended nearly, as follows: A little west of North Sudbury, Sudbury Centre, and South Sudbury, or, more specifically, by the Moses Mossman place, across the Poor Farm, by the east bank of Willis's Mill Pond, across or just east of Blandford's Pond, over the Walter Rogers place, and a little west of Hunt's Bridge. From this easterly limit, it extended to the town's western boundary. Oct. 27, 1651, John Sherman and others were appointed to lay out this land. The following record indicates how the money was raised to meet the expense of this work, and also a rule that was agreed upon for the apportionment of the land: —

Nov. 27, 1651. "It is agreed in a public town meeting warned for that purpose, that the rate now to be levied for the payment of John Sherman and others for laying out the two miles westward joining to our former bounds which was last granted by the Court for our enlargement shall be paid

by the inhabitants every man to pay alike, the same in quantity and when that the two miles shall be layed out that
every man shall enjoy a like quantity of that land."

About two years later a dispute arose relative to the manner in which the two-mile grant was to be divided. "Two
ways were proposed, neither of which gave satisfaction; the
first was to divide them equally to every man; the other was
to divide by estate or family — to every man four parts — to
every wife, child or servant bought or brought up in the
family one part."

On Jan. 4, 1655, at a selectmen's meeting it was "voted
to take some means to get the new grants laid out;" and it
was also agreed "to keep a herd of cattle upon the land the
next summer." Thus the subject of the new grant was a
prominent one, and how to apportion it was an important
matter. At length the plan was adopted of dividing it
into squadrons, the arrangement of which was as follows:
"The south east was to be the first, the north east the
second, the north west the third, and the south west the
fourth." It was voted there should be a highway extending
north and south, "30 rods wide in the new grant joining to
the five miles first granted;" also, "Voted that there should
be a highway 30 rods wide, from south to north, paralel with
the other said highway in the middle of the remaining tract
of land."

The records further state, that, as there was a pond in the
third and second squadrons, "so that the middle highway
from south to north cannot pass strait," it was voted to have
it "go round the pond." These squadrons were subdivided
into parcels of equal size, each containing one hundred and
thirty acres, and were apportioned to the people by lot. It
was voted that "the first lot drawn was to begin at the
south side of the first squadron running east and west
betwixt our highways; the second lot to be in the north
side of the first, and so every lot following successively as
they are drawn till we come to Concord line and so the first
and second squadron."

Persons who received parts of this land, and the order of
receiving it, are thus given in the records: —

John Blanford	1
Thomas Noyes	2
Walter Hains	3
William Kerley	4
Joseph Freeman	5
Henry Curtis	6
Mr. Brian Pendleton	7
Thomas Rice	8
Edward Rice	9
Mr. Herbert Pelham	10
L[t] Edmund Goodenow	11
Robert Davis	12

These twelve lots written, are the first squadron, the first of them joining to the country land on the south, and the last of them joining to Lancaster highway on the north, each lot containing one hundred and thirty acres, the length being nearest hand east and west, the breadth north and south.

The second squadron are:

William Ward	13
Josiah Hains	14
Henry Loker	15
John How	16
Edmund Rice	17
Philemon Whale	18
John Loker	19
Mr. Edmund Browne	20
John Parmenter, Dea	21
John Maynard	22
Robert Darnill	23
Thomas White	24
Richard Newton	25
John Reddicke, part of his	26

These thirteen lots and a part afore written are the second squadron, the first whereof being William Ward's who joineth to Lancaster highway on the south, the last being part of Sargent Reddicke's lot which joineth to Concord line on the north all this squadron of lots, with the other aforegoing, being bounded on the east by a highway thirty rods wide, and part of the two miles last granted to Sudbury each lot containing one hundred and thirty acres; third squadron are as followeth : —

John Ward	27
Peter Kinge	28
John Smith	29
Hugh Griffin	30
Henry Rice	31
John [——]	32
Robert Beast	33
William Kerley Sen	34
John Wood	35
John Rutter	36

Mr Wm Browne his farm of two hundred acres, and his lot of one hundred and thirty acres, being granted to be in the north west angle beyond Asibath river before the lots were laid out. Also the other part of Sargent Reddicke's lot joining to Mr. William Browne's farm on the north.

Solomon Johnson Sen	37
John Toll	38
Widow Goodenow	39

The thirteen lots last written with Mr. Wm Browne's farm and lot and the part of Sergent Reddicke's lot, are the third squadron. Mr. Browne's farm joineth to Concord line on the north, and the widow Goodenow's lot joineth the same said Lancaster highway on the south, the said squadron of lots and farm being on the east the middle highway thirty rods wide and the second squadron, and butting on the west upon the wilderness.

The fourth squadron are as followeth : —

John Moores	40
John Woodward	41
John Grout,	42
John Bent Sen,	43
Thomas Goodenow	44
Thomas Plympton,	45
John Haines,	46
Mr Peter Noyes,	47
Mr William Pelham	48
John Parmenter Junior,	49
Thomas Kinge	50
The Cowpen land being one hundred and thirty acres	51

These above eleven lots going with the cowpen land, are the fourth and last squadron, the first [one] of [which] being [that of] John Moores, who joineth on the north the same said Lancaster highway, the cowpen being the last, which joineth on the south to the wilderness the said eleven lots and cowpen butting on the east the aforesaid + highway and first squadron and butting on the west the wilderness. Also let it be remembered that the long highway from south to north goeth at the west end of the pond through the lands of John Toll and Solomon Johnson, and is twelve rods wide at the narrowest, which way the said John Toll and Johnson have sufficient allowance.

This land, laid out so regularly, was good property. Some of the most substantial homesteads of the town have been, and still are, upon it. The names of Howe, Parmenter, Woodward, Moore, Browne, Walker, Noyes, Balcom, and Rice, of the older inhabitants, and, later, of Fairbanks, Stone, Willis, Smith, Hayden, Maynard, Perry, Bowker, Vose, Brigham, and others, — all had residences there. The possession of this new grant territory, and its early apportionment, would serve naturally to keep the people in town. It opened new resources to the settlers by its timber lands; and the circuitous course of Wash Brook gave meadows and mill privileges which the people were not slow to improve. Probably the earlier settlers of this tract went from the east side of the river as into a new country or wilderness. There they erected garrisons; and that there were in this territory at least three of these houses indicates the exposed condition of the place at the time of its early occupation by the English. "Willis," the largest pond in town, a part of "Nobscot," the highest hill, and the most extensive timber tracts, are in this new grant. In it have been located no less than five saw or grist mills. From this territory was taken part of the town of Maynard, and in it were located for years two out of five of the old-time district school-houses. The Wayside Inn and the Walker Garrison are still there; and although the stirring scenes of the old stage period, which gave liveliness to the one, and the dismal war days, which gave importance to the other, have passed away, yet there remains a thrift and prosperity about the substantial farms of the ancient new grant lots that make this locality one of importance and interest.

THE THIRTY-ROD HIGHWAY.

But, while these new lands proved so beneficial to the town, the "Thirty-Rod Highway" in time caused considerable trouble. It was laid out for the accommodation of the owners of lots, and, as the name indicates, was thirty rods wide. The unnecessary width may be accounted for as we account for other wide roads of that day: land was plentiful, and the timber of so large a tract would be serviceable to the town.

But the width tended to cause disturbance. The land was sought for by various parties, — by abuttors on one or both sides, it may be; by those dwelling within the near neighborhood; and by such as desired it for an addition to their outlying lands, or a convenient annex to their farms. The result was that to protect it required considerable vigilance. Encroachments were made upon it, wood and timber were taken away, and at successive town-meetings what to do with this Thirty-Rod Highway was an important matter of business. But at length it largely ceased to be public property. Piece after piece had been disposed of; some of it had been purchased by private parties, some of it exchanged for lands used 'for other highways, and some of it may have been gained by right of possession.

But, though so much of this road has ceased to be used by the public, there are parts still retained by the town and open to public use. The Dudley Road, about a quarter of a mile from the William Stone place, and which passes a small pond called the Horse Pond, tradition says is a part of this way. From near the junction of this with the county road, a part of the Thirty-Rod Way runs south, and is still used as a way to Nobscot. On it, tradition also says, is the Small-Pox Burying-Ground at Nobscot. A part of this road, as it runs east and west, is probably the present Boston and Berlin Road, or what was the "Old Lancaster Road." Other parts of this way may be old wood-paths that the Sudbury farmers still use and speak of as being a part of this ancient landmark.

"OLD LANCASTER ROAD."

This road, which was at first called the "Road to Nashuway," probably followed an ancient trail. In 1653 it was "agreed by the town that Lieutenant Goodenow and Ensign Noyes shall lay out the way with Nashuway men so far as it goes within our town bound." A record of this road is on the Town Book, and just following is this statement:—

"This is a true copy of the commissioners appointed by the town taken from the original and examined by me.

"HUGH GRIFFIN."

This record, which is among those for 1646, by the lapse of time has become so worn that parts are entirely gone. It is supposed, however, that some of the lost parts have been restored or supplied by the late Dr. Stearns. We will give the record, so far as it can be obtained from the Town Book, and insert in brackets the words that have been supplied from other sources : —

RESIDENCE OF JOSEPH C HOWE.

We whose names are hereunto subscribed appoint[ed by] Sudbury and the town of Lancaster to lay out the high[way over the] river meadow in Sudbury near Lancaster to the [town] bound according to the Court order, have agreed as follows [viz] That the highway beginning at the great river meadow [at the gravel] pitt shall run from thence [to the northwest side of] Thomas Plympton's house, [and from thence] to timber swa[mp as] marked by us and so on to Hart Pond leaving the [rock] on the north side of the way and from thence to the extreme [Sudbury bounds] as we have now marked it the breadth of the way is to be the gravel pitt to the west end of Thomas Plympton's lot and . . . rods wide all the way to the utmost of Sudbury bound and thence upon the common highway towards Lancaster through Sud[bury] therefore we have hereunto set our hand the 22ⁿᵈ day of this pres[ent month]

EDMUND GOODENOW

Date 1653

THOMAS NOYES

WILLIAM KERLEY

This road has for many years been a landmark in Sudbury; but the oldest inhabitant cannot remember when, in its entire length, it was used as a highway. Parts of it were long since discontinued, and were either sold or reverted to the estates of former owners. In 1806, an article was in the warrant " to see if the town would take any measures for opening the road called ' Lancaster Old Road ' at a gate a little north of Curtis Moore's dwelling house thence running southerly till it comes into the road leading from the mills to the meeting house." The road here referred to is probably that which comes out by the present Horatio Hunt place, about midway of the two villages. This record shows the track of the road from its intersection with the present meeting-house road to the point referred to as being " a little north of Curtis Moore's dwelling house ; " and, from that point, it probably continued along the present travelled way to the Berlin road. Its course east of the Hunt place, so far as we can judge from tradition, record, visible traces, and the lay of the land, took the following course: Going easterly a few rods, it goes southerly, and at a point about a quarter of a mile easterly of the Wadsworth Monument it takes a southeasterly course, and intersects the present Graves Road at the junction of two roads, near the William Jones place. It then, we believe, ran northeasterly over the length of the ridge, by what is still a rude wood-path, and came out on the eastern slope of the hill, near the Albert Haynes place, where Mr. Plympton once kept a grocery store. A little east of this, and south of the Elbridge Bent place, there are traces of a road, that for a little distance has a stone-wall ou either side, and which comes out a little south of the western end of the northern causeway, or at a point a little south of where the Water-row Road intersects the road going from Sudbury Centre to Wayland. Some have placed that part of this road which is east of the Graves Road a little further south, — that is, along the south side of the hill, rather than upon it, — but we believe the nature of the meadow at the east, and the absence of all trace of the road in the valley, together with traces of an ancient road through the woods on the hill and also near the Elbridge Bent place, are evidences that it took the course first described. Probably mistakes have been made relative to the course of this road west of Sudbury Centre, from the fact that formerly there were two Lancaster roads. (See map of 1794.)

The two-mile grant was hardly disposed of, and the Laucaster Road laid out, before there was a plan for the formation of a new plantation. The result was the settlement of the town of Marlboro. (See Chapter IX.) But the loss of population did not materially affect the prosperity of the town or delay the progress on the west side.

THE HOP-BROOK MILL.

In 1659 a mill was put up, where the present Parmenter Mill stands in South Sudbury. This mill was erected by Thomas and Peter Noyes. In recognition of the serviceableness of their work to the community, the town made them a land grant, and favored them with such privileges as are set forth in the following record : —

Jan. 7th 1659. Granted unto Mr Thomas Noyes and to Mr Peter Noyes for and in consideration of building a mill at Hop brook laying and being on the west side of Sudbury great river below the cart way that leads to Ridge meadow viz: fifty acres of upland and fifteen acres of meadow without commonadge to the said meadow four acres of the said fifteen acres of meadow lying and being within the demised tracts of uplands; Also granted to the above named parties timber of any of Sudbury's common land, to build and maintain the said mill. Also the said Thomas and Peter Noyes do covenant with the town for the foregoing consideration, to build a sufficient mill to grind the town of Sudbury's corn; the mill to be built below the cart way that now is leading to Ridge meadow, the said Grantees, their heirs and successors are to have nothing to do with the stream above four rods above the aforementioned cartway of said mill to be ready to grind the corn by the first of December next ensueing, and if the said grantees, their heirs or assigns shall damage the highway over the brook, by building the said mill, they are to make the way as good as now it is, from time to time, that is to say, the above specified way, over the Mill brook of said Thomas Noyes and Peter are also to leave a highway six rods wide joining to the brook from the east way that now is to the Widow Loker's meadow. (Town Records, Vol. I.)

While the new mill was being built, a way was being made to it from the causeway, as we are informed by the following record, dated Feb. 7, 1659 : —

We the Selectmen of Sudbury, finding sundry inconveniences, by reason of bad and ill highways not being passable to meadow lands and other towns, and finding the law doth commit the stating of the highways to the prudence of the selectmen of towns, we therefore being met the day and year above written, on purpose to view the highways in the west side of Sudbury river, and having taken pains to view them, do we say, conclude and jointly agree that the highway from the Gravel pits shall go through the land newly purchased of Lieut. Goodenow to that end, and from thence down the brow of the hill the now passed highway, unto the place where the new mill is building, that is to say, the way that is now in occupation, we mean the way that goeth to the south and Mr Beisbeich his house, we conclude and jointly agree, that the way to the meadows, as namely, the meadow of John Grout, Widow Goodenow, John Maynard, Lieut. Goodenow, shall go as now it doth, that is to say, in the hollow to the said meadows, the highway to be six rods wide all along by the side of the said meadows.

The new road here mentioned is, probably, mainly the same as that leading from the old causeway, or Gravel Pit, to South Sudbury to-day. Until within about a century it passed round the southern brow of Green Hill. This road was probably part of a path or trail that had been travelled before. This is indicated both by the circumstances and the language of the record. It is not improbable, that, before the formal recognition or laying out of this road, a part of it was a way from the Gravel Pit, or end of the long cause-

way, to Lieutenant Goodenow's, southeasterly of the present
Coolidge place, and extended from that point to Lanham, and
was the road travelled by Thomas Read and others of Lanham to the meeting-house.   There is still an old lane easterly
of the Cooledge Farm, marked by fragments of wall, which
may have been a part of the way to the old Goodenow Garrison.   It is not improbable that this lane extended as a pathway along the margin of Lanham Meadows to Lanham.   If
this was the case, then the land spoken of as purchased of
Lieutenant Goodenow, for the "new mill" road, may have
extended, from the point where this lane leaves the present
county road, along towards Green Hill; and the "now passed
highway" mentioned may have been the road in South Sudbury called the "old road," which, it is conjectured, was a
part of the path leading from South Sudbury to the old Lancaster trail.   (See period 1675–1700.)   Or, in other words,
two ways may be referred to in the records as making a part
of this new road; one, a portion of the path leading from the
old Lancaster trail to the southwest part of the town, which
was probably travelled by those living in the vicinity of Nobscot, as they passed to the east part of the town; the other,
an early path by the Goodenow Garrison to Lanham.

NEW MEETING-HOUSE.

While the town was making improvements on the west
side of the river, it was active on the east side also; and one
of the important works there, in this period, was the erection
of a new meeting-house.   Whether the people had outgrown
the old one, or desired a better, is not stated; but it is a mark
of thrift, or of increase, that they proposed to build anew.
That more room was wanted, is indicated by this record, in
1651: "It was agreed by the town that Edm^d Rice Senior,
William Browne, John Reddicke and Henry Rice that they
four shall desire the Pastor's approbation to build galleries
in the old meeting-house, and if the Pastor do consent, then
the town doth hereby give full power to the Pastor and these
four men to continue the work, and to let it out to workmen."

Probably these galleries were never put in, as they soon afterwards commenced building a new meeting-house. Before, however, it was decided to build anew, various plans were suggested relative to the enlargment and improvement of the old one. In 1650 it was ordered that the deacons should "mend the meeting house and make it comfortable." One plan was to enlarge it by the addition of "13 foote at the end of it," and that the committee should "finish the back side which enlargement is for a watchouse." A plan a little later was that the meeting-house "be enlarged by building 10 foote on the foreside of it all the length of the meeting house to be built with two gable ends in the front; and Mr. Brown the Pastor doth promise to give twenty shillings toward the work; the former order for enlarging the meeting house at the north west end is hereby repealed. It is also ordered that the back side of the meeting house be made hansom."

On Dec. 10, 1651, the town succeeded in passing a vote for the erection of a new meeting-house, the vote standing twenty-five for and fourteen against it. But this vote was repealed at a meeting January 23 of the same year (Old Style), together with all orders for the repairing or alteration of the old one. The following year it was "agreed that the meeting house shall be made use of for a watch house until some further course be taken by the town." At length it was again decided to build a new meeting-house; and in 1652 a contract was made for the work.

This contract is on the Town Records, but has become considerably worn and defaced, so that parts are almost or quite unintelligible. There is, however, a copy in the "Stearns Collection," which, with some slight immaterial alterations, is as follows: —

The town agreed with Thomas Plympton Peter King & Hugh Griffin to build a new meeting house which was to be forty feet long & twenty feet wide measuring from outside to outside, the studds were to be 6 inches by 4 to stand for a four foot clapboard. There were to be 4 transom windows five feet wide & 6 feet high, and in each gable end a clearstory window, each window was to be 4 feet wide and 3 feet high. There were to be sufficient dorments across the house for galleries if there should afterward be a desire for galleries the beams to be 12 inches by 14 and the ground sills were to be of white oak 8 inches square. The posts were to be a foot square, and the 2 middle beams to be smoothed on three sides and the lower corners to be run with a *bowkell.* They the said Plympton King & Griffin are to find timber to fell, hew, saw, cart, frame, carry to place & they are to level the ground and to find them sufficient help to raise the house, they are to inclose the house with clap boards and to lyne the inside with cedar boards or otherwise with good spruce boards, & to be smoothed & over lapped and to be lyned up the windows, & they are to hang the doors so as to bolt. One of the doors on the inside is to be sett with a lock. They are to lay the sleepers of the doors with white oak or good swamp pine, & to floor the house with plank. They are to finish all the works but the seats, for which the town do covenant to give them * * * * 5 pound 20 to be paid in march next in Indyan [corn] or cattle, 30 more to be paid in Sep' next to be paid in wheat, butter, or money & the rest to be paid as soon as the work is done in Indyan corn or cattle the corn to [be] merchanta-ble at the price current.

    Witness EDMD. GOODNOW
         THOMAS NOYES

    The new building was to be erected on the site of the old one. The town ordered " that the carpenters should provide 12 men to help them raise the meeting house," for which they were to be allowed half a crown a day. The roof was to be covered with thatch, and the workmen were to have " the meadow afterwards the minister's to get their thatch upon." In 1654 a committee was appointed " to agree with some-body to fill the walls of the meeting house with tempered clay provided they do not exceed the sum of 5 pounds 10 shillings." The parties who were to build the house were employed " to build seats after the same fashion as in the old meeting house," and they were to have for every seat one shilling eight pence. The seats were to be made of white oak, " both posts and rails and benches." In 1655 the pas-tor and Mr. Noyes were empowered " to appoint a man to remove the pulpit and the deacons' seat out of the old meet-ing house into the new meeting house." Hugh Griffin was appointed for the work, and was ' to have 18 shillings for the work if the work is done this week or next according to the pastor's approbation."

    The records also state that " upon the pastor's request the town hath granted that he shall have liberty for to set up the seat for his wife in the new meeting house under the window by the pulpit."

Dec. 27, 1655, it was voted that the meeting-house should be seated with new seats, "that the seats now brought into the meeting house shall be carried out again and the select men shall have power to place men in the seats when they are built."

The new building being brought to completion, the people probably left the little first meeting-house that the deft hands of John Rutter had reared, and went into this with hearts thankful for new comforts and conveniences. It may, however, have been with some reluctance that they left the old meeting-house, as around it doubtless clustered memories both glad and sad; for it had sheltered them in times of united worship in their earlier experience in Sudbury; when they had special need of divine support as strangers in a wilderness country, there they met, and together found strength for their trials and toils, and grace which brought patience and faith. Surely the old meeting-house was a place only to be exchanged for another, as that other brought new comforts and was better adapted to meet their needs. Thus at the beginning of this period the town was in a thrifty condition, and had a fair prospect of speedy development and future prosperity. Civilized life was casting its brightness over the hills and along the valleys, and the scattered corn and wheat fields were gladdening the plains, which were being dotted on both sides of the river with pleasant homesteads. The young people who early came to the settlement were now coming into the full strength of sturdy manhood and womanhood; and all had been sufficiently long in the country to know what it required of them and what they might expect from it. No outbreak had as yet occurred between the white man and his copper-colored brother of the woods, and both Nature and her children worked together in harmonious relations to bring plenty and peace. There are various small matters on record which indicate that the town looked well to its minor relations or interests, and exercised a vigilant watchfulness in making provision for whatever called for its

care. The following are the records of some of these matters.

March 6, 1650, it was ordered " that the town rate of ⅔
now to be raised for the payment of the town debt shall be
paid in corn." The same year it "ordered, a rate for the
town pound to the value of 10 pound shall be leved to be
paid in wheat 5 bush butter 6ᵈ, and ⅔ shall pay as much as a
bushel of wheat."

A controversy was going on about this time with regard
to the Sudbury and Watertown bounds, and the town made
" provision to prevent the encroachments of Watertown; "
and a committee was appointed " to seek for the stopping of
Watertown proceedings in coming too near our bound."
The same year it was ordered that " a part of the town rate
should be appropriated for the drum and halberd," and a
rate was assessed "for repairing the Bridge, and Hugh Griffin was to have some pine poles for the staying of the same."
In March, 1654, the controversy about the territorial bounds
between Sudbury and Watertown was ended by the establishment of a boundary line between the two towns, by
agents appointed from both places. In 1655, "the line of
the New Grant was run by John Ruddock, Thomas Noyes,
and John Howe."

But while the town was growing and increasing in strength,
a controversy occurred which was of a somewhat serious character. Questions arose relating to the division of the " two-
mile grant," to the title of parties to certain lands, and to
rights in the east side cow common. The controversy concerning this latter subject was in relation to " sizing" or
" stinting" the common. It was specified when this land
was reserved, that it "should never be ceded or laid down,
without the consent of every inhabitant and townsman that
hath right in commonage; " and the rule for pasturing cattle upon it was, " The inhabitants are to be limited in the
putting in of cattle upon the said common, according to the
quantity of meadow the said inhabitants are rated in upon
the division of the meadows." The rule of allowance on
this basis was as follows : " For every two acres of meadow
one beast, that is either cow, ox, bull or steer, or heifer

above a year old, and every horse or mare above a year old to go as one beast and a half, and every six sheep to go for one beast, and that all cattle under a year old shall go without sizing." The endeavor to define rights of commonage, or the relation of the individual to this piece of town property, proved a difficult task. As might be expected among a people of positive natures, strong opinions were entertained, and decided attitudes were taken concerning a matter of individual rights. The affair was not wholly confined to the town in its social and civil relations, but the church became connected with it. The result was that a council was called to adjust ecclesiastical matters, and advice was also sought and obtained of the General Court.

It is not our purpose to give all the details of this once memorable case. We will, however, state a few facts that may suggest something of its general character. The case came before the people by a call in town-meeting for a vote as to whether they considered " the act of the selectmen in sizing the commons a righteous act." The affair not being satisfactorily adjusted in town-meeting, all the issues concerning the controversy, whether related to the cow commons or other matters in dispute, were laid before a committee of the Colonial Court. In answer to a petition of Edmund Brown, Peter Noyes, Jr., Walter Haynes, and divers others of Sudbury, the Court ordered that Maj. Simon Willard, Ensign Jn° Sherman and Mr. Thomas Danforth should be a committee " to hear and determine the difference between all or any of the inhabitants of Sudbury in reference to what is mentioned in the petition which petition is on file." (Colonial Records, Vol. IV., p. 228, date 1655.) The committee met at the ordinary kept by,John Parmenter, and the questions which came before them were as follows: first, as to the right or title of certain individuals to certain lands, and specifically as to some held by Rev. Edmund Brown and Hugh Griffin; second, as regarding the right of suffrage exercised by some not considered town inhabitants; third, as regarding the right of sizing or stinting the common; fourth, as regarding the act of defacing the town records. The committee appointed by the Court

to adjust matters rendered this report: "Concerning the title
of lands appropriated to several inhabitants . . . we do not
find just cause to make valid their claims;" and as concerns
the land held by Mr. Brown the pastor of the Church there
touching a part thereof some objection has been made and
clamoring report laid against him, we do not find any just
ground for the same." The committee concluded his titles
were good, and confirmed them. Concerning the stinting of
the common within the compass of the five miles, the committee concluded that the rule was " not as clear as desirable ; " and they made the following recommendations, which
are given mainly in their own words: That, in the rule for
stinting the common, respect should be had for both those
whose estates had been weakened and those which had been
prospered, that those of the former class should be considered and proportioned according to their several allotments
of meadow, which gave them their right in the other part
of the common already determined, the rule for which was
in the Town Book, folio 27, and there was no disagreement about, and those of the latter class, namely, whose
estate had been prospered, should be considered and proportioned according to the invoice of their estates given in for
the county rate last past, without any respect-had to their
meadow formerly allotted them. The committee also declared that no person should have power to vote about the
common " but such as have been allowed as free inhabitants
of the town or have come upon the right of some that were
so allowed." Since the committee found that the records,
folio 58, touching the case, had been " crossed and defaced,
they censured the act, and recommended that they be kept
by the recorder of the court until there be a loving com-
posure and agreement for former differences and a mutual
choice of a fit person to keep the same." As some complaint had been made in reference to the title of Hugh Griffin's land, they stated that they considered his title valid.
They finally concluded that every "allowed inhabitant of the
town should have his commonage according to his meadow
or invoice of his estate at his pleasure ; " and that no person
who is not an allowed inhabitant, or had meadow, in case of

voting should have any claim to commonage. The people of Sudbury expressed full assent to the report of the commissioners, and returned "hearty thanks unto them for their paines faithfulness and love expressed." The council of churches having also met and considered the case, a formal adjustment of matters was made, and again things moved on in their accustomed way. "John Parmenter having expended the sum of 17-5-12 in entertaining both the council and committee appointed to end their differences, the Court orderes the said charges to be borne by all the town."

CHAPTER XI.

1675–1700.

Philip's War: Sources of Information; Cause and Nature. — Defensive Measures by the Town: Garrison-Houses; Militia. — Defensive Measures by the Colony. — Services of the Town outside its Limits; List of Men Impressed. — Swamp Fight. — Services of Ephraim Curtis among the Nipnets: As a Messenger with Proposals of Peace; As a Guide in Captain Hutchinson's Expedition. — Signs of Indian Hostilities in and about the Town. — Edmund Brown's Letter. — Night Attack on the Indians, and Death of Netus.

> Over the hillsides the wild knell is tolling,
> From their far hamlets the yeomanry come;
> As thro' the storm-clouds the thunder-burst rolling
> Circles the beat of the mustering drum.
> O. W. HOLMES.

THE last quarter of the seventeenth century began dark and threatening to the colonists. A memorable Indian war was at hand, and gloomy and portentous was the outlook as the year 1675 set in. Sudbury, on account of its frontier position, was to be badly harassed by the enemy; and perhaps no New England town became more prominent than this in the annals of that remarkable period.

But, notwithstanding the prominence of Sudbury in this remarkable conflict, there is little information pertaining to it in the records of the town. This absence of information, however, is not very remarkable. The town books were for town business, and the military movements of that period largely related to the colony. The sources from which mainly we derive information are papers preserved in the State archives, historians of the period, and a valuable paper recently discovered among the old Court files. The paper last mentioned consists of a petition presented by the inhabitants of Sudbury to the General Court assembled Oct. 11, 1676. This document settles the date of the Sudbury fight, and gives in detail some of the events connected with Philip's attack on the town. We shall refer to it as " The Old Petition."

Before commencing the narrative of the war, we will consider briefly the cause and nature of it. This war originated with and was conducted by Philip, a Wampanoag chieftain. Ilis aboriginal name was Metacomet, but he was called Philip by Governor Prince, because of his bravery. Philip was a son of Massasoit, a friend of the Pilgrims at Plymouth, and lived at Mount Hope, near Bristol, R.I., a place on the west side of Mount Hope Bay. The Indian name of the place was Pokanoket. Metacomet, unlike his father, distrusted the English. He feared the gradual encroachment upon his broad forests betokened no good ; and he sought to check the English advance and increase by a devastating war. To accomplish his object, he sought alliance with most of the tribes of New England, and so far succeeded that a large portion of them were engaged in the hostilities that followed. With his combination of tribes, Philip had the material to do great mischief.

Probably of all the foes that New England ever encountered, Philip of Pokanoket was most dreaded ; and this war was the most destructive of any Indian war waged for the same length of time in this country. Villages and hamlets faded before his savage force ; homes became smouldering ash-heaps; and lands, smiling in the sunlight of civilized life, were left forsaken and desolate, again to be draped in the old forest shade.

Besides the usual ferocity expected in an Indian combatant, the peculiar characteristics of the time and place aggravated the unhappy situation of the settlers. The wild condition of the country, the isolation of dwellings, the slow communication of place with place, — all these were circumstances suited to arouse feelings of distrust, and to stir the inhabitants to a state of alarm. They were subjected to constant expectation of sudden Indian attack. Any sign might forebode the approach of the foe, and send the people to the shelter of their friendly garrisons. The strange foot-print of a moccasin on the outskirts of an outlying field, the freshly made trail in the forest, the mysterious smoke rising above the distant woodlands, or the dull sound of a gun in the thicket, were omens mysterious and strange. Besides the arousing of apprehension by signs of a material character, the situation was such that the superstitious nature of the inhabitants was wrought upon to an unusual degree. It was thought there were mysterious prognostications of what was to come. Strange omens were supposed to be seen in the sky, and wild, rushing sounds heard over the tree-tops, which were considered ominous of evil. So marked, indeed, were these circumstances, that perhaps the impressions made were different from those of any other war in New England.

Long after its devastations had ceased, the tale of Philip's raids was rehearsed by the farm-house fireside; tradition passed the story of the times to posterity; children received it from the lips of the parent who had heard, while within garrison walls, the wild whoop from the woods, or witnessed the skulk of the savage along forest, bramble, and rock. It was a wild, weird story to tell, and late listeners lingered about the bright hearthstone, and left with reluctance the warm kitchen precinct for the remote chamber beneath the old roof.

For a better understanding of the particular relation of this war to Sudbury, we divide the subject thus: —

First, the defensive condition of the town when the conflict set in.

Second, The part its citizens took in military operations outside the town limits.

Third, the Indians' near approach, their repulse, and the death of Netus.

Fourth, the attack on the town and the defense of the garrisons.

Fifth, the contest at the causeway and old town bridge.

Sixth, the battle at Green Hill, or the Sudbury fight.

DEFENSIVE MEASURES.

The principal means of defense in this war were the garrison-houses. These were not always under colonial authority, but were often private dwelling-places conveniently located. They were sometimes a rendezvous for the town's militia in times of expected attack, and used occasionally to shelter colonial soldiers when sent to a beleaguered place. Some of these garrison-houses were built strong, for the purpose of defense, while others were built in the ordinary way, and fortified when the danger became imminent.

Sudbury had several of these places of defense, a knowledge of which has come down to us, namely: The Brown Garrison, the Walker Garrison, the Goodenow Garrison, the Haynes Garrison, two others whose names are now unknown, and a block-house. Of these places we give the following information, derived from personal knowledge, record, and tradition: —

THE BROWN GARRISON.

This stood on the present estate of Luther Cutting, about a dozen rods southeasterly of his residence, or a few rods east of the Sudbury and Framingham road, and about a half mile from the town's southern boundary. It had a gable roof, was made of wood, and lined with brick. It was perhaps built by Major Thomas Brown, and was owned and occupied by the descendants of the Brown family till a mod-

THE BROWNE GARRISON HOUSE.

om an original painting by A. S Hudson, from descriptions given by person
once familiar with it.

ern date. It was demolished about thirty-five years ago, when in the possession of Mr. Conant.

THE WALKER GARRISON.

The Walker Garrison-house is in the west part of the town, a little south of the Massachusetts Central Railroad, on the Willard Walker estate. This building is a curious structure, with massive chimney, large rooms, and heavy frame-work. It is lined within the walls with upright plank fastened with wooden pins. It may have been erected by Thomas Walker, whose name, with others, is subscribed to "The Old Petition."

THE GOODNOW GARRISON.

This garrison stood a little southeasterly of the present Coolidge house, or a few rods northeast to east of the East Sudbury railroad station, and perhaps twenty or thirty rods from the South Sudbury and Wayland highway. A lane formerly went from the road to a point near the garrison. This house was standing about three-quarters of a century ago. Tradition states, that an old building a few feet square stood by it, which was called "the old barrack," and was removed to the Farr Farm. An old inhabitant, — C. G. Cutler, — who had been to the house in his early life, informed the writer that there was no mistake about this being the Goodnow Garrison; for years ago it was generally considered so by the community.

THE HAYNES GARRISON.

This garrison stood on the Water-Row Road, by the margin of the river meadow, a little northerly or northeasterly of the Luther Goodenow house. It was about an eighth of a mile from the Wayland and Sudbury Centre highway, two or three rods from the road, and fronted south. In later years it was painted red. In 1876 it was still standing, but has since been demolished. It is supposed to have been erected by Walter Haynes, and was probably the place which, in the early records of the town, was repeatedly referred to as "Mr. Haynes' old house."

One of the buildings which common tradition says was a garrison, but whose name is unknown, stood near the Adam How place, about twenty-five rods northwest of the house. It was one story high, and had a room at each end. For a time it was owned and occupied by Abel Parmenter, and was torn down years ago. It is stated by tradition, that, when the Wayside Inn was built, the workmen repaired to this house at night for safety.

The garrisons previously mentioned were named from their early occupants. Parmenter was the name of the first occupant of this house of whom we have any knowledge; if he was the first, then doubtless this house was formerly known as the Parmenter Garrison.

The other garrison, the name of which is unknown, was north of the Gulf Meadows, and on or near the present Dwier Farm (Bent place). Tradition concerning this one is less positive than concerning the other. An old inhabitant, once pointing towards the old Bent house, said, "There is where the people used to go when the Indians were about." It is quite evident that the Bent house was not a garrison, for that was built about a century ago; but across the road southwesterly there are indications that some structure once stood, which may have been a garrison.

THE BLOCK-HOUSE.

The block-house stood in the north part of the town, on the Israel Haynes Farm. It was situated, perhaps, from thirty to fifty rods southwest of the house of Leander Haynes, on a slight rise of ground. It was small, perhaps fifteen feet square, more or less, and so strongly built that it was with difficulty taken to pieces. It was demolished about three-quarters of a century ago, when owned by Mr. Moses Haynes. Mr. Reuben Rice of Concord, a relative of Mr. Haynes, when over ninety years of age informed the writer that when it was torn down he chanced to be passing by, and looked for bullet-marks, and believed he found some. He stated there was no mistake about the house being used as a garrison.

There may have been garrisons in town about which tradition is silent; and doubtless other dwellings were put in a defensive attitude when Indian hostilities began. It is stated that "many houses were fortified and garrisoned." On the east side we have heard of no garrisons, but Rev. Edmund Brown fortified his house. In a letter sent to the Governor, Sept. 26, 1675, he states as follows: "I have been at a round charge to fortify my house, and except finishing the two flankers and my gate have finished. Now without four hands I cannot well secure it, and if for want of hands I am beaten out, it will be very advantageous to the enemy, and a thorn to the town." The men asked for were granted him; and his house afforded a place of defense to the inhabitants of that locality, who were directed to resort to it in time of peril. After the war began the meeting-house was made a place of security, and fortifications were constructed about it.

Such were some of the means provided for protection in the coming conflict. These were the strongholds that stout hearts defended. In view of their service, it is unfortunate that these relics have to such an extent been destroyed. But, as we have stated, only one remains. With regard to the others, all that can now be done is carefully to mark the site and preserve the traditions concerning them.

MILITIA.

Beside the garrison-houses, the town had a small force of militia. Says "The Old Petition": "The strength of Our towne upon yᵉ Enemy's approaching it, consisted of eighty fighting men." These men were able bodied and strong for the work of war, liable to do duty for either country or town; while others, younger and less vigorous, could stand guard and do some light service. When the war was fairly begun, the town's force was replenished by outside help. So that, with the people collected in garrisons, and the armed men able to fight in a sheltered place, a stout defense could be maintained against a considerably larger force.

COLONIAL MEASURES OF DEFENSE.

Beside the defensive measures adopted by the town, there were also others devised by the colony. The cause was a common one. If the frontier towns were left unprotected, the seaboard settlements would be rendered unsafe. Some of the defensive measures adopted by the colony, in which Sudbury shared, are set forth in the following papers: —

CAMBRIDGE, 28: 1 mo. 1676.

In obedience to an order of the Honorable Council, March, 1675-6, appointing us, whose names are underwritten, as a committee to consult the several towns of the county of Middlesex, with reference to the best means of the preservation of our out-towns, remote houses, and farms, for their security from the common enemy, we having sent to the several towns to send us their apprehensions by some one meet person of each town, this day we consulted concerning the same, and have concluded to purpose as followeth.

1. That the towns of Sudbury, Concord and Chelmsford be strengthened with forty men apiece, which said men are to be improved in scouting between town and town, who are to be commanded by men of prudence, courage and interest in the said towns, and the parties in each town are to be ordered to keep together in some place commodious in said towns, and not in garrisoned houses; and these men to be upon charge of the country.

2. That for the security of Billerica there be a garrison of a number competent at Weymessit, who may raise a thousand bushel of corn upon the lands of the Indians in that place, may be improved daily in scouting and ranging the woods between Weymessit and Andover, and on the west of Concord river on the east and north of Chelmsford, which will discover the enemy before he comes to the towns, and will prevent lurking Indians about our towns. Also that they shall be in a readiness to succor any of these towns at any time when in distress; also shall be ready to join with others to follow the enemy upon a sudden after their appearing.

3. That such towns as Lancaster, Groton, and Marlborough, that are forced to remove, and have not some advantage of settlement (peculiar) in the Bay, be ordered to settle at the frontier towns, that remain, for their strengthening; and the people of the said towns to which they are appointed, are to see to their accommodation in the said towns.

4. That the said towns have their own men returned that are abroad, and their men freed from impressment during their present state.

5. That there be appointed a select number of persons in each town of Middlesex, who are, upon any information of the distress of any town,

forthwith to repair to the relief thereof; and that such information may be seasonable, the towns are to dispatch posts, each town to the next, till notice be conveyed over the whole country, if need be.

Your humble servants,

HUGH MASON,

JONATHAN DANFORTH,

RICHARD LOWDON.

Another paper, setting forth suggestions for defensive measures, is the following: —

For the better securing our frontier towns from the incursion of the enemy, it is ordered by this Court, and authority thereof, that in each and every of these towns hereinafter mentioned, respectively, shall be allowed for their defence a sutible numbers of soldiers, well armed and furnished with ammunition fit for service; the number or proportion in such towns to be as follows, viz.

Groton,	20 men.	Weymouth,	15 men.
Pawtucket,	— men.	Billerica,	20 men.
Sudbury,	30 men.	Andover,	20 men.
Braintree,	15 men.	Concord,	20 men.
Bradford,	10 men.	Milton,	10 men.
Haverhill,	20 men.	Hingham,	20 men.
Chelmsford,	20 men.	Dedham,	20 men.
Medfield,	30 men.		

And it is further ordered, that each and every of the towns above mentioned, shall well and sufficiently maintain their several proportions of men with suitable provisions, respecting diet, at their own proper cost and charge during the time of their service.

These garrison soldiers, together with those who are to be in the prosecution of the enemy, are to be raised out of the four counties in which the garrisons are to be settled, and that these soldiers that are raised out of the garrison towns, shall be allowed them in part of the garrison, according as their proportion shall be, and that the settling of these garrisons in the respective towns, as to the place, and also the commander-in-chief, together with direction for the improvements of said garrisons to the best advantage for the security of towns and persons, it shall and is hereby left to the committee of militia in the several towns, who are hereby required and impowered to act therein according to this order. And this to be instead of a line of garrisons formerly proposed.

The deputies have past this with reference to the consent of the honored magistrates hereto. WILLIAM TORREY, Clerk.

Still another paper, showing the country's alarming condition, and the effort made by the colony to meet it, is the following: It was ordered, May 3, that each of the frontier towns be "divided into so many parties as a meete number may each day by turns be sent forth vpon the scout wth whom a party of Indians at the charge of the county shall be joined." (Colonial Records, Vol. V., p. 79.) These were to be managed by suitable commanders appointed by the military committee, and the soldiers who were absent "in service appertaining to sayed townes" were to be returned home and freed fiom the impress. In connection with said order, Sudbury was mentioned. Six others only were given. It was also ordered, at the same time, that when any town was assailed by the savages the chief commander, if present in any town, shall "send forth with what ayde can be spared with safety at home, for the security of the distressed." It was also ordered, — lest the frontier towns be endangered by persons leaving them in an exposed condition, — that no person "who is by law engaged to trayne, watch, ward or scout, is to leave the town he is an inhabitant of, without the consent of the committee of mellitie, or vpon their denial of the council of the commonwealth." Also, no party capable of doing garrison duty was to absent himself without the leave of the garrison commander. The Court also ordered, that soldiers should be employed daily "in scouting and warding, to prevent the skulking of the enemy about the sayd townes, and to give tymely notice of approaching danger, and also that the brush in highways and other places [judged necessary] be cut up;" "such persons, youth, &c." as were not in "traine bands, and exempt by law," were to be under obligations " to attend command for that service."

Thus the inhabitants of the frontier towns were to remain at their posts, and fight. If they fled to the forest, it was a lurking place for the foe; if they ventured for security to the seaboard settlements, they were liable to seizure and exile. All they could do was to gird themselves for the contest, and, gathered about their cordon of garrisons, await the coming foe.

SERVICES OF SUDBURY OUTSIDE ITS OWN TERRITORY.

The people did not have long to wait inactive about their garrisons; for though at the beginning of the war the town of Sudbury was not attacked, as the Indians chiefly confined hostilities to the county of Plymouth, yet it was soon called upon to send aid to other places. Nov. 22, 1675, a warrant came from Major Willard to John Grout, Josiah Haynes and Edmund Goodnow, who called themselves the "humble servants the militia of Sudbury," requiring the impressment of nine able men to the service of the country. They state to the Governor and Council that they have impressed the following men, namely: William Wade, Samuel Bush, John White, Jr., Thomas Rutter, Peter Noyes, Jr., James Smith, Dennis Headly, Mathew Gibbs, Jr., and Daniel Harrington; but that they wish to have them released. Joseph Graves, master of Harrington, states that his servant had not clothing fit for the service; that he was well clothed when he was impressed before, but that he wore his clothes out in that service, and could not get his wages to buy more. The service that he was formerly impressed for was the guarding of families in "Natick Bounds." One of those families is supposed to be that of Thomas Eames, which was attacked by the Indians near the outbreak of the war. (See Chapter II.) A further reason for their release from this service is found in the following extracts from their petition: "Considering our condition as a frontier town, and several of our men being already in the service, our town being very much scattered;" furthermore, that, several families being sickly, no use could be made of them for "watching, warding, scouting or impress, whereby the burden lies very hard on a few persons."

But, notwithstanding the imperiled condition of the people, we find that the town was represented a few weeks later in the "swamp fight," which was one of the hard-fought battles of the war. This conflict occurred Dec. 19, 1675, in what is now Kingston, R. I. At this place the Narragansett Indians had a stronghold that the English resolved to attack. For this purpose an expedition of one thousand men was fitted out from the united colonies of Massachusetts, Plymouth, and Connecticut, under command of Major Josiah Winslow, Governor of the Plymouth Colony. The march of the expedition was in winter, and heavy snows impeded the progress of the troops. The fort, for one built by Indians, was unusually strong. It was situated on a few acres of upland, in a swampy morass. The work was constructed of pallisades, surmounted by brush work, and the way to it was by fallen trees, which could be protected by firing from a block-house. As the English charged over this bridge, they were swept by the fire of the foe in a murderous manner, and before the fight was over seventy of the English were slain, and one hundred and fifty were wounded, while the Narragansetts, it is supposed, lost about one thousand. Sudbury was represented in Captain Mosely's company, which company, together with Captain Davenport's, it is said, led the van. Among the nine of Captain Mosely's men who were wounded was Richard Adams of Sudbury.

Not only did Sudbury furnish its quota of militia, but it supplied farther aid to the colony by the services of Lieut. Ephraim Curtis, the famous guide and scout. Mr. Curtis was a carpenter by trade, and at this time about thirty-three years of age. He had an intimate acquaintance with the country and its native inhabitants, and could speak their language with fluency. One prominent service that he performed was in acting as a messenger of the colonial authorities to the Nipnet Indians, who inhabited western and central Massachusetts. Supposing that an alliance of those Indians with Philip had not already been made, or that, if made, it might be broken, the authorities selected Ephraim Curtis to go among them and make overtures of peace. In giving information to the country of what had been done to avert the war, the authorities state as follows: " When our forces were sent out against Philip, We to satisfy and secure them, (the Nipnets), sent them, by Ephraim Curtis, a declaration with the public seal, that we had no design or intent to disturb them or any other Indians, that would remain in the plantation peaceable. Which message and messenger were rudely entertained by many of them there assembled, and the

messenger much endangered by the younger men, and not
with any satisfaction by the sachems, as the event showed."
Lieutenant Curtis went on more than one expedition to the
Nipnets. June 25, he was sent "to make a perfect discovery
of the motions of the Nipmug Indians." In a letter to the
colonial authorities, dated July 4, he says that he delivered
the letter to the committee at Brookfield, and from there
went directly to the Indians, whom he found at the same
place where he had met them before. The task undertaken
by Curtis in carrying out his embassy was dangerous in the
extreme, and his thrilling experiences as set forth in a letter
addressed to the Governor and Council, July 16, show a
sagacity and daring unsurpassed even in those heroic times.
We will give this letter in substance, quoting verbatim as
far as space will allow : " Whereas your Honors employed
your servant to conduct and also to make a perfect discovery
of the motions of the Nipmugs and western Indians, Your
Honor may be pleased here to see my return and behaviour."
After giving some incidents of the journey before he reached
Brookfield, he goes on to say, that, entering the woods, they
proceeded westward, till they discovered an Indian trail,
which they followed many miles, till they came to " the low
river by Springfield old road." He says, " Here we saw new
footings of Indians, and so, looking out sharp, in about two
miles riding we saw two Indians, which when I saw, I sent
the Indians that were with me from Marlborow, to speak with
them, but as soon as they had discovered us, they ran away
from us, but with fast riding and calling, two of our Indians
stopped one of them, the other ran away. We asked this
Indian, where the other Indians were. He being surprised
with fear, so he only told us that the Indians were but a
little way from us. So then I sent the Marlborow Indians
before, to tell them that the messenger of the Governor of
the Massachusetts was coming with peaceable words, but
when he came to them they would not believe him." Mr.
Curtis describes their place of encampment as being an
island, in area about four acres, encompassed by a broad,
miry swamp. Before reaching the river there met them at
least forty Indians, some with their guns on their shoulders,

others with them in their hands ready cocked and primed;
and most of those next to the river presented at them.
He addressed them in the name of the Governor, whom he
called his master, the Great Sachem of the Massachusetts,
and required them to own their fidelity. He informed them
that he came not to fight or to hurt them, but as a messenger
from the Governor. He states that there was a great uproar
among them, and some would have him killed. Says he,
"I requested their sachems to come over the river, but they
refused, saying that I must come over to them. My company was something unwilling, for they thought themselves
in very great danger where they were. I told them we
had better never have seen them, than not to speak to the
sachems, and if we ran from them in the time of this tumult
they would shoot after us, and kill some of us. So with
much difficulty we got over the river, and moist meadow, to
the island where they stood to face us at our coming out
of the mire, many Indians with their guns presented at us
ready cocked and primed, so we rushed between them and
called for their sachems. Still the uproar continued with
such noise that the air rang. I required them to lay down
their arms, and they commanded us to put up our arms
first and come off our horses, which I refused to do. With
much threatening and persuasion at last the uproar [ceased].
Many of them said they would neither believe me nor my
master, without he would send them two or three bushels of
powder. At length I spoke with their sachems which were
five, and their other grandees, which I think were twelve
more. Our Natic Indians seemed to be very industrious, all
this time to still the tumult, and so persuade the Indians,
and as I came to speak with the sachems we dismounted
and put up our arms." Mr. Curtis says their number was
about two hundred. (State Archives, Vol. LXVII., p. 215.)
Thus important and perilous was the work in which Curtis
engaged for the colony; and that he was selected for the
undertaking indicates the confidence of the authorities in
both his courage and sagacity. It may be in connection with
work among the Nipnets that the following order came to
the constables of Sudbury, July 16, directing them " to im-

press two or three valuable horses with men and arms as Ephraim Curtis shall require." These were to be delivered to Curtis, and to accompany him, with two or three "able and confiding Indians which Captain Gookin will provide to go with him on the country's service." The order was to be carried out with all speed. If the carrying out of this order related to work among the Nipnets, then more than one Sudbury citizen participated in it and encountered its perils.

Still another service that was rendered by Curtis was in connection with the ill-fated expedition sent out under command of Capt. Edward Hutchinson. July 27, 1675, Captain Hutchinson was ordered to take with him Capt. Thomas Wheeler of Concord, and a score or more of his troop of horse, Ephraim Curtis as a guide, and three Christian Indians as interpreters, and forthwith to repair to the Nipmuck country, to ascertain the movements of the Indians. The company went from Cambridge to Sudbury, July 28, 1675, and August 1 they arrived at Brookfield. They there learned that the Indians were about ten miles away. Messengers were sent to inform them of the approach of the English with friendly intentions. An interview was had with the sachems, who promised to meet the English near Brookfield the next morning. At the appointed time the English repaired to the place agreed upon, but the Indians were not there. It was considered inexpedient to follow them further; but, urged by the people of Brookfield, they proceeded, contrary to the advice of their guides, several miles, to a place near a swamp, when they found themselves in an ambuscade. The Indians, consisting of two or three hundred, suddenly attacked the little company, killing eight and wounding three. Among the killed was Sydrack (or Shadrack) Hapgood of Sudbury, and among the wounded were Captains Hutchinson and Wheeler. A retreat was at once made to Brookfield; and, having reached there, the soldiers entered one of the strongest houses and prepared for defense. Ephraim Curtis and Henry Young from Concord were sent to acquaint the Council at Boston of their imperiled condition. The brave emissaries started at once on their venturesome mission; but the town was so beset with the savages

that they were forced back to the garrison.   Soon afterwards
the house was assailed with great fury.   Young, looking
from the garret window, was shot and mortally wounded.
The night that followed was terrible.   The shot pelted on
the walls like hail, and the Indians attempted to set the
building on fire.   The situation was critical, the ammunition
was growing scant, and unless something was done to bring
relief all would inevitably be killed or taken captive.   The
undertaking was extremely hazardous.   To succeed required
a man of great courage and endurance, with a sagacity sufficient to outmatch the foe.   Few were fit for such a service,
even if any could be found to serve.   But the task was to
fall upon some one, and the man selected was Ephraim Curtis.   Again the bold adventurer set forth from the garrison,
a lone soldier, to rely on his prowess and a protecting Providence to shield him on his course.   Captain Wheeler in his
official report states of the affair as follows: "I spake to
Ephraim Curtis to adventure forth again on that service, and
to attempt it on foot as the way wherein was the most hope
of getting away undiscovered.   He readily assented, and
accordingly went out; but there were so many Indians every
where threatened, that he could not pass, without apparent
hazard of life, so he came back again, but towards morning
the said Ephraim adventured forth the 3d time, and was fain
to creep on his hands and knees for some space of ground
that he might not be discovered by the enemy, but through
God's mercy he escaped their hands, and got safely to Marlboro, though very much spent and ready to faint by reason
of want of sleep before he went from us, and his sore travel
night and day in that hot season till he got thither."   On
arriving at Marlboro he met Major Simon Willard and Capt.
James Parker of Groton, with forty-six men, who were there
to scout between Marlboro, Lancaster, and Groton.   These,
on receiving intelligence of affairs at Brookfield, hastened at
once with relief.   They arrived August 7, just in season to
rescue the survivors.   After this narration, it is unnecessary
to speak of the bravery of this Sudbury scout, or the value
of his services to the country.   It was a forlorn hope upon
which he went forth, and none better than he knew the haz-

ardous nature of his task, or the sad consequences of capture. Many weary miles of travel lay between him and the seaboard settlements, but, tired and faint, he sped on his way till he had faithfully discharged his trust, and sent the rescuers to his beleaguered comrades.

But the time was near when Sudbury was to need all her resources for the defense of her own territory. The foe that hitherto largely operated in the county of Plymouth was soon to invade that of Middlesex, and make Sudbury the scene of most important events. The first approach of the Indians to the town and its vicinity with hostile intent was, we judge, in small bands, which ranged the forest in an independent way, or which acted as detachments to spy out the land. These scouting parties alarmed the inhabitants, who sent messages to the colonial authorities, with a statement of facts and request for relief. The indications are that the colonial authorities did not anticipate that great peril was so near. After the defeat of the Narragansetts in the swamp fight, it was supposed that the Indians were in a crippled condition, and that the devastating effect of that fight would tend to discourage and keep them in check. To so great an extent was a sense of security felt by the authorities, that in some cases soldiers were dismissed from the garrison-houses. Captain Brocklebank, who was stationed at Marlboro, asked to be dismissed from that place, stating that he had little to do. But the weakness of the enemy was evidently overestimated ; and it was not long before the frontier towns were made aware that a formidable foe was near. Feb. 23, 1675, Hugh Clark stated to the Council, that he " being the last week upon the scout with Capt. Gibbs, about Lancaster, Concord and Sudbury, found several houses deserted, having corn in them, and cattle about them, belonging to the late inhabitants thereof, who for fear left their habitations." He states that they found at least about sixty bushels of corn in one house. And he assured the Council that "it would be of advantage to the Indians and straighten the English unless something is done to prevent it."

The Rev. Edmund Brown, who, as we have before noticed, fortified his house, sent information to the authorities by

Ensign Grout about the presence of a lurking enemy in Sudbury. He says: " It is reported that our woods are pestered with Indians. One Adams within our bounds was shot at by a lurking Indian or more. He was shot through the coat and shirt near to the arm pit. One Smith walking the woods was assailed by 3 or 4 Indians, whom he discovered swooping down a hill toward him, but Smith saved himself by his legs. One Joseph Freeman coming up about 4 mile Brook discovered two Indians, one in the path presenting his gun at him in the way (in a bright moonlight night), but Freeman dismounting shot at him, and mounting rode for it. One Joseph [Shaley] coming home from Marlboro on Thursday last discovered Indians in our bounds, one of which made a shot at him, the bullet passing by him, but being mounted and riding for it he escaped. One Joseph Curtis, son to Ephraim Curtis on Saturday last heard 3 volleys of shot made by Indians between us and Weston. This being to long, Ensign Grout can give a full narrative to your Honor and Councill. The consideration of all which I hope will excite you : : : to order that these woods may be scoured and that our town of Sudbury a frontier town may be enabled to contribute aid therein and defend itself with its quantity of men, I humbly move. And this I shall [present] unto the Honorable Councill that we may not have men pressed out of our small town." Date, " Sudbury 26th 7th mo." In another letter dated " Sudbury 7th of 12th mo. 75," Mr. Brown refers to a late order of the authorities dismissing garrison soldiers, and requests that John Gleason, who had been impressed but returned in safety, might be at his disposal. He also speaks of Zenias Parmenter, whom they " were pleased to free from impress." He objected to having his guard dismissed, on any general order for the dismissal of garrisons, since he maintained it at his own expense.

Thus, towards the close of 1675, Sudbury and its vicinity felt a sense of insecurity, because of a lurking foe. The indications are, that before the Indians made an advance in great force they came in small detachments or bands, doing occasional mischief, and keeping the inhabitants in

a state of suspense. No one was safe who went abroad
unarmed; and those living in the more exposed localities
had even abandoned their homes. In the instance related
by Hugh Clark, the flight was precipitous, the corn being
left in the crib. But it was not long after these evidences
of a mere scattered foe before there were indications that the
town was to suffer a more general attack by a considerably
increased force. In the towns beyond its western border
more or less havoc had already been made, and one after
another of them had already succumbed. Feb. 10, 1675,
Lancaster suffered by the loss of fifty killed or taken captive; and the same month a requisition was made upon Concord and Sudbury requiring them "forthwith to impress 8
carts in each town for the bringing down of goods of such
persons of Lancaster as being bereaved by the late hand of
God are disabled from continuing there." By March 13,
Groton was made desolate, and forty dwellings were burned;
and Marlboro alone remained between Sudbury and the vast
wilderness that sheltered the foe. The first blow that fell
on the town, that has been noted by historians of that day,
was on the 10th of March, 1676. Says Mather, "Mischief
was done, and several lives were cut off by the Indians. An
humbling Providence, inasmuch as many churches were this
day fasting and praying." This attack on the town was evidently sufficient to put the people more on their guard, and
the better prepared them to meet the great force which was to
assail them in the following month. It was about three days
before this attack of March 10 that Rev. Edmund Brown's
letter was dated, in which he writes to the authorities, and
mentions the "eminent danger yet remaining over our heads
which occasions divers of our towns to make address for
some grant and with good success." Eleven days after this
attack, "at the motion and request of Ensign Grout of Sudbury, on behalf of Lieut. Ephraim Curtis, it was ordered that
the said Curtis, together with any other volunteers which
shall join with him, shall march under his command into the
woods, and endeavor to surprise, kill, or destroy, any of the
Indians our enemies : : : and he may expect such encouragement as the late order of the General Court directs."

THE NEAR APPROACH OF THE INDIANS, THEIR REPULSE,
AND THE DEATH OF NETUS.

While the prospect was thus threatening, the design of
the Indians for a season was effectually stayed, and a disastrous invasion prevented, by a bold move made by the inbah-
itants of the town.   The event referred to occurred March
27, 1676.   A force of savages, near three hundred in number, were within about a half mile of Sudbury's western
boundary.   The force was led by Netus, the Nipmuc captain.   (See Chapter II.)   This band was intent on mischief.
It was on the trail for prey.   Flushed with the expectation
of easy victory, they waited the dawn of day to begin their
foul work, and seize such persons and spoil as were found
outside the garrisons.   On Sabbath night they made their
encampment within half a mile of a garrison.   Their mischievous course through the previous day had been so little
opposed that they felt secure as if in a world of peace.   But
the English were on their track.

Intelligence of their presence at Marlboro had reached
Sudbury, and a movement was made to oppose them.   A
score of bold citizens set forth for the beleaguered place.
On their arrival at Marlboro they were reinforced by twenty
soldiers, who were taken from the garrisons, and the two
forces went in search of the enemy.   Before daybreak they
discovered them asleep about their fires.   The English, in
night's stillness, crept close upon the camp.   Wrapped in
slumber, and unsuspicious of what was so near, the Indians
were suddenly startled by a destructive volley from an unexpected foe.   The English took them by complete surprise.
So effectually had they directed their fire that the Indians
speedily fled.   About thirty of their number were wounded,
of whom it is said fourteen afterwards died.   Not only were
the Indians numerically weakened, but demoralized somewhat by such a bold and unlooked-for assault.   Probably
this act saved Sudbury for a time.   Netus was slain, and for
near a month there was a cessation of hostilities within and
about the town.

As the importance of this event is considerable, and the

evidence is quite clear concerning it, we will present the narrative as given by several authorities. Says Mather: "March 27th some of the inhabitants of Sudbury being alarmed by what the Indians did yesterday to their neighbors in Malbury, apprehending that they might come upon the enemy unawares, in case they should march after them in the night time, they resolved to try what might be done, and that, not altogether without success, for toward the morning whilst it was yet dark, they discovered where the Indians lay by their fires. And such was their boldness, as that about 300 of them lay all night within half a mile of one of the garrison houses, in that town where they had done so much mischief the day before. Albeit the darkness was such as an English man could not be distinguished from an Indian; yet ours being 40 in number discharged several times upon them, and (as Indians taken at that time do confess) God so disposed of the bullets that were shot at that time, that no less than thirty Indians were wounded, of whom there were 14 that died, several of which had been perpetrators in the late bloody tragedies. They fired hard upon the English, but neither killed nor wounded so much as one man in the skirmish."

Captain Brocklebank, garrison commander at Marlboro, states thus in his report to the colonial authorities: "Sabbath day night there came about 20 men from Sudbury, and we out of the several garrisons drew 20 more, and in the night time they went out to see if they could discover the enemy and give them some check." He states, that "they found them by their fires, and fired on them, and they ran away; but their number being few, and not knowing the number of the enemy, but apprehending by their noise and firing at them that the force of the enemy was considerable, they returned home without the loss of any men or wounds from the enemy, and only one man had his hand shattered by the breaking of a gun."

Thus straightforward and plain are these authorities in their description of this nightly encounter. No better evidence could be desired than Captain Brocklebank's letter. From these narratives we are informed that the people of

Sudbury formed this bold project; that a score of her brave citizens went forth to stay the course of the Indian invaders; that they went beyond the limits of Sudbury into a neighboring town that had already been attacked by the foe; and that, upon receiving aid from a government official in command of the garrison, they made this successful assault. There is no evidence that when they started they had any assurance that reinforcements would be afforded them. They knew the enemy were in force at Marlboro, and courageously marched to check their advance. Whether the reinforcements that they received at Marlboro were citizens of that town, or some of the soldiers who were sent there by the government, we are not informed. We know that Captain Brocklebank was a government commander, and that a part of the Marlboro garrison were government men, some of whom subsequently accompanied Captain Brocklebank to the Sudbury fight.

That Sudbury people in this affair acted not simply in their own defense is implied in "The Old Petition," in which it is stated that "the Indians in their disastrous invasions were resolved by our ruine to revenge yᵉ reliefe which our Sudbury volunteers approached to distressed Marlborough, in slaying many of yᵉ enemy & repelling yᵉ rest."

CHAPTER XII.

1675-1700.

Philip's War. — Indian Invasion; Date. — Number of the Enemy. — Philip's Preparation. — Indian Powwow. — Movements of the English. — General Attack on the Town. — Assault on the Haynes Garrison. — Hostilities on the East Side. — Resistance of the English. — Arrival of Reinforcements; Concord Company, Watertown Company. — The Indians Driven Over the Causeway and Bridge. — Attempt to Reinforce Captain Wadsworth. — Description Given in " The Old Petition."

> Up the hillside, down the glen,
> Rouse the sleeping citizen;
> Summon out the might of. men!
> It is coming, — it is nigh!
> Stand your homes and altars by;
> On your own free thresholds die.
>
> WHITTIER.

HAVING noticed the course of hostilities in and about Sudbury by scattered detachments and skulking squads of Indians, we will now consider a more prominent event of the war, — namely, the attack upon the town by King Philip, with one of the most formidable forces that he ever led along the New England frontier. We have found no evidence that, up to April, 1676, Philip himself ever visited the place; but in the final assault the great chieftain directed his warriors in person. At the time of the invasion there was nothing west of Sudbury to obstruct his course. The last town was Marlboro, and this was devastated as by a close gleaner in the great field of war. The people had almost wholly abandoned the place; the dwellings were reduced to ash-heaps, and a few soldiers only were quartered there to guard the road to Brookfield and the Connecticut. Sudbury at this time was the objective point of King Philip. That he had a special purpose in assailing the place, other than what led him to conduct the war elsewhere, is implied in " The Old Petition," in the words before quoted, where the object of revenge is mentioned. Certain it is, he had a strong force, and fought hard and long to destroy the place.

DATE OF PHILIP'S ATTACK ON THE TOWN.

Before entering, however, on the details of the conflict, we will notice the time at which it occurred. Previous to the discovery of " The Old Petition," two dates had been assigned, namely, the 18th and the 21st of April. Various authorities were quoted in support of each. So important was the matter considered, that a committee was appointed to examine evidence on the subject. The committee reported in favor of the 21st. (Report of Kidder and Underwood.) Notwithstanding this decision, opinions still differed ; but the discovery of " The Old Petition " has fully settled this matter, and established beyond question that the date of Philip's attack on the town and the garrisons, and the " Sudbury Fight," was the 21st. We can understand how, before the discovery of this paper, opinions might vary ; how an historian might mistake as to a date, and a monument might perpetuate the error. When President Wadsworth erected a slate-stone at the grave of Captain Wadsworth, the date inscribed might have been taken from the historian Hubbard, who might have received it from an unreliable source. But we can hardly suppose that a mistake could occur in the paper above referred to concerning the date of this event. This paper is a calm, deliberate document, signed by inhabitants of Sudbury, and sent to the Colonial Court less than six months after the invasion by Philip. It gives the date of the invasion in the following words : " An Account of Losse Sustained by Severall Inhabitants of ye towne of Sudbury by ye Indian Enemy 21st April 1676."

NUMBER OF THE ENEMY.

Philip arrived with his force at Marlboro on or about the 18th of April, and soon started for Sudbury. The number of his warriors has been variously estimated. In the " Old

Indian Chronicle" it is given as "about a thousand strong." Gookin states, in his history of the Christian Indians, "that upon the 21st of April about mid-day tidings came by many messengers that a great body of the enemy not less as was judged than fifteen hundred, for the enemy to make their force seem very large there were many women among them whom they had fitted with pieces of wood cut in the forms of guns, which these carried, and were placed in the centre, they had assaulted a place called Sudbury that morning, and set fire of sundry houses and barns of that town . . . giving an account that the people of the place were greatly distressed and earnestly desired succor."

Besides Gookin's statement as to the presence of squaws in the company, we have the authority of Mrs. Rowlandson, who mentions an Indian that went to the Sudbury fight accompanied by his squaw with her pappoose upon her back. Mrs. Rowlandson was the wife of Rev. Mr. Rowlandson of Lancaster, and was made captive in the attack on that town. She went with Philip to Sudbury, and became a witness to some of the sad scenes there, which were published in a book entitled "Mrs. Rowlandson's Removes."

Other evidence of the size of Philip's force is found in the "Old Petition," which says, "Let ye Most High have ye high praise due unto him, but let not ye unworthy Instruments be forgotten. Was there with vs any towne so beset since ye ware begun, with twelve or fourteen hundred fighting men, warriors, sagamores, from all Parts with their men of Arms?"

THE PREPARATION.

Before the Indians went to Sudbury they made careful preparation. Says Mrs. Rowlandson, " They got a company together to pow-wow." The manner as she describes it is as follows : —

There was one that kneeled upon a deer skin with a company round him in a ring, who kneeled striking upon the ground with their hands and with sticks, and muttering or humming with their mouths. Beside him who kneeled in the ring there also stood one with a gun in his hand. Then he on the deer skin made a speech, and all manifest an assent to

it, and so they did many times together. Then they bid him with a gun,
go out of the ring, which he did, but when he was out they called him in
again, but he seemed to make a stand. Then they called the more ear.
nestly till he turned again. Then they all sang. Then they gave him
two guns, in each hand one, and so he on the deer skin began again, and
at the end of every sentence in his speaking they all assented, and humming or muttering with their mouths, and striking upon the ground with
their hands. Then they bid him with the two guns go out of the ring
again, which he did a little way. Then they called him again, but he
made a stand. So they called him with greater earnestness. But he
stood reeling and wavering as if he knew not whether he should stand or
fall, or which way to go. Then they called him with exceeding great
vehemence, all of them, one and another. After a little while he turned
in, staggering as he went, with his arms stretched out, in each hand a
gun. As soon as he came in they all sang, and rejoiced exceeding
awhile, and then he upon the deer skin made another speech, unto which
they all assented in a rejoicing manner, and so they ended their business
and forthwith went to Sudbury fight.

The foregoing statements plainly show that a large force
was being led to Sudbury. The great chieftain doubtless felt
sure of his prey. Mrs. Rowlandson says, " To my thinking
they went without any scruple but that they should prosper
and gain the victory." Philip was not aware of the strong
reinforcements which were to be sent to the town's relief.
The tramp of Wadsworth and his company had not as yet
reached his ears. For aught he knew, the forest resounded
with only the tramp of his own stalwart men.

But, while the Indians were preparing for the attack, the
English were by no means idle. Things were fast being put
in readiness to meet the worst. The blow received was to
be returned, and the spoils of conquest were to be dearly
obtained. Notwithstanding the customary cunning of the
Indians, and their usual sly way, the attack in this instance
was not an entire surprise. Their coming was announced by
several acts of hostility on the day previous to the general
assault. According to tradition, they began their marauding
by burning several houses and killing several inhabitants.
Among the slain were a Mr. Boone and son, and Mr.
Thomas Plympton, who was endeavoring to conduct them,
with some of their goods, to a place of safety. This skir-
mishing on the outskirts put the people on their guard, and

warned them to flee for their lives. It showed the hostile intent of the enemy, and the necessity of making haste if they would escape capture or death. Adequately to describe the state of affairs in Sudbury on the eve of this Indian invasion would be a difficult task. We may, however, conjecture that the scene was a thrilling one, and that it was a time of uncertainty and anxious suspense to the inhabitants. What had come upon others was about to come upon them. The dismal intelligence of disaster to far-off settlements was to be made more vivid by the same dread foe in their midst. It was their dwellings that were soon to be ash-heaps, their herds that were to be spoils of war, their fields that were to suffer invasion. The wild omens were to bring presaged wrath to *their* doors; and the warm homes once smiling with comfort were to be forsaken and left to the foe. With but a partial realization of what was to come, we may conclude that Sudbury was never before or since so astir. There were men struggling for life; families hurrying together to the shelter of garrisons, with whatever of household goods they could snatch; loving ones bearing the feeble and sick in their arms, and all rushing to a place of safety. From hither and yon flocked the company. Again and again the latch-string was flung loose from the garrison, as one by one new arrivals came in. None knew when they abandoned their homes that they would see them again, nor that they themselves would ever reach a safe place. The Indian invader was hard by their track. He might spring any moment upon them. Each object might be his place of concealment. He lurked by the woody wayside, he crept along the margin of the open lands; and on the outskirt of the woodland he peered to get a sight at some late refugee whom he might bear away as his prey.

Within the garrisons the scenes were also, doubtless, of a stirring character. These places were soon to be isolated. Communication with them was to be cut off. They were to be surrounded by a fierce horde of beleaguering savages; and before help could arrive the doors might be battered by tomahawks, or the torch be applied to the wall. Anxiously might those who had entered these places watch and await coming events; eagerly may they have looked to catch a glimpse of their belated townsmen who might be coming from the more exposed outskirts, or who, like the brave Thomas Plympton, had gone forth to bring to the garrison the dwellers on lonely homesteads. The sound of firing over the distant woodlands; the smoke rising in clouds upon the far-off horizon; occasional new arrivals from different localities, bringing evidence of the near approach of the Indians, — all these would present a scene of a startling character; and as the night shadows of April 20 crept about the lonely garrisons, those within had no assurance but that it was as the darkness of the shadow of death.

But, though the scene was thrilling and one of anxious suspense, it was nevertheless one of courage and hope. From what we know of the character of the Sudbury inhabitants, and of their conduct when the attack was begun, we conclude that in those hours of ingathering there were hearts full of determination, and that plans were laid for a successful defense. Doubtless the ammunition was carefully looked to and put in a convenient place, the flints scraped, the priming-wire used, and every aperture in the garrison walls closed and secured, except such as were left to fire from.

Beside the regular force of the town's militia who were to assist in defense of the garrisons, it is supposed some militia were present from other places. Some men from the force of Captain Brocklebank, the garrison commander at Marlboro, are supposed to have been there. Of twelve soldiers who went from Rowley, and did service in Sudbury, seven returned to their homes; and it is hardly supposable that so many should have escaped if in the Wadsworth fight. We presume, therefore, with the historian of Rowley, that they helped man these garrisons.

THE ATTACK.

During the night of the 20th of April, Philip advanced his forces, and took positions for the coming day. The Indians possessed such a knowledge of the country as enabled him to do this to advantage. Every path through the woodland had been trod by the moccasined foot; every log crossing or rude bridge, from the Connecticut to the river at Sudbury, were on old and well-worn trails. Among the invaders were some who had lived thereabouts for years, or had ranged the forest for game, or frequented the Musquetahquid (Sudbury River) for fish. From these Philip might obtain information of the country, and thus be enabled to lay his plans. This doubtless was what he did. Probably every homestead, however humble, was noted ; every highway guarded, and every wood-path carefully watched. No lone haystack in secluded meadow nook, no rude shelter for cattle, no rough shed for the sheep, escaped the vigilance of his roving marauders as in night's stillness they ranged through the town. As they reconnoitred about the garrisons, they doubtless noticed each object from which they could direct their fire, and each way of approach and retreat.

Of the movements of the Indians the English probably knew but little as the night wore on. The soft tread of the moccasin, as the dusky squad stole silently about these strongholds, was too gentle for even the ears of such anxious listeners in the ominous stillness of that solitude. Even the slow-moving bush which may have hidden from view some adventurous savage, as he approached a little nearer to reconnoitre the place and discover its weak or strong points, though it aroused suspicion of a lurking foe, yet revealed nothing of his number or strength, nor of the squad in concealment near by, who awaited the whispered report of their comrade. No night-fires lit the heavens with their lurid glow, disclosing the foe's intent. His dark encampment was doubtless within the dense pines, where he lay on his evergreen couch until called forth by the signal of daybreak. The stillness of nature and of man were both there. It was the calm that foreboded a storm which was to burst upon man and his dwelling, the herd and its stall.

But the silence soon broke. With the morning the mystery cleared. It was early discovered by the inhabitants that during the night-time the Indians had gotten possession of everything in the west part of the town but the garrisons, and that they had become so scattered about in squads, and had so occupied various localities, that at a given signal they

could strike a concerted blow. Says the "Old Indian Chronicle," "The houses were built very scatteringly, and the enemy divided themselves into small parties, which executed
their design of firing at once." The smoke of dwellings
curled upward on the morning air, the warwhoop rang out
from the forest, and from the town's westerly limit to the
Watertown boundary the destructive work was begun. It
is said by tradition that the Indians even entered the Watertown territory, and set fire to a barn in what is now Weston.

About the time of firing the deserted houses, the Indians
made their attack on the garrisons. The detachments for
this work were probably as specifically set apart as were
those for burning the dwelling-places; and doubtless hours
before daybreak the foe lay concealed in their picked places
ready to pour their shot on the wall. The attack on the
Haynes house was of great severity. The position of the
building favored the near and concealed approach of the
enemy. The small hill at the north afforded a natural ram-
part from which to direct his fire; behind it he could skulk
to close range of the house, and drive his shot with terrible
force on the walls. There is a tradition, that, by means of
this hill, the Indians tried to set the building on fire. They
filled a cart with flax, ignited, and started it down the
hill towards the house; but before it reached its destination
it upset, and the building was saved. Tradition also states
that near the house was a barn, which the Indians burned;
but that this proved advantageous to the inmates of the garrison, as it had afforded a shelter for the Indians to fire from.
Probably this barn was burned with the expectation of setting fire to the house.

But it was not long that the Indians were to fight at
close range. The bold defenders soon sallied forth, and
commenced aggressive warfare. They fell on the foe,
forced them back, and drove them from their "skulking
approaches." Could Philip have spared reinforcements at
this critical time, he doubtless would have readily done so,
rather than suffered defeat at this garrison. But his main
force was lying in wait at Green Hill for Captain Wadsworth, other detachments were plundering on the east side,

THE HAYNES GARRISON HOUSE.
From original painting by A. S. Hudson.

and some were besieging other garrisons. The force needed
at different localities prevented a concentration at any one
point. Thus the day was won at the Haynes house. In
the skirmish the Indians suffered considerably, while the
English lost but two, and that through their own indiscretion.

While the conflict was going on, the inmates of the garrison showed stout hearts and commendable coolness and courage; even the women manifested but little, if any, timidity.
Perhaps they served in opening and closing the apertures
to the garrison, when the musket was thrust out and withdrawn; they may have swabbed the foul guns, wiped the
priming-pan, and scraped the flints; they may have stood,
powder-horn in hand, with the powder all poured for the
charge, and the tow wadding all torn for the ramrod's ready
work. Such was the work at the old Haynes Garrison, —
the noble work of a noble company.

The service at the other garrisons was probably all that
was needed. That none of these houses were captured is
enough to indicate a stout and manly defense. They were
all coveted objects of the enemy, and plans for the capture
of each had been carefully laid. That all the garrisons did
both defensive and aggressive work is shown by "The Old
Petition," which says, "Our Garrison men kept not within
their Garrisons, but issued forth to fight yᵉ Enemy within
their skulking approaches." Thus manly was the defense of
the garrisons during the long morning hours of that eventful
day. From the dawning till noon the clouds gathered and
broke over those frail, scattered fortresses. All about them
was confusion and turmoil; in various directions the dense
smoke-cloud drooped its dismal drapery over smouldering
homesteads; and on the ears of the beleaguered inhabitants
frequently broke the wild yell of the foe. But still they
fought on, with none near to assist them. No drum-beat
announced the approach of reinforcements. They might not
have known that relief parties had started. The tramp of
Wadsworth and his company, as they passed through to
Marlboro the preceding night, might have been mistaken for

the tramp of the foe; and nothing, for aught they knew, awaited the garrisons but to win the victory alone.

HOSTILITIES ON THE EAST SIDE.

While the conflict was raging around the garrisons on the west side, there was by no means inactivity on the east side. The condition of things was critical there also; the circumstances in the two places, however, were different. The east side was so protected by the high water, which at that time covered the meadows, that the savages would naturally be more cautious in their mode of attack; with a crossing only at the town bridge and causeway, it would be unsafe to scatter their forces very much, or to venture far from the place of retreat; nevertheless they invaded the territory, and commenced their mischievous work by plundering dwelling-houses. They doubtless intended to take what spoils they could carry away, and then burn the place; but they were effectually checked in their work. The inhabitants fell upon them with fury. They beat them from the very thresholds of their humble homes, and snatched the spoil from their savage clutch; they even forced them to retreat on the run, and seek safety in precipitous flight.

During the progress of the conflict the women and children were probably at the stockade of Rev. Edmund Brown, at Timber Neck. This stockade was sufficient to shelter all in that neighborhood. It was admirably situated as a place of defense: being at the junction of Mill Brook and the river, at high water it had but two sides of attack, and the Indians could only reach it by a circuitous course. From these circumstances it is hardly probable that it would require many soldiers to man this stockade; hence more could be spared to defend their homes. But all that could be spared made a very small company at best.

The entire defensive force of the town being but about eighty militia men, with a few added who had come from outside, we may conclude that the fighting was largely done by a few. Says "The Old Petition," "The enemy was by few beaten out of houses which they had entered and by a few hands were forced to a running fight which way they

could, yᵉ spoil taken by them on yᵉ East side of yᵉ river was
in great parᵗᵉ recovered." This gives an outline of the facts,
which, like the rest of " The Petition," suggest various possible and probable details of the conflict; and the conjecture
is by no means extravagant, that those morning hours on
both sides of the river witnessed scenes of daring by those
brave little companies unsurpassed in the annals of King
Philip's War.

Before leaving this part of the subject, we will quote from
" The Old Petition," which to an extent has furnished the
facts from which the foregiven description has been taken:
" The Enemy well knowing Our grounds, passes, avenues,
and situations, had near surrounded Our town ni yᵉ morning
early (Wee not knowing of it) till discovered by fireing severall disserted houses; the Enemy with greate force & fury
assaulted Deacon Haines' house well fortified yet badly scit-
uated as advantagous to yᵉ Enemy's approach & dangerous
to yᵉ Repellant yet (by yᵉ help of God) yᵉ Garrison not
onely defended yᵉ place frō betweene five or six of yᵉ clock
in yᵉ Morning, till about One in yᵉ Afternoon but forced
yᵉ Enemy with considerable slaughter to draw off. Many
Observables worthy of Record hapened in this assault, vizt:
that noe man or woman seemed to be possessed with feare;
Our Garrisonmen kept not within their Garrisons, but issued
forth to fight yᵉ Enemy in their sculking approaches: We
had but two of Our townes men slaine, & yᵗ by indiscretion
none wounded."

ARRIVAL OF REINFORCEMENTS.

While the town's inhabitants were defending the garrisons, and at the same time endeavoring to prevent the savages from further plundering their dwellings and making off
with the spoils, reinforcements were approaching the town
from several directions. Among the principles of action
proposed by the authorities at the beginning of the war was,
that one town should assist another with what men it could
spare, on the giving of a general alarm; so it was in the
case before us. Intelligence of the enemy in the neighborhood of Sudbury spread rapidly to surrounding places, and

men hastened from Concord and Watertown, and were sent by the colonial authorities from the vicinity of Boston. As each of these three reinforcements had a history of its own, we will describe them separately.

THE CONCORD COMPANY.

This consisted of " twelve resolute young men," who endeavored to render assistance in the neighborhood of the Haynes Garrison-house. Before they had reached it, however, and formed a junction with the citizens of the town, they met with a melancholy fate in the neighboring meadow. The account of the affair is thus given by Mr. Shattuck in the Concord history, which account, he states, is preserved by tradition : "Arriving near the garrison-house of Walter Haynes, they observed several squaws, who, as they drew near, danced, shouted, powwowed, and used every method to amuse and decoy them. Eleven of the English pursued and attacked them, but found themselves, too late, in an ambuscade, from which a large number of Indians rushed upon and attacked them with great fury. Notwithstanding they made a bold resistance, it was desperate, and ten of them were slain. The other escaped to the garrison, where the neighboring inhabitants had fled for security, which was bravely defended."

Of those who were killed at this time belonging to Concord, Shattuck's history gives the following names : James Hosmer, Samuel Potter, John Barnes, Daniel Comy, and Joseph Buttrick. The Middlesex Probate Records have the following concerning James Hosmer, in connection with the settlement of his estate : " being slayne in the engagement with the Indians at Sudbury on the 21st of the second month [April] in the year 1676." In the Middlesex County Probate Records are also the following names of soldiers slain in Sudbury, April 21 : David Curry and Josiah Wheeler of Concord, and William Haywood of Sudbury. Says the Old Indian Chronicle : " They were waylaid and eleven of them cut off." Says Hubbard of this affair : " These men at the first hearing of the alarm, who unawares were surprised near a garrison-house, in hope of getting some advantage upon a small party of the enemy that presented themselves in a meadow. A great number of the Indians, who lay unseen in the bushes, suddenly rose up and intercepting the passage to the garrison-house, killed and took them all."

The men thus slain on the meadow were left where they fell until the following day, when the bodies were brought in boats to the foot of the old town bridge and buried. Two of the parties who helped perform the work of burial were Warren and Pierce of the Watertown company. The following is their description of the scene, as given in a petition to the General Court: "On the next day in the morning, so soon as it was light, we went to look for the Concord men who were slain in the River meadow, and there we went in water up to our knees, where we found five, and we brought them in canoes and buried them there." The spot mentioned here as the burial place is, we conjecture, on the northerly side of the town bridge, on the eastern bank of the river. This supposition is based on the fact that it was high water on the meadow at that time, and hence this place was probably the only one suitable for burial. A monument to this brave relief company would be very appropriate, and serve to mark a locality which on that day was full of stirring events.

THE WATERTOWN COMPANY.

The reinforcements from Watertown were more fortunate than those from Concord, and were spared to assist in saving the town. This company was under the command of Capt. Hugh Mason, a bold and gallant commander. Captain Mason was of a committee of four appointed March 15 to provide for the defence of the frontier towns of Middlesex county. At the head of forty Watertown men he had marched previously to the relief of Groton. He was now prompt to meet the foe at Sudbury, and, although seventy-five years old, he came in a timely manner.

These reinforcements probably arrived some time before noon. As the attack began about daybreak, and took the inhabitants of Sudbury somewhat by surprise, it is hardly probable that the news would reach Watertown until the

morning was well advanced. Watertown was the border
town on the east. The part now Weston was called the
"Farmers' Precinct." At this locality the sound of guns
could without doubt be heard, and the smoke rising over
the woods in dark ominous clouds might bespeak what was
befalling the neighborhood. Moreover, the intelligence may
have reached Watertown by couriers, who carried it to Boston, arriving there about midday.

When Captain Mason reached Sudbury, about two hundred Indians were on the east side the river engaged in mischievous work. The little company of town's people who
could be spared from the stockade was too small to drive
them back over the river. The best they could do was to
keep them from too close range of their little stronghold,
and save a part of their property and dwellings. But when
these reinforcements arrived, the united forces compelled the
foe to make a general retreat. Whereas, before the arrival
of reinforcements, the Indians, as stated in "The Old Petition," " were by few beaten out of houses which they had
entered and were plundering, and by a few hands were
forced to a running fight," they were now driven beyond
the causeway and bridge.

The contest that preceded this retreat of the savages was
doubtless severe. Two hundred Indians were a force sufficient to offer stubborn resistance. They were near a large
force held in reserve by King Philip on the west side of the
river, and might at any time receive reinforcement from
him; and if they could hold the causeway and bridge, the
day might be won. On the other hand, the English had a
vast deal at stake; if the foe was forced over the stream, the
east side would for a time be safe. They could defend the
narrow causeway and bridge, while the high water would
protect their flanks. Such were the circumstances that
would cause each to make a hard fight. But the English
prevailed. The foe was forced back, and the bridge and
causeway were held, so that they could not repass them.

But the English did not stop with this victory; though the
day was won here, the contest still waged on the west side.
From beyond Green Hill, about two miles westerly, came

the sound of combat; and they knew that Captain Wadsworth and his company, who passed through Watertown on their way to Marlboro, were engaged in stern conflict. The scent of battle as it came borne on the April breeze, the dull sound of the distant firing, and the outlying detachments sent to keep reinforcements away, indicated that the contest at the hill was hot. But, undaunted, the English pushed forward. Beyond the bridge and the causeway, up the slope of the hill, perhaps by the Old Lancaster Road, they moved on to the work of rescue; but they failed in the accomplishment of their object. The Indians were too many for that small company. Notwithstanding their courage, they had but limited strength. The Indians endeavored to surround them, and being forced to retreat they sought refuge in the Goodnow Garrison. There they remained until nightfall, when they again sallied forth; but this time it was not to meet the enemy. The conflict was over. The disastrous day was done. Night covered as with a friendly mantle the terrible scene; its shadows were unbroken by the flash of guns, and its stillness undisturbed by the rude sounds of war. The foe had retired, their victims lay dead where they fell, and a "few surviving comrades" were all they could bear with them to the east side settlement.

Thus noble was the work of that company; and the peril attendant upon the undertaking is indicative of the courage with which they entered upon it. Major Gookin, in his "History of the Christian Indians," states concerning this affair as follows: "Upon April 21, about midday, tidings came by many messengers that a great body of the enemy had assaulted a town called Sudbury that morning. Indeed (through God's favor) some small assistance was already sent from Watertown by Capt. Hugh Mason. These with some of the inhabitants joined and with some others that come in to their help, there was vigorous resistance made, and a check given to the enemy, so that those that were gotten over the river were forced to retreat, and the body of the enemy were repulsed, that they could not pass the bridge, which pass the English kept."

Says Warren and Pierce, who were of the Watertown

company: "But we who were with them can more largely inform this Honored Council, that as it is said in the petition that we drove two hundred Indians over the river, we followed the enemy over the river . . . and with some others joined and went to see if we could relieve Capt. Wadsworth upon the hill, and there we had a fight with the Indians, but they being so many of them, and we stayed so long, that we were almost encompassed by them, which caused us to retreat to Capt. Goodnow's Garrison, and there we stayed it being near night till it was dark."

We have found no list of Watertown soldiers with the express statement that they served at Sudbury, but we give the following names of men who were impressed from that town in November, 1675, for the defense of the colony, and who were returned by Captain Mason as "rationally most fit to goe upon the servis": "Daniell Warrin, Sr., John Bigulah, Sr., Nathaniel Hely, Joseph Tayntor, John Whitney, Sr., George Harrington, William Hagar, Jr., John Parkhurst, Michael Flagg, Jacob Bullard, Isaac Learned, Joseph Waight, George Dill, William Pierce, Nathaniel Sangar, Moses Whitney, John Windam, Joseph Smith, Nathaniel Barsham, John Barnard."

CHAPTER XIII.

1675–1700.

Philip's War. — The Sudbury Fight. — Number of Men in Captain Wadsworth's Company: The Arrival at Marlboro; The Return to Sudbury. — The Ambuscade: Place of It. — Philip's Plan of Attack. — Number of Indians. — The Battle. — The Forest Fire. — Retreat of the English. — Refuge in Hop Brook Mill. — Number of the English Slain. — Philip's Loss. — Treatment of Captives. — Rescue of the Survivors. — Burial of the Dead. — Place of Burial. — Biographical Sketches: Captain Wadsworth, Captain Brocklebank. — Roxbury Men. — Concord Men. — Marlboro Men. — The Christian Indians. — Movements of the English after the Battle. — Sudbury's Loss.

> Fast on the soldier's path
> Darken the waves of wrath;
> Long have they gather'd, and loud shall they fall;
> Red glares the musket's flash,
> Sharp rings the rifle's crash,
> Blazing and clanging from thicket and wall.
>
> O. W. HOLMES.

WHEN the intelligence reached Boston that the Indians had invaded Marlboro, the Council sent to its relief a company of soldiers under command of Capt. Samuel Wadsworth of Milton. The number in this company has been variously estimated. Mather sets it at seventy; "The Old Indian Chronicle" says, "Wadsworth being designed of a hundred men, to repair to Marlboro, to strengthen the garrison and remove the goods." Hubbard says, "That resolute, stout hearted soldier, Capt. Wadsworth . . . being sent from Boston with fifty soldiers to relieve Marlboro." It is not remarkable that estimates should differ with regard to the number in this company, since all the men who accompanied Wadsworth from Boston were not in the engagement at

233

Sudbury. When Captain Wadsworth reached Marlboro he exchanged a part of his younger men, who were wearied with the march, for some at the garrison, and accompanied by Captain Brocklebank, the garrison commander, started back to Sudbury. Lieutenant Jacobs, who commanded the garrison in the absence of Brocklebank, in reporting to the authorities in regard to the number of men left with him, states as follows: "There is remaining in our company forty-six, several whereof are young soldiers left here by Captain Wadsworth, being unable to march. But though he left a part of his men he took some from the garrison at Marlboro." From what we know of the fate of a large part of this company, and the circumstances attendant upon the expedition, we conclude the number engaged in the Sudbury fight was not much over fifty. If twenty-nine men were found slain after the battle, and fourteen escaped, and about a half dozen were taken captive, the number would not be far from the foregoing estimate.

Captain Wadsworth arrived at Marlboro some time during the night of the 20th. Upon ascertaining that the Indians had gone in the direction of Sudbury, he did not stop to take needed refreshment, but started upon the enemy's trail. Hubbard says, "Understanding the enemy had gone through the woods towards Sudbury, this unwearied company, before even they had taken any considerable rest, marched immediately back towards Sudbury [East Sudbury], that lies ten miles nearer Boston." Says Gookin (" History of Christian Indians"), "He [Wadsworth] understanding that the enemy had attacked Sudbury, took a ply of his men, about six files, and marched for their relief, with whom Capt. Broklebank, who kept guard at Marlboro went. Taking this opportunity as a good convoy, to speak with the council. Capt. Wadsworth being a valient and active man and being very desirous to rescue his friends at Sudbury, marched in the night with all the speed he could." Says Lieutenant Jacobs, in his official letter, of Wadsworth's departure, " Although he had marched all the day and the night before, and his men much wearied, yet he hastened back again, and was accompanied by Capt. Broklebank, commander of the garrison of

Marlboro with the small number he durst spare out of his garrison." (Date April 24, 1676. State Archives, Vol. LXVIII., p. 227.)

The English encountered no Indians until they had gone some distance into Sudbury territory, when they came upon a small party, who fled at their approach. Captain Wadsworth with his company pursued until they found themselves in an ambush, where the main body of Philip's force lay concealed.

THE BATTLE-FIELD.

Before considering the battle which followed, we will give some description of the place where it occurred. This place was at what is now South Sudbury, a little northeasterly of the village, and on the westerly side of Green Hill. The ambush was probably laid near the foot of the hill, a few rods east of the place where Wadsworth was buried. At this point there was, until within a very few years, an old path through the woods (see map), which we conjecture once led from the Hop Brook Mill to the Old Lancaster Road, and may have been the way travelled to that mill, and to the westward of it, before the construction of the new road that was built in 1659. This road, in our recollection, extended to the edge of the cleared land on the Joseph Richardson farm (present Newton place), but since the clearing up of the woods in that locality it has almost or quite disappeared. We conjecture that at or along this path the battle began. This we think is indicated by several circumstances.

First, it was very near the spot where the slain soldiers were buried. The burial-place would naturally be not far from the greater number of the slain, or about midway of the battle-field, unless the nature of the ground was such as to make it inexpedient to dig the grave there. From the top of Green Hill to near the spot where the soldiers were buried is hard, rocky ground, while at the place of burial was easy digging; and, moreover, being of sandy soil, it may have been covered with but small, scanty shrubbery, and been a sunny spot in the woods quite suitable for the purpose. It is not therefore unlikely, if the main part or all of the slain were scattered from about the foot to the summit of the hill, that they were carried to that spot for interment.

Second, it was not far from the foot of the hill, which the English ascended as the battle advanced. The space fought over could not have been great, since every foot of it was hotly contested, and the engagement lasted but a few hours. The distance from the path at the foot of the hill to the summit, where the English made their stand, was about an eighth of a mile. Therefore we judge the battle began on or near the path.

But the one thing which more than any other may indicate the place of ambush was the probable plan of King Philip. This plan was to intercept Captain Wadsworth before he could reach the east side, or get into the neighborhood of the Goodnow or Haynes Garrisons. To do this, he would naturally allow the English to pass on to Marlboro during the night undisturbed, and then conceal his force to intercept him on his return. The wily chieftain knew that his return was only a matter of time, and he hastened to get his ambush in readiness for him. But, to have the plan a success, it was all-important to choose the spot where Wadsworth would be most likely to pass. To the westward of Hop Brook it might be hard to determine what way the English would take. But it was probable they would so direct their course as to cross Hop Brook at the bridge, near Noyes' Mill (South Sudbury), since at that season of the year the stream might be swollen so as to make it difficult to pass it at any other place. At some point easterly of the bridge, then, the ambush would naturally be laid.

But from Hop Brook to the east side, as before noticed, there were two ways: one, a part of the Old Lancaster Road north of Green. Hill, connected with Hop Brook Mill by the wood-path before mentioned; the other, the "new road," which went south of Green Hill. As it was uncertain which of these roads Wadsworth would take, Philip would naturally lay his ambuscade upon the path which we have conjectured connected these two highways (see map); so that if Wadsworth went by way of the Lancaster Road he would fall into the ambush, and if he went by the south road Philip

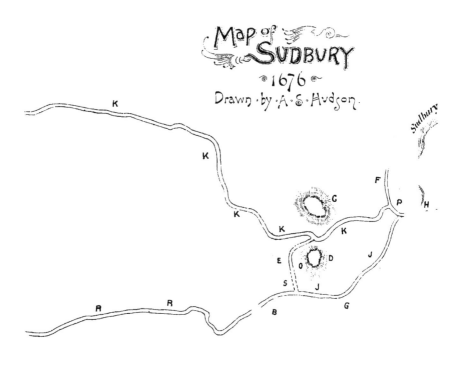

Map of
SUDBURY
1676
Drawn by A. S. Hudson.

would lead him into the fatal path by decoys. This is what we suppose Philip did. He allowed Wadsworth to pass to Marlboro at night, then selected a place by this path in which to conceal his men. Wadsworth, all unsuspicious of his plan, had probably passed the Hop Brook Bridge, and was passing by the south road to East Sudbury, when the Indian decoys turned him from his course, and led him to the place of ambush.

The following statements from several well-known authorities favor the foregoing suppositions. Says " The Old Indian Chronicle," " When they arrived within a mile and a half of Sudbury, the enemy having hid themselves behind the hills, sent forth two or three to cross the march of our forces, and being seen to counterfeit themselves affrighted and fly, whereby to trepan our men into their ambuscade, which mischievous plan succeeded according their to wishes." Hubbard says, " Being come within a mile of the town, we espied a party of Indians not far from them, about a hundred, not more as they conceived. These they might easily deal with, who turning back awhile drew Capt. Wadsworth and his company above a mile into the woods." Says Gookin, " Being spent and weary with travel and want of rest Capt. Wadsworth fell into the enemy's ambushment on the morning, and the enemy being numerous encompassed him round."

It is noticeable by these statements, that the distance that these men were decoyed is variously estimated at from a mile to a mile and a half. This does not exactly correspond with the distance between the supposed place of ambush and the aforesaid roads. But they may have been allured by a circuitous course, or the distance mentioned by these authors may have been a loose estimate. It would not be strange if authors should be somewhat inexact on a point like this. It was an unfamiliar locality to them. If they received information from survivors of the fight, the place also was strange to them, and they might think the distance over which they were led by decoy to be greater than it in reality was; and as in the case of the date of the fight, one historian might transmit another's mistake. If our conjectures, then, are correct, we think these soldiers were allured from some point on

the road from Hop Brook to East Sudbury to a spot near
the place of their burial.

THE AMBUSCADE.

The force that lay in ambush is supposed to have been
quite strong. Gookin speaks of "the enemy being numerous." "The Old Indian Chronicle" speaks of it as about a
thousand. The latter estimate is probably not far from
right. If two hundred Indians were engaged about the old
town bridge, and if Philip entered Sudbury with towards
fifteen hundred, about one thousand may have been in ambush. As the foe appeared, the English pursued, and followed hard as they withdrew. That they should do this
unsuspicious of peril may be a matter of some surprise.
Captain Wadsworth was not inexperienced in Indian warfare; before this he had been on their trail. When Lancaster was assailed, he had gone to its relief. It might
seem strange, then, that he should be led into ambush,
when aware of Indian strategy, and accompanied by Captain Brocklebank, who could advise him of King Philip's
strength.

A little reflection, however, may diminish surprise. If
one hundred Indians, as is stated by Hubbard, at once hove
in sight, the English may have considered it King Philip's
main force. These by their flight may have acted surprised.
They were in the vicinity of the place whither, it is said, the
Indians had gone. Wadsworth was not far from two of
Sudbury's garrisons, and not far from the outskirts of the
east side settlement. He may have heard the sound of guns
in different directions, and especially the firing at the old
town bridge; this, perhaps, led him to suppose Philip's
forces much scattered about, and that what he saw was the
nucleus of his powerful host. It is not, then, very remarkable if he was thrown off his guard, and that he considered
that but little caution was required.

But the pursuit was fatal. The Indians retreated until
the place of ambush was reached. Then suddenly the foe
opened his fire from a chosen place of concealment, where
each man had the opportunity of working to advantage. By

these means the trap was sprung. Simultaneous with this sudden onslaught of the ambushed foe an attempt was made to surround the English. Mather says that, " a great body of the Indians surrounded them." Hubbard states, " On a sudden a great body of the enemy appeared. About five hundred as was thought compassed them around." This was shrewd on the part of Philip. The first move of the English would naturally be to regain the main path, and make for the highway so near at hand. A short run to the northerly would lead Wadsworth to the Old Lancaster Road, or a quick retreat southerly would soon bring him to the road from Hop Brook to East Sudbury; while one of these ways would bring him to the town bridge and the old Haynes Garrison, and the other to the Goodnow Garrison. It might, then, be expected that Philip would cut off the retreat.

But, though suddenly surrounded and beset on all sides, they maintained a most manly defense. It may be doubtful if there is its equal in the annals of the early Indian wars. From five hundred to one thousand savages, with Philip himself to direct their manœuvres, pouring their fire from every direction, and this against about four-score of English, hard marched, in an unfamiliar locality, could do deadly work. Yet there is no evidence of undue confusion among the ranks of the English.

The sudden onslaught of the savages was attended, as usual, with shoutings and a horrible noise, which but increased the threatening aspect, and tended to indicate that things were worse than they were. In spite of all this, the brave company maintained their position, and more than held their own. Says Mather, " They fought like men and more than so." Says " The Old Indian Chronicle," " Not at all dismayed by their numbers, nor dismal shouts and horrid yellings, ours made a most courageous resistance." Not only was the foe kept at bay, and the English force mainly kept compact, but a movement was made to obtain a better position; hard by was the summit of Green Hill, and thitherward, fighting, Wadsworth directed his course. This he reached, and for hours he fought that furious host, with such

success that, it is said, he lost but five men. Says "The Old
Indian Chronicle," "Having gained the top of the hill, they
from thence gallantly defended themselves, with a loss of
five men, near four hours." Hubbard informs us that "the
Indians forced them to the top of an hill, where they made
very stout resistance considerable while." Thus successfully
was the battle waged by the English, despite circumstances
and the strength of the foe.

THE FOREST FIRE.

But a new element was to be introduced. The fight had
doubtless been prolonged far beyond what Philip had at first
supposed it would be. Desperate in his disappointment that
the English had not surrendered, they again resort to strategy to accomplish their work. The day was almost done.
Philip's force had been decimated by Wadsworth's stubborn
defense. Darkness was soon to set in, and under its friendly
concealment the English might make their escape. New
means were to be employed, or the battle to the Indians
was lost, and the fate of Philip's slain warriors would be un-
avenged. Wadsworth might form a junction with the soldiers at the east side of the town, or make his way to the
Goodnow Garrison just beyond Green Hill. A crisis was at
hand. Philip knew it, and made haste to meet it. The
fight began with strategy, and he sought to close it with
strategy. He set fire to the woods, the leaves of which at
that season are sometimes exceedingly dry; and the flames,
fiercely fanned in the April breeze, drove Wadsworth from
his advantageous position. The English were forced to fly
before the devouring element. Says "The Old Indian
Chronicle," "The cowardly enemy disheartened by so many
of their fellows slain in the first attack, not daring to venture close upon them, yet that we may not think these bar-
barians altogether unacquainted with strategem, nor so silly
as to neglect any advantages, at last they set the woods on
fire to the windward of our men, which by reason of the
wind blowing very hard, and the grass being exceedingly
dry, burnt with a terrible fierceness, and with the smoke and
heat it was like to choke them, so that being no longer able

at once to resist the approaching fire, and the cruel enemy, they are forced to quit that advantageous post in disorder." The historian Hubbard says nothing about the fire; he states, however, "The night drawing on, and some of the English beginning to scatter from the rest, their fellows were forced to follow them so as the enemy taking the chase, pursued them on every side as they made too hasty a retreat." That Hubbard mentioned no fire may naturally occasion surprise; but the silence of one historian concerning an event should not invalidate the affirmation of it by another, especially since by a little reflection it may be a matter of surprise that the English should retreat in such haste without the menace of some new peril, when night's friendly help was so near. The statement then of one author, with no reason to doubt his veracity, but a strong presumption to confirm his words, may remove any doubts that might be suggested by the silence of others.

THE RETREAT.

With this new combination of forces pressing hard upon them, nothing was left but retreat. But the results of the retreat were disastrous and exceedingly sad. There is something melancholy indeed attendant on that precipitous flight. For hours, shoulder to shoulder, those men had manfully stood. Inch by inch they had gained the hill-top. The wounded had likely been borne with them, and laid at their protectors' feet; and the brave company awaited night's friendly shades to bear them gently to a place of relief. But they were to leave them now in the hands of a foe less merciful than the flames from which they had been forced to retire. Their defenders had fired their last shot that would keep the foe at bay, and in hot haste were to make a rush for the Hop Brook Mill. It was a race for life; a gauntlet from which few would escape.

Historians agree that the rout was complete. Hubbard mentions the too hasty retreat, "by which accident, being so much overpowered by the enemy's numbers, they were most of them lost." Says "The Old Indian Chronicle," "The Indians taking advantage of [the rout] came in upon them like so many tigers, and dulling their active swords with excessive numbers obtained the dishonor of a victory. Our two Captains after incomparable proof of their resolution and galantry, being slain upon the place with most of their men." So closed the scene on Green Hill, as the fitful gleam of the forest conflagration lighted the night shadows and revealed the terrible work.

The flight of the men to the mill was doubtless attended with fearful loss. It was situated at what now is South Sudbury village, on the site of the present Parmenter Mill. The distance from the top of Green Hill is from a quarter to half a mile. This distance was enough to make the slaughter great. A break in the ranks, and the foe could close in, and the tomahawk and war-club could do a terrible work. It is said that a small company broke away from the enemy. Says "The Old Indian Chronicle," "But those few that remained escaped to a mill which they defended until night." This statement indicates that the rout began before night, while Hubbard says "the night drawing on." This disparity of statement is slight. Each may mean the same thing, if the rout occurred about night, as it probably did. We would expect Philip's strategy to be employed before the day closed, as he wished to scatter the English before darkness afforded the means of escape. Gookin informs us that "Wadsworth's men were generally cut off, except a few who escaped to a mill which was fortified but the people were fled out of it, and the enemy knew not of their flight." Other authorities give different estimates. Hubbard states, "scarce twenty escaping in all."

Thus closed that tragic day. The firing had ceased. Silence settled with the nightfall over that usually peaceful spot; yet night's natural stillness was not undisturbed. The shouts of the captor as he exultingly looked over his fallen foe, the groans of the wounded white man and savage, the gathering of Philip's scattered forces, each to narrate the deeds of that eventful day, the blaze of the Indian's night-fire, and the strange forms that flitted to and fro, — all together might present a scene that was dismal, weird, and strange.

LOSS OF THE ENGLISH.

As to the number of English slain, accounts somewhat differ. This is not strange, when men differ as to the number engaged. Mather says "that about fifty of the men were slain that day." Gookin speaks of "thirty-two besides the two captains." Hubbard says, "So as another captain and his fifty perished that time of as brave soldiers as any who were ever employed in the service." Lieut. Richard Jacobs of the garrison at Marlboro, in his letter to the Council, dated April 22, 1676 (Vol. LXVIII., p. 223, State Archives), says, "This morning about sun two hours high ye enemy alarmed us by firing and shouting toward ye government garrison house at Sudbury." He goes on to state that "soon after they gave a shout and came in great numbers on Indian Hill, and one, as their accustomed manner is after a fight, began to signify to us how many were slain; they whooped seventy four times which we hope was only to affright us, seeing we have had no intelligence of any such thing, yet we have reason to fear the worst, considering the numbers, which we apprehend to be five hundred at the most, others think a thousand." The Indians informed Mrs. Rowlandson that "they killed two captains and almost an hundred men." She states, "One Englishman they brought alive with them, and he said it was too true, for they had made sad work at Sudbury."

Thus, according to the various accounts, by far the greater part were slain. There is one thing which goes to show, however, that Mather may not be far from correct, — that is the evidence of the exhumed remains. When the grave was opened a few years ago, parts of the skeletons of twenty-nine men were found. We can hardly suppose, however, that these were all the slain. Some who were wounded may have crawled away to die. Others, disabled, may have been borne from the spot by the foe; and in various ways the wounded may have been removed, to perish near or remote from the field of battle.

According to the testimony of Mrs. Rowlandson, the bodies of the slain were plundered. She remarks, that, "after the

master came home, he came to her and bid her make a shirt
for his pappoose of a pillow-bier." She says also, "About
that time there came an Indian to me and bid me come to
his wigwam that night, and he would give me some pork
and ground nuts. I did, and as I was eating, another Indian
said to me, he seems to be your good friend, but he killed
two Englishmen at Sudbury, and there lie the bloody clothes
behind you, I looked behind me, and there I saw the bloody
clothes behind me with bullet holes in them." No signs
of equipments or attire were found in the grave when the
remains were disinterred; and it is probable that the slain
were stripped by the savages, and the garments and equipments were carried away.

LOSS OF PHILIP.

As to the number of savages slain on that day, we can
hardly expect to obtain any accurate knowledge. The
Indians would intend to leave no traces of what havoc
the English had made. They would likely care for their
wounded, and remove or conceal their dead. Tradition
states ("History of Framingham"), that one of the sons of
Eames of Framingham was present as a captive at the attack
on Sudbury, and he is said to have reported that the Indians
suffered severely by the fire from the garrison; and that an
aged squaw lost six sons, all of whom were brave and distinguished warriors.

From all the circumstances, there is space for fair inference that their loss was large. Wadsworth and Brocklebank
were bold and sagacious men; their soldiers were doubtless
valiant to a great degree. During those hours of defensive
work there is little doubt but the ranks of King Philip were
greatly thinned. Encompassed as the English were by hundreds of combatants eager to rush in and close the contest
with hatchet and club, it is safe to infer that only an effective
and quickly repeated fire, such as would be deadly to many,
would keep such a host at bay. The very fact that Philip
by daybreak withdrew, after his destructive work at Green
Hill, is a presumption that he was in a crippled state. Without losses so severe as to make it utterly unwise to push on,

flushed by Wadsworth's defeat, he would naturally move forward to destroy the east side settlement, and go with conquering march toward the sea. But he retraced his steps westward.

A further evidence that the havoc in Philip's force was great, is the statement of Mrs. Rowlandson, "that they came home without that rejoicing and triumphing over their victory which they were wont to show at other times; but rather like dogs (as they say) which have lost their ears, yet I could not perceive that it was from their own loss of men. They said they lost not above five or six. And I missed none, except from one wigwam. When they went they acted as if the devil had told them that they should gain a victory, and now they acted as if the devil had told them they should have a fall. Whether it were so or no, I cannot tell, but so it quickly proved, for they quickly began to fall, and so they held on that summer till they came to utter ruin. They came home on a Sabbath day, and the powwow that kneeled upon the deerskin came home, I may say, without any abuse, as black as the devil." She further states that "it was their usual manner to remove when they had done any mischief, lest they should be found out; and so they did at this time. We went about three or four miles, and there they built a great wigwam, big enough to hold one hundred Indians, which they did in preparation to a great day of dancing. They would now say among themselves that the governor would be so angry for the loss at Sudbury that he would say no more about the captives."

Hubbard says, "It was observed by some (at that time their prisoners, since released), that they seemed very pensive after they had come to ther quarters, showing no such signs of rejoicing as they were usually wont to do in like cases. Whether from the loss of some of their own company in that day's enterprise (said to be an hundred and twenty) or whether it were the devil in whom they trusted, that deceived them, and to whom they paid their addresses the day before by sundry conjurations of their powwows, or whether it were by any dread that the Almighty sent upon their excreable Blasphemies which 'tis said they used in the

torturing of some of their poor captives (bidding Jesus come
and deliver them out of their hands from death if He could)
we leave as uncertain, though some have so reported. Yet
sure it is, that after this day they never prospered in any
attempt they made against the English, but were continually scattered and broken till they were in a manner all consumed."

As ultimate authority in this, as in other matters, we
refer to "The Old Petition," in which it is stated as follows of the Indians slain: "Secondly, yᵉ service pformed at
Sudbury by yᵉ help of yᵉ Almighty whereby yᵉ Enemy lost
some say 100, some 105, some 120, and by that service much
damage prevented from hapning to other places whereby yᵉ
Country in Generall was advantaged, reason requires some
favorable considerations to yᵉ servants of Sudbury. For if it
be considered what it hath cost our Country in sending out
some forces some of which p ties have not returned with
yᵉ certaine newes of such a number slaine as with us."

These things indicate that Philip's loss was severe. He was
stayed in his course; he was unable to reinforce his outstand-
ing detachments in their attempt to destroy the town, and he
quickly made his retreat. Wadsworth did not die in vain.
Not only did he help save the east side settlement, but, keeping the foe hotly engaged for hours, he crippled their force
to such a degree that they abandoned their plans of conquest
in that vicinity.

THE CAPTURED.

But the sad story is not wholly told when we speak of the
slain. The tragedy was not complete when the surviving
few had left the field and taken refuge in the mill. Some
were captured alive. These were subjected to such atrocious
treatment as only a savage would be expected to give. Says
Hubbard, "It is related by some that afterwards escaped
how they cruelly tortured five or six of the English that
night." Mather says, "They took five or six of the English, and carried them away alive, but that night killed them
in such a manner as none but savages would have done, . . .
delighting to see the miserable torments of the wretched
creatures. Thus are they the perfect children of the devil."

THE SURVIVORS.

The few English who escaped to the mill found it a place of safety. Says tradition, this was a fortified place, but it was then left in a defenceless condition. This latter fact the Indians were ignorant of, hence it was left unassailed. The escaped soldiers were rescued at night by Warren and Pierce, with some others, among whom was Captain Prentis, "who coming in the day hastily though somewhat to late to the relief of Capt. Wadsworth having not six troopers that were able to keep way with him fell into a pound or place near Sudbury town end, where all passages were stopped by the Indians." Captain Cowell also gave assistance, and thus these weary, war-worn men, the remnant of the gallant company that fought on that memorable day, were conducted to a place of safety.

BURIAL OF THE DEAD.

The morning light of the 22d of April broke upon a sad scene in Sudbury. The noise of the battle had ceased, and the fires had faded away with the night-shadows. Philip had betaken himself from the field of his hard-earned and unfortunate victory, and nothing of life was left but the leafless woods, and these charred as if passed over by the shadow of death. It was a scene of loneliness and desolation. The dead, scalped and stripped, were left scattered as they fell; while their victors by the sunrising were far on their way back over the track which they had made so desolate. This scene, however, was shortly to change. Warm hearts and stout hands were pushing their way to see what the case might demand, and if possible render relief.

Before nightfall of the 21st, so far as we have learned, little, if any intelligence was received by the parties who had rushed to the rescue, of the true state of things about Green Hill. Wadsworth and Brocklebank were encompassed about by the foe, so that no communication could be conveyed to the English, who anxiously awaited tidings of their condition. It was known at the easterly part of the town that hard fighting was in progress at or near Green Hill. The

shouting, firing, and smoke betokened that a battle was in
progress, but how it would terminate none could tell. After
the Sudbury and Watertown men had driven the Indians
over the river, they strove hard to reach the force on the
hill.　Says Warren and Pierce, in their petition : " We who
were with them can more largely inform this Honored Council that as it is said in the petition, that we drove two hundred Indians over the river and with some others went to
see if we could relieve Capt. Wadsworth upon the hill, and
there we had a fight with the Indians, but they being so
many of them, and we stayed so long that we were almost
encompassed by them, which caused us to retreat to Capt.
Goodnow's garrison house, and there we stayed it being near
night till it was dark."

But another force had also striven to reach the town,
and join in the work of rescue. This was a company from
Charlestown, commanded by Captain Hunting.　Of this
company, Gookin says ("History of Christian Indians") :
" On the 21st of April, Capt. Hunting had drawn up and
ready furnished his company of forty Indians at Charlestown.　These had been ordered by the council to march to
the Merrimac river near Chelmsford, and there to settle a
garrison near the great fishing places where it was expected
the enemy would come to get fish for their necessary food."
But, says Gookin, " Behold God's thoughts are not as ours,
nor His ways as ours, for just as these soldiers were ready to
march upon the 21st of April, about midday, tidings came by
many messengers that a great body of the enemy . . . had
assembled at a town called Sudbury that morning."　He
says " that just at the beginning of the lecture there, as soon
as these tidings came, Major Gooken and Thomas Danforth,
two of the magistrates who were there hearing the lecture
sermon, being acquainted, he withdrew out of the meeting
house, and immediately gave orders for a ply of horses belonging to Capt. Prentis's troop under conduct of Corporal Phipps,
and the Indian company under Capt. Hunting, forthwith to
march away for the relief of Sudbury; which order was accordingly put into execution.　Capt. Hunting with his Indian
company being on foot, got not into Sudbury until a little

within night. The enemy as is before [narrated] were all retreated unto the west side of the river of Sudbury, where also several English inhabited."

But though the rescuing parties were either repulsed, or too late to render assistance at the fight, they were on hand to bury the dead. Says Warren and Pierce: "After burrying the bodies of the Concord men at the bridge's foot, we joined ourselves to Capt. Hunting and as many others as we could procure, and went over the river to look for Capt. Wadsworth and Capt. Broklebank; and we gathered them up and burried them."

The manner in which this burial scene proceeded is narrated thus by Mr. Gookin ("History of Christian Indians"): "Upon the 22nd of April early in the morning over forty Indians having stripped themselves and painted their faces like to the enemy, they passed over the bridge to the west side of the river without any Englishmen in the company, to make discovery of the enemy (which was generally conceded quartered thereabout), but this did not at all discourage our Christian Indians from marching and discovering, and if they had met with them to beat up their quarters. But God had so ordered that the enemy were all withdrawn and were retreated in the night. Our Indian soldiers having made a thourough discovery and to their great relief (for some of them wept when they saw so many English lie dead on the place among the slain), some they knew, viz, those two worthy and pious Captains, Capt. Broklebank of Rowley and Capt. Wadsworth of Milton, who with about thirty two private soldiers were slain the day before. . . . As soon as they had made a full discovery, [they] returned to their Captains and the rest of the English, and gave them an account of their motions. Then it was concluded to march over to the place and bury the dead, and they did so. Shortly after, our Indians marching in two files upon the wings to secure those that went to bury the dead, God so ordered it that they met with no interruption in that work."

Thus were the slain soldiers buried on that April morning, in the stillness of the forest, far away from their kindred, friends, and homes. Those, who through inability had failed to defend them in the day of battle, now tenderly took them to their last long resting-place. A single grave contained them. Though scattered, they were borne to one common place of burial, and a rough heap of stones was all that marked that lone forest grave. Such was that soldiers' sepulchre, a mound in the woods, left to grow gray with the clustering moss of years, yet marking in its rustic simplicity one of the noblest and most heroic events known in the annals of King Philip's War. They sleep —

> "While the bells of autumn toll,
> Or the murmuring song of spring flits by,
> Till the crackling heavens in thunder roll,
> To the bugle-blast on high."

PLACE OF BURIAL.

The grave was made on the westerly side of Green Hill, near its base, and was in the northeast corner of the South Sudbury cemetery before its recent enlargement. In our recollection, the grave was marked by a rude stone-heap, at the head of which was a plain slate-stone slab. The heap was made of common loose stones such as a man could easily lift, and was probably placed there when the grave was made. It was perhaps three or four feet high, and a dozen feet wide at the base. The slab was erected about 1730 by President Wadsworth of Harvard College, son of Captain Wadsworth. As we remember the spot, it was barren and briar-grown; loose stones, fallen from the top and sides of the mound, were half concealed in the wild wood grass that grew in tufts about it. It remained in this condition for years, and the villagers from time to time visited it as a place of interest.

In the year 1851 the town agitated the matter of erecting a monument, and the Legislature was petitioned for aid, which was granted. But the monument does not mark the original grave. The committee who had the matter in charge located it about fifty feet to the north. The old grave was at, or about the turn of the present avenue or path, at the northeast corner of the Adam Smith family lot, in the pres-

THE WADSWORTH GRAVE,
So Sudbury
From an original painting by A S Hudson.

ent Wadsworth Cemetery. After it was decided to erect the monument in its present position, the remains of the soldiers were removed. The grave was opened without ceremony in the presence of a small company of villagers. It was the writer's privilege to be one of the number, and according to our recollection the grave was about six feet square, in which the bodies were placed in tiers at right angles to each other. Some of the skeletons were large, and all well preserved.

In connection with the events just described, we will give a few facts concerning some of the men engaged in them.

CAPT. SAMUEL WADSWORTH.

Capt. Samuel Wadsworth was the son of Christopher and Grace Wadsworth of Duxbury. He was supposed to be their oldest child. It is stated that when he died he was forty-six years old, but this is uncertain. He married Abigail Lindall of Duxbury, and owned lands at one time in Bridgewater, which were a part of a grant to his father. These lands comprised one sixty-fourth part of Bridgewater when it included most of Hanson and Abington. In 1685 Captain Wadsworth's share is entered upon the Bridgewater records under the name of Widow Wadsworth. About 1660 Captain Wadsworth bought several hundred acres of land in Milton. A part of this estate was retained in the family to the eighth generation. His family consisted of six boys and one girl. His wife lived on the homestead many years after his death. Captain Wadsworth was an influential citizen, and took an active part in affairs both political and religious. At the time of Philip's War he was a captain in the militia of Milton. He was considered "a resolute, stout-hearted soldier," and "one worthy to live in our history under the name of a good man." (Genealogy of the Wadsworth Family).

CAPT. SAMUEL BROCKLEBANK.

Capt. Samuel Brocklebank was a citizen of Rowley, Mass. He was born in England about 1630. A few years after his arrival in this country, his mother, who was a widow, came over, accompanied by two children. Samuel Brocklebank shortly after becoming of age was chosen a selectman, and continued to hold important town offices until his death. He became a deacon of the church Feb. 18, 1665. In 1673 the Council appointed him captain of militia, and after the breaking out of Philip's War he was stationed at a government garrison at Marlboro, where he had command of some colonial soldiers, and from which place he went with Captain Wadsworth to Sudbury. At the time of his death he was about forty-six years old. He left a widow and six children, Samuel, Hannah, Mary, Elizabeth, Sarah, and Joseph. Captain Brocklebank was an estimable citizen, a brave soldier, and a fit associate of Captain Wadsworth in his perilous work.

Lieutenant Sharp of Brookline and Lieut. Samuel Gardiner of Roxbury were, it is stated, brave and efficient men. And all the soldiers who were slain on that disastrous occasion were, we are informed, as brave soldiers as any who were engaged in the service at that time.

ROXBURY MEN.

The following is a list of the Roxbury men who were of Captain Wadsworth's company, and killed at the Sudbury fight: Thomas Baker, Jr., John Roberts, Jr., Nathaniel Seaver [or Leason], Thomas Hawley [or Romley], Sr., William Cleaves, Joseph Pepper, John Sharpe, Thomas Hopkins, Samuel Gardner.

CONCORD MEN.

John Barnes lived in Concord in 1661, and married Elizabeth Hunt in 1664.

Joseph Buttrick was a son of William Buttrick, who came to New England in 1635, and died in 1698, aged eighty-two. His second wife was Jane Goodnow of Sudbury.

James Hosmer was the oldest son of James, who came to Concord among the first settlers, and died in 1685. James, the son, married Sarah White in 1658. His widow married Samuel Rice.

Samuel Potter was son of Luke Potter, one of the first settlers at Concord and deacon of the church there. Samuel married Sarah Wright in 1675.

MARLBORO MEN.

In Hudson's " History of Marlboro " it is stated that the records of that town give the names of John Howe, Henry Axtel, and Eleazer Ward as being slain by the Indians in Sudbury; but whether in the Sudbury fight with Wadsworth, or not, is not known.

John How was a son of John How, one of the petitioners for the Marlboro Plantation. He was born in 1640, probably in Sudbury, and married in 1662.

Henry Axtel was one of the proprietors of Marlboro at the time of its incorporation, and drew his land in the first division. He married in 1665, and was slain by the Indians between Sudbury and Marlboro, April 20, 1676.

Eleazer Ward was born near 1649, married Hannah Rice, lived in Sudbury, and was killed by the Indians upon the highway between Sudbury and Marlboro, April 20, 1676.

THE CHRISTIAN INDIANS.

In connection with what has been said of the English who were in this battle, we will give a few facts concerning the Indians who came to the rescue under Captain Hunting. These were a detachment of the Christian Indians who had been placed on Deer Island' by the colonial authorities, after the outbreak of the war. Years before, they had been gathered by Rev. John Eliot into several villages, where they lived peaceably among themselves, and on friendly relations with the whites. Their character and conduct was such as showed the civilizing influence of Christianity, and the power of the gospel to uplift and bless their race. But a few acts by a few recreant and unfaithful ones aroused the suspicion of the English against them all, so that, instead of allowing them to be their allies, they exiled them to an island in Boston harbor. But as the war progressed, their assistance was needed; and at the request of Mr. Eliot and General Gookin, the Governor and Council allowed a detachment to be placed under the command of Captain Hunting, and sent at once to Sudbury. In this service they showed their bravery and faithful attachment to the English. When they crossed the river, to discover the enemy's movements on the west side, they knew not but what Philip was in ambush for further prey, but they moved forward, and went beyond Green Hill; and when in the solitude of the forest they beheld those prostrate forms, their stern spirits were melted, and it is said, they wept.

MOVEMENTS OF THE ENGLISH AFTER THE FIGHT.

The dead having been buried, the English repaired, according to Warren and Pierce, to Nobscot to bring the carts into "Sudbury towne." These carts are probably the same as those mentioned by Gookin, when he says, " At the same time [that is, at the time the survivors of this fight were secreted in Noyes's Mill] Captain Cutler of Charlestown, with a small company," — according to Hubbard, eleven, — " having the convoy of some carts from Marlboro that were coming to Sudbury, having secured his carriage at a garrison house, escaped narrowly being cut off by the enemy." The same author goes on to state, that the enemy " at that time cut off some English soldiers that were coming down under the conduct of one Cowell of Boston, that had been a convoy to some provisions at Quaborg Fort." Other soldiers were soon on the march to the spot, the country having been aroused by this disaster to Wadsworth.

On April 22, 1676, it was ordered by the Council, " that the majors of Suffolk and Middlesex issue out their orders, Maj. Thomas Clark to the Captain of the troop of Suffolk, to raise forty of his troops, well attended, and completely armed with fire arms, and furnished with ammunition, under the conduct of Cornet Eliot, [and] such officers as he shall choose to accompany him, forthwith to visit Dedham, Medfield, and so to Sudbury ; and Major Daniel Gookin to issue out by order a like number of troops out of Middlesex troops, under the conduct of Thomas Prentis, or such as he shall choose, to visit Concord, Sudbury, and so to Medfield."

The order to Cornet Eliot was, " You are ordered and requested to take forty of the troop, and so many as you can suddenly raise, and march with them into Sudbury, and inquire of their present distressed condition, and of the interring of the dead bodies, as also of the enemy's motion, and place of their rendezvous, and if you have opportunity you are to distress, kill, and destroy the enemy to the uttermost, taking good heed lest, through any neglect, or too much adventurness, you hazard the lives of the men by their sudden surprisal of you. You are also to visit Medfield, and make report of what you find to the Council, and in so doing this shall be your warrant."

Thus, after this disastrous battle, the English were on the move; but the Indians had departed westward. As we have noticed by the letter of Lieutenant Jacobs, they passed through Marlboro on the morning of the 22d, when the sun was about two hours high. This was Philip's westward retreat. He never retraced his footsteps. Sudbury was the last eastward town in his march. As a conqueror he could go no farther. On April 21 his sun had reached its meridian; on the 22d it turned towards its setting. His host was broken; the ranks of his warriors began to thin; and when he returned to his home at Mount Hope, it was to be hunted and harassed; and Aug. 12, 1676, he fell by the hand of one of his race.

SUDBURY'S LOSS.

The war with King Philip left the town in a weakened condition. Even had the people sustained but little direct loss, their prosperity would naturally have been checked by the imperiled state of the community; but the actual loss to the people in property was considerable, as is indicated by various petitions, in which they set forth their circumstances. In 1677, some inhabitants of Marlboro, Lancaster, and Sudbury sent a petition to the Court, asking that a certain tract of land lying about Marlboro, called by the Indians Whipsuffrage and Ocogooganset, might be given them. The reason of this request was, as they say, " Because many of which Indians in our late war have proved very perfidious

and combine with the common enemy," and because we having been "upon ye Country's service, and hazarded our lives
against ye common enemy, have suffered much damage by
being driven from our habitation, and some of our habitations burnt." (State Archives, Vol. XXX., p. 240.)

But we are not left to general statement of the material
loss sustained, for the specific damage to each individual's
property is given in " The Old Petition." The first part of
the petition, together with a list of the losses, which we give
here verbatim, is as follows: —

To ye Honb'e ye Governor Magistrates & Deputies of ye Genl Court
    assembled at Boston ye 11th Octobr 1676.
    The humble Petition of yor poore, distressed Inhabitants of Sudbury
Humbly Showeth.
    That whereas yor impoverished Petitionrs of Sudbury have received
intelligence of a large contribution sent out of Ireland by some pious &
well affected p sons for ye reliefe of their brethren in New England by ye
hostile intrusions of ye Indian Enemy, and that upon this divers distressed towns have presented a list of their losses sustained by fireing
and plundering their estates. Let it not seem presumption in yor poore
Petitionrs to p'sent a list of what Damages are sustained by yor enemies
in his attempts; hoping that or lott will be considered among Our brethren of ye tribe of Joseph; being encouraged by an act of Our Honble
Genll Court; that those who have Sustained considerable damage should
make addresses to this prsent session.
    An Accompt of Losse Sustenied by Severall Inhabitants of ye towne
of Sudbury by ye Indian Enemy ye 21st Aprill 1676.

	L	S	D
Mary Bacon formerly ye Relict of Ensign Noyes	140	00	00
Thomas Plimpton	130	00	00
Deacon John Haines	180	00	00
Seg Josiah Haines	190	00	00
Capt James Pendleton	060	00	00
John Goodenow	150	00	00
William Moores	180	00	00
Edward Wright	100	00	00
Elias Keyes	060	00	00
John Smith	080	00	00
Samuell How	140	00	00
Mr Pelham	050	00	00
Mr. Stevens	015	00	00
Corporall Henry Rice	180	00	00
John Allen	060	00	00
James Roose	070	00	00

John Grout jun[r]	060 : 00 : 00
Thomas Rice	100 : 00 : 00
Widd Whale	024 : 00 : 00
Henry Curtice	200 : 00 : 00
John Brewer	120 : 00 : 00
Jacob Moores	050 : 00 : 00
Henry Loker	100 : 00 : 00
Joseph ffreemon	080 : 00 : 00
Joseph Graves	060 : 00 : 00
Peter King	040 : 00 : 00
Widd Habgood	020 : 00 : 00
Benjamin Crane	020 : 00 : 00
Jhomas wedge	015 : 00 : 00
John Blanford	010 : 00 : 00
Thomas Brewer	010 : 00 : 00
Richard Burk	010 : 00 : 00
Thomas Reade	003 : 00 : oo
Wholl Sum	2707 : 00 : 00

Beside y[e] uncovering y[e] Many houses & Barnes & some hundred of Acres of lands which are unimproved for feare of y[e] Enemy to Our greate loss & Damage — (Signed)

Edm Browne	Joseph [——]
Edm Goodnow	Peter Noyes
John Grout	Jonathan Stanhope
John Haines	Edward wright
Josiah Haines	Jabeth Browne
Thomas Read	John Grout jun[r]
Peter King	Joseph Graves
John Ruter sen[r]	Tho Walker
Joseph Noyes	John Blanford
John Goodnow	John Allen
Mathew Gibs	Henry Curtis
Thomas wedge	Jacob Moores
Benjamin Crane	John Brewer
Zecriah Maynard	James Ross
Joseph Moore	Richard Burk
John Parminter	Thomas Brewer
Henry Loker	Samuell How.

The contribution to which the petition refers was called " The Irish Charity Donation or Fund." The gift was made in 1676, for the people in the Massachusetts, Plymouth and Connecticut colonies who had suffered in King Philip's War. It was " made by divers Christians in Ireland for the relieffe

of such as are Impoverished, Distressed and in Nessesitie by
the late Indian wars;" sent by the "Good ship called the
Kathrine of Dublin." Rev. Nathaniel Mather, the brother of
Increase, is supposed to have been a means of procuring the
fund. The proportion received by Sudbury was for twelve
families, forty-eight persons, 7*l.* 4*s.* 0*d.* This was to be delivered to the selectmen of the several towns in meal, oat meal,
and malt at 18*d.* per ball, butter 6*d.* cheese 4*d.* per pound.

The following is another section of the same petition: —

Furthermore prmitt yor humb^{le} Peticon^{rs} to present a second motion.
And let it be acceptable in ye eyes of this Our Grand Court vizt:

That whereas by an Act of Our late Genll Court ten rates are leavied
upon Our towne amounting unto 200^{lb}: as appeareth p warrant from Our
Treasurer, which said sum was leavied by Our Invoyce, taken in ye yeare
before Our greate damage susteyned. It is ye humble & earnest request
of yor Petition^{rs} to commiserate Our Condition, in granting to us some
abatement of ye said sum for ye ensueing consideration, Vist: ffirst Our
towne to pay full for theire estates then taken which in greate pte they
have now lost by ye enemy's invasion may seem not to savor of pitty no
not of equity

.   .   .   .

Is it not reason^{les} that this service soe beneficiall should not be considered with some reward which may not easily be esserted (sic) by issuing
forth an Act of yor grace in a suitable abatem^t of ye said sum leavied
with ye conferring of a Barrell of Powder & suitable shott in regard that
yor Petioners have spent not only their owne stock or others but much
of ye Towne stock.

In response, "the Court judged meet to order that Sudbury be allowed and abated forty fower pound ten shillings
out of ye whole sume of their ten county rates." (Colonial
Records, Vol. V., p. 124.)

CHAPTER XIV.

Revival of Prosperity after Philip's War. — Payment for Fortification of the Meeting-House — Erection of Saw-Mill at Hop Brook. — Death of Rev. Edmund Browne; Place of Burial; Historical Sketch. — Settlement of Rev. James Sherman. — Purchase of Parsonage. — Building of New Meeting-House. — Political Disturbances. — Change of Charter. — Administration of Sir Edmund Andros. — Indian Hostilities. — The Ten Years War. — Distribution of Ammunition. — Petition of Sudbury. — Phipps Expedition. — Sudbury Canada Grant. — Witchcraft. — Samuel Paris; Historical Sketch. — Incorporation of Framingham. — Miscellaneous Matters.

> The land lies open and warm in the sun,
> Anvils clamor and mill-wheels run;
> Flocks on the hillsides, herds on the plain,
> The wilderness gladdened with fruit and grain.
>
> WHITTIER.

THE war with King Philip being ended, the way was opened for renewed prosperity. New buildings went up on the old estates, the garrisons again became quiet homesteads, and the fields smiled with plentiful harvests. An early movement was made to meet indebtedness caused by the war. March, 1676–7, it was ordered, "that the rate to be made for the fortification about the meeting house of this town shall be made by the invoice to be taken this spring, leaving out all strangers and sojourners, and that the logs there used be valued at two shillings six pence each, boards five shillings six pence per hundred foot, and every man's day's work at 18ᵈ." A little later, Feb. 26, 1677, it was ordered, "that such persons as have brought in logs for fortification of the meeting house, do bring in their account of logs, and all persons an account also for their days' work done thereupon unto the town clerk between this and the next town meeting now appointed to be the 11th of March next, and such as do not, shall lose both their logs and work, for the town will wait upon them no longer."

ERECTION OF SAW-MILL.

Another movement that denotes the town's activity and recuperative power was the erection of a saw-mill. A town record, dated March 26, 1677, informs us it was ordered that " Peter King, Thomas Read, Sen., John Goodenow, John Smith and Joseph Freeman have liberty granted them to build a saw mill upon Hop Brook above Mr. Peter Noyes's mill, at the place viewed by the committee of this town chosen the last week, which if they do, they are to have twenty tons of timber of the common lands for the building thereof, and earth for their dam, and also they are to make a small dam or sufficient causage so as to keep the waters out of the swamp lands there, provided also that if Mr. Peter Noyes shall at any time throw up his corn mill they do in room thereof set up a corn mill as sufficient to grind the town's corn and grain as Mr. Noyes's present mill hath done and doth, and see to maintain the same, and whenever they or any of them their heirs, executors, administrators, Assigns, or successors, shall either throw up their said corn mill or fail to grind the towns corn and grain as above said, the towns land hereby granted shall be forfeited and returned to the town's use again, and lastly the said persons are not to pen up the water, or saw at any time between the middle of April and first of September, and they are also to make good all the highway that they shall damage thereby."

DEATH OF REV. EDMUND BROWNE.

The town had not moved far on the road to renewed prosperity before another calamity came. This was the death of its pastor, Rev. Edmund Browne, who died June 22, 1678. The first intimation we have on the town records of Mr. Browne's sickness is the following : " Ordered, that next Lord's day there be a free contribution [asked] and collected by Deacon Haines for and towards carrying and charge of

Preacher (upon the sickness of Mr. Edmund Browne, Pastor) that the pulpit might be supplied notwithstanding, after the best manner that may be obtained." Captain Goodenow, Deacon Haines, Mr. Joseph Noyes and Peter King were empowered to be a standing committee during the pastor's sickness, and ordered " to take care that this town be supplied with able Preachers whilst the Pastor is not able to officiate." "The following named persons offered themselves for the 1st month to travel with horse and weekly to fetch and return Preachers for the supply of the town, at least every Lord's day. 1st Peter Noyes, Joseph Parmenter, 2d Tho. Brown, Joseph Moore, 3d Jno Goodenow, Joseph Graves, 4th Samuel How, Thomas Read, Jr."

We have discovered no record, and are aware of no tradition, relating to Mr. Brown's burial or place of interment. He may have been buried in the old yard in Wayland, and the grave may have been left unmarked, or the stone may have been broken or fallen, and been removed. It has been conjectured that his remains were placed in some tomb in or about the city of Boston. The writer has examined copied inscriptions on the stones of some of the older graveyards of Boston, but has discovered there no name which could be that of the first pastor of Sudbury. In Sewall's Diary is the following entry: " Monday, May 9th, 1709. Major Thomas Brown Esq. of Sudbury was buried in the old Burying place. Bearers, Cook, Sewall, Hutchingson, Townsend, Jas Dummer, Dudley, Scarves and Gloves." " The old Burying place " was that of King's Chapel, Boston. The wife of Major Thomas Brown was buried in the East Side Burying-ground, Sudbury. If Major Brown was not buried with his wife, but it was considered important that his remains should be taken to Boston for interment, the same may have been the case with Edmund Browne.

In the death of its first pastor the town met with a great loss. It is true, he was nearly or quite fourscore years old, but judging from his activity in the Indian war, in fortifying his house, and sending messages to the Colonial Court, he was still energetic and robust. Moreover, he had been with the people from the beginning of the settlement; he had passed with them through the desolations of a terrible war, and had been a sharer of their joys and sorrows for many years. From what we know of him, we judge him to have been a warm friend of the truth, and an ardent defender of the Christian faith. It is certainly creditable to him, that, after such a long pastorate, his people were of a character to empower their committee to provide "an able Orthodox Preacher," after he was taken ill.

Mr. Browne came from England in 1637, and, according to Mather, was ordained and in actual service in that country before he came to America. He was a freeman of Massachusetts Bay Colony, May 13, 1640. He married, about 1645, Anne, widow of John Loveren of Watertown, but left no children. He was a member of the synod that established "The Cambridge Platform," 1646–8; was on the council that met in 1657 to settle the difficulties in Rev. Mr. Stone's church, Hartford; preached the artillery election sermon in 1666; and his name is attached to the testimony of the seventeen ministers against the proceedings of the three elders of the First Church, Boston, about 1669.

Mr. Browne was quite a land owner, his real estate, as it is supposed, amounting to three hundred acres. His early homestead at Timber Neck had originally belonging to it seventy acres. He received from the General Court a grant of meadow land situated in the present territory of Framingham, and from time to time became possessed of various lands both within and without the town. Mr. Brown hunted and fished, and it is said was a good angler. He played on several musical instruments and was a noted musician. In his will he speaks of his "Base Voyal" and musical books and instruments. He was much interested in educating and Christianizing the Indians, and at one time had some of them under his special care. His library was for those times quite valuable, containing about one hundred and eighty volumes. He left fifty pounds to establish a grammar school in Sudbury; but by vote of the town, in 1724, it was diverted to another purpose. He also left one hundred pounds to Harvard College.

SETTLEMENT OF REV. JAMES SHERMAN.

The town was not left long without a pastor. It soon called the Rev. James Sherman, who had preached during the illness of Mr. Browne. May 6, 1678, "it was ordered that the committee engage the service of Mr. James Sherman that hath officiated in the town in that kind to continue in that work till the first of September next, or longer as they shall see cause, or till further order from the town." May 20, on a "training day," it was decided that Mr. Peter King was to entertain Mr. Sherman, and to have six shillings per week "for his diet, lodging, attendance, and horse."

Active measures were immediately taken to provide the minister with a house. The town bought of John Loker the east end of his house, standing before and near the meeting-house, and his orchard, and the whole home lot of about four acres; it also bought of him the reversion due to him of the western end of the house that his mother then dwelt in. This part of the house was to be the town's property at the marriage or death of the said Widow Mary Loker. For this property the town was to pay John Loker fifty pounds. (See p. 116.) The Widow Loker appeared at town-meeting, and surrendered all her reversion in the western end of the house to the town, reserving the liberty to have twelve months in which "to provide herself otherwise." She also promised in the meantime "to quit all egress and regress through the eastern end of the house and every part thereof." In consequence of this the town agreed to pay her annually — that is, till she should marry or die — twenty-five shillings, money of New England. The town also voted to raise twenty-five pounds with which to repair the house. The records inform us, that "the said town doth freely give and grant unto Mr. James Sherman, minister of the word of God, all that house and lands which the said town bought lately of John Loker, and twenty pounds to be paid him in [country] pay towards the repair of the said house, and also twenty pounds more to be paid him in money, for and towards the purchase of the widow Mary Loker's lot that lies adjoining to it, when she shall have sold it to the said Mr. James Sherman, and also six acres of common upland lying on the back side of the town at the end of Smith field, and also six acres of meadow ground some where out of the common meadows of this town. These foregoing particular gifts and grants the said town doth engage and promise to the said Mr. James Sherman minister and his heirs . . . in case he shall settle in this town and live and die amongst them their Teaching Elder. But in case the said Mr. Sherman shall not carry out the constant work of preaching in and to this town, during his life, or shall depart and leave this town before his death, then all the premises shall return to the said town's hands again to be at their own dispose forever, only they are then to pay to the said Mr. Sherman all the charges he hath been out for the same in the meantime, as [they] shall be judged worth by indifferent men mutually chosen, unless both parties shall agree therein among themselves."

The town also agreed to pay Mr. Sherman eighty pounds salary; twenty pounds of this were to be paid him in "money, twenty pounds in wheat, pork, beef, mutton, veal, butter, or cheese, or such like species at country price, and the remaining forty shall be paid him in Indian Corn and Rye, or Barley or Peas, all at country prices." He was to have five pounds added per annum to his salary for the cutting and carting home of firewood. He was also to have the use of the minister's meadow lands, and could pasture his cattle on the common land, and have firewood and timber from the common land of the town.

The 30th of October, 1678, " the said Mr. James Sherman did then and there freely and fully declare before the town his acceptance of all that which the said town had granted and done in all respects as is before written, in consideration thereof for his part he did promise the said town, that he would live and die in the constant and public discharge of this duty, by preaching the word of the Lord unto them, and in the faithful administration of all the ordinances of Christ amongst them ; which the Inhabitants of the said town accepted of ; and said Mr. Sherman also declared there that if the mint house should be put down so that money cannot be had he should neither expect nor desire any part of his salary in money."

Thus the town secured the services of Mr. Sherman, and provided him with a place of residence; and within a year after the death of Mr. Browne, the church was again equipped for work. Mr. Sherman was son of Rev. John Sherman of Watertown. He married Mary, daughter of Thomas Walker of Sudbury, and had two sons, John and Thomas. He was ordained in 1678, and was dismissed May 22, 1705. After leaving the pastoral office he remained in town for a time, occasionally preaching abroad. Afterwards, he practiced medicine in Elizabethtown, N. J., and Salem, Mass. He died at Sudbury, March 3, 1718.

NEW MEETING-HOUSE.

During the pastorate of Mr. Sherman, the town took measures for the erection of a new house of worship. Oct. 6, 1686, "it was determined, ordered, and voted, that a new meeting house be built within this town with all convenient speed, after such manner as shall be resolved upon by the town." "It was ordered that the said new meeting house shall be erected finished and stand upon the present Burying place of this town and on the most convenient part thereof or behind or about the old meeting house that now is."

The business of building the meeting-house was entrusted to Deacon John Haines, between whom and the town a covenant was made at a town-meeting, Jan. 10, 1685. It was to be raised on or before the first day of July, 1688; and for the work Mr. Haines was to have two hundred pounds, — one hundred and sixty pounds of it to be paid in "country pay and at country price," and the other forty pounds to be paid in money. The country pay was to be in "good sound merchantable Indian corn, or Rye, or wheat, or barley, or malt, or Peas, or Beef, or Pork, or work, or in such other pay as the said Deacon Haines shall accept of any person."

The meeting-house was to be "made, framed and set up, and finished upon the land and place appointed by the town on the 6th of October last past, in all respects for dimentions, strength, shape, . . . and conveniences, as Dedham meeting

house is, except filling between studs ; but in all things else
admitting with all in this work such variations as are particularly mentioned in the proposition of Corporal John Brewer
and Sam¹ How." The town was to help raise the building,
the clapboards were to be of cedar, the inside to be lined
with either planed boards or cedar clapboards, and the windows were to contain two hundred and forty feet of glass. It
was voted, "that Leut. Daniel Pond shall be left to his liberty whether he will leave a middle alley in the new meeting
house, or shut up the seats as they are in Dedham meeting
house, provided always that the seats do comfortably and
conveniently hold and contain seven men in one end of the
seats and seven women in the other end of the seats."

At a town-meeting, Feb. 13, 1687–8, "a committee of
eleven men were chosen to receive the new meeting house
of Deacon John Haines, when it is finished according unto
covenant made between him and the town," and also "to
appoint persons how and where to sit in the meeting house."
It was voted, "that the most considerable rule for seating of
persons in the meeting house shall be by what they pay to
the building thereof, excepting in respect to some considerable persons or to age and other considerable qualifications."
It was voted that there should be "a good, sufficient and
strong ladder placed at the meeting house with as much
speed as may be, to prevent whatsoever occurrence may happen." "Mary Loker was to have one pound fifteen shillings
for the year ensuing for sweeping the new meeting house
and keeping it clean." It was voted, that "there should be
a convenient place for the storing of the ammunition of the
town over the window in the south west gable. The dirt
on the north east and south east side of the new meeting
house was to be moved and placed at the foreside of it, and
the ground was to be raised to within four or five inches of
the sill, and to cover it with gravel and make a convenient
way in at the door."

A few years after this meeting-house was built a bell was
provided for it. It cost "twenty and five pounds in money."
John Goodenow and Edward Wright paid this, and they
bought the bell of Caleb Hubbert of Braintree. It was voted

that John Parmenter should sweep the meeting-house from April 1, 1696, to April 1, 1697, for fourteen bushels of Indian or twenty shillings in money. The building being completed, a committee was chosen "to go to Dedham and clear up accounts with and obtain a discharge from Lieut. Daniel Pond concerning our new meeting house."

CIVIL AND MILITARY DISTURBANCES.

While the people of Sudbury were endeavoring to repair their misfortunes, they worked at a disadvantage. The country was by no means quiet. Disturbances, both civil and military, embarrassed the land. Kings in rapid succession ascended the British throne. In 1685 came the death of King Charles, who was succeeded by James II., who was followed by William of Holland. Change in England meant change in America, and change in America meant change in the colonial towns. For some time there had been a controversy concerning the colony's charter. In 1685 it was declared that this charter was forfeited. The liberties of the people passed into the hands of the King of Great Britain, and the colony was called to submit to such form of government as Charles II. and James his successor saw fit to allow. But the people yet hoped to resume the old charter. Events, however, proved that these hopes were vain. In 1692 a new charter was brought to Boston by Sir William Phipps, and from a colony Massachusetts passed to a province, which included Nova Scotia, New Hampshire, Plymouth, Massachusetts, and Maine. With this change came new relations and laws. The new charter gave the governor extended power. He had the appointment of all the military officers, and, with the consent of the Council, the judicial also. He could call or adjourn the General Court, and no act of government was valid without his consent. But before the completion of this list of events, the community was agitated by a usurpation of power unsurpassed in the history of the colony.

In 1686, Sir Edmund Andros was commissioned by King James to succeed Dudley as colonial governor. Andros proved a pernicious ruler, whose despotism was not long to be borne. Among his arbitrary acts was imprisonment without trial, unjust and oppressive taxation, denial of the right of *habeas corpus* and the right of the people to hold their town-meetings. But the act which perhaps threatened the greatest embarrassment was that relating to real estate. The people were informed that they had unsound claims to their lands, and that the titles to them were void. Notwithstanding Indian deeds were produced, they were told these were " worth no more than the scratch of a bear's paw." Although King James is said to have commanded, that " the several properties according to the ancient records " should be continued to the people, yet the commission to Andros intimated his intention of assuming the whole "real property " of the country, and that landed rights were to be granted the people on such terms as the king might demand.

The result was a general embarrassment, and on April 18, 1689, there was a revolt and resort to arms. A council of safety was formed, and there met in Boston the 22d of May, the representatives of fifty-four towns. Sudbury sent Peter King as its delegate. He was instructed " to consult with the council sitting," and directed " not to resume the former charter government only that the present council should stand until we receive orders from his Royal Highness the Prince of Orange, and that the prisoners in durance be safely kept until such time as they may be brought before lawful justice." Forty of the representatives of the fifty-four towns voted in favor of resuming the old charter. This, however, being opposed by Broadstreet, the president, and also by many of the old magistrates, it was agreed to resume only the government chosen in 1686 under the charter, until further orders were received from England. Forty delegates voted for this measure, and Mr. King of Sudbury was among the number. The dissolution of the old charter was in 1686. On May 26, 1689, a ship brought the news of the proclaiming of King William and Queen Mary; and the arrival of the charter for a province was in 1692.

Thus, when the country was stirred by civil commotion,

the town took its appropriate part; and, despite the bustle and stir in these important matters of state, it pursued its steady way. The persons who served from Sudbury in the General Court from the deposition of Andros, in 1689, were Peter King, Peter Noyes, John Haynes, Joseph Freeman. (Mass. Hist. Coll., Vol. XXIV., p. 289.)

THE TEN YEARS WAR.

The disturbing elements of this period were not confined to civil relations. The border settlements were exposed to the sudden assaults of the savages, who needed only a pretext or an opportunity to commence their depredations. An occasion was soon afforded. About 1689 hostilities broke out among the settlements of New Hampshire and Maine, and the county of Middlesex was called upon to send its troops and munitions of war to the ravaged districts between the Penobscot and Merrimac. But a war of greater proportions soon threatened the colony, and which was to be of a duration, not of months, but of years. This war, waged between England and France, and known as King William's, or the "Ten Years War," for about a decade of years, menaced the frontier towns of New England. The work of devastation was soon commenced, and revived the associations of by-gone years. The musket was once more to be shouldered and the sword unsheathed in defense of imperiled firesides and the arbitrament of disputed rights.

French authorities, with the sanction of the governor general of Canada, sought an alliance with the Indians, and the French and savages combined made the border a perilous place. But the war affected the New England colony in general. Levies were made on the towns for men to man the outposts and to go on expeditions of an aggressive and hazardous nature. During these years of hostility Sudbury was less exposed than in the war with King Philip. Her greatest trial was from sudden incursions, and a liability to large drafts on her weak resources. It is recorded in the town book, that, in 1688, there was a distribution of the stock of ammunition. The following statement is accompanied by a list of persons who took the stock in charge: —

The names of those persons as have taken the public stock of ammunition into their hands, and have agreed to respond for the same in case that it be not spent in real service in the resistance of the enemy are as followeth.

Captain Thomas Brown
John Goodenow
Lieut. John Grout
Ensign Jacob Brown
Peter King
Lieut. Edward Wright
John Rice
Mr. Thomas Walker, Sr.
Thomas Reade, Sr.
Deacon John Haines
Lieut. Josiah Haines
Sargent Joseph Freeman
Corp. John Brewer
Joseph Curtis
Mr. Joseph Noise
Joseph Moore
Zachariah Maynard
Sargent John Rutter
Jonathan Stanhope
Corp. Richard Taylor
Corp. Joseph Gleason
Jonathan Rice
Thomas Plympton.

Benjamin Moore
Samuel How
Matthew Gibbs
Mr. Hopestil Brown
Daniel Stone
Corp. John Bent
Corp. Henry Rice
Mr. William Brown
Mathew Rice
John Allen
Mr. Peter Noyes
Widow Mary Rice
John Parmenter
Mr. James Sherman
Stephen Blandford
John Grout, Jun.
Thomas Knapp
Benjamin Parmenter
Sarjeant James Barnard
John How.

The most of the persons thus named had allowed them a little over four pounds of powder, a little over thirty-three pounds of shot, and thirteen flints. About two years from this date, 1690, an order came to Major Elisha Hutchinson, commander of the forces, to detach "18 able soldiers well appointed with arms and ammunition out of the several companies of his regiment to rendezvous at Sudbury upon Tuesday the 27th of May with six days provisions a man."

These things indicate a harassed condition of the country, and perhaps a near approach of the foe to Sudbury. Nothing, however, so forcibly sets forth the military service of the town in those times as a paper bearing no date, but found in the State Archives among others belonging to that period. The document, which is in the form of a petition, is as follows : —

To the honorable Governor, Deputy Governor, and to all our honored
Magistrates and Representatives of the Massachusetts Colony,
now sitting in General Court in Boston.

The humble petition of us who are some of us for ourselves, others
for our children and servants, whose names are after subscribed humbly
showeth that being impressed the last winter several of us into dreadful
service, where, by reason of cold and hunger and in tedious marches
many score of miles in water and snow, and laying on the snow by night,
having no provision but what they could carry upon their backs, beside
hard arms and ammunition, it cost many of them their lives. Your humble petitioners several of us have been at very great charges to set them
out with arms, and ammunition, and clothing, and money to support
them, and afterwards by sending supplies to relieve them and to save
their lives, notwithstanding many have lost their lives there, others came
home, and which were so suffered, if not poisoned, that they died since
they came from there, notwithstanding all means used, and charges out
for their recovery, others so surfeited that they are thereby disabled
from their callings. Likewise your humble petitioners request is that
this honored court would grant this favor that our messengers may have
liberty to speak in the court to open our cause so as to give the court
satisfaction. Your humble petitioners humble request is farther that
you would please to mind our present circumstances, and to grant us
such favors as seems to be just and rational, that we may have some
compensation answerable to our burden, or at least to be freed from farther charges by rates, until the rest of our brethren have borne their
share with us, and not to be forced to pay others that have been out but
little in respect of us, whereas the most of us have received little or nothing but have been at very great charges several of us. If it shall please
this honorable General Court to grant us our petition we shall look upon
ourselves as duty binds us ever pray.

John Haynes Sen.	Thomas Walker
Joseph Noyes Sen.	John Barrer
Peter Haynes Sen. [or Noyes]	Samuel Glover
Mathew Rice	Joseph Gleason sen
John Allen	Thomas Rutter
Mathew Gibbs sen	Joseph Rutter
Thomas Rice	Benjamin Wight
James Rice sen	Peter Plympton
Joseph Curtis	Israel Miller
Josiah Haynes sen.	Stephen Cutts

(State Archives, Vol. XXXVI., p. 59.)

This petition presents a story of sorrow. The service
referred to was, it is supposed, in connection with the ill-
fated expedition of Sir William Phipps in 1690. In this

expedition Sudbury was represented by a company of men, some of whom were from Framingham. A large force, consisting of forty vessels and two thousand men, most of whom were from Massachusetts, was fitted out for the capture of Quebec. The fleet sailed from Boston, and the land forces marched by way of Montreal and the lakes. But the great enterprise failed. Gotten up in haste, it was poorly prepared, and its military stores were but scant. Being late in the season, unfavorable weather prevailed, the small-pox set in, and the expedition came back with its object unachieved. It is said that many more died of fever after the expedition returned to Boston. But this was not all. The money in the treasury was insufficient to pay the soldiers, and for the first time in the history of the country paper money was issued; but from this the soldiers obtained only from twelve to fourteen shillings to the pound.

Years after the Phipps expedition, survivors or their heirs petitioned the Court for land grants, and received them. These lands were called Canada grants. In answer to such a petition, Sudbury received land in Maine, which was called the Sudbury Canada grant. This grant now makes the towns of Jay and Canton. (New England Historical Antiquarian Register, Vol. XXX., p. 92.) The names of the petitioners for the foregoing grant have been preserved in a paper which bears date " Oct ye 26th 1741." The list was given in connection with what was called " A lift tax of fifteen shillings a man." A few of these names are as follows: Ward, Graves, Stone, Rice, Bridges, Newton, Walker, Woodward, Joseph Rutter, Gibbs, Peter Bent, Brewer, Samuel Paris. The petitioners were formed into a society, having Capt. Samuel Stone, treasurer, and Josiah Richardson, clerk, both of Sudbury.

Thus along from 1688 till the declaration of Peace at Ryswick, Dec. 10, 1697, there was inconvenience and loss. On the 27th of July, 1694, a detachment of the Abenakis, under the Chief Taxous, crossed the Merrimac, and assailed Groton, where the Indians killed twenty-two persons and captured thirteen. In August, 1695, a sudden descent was made on Billerica, in which fifteen persons were killed or

THE WALKER GARRISON HOUSE.
See page 199.

captured. Lancaster suffered in 1692, also in 1695, and in September, 1697, the Indians again entered the town. Thus near lurked the troublesome foe, and Sudbury doubtless felt its insecurity when it learned of these savage incursions in the neighboring towns. The following record on the Town Book bears testimony to this sense of insecurity: "Also agreed to call the town together for the choice of all town officers next lecture day at twelve of the clock, and it being a troublesome time with the Indians but few appeared."

WITCHCRAFT.

Another source of disturbance towards the last of the century was the witchcraft delusion. Supposed cases had occurred before in the Massachusetts Colony, and persons had been executed whom it was said had the power to bewitch men; but in 1692, it broke out with renewed violence, and strangely disturbed society. We know of no alleged cases in Sudbury; but a person prominently connected with Salem witchcraft subsequently went to Sudbury, and dwelt there until his death. This was the Rev. Samuel Paris, the first minister of what was then Salem Village, but now the town of Danvers. In view of this fact, a few words concerning the matter and Mr. Paris' sad history may not be amiss.

The Salem witchcraft delusion began in Mr. Paris' family. During the winter of 1691-2 a company of young girls were accustomed to meet at his house and practice fortune-telling, necromancy, and magic. It is stated they attained some skill in this matter, and that after a while they ascribed to it supernatural agency. The community became alarmed, and the physician called them bewitched. Two of these girls were of Mr. Paris' household, — one a daughter, the other a niece, neither of them over eleven years of age. The complaints made were similar to those made years before by the children of John Goodenow of Boston. An Indian woman named Tituba, who had been brought from New Spain, lived in Mr. Paris' family. Tituba was accused of being the witch, and of bewitching these children. She confessed, and claimed to have confederates. Had the children of Mr.

Paris been unnoticed, or the matter brushed lightly by, perhaps it had stopped right there; but they were pitied, and shown special attention, and new cases soon occurred. The work of accusation and suspicion went forward, and rapidly spread, until it reached fearful proportions. Scores were apprehended, tried, and condemned, until men knew not when they were safe.

The delusion was soon dispelled, and society resumed a more tranquil state; but as the darkness broke it left bitter regrets; for the light shone on a record as sad as any in the annals of the Massachusetts Colony. From Mr. Paris' position, as pastor of the Salem Village Church, he may have come in contact with cases in a perfunctory way which gave him unpleasant publicity. In 1695 a council met at Salem Village to confer about the witchcraft matter as related to Mr. Paris and his people. Shortly after this he left the church and the place. He became a trader, went to Watertown, then Concord; but his stay in each place was short. He then went to Dunstable, where for a few months he preached. He at length went to Sudbury, and died there about 1720. Thus originated the Salem witchcraft, and thus passed away the man who received notoriety by it.

Moral. — Deal not with familiar spirits. "Resist the devil, and he will flee from you." Leave necromancy, magic, and all the black arts, and seek more substantial and sensible things.

HISTORICAL SKETCH.

Mr. Paris was the son of Thomas Paris of London. He went to Harvard College, but did not remain to graduate. Before preaching at Salem Village he preached at Stowe. He was twice married, his first wife dying in 1696, at about the age of forty-eight, his second wife in 1719. His first wife was buried at Danvers; her grave is marked by a headstone upon which is the following verse, after which are the initials of Mr. Paris: —

> Sleep Precious Dust, no stranger now to Rest,
> Thou hast thy longed wish, within Abraham's Brest,
> Farewell Best Wife, Choice Mother, Neighbor, Friend,
> We'll wail thee less, for hopes of thee in the end.

Mrs. Paris, it is said, was a good woman. Mr. Paris left several children. His daughter Dorothy, born 1700, became the wife of Hopestill Brown of Sudbury. Another daughter married Peter Bent. His son Noyes Paris, born 1699, took his first degree at Harvard College, 1721. His other son, Samuel, was born 1702.

After Mr. Paris came to Sudbury, we conclude that for a time he taught school there. The records state, that in 1717, Mr. Samuel Paris was to teach school four months of the year at the school-house on the west side of the river, and the rest of the year at his own house. If he was absent part of the time, he was to make it up the next year. In Book III., Sudbury Records, we have the following statement, with date May 25, 1722: "These may certify that ye 28 pounds that ye town of Sudbury agreed to give Mr. Samuel Paris late of Sudbury, for his last yeares keeping school in sd town, is by Mr. John Clapp treasurer for said town by his self and by his order all paid as witness my hand John Rice excuter of ye last will and Testament of ye sd Mr. Paris."

There are graves of the Paris family in the old burying-ground at Wayland. Towards the southeast side of it stands a stone with the following inscription: "Here lyes ye Body of Samuel Paris, Who Died July 27th 1742 in ye 8th year of his age." On another stone is marked: "Here lyes ye Body of Mrs. Abigail Paris who departed this life February ye 15th 1759 in ye 55th year of her age."

INCORPORATION OF FRAMINGHAM.

At the close of the century, Sudbury lost a portion of the inhabitants who dwelt upon its southern border and were identified with the town. This loss was occasioned by the incorporation of Framingham in 1700. A petition was presented to the Court in 1792-3 (State Archives, Vol. CXIII.) by these people and others, who state, that they are "persons dwelling upon sundry farms lying between Sudbury, Concord, Marlboro, Natick, and Sherborn, and westerly in the Wilderness." They say they "have dwelt there about forty years, and are about forty families, some having built, and some building." They also say they "have endeavored to attend public worship some at one town, some at another;" and they ask to be made a township, and have the privileges usually accorded in such cases. The Court granted the request of the petitioners, and ordered that the farms adjacent to Framingham should be annexed to the proposed new town; and the people of Framingham having asked the Court "that the line between s^d annexed farms and Sudbury be accepted," the request was granted. Some of the names attached to the petition are still familiar in Sudbury, viz.: Bent, Stone, Rice, Gleason, Walker, and How.

STATISTICS.

The population of the town toward the beginning of this period is indicated by the fact that in 1679 six tything-men were appointed, who were "to inspect from ten to thirteen families each." The following is a report made at a selectmen's meeting, in 1682, of improved land in and bordering upon the town: "Lands of persons dwelling in the town, 3896 acres. List of lands in town of persons dwelling elsewhere up and down the country, 2522 acres. List of men's lands bordering about or near the town, amounted to 5130 acres, in which Mr. Danforth's lands and Mr. Gookin's lands were not cast, because the contents were not certain."

These were sent, together with the list of troopers in and about town, by Deacon Haines, commissioner, to Cambridge. The list of troopers that the town clerk made a rate upon, as mentioned with date 1683, is eighteen; and with date 1682 we have the county's money rate mentioned as follows: "The part to be collected on the east side the river, 5^{lbs} : 4^s : 5^d; on the west side the river, 4^{lbs} : 8^s : 0^d."

Some little attention was given to matters of education in this period, as indicated by a selectmen's report dated March 30, 1680. On Oct. 2, 1692, John Long was chosen as "a wrighteing school master, to teach children to wright and cast accounts." Mr. Long continued to serve the town as schoolmaster for several years.

Thus closed the century in which the town of Sudbury had its beginning. It was a diversified history, in which the light and shadow alternately played on the scene. But the power of a protecting Providence kept the people safe amid every trial and danger, and brought them forth with a prosperity and strength which fitted them for the important events of the future. Probably but few, if any, who were of the original grantees in 1638, entered upon the scenes of the eighteenth century; but their children and children's children were to continue their work, and project their influence into far-off years; and as we continue the narrative, and consider the subsequent events in this history, we may see how the fathers lived in their sons.

CHAPTER XV.

1700–1725.

Educational Advantages; Why so small.— School Laws by the Province. — Town Action. — Grammar School; Location. — Mixed Schools. — Masters. — School-Houses. — Ecclesiastical Matters. — Dismission of Rev. Mr. Sherman. — Ordination of Rev. Israel Loring. — Division of the Town into Two Precincts; Petitions, Remonstrances, Decision of the Court, Subsequent Action of the Town. — Call of Mr. Loring by the People of the West Precinct; His Acceptance. — Renewal of the Church Covenant by the People of the West Side; Subscribers Thereto. — Settlement of Rev. Mr. Cook in the East Parish. — Building of a Meeting-House on the West Side; Location. — Removal of the East Side Meeting-House; New Location.

The wealth of thought they knew,
And with a toil-blest hand
The path of learning, broad and free,
Sped through our favored land.
MISS SIMES.

A PROMINENT feature in Sudbury at the beginning of the eighteenth century was the attention given to schools. Hitherto comparatively little had been done in this matter. As has been stated, means were provided for moral instruc-

tion, but the opportunities for acquiring more than the rudiments of secular knowledge were extremely meagre. The
causes of this were various. It was not an educational age,
there was but one college in the Massachusetts Bay Province; teachers at that day were scarce, and without proper
instruction there was but poor encouragement to establish
public schools. Moreover, it was an age of economy. Careful expenditure was a necessity in that tax-burdened and impoverished period. Society was bearing the burdens incident
to the waste of successive wars. Specie was scarce and commodities dear. To procure things needful for every-day life
payment in country produce was often made. Sometimes
town taxes were paid in wares. In 1687 the taxes of Hingham were paid in pails. In 1693 those of Woburn were paid
in shoes. Various were the expedients that the towns employed to meet necessary calls that were made upon them.
No wonder that in such times schools were neglected. It
would not be strange if men were unmindful of every demand
but those of stern necessity.

But in 1692 a law was enacted, that every town in the
province having fifty householders, or upwards, should be
"constantly provided of a schoolmaster to teach children
and youth to read and write; and where any town or towns
have the number of one hundred families or householders,
there shall also be a grammar school set up in every such
town, and some discreet person of good conversation, well
instructed in the tongues procured to keep such school."
Any town neglecting this requirement one year was liable
to be fined ten pounds. In 1701 the Provincial Court passed
an additional school act, stating, concerning the former one,
that it was "shamefully neglected by divers towns, and the
penalty thereof not required tending greatly to the nourish-
ment of ignorance and irreligion, whereof grievous complaint
is made." For neglecting this second law the penalty was
made twenty pounds. This also proved quite insufficient for
its purpose, for it was stated "many towns . . . would incur
the penalty and pay for the neglect of the law rather than
maintain the school required." In 1718 the Court enacted
that the fine should be thirty pounds in the case of towns

that had one hundred and fifty families, forty pounds in the case of towns of two hundred inhabitants. There was certain provision made by the law of the province by which the schoolmaster was to be maintained. He was to have a convenient house and competent salary. It was also provided that the instructor should be an actual schoolmaster; the town minister was not to act as a substitute.

Such were some of the school laws at the beginning of the eighteenth century. That they affected town action is probable; and very likely they exerted a powerful influence in procuring better schools in Sudbury. The records inform us that Jan. 1, 1702, the town voted that a rate should be made "to pay the 5 pounds the town was fined for want of a school master." This is the only time we hear of the town's receiving the penalty. On the contrary, there is ample evidence of diligent endeavor to meet the law. Nov. 17, 1701, at a town-meeting, "it was voted to choose Mr. Joseph Noyes as a grammar school master for one year. . . . Also chose Mr Wm Brown and Mr. Thomas Plympton to present the said school master unto the Rev. ministers for their approbation of him, which are as followeth, Mr. James Sherman, Mr. Joseph Esterbrooks, Mr. Swift of Framingham." This Reverend Committee duly met, and examined the candidate, and reported as follows, Nov. 21, 1701: "We the subscribers being desired by the town of Sudbury to write what we could testify in concerning the justification of Mr. Joseph Noyes of Sudbury for a legall Grammar School master, having examined the said Mr. Joseph Noyes, we find that he hath been considerably versed in the Latin and Greek tongue, and do think that upon his dilligent revisal and recollection of what he hath formerly learned, he may be qualified to initiate and instruct the youth in the Latin tongue. JOSEPH ESTERBROOKS, JOHN SWIFT."

On the strength of this careful approval and guarded recommendation, the successful candidate went forth to his work. He did not, however, long retain his position. For some cause not mentioned, the place soon became vacant; and February of the same year Mr. Picher became Mr. Noyes's successor. The contract made with Mr. Picher was as follows: "It is agreed and concluded that the town will and doth grant to pay unto Mr. Nathaniel Picher six pounds in money in course hee doth accept of the Towne's choice as to be our Grammar scool master, also for one quarter of a yeare, and to begin ye third of March next ensuing, and to serve in the place the full quarter of a yeare, one half of the time on the east side of the River, and the other half of the time on the west side of the river. This Grammar scool master chosen if he accepts and doth enter upon the work it is expected by the above said Towne, that he should teach all children sent to him to learn English and the Latin tongue, also writing and the art of Arithmatic." In 1703 it was voted to pay Mr. Picher for service done that year twenty-eight pounds, "he deducting a months pay . . . for his being absent one month in summer time from keeping of scool, which amounth to twelfeth part of time;" "also voted and agreed as a free will, to give unto Mr. Picher two days in every quarter of his year to visit his friends, if he see cause to take up with it." In 1711, Lieut. Thomas Frink and Quartermaster Brintnall were "to agree with sum person who is well instructed in ye tongues to keep a scool." His pay was not to exceed thirty pounds.

These records show something of the expense of a grammar school in the olden times; they also give hints of the character, duty, and pay of the teachers; and of the manner of selection and examination. We have no means of knowing the proficiency attained by the pupils in those grammar schools; but with so much careful painstaking, and so large an expenditure of money, we may presume that something more than the mere rudiments were obtained.

The place of the school was changed from time to time. In 1702 it was voted "that the scool master should keep ye scool on ye west side of ye river at ye house of Thomas Brintnell, which is there parte of time belonging to ye west side of ye river." The custom of changing the place of the school was continued for many years; for we find the following record as late as 1722: "Voted by the town that ye scool master shall keep scool one half of ye time on ye west side of ye river in Sudbury, voted by ye town, that ye scool master shall keep

yᵉ first quarter at yᵉ scool house at yᵉ gravel pitt, voted by
yᵉ town that yᵉ second to bee keept on yᵉ east side yᵉ river as
Near yᵉ water as may be conveniant, voted by yᵉ town that
yᵉ third quarter to be keept at yᵉ house of Insign John
Moore, voted by yᵉ town that yᵉ fourth quarter to be keept
at yᵉ house of Clark Gleason." In the year 1717, Samuel
Paris was to keep school four months of the year at the
school-house on the west side of the river, and at his own
house the rest of the year. If he was away part of the time,
he was to make it up the next year.

But in addition to these means for obtaining advanced
instruction, there were schools of a simpler character. About
the time that provision was made for a grammar school, we
read of "masters who were to teach children to rede and
wright and cast accounts." This was done in 1701, at which
time the town "voted and chose John Long and John Balcom" for the purpose just stated, and to pay them for one
year thirty shillings apiece. From this time repeated reference is made in the records to schools of a primary or mixed
character.

Among the schoolmasters who served before 1750, are
William Brintnal, Joseph Noyes, Nathaniel Picher, Jonathan
Hoar, Samuel Paris, Nathaniel Trask, Jonathan Loring, John
Long, John Balcom, John Mellen, Samuel Kendall, Ephraim
Curtis, and Zachery Hicks. Some of these taught for a suc-
cession of terms or years. William Brintnal taught a gram-
mar school as late as 1733–4, and receipts are found of Samuel
Kendall in 1725 and 1736.

Prior to 1700, school-house accommodations were scant.
There was no school building whatever. In 1702 "the town
agreed that the school should be kept at the meeting house
half a quarter and the other half quarter at the house of
Benjamin Morses." But it is a law of progress that improvement in one direction suggests improvement in another; so
with better schools better accommodations were sought for.
Jan. 1, 1702, the "town voted and paste into an act, to have
a convenient scool hous;" also voted "that the scool house
that shall be built by the town shall be set and erected as
near the centre of the town, as may be conveniantly set upon

the town's land;" also "that it be twenty feet in length,
: : : eighteen feet in breadth, seven feet from the bottom of
the cell to the top of the plate, a large chimney to be within
the house, the house to be a log house, made of pine, only
the cells to be of white oak bord and shingles to be covered
with.   Also the chimney to be of stone to the mortling and
finished with brick.   This was paste into an act and vote
Jan. 15th 1701–2."   At another meeting it was decided "that
there should be two scool houses;" that they should be of
the same dimensions; and "that the one on the east side
should be set near to Enoch Cleavland's dwelling house."
It was afterwards voted that "the scool houses should be
builte by a general town acte and that the selectmen should
make a rate of money of 20 pounds for their erection."   One
of the houses was to be placed "by Cleafflands and the other
near unto Robert Mans."   In 1711 the town voted to have
but one school-house, and this school-house was to be built
at "ye gravel pitt."   "Ye scool house" here mentioned was
"to be 20 foot long, 16 foot wide, six foot studd, nine foot
and a half sparrl.   Ye sills to be white oak ye outside, to be
borded, and ye bords to be feather edge.   Ye inside to be
birch and borded with Ruff bords, lower and uper flower to
be bord and a brick Chemne, and two glass windows 18
Enches square per window, and the Ruffe to be borded and
shingled."   It was to be ready for a school by the last of
May, 1712.   Joseph Parmenter was to make it, and have for
pay fourteen pounds.

The evidence is that the desire for school privileges spread,
and that the extremity of the town soon sought for increased
advantages.   April 17, 1719, the town was called upon "to
see if it will grant the North west quarter of the towns petition, they desiring the school master some part of the time
with them."

The above records comprise the most important ones relating to schools during this period.   As we leave these educational matters, some reflections arise concerning their relation
to the town's future and far-reaching history.   They were
the beginnings of great and long-lasting influences.   Those
humble houses of the early New England schools were the

town's nurseries of useful knowledge. In them minds were disciplined for that active period which, before the century closed, was to shape the country's career, and make of the colonies a great cluster of states. What a work was wrought within them! What responsibility was upon those who had charge of these far-back beginnings! We have found nothing on the records to indicate what methods were employed in governing or teaching; but there is abundant room for the supposition that those who founded and those who taught these schools feared God; and that they considered his Word a book suitable to be read and taught in all places of learning. No wonder, that, with such a beginning, our common schools have had such great success; and that the influences that survived those times, manners, and men should have such large and lasting results.

ECCLESIASTICAL MATTERS.

As in educational matters, so in those pertaining to the church, we find the period prolific in change. Great and important events transpired relating to the meeting-house, the minister, and the people. The first change was the dismission of the pastor. On May 22, 1705, the pastoral relation between Rev. James Sherman and the people of Sudbury was dissolved. But not long was the church left pastorless. The same year of Mr. Sherman's removal a town-meeting was held, in which it was voted "y^t ye town will chose a man to preach ye word of God unto us for a quarter of a year." The Rev. Israel Loring was chosen for the term mentioned. He began to preach in Sudbury, Sept. 16, 1705; and the result was he was ordained as pastor, Nov. 20, 1706.

After the settlement of Mr. Loring ecclesiastical matters were not long in a quiet state. A new subject soon engrossed public attention. There was an attempt made to divide the town into two parochial precincts. The west side people doubtless loved the little hillside meeting-house, about which were the graves of their friends, and whose history was associated with so much of their own. Their fondness for it had doubtless increased as the years passed by, and there clus-

tered about it memories of things the sweetest and the sad-
dest that had entered into their checkered experience.   Here
their children had been offered in baptism; here had been the
bridal and the burial, the weekly greetings and partings, the
exchange of intelligence of heart and home.   It had been the
place for prayer and the preached word; a place of watch
and ward, and a place of resort in times of danger.   But notwithstanding their fondness for the sacred spot, they were
too practical a people to allow sentiment to interfere with
their true progress, and what they believed to be their spiritual good.   With their slow means of transit, and the rough
roads of that period when at their best, it was a long and
weary way they had to travel every Sabbath day; but when
the roads became blocked with the drifting snow, or the river
was swollen with floods, then it was sometimes a perilous
undertaking to reach the east side meeting-house and return.
In that primitive period the people of Sudbury did not desire
even a good excuse to keep them from public worship; they
were Puritanic in both precept and practice.   They would
allow no small obstacle to cheat their soul of its rights; but
if there were hinderances in the way to their spiritual helps,
they required their immediate removal.

Hence, a movement was inaugurated to divide the town,
and make of it two precincts, in each of which there should
be a church.   A primary act for the accomplishment of this
purpose was to obtain the consent of the General Court.   To
do this a petition was presented, which, as it tells its own
story, and sets forth the entire case, we will present : —

Petition of the West Side people of Sudbury to Governor Dudley and
    the General Assembly.
    The petition of us who are the subscribers living on ye west side of
Sudbury great River Humbly showeth that wereas ye All wise and over
Ruling providence of ye great God, Lord of Heaven and Earth who is
God blessed forever moore, hath cast our lott to fall on that side of the
River by Reason of the flud of watare, which for a very great part of the
yeare doth very much incomode us and often by extremity of water and
terrible and violent winds, and a great part of the winter by ice, as it is
at this present, so that wee are shut up and cannot come forth, and many
times when wee doe atempt to git over our flud, we are forced for to seek
our spiritual good with the peril of our Lives.

Beside the extreme Travill that many of us are Exposed unto sum 3 : 4 : 5 : 6 miles much more than a Sabbath days Jurney, by Reason of these and many more objections, to many here to enumerate, whereby many of our children and little ones, ancient and weak persons, can very Rarly attend the public worship. The considered premises we truly pray your Excellency and ye Honorable Council and House of Representatives to consider and compassionate us in our Extreme suffering condition, and if we may obtain so much favor in your Eyes as to grant us [our presents] as to appoint us a Commity to seé and consider our circumstances and make report thereof to this honorable Court. And your pore petitioners shall ever pray.

Sudbury, January 15th 170$\frac{4}{7}$

John Goodnow.	John haynes. Jr.
John haines	Robert Man his mark
John Brigham	Benjamin wright.
William Walker.	David Haynes.
George Parmenter.	Prefer haines.
David how.	Thomas Brintnal.
George Parmenter, Jr.	Edward Goodnow his mark
Joseph Parmenter.	John Goodenow, jr
John brigham.	Ephraim Garfield, his mark.
Samuel willis.	Thomas Smith, Junior.
Joseph willis	Jonathan Rice.
Richard Sanger.	
Tho: Smith	
Joseph Hayes [Haynes]	
timothy gibson, Jr	
Joseph F. Jewel (his mark).	
Isaac Mellen	
Melo C. Taylor. (his mark).	
John Balcom.	
Joseph Balcom.	

(State Archives, Vol. II., p. 221)

It was ordered that the town of Sudbury be served with a copy of the petition, and notified to attend the next session of the Court, and present objections if they had any. At a town-meeting in Sudbury, Oct. 4, 1707, a committee was chosen to attend the General Court, and give answer to the above petition. The committee was composed as follows: " Mr Joseph Noyes, Lieut. Hopll Brown, Ens. Samll King, Mr. James Barnard, Mr. Noah Clapp, Mr. Thomas Plympton." This committee duly appeared to present a protest to the west side petition. The following are their words of remonstrance : —

The committee chosen humbly showeth,

That whereas a petition hath been presented to this Hon. Court in their late session by a Small number of persons Dwelling on the westerly side of the river in Sudbury, (though Privately carried on)

Praying that these may be a precinct by themselves &c. we do Humbly offer to your Judicious consideration

That the number thus Petitioning is but Small and that others Inhabiting on the westerly side of said River a number near Equal to them, Do oppose the same Looking on such a motion by their neighbors att this Time Especially to be Unseasonable and unreasonable, considering 1.) the Great Expense that we have of Late been att: Occasioned by the deposition of our Late, and the Settling of our Present Minister. (2.) The vast Expenses attending the same, calls and may call for, Obliges us to Request that the Division Petitioned for, may be suspended, we deem ourselves incapable of affording,

1st Two Orthodox minister's Gospel maintainance, 2nd we are Ready to afford to our neighbors what help we can in making the Causway, (so much complained of) passible in ordinary floods, by allotting to every man his quota or proposition to raise, which would be much for the Benefit of Travellers, as well as ourselves.

Finally there are also some of those who now petition for division : that did complain, and declare that the Salary granted to our present minister was so Great that the town was not able to perform it, and if they Plead their remoteness from the public worship of God : we humbly offer that if the meeting house be placed in the Centre of the Inhabitants on the westerly side of the river (where we may expect it will be), many of their dwellings will be as Remote from the meeting house as they are now,   We might bring many more objections which might be of weight, but shall add no more, but leave these to the Judicious consideration of this Honourable Courte, and follow these our Representatives with our petitions to the High Court of Heaven, that this Honouable Court may be so directed in this and in every affair before them, that Gods Glory and the Prosperity of Religion may be promoted, and we, your most humble and obedient servants, may have ever cause to pray &c.

Sudbury. October. 29th: 1707.

Joseph Noyes,   James Barnard,
Thomas Plympton,   Noah Clapp,
Samuel King.

(State Archives, Vol. II., p. 227.)

The following names are signed to the original document:

WEST SIDE INHABITANTS.	EAST SIDE INHABITANTS.
Hop^{ll} Browne	John Rice
Tho': Plymton	Joseph Gleason S^{er}
Sam^{ll} Wright,	Matt^{w} Stone
Joseph Goodenow	Sam^{ll} Graves
John Moore	Jo^{s} Chamberlim
Matt^{w} Gibbs	Jo^{s} Moore S^{er}
Noah Clapp	Jo^{s} Moore
Joseph Stanhope	Jo^{s} Noyes
John Gibbs	Jo^{n} Long
William Arnold	Benj parmento^{r}
Thos Read Ju^{r}	Isaac Stanhope
Josiah Hayden	John Allin
Go^{s} Steenens	John Parmintor
Thos Cuttler	Edmund Rice
John Rice	Matt^{w} Rice
widow Sarah Bowker (⫾) her mark	James Brewer
Benj Moore	Nat^{ll} Moore
Nath^{ll} Rice	Thos Brown
wid: Arabella Read	Ephaaim Rice
John Burk	Isaac Gleason
Ephranin Pratt	John Graues
Peter Plymton	John Grout
Thos Read	James Ross
Joshua Hayns	Thos ffrinke
	Geron Jennison
	Ebe^{r} Rice
	Sam^{ll} Allin
	Jon^{t} Rice
	Joseph Gleason J^{r}
	John abbutt
	John Adams
	Sam^{ll} King
	Jon^{t} Griffin
	Ephraim Curtiss
	John Loker
A True Coppy	Thos Moore

After hearing both petition and remonstrance, the Court ordered that a committee should be sent, and report what the case required. This committee was made up of Capt. Samuel Checkley, [Capt.] Thomas Oliver, and Capt. Jonas Bond. These parties " were to join with such as the hon-

ourable board should nominate, and they were to go upon
the parish and hear what was for or against, notifying the
town at least a week beforehand." John Phillips and Joseph
Lynde, Esq., were named a committee of the board for the
office aforesaid, and the petitioners were to pay the charges
of the committee. The report of these parties was rendered
May 13, 1708. It was in substance, that they considered
" the thing was necessary to be done, but their opinion is,
that now by reason of the [grievous] times not so conveniant."

But the petitioners were not to be baffled by an answer
like this. Accordingly, again they presented their case by
another petition, dated May 26, 1708–9. This second petition sets forth the case thus : —

The Humble Petition of Several of the Inhabitants of the town of Sudbury, on the west side of the River.

To Court session assembled May 26th 170⅝ showeth that your Petitioners lately by their Petition to the Great and General Assembly, represented the hardships & Difficulties they Labored when by reason of
their distance from the meeting house and the difficulty of getting over
the water and Some times Impossibility, there being three hundred and
sixty five on that side and sometimes in the winter not one of them can
possibly go to meeting, the East and West sides are Equal in their payments to the minister and therefore praying they might be made a Precinct and have a meeting house and minister of their side of the River,
wherupon the petition was refered to a committee who upon Consideration of the premises (as your petitioners are Informed) have made a
Report to this Great and General assembly that the thing was necessary
to be done, but their opinion is that now by reason of Troublesome
Times not so Conveniant.

Your [Petitioners] thereupon humbly pray that this great and General
assembly would please to Grant them the Prayer of their petition, that
they may be Empowered to build a meeting house and have a minister
settled on their side, in such time as to this Great and General Assembly shall seem meet and Yoᵣ Petitioners (and as in duty bound) shall
pray,　　　　　John Brigham, John Balcom.　In behalf of ye rest.

This petition was more successful, and obtained, in part
at least, what it sought ; and the following, read in council,
the 28th of May, 1708, and read a second time and concurred
in, June 24th, the same year, was ordered : —

Notwithstanding the present difficulties represented by the committee, If the Inhabitants on West side the River think themselves able to Erect a meeting House and support a minister and shall present a Subscription to this Court amounting to fifty pounds per annum for his maintenance during the first seven years,

That then the Prayer of their Petition be Granted, to bee a Parish or Precinct by themselves. And that they have liberty to erect a meeting house for the Public worship of God, and to invite and procure a Learned Orthodox minister of good conversation to preach to them.

Always Saving Inviolate, and in no ways Infringing the Contract and agreement of the Town made with Mr. Loring, the present minister, and his maintenance, to be duly paid him accordingly, until the Town in General shall make other Provision or the Court take further Order.

But, although the petitioners received permission to build a meeting-house, years elapsed before they availed themselves of the privilege. Meanwhile the subject was more or less agitated. Various measures for the adjustment of matters were proposed, and failed. At one time there was action by the town, at another by the Court. In 1712–13 there was a town-meeting, " to see if the town will do any thing to bring the house into ye center of ye town, or within a quarter of a mile of ye centre, or as near ye centre as may be conveniant, ye town of Sudbury being seven miles long, and ye meeting house as it now standeth but about a mile and half from ye east end of said town."

In December, 1715, a committee was appointed by the Court, who assigned a place for the meeting-house. Tradition states that a spot about a mile northeasterly of Sudbury Centre, and not far from the Thomas Plympton estate, was once designed for the meeting-house. This may have been the place assigned by the committee of 1715. In 1720 the town voted to remain an entire town ; to have a meeting-house on the west side of the river sufficiently large to accommodate all, and to have it built at or near the Gravel Pit.

June 9, 1721, it was ordered by the General Court that "a new meeting house be erected, built, and finished upon the place assigned by a committee assigned by ye s^d Court, in Dec. 1715, and that ye old meeting house be put into good repair." At a town-meeting, Dec. 26, 1721, held at the house of Mr. George Pitts, it was agreed " to grant 24 pounds for preaching for the present on the westerly side of the river." It was also decided at that meeting to choose a committee to present a petition to the General Court, " that ye west side inhabitants may have liberty to place their meeting house on ye rocky plaine ; " which request was granted.

The preliminary work of forming two parochial precincts was now completed ; it only remained to adjust ecclesiastical relations to the new order of things, and provide whatever was essential to its success. The church was to be divided, ministers secured, and a meeeting-house built. All these came about in due time. After the decision, in December, 1721, " to have the preaching of the word amongst us," and the granting of money to meet the expense, Rev. Mr. Minot was invited to preach six Sabbaths in the west precinct. It may be that about this time Mr. Loring preached some on the west side, since on the town debt, as recorded April 9, 1722, there stands this statement : " To Mr. Israel Loring to ye supporting ye ministry on both [sides] ye river in Sudbury 80. 0. 0."

But more permanent arrangements were soon made. On the 6th of June, 1722, they extended a call to Rev. Israel Loring, and offered "£100 for his settlement." July 10, Mr. Loring responded to the invitation in the following words : " To the Inhabitants of the west Precinct in Sudbury : I accept of the kind invitation you have given me to come over and settle and be the minister of the Westerly Precinct." A few days after the above invitation the east side invited him to remain with them, and took measures to provide for " their now settled minister, Mr. Israel Loring." The day after replying to the first invitation, he wrote to the east side people informing them of his decision to leave them and settle in the west precinct. Mr. Loring moved to the west side, July 25, 1723. (Stearns' Collection.) He lived about a mile toward the north part of the town, in what was afterwards an old red house, on the William Hunt place that was torn down some years since. He subsequently lived at the centre, on what is known as the Wheeler Haynes place.

THE LORING PARSONAGE, Sudbury Centre.

The church records by Mr. Loring state as follows: " Feb. 11, 1723. The church met at my house, where, after the brethren on the east side had manifested their desire that the church might be divided into two churches, it was so voted by majority." At the time of the division of the church, the number of communicants on the west side was thirty-two males and forty-two females. (Stearns' Collection.) The Church Records went into the possession of the West Parish. On March 18, 1724–5, the west side people "entered into and renewed" a "holy church covenant," to which were subscribed the following names : —

Israel Loring	David Haynes.
Hopestill Brown	Peter Plympton.
James Haynes Senr	Noah Clap
John Clap Senr	Ephraim Pratt
Thomas Read Senr	Joseph Noyes
Peter Haynes.	John Moore.
Benjaman Wright,	Daniel Estabrooke
Joseph Goodenow	Hopestill Brown Jun.
John Rice,	James Craige,
Samuel Willis.	Joseph Brown.
Thomas Read Jun.	Jonah Haynes.
John Brigham,	Micah Stone.
John Haynes.	Ebenezer Dakin. out of town.
David Parmenter,	John Clap Jr.
Joseph Gibbs, dismissed,	Peter Noyes,
David Maynard.	James Haynes.

While ecclesiastical matters were in process of adjustment on the West side, they were progressing towards a settlement on the East side also. It is stated that the East Precinct was organized June 25, 1722. (Temple.) When the effort to secure the services of Mr. Loring proved futile, a call was extended to Rev. William Cook, a native of Hadley, Mass., and a graduate of Harvard College. The call being accepted, Mr. Cook was ordained March 20, 1723, and continued their pastor until his death, Nov. 12, 1760. (See period 1750.-1775.) The town granted eighty pounds to support preaching on both sides of the river for half a year.

NEW MEETING-HOUSES.

An important matter in connection with the new order of
things was the erection of new meeting-houses. This work
received prompt attention. "At a town meeting January
22: 172⅔ the town granted five hundred pounds to build a
new meeting house on the west side, and repair the old one
on the east side, three hundred and eighty pounds for the
new, and one hundred and twenty pounds for the repairing
the old on the east side." The sum for repairing the old
house was at a subsequent meeting made one hundred and
fifty pounds. That this grant of the town was followed up
by speedy action is indicated by the following receipt, dated
Sudbury, May 31, 1725 : —

Received of Deacon Noah Clap treasurer for the town of Sudbury,
ten pounds four shillings and four pence, in full of all accounts relating
to the building of the new meeting house in the west precinct of said
Sudbury.

This ten pounds, four shillings, and four pence, and former receipts
of money, making the sum of four hundred pounds, we say received
by us.　　　　　　　　　　　　　　　ABRAHAM WOOD,
　　　　　　　　　　　　　　　　　　JOSEPH DAKIN.

The meeting-house in the West Precinct was placed on
the site of the present Unitarian Church in Sudbury Center.
The location was probably selected because central to the
inhabitants of the West Precinct. The following town record is interesting, not only because it relates to the location
of the meeting-house, but to other familiar landmarks in the
vicinity : —

Sudbury. June 12: 1725. laid out to the right of Briant Pendleton,
sixteen acres and one hundred and forty rods on and adjoining to the
Pine Hill, near to and Northwesterly of the meeting house on Rocky
Plain in the west precinct in said Sudbury, southerly partly by a highway, or road leading from Pantry towards Mr. Wood's mills (at South
Sudbury), along by said meeting house, partly by land laid out for a
burying place and accommodations for and about said meeting house,
and partly by Lancaster road, westerly by land claimed by the Grouts
and northerly bounded by land claimed by James Craigs. In part and
partly by land claimed by the Maynards, and easterly bounded by said
Maynards land.

There is no evidence that when the West side meeting-house was built there was so much as a humble hamlet at Rocky Plain. The presence there at that time of a single house is all that is indicated by tradition or record. In several instances the records state something about "yᵉ new house on rocky plain." In May, 1722, there was a town-meeting at the new house on Rocky Plain. Oct. 11, 1722, "a meeting was held at the new house on rocky plain" to attend to matters relating to a new meeting-house. The first town-meeting that was held in the new church edifice was on Aug. 5, 1723. At that time it was voted to have the warnings for town-meetings for the future posted on both sides of the river at the two houses of worship.

Near the spot selected for the meeting-house was the burying-ground set apart by "yᵉ Proprietors of yᵉ undivided lands" in 1716–17. (See p. 121.) This reservation may have influenced the people in the selection of Rocky Plain for the new meeting-house; and the erection of the meeting-house there probably determined the location of the central village of the West Precinct, and in later years of the town of Sudbury. Furthermore, if the town at this time had decided to remain one parish, and erected a meeting-house near the Gravel Pit, for the accommodation of all, the principal village would have been gathered in that locality, and the town might have remained undivided to this day.

After the setting off of the West parish, it was considered advisable to move the East side meeting-house nearer the centre of the East Precinct. Jan. 29, 1721–2, "the town by a vote showed its willingness and agreed to be at the charge to pull down yᵉ old meeting house and remove it south and set it up again." At the same meeting they chose a committee to petition the General Court for permission. In a paper dated Dec. 28, 1724, and signed by Mr. Jennison, Zechariah Heard, and Phineas Brintnal, it is stated that they were "the committee who pulled down and removed the old meeting house in the East Precinct of Sudbury." About 1725 was recorded the following receipt: "Received of Mr. John Clap, late treasurer of the town of Sudbury, the sum of four hundred pounds in full, granted by said town to carry on the building of a meeting house in the East Precinct in said town. We say received by us, Joshua Haynes, Ephraim Curtis, John Noyes, Samuel Graves, Jonathan Rice, Committee." This building was located at what is now Wayland Centre, on the corner lot just south of the old Town House. The town instructed the committee "to make it as near as they can like the new house in the West Precinct, except that the steps "are to be hansomer:" it was also to have the same number of pews. There is on record the following description of material used for one of the pulpits, together with the price: —

Seaming fringe	$0 = 10 = 0$
4 Tassels.	$1 = 4 = 0$
2 yards very fine Silk Plush	$2 = 0 = 0.$
$1\frac{3}{4}$ yds Tickn for the Cushn	$0 = 7 = 7.$
4 lbs. finest feathers, a. $\frac{2}{3}$ 8 :	$0 = 11 = 3.$
Making Cushn Pill & filling	$0 = 1 = 6.$

Thus at last both precincts were provided with new meeting-houses, and a matter was settled that had occasioned much interest and more or less activity for nearly a quarter of a century. Doubtless participants in the affair at the beginning and during its progress had passed away, and before its settlement worshipped in a temple not made with hands, whose Builder and Maker is God. The intercourse between the two precincts was pleasant, and for a while the ministers exchanged once a month. For years the salaries of the two pastors were equal, and again and again is there a receipt on the town book for eighty pounds for each.

CHAPTER XVI.

1700-1725.

Queen Anne's War; Attendant Hardships. — Father Ralle's War; Eastern Expedition, List of Sudbury Soldiers. — Ranger Service; Its Nature. — Death of Samuel Mossman. — Imperilled Condition of Rutland. — Death of Rev. Joseph Willard by the Indians. — Petition for Assistance. — List of Sudbury Soldiers at Rutland. — Captain Wright's Letter. — Lieut. William Brintnall; His Letter. — Province Loans. — River Meadow. — Causeway. — Roads. — Miscellaneous.

> Straggling rangers, worn with dangers,
> Homeward faring, weary strangers
>   Pass the farm-gate on their way;
> Tidings of the dead and living,
> Forest march and ambush giving,
> Till the maidens leave their weaving,
>   And the lads forget their play.
>   WHITTIER.

WHILE ecclesiastical matters were in process of adjustment in Sudbury, and business was being transacted to further the blessed gospel of peace, the community was again stirred by the rude sounds of strife. The red hand of war was once more outstretched for destruction, and requisitions for both material and men were again made on the New England towns. The first war of the period was Queen Anne's, so called from Anne of Denmark, who had ascended the throne of Great Britain. It was waged between England and France, and, like that of King William, continued about ten years. The province, to an extent, conducted the war by campaigns. In 1704, Col. Benjamin Church marched to make an attack on Acadia. He commanded a force of about five hundred men, and designed also to attack the Indians of the

Penobscot and Passamaquody. In 1710 an expedition was formed, commanded by General Nicholson, which recovered Port Royal. In 1711 a campaign was arranged for the capture of Quebec. For these, and other warlike undertakings, the resources of the provincial towns were drawn upon; and the taxation, deprivation, and loss attendant on these successive drafts became a grievous burden.

During these years Sudbury had its part to bear. Although, being removed from the border it did not suffer attack, it had seasons of suspense. In 1706 it was rumored that a large force was coming to New England; and Chelmsford, Groton, and Sudbury were alarmed. The next year the enemy approached Groton and Marlboro, but still left Sudbury unmolested. The town is mentioned in a province resolve of May, 1704–5, where it is ordered "that such and so many of the soldiers enlisted in the military companies and troops within the respective towns and districts herein after named, shall each of them at [his] own charge be provided with a pair of good serviceble snow shoes, mogginsons, at or before the tenth of November this present year, which they shall keep in good repair and fit for the service." (State Archives, Vol. I., p. 247.)

The testimony of the town concerning the hardship of the period is given in a protest before quoted, in which the people set forth, as a reason why the parish should not be divided, "the Vast Expenses which the present wars and expeditions attending the same calls and may call for."

Peace came in 1713, by the treaty made at Utrecht, and for a time the land had rest.

But the cessation of Indian hostilities that followed Queen Anne's War and the Peace of Utrecht was not long continued. The war-path was soon again to be trod by the savage, and his freshly made trail was to be followed by the white man to bring back the captives or recover the spoil. The cause of the second war of this period was the encroachments of the savage tribes in the east. The Indians in the eastern part of the province (Maine), instigated, as is supposed, by the Governor General of Canada, and by the Jesuits coming among them, sought to prevent English inhabitants from a reoccupation of the former settlements. For this object, the Cape Sable and Penobscot Indians joined with the tribes of the Kennebeck and Saco.

This savage alliance meant hardship to the frontier whites. Predatory bands of the foe lurked in the dark woodlands, and parts of the province were again kept on the watch. Sudbury was in no instance assailed, but its soldiers did service in other parts. It had men in the eastern expedition, which was fitted out in 1724, to operate against the Indians on the Kennebeck. Upon this river, at Norridgewock, there was an Abenaki village, which had been to the English a source of trouble, and it was determined to destroy it. When the troops arrived, the place was found in an unguarded condition. Ralle, the Jesuit missionary, who had been the chief instigator of the Indian atrocities, fell dead in the furious affray. The chiefs Mogg and Bomazeen also perished, and the tribe was vanquished. Among the soldiers in the eastern expedition are the following, who were in three different companies : —

Elijah Willis,	Jas. Maynard,
Isaac Rice,	Bartho Stephenson,
John Gould, Sargent,	Joseph Woodward,
John Barker, Clerk,	Nathan Walker.
Thomas Gates.	

(State Archives, Vol. XCIII., pp. 131–46)

RANGER SERVICE.

Sudbury rendered the country service, not only by its soldiers in the conspicuous campaign, but also by its rangers in a less ostensible service, made up of such marchings and scoutings as helped to harass and hinder the foe. They ranged the frontier as a faithful border guard, and stood between homestead and savage invaders, who lurked ready to swoop down on the defenseless home, and make captive or kill the inmates.

In this service one of the Sudbury men lost his life under peculiarly sad and touching circumstances. Says the narrator : " At evening one of our men viz : Samuel Mossman of

Sudbury, being about encamping, took hold of his gun that stood among some Bushes, drew it towards him with the muzzle towards him, some Twigg caught hold of the Cock, the Gun went off and shot him through, he died immediately." (Letter of John White to the authorities. State Archives, Vol. LXXII., p. 230.) Thus a lone grave in the wilderness was prepared for a soldier of Sudbury. What other instances of accident, hardship, and loss may have been sustained in service like this, there are none now to relate; but the very nature of this border warfare is suggestive of hardship, of hair-breadth escapes, of exposure to wilderness perils, to rough weather and the tricks of a wary foe.

One place in which Sudbury soldiers did valuable service at this time was Rutland. This town was frontier territory, and for thirty years had suffered more or less from savage incursions. As has been noticed, it was settled largely by people from Sudbury (see Chap. IX.); and naturally the town would be interested in their kinsmen or former citizens.

About the time of which we write, several of the inhabitants had been killed or captured. Among the former was their minister, Rev. Joseph Willard. The circumstances attending this death were peculiarly sad. Mr. Willard had been called to the ministry of the Rutland church, and was to have been ordained in the fall. One day in August, being out with his gun hunting, or to collect fodder for his cattle, he was suddenly beset by two Indians. They fired upon him, but without effect. He returned the fire, wounding one of them; the other closed in for a hand-to-hand fight, when three more Indians came to his assistance, and together they gained the mastery, and killed and scalped their victim.

Such was the exposed condition of the early settlers at Rutland in this gloomy period. February, 1724–5, they sent a petition to Governor Dummer for help, in which they stated that "the summer previous they laboured under great difficulty & hardship by reason of the war with the Indian enemy, and not being able to raise their corn and other provisions, so that they were obliged to travel near twenty miles for the same, and purchase it at a very dear rate, which render it very difficult to subsist themselves and their families, more especially ye soldiers posted there." They desired that more might be added to the five soldiers already allowed them.

This indicates the imperilled condition of the place. Predatory bands were lurking about it. The woodlands were a covert from which the savage might suddenly sally, and in whose dark forest retreat he might safely secure his prey. At any time the people might suffer attack. Their harvest, their homes, their households, were alike liable to be devastated and swept away. But strong men were sent to defend them, stout hearts were soon there ; and to a large extent these came from the town of Sudbury. Again and again were detachments sent from the place. Some of the soldiers for this service were under the command of Capt. Samuel Willard. In his journal he speaks of mustering at the town of Lancaster one day, and moving on to Rutland the next; of laying by in foul weather, of marching back and forth through the country, and of seeing and following the signs of Indians. The service spoken of was from July to August, 1725. In the course of his narrative he speaks of William Brintnall being sick, and of David How being lame, both of whom he sent home. (State Archives, Vol. XXXVIII., pp. 109, 110.) These two men were soldiers from Sudbury. Another commander under whom the Sudbury soldiers served was Capt. Samuel Wright. (See p. 170.) On a muster-roll of Captain Wright, read in Council, June 17, 1724, are the following names of Sudbury men who had served for several months : —

Daniel How, Lieut.	Hugh Ditson,
Corp Joseph Bennet,	Wm Thompson,
John Norcross, Gentl.	Jon^a Stanhope,
Isaac Gibbs,	Daniel Bowker.
Amnill Weeks, servant to Samuel Stevens.	

In another muster-roll, consented to in 1724, are the following names: Samuel How, Sergt. Joseph Bennet, Corp.

Hugh Ditson, William Thompson, John Ross, son to James Ross, Amnil Weeks, servant to Samuel Stevens. In another muster-roll of Captain Wright, examined in 1725, are the names of Serg. Daniel How, Mark Voice [Vose], Daniel Mackdonald, Richard Burk. Other rolls examined in 1725 have the names of Daniel Bowker, Abner Cutler, Charles Adams, Elias Parmenter, and Pegin, a Natic Indian. (State Archives, Vol. XCI.)

It was in the year 1724 that an occurence took place which shows the perils of the times, and the nature of the service to which our rangers were called. Says Captain Wright in a letter to the Court: —

These are to inform your Honors that what I feared is come upon us for want [of men] to guard us at our work, this day about 12 o'clock five men and a boy [were] making hay in the middle of the town.

A number of Indians surrounded them and shot first at the boy which alarmed the men, who ran for their guns, but the Indians shot upon them, and kept them from their guns, and shot down three of the men and wounded another in the arm, who got home, the fifth got home without any damage.

The men that are killed are James Clark, Joseph Wood, Uriah Ward, the boy missing is James Clark.

(State Archives, Vol LXXII.)

This matter-of-fact report of Captain Wright is vividly suggestive of the nature of that period. The border settlements knew not when they were safe. There was poor encouragement to sow if a foe might destroy the harvest or keep the husbandman from its safe ingathering. Yet so it was. Spring with its sunshine and showers might warm and mellow the soil, the field be well sown, the midsummer ripen the crops, and the time of harvest promise gladness and plenty. A noontide stillness rests on the fruitful fields. The warm, mellow haze of the early autumnal day enwraps nature about, and the landscape is tranquil in the mild air of a New England Fall. All is quiet, save for the motion of the busy harvesters as, moving about amid the rustling maize, they cut the stalks or gather the corn. But the whole scene may suddenly change; like the haymakers mentioned by Captain Wright, so these harvesters, all unconscious of what is near, may be startled by the rushing of savage feet, and, before they can make any defense, be slain or carried captive to a far-off place.

Before the service closed, William Brintnall, whose name has been prominent on the muster-lists, was assigned to the leadership of the little company who was to guard Rutland, going there as lieutenant. The following is a letter written by him to the Governor : —

RUTLAND, August 19th 1725.

Honored sr. After my duty to you presented, these are to inform your Honors, that by virtue of the Order I received from you to go to Rutland in quest of the Indian Enimies, and Scout about the meadow, with twelve volunteers, I have accordingly obeyed said orders, by having the twelve men, Eight of which are Capt. Willard's men, and Four who I Enlisted and came to Rutland with these on friday Last, and have Ever since scouted and guarded the meadow, for ye people in their getting of hay, we have discovered no signs of Indians as yet, but Expect them dayly, for Ensign Stephens is arrived with his son from Canada, and saith that ye [there] was a company designed for New England, when he came from Canada. he intends to be at Boston with your Honor on Monday next. all at present. I remain your Honor's Ever Devoted Lieut.   WM BRINTNALL.

The new men who I enlisted are

Samull Goodenow,	Paul Brintnall,
Benj. Dudley,	Jonathan Bent.

Capt. Willard's men are

William Brintnall,	Joshua Parker,
Danel How,	Jacob Moore,
Cyprian Wright,	James Nutting,
Delivce Brooks,	Thomas Lamb.

(State Archives, Vol. LXXII., p. 258)

According to the muster-roll of Sergeant Brintnall, he and his company of volunteers served from Aug. 17, 1725. Their pay was four shillings per day, the time of service ten weeks and two days, and their duty to serve as a guard about Rutland. William Brintnall taught school in Sudbury shortly before his enlistment in the above service. On the town book is the following record: " Received of the Constable of Sudbury, by order of the town Treasurer, all that was Due to me for keeping the school in the year 1722: 1723: 1724. Signed per William Brintnall Sudbury, Sept. 8, 1726."

One of the last prominent military acts of this period was
the disastrous defeat of John Lovewell of Dunstable, by the
Pigwackets, at the present town of Fryeburg, Me. At about
this date the tribes ceased hostilities. For a time the war-
path was abandoned, and it was again safe for the defenseless traveller to take the forest trail.

PROVINCE LOANS.

In order to meet the exigencies of the times, in the year
1721 the General Court issued a loan to the amount of fifty
thousand pounds. This was to be distributed among the
several provincial towns, in what were called bills of credit.
The distribution was according to the taxes paid by the
towns, and was to be returned to the public treasury within
a certain length of time. That Sudbury took her share of
the loan is indicated by several payments which were successively made and a record of receipts received. Of these
the following is a specimen : —

BOSTON August 2 : 1720.

Received of the Trustees of the town of Sudbury by Mr. Daniel
Haynes, one hundred and one pounds, twelve shillings, being the first
fifth part of their proportion to the £50,000. Loan.

Per. ALLEN, Treasurer.

From time to time other fifths were paid, and receipts rendered therefor, until Aug. 12, 1730, when the last fifth was
paid, and a receipt in full was received. The loan of 1721
was followed by another a few years later to the amount
of sixty thousand pounds. The order authorizing it was enacted in 1728, and was called "an act for raising and settling
public revenues for and defraying the necessary charges of
the government by an emission of £60,000 in bills of credit."
(Felt's "Historical Account of Massachusetts Currency,"
p. 84.) Sudbury had a share in this loan also.

While the attention of the people in this period was largely
engrossed with educational, ecclesiastical, and military matters, the regular, routine business of the town was not neglected. Aug. 11, 1702, "it was voted, that the Towne would

send a pettione to the general cort concerning our River meadows, that are much damnified by reason of many stoppages, that the Generall Cort would ease us of our tax, or choose a committee to see if it may be helpt, the pettione to be sined in the name of the towne." This vote was carried out, and a petition was sent to the Court jointly by Concord and Sudbury. In it they state that they had sustained —

Grate damage by reason of the water lying on sd meadow whereby they are much straitened and incapacited to bear Town and county charges, and maintain of their families, and something hath been done in order to the Lowering of the water by Removing Rocks and bars of sand, and formerly there hath been a committe sent up by the general court to view the sd meadow, and they have found the stoppage of water may be cleared, but by reason of different apprehensions it hath Layne ever since, we therefore humbly pray the Hon¹ Court that it impower a committee to see that the work be done forthwith, that so the present opportunity may not be neglected, and to set us a way that those persons concerned in sd meadow may beare an equal proportion in sd work. The court resolved to appoint a committee of persons in Concord, Sudbury and Billerica fully empowered to order and determine what may be necessary for clearing sd meadow.

In 1710 the town voted to petition the General Court to make the long causeway "a county road." Feb. 22, 1714–15, it was requested "to see what method the town will take for mending and raising the causeway from the Town Bridge to Lieut. Daniel Haynes." On June 2, 1720, it was requested "to see if the town will raise the causeway from the Gravel pit as far as Capt. Haynes'es old place, proportionally to the aforesaid Long Causeway when mended."

Feb. 25, 1714–15, the town ordered that it would choose a committee of three men to join with Concord to view the obstructions and stopages in the great river.

In 1723–4 a way was laid out from Lanham to the west meeting-house. According to the records, "the latter part of said way, bounded as follows, viz. through the ministerial land, near the southwesterly corner, and so on, something northwesterly. From thence it went, in a straight line, to Nathaniel Rice's, and so northerly, to the highway leading to Lancaster, near the new meeting house." It is now known as the Old Graves Road, so called from a house which stood just south of the Old Lancaster Road, at its intersection with this one.

Dec. 14, 1715, the town voted that "there be a horse bridge built on Assabeth river : : : and that the selectmen do order that ye bridge be erected and built over assabath river between ye land of Timothy Gilson and Thomas Burt's land." In 1717–18 the town voted that it would have "a New bridge built over Sudbury river where the old bridge now stands, at the end of the long Causeway."

About 1715 a statement is made in relation to three pounds for providing "a burying cloth, for ye towns use."

In 1722 there is reference to two padlocks, — one for the pound, another for the stocks, — indicating that the unruly were subject to restraint and discipline.

May 13, 1723, it was voted to choose a committee to present a petition to the General Court "to prevent ye stopage of ye fish in Concord and Sudbury river."

CHAPTER XVII.

Highways. — Bridges. — Schools. — Movement for a New Township; Remonstrances — Petition Relating to the River Meadows. — Sale of Peter Noyes's Donation of the Hop Brook Mill. — Gratuities to the Ministers. — Miscellaneous Matters.

The years with change advance.
TENNYSON.

THE period upon which we now enter was an eventful one throughout the whole country. Three governors, Burnett, Belcher, and Shirley, bore rule. Burnett died in 1729, Belcher left office in 1740, and Shirley entered upon the office in 1741. During the latter part of this period war again called to the front the provincial forces, and the towns were to hear its stern voice and to feel its rude shock. Before, however, the season of strife set in, there was a brief season of peace. During this respite the town made advancement. The tokens of increasing prosperity were manifest in the construction of highways and bridges, and the attention given to miscellaneous matters.

HIGHWAYS.

Of these improvements we will notice, first, those relating to highways. This subject had more prominence than in the preceding period, the reasons for which are obvious; as time passed on new clearings were made upon which to locate new homes, and new homes perhaps demanded new roads. The last period was one of war; new facilities may have been postponed till better times. Furthermore, the formation of the west precinct doubtless called for new roads. With a meeting-house at Rocky Plain, and a community beginning to gather, new paths were to be opened to it.

In 1735-6 a way is mentioned as "beginning at Marlborough road, at Mr. Abraham Woods shop until it comes
to Lieut. John Haynes." About the same time is the statement of a change of highway from Whale's Bridge over
Pine Plain (Wayland), a part of which way is spoken of in
connection with Jonathan Grout's land. In 1736 a new
highway is spoken of over Pine Brook at John Grout's.
In 1733 the town accepted of a road "laid out by Samuel
Dakins to Concord line, and so into the road leading to Stow
by Mr. Jonathan Browns in sd town." Also at the same
meeting "a way for the upper end of little Gulf at Mr.
Samuel Noyes land by David Maynards to Pantry Bridge."
In 1734 a way was laid out "from Landham to Sudbury part
of the way to go through the land of John Goodnow and
part land of Isaac Reed." About 1735-6 a way is spoken of
"from Landham to the Clay pits on the east side of Paul
Brintnal's barn." During this period "Zackriah Hurd was
to make a new way lastly laid out by John Grout's by a
Jury," "a substantial, passable County Road." In 1742 a
highway was "accepted for the County road by the town
bridge to Sedge meadow." The next year Eliab Moore was
allowed "to set up gates or bars and fence from the highway
leading from the town bridge to Sedge meadow." Towards
the end of the period a highway is spoken of "from Honey
Pot Brook through Jabez Puffer's land." In 1728 the town
accepted of a highway "from the centre road by the house
of Joseph Moore by the training field till it come into the
Concord road." In 1729-30 it was voted "to accept the
way laid out from Thomas Smiths to the west meeting
house." This was to go "through Pantry." In 1730 mention is made of a way from "Non sidge round hill by Peter
Bent's into town." Also a highway is spoken of from
Lancaster road "beginning at Mr. Peter Plympton's land
leading into Gulf neck, by David Parmenters and Uriah
Wheelers, by the training field, and so into same road at
Lake end." A way is also spoken of in 1729, in the east
precinct of Sudbury, "from Non Such Round hill to the
meeting house in said Precinct." In this period there is
mentioned a road "from the New bridge, by Mr. Joseph

Stones In sd Towne to the road leading to Framingham by Mr. Benjamin Stones In sd town."

As might be expected, when so much attention was paid to the highways, the causeways and bridges were not neglected. In 1733 two men were to repair the bridge at the east side of the causeway, " so as ye said butments may not be washed down or be carried away by ye floods as in times past." In 1735 new plank was provided "for the Grat bridg at the East End of the Long Causewa." About 1743 a subscription was made for a bridge between the land of "John Haynes on the west side the river and John Woodward on the east side the river, and Mr. Edward Sherman and John Woodward, agreed, if the subscribers would erect the bridge, to give a good and conveniant way, two rods wide through their land." In 1747 Jonathan Rice rebuilt Lanham Bridge, and received for the same five pounds. The next year there is a record as follows : " To Matthew Gibbs for Rum & for raising Landham Bridge 12 Shillings." In 1726–7 it was voted to expend on the "long causeway from the town bridge to the gravel pit one hundred pounds." In 1729 the town voted to build a new bridge at the east end of the long causeway. In connection with this record we have the two following of about the same date : that "part of the effects of the old meeting house " was to be paid toward the building of the bridge over Sudbury River. The other is this report of the committee chosen by the town to build a bridge at the eastern end of the long causeway : " To David Baldwin for frame of Bridge, 37 pounds. To twelve men to raise said bridge, who went into ye water 3 pounds." Other items were given, among which is this : " For Drink &c. 5ˢ 1ᵈ." (Date, 1729.) On the town records, dated Nov. 28, 1730, is the following : " Received of the selectmen of said town [Sudbury] four pounds and ten shillings in full discharge for building a bridge for said town over the brook by Mr. Abraham Woods in Sudbury [South Sudbury]. I say received per John Goodnow."

EDUCATION.

During this period educational advantages were on the gain. In 1732 a school-house was built on the east side.

In 1735 the town voted thirty pounds for the support of
public schools. The next year the town granted twenty
pounds for the out-schooling in said town, three parts for
the west and two for the east side of the river. In 1733 the
committee were instructed " not to exceed sixty pounds for
the schools ye year ensuing." In 1734 it voted thirty pounds
for the grammar school in Sudbury; also voted that their
representative present a petition to the General Court in
behalf of the town for a school-farm in some of the unappropriated land. In 1734 it "granted 30 pounds to support
schools at the school house, and twenty pounds for and
towards schools in the out parts or quarters of s⁴ town for
that year.' In 1735-6 Amos Smith asked to have the grammar school removed into the several out-parts of the town
"for the futer;" but the town voted in the negative. In
1740 it was ordered that the grammar school should be kept
" in the five remote corners of the town, as it hath formerly
been from the 8ᵗʰ day of December until ye end of October
next." In 1747 the town voted that the schools should be
kept at five places, " at the school house near Nathan Goodnow's, at that near Israel Mosses, and at or near the house
of Mr. Elijah Haynes, at or near the house of Dea. James
Brewer as can conveniantly Bee, and yᵉ school belonging to
yᵉ farm near Mr. Smiths." Thus former school privileges
were still kept up, while new opportunities were extended to
districts more remote.

MOVEMENT FOR A NEW TOWNSHIP.

While the town was thus making perceptible progress,
and the tokens of wholesome prosperity were appearing here
and there, an occurrence arose which was thought to be portentous of undesirable things. This was an attempt, in the
year 1739-40, by a portion of the Sudbury inhabitants to
colonize and become a new town. The movement was made
jointly by parties from Framingham, Sudbury, Marlboro, and
Stow. A petition was sent by them to the General Court,
March 14, 1739, in which they ask to be made a "separate
Township, invested with proper liberties and privileges, and
as such proposing our centre at a pine tree with a heap of

stones round it." The reasons they gave were that "we have for a long time been greatly incommoded, and labored undere great difficulties as to an attendance on ye means of grace, publickly dispensed, by reason of ye great distance from ye place of ye public worship in ye towns to which we respectively belong, some of our houses being three, four, five and six miles therefrom, and ye roads very difficult especially at some seasons of ye year." They further state " we apprehend ourselves capable by the blessing of Heaven on our lawful endeavor to support ye charges y^t may accrue." This was signed by forty-three persons. The Court received the petition, and by an act of the House of Representatives, March 14, 1739, it was ordered that the petitioners "serve the towns represented by it with a copy of the petition, that they might be present at the next May session, and show cause, if they had such, why it should not be granted." (State Archives, Vol. XII., p. 137.)

Sudbury was duly represented at the appointed time. The town voted, May, 19, 1740, "that Capt. John Haynes & Mr. John Woodward Be a committee fully impowered in the town's behalf To go to the Great & General Court or assembly to give our reasons why ye prayer of the Petition of Sundry inhabitants of Sudbury, Framingham and Stow should not be granted as set forth in the petition." When the case was called up by the Court, the delegates in behalf of the town presented the protest. In the document that contains it they set forth several reasons why the petition of David Howe and other inhabitants of Sudbury, Marlboro, Framingham, and Stow, dated March 14, 1739, should not be granted. They state that "there in an uncertainty" about the petition; that the town does not know what damage it is likely to sustain by loss of population or land; that to weaken the town would tend to discourage the ministers, who have several times applied for more salary, which would very readily be granted if the ability of the town would admit of the same. They refer to the —

. Very great charge that the town hath lately been at in building 2 meeting houses, 2 school houses, and settling 2 ministers together with several great bridges and sundry long and difficult causeways, which with the continual accompanying changes of the said town, make the burthen in a great measure insupportable on many of the inhabitants, and if any should be taken from said town, it would make the burthen still heavier.   That the meeting house on the west side of Sudbury river was placed by a committee of this Hon. Court, where the Petitioners desired it, and that they signed to the place where the meeting house now standeth with their own hands, and yet many of the inhabitants on the west side of said River, live at a greater distance, from the west meeting house than any of the Petitioners.   The very great difficulties that the town of Sudbury is under by reason of the floods that in the summer season often overflow our meadows, and so damage our hay and grain, that makes many of the inhabitants of said town so weak, that instead of bearing charges in the town apply themselves for relief, all which reasons and considerations lay the town of Sudbury under a necessity of claiming those privileges granted to them by the Royal Charter in the following words, viz.   That all and any land, tenements, hereditaments, and all other estate, which any person or persons, or bodies, politic or Corporate Towns, do hold or enjoy or ought to hold and enjoy, within the bounds aforesaid, by or under any grant or estate duly made or granted by any General Court formerly held, or by any other lawful right or title whatever shall be by such Towns their Respective Heirs, successors, assigns, forever hereafter held and enjoyed according to the Import and patent of such respective grant.

We therefore pray this Hon. Court to take the Premises into ye wise consideration and dismiss the before recited Petition, and so resting we Crave leave to subscribe our Selves your Excellency's and Honor's most humble servants, who as in duty bound shall ever pray.

JOHN HAYNES) Committee
JOHN WOODWARD) for
) Sudbury.

A remonstance to the petition was also sent by the town of Framingham, and the request of the petitioners for a new township was not granted.

RIVER MEADOWS.

July 15, 1742, a petition was presented, signed by Israel Loring and about seventy-five others, relating to the river meadows.   It was directed to His Excellency, William Shirley, Esq., Captain General and Governor, and was as follows : —

The petition of us who are the subscribers, who are the major part of owners and propriters of the meadows lying upon the river called Concord and Sudbury River, Humbly showeth, that wheras your petitioners have and do often times suffer very great damages both in our hay as well as our grass, by reason of the floods which hath and do very often over flow and stand a long time upon our said meadows, and great cause whereof as we humbly conceive in the many bars and stoppages which are in the river, and sundry of these within the bounds of Concord and Sudbury, whereof our humble request is that your Excellency and Honors would be pleased to appoint for a relief, as in your great wisdom you shall think best, commissioners of sewers (as the law directs in such causes) with full power to act and do for our relief what may be thought by them in our case needful and necessary for the removal of said bars and stoppages that are in the said river &c, all which is humbly submitted, and your petitioners as in duty bound shall ever pray. (State Archives, Vol. CV., p. 209.)

There was a further list of sixty-two names given in an additional part, dated December, 1742, accompanied by a statement that the signers did not have opportunity to sign the first petition.

SALE OF HOP BROOK MILL.

In 1699 the town chose a committee to receive a donation given by Mr. Peter Noyes, late of Sudbury, to the poor of the town. This donation consisted of his mill. After the town took possession of this property, it was leased for a term of years to Mr. Abraham Wood. On the town record is the following reason for granting this lease : —

Wheras the towne taking into consideration the gift that Ensign Peter Noyes hath given to ye poore of our towne namely ye mills, commouly called by ye name of ye new mills, with ye lands and privilleges belonging to ye same and being sensible that ye letting of it yearly, will be a means to bring ye sd mills and housen to decay and in time utter ruine, in which will be a great wrong to our poore, and that will not answer ye end of ye (Townes) doner, Therefore in respect to both [him] and our own good which is involved in ye same, we therefore by a vote, grant liberty to them that are concerned as to ye disposal of said gift, to dispose of it for years as they shall see cause for ye benefit and in behalf of ye poore of ye towne of Sudbury.

March ye 19th, 1700. This was passed into an act by ye towne by a magger vote.

In 1728-9 it was voted to sell the mills, and give a deed in the name of the town. The heirs of the donor had laid claim to a considerable part of his gift ; a lawsuit had com-

menced, and the town had voted money to defend the property ; the town, therefore, voted to sell the same for the
sum of seven hundred pounds. The money was to be put
on interest for the use of the poor, and to be disposed of by
the selectmen and ministers. The property was purchased
by Messrs. Abraham Wood, Sen., and Abraham Wood, Jr.
The following record was made concerning the sale : " These
may certify that the subscribers, selectmen of the town of
Sudbury, have received the bonds or security given by Mr
Abraham Wood Sen. and Abraham Wood Jun. for seven
hundred pounds Province Bills, in full of and at the hands
of Noah Clapp, Uriah Wheeler, and John Hayns. Barin
date Mar. 13th 1728 : 9. "

In 1730–1 the town petitioned the General Court " that
the Great Bridge over Charles river may not be built, but a
ferry erected instead."

The four records following show the kindness the town
exercised towards its ministers : In 1733 it voted to give
Rev. Mr. Cook twenty pounds in money towards making up
for the loss of his barn, which it is said was agreeable to a
petition of some inhabitants of Sudbury ; it also voted, at
the same meeting, to give the ministers a gratuity of forty
pounds each for the year ; in 1734 the town voted that Rev.
Mr. Minot should have five pounds for preaching three days
when Mr. Loring was lame ; in 1735 the ministers were to
have so much as to make their salaries, including the wood,
a hundred and fifty pounds each of them.

In 1739 an article was in the warrant " to see if the town
will grant money to provide more ammunition to the town's
stock."

In 1740 the town " voted to procure another meeting house
bell as good as the one they had."

In 1741 the following items were inserted in the town
book : " To Dr Roby for medicine administered to Frank,
negro woman." " Granted ten pounds for cutting and clearing the brush growing or standing around the west meeting
house." Granted twenty pounds for the relief of the [poor
of the] town. " Granted to Joseph Muggins and Joseph

THE WOODS OR ALLEN HOUSE.

The oldest house in South Sudbury, and the author's birthplace.

Goodnow, to take the care of, and sweep the meeting houses in s^d town, and take care of the two school houses in s^d town, at forty shillings apiece, old tenor, End the year ensuing." "To Thomas Reed for what he did for Frank, Negro, in ye time of her last sickness."

In 1746–7 "a committee was chosen to show cause to the General session why the wife and children of Edward Joyu should not be deemed inhabitants of the town."

In 1747 "an agent or agents were appointed to prosecute such person or persons as have Broken the meeting house Bell Belonging to said Town, now hanging in the School house near the East meeting house, In said town."

CHAPTER XVIII.

1725–1750.

Third French and Indian War. — Sudbury Soldiers at Cape Breton. — Fort No. 4, N.H. — Capt. Phineas Stevens. — Sketch of His Life. — His Service in Connection with the Building and Defense of the Fort. — Capt. Josiah Brown. — Engagement with French and Indians about the Fort. — Petition of Captain Brown. — Petition of Jonathan Stanhope. — Battle between the Forces of Captain Stevens and General Debeline. — Expedition of Captain Hobbs. — Battle between the Commands of Captain Hobbs and Chief Sackett. — Sketch of Capt. Josiah Brown. — List of Captain Brown's Troopers.

He cometh unto you with a tale which holdeth children from play, and old men from the chimney-corner. — SIR PHILIP SIDNEY.

HAVING considered the records of a short interval of peace in this period, we again turn to the annals of war. England and France were again to engage in strife. This war has had various names. It has been called in America "King

George's War," but in England " The War of the Austrian
Succession." It has also been called "The Cape Breton
War," and " The French and Indian War." The latter term
is appropriate, but might tend to mislead, since other wars
have occurred with these parties. A suitable term for it may
be " The Third French War."

The war was declared in 1744, and continued till the
peace of Aix-la-Chapelle, in 1748. Its principal event was
the capture of Louisburg, a French stronghold at Cape Breton, which had been called, because of its strength, the
Gibraltar of America. It had been built since the peace
treaty of Utrecht, at great expense, but after a forty-nine
days' siege it fell into the hands of the English. The troops
for its capture were from Massachusetts, Connecticut, Rhode
Island, and New Hampshire. The men suffered much before
the place surrendered, but when the work was at length
accomplished there was rejoicing throughout the province.
Sudbury soldiers assisted at the capture of this place. The
following is a list of some of the men : —

Samuel Osborne, Silas Balcom, John Underwood, Samuel Balcom,
John Rice, Reuben Vose, Ruben Moore, John Nixon [at this time of
Framingham, afterwards of Sudbury], Lieut Estabrook, Lieut. Augustus
Moore, Abijah Walker, Micah Parmenter, Jas Balcom, Eben Mossman,
James Balcom.

Besides service in connection with this prominent event in
the war, there was another service with which Sudbury soldiers were connected, which, though less prominent than the
one just mentioned, was of vast importance to the country.
This was the work of a border guard, or manning the frontier forts. As in other contests between England and France,
when hostilities broke out in America there was a wild border
conflict with a mixed savage and civilized foe. Tribes not
friendly to the English, nor bound to them by treaty allegiance, hastened to aid their old allies, the French, in Canada, and strewed their pathway thither with sad marks of
their mission and of their impatience to begin the strife.

A confederation thus formed by the Indians and French
meant terror to the English frontier. Predatory bands of

savages again took the trail. The woodlands again resounded with their rude shouts; and the sunny hillsides and fair intervales by the northern New England streams were again trod and retrod by the Indian in his sly search for human prey.

To protect these defenseless places, and form a rendezvous into which the people could flee, and at the same time furnish quarters for such a military guard as might be sent to intercept the foe, was of very great importance. To accomplish these objects there was erected by the province and the towns a cordon of block-houses and forts. Several of these were situated in the vicinity of the Connecticut River, of which the most northerly was called No. 4, and was at what is now Charlestown, N.H. This fortification was notable for the frequent attack and repulse of the enemy. It was in the direct track of the French and Indians as they swept down from Canada, by way of Lake Champlain and Montreal, on their way to the frontier towns of Massachusetts. To take this fort was considered of great importance by the enemy, who hovered about it as a coveted prize; and it was of equal importance to the English to retain it.

In the holding of this wilderness fortress, and in military operations in the vicinity, Sudbury soldiers had a prominent share. The commander of the fort was Phineas Stevens, a native of Sudbury; he was a noted Indian fighter, and an ambassador to Canada to negotiate for the ransom of prisoners.

CAPT. PHINEAS STEVENS.

Mr. Stevens was born Feb. 20, 1706 (see Chap. IX.), and went to Rutland with his father, Dea. Joseph Stevens, about 1719. Aug. 14, 1723, he was taken captive by the Indians, and carried to Canada. He was afterwards redeemed, and taken home. In 1734 he married his cousin, Elizabeth Stevens, of Petersham, Mass. He lived for a time at Rutland, and moved from there to Charlestown, N.H. He was a prominent citizen of that place, in both civil and military matters, in its early history. His name was on the proprietors' book about 1743 as a petitioner for a proprietors' meeting; and the same year he was on a committee for providing a "learned and orthodox minister to preach the Gospel." The same year he received a commission as lieutenant of militia from Governor Wentworth of New Hampshire. In 1744 he was commissioned by Governor Shirley of Massachusetts as lieutenant of volunteers for the defense of the frontier. The next year he was appointed by the same authority as captain for service against the French and Indians.

Captain Stevens was repeatedly commissioned to go to Canada to negotiate for the deliverance of prisoners. In 1752 he negotiated for the deliverance of John Stark of New Hampshire, who was afterwards General Stark who commanded the continental forces at the battle of Bennington. The ransom of Stark was an Indian pony, valued at one hundred and three dollars. This amount was paid back by Stark in money, which he earned as a hunter on the Androscoggin, Maine.

Since to narrate all the services of Captain Stevens at No. 4 and elsewhere in this war would take considerable space, we will only present a few facts which may set forth something of his military history and the arduous nature of his work. A settlement was begun at No. 4 about 1740, and shortly afterwards Mr. Stevens went there and became one of the three proprietors who settled the place. At that time No. 4 was the most advanced post of English civilization in the northwest. It was surrounded by dense forests, and much exposed to the French and Indians in their incursions from the north. The foe to which the people were exposed was exceedingly fierce and cruel. Such a combination of bad qualities as was manifested by the enemy that came from Canada was seldom seen.

FORT NO. 4.

About three years after the settlement began, the prospect of war was so great that the proprietors of No. 4 held a meeting and decided to erect a fort, and made an assessment to meet the expense. Lieutenant Stevens was one of the assessors to apportion the sum of three hundred pounds towards the work. He was also one of a committee appointed to keep the fort in repair, and "to take care that no person come to dwell in any of the houses within the fort but such as they the said committee shall approve." The fort was built under the direction of Col John Stoddard of Northampton, Mass., who had formerly superintended the building of the block-house at Fort Dummer in central Massachusetts. The fort contained about three-quarters of an acre, was built in the form of a square, and had about one hundred and eighty feet on a side. The walls were made of squared timbers, and put together after the manner of a log-house. Inside the enclosure were houses, which were owned by private parties previously to their enclosure in the fort, but were bought up and afterwards called province houses. One of these belonged to Lieutenant Stevens, for which he received thirty-five pounds. These houses were placed against the walls of the fort, and so arranged that they could at once be put in a state of defense if the enemy got inside the fort. On the north side the fort had a stockade of timbers about a foot in diameter, which were placed end-wise in the ground, and were about twelve feet high.

New Hampshire having but little interest in defending a place so far from their other settlements, and Massachusetts feeling under no obligations to protect them, because outside her limits, the little company provided its own means of defense. The assistance subsequently rendered by Massachusetts was on account of the protection afforded by this fort to her settlements on the south.

The fort was scarcely finished when war was declared by England against France and Spain. A few soldiers were stationed to defend the little stronghold, and Capt. Phineas Stevens was placed in command. In the early part of the war the fort was unmolested; but April 19, 1746, about forty French and Indians came into the vicinity, and did disastrous work. Several men were captured, and a saw and grist mill was burned. May 2d another raid was made, and one man was killed. On May 24th, Capt. Daniel Paine of Dudley, Mass., was sent to assist in defending the place. Shortly after his arrival, some of his men ventured out to see the place where the man had been killed a few days before, when they were suddenly assailed by the savages, who killed five of them and captured one. Captain Stevens with a few men rushed to the rescue. He engaged the savages, and forced them to retire, as it is supposed, with the loss of several men. At about this time Captain Stevens was reinforced by a troop of horse from Sudbury, under command of Capt. Josiah Brown.

SERVICES OF CAPTAIN BROWN'S COMPANY.

On the 17th of June, shortly after their arrival, this company was called into action, and had a severe engagement with the enemy in a meadow not far from the fort. The following is an account of the affair published July 1, 1746:

We hear that on Thursday, the 19th, ult, at a plantation called No. 4, Capt. Stevens, of the garrison there, and Capt. Brown, of Sudbury, with about fifty men, went out into the woods to look for horses and, coming near a causeway there were obliged to pass, their dogs being on the hunt before them, and barking very much, they suspected some Indians were near; whereupon, keeping a good lookout, they discovered a great number of them, supposed to be a hundred and fifty, lying in ambush, waiting for them on the other side; so that if they had passed over, in all probability, most of them might be cut off.

The Indians on finding themselves discovered, suddenly started up, and a smart engagement immediately ensued, in which, it is supposed, that the English fired first and engaged them so closely and briskly that they soon drew off, and being followed by our men retreated into a large swamp; whereupon the English returned to the garrison, not caring to venture, after such numbers, into so hazardous a place. (Farmer & Moore, Vol. III., p. 294.)

Captain Brown, in a petition to the General Court in behalf of himself and his troops, states as follows concerning this battle : —

That whereas on the 19th day of June 1756 in his Magestie's service, at a place called No. 4, on the western frontier, the said Josiah Brown with his troop had a very warm and dangerous engagement with a numerous party of the Indian enemy, together with painful travel, and with other hardships and difficulties attending. In which engagement by good evidence and the most certain accounts we can get a considerable number of said enimies were slain and others sore wounded. [The purport of the petition was that the Court might afford them such "encouragement" as it thought best.]

By order of said troop, at their meeting on the 25th Dec. 1750.

(State Archives, Vol. LXXIII., p. 733)   JOSIAH BROWN.

Captains Stevens and Brown had no men killed outright in this engagement, but Jedediah Winchell was mortally wounded and shortly afterwards died. Jonathan Stanhope, David Parker, and Noah Eaton were wounded. Stanhope was from Sudbury, and Eaton from Framingham. Mr. Stanhope subsequently presented two petitions to the General Court, one of which is as follows : —

In the battle with the Indians at No 4, June 19, when I was a Trooper in his majesty's service, I received a shot which broke my arm all to pieces, and caused me great pain, and cost for the injuries, and has incapacitated me from obtaining a subsistance for myself, and I have very little hopes of ever having the use of it again. The account of the time I have lost and expenses which I have been exposed to since I was wounded is as follows :

To sixteen weeks at said No. 4, when I lay confined with my wound to the first months when I had Province billeting at 6–3 per week besides said billeting £1. 5. 0
To 12 weeks more when I found myself altogether and had no Province pay nor billeting at 12–6 pr wk. . . . 7. 10. 0
And to my son's attending on me then and finding himself from the 23d of June to the 17th of October following, being 16 weeks and 3 days: to my son's nursing and attending me the said 16 weeks, at 5 per week 4. 2 6
And to 9 weeks board when he had neither Province pay nor billeting at 7–6 per week 3. 7. 6

£16. 5. 0

At the close of military operations, in 1746, Massachusetts withdrew most of her soldiers stationed in the vicinity of the Connecticut River in New Hampshire. The chief reasons for this were that the place was outside her own limits, and that New Hampshire refused to co-operate in defending it. No. 4 being deprived of troops, it was for a time abandoned. The people in the vicinity were obliged to leave their homesteads, and take refuge in the older settlements. During the winter that followed the evacuation of No. 4, the enemy did not venture far from their quarters in Canada. Meanwhile an effort was made to again man the deserted forts. A prominent person in the furtherance of this project, it is supposed, was Captain Stevens. He communicated with Governor Shirley, and stated that a force of one hundred men should be sent to several of the frontier posts to "go and waylay the streams the enemy come upon when they issue out from Crown Point." The authorities did not grant the request by allowing all the men that were asked for, but only so many as it was thought would repel an attack made on the forts. The matter of taking measures for such agress-ive work as was proposed by Stevens was deferred.

ATTACK OF GENERAL DEBELINE.

In March, 1747, Captain Stevens was ordered to go with thirty men and take possession of No. 4. He arrived there on the 27th. A few days later the place was furiously assailed by the French and Indians, under the leadership of General Debeline. Captain Stevens, in his report made to Governor Shirley, dated April 9, 1747, gives the following account of the attack : —

Our dogs being very much disturbed, which gave us reason to think that the enemy were about, occasioned us not to open the gate at the usual time ; but one of our men, being desirous to know the certainty, ventured out privately to set on the dogs, about nine o'clock in the morning; and went about twenty rods from the fort firing off his gun and saying, Choboy to the dogs. Whereupon, the enemy, being within a few rods, immediately arose from behind a log and fired : but through the goodness of God, the man got into the fort with only a slight wound. The enemy being then discovered, immediately arose from their ambush-ments and attacked us on all sides. The wind being very high, and everything exceedingly dry, they set fire to all the old fences, and also to a log-house about forty rods distant from the fort to the windward ; so that within a few minutes we were entirely surrounded with fire — all which was performed with the most hideous shouting and firing, from all quarters, which they continued, in a very terrible manner, until the next day at ten o'clock at night, without intermission ; during which time we had no opportunity to eat or sleep. But notwithstanding all their shoutings and threatenings, our men seemed not to be in the least daunted, but fought with great resolution; which, doubtless, gave the enemy reason to think we had determined to stand it out to the last degree. The enemy had provided themselves with a sort of fortifica-tion, which they had determined to push before them and bring fuel to the side of the fort, in order to burn it down. But instead of performing what they threatened, and seemed to be immediately going to undertake, they called to us and desired a cessation of arms until sunrise the next morning, which was granted : at which time they would come to a parley. Accordingly the French General Debeline came with about sixty of his men, with a flag of truce, and stuck it down within about twenty rods of the fort in plain sight of the same, and said if we would send three men to him he would send as many to us, to which we complied. The General sent in a French Lieutenant with a French soldier and an Indian.

Upon our men going to the Monsieur, he made the following proposals, viz. — that in case we would immediately resign up the fort, we should all have our lives and liberty to put on all the clothes we had, and also to take a sufficient quantity of provisions to carry us to Montreal, and bind up our provisions and blankets, lay down our arms and march out of the fort.

Upon. our men returning, he desired that the Captain of the fort would meet him half-way, and give an answer to the above proposal, which I did, and upon meeting the Monsieur, he did not wait for me to give an answer, but went on in the following manner, viz. — that what had been promised he was ready to perform, but upon refusal he would immediately set the fort on fire, and run over the top, for he had seven hundred men with him, and if we made any further resistance, or should happen to kill one Indian, we might expect all to be put to the sword. "The fort," said he, "I am resolved to have or die. Now do what you please, for I am as easy to have you fight as to give up." I told the General, that in case of extremity his proposal would do; but inasmuch as I was sent here by my master, the Captain General, to defend this fort, it would not be consistent with my order to give it up unless I was better satisfied that he was able to perform what he had threatened; and furthermore I told him that it was poor encouragement to resign into the hands of the enemy, that upon one of their number being killed, they would put all to the sword, when it was probable that we had killed some of them already. "Well," said he, "go into the fort, and see whether your men dare to fight any more or not, and give me an answer quick, for my men want to be fighting." Whereupon I came into the fort and called all the men together, and informed them what the French General said, and then put it to vote which they chose, either to fight on or resign; and they voted to a man to stand it out as long as they had life. Upon this, I returned the answer that we were determined to fight it out. Upon which they gave a shout, and then fired, and so continued fighting and shouting until daylight the next morning.

About noon they called to us and said " Good morning," and desired a cessation of arms for two hours that they might come to a parley; which was granted. The General did not come himself, but sent two Indians, who came within about eight rods of the fort and stuck down their flag and desired that I would send out two men to them, which I did, and the Indians made the following proposal, viz. — That in case we would sell them provisions, they would leave and not fight any more; and desired my answer, which was, that selling them provisions for

money was contrary to the laws of nations, but if they would send in a
captive for every five bushels of corn, I would supply them. Upon the
Indians returning the General this answer, four or five guns were fired
against the fort, and they withdrew, as we supposed, for we heard no
more of them.

In all this time we had scarce opportunity to eat or sleep. The cessation of arms gave us no matter of rest, for we suspected they did it to
obtain an advantage against us. I believe men were never known to
hold out with better resolution, for they did not seem to sit or lie still
for one moment. There were but thirty men in the fort, and although
we had some thousands of guns fired at us, there were but two men
slightly wounded, viz. John Brown and Joseph Ely. (Saunderson's
"History of Charlestown, N H.")

In the course of the year 1747 the people living near the
Connecticut River suffered much from the enemy's incursions. As they could obtain little or no aid from New
Hampshire, they again applied to Massachusetts. In February, 1748, the authorities allowed one hundred men each
for Forts Massachusetts and No. 4; and directed that orders
be issued to the commanding officers in those garrisons that
a suitable number of men should be employed, until the
following October, to intercept the French and Indians in
their march to the frontier. At the same time a bounty was
offered of a hundred pounds for an Indian scalp. Captain
Stevens was again appointed to command at No. 4, and Capt.
Humphrey Hobbs, another brave officer, was made second in
command.

Shortly after Captain Stevens assumed command of No. 4,
on March 15th, a party of Indians attacked some men near
the fort who were out to gather wood. Captain Stevens sallied forth to the rescue, but no general engagement occurred,
as the enemy, which consisted of only a small company, left
the place, after killing, in their first onset, one person and
wounding another and taking captive a third. As the spring
advanced Captain Stevens and his men were engaged more
or less in marchings and scoutings in the vicinity of No. 4,
and from there to Fort Dummer in the central part of Massachusetts. June 24 forty men, under command of Captain
Hobbs, started on a scouting expedition, designing to march
through the wilderness to Fort Shirley, in Heath, Mass.

After being out two days, they had an engagement with
the Indians, which, it is said, lasted four hours, and in
which one of the Sudbury soldiers was wounded. The following account of the battle is from Saunderson's "History
of Charlestown, N.H."

BATTLE BETWEEN CAPTAIN HOBBS AND CHIEF SACKETT.

Capt. Hobbs started out from No. 4, on the 24th of June. During the
first two days of his march, he met with no interruptions, except such as
were occasioned by the natural difficulties of the way. On the 26th, it
being Sunday, after travelling a little distance, he halted at a place about
twelve miles north-west of Fort Dummer, in the precincts of what is now
the town of Marlborough, to afford his company an opportunity to
refresh themselves; and though he did not dream that he was pursued,
or that the enemy was any where near, he still posted a guard on his
trail, like a true officer, as carefully and circumspectly as if danger had
been apprehended. The party then took possession of a low piece of
ground, covered with alders intermingled with large trees, through which
flowed a rivulet, and without any anticipaton of being disturbed, had
begun regaling themselves at their packs.

But, as was too frequently the case in those times, danger was nigh,
though they had no apprehension of it; for a large body of Indians had
discoverd their trail, and made a rapid march for the purpose of cutting
them off. Sackett, their chief, (reputed to be a half-blood,) was not only
a courageous and resolute fellow, but was distinguished for a sagacity
that rendered him no common antagonist.

Apparently certain of victory, on account of his numbers, which fore-
stalled the necessity of a wily approach, he dashed down upon the trail
of Hobbs, driving in the guards which he had posted in his rear, and
instantly commenced an attack upon his main force with all the yells
and demonstrations of a savage warfare.

Hobbs, though taken by surprise, was not in the least deprived of his
self possession.

An old Indian fighter as he was, whose men were under a perfect
discipline, it took but a moment to form them for action, and but a moment more elapsed before each, by the advice of his commander, had
selected the cover of a large tree, and stood ready to repel any assault
of their oncoming foe. Confident of success, on account of the superiority of their numbers, which were more than four to one, to the force
under Hobbs, the enemy without seeking cover, rushed forward with
terrible shouts, as if they had determined at the outset to bear down all
resistance; but being met by a well directed fire, by which several of
their number were killed, their impetuosity received such a check as to
cause them to retreat for shelter behind the trees and brush.

The conflict which then followed between the parties, in which the sharp-shooters bore a prominent part, was of the most exciting nature. The two commanders had been known to each other in times of peace, and were both distinguished for their intrepidity.

Sackett, who could speak English, frequently called upon Hobbs, in tones that made the forest ring, to surrender; and with threats in case of refusal that he would annihilate his force with the tomahawk.

Hobbs, with a voice equally loud and defiant, challenged him to come on and put his menace, if he dared, into execution. The action continued for four hours, Hobbs and his force displaying throughout the most consummate skill and prudence, and neither side withdrawing an inch from its original position. The Indians, during the fight, not unfrequently approached the line of their adversaries, but were as often driven back to their cover; the fire of the sharp-sighted marksman opposed to them being more than they could endure. Thus the conflict continued, till, finding that his own men had suffered severely in the struggle, and that the resistance of Hobbs and his men was not likely to be overcome, Sackett retired and left them the masters of a well fought field.

The company of Capt. Hobbs was so well protected that only three, Ebenezar Mitchell, Eli Scott, and Samuel Gunn, were killed. The wounded were Daniel McHenney of Wrentham, who had his thigh broken by a ball, by which he was disabled for life; Samuel Graves, Jr., of Sunderland, a brave lad of seventeen years of age, who was shot through the brain in a horrible manner, yet recovered, but not so as to be afterwards capable of business; — also slight wounds were received by Nathan Walker of Sudbury, and Ralph Rice. Many of the enemy were seen to fall, especially when they left their cover and advanced. Yet, though their loss was undoubtedly great, so effectually was it concealed that its extent was never ascertained. After the retirement and disappearance of the Indians, Captain Hobbs and his men remained concealed till night, apprehending another attack; but, as the darkness fell around them, discovering no signs of the enemy, they gathered up their packs, and took their dead and wounded, and after burying the former under some logs, about half a mile from the scene of action, and conducting the latter to a more conveniant place, about two miles distant, they encamped for the night. They arrived at Fort Dummer the next day, which was the 27th, at four o'clock in the afternoon, whence they sent their wounded to Northfield where they could receive the needed medical aid.

Nathan Walker recovered and arrived safely home. He afterward petitioned the General Court for assistance. In the petition he states that he was a soldier in the Province service under the command of Capt. Hobbs, and that on June 26th, 1748, in a fight with the Indian and French enemy, he was wounded in the arm. (State Archives, Vol. LXXIII., p. 620.)

Capt. Josiah Brown, the commander of the troop which went from Sudbury to assist in the defense of Fort No. 4, was a brave soldier and worthy man. The following is a brief sketch of his life, together with two lists of men who belonged to his troop before the war began and also towards its close. As some of the names are in both lists, perhaps they served through the intervening years, and were present at the defense of No. 4. The troop of 1747–8 was called into service that year, September 23, and served a short time.

CAPT. JOSIAH BROWN.

Mr. Brown was a prominent citizen of Sudbury. He passed through all, or nearly all, the grades of town office; and his name is also conspicuous in the annals of the church. In 1757, Josiah Brown, Samuel Dakin, and Jabez Puffer were chosen delegates to assist in settling the difficulty between the church in Leominster and their pastor. The first two were brave captains in the war against the French and Indians; the first was prominent at Fort No. 4, the other was killed near Fort Edward in 17£8. (See period 1750–1775.) As a token of his regard for the West Side Church, Mr. Brown gave it a piece of land, the proceeds of which, it is stated, were sufficient for the supply of the elements for communion. He was one of the signers of the church covenant in 1724–5.

SUDBURY June 4th 1739

A list of the Gentlmen of the Horse under the command of Capt. Josiah Brown

Trum: Jonathan Belcher,	Nathaniel Seaver
Cor. Josiah willas [willis]	Cor. Daniel Winch
Cor. Daniel Gregory,-	Bezebeal Frost
Cor. Edward Moore	Benja Whitten
Benony Prat	Cornelus Wood
David How	David Stone
Danil Goodenow	Eliph{a} wheler
David Maynard Jr.	Ebenezer Puffer.
Elijah Bent	Elijah Smith
Ebenezer Heminway	Edmond Parmenter
Ecobad Heminway	Hezekiah Moore

Ephriam Puffer   James Crage
Hopestill Browne   Joseph Parmenter
John Cheney   Nathaniel Rice
John Heminway   Phinehas Gibbs.
Jabez Mead   Sam¹ Heminway
John Maynard Jr.   Sam¹ Browne
Nathan Loring   Jabez Puffer
Robert Seaver   Jonathan Maynard
Sam¹ Brigham   Jonathan Puffer
Timothy Sternes   Philis Part
John Bent   Sam¹ Stone
[Isaac] Reed   Solomon Parmenter Jr.
Thomas Winch Jr.

Muster roll of Brown's company 1747–8.

Josiah Brown Capt   Micah Gibbs
John Noyes Cornet   Joseph Brintnall
Dan¹ Stone Clerk   John Brigham
Jonᵃ Belcher Trumpeter   Wᵐ Hunt
Nathaniel Seaver   Matthew Gibbs
Phinehas Gibbs   Henry Smith
Sam¹ Brown   David Maynard
Jonathan Maynard   Samuel Maynard
Isaac Reed   Isaac Brewer
Joseph Reed   Obediah Moore
Wᵐ Brown   Nathan Walker
Dan¹ Stone   Joseph Greene
John Bruce   Isaac Brintnall
——— Parmenter   Henry Loker
John Gould

Other names are

Thomas Winch   Sam¹ Giles
Dan¹ Gregory   Beng Eaton
James Peterson   Sam¹ Frost
Thomas Biglo   Elias Whitney
Thomas Winch   George Whitney
Samuel Winch   Sam¹ Whitney
Josiah Hoar.

CHAPTER XIX.

1750-1775.

The Work-House. — Regulations of it. — Pest-House at Nobscot. — Graves of Small-Pox Victims. — Pest-Houses on the East Side. — Graves of Victims. — Inoculation for the Disease. — Statistics Relating to It. — Highway Work. — Lottery for Repairing the Causeway. — Schools. — School-Houses. — Fourth French and Indian War. — Causes of It. — Lists of Sudbury Soldiers in Various Campaigns. — First and Second Foot Companies. — Alarm List. — Troops of Horse. — Battle at Half-Way Brook. — Death of Captain Dakin. — Sketch of his Life. — Covenant. — Correspondence. — French Neutrals. — Death of Rev. William Cook. — Settlement of Rev. Josiah Bridge. Death of Rev. Israel Loring. — Sketch of His Life. — Settlement of Rev. Jacob Bigelow. — Division of West Part into Wards. — Powder House. — Noon Houses. — Pound. — Measures to Suppress Swindling.

> Over the roofs of the pioneers
> Gathers the moss of a hundred years ;
> On man and his works has passed the change
> Which needs must be in a century's range.
>
> WHITTIER.

BETWEEN 1750, and 1775, the country was in an unsettled condition. Events of a stirring character transpired, and the times were productive of lasting influences. Peace prevailed when the period began, but was very short-lived. The treaty of Aix-la-Chapelle, made in 1748, was of little avail to hold England and France in friendly relations. After the lapse of about a half-dozen years, war was again declared, and hostilities in America broke out anew. The close of the period also was stormy. It was just before the Revolutionary War. The provinces were in process of preparation for that far-famed struggle from which they were to emerge a new nation. Before, however, entering upon military matters, we will notice some of the civil events of the period.

THE WORK-HOUSE.

In 1753, a movement was made to establish a work-house in Sudbury. At the above-named date a vote was taken, when " it passed very fully in the affirmative, that it [the town] would provide a Work House in sd town, that Idle & Disorderly People may be properly Employed." Ephraim Curtis, Joseph Brown, and Ebenezer Roby were a committee in the matter. In process of time the project thus begun was accomplished. March 17, 1762, the town decided "to hire some suitable house for a Work House that the Idle Persons in sd Town might be kept to Labor." Pursuant to vote, a building was rented of Isaac Reed, for which he was to receive two pounds eight shillings. In 1765, the town " voted to give Mr. Reed two pounds eight shillings for his house (and garden spot) & his putting sd house in good Tenantable Repair." In 1763, the town chose "overseeis of the poor for sd house," and Mr. Isaac Reed was of this board.

WORK-HOUSE REGULATIONS.

At a quarterly meeting of all the Overseers of the Poore in Sudbury at the work house in said Sudbury on the first Tuesday of the month, April, Anno Domini 1763, in order to inspect the management thereof and for ordering the Affairs of the said House when we the said overseers were Duely and lawfully meet together at the said work house, and after Due and mature consideration, we Came into the Folowing needfull Rulls and orders for the Regulation of the said house, and those Idle Persons that are by Law or may fall under our Inspection.

Which Rules & orders are as followeth. 1stly That every one of the overseers Shall Punctually meet at the Said work house, at the times set for their monthly or Intermediate Meetings, and in Case of their not attending or unseasonably attending, Shall forfitt and pay to the sd overseers and for their use, the Sum of Two Shillings Lawfull money, and in Case he or they Shall neglect or Refuse to pay the Same or to Shew any Reasonable Excuse for his neglect, the Same Shall be Recovered from him or them by their Clark by Distress and Sale of his or their Goods, the Clark observing the Same Rulls that Constables are by law obleged to Do in making Distress for their Rates.

2ndly. That when any Parson whome we Shall Judge Doath Fall under our Immediate care and Inspection Shall be by a Summon under the hand of our moderator or Clark Duly Sent to him Setting forth the time for his appearance before us at the said work house, and Shall not

Punctually apeare before us the said Overseers, at the said work house, that then and in that Case, a warrant under the hand and Seal of our said Clark Shall Isue out Dyrected to the master of the said work house or to the Constable of the s^d Towne of Sudbury forth with Requiring them to apprehend the body of the s^d Contemptous Parson and Cause him or her to appear before us, the s^d overseers, at the said work house, that he or she may be Proceeded with or Punished for his or her Contempt, by being publickly whipped at the whipping post at the work house not Exceeding Ten Stripes or otherways as the Said Overseers Shall then order, and be Subject to pay to the officer that Shall have served the s^d warrant his fees by Law allowed him, the Service of which Summons Shall be found by Giving him or her Summon in form aforesaid or Leaving same at his or her Last or usual place of abode, by any Constable of s^d Sudbury or any one of the Overseers who Shall make Return of ye s^d Summons to the s^d Overseers at the time therein ordered.

As evidence of further modes of discipline employed in this period, we find that, in 1760, the town allowed payment to Colonel Noyes for making stocks, and also for four staves for the tything-men. In the warrant for a town-meeting in 1757, is the following article: "To see what the town will do with regard to Dido a Negro woman who is now upon charge in this town." With regard to this Dido the town ordered the selectmen "to make strict inquiries who brought Dido into town."

SMALL-POX HOSPITALS.

Another institution introduced into the town in this period was the pest-house. There is in the Stearns' "Collection" a document, without date, that is presumably a petition to the selectmen, asking that a town-meeting be called —

As soon as may be by Law, for the Purchase of and Erecting a House or houses for the conveniance of taking the Small Pox by Inoculation, for the better Security of the Good Citizens of s^d town, [to] do or act as the Town shall Judge proper when met.

As in duty Bound

Jno. Goodenow	Jonathan Bent,
Luther Richardson,	Jotham Goodenow,
Elisha Goodenow,	Israel How,
Elisha Moore,	Caleb Wheeler.
Silas Goodenow,	
Joel Goodenow.	

Probably the above petition antedates the record given
below, dated " Oct. 14, 1761: Town Dr. To Mr. Isaac Reed
for sledding wood and assisting to repair a House, for those
who may have the small pox." Tradition points to several
localities, which at that time were within the town limits,
where pest-houses were situated. The site of one of these
is at Nobscot Hill. On the eastern side of the hill, on land
owned by Mr. Hubbard Brown, and a short distance from a
small pond, are the graves of the small-pox victims. They
are clustered together, beneath a small growth of pines that
are now scattered over that briar-grown spot; and the wind,
as it sweeps through the branches of this little pine grove,
and the occasional note of the wild-wood bird, alone break
the stillness and disturb the loneliness of that forest burial-
place. On a stone that marks one grave is the following
inscription : —

IN MEMORY

OF

MR BUCKLEY HOW,

SON OF

MR BUCKLEY HOW

OF

HUBARDSTON

WHO DIED OF THE SMALL POX,

NOV. 14th 1792

IN THE 21st YEAR OF HIS AGE.

———

MR BUCKLEY HOW.

Just how many graves are about this spot we have no
information, but a former owner of the land, Mr. Edward
Brown, conjectured, as he mowed the brush thereabouts
many years ago, that there were at least eight or nine
well-defined graves there. This burying-place, as we have
said, is on a part of the Thirty-rod Highway. The small-
pox hospital at Nobscot, tradition says, was in the " Nixon
pasture," which is the large field on the northern slope of
the hill; and the same authority asserts that the house in
which John Nixon once lived, and which was on his farm,

was the building used for the hospital. Tradition also says that the Browns, who at that time dwelt at a place just west of the residence of Hubbard Brown, were accustomed to carry milk to a designated spot, and put it in vessels left there to receive it by those in charge at the hospital.

In the north part of Sudbury there are several graves of persons who died of small-pox. Three of them are on the plain, a mile west of the old Pratt Tavern; but they were levelled down by a person who came into possession of the place about 1825. Other graves are on the farm south of Mr. Jonathan Rice's Tavern, in the northwest part of the town. There is another at Bridle Point, just east of the bridge near the railroad crossing.

There were two pest-houses on the east side; one on "the Island," and the other at the northeasterly part of the present town of Wayland, not far to the northerly of the Sumner Draper estate. There is a field in that vicinity still called the "pock pasture." On the Draper farm, not far back of the dwelling-house, are the graves of other victims of this dreaded disease. The following inscriptions are taken from stones that mark these graves: —

IN MEMORY OF

MR. ZEBADIAH ALLEN

WHO DIED OF THE SMALL POX —

JUNE 2, 1777

AGED 75 YEARS.

IN MEMORY OF

MARY, WIFE OF

MR. ZEBADIAH ALLEN

WHO DIED OF THE SMALL POX

JUNE 7, 1777

AGED 75 YEARS.

These hospitals were designed especially for persons who desired to be inoculated for the disease with the virus of a small-pox patient. This method of treatment was introduced about 1721. For a time it met with great prejudice, but

at length it gained ground, and many people incurred the
risk involved in having the disease in this way, which, with
proper treatment, was said to be very light, rather than the
risk of taking it in the ordinary way by contagion. The following statistics, taken from Rev. Israel Loring's "Diary,"
will tend to show with what reason society believed in this
method : —

July 19th 1764. Persons who have had the small pox in Boston in
the year 1764. : : : : .

In the natural way —	Whites —	644
	Blacks,	55
	Total,	699
Died —	Whites,	102
	Blacks,	22
	Total,	124
By inoculation	Whites,	4690
	Blacks,	207
	Total,	4897
Died,	Whites,	43
	Blacks,	3
	Total,	46

Removed into the country to avoid the disease, 1537.

This old manner of practice is now among the things that
were ; and with it the pest-houses, too, have passed away.

HIGHWAY WORK.

In 1751, it was voted that in highway work " eight hours
shall be accounted for a days work," " two shillings shall be
a day's wages for a man, or so in proportion to an hour ; "
also " that one shilling be allowed for a good yoke of oxen
a day."

In 1756, a proposition was started to raise money by way
of a lottery to repair the long causeway from the town bridge
to Lieut. Benjamin Estabrook's. When it came to town-
meeting it "passed in the negative." In 1758, the town
again proposed to raise and repair the long causeway, and

THE SUMMER RESIDENCE OF HON, HOMER ROGERS.
Biographical Sketch, page 619.

two short ones towards Lieutenant Estabrook's, and to do it by means of a lottery. To this proposition a formal remonstrance was presented, in which it was stated that the raising of the causeway would damage the meadow, by causing the water to flow back ; that there was " a good bridge over the river where people may travel at all seasons of the year, from Boston to Marlboro;" and that there is not " one foot of fall in said river for twenty-five or thirty miles." This remonstrance, however, did not prevent the ultimate accomplishment of this project. At a March meeting, 1758, the town voted to petition the General Court for leave to repair and raise the causeway by lottery, and chose the following committee to attend to the work: Col. John Noyes, William Baldwin, and Col. Josiah Brown. The Court gave its assent, and made specifications and conditions as to how the scheme should proceed. One of the conditions was that drawing lotteries was not to continue over fifteen days, exclusive of Sunday. In these lotteries the town took ventures. In 1761 " the town voted to take the tickets in Sudbury Lottery third class, that shall remain unsold in the manager's hand, when the drawing 1st Lottery shall commence, : : : and ordered the tickets that remain unsold aforesaid to be lodged with the Town Treasurer, on the day the Lottery commences drawing." The town lost by this venture, as May 11, 1761, it "granted 27lbs 12s Lawful money, to defray the loss the town sustained by the tickets which the town voted to take, and ordered the assessors to vote it into a rate forthwith, and each person to have the liberty to work out his rate, provided he or they work it out at or before the time set for working out sd rate, and to be under the regulation of the managers of sd Lottery." In October of the same year the question came up as to taking tickets in Sudbury lottery fourth class that should remain unsold in the hands of the managers when the drawing began. " The vote passed in the negative."

In 1653, it was " voted to accept of a highway laid out from Peletiah Deans North east corner, unto ye town way leading from the Training field by Ephraim Curtis, Esq. by Lt. Rice's to Weston." The same date a road was laid out from " Mr. Jonathan Griffin's Corner, running southwesterly into the way by Mr. Eliab Moor's North Corner, formerly Mr. John Adams'." In 1769, the town " granted money to improve a road lately laid out from Rev. Josiah Bridges, to the school house near the East meeting house." The school-house was the old Newell Heard store, and the road referred to, was the present way from the Wellington place by H. B. Braman's into Wayland Centre. In 1773, the town took action to see if it would discontinue the road " leading from Dr. Roby's [now Warren Roby's] to Zecheriah Briant's [now H. B. Braman's] lying between the two county roads." This was a travelled road before the laying out of the one last mentioned. It had its course from near the old Roby house, just west of Mr. Braman's, along the ridge toward Bridle Point. In 1774, the town accepted " a way laid out from Samuel Goodnow's dwelling house to the Lancaster road." The same date the town accepted a way " laid out from Lancaster old road to Lt. Joseph Willis' gate by the widow Brigham's dwelling house." In 1774, the town accepted a road " laid out from Mr. Thomas Walker's land leading to the west meeting house." In 1771, money was granted " to widen the causy at Iron Works meadow." Jabez Puffer, John Balcom, and Joseph Willis were chosen a committee.

SCHOOLS.

While the town was advancing in means for the public convenience and safety, educational matters were progressing also. In 1751, the selectmen agreed " with Mr. Wm Cook [only son of Rev. Mr. Cook] to keep a grammar school . . . for six months, beginning the school the first day of November; and also to teach children & youth to Read English and wright and Instruct them in Rethmetick, and to keep the school in the Town School House as the Selectmen shall from time to time order For the sum of Twelve pounds Exclusive of his Board." It was voted that year that the grammar schools should 'be kept in the two town school-houses by each meeting-house. This shows us where two of the town school-houses stood at that time; and this, with other records, show that school matters were at that time conducted by the Board of Selectmen. Another record of 1756 shows where two other school-houses stood, inasmuch as the town voted that year that the grammar school should be kept at four places, — " two at the school houses near the meeting house, one at the school house near Joseph Smith's, and the other at that near Nathan Goodnow's." John Monroe was to keep the school, and have five pounds thirteen shillings four pence for a quarter, and the town was to pay his board. Other school-houses were also alluded to in the following record made the same year: " The town voted 14 pounds for a reading and writing school, and that it should be kept at four places, viz, at the school house near Samuel Puffer's [perhaps the Pantry school], at the one near Deacon Rice's, at the one near Joseph Stanhope's, and the one near the house of Jonas Brewer."

In 1755, the town " voted for Grammar school 30 pounds, three fifths to be spent on the west side, and two fifths on the east side the river; for the west side the school was to be kept at the farm." In 1752, it " voted for the support of the Grammar school in sd town the year ensuing 37 pounds 6 shillings 8 pence." The school was to be held in five places, — " two on the east side the river and three on the west, in places as followeth. In the school house near the house of Mr. Joseph Smith, and in a convenient place or near the house of Dea Jonas Brewer as may be, or in a convenient place as near the house of Mr. Edward More as may be, and in a convenient place as near the house of Lt Daniel Noyes as may be, and in the school house near to and northerly from the house of Dea Jonathan Rice all in sd town." The same year the town voted that " the Reading & writing school should be kept In the two Town school houses the year ensuing." During this period several school-houses were built, which stood about half a century. In 1705, it was " voted, that the School house near [the] East meeting house [should] be improved, [and] to build a new school house near said meeting house." This may have been afterwards the Newell Heard store. Besides school-houses repaired and built, an attempt was made to supply them with fuel at the town's expense. It is recorded, that, March

1, 1774, the town voted "to see if [it] will order that the several school houses in said town shall be supplied with wood for the future at the charge of the town, agreeable to the petition of Jacob Reed and others." "The article passed in the negative."

FOURTH FRENCH AND INDIAN WAR.

The peace that followed the treaty of Aix-la-Chapelle was of short duration. But a few brief years elapsed before the thunder tones of a terrible conflict burst on the ears of a startled land, and sent a shudder to hearts and homes. For the fourth time the English and French were to cross their weapons in an inter-colonial war. For years the two nations had been expanding in population and power on the American shores, and during this interval they had been fanning the old flame of jealousy which had its origin far back in a feudal age. Each was desirous of supremacy on this side the Atlantic, and to obtain it each was strengthening its lines for aggressive and defensive work. The one power worked on the seaboard, and extended its operations from the Penohscot a thousand miles south; the other stretched its lines of defense along the far-distant interior, and dotted the valley of the St. Lawrence River, the margins of the Mississippi and far-distant lakes, even to the borders of the Gulf of Mexico, with its trading-posts, its strongholds, and its papal missions. These powers sought the same common prize, — the conquest of the country. Already the English claimed that part of it south of the latitude of the north shore of Lake Erie, and westward to the far-off Pacific, by right of charter. Already the Frenchman disputed this right, and claimed the interior as it bordered the Mississippi River and its tributaries, by right of exploration and settlement. Which was to be the permanent title was to be settled, not by diplomacy, but by the arbitrament of the musket, tomahawk, and torch. The French early prepared for this mode of adjusting their claims. More than sixty fortifications had been constructed by them prior to 1750. The English, made suspicious by the erection of garrisons, and knowing the sig-

nificance of trading-posts in the interior of the country, prepared to arrest the course of the foe.

Before, however, a settlement was effected a long and
severe war ensued ; so severe, indeed, was the struggle, that
long after the period was past its events were prominent in
the annals of New England. Tradition kept them alive as
the years rolled by, and the wild scenes set forth by survivors
became the subject of ballad and song. Long after the
struggle had ceased, tales of those times were recited by the
blazing hearth, as, gathered by the fitful fire-light, groups
of listeners gave ear to the thrilling rehearsal, while they
watched the changeful glow of the coals as they crackled
and crumbled on their ashen bed. The snow-shoes, brought
down from the garret, where they had long lain amid the
dust of that mystic place, were reminders of the cold, rough
march, and the noiseless procession of rangers, as they sped
over the pathless snow. The bright fire-light, as it flickered
up the chimney's broad flue ; the mossy wood, newly cut, in
the corner, — all were alike suggestive of forest adventure,
of the lone sentinel guard in the dark, deep shade, and of tales
told by the light of camp-fires in places far from home.

The war was to a large extent carried on by expeditions
or campaigns, the object of which was to capture the strongholds of Canada. We will give lists of Sudbury soldiers who
were in these campaigns.

CROWN POINT EXPEDITION.

In 1755, a regiment was raised, and placed under command
of Col. Josiah Brown of Sudbury, for the purpose of prevent-
ing the encroachments of the French about Crown Point and
upon "Lake Iroquois, commonly called by the French, Lake
Champlain." The regiment belonged to the command of
William Johnson. The following is a list of the field and
staff officers : —

Josiah Brown, Col.	Samuel Brigham, Surgeon.
John Cummings, Lt. Col.	Benjamin Gott, Surgeon's Mate
Steven Miller, Major	David Mason, Commissary
Samuel Dunbar, Chaplain	Joseph Lovering, Adjutant

Sept. 10, 1755, Samuel Dakin received a commission as captain of foot in this regiment. The muster-roll of his company contains forty-eight names, of which the following are supposed to be from Sudbury: —

Capt. S. Dakin	Sam¹ Grout
Elisha Cutler	Jason Gleason
Silas Clapp	Abel Farrar
Moses Puffer	Josiah Barker
Nath¹ Eveleth	Ephriam Woods, Jr.
Sam¹ Gibbs Jr	Samuel Estabrook
Sam¹ Burbank	Lt. Joseph Baker
Joseph Sherman	Jonᵃ Barrett

Sudbury men in a second list of Capt. Samuel Dakin's Company, 1755: —

Samuel Grout sergt.	Samuel Mead, Jr.
David Eveleth corp¹	Jason Gleason
Jonathan Bent	Nathaniel Gibbs
Silas Clapp	Samuel Burbank
Silas Puffer	Moses Jones
Joseph Maynard	Charles Wetherbe
Wᵐ Skinner	Abijah Brigham
Simon Maynard	Josiah Sherman
Jedediah Parmenter	Josiah Walker.

Sudbury men in Capt. Jonathan Hoar's company, 1755: —

Adam Gilbert	Charles Roiley
Uriah Choochett	Jonathan Stanhope.

Sudbury men in the Crown Point expedition of 1756, in Capt. Ebenezer Newell's company: —

John Nixon Lieut. [Fram]	Micah Grout
Ensign Joseph Brintnall	Leavitt How
Warren Goodenow	Isaac Goodenow
Ezra Barker	

Sudbury men in Capt. John Nixon's company, 1756: —

Samuel Parmenter	Samuel Putnam
Phinehas Haynes	Wᵐ Puffer
Samuel Burbank	Jonᵉ. Maynard
Eph. Hayden	

Sudbury men in a third list of Capt. Samuel Dakin's company : —

Samuel Grout	Joseph Sherman
David Evelith	Jonathan Bent
Silas Clapp	Joseph Maynard
Wm Skinner	Silas Puffer
Jedediah Parmenter	Simon Maynard
Samuel Mead Jr.	Jason Gleason
Nathaniel Gibbs	Moses Stone
Samuel Burbank	Abijah Brigham
Charles Wetherbe	

Sudbury men in other lists are as follows: Crown Point expedition in Capt. William Jones' company, Colonel Thatcher's regiment : —

Jonas Balcom	Miles Realy
Ebenezer Woodis	Nathaniel Hayden
Leavitt How	Nathan Maynard
Oliver Grout	Jonas Gibbs
Benjamin Gleason	Solomon How
Joseph Mungry	Nathan Smith
Micah Grout	

In Col. John Jones' regiment for the invasion of Canada, under command of General Amherst : —

Joel Clapp	Daniel Parmenter
Silas Hemenway	Isiah Parmenter
Joseph Green	—— Cole
Ebenezer Wooddis	Samuel Putman
Andrew White	

In Capt. Josiah Richardson's company, Col. Joseph Buckminster's regiment : —

Jonas Balcom	Miles Realy
Joseph Muzzy	Nathaniel Hayden
Leavet How	Nathan Maynard
Micah Grout	

In the company of Capt. John Nixon of Sudbury, 1761 : —

Isaiah Parmenter, Serg^t	Uriah Gibbs.
Ebenezer Woodes, Corp^l	Moses Haynes

Caleb Clark
Nathaniel Cutter
Benjᵃ Cutter
Benjᵃ Clark
Wᵐ Daniels
Josiah Everton.
Ephraim Goodnow Jun.
Thomas Green

Ephraim Hayden
Isaac Lincoln
Jesse Putnam
John Putnam
Daniel Parmenter
David Rice
Elijah Willis.

In Capt. Moses Maynard's company : —

Oliver Gould

Benjamin Gleason

Others in the service : —

John Rutter.
Josiah Baldwin.
Josiah Pratt.

Samuel Graves
Daniel Wyman.

Lieut. Samuel Curtis and eighteen men joined Capt. Samuel Dakin's company in the expedition to Canada in 1758.

The following lists contain the names of the active militia force of Sudbury, April, 1757. Many whose names are in these lists engaged in one or more of the campaigns as the war progressed, and then returned to exchange the musket or sword for the implements of peaceful pursuits, still holding themselves in readiness at their country's call to place their names again on the muster-roll : —

A List of The Officers and Soldiers of the First Foot Company in Sudbury under the command of Capt. Moses Maynard, Lᵗ Joseph Curtis and En. Jason Glezen.

Sarg John Rice
　" Israel Rice
　" Samuell Russell
　" Isaac Cutting.
Corpˡ Jonathan Underwood
　" Nehemiah Williams
　" Josiah Farrar
　" Samˡ Fisk
Drum. John Combs.
　" Wᵐ Russell.
Joseph Smith

Abraham Jenkens Jun.
Ebenezer King
Joseph Trask
Thomas Allen Jun
Elijah Rice
John Parmenter Jun
Grindly Jackson
Caleb Moulton
Bezaleel Moore
Timothy Underwood
Phineas Gleyen

Shemnel Griffyn
Joseph Rutter
Samu^{ll} Abbott
Randall Davis Jun
Wm Moulton
John Parmenter
Saml Gould Jun.
Ephraim Smith
Jonathan Graves
Jacob Alderick
Saml Livermore
Charles Wetheaby
Wm Ravis
David Bent
Isaac Damon
James Davis
Henery Coggin
Wm Dudly
Micah Rice
Isaac Wetheaby
Jonathan Belcher
Ephraim Abbott
John Allen
Benj^a Glezen

Samu^{ll} Griffyn
Micah Maynard
Wm Grout
Edwd Sharmon Jun
John Walker
John Meriam
Edmond Rice
Jason Glezen
Elijah Ross
John Morffet
Benj^a Cory
Ebenezer Staples
Saml Pool
Zebediah Allen Jun
Josiah Maynard
Jonas Woodward
Benj^a A. Williams
David Patterson
David Stone
Jason Glezen Jun
Thomas Bent Jun
Thadeus Russell
James Ross
Wm Sanderson

A true Copy taken Apr. 25, 1757

SAM^L CURTIS, Clerk.

A true list of the 2ond Foot Company in Sudbury under command of Cap^{tn} Josiah Richardson taken by Ezekiel How Clerk, April ye 25th 1757.

Capt. Josiah Richardson
Lef^{nt} Abijah Haynes
Ensⁱⁿ Jabez Puffer
Serg^t Joseph Willis
Serg^t Elijah Smith
Serg^t Corneleas Wood
Serg^t David Moore
Corp Joseph Stanhope
Corp Samuell Eaton
Corp Oliver Dackin
Corp Josiah Richardson Jun.
Drum. Jessie Willis
    "   Wm Rice Jun.
John Rice
John Reamos
Jonas Gibs
John Jacob Cibellar

Wm Skiner
Wm Gibs
Wm Hayden
Isaac Hunt Jun
Jeams Wier
Ephriam Rice
Ephriam Goodenow
Elijah Parmenter
Ezekiel Parmenter
Ephriam Hayden
Edmond Goodenow
Eben^r Burbank
Eben^r Woode
Geo. Wheller
Geo. Mossmon
Joseph Maynard Jun
Jeames Carter

Leavit How

Micah Goodenow

Michall Mellong

Morris Clarrey

Micah Parmenter

Micah Grout

Miells Rayley

Mosies Rice

Nathan Moore

Nathaniel Gibs Jun.

Nathaniel Muzzey

Norman Saever

Nathaniel Cuter

Rowen Boogrill

Reubin Willis

Richard Ralley

Reubin Norse

Oliver Mors

Peletiah Parmenter

Edward Bointon

Patrick Roach

Simeon Harris

Samuiell Parmenter

Samuiell Osbon

Samuiell Brigham

Samuiell Dackin Jun

Samuiell Burbank Jun

Samuiell Puffer Jun

Samuiell Knight Jun

Silas Balkom

Silas Puffer

Silas Smith

Samuiell Putnam

Thomas Goodenow

Thomas Walker Jun

Uriah Parmenter Jun

Wᵐ Parmenter

Daniel Noyse Jun

James Haynes

Isaack Linckon

Jeames Thompson

Jonathan Maynard

Josiah Haynes

John Mossman

Jonas Hallden

Jonas Hayden

Isrial Haynes

Jeams Puffer

Jonal Balcom

Josiah Rice

John Willis

John Burbank

Josiah Bennit Jun

Jonathan Haynes

Jonathan Rice Jun

John Goodenow

John Puffer

Jeams Puffer Jun

Joseph Muzzey Jun

Aron Haynes

Abijah Walker

Ambrus Tower

Asa Smith

Asiell Clap

Aron Johnson

Abel Brown

Aron Eams

Andrew White

Benimin Tower

Beniman Berry

David Maynard Jun

Daniell Clap

Daniell Bowken

David Clark

Daniell Parmenter

There was also in Sudbury what was called an Alarm List. This included persons between the ages of sixteen and sixty, who were ordinarily exempt from military duty, but were liable to be called upon in emergencies. The following are the names on an Alarm List which is supposed to have been commanded by Capt. Thomas Damon.

List of those persons who are obliged to appear on an alarm, between the ages of 16 and 60 in the First foot Company in Sudbury. Apr 25. 1757

SAMUEL CURTIS, Clerk.

Ebenezer Roby, Esq.	Zebediah Allen
Wm Cook Jun	Paul Brintnal.
Wm Baldwin	Hopstill Bent,
Ebenezer Roby Jun.	Joseph Beal.
Abial Abbott	Joseph Sharmon,
Isaac Baldwin	James Brewer jun.
Naham Baldwin	Eliakim Rice.
John Ross.	Benjaman Dudley
Zecariah Briant.	Samuel Parris.
Benjn Briant	Peter Bent Jun
Benjn Ball	Thomas Graves
Daniel Wyman	Isaac Woodward
James Patterson	Thomas Jenkinson
Thomas Bent	David McDaniels
Joseph Goodnow	Daniel Moore Jun
Elijah Bent	Amos Brown
Cor. Thomas Damon	Jonathan Patterson
James Graves	Elisha Rice Jun.
Amos Sanderson	Peter Briant
Ezra Graves	David Sharmon
Joseph Livermore	Josiah Haynes
Isaac Rice	Isaac Stone
Peter Bent	Jonathan Griffin.

In August, 1757, the men on both the Active and Alarm Lists were mustered for service. The year had been one of disaster to the English and American forces; and, on August 3, General Montcalm with about nine thousand French and one thousand Indians besieged Fort William Henry, which he captured after a six days' siege, during which time it was gallantly defended by Colonel Monroe with a force of twenty-three hundred and seventy-two men. The report of the disaster was sad intelligence to New England and consternation prevailed. The militia were called to arms, and soon a large part of those on both the Active and Alarm Lists were on their way towards Fort William Henry; but Montcalm not taking advantage of his victory in the way that was expected, in about two weeks the troops returned.

The following are the officers of a troop of horse in
Sudbury in 1762 : —

> Capt. John Noyes
> 1st Lieut. Israel Moore
> 2ond Lieut. Richard Heard
> Cornet, Jonathan Parmenter
> Quarter Master, Samuel How.

Officers of the troop of horse in Sudbury in 1771 : —

FIRST COMPANY.	SECOND COMPANY.
Capt. Joseph Curtis	Capt. Aaron Haynes
1st Lieut. Micah Maynard.	1st Lieut. Daniel Bowker
2ond Lieut. Ebenezer Staples.	Ens. James Puffer.
Ens. Samuel Choate	

THIRD COMPANY.
Capt. Samuel Knight
1st Lieut. Moses Stone

The foregoing lists indicate that the town was well represented in the last French war, and that its militia force was
quite strong. Some of the officers whose names are given
were prominent citizens. Col. Josiah Brown has been mentioned in connection with military operations of a preceding
period. Capt. John Nixon, who in 1759, is mentioned as a
citizen of Sudbury, was, subsequently, General Nixon of
Revolutionary fame. Other of her soldiers who became
efficient officers in the Revolutionary War received their first
lessons in military tactics in this severe school.

In one of the expeditions of this war, the town sustained
the loss of Capt. Dakin and several others of its citizens, who
were killed by the Indians at Half-Way Brook, near Fort
Edward, July 20, 1758. At the time of this event, Capt.
Dakin and his company were connected with the expedition
of General Amherst against Crown Point. The following
brief account of the attendant circumstances are stated in a
diary kept by Lieut. Samuel Thomson of Woburn : —

"July 20, Thursday in the morning, 10 men in a scout
waylaid by the Indians and shot at and larmed the fort and
a number of our men went out to assist them, and the enemy
followed our men down to our Fort, and in their retreat,

Capt. Jones and Lieut. Godfrey were killed, and Capt Lawrence and Capt. Dakin and Lieut. Curtis and Ens^n Davis, and two or three non-commissioned officers and privates, to the number of 14 men, who were brought into the Fort, all scalped but Ens^n Davis, who was killed within 30 or 40 rods from the Fort: and there was one grave dug, and all of them were buried together, the officers by themselves at one end, and the rest at the other end of the grave; and Mr. Morrill made a prayer at the grave, and it was a solemn funeral; and Nathl Eaton died in the Fort and was buried; and we kept a very strong guard that night of 100 men. Haggit [and] Wm Coggin wounded."

Then follows a list of the killed, beginning, —

> Capt. Ebenezer Jones of Willmington
> Capt   Dakin of Sudbury
> Lieut Samuell Curtice of Ditto
> Private   Grout of do

"We have also an account that there are seven of our men carried into Ticonderoga, which make up the number of those that were missing.

"21. Friday, in ye forenoon a party of about 150 went out to find more men that were missing, and we found 4 men who were scalped, and we buried them, and so returned: and at prayer this evening we were Laromed by a false outcry. Nicholas Brown died and was buried; and Moses Haggit died."

As Jonathan Patterson and Nathaniel Moulton of Sudbury are reported missing, they may have been among the number above referred to.

The following epitaph of Captain Dakin was written by William Rice, Esq., who was his orderly sergeant.

> Good by, Capt. Dakin Samuell.
> In a battle near Lake George he fell.

In the death of Captain Dakin, a loss was sustained by the town, the church, and the province. The following sketch contains some facts concerning his life,

SKETCH OF CAPTAIN DAKIN.

Samuel Dakin was a son of Deacon Joseph Dakin, whose father, Thomas, settled in Concord prior to 1650. In 1722, he married Mercy Minott, daughter of Colonel Minott who built the first framed house in Concord. The farm of Captain Dakin was in the northern part of Sudbury, on the road running northerly to Concord, his house being very near the town boundary. As early as 1745, he was appointed ensign of the second company of foot in Sudbury, of which Josiah Richardson was captain and Joseph Buckminster was colonel. Sept. 10, 1755, he received the commission of captain in Col. Josiah Brown's regiment. In May, 1758, he received an order from Ebenezer Nichols to be present with his company at Worcester on the 25th, and to furnish his men with " Bounty for Biliting." From Worcester he proceeded to Fort Edward, where he probably arrived about the middle of June, and in the vicinity of which he remained till his death, which occurred as before described. Captain Dakin was not only valiant in his country's service but valiant in the army of the Lord as well. His character as a Christian is indicated by the following covenant, copied from the original, which is still in the possession of one of his descendants.

COVENANT.

O, Thou Glorious God! Thou hast promised mercy in Christ Jesus, if I turn to Thee with my whole heart. I therefore upon the call of the Gospel, do come and throwing down my weapons of rebellion, do submit to Thy mercy, as Thou requirest as the condition of my acceptance with Thee, that I put away mine idols and be at defiance with Thine enemies, which I acknowledge I have wickedly sided with against Thee, I do now from my heart renounce them all, firmly covenanting with Thee not to allow myself in any known sin, but constantly to use all means that I know Thou hast prescribed, for the death and destruction of my corruptions, and as my heart has been running after this world and sin and vanity, I do now resign it to Thee that made it, protesting before Thy Glorious Majesty, that it is the firm resolution of my heart and that I do unfeignedly desire grace from Thee, that when Thou shalt call me here-unto, I may practice this my resolution, and by Thine assistance, to forsake that which is dear to me in this world, rather than turn from Thee to the ways of sin, and Thou wilt enable me to work against all temptations, whether in prosperity or in adversity, lest they draw my heart from Thee. O, Glorious God, I would again come before Thee with all possible veneration bowing myself at the feet of Thy Glorious Majesty. I do here take the Lord Jehovah, Father, Son and Holy Spirit, for my portion and chief good, and do give up myself body and soul for service to serve Thee all the days of my life I do here upon the bended knees of my soul, accept of Jesus as the only way by which sinners have access to God. I do this day take the Lord to be my Lord, and Jesus Christ to be my Saviour, resolving to serve Thee in all my affairs. I do renounce my former righteousness, and take Thee to be " The Lord my right-eousness " and am willing to take my lot as it falls, as to the goods of this world, leaving all my concerns with Thee, verily supposing that nothing separate me from the love of Jesus Christ my Lord and dear Redeemer, and from this day I shall be bold to call the Lord Jehovah my Father, and Jesus Christ my Redeemer, and the Holy Ghost my sancti-fier, hoping that my God will suffer no allowed sin to make void this covenant, and this covenant that I have made on earth, may it be ratified in heaven. Amen & Amen.

July 27th 1753. memorandum.

This day renew this covenant having often broken it. The Lord accept me again for his great mercy sake in Jesus Christ.

Sept. 29th 1756. memorandum.

This day renew this covenant, having often broken it, although nothing hath failed on God's part and now going on an Expedition against the enemy at Crown point, I have given myself up wholly to God to be at His disposal in life or death, and O that God would accept of me again for Jesus Christ's sake.

　　　　　　　　May 23d 1758.　memorandum.

This day renew this covenant with God, and while going on an expedition against Canada I have left myself wholly in the hands of God, to be at His disposal in life or death.

　　　　　　　　　　　　　　SAMUEL DAKIN.

Captain Dakin's character is also shown by the following extracts from letters to his wife while he was serving in the Canada campaign. In a letter dated Sept. 26, 1755, he says: " I am in good health and my company are so obedient to me and so loving one to another that it makes my life exceeding comfortable and pleasant. I have never yet heard one thwarting word in my company, but they seem all to have a brotherly care one for another, and have never heard one profane word among them, and their forwardness to attend religious exercises is delightful to me so that I have many mercies."

In a letter of June 10, 1758, he speaks of the condition of his company, and says: "they are all well, and I hope I shall be very happy in my company, and they are very ready to attend prayers and singing of Psalms which we have practiced on our journey."

July 11, 1758, in writing from Lake George he says: "And now my dear wife and children, I desire you would not distress yourselves about me but commit me in your prayers to God to be wholly at his disposal and I hope by his preserving providence I shall after awhile rejoice with you again in my own house; but if not I hope we shall all rejoice together in heaven which will be spiritually better." Before he closes his letter he asks for their prayers for himself, his men, and the whole army.

Such are some extracts from the correspondence of this Christian soldier. They serve, not only to set forth the character of the man, but of an officer in the military service of those times. Surely, if Captain Dakin was a representative of that generation of men, no wonder that the cause for which they fought was at last triumphant. His descendants have been prominent citizens of Sudbury. Levi and Thomas, grandson and great grandson, were deacons in the Congregational Church.

Not only were the New England towns called upon to furnish men for the war, but their equipment and mainten- ance also when in the field. As the soldiers to an extent enlisted for single campaigns, repeatedly, the expense of fitting out demanded new contributions. This condition of things occasioned heavy taxation and the issuing of bills of credit by the government. Besides the money provided by the public for the prosecution of the war, some means were furnished by the merchants, farmers and others for the encouragement of enlistments.

FRENCH NEUTRALS.

Among other services rendered by the towns was the maintenance of what were termed French Neutrals, the people whom Longfellow has described in his poem, "Evan- geline." As Sudbury had some of these to care for, a few words relative to their general history may be appropriate. Upon the cession of the province of Nova Scotia by France to the British in 1713, a colony of about seven thousand French Roman Catholics became subjects of Great Britain. These colonists were allowed to remain on the land they had occupied, on condition of their taking the oath of allegiance to England. The oath was taken with the qualification that, in case of war against France, they were not to take up arms against their own countrymen. It was thus they acquired the name of French Neutrals. But it was alleged that, during the war which began in 1755, they furnished the French and Indians with substantial aid, thus enabling them the better to harass the English, that three hundred of them were found in arms at the taking of Fort Beau- Sejour, and that although an offer was made to such as had not resorted to arms to still hold their estate on taking the oath of allegiance without qualification, yet they one and all refused to do so. In view of this attitude, the English believed that the public safety required their removal from the province. If they were taken to Canada they would still be enabled to assist the French. It was, therefore, determined to convey them to different parts of the British Colonies. The plan of removing them was largely intrusted to the forces of Massachusetts under command of Lieutenant-Colonel Winslow.

At an appointed time, the people were called into the different ports "to hear the King's orders." About four hundred of their best men assembled at the village of Grand Pré. A guard being placed about the church where they were, Colonel Winslow made known his sad errand.

One thousand of these French Neutrals arrived in the Massachusetts Bay Province and were supported at public expense. Different towns, among which was Sudbury, had their quota to care for. Repeatedly is there a record of supplies furnished them by the town. The following is a general statement of some of these, and also a bill of attendance and medicine furnished by Dr. Roby, one of Sudbury's old time physicians.

An account of what hath been expended by s^d Town of Sudbury on Sundry French Persons sent from Nova Scotia to this province and by s^d government to Town of Sudbury.

The subsisting of Eighteen persons ten days — six persons three weeks, and four persons twenty-three weeks, the whole amounting to one hundred and twenty-seven weeks for one person charged at four shillings week for each person £25 — 8^s

Ephraim Curtis	Ebenezer Roby
Josiah Brown	Josiah Haynes
John Noyes	Samuel Dakin
Elijah Smith.	Selectmen.

Some of them being sick a great many comers and goers to visit them made the expense the greater even thirteen or fourteen at a time for a week together.

State Archives, Vol. XXIII., page 98.

MASSACHUSETTS PROVINCE.

For medicine and attendants for the French Neutrals from Nova Scotia.

1755, Dec. 11 — To Sundry Medicines for French young woman — 27 — To Do. for girl 6^d

1756, Mar. 22, — To Sundry Medicines and Journey in the night west side the River — 0-5-8

To Sundry Medicines Journey west side 0-4-0

To Do. 4^s To Journey and Medicines 0-7-0

To Do. $\frac{1}{6}$ for the old Gentleman when he fell off the House and was greatly bruised and sick of a fever the clavicula being broke.

May, 1756, To medicine and attendants for the old Gentleman, the whole month of May and his wife greatest part of the time himself when dangerously sick of a fever, violent coughs and are still remaining in a low languishing condition.

N. B. The above old gentleman and wife have been in a low languishing condition all the spring and have had no more doctoring than what has been of absolute necessity.

State Archives, Vol. XXIII., page 97.

Melancholy, indeed, was the fate of those ancient Acadians. Although the circumstances were such that the English may have considered their removal a military necessity, yet the fact remains that sorrow and hardship attended their exile. They were strangers in a strange land. Their pleasant homes were abandoned, and with their lands passed into the hands of another race.

" Waste are those pleasant farms and the farmers forever departed ;
Scattered like dust and leaves when the mighty blasts of October
Seize them, and whirl them aloft and sprinkle them far o'er the ocean."

Feb. 10, 1763, a treaty of peace was signed at Paris, and the long, arduous struggle between the two great nations ceased. The announcement brought great joy to New England. Days of public thanksgiving were observed, and praise was offered unto Him " from whom all blessings flow." No longer was Canada to be a place from which a foe could sally forth to harass the exposed frontier, and to which he could return with his captives and booty. The same flag was to float over New England and beyond the northern border, and the Canadian fortresses were to be manned by English or American soldiers.

In yet another way did this war bring its benefits to Americans. It gave them a knowledge of the military tactics of Europe, by which they were the better able to cope with the British when, in after years, they met them on the memorable fields of the Revolutionary War.

About ten years after the close of the war both precincts lost their pastors. The first that died was Mr. Cook, who passed away in 1760. That year the town voted " sixty-five pounds to each of the Rev^d ministers for the year ensuing including their salary and fire wood; in case they or either of them should decease before the expiration of the year, then they or either of them to receive their salary in proportion during the time they shall live and no longer."

This may indicate that their death was anticipated. Another record indicates that Mr. Cook had been sick some time when this vote was passed, as the town book goes on to state, "The same meeting granted thirty-three pounds, six shillings six pence to pay persons who had supplied the pulpit in Mr. Cook's confinement, and also granted thirty pounds more to supply the pulpit during his sickness, and chose a committee to provide preaching in the meantime." May 11, 1761, the town appropriated seventeen pounds, six shillings, eight pence " out of the money granted for the Rev. Mr. Cook's salary in the year 1760, to defray the Rev. Mr. Cook's funeral expenses."

Mr. Cook had one son who taught the grammar school for years in Sudbury, and died of a fever in 1758. After the decease of Mr. Cook, another minister was soon sought for on the east side. A little disturbance, and perhaps delay, was occasioned by a petition sent to the General Court relating to the settlement of another minister on the east side the river. But the matter was amicably adjusted by a vote of the town; whereby it decided " not to send an agent to the General Court to show cause or reason why the petition of Deacon Adam Stone and others relating to the settlement of a Gospel minister on the East side the river should not be granted." The town furthermore voted, that the " prayers of the petition now in Court should be granted, Provided the Court would Grant and confirm the like Privilege to the West Church and Congregation when there shall be reason. John Noyes Moderator."

The way cleared of obstructions a new pastor was soon found. Choice was made of Rev. Josiah Bridge. Oct. 14, 1761, Capt. Moses Maynard was allowed twelve shillings " for his travel to Lunenburg to wait on Mr. Bridge ; " and, at the same meeting, it was " voted to grant to Mr. Bridge his settlement and salary as he had contracted with the East

Precinct for, and ordered the assessors to assess the inhabitants of the town for the same."

Delegates were duly chosen by the West Side Church, Nov. 3, 1761, to attend Mr. Bridge's ordination, — Deacon Haynes, John Haynes, Josiah Richardson, and Cornelius Wood. Mr. Bridge was a native of Lexington, and graduate of Harvard College in 1758. He was ordained Nov. 4, 1761, and died June 19, 1801, aged sixty-two, and in the fortieth year of his ministry. A few years after Mr. Cook's decease Rev. Mr. Loring also passed away, his death occurring March 9, 1772.

The West Church voted, April 7, 1772, "to set apart Thursday next as a day of Fasting and prayer to seek ye direction and blessing of heaven on the endeavor to settle another Gospel Minister among them." Also, "voted that the Rev. Mr. Stone of Southboro, Rev. Mr. Bridge of the East Precinct, Rev. Mr. Bridge of Framingham, and Rev. Mr. Swift of Marlboro be requested to give their presence and assistance. Exercises to commence at 10 o'clock." May 6, 1772, the town "granted Eighteen pound Lawful money for to pay the charge of Rev. Mr. Loring's Funeral," also at the same date it was "voted that the remainder of the [money] granted to pay the Rev. Mr. Loring's salary should be applied for supplying the pulpit."

SKETCH OF MR. LORING.

The service of Mr. Loring in the church at Sudbury was long and fruitful. He died in the ninetieth year of his age and the sixty-sixth year of his ministry. It was said of him that "as he earnestly desired and prayed that he might be serviceable as long as he should live, so it pleased God to vouchsafe his request, for he continued to preach 'till the last Sabbath but one before his death, and the next day prayed in the town meeting, which was on the 2nd day of the month. The night following he was taken ill, and on the 9th of March 1772, he expired." Mr. Loring had pious parentage. His father, Mr. John Loring of Hull, came from England, Dec. 22, 1634. It has been said of him that, like

Obadiah, " he feared the Lord greatly." His mother was also religious, and " prayed with her family in her husband's absence." Mr. Loring was born at Hull, Mass., April 6, 1682. It is supposed he was converted in his youth. He graduated at Harvard College in 1701. He began to preach at Scituate, lower parish, Aug. 1, 1703, and preached first at Sudbury July 29, 1705. In the year 1723, on the 25th of July, he removed to the west side of the river, where he continued in service until flesh and strength failed. He left two sons and four daughters, his son Jonathan having died some years before the death of his father. Elizabeth, born Nov. 16, 1712, married Richard Manson of Sudbury, June 6, 1746. Mary, born Sept. 14, 1716, married Elisha Wheeler, and died, Jan. 22, 1801. Nathan, born Nov. 27, 1721, married Keziah Woodward, Dec. 31, 1747, who died July 28, 1754. He married a second time, and died April 25, 1803. " He was a farmer, and lived on the place afterwards owned by Loring Wheeler 1st." On the fidelity of Mr. Loring's ministry we need offer no comments: his works are his memorials. At the time of his installation at Sudbury the church numbered one hundred and twenty, — forty-one males and seventy-nine females. During his ministry four hundred and fifty were added to it; of these, forty-two males and seventy-two females were added before the division of the church, and, after the division, there were added to the West Church one hundred and twenty-nine males and two hundred and seven females. The whole number of children baptized by Mr. Loring in Sudbury was fourteen hundred.

It has been said concerning his service on the West Side, " Thus did this excellent and venerable man thro' a long series of years, burn and shine in eminent Piety, indefatigable Dilligence, faithfulness, and distinguished usefulness of truly primitive stamp. Heu Pietas ! heu prisca Fides !" It is said, further, that he was " honored and revered by all whose regards were worth receiving ; and for a great number of years was the head and the glory and delight of the ministry." Beside these substantial testimonials of merit, he has left various publications which also set forth his worth. Some of these printed works are as follows: —

" The nature and necessaty of the New Birth. (a sermon.) Printed for and sold by D. Henchman, over against the British meeting house. MDCCXXVIII."

" Serious thoughts on the miseries of hell. (Preached at Sudbury, Sunday, Feb. 20, 1731-2.)"

Several other sermons on important religious subjects were published, also an election sermon, of date 1739; a convention sermon, 1742, and others not mentioned here, making in all eleven publications. He also kept a succession of diaries, some of which are still extant. They are closely written and somewhat hard to be read, but contain valuable matter that pertains to the affairs of both province and town. Mr. Loring was a strong Calvinist, an earnest preacher and somewhat noted minister. It is said he did not like the ways of Mr. Whitefield, the evangelist, and the excitement attendant upon his revivals; and this, together with some other matters, led to some unpleasantness for a time. He was fine looking, tall, slender, and of dark complexion. When he lived on the East Side, he occupied the parsonage which the town provided for Mr. Sherman. In 1778, the town voted " to give to Mr. Isreal Loring our present minister ye 4 acres of land and ye building now upon it y^t ye bought of John Loker to him and his heirs forever, on y^{esd} Mr. Isreal Loring relinquishing ye £50 which ye town granted him." (See Chapter XV.)

Thus lived and died a good and great man; but " though dead he yet speaketh."

" The precious memory of the just
Shall flourish when they sleep in dust."

After the death of Mr. Loring, the church did not remain long dependent upon a temporary supply. On July 27, 1772, it proceeded to select a Gospel minister, and the Rev. Jacob Bigelow was unanimously chosen. He was to have a salary of seventy-four pounds. He was ordained Nov. 11, 1772. The following churches were represented on the occasion of ordination : East Precinct, Josiah Bridge ; Waltham, Jacob Cushing; Weston, Samuel Woodward; Sherburn, Elijah Brown; Framingham, Matthew Bridge; Lexington, Jonas Clark ; Westborough, Ebenezer Parkman.

MISCELLANEOUS.

For a time preceding the Revolution, the West Side was divided into the North and South Wards. In 1765, Richard Heard offered to collect the taxes on the East Side the river for three pence per pound if they would appoint him collector and constable ; and Aaron Haynes offered to collect them for the North Ward, West Side, and Jedediah Parmenter for the South Ward at the same rates.

In 1765, the town " voted to build a new stone pound between Lieut. Augustus Moors' dwelling house at the gravel pit, on Col. Noyes land which he promised to give the town to set a pound on by Dead." The pound was to be " 30 feet square from Enside to Enside 6 ft high with pieces of timber locked together round the top 8 inches square, for six pounds and the old pound."

In 1771, the town voted to build a powder-house in which to keep the town's stock of ammunition. It granted for this object " 7 pounds 9 shillings and 4 pence, and agreed with Col. John Noyes to build it, and place it near or on Wm Baldwin's land near Major Curtis'." Another record of the same year states that " the town voted to erect the powder house on the training field near Mr. Elisha Wheelers." In 1773, it " voted to remove the powder house to some suitable place on or near the gravel pit hill, and chose a committee to remove the same, if the committee should think the house will be sufficient for the use it was built for, and rough cast and underpin said building."

In 1772, the town " gave leave to John Balcom, Joseph Willis, Abijah Brigham, and Jonathan Smith, to set up a small House on the town land near the west meeting house for the people to repair to on the Sabbath day." There may have been other similar buildings erected near. They were intended as a convenient resort for the people, during the interval between services on Sunday, for the purpose of warming themselves and eating their dinners.

May 17, 1773, the town chose a committee " to consider and report what is proper to be done in order to suppress that set of men in this town, who make it their business to trade with and cheat strangers." The committee reported as follows : —

" That for the benefit of the public, the names and character of the persons belonging to and residing in Sudbury hereafter named . . . . are persons who go about the country and cheat honest men by purchasing their horses, cattle and other effects, by telling fair stories, and promising short pay, should be published in the several newspapers, that the Public may be cautioned against trading with or trusting them on any account."

The town accepted of the report, and chose a committee to find out the persons who aided and assisted in the work, " by purchasing the horses and cattle &c at a low price which they know are obtained in such a clandestine way and manner, that their names may be exposed in like manner. Also voted, that the town Clerk send an attest copy to the several Printers in the town of Boston, to be printed for the benefit of the public."

CHAPTER XX.

1775-1800.

War of the Revolution. — Causes of It. — Attitude of the Town Relative to the Stamp Act. — Instructions to the Representative Concerning It. — Report of the Committee Relative to the Importation of Tea. — Patriotic Resolutions of the Town. — Instructions to its Representatives. — An Old Document Descriptive of the Times. — Military Preparations. — Choice of Militia Officers. — Organization of Minute Companies. — Names and Captains of Companies. — Muster Rolls. — Equipments. — Drill. — Call Roll of Captain Nixon's Company. — Military Stores Removed to Sudbury. — The Alarm. — The Mustering and March. — The Arrival at Concord. — The Encounter at the North Bridge. — Retreat of the British. — The Pursuit. — Encounter at Merriam's Corner. — At Hardy's Hill. — Incident. — Sudbury's Loss. — Sketch of Deacon Josiah Haynes. — Sketch of Mr. Asahel Read.

> Far as the tempest thrills
> Over the darken'd hills,
> Far as the sunshine streams over the plain,
> Roused by the tyrant band,
> Woke all the mighty land,
> Girded for battle from mountain to main.
> O. W. HOLMES.

THE period from 1775 to 1800, in this country, may truly be termed the period of the Revolution. It witnessed the commencement and close of armed opposition to the British Crown, and the establishment, in America, of a new nationality. In the work of overthrowing the old and establishing a new government, the several provincial towns had a common concern; each supplied its quota and each stood ready to respond to the country's call. Sudbury, on account of its situation and size, bore a prominent part. It was the most populous town in Middlesex County; its territory was extensive, and for a time in close proximity to the seat of war: for these reasons, much was expected of it, and its patriotism was equal to the demand. Before a consideration in detail of the part taken by the town in this stormy period we will notice in brief the causes of the war. The thirteen original States were, for the most part, settled by English emigrants. They loved the mother country, its institutions and laws, and had no desire to throw off allegiance so long as England respected their rights. The two countries had stood together on the fields of successive wars, they had things in common to be shared and kept, — one language set forth their traditions, one literature contained their history and laws. It was natural and desirable that they should have but one flag and sustain one general government. But causes worked to alienate and bring about a final rupture. The colonies were oppressed with excessive taxation, denied the rights of their ancient charters, refused representation in council and the right of petition at court. Misguided and rash officials were placed in their midst, and they were subject, in various other obnoxious ways, to checks on their peace and prosperity.

Before hostilities broke out, protests were repeatedly presented to the Crown against its despotic proceedings; but the colonies had little hope of English concession, hence, great activity prevailed in council, and the people prepared to meet the worst. Resolutions were passed, and such plans laid for aggressive and defensive measures as the exigencies of the province required. In these measures Sudbury had her share. The town was usually present, by delegates, in response to all calls, and her vote was stanch for the continental cause. In 1770, the people manifested their hearty appreciation of the agreement of merchants in Boston " to stop the importation of British goods, and engaged for themselves and all within their influence, to countenance and encourage the same." At an early day, they chose a committee to prepare and present instructions to Peter Noyes, Representative to the General Court, in regard to the Stamp Act, which set forth their opinions very strongly concerning that petty piece of tyranny. Record after record appears on the Town Book, of resolutions and acts that show how posi-

tive the people were in their patriotism, and how pronounced
they were in declaring it.   These are of such a character
that to give a few of them will suffice.

1773.   The Town being met, the committee appointed by the town
to take into consideration the affair relating to the Tea sent here by the
East India Company, reported as follows, viz." —

Taking into Consideration the late Conduct of administration, together with an act of Parliament enabling the East India Company to
export their Teas unto America Free of all Duties and Customs, Regulations and penalties in America as are provided by the revenue Act;
we are justly alarmed at this Detestable Craft and Policy of the Ministry to deprive us of our American Liberties Transmitted to us by our
Worthy Ancestors, at no less expense than that of their Blood and
Treasure.   That price our Renowned Forefathers freely paid, that they
might transmit those Glorious Liberties as a free, full, and fair inheritance to Posterity, which liberties through the Indulgent Smiles of
Heaven, we have possessed in peace and Quietness, till within a few
years Past (Excepting in the reign of the Detestable Stewarts) but now
Behold! the pleasing scene is changed, the British ministry, assisted
by the Inveterate Enemies to American Liberty on this as well as on
the other side of the Atlantick, Combining together to Rob us of our
dear Bought freedom; have Brought us to this sad Dilemma, either to
resolve like men in defense of our just Rights and Liberties, or sink
under the weight of their Arbitrary and unconstitutional measures into
a State of abject Slavery.   Therefore as Freeborn Americans Intitled
to all the immunities, Liberties and Privileges of Freeborn Englishmen,
we look upon ourselves under the Strongest Obligations to use our
utmost Exertions in defense of our just Rights in every constitutional
method within our Power, Even though the Cost of the Defense should
equal that of the purchase.   Therefore resolved

1st That as we are entitled to all the Privileges of British Subjects,
we have an undoubted and exclusive Right to Grant our own monies
for the support of Government and that no Power on Earth has a right
to Tax or make Laws binding us, without our consent.

2dly That the British Parliament laying a Duty on Tea Payable in
America, for the express purpose of Raising a Revenue, is in our
opinion an unjust Taxation, and that the specious method of permitting
the East India Company to export their Teas into the Colonies, has a
direct tendency to rivet the Chain of Slavery upon us.

3dly. That we will lend all the aid and assistance in our Power in
every Rational Method, to hinder the Importations of Teas, so long as
it is subject to a duty; and that this Town are well pleased with, and
highly approve of that Resolution in particular entered into by the
Town of Boston, viz that they will not suffer any Tea to be imported
into that Town while subject to an unrighteous Duty; and it is the

desire and expectation of this Town that said resolution be not relaxed in any Degree; which if it should it would much lesson that confidence (which we hope we may justly say) we have reason to place in that respectable metropolis

4[thly] That the Persons appointed by the East India Company to receive and vend their Teas (by their obstinate refusal to resign their odious Commission) have shown a ready disposition to become the Tools of our Enemies, to oppress and enslave their Native Country, and have manifested such stupidity and wickedness to prefer private Interest to the good of their Country, and therefore can expect no favor or respect from us ; but we leave them to accumulate a load of Infamy, proportionate to their vileness.

5[a] That whoever shall sell, buy, or otherwise use Tea, while subject to and poisened with a Duty, shall be deemed by us Enemies to their Country's welfare ; and shall be treated by us as such. The Town by their Vote Ordered the foregoing resolves to be recorded in the Town Book, and a Copy of the same to be forwarded to the Committee of Correspondence at Boston, with our sincere thanks to that Respectable Town, for their Manly Opposition to every minsterial measure to enslave America.

Thomas Plympton, Ezekiel Howe, John Maynard   }
Sampson Belcher, Phinehas Glezen, Josiah Langdon } Committee

With like spirit the town expressed itself in the following instructions to Peter Noyes, its Representative to the Court:

Sir, you being chosen by the inhabitants of this town to represent them in the Great and General Court or Assembly of their Province, we think proper at this critical Day, when our invaluable rights and privileges are so openly invaded to give you the following instructions.

That you invariably adhere to and steadfastly maintain (so far as you are able) all our Charter Rights and Priveleges and that you do [not] consent to give them or any of them up, on any pretense whatever. That you make use of all your influence, that some effective method be devised and pursued for the restoration of our violated rights and redress of all our grievances. That you use your endeavors that the Governor be prevailed upon to make a grant for the payment of our agent chosen by the Representative body of the Province to present our complaint to the ears of our King

John Maynard.   }
Sampson Belcher. |
John Balcom. |
W[m] Rice, Jr.   } Committee.
Phineas Gleason. |
Aaron Merriam. J

Nov. 14, 1774, the town voted " their approbation of the several measures of the Provincial Congress so far as has been communicated to them." It also voted, at the same meeting, " to choose a committee to observe the conduct of all persons touching the association agreement entered into by the Continental Congress, whose business it shall be to see the articles contained therein are strictly adhered to by the inhabitants of this town."

In 1774, the town chose Thomas Plympton, Capt. Richard Heard, and James Mossman to represent it at the proposed Provincial Congress. The records just quoted are a few from many that show the fidelity of Sudbury to the great cause of freedom in those tumultuous times. It was decided as to the true principle of action, and equally prompt and consistent in carrying it out. Enough has been said to show the town's place in that preparatory period that led to the clash of arms ; but we will quote a paper written by a Revolutionary soldier of Sudbury, which shows the spirit of the age and gives a synopsis of events and the way in which they were viewed by one living in town at the time of their occurrence ; and although, in presenting this paper, we may anticipate some of the events we are about to narrate, yet we think it proper to do this, rather than make a break in a paper so valuable both to local and general history.

" The Causes that led the Colonies to Take up armes Against the Mother Country is proper to be Shown To Prove the Necessity the Colonies were under to resist the oppressive Measures which the Colonies were laid under ; namely the stamp act ; on the Stamp act Being Repaled, an act called the Declaritory act, more oppressive and Hostile to American Rights than any thing that had Preceded it. A Cargo of Tea was consigned To the Friends of the Royal Governor Hutchinson with a duty [of] three pence on a pound, but the inhabitants of Massachusetts [being] Determined not to pay that Duty, a Party of men. in Disguise Entered on bord the Ships and Destroyed Three Hundred and Forty Two Chests of Tea. After these proceedings were received in England The Excitement was very strong

against Massachusetts and Particularly against Boston,
which was considered The seat of Rebellion. A Bill was
then Brought forward that was called the Boston Port Bill;
the Port of Boston was Precluded the Privelege of Landing
and Discharging or Loading and Shiping goods. The words
Whigs and Tories was introduced about this Time. To the
Honor of Sudbury there was Not any of the latter Class to
be found within the limits [of] Sudbury.

"The People were Carfull to Promote men that were
Strongly opposed to British Tireny. The Town of Boston
Passed a vote to stop all importation from Great Britain and
the West Indies.

"Requesting the other Colonies to fall in with the same
Resolve, Many of the inhabitants of . . . signed a Resolve
not to buy any imported goods. Most Noted Men in Boston
that took the lead . . . were James Otis John Hancock
and Samuel Adams; in September 1774 Ninty of the Representatives of Massachusetts Met at Salem and formed
What was Called the Provincial Congress and adjourned to
Concord. Here they chose John Hancock President, and
drew up a Plan for the immediate Defense of the Province
By appointing officers, also Pased a Resolve to get in
Readiness to Compose an Army at the shortest Notis and
called Minute men. The minute company in Sudbury was
commanded by Capt John Nixon afterwards General, the
North Melitia Company was commanded [by] Capt. Aaron
Haynes The South By Capt. Moses Stone, the orders were
for Every man to be supplied with a Gun and Bagnet
Cartrege Box and 36 Rounds, our •Guns to [be] Kept in
Good Repair. The men that were freed by Ege from doing
Military Duty formed themselves into a Company Called the
Alarm Company Commanded by Capt. Jabez Puffer. Train-
ings were as often as once a week the three fall months, in
the winter Not so often. The young Men In the Winter
months made a Practis of calling on their officers Evenings
and going through the Manual Exercise In Barn Flours. I
have exercised many a Night With my Mittens on. Such
was the Patriotic sperit that Reigned in the Brest of Every
True American Never to stain the Glory of our worthy

Ancestors but like them Resolve never to part with our birthright. To be wise in our deliberations and determined in our Exertions for the preservation of our libertys, being Irritated by Repeated Injuries and Striped of our inborn rights and dearest Priveleges; The Present Generation may view those Transactions with surprise; every Rational mind must feel satisfied of the overruling hand of Providence. To bring about the great event here we must Cast our Eyes on the Father of Mercies with a full belief that He would Make his arm beare For us as he did for our Ancestors that we should be Enabled to Defend and Maintain our Rights Boath of a Civil and Religious Nature. With these impressions Strongly impressed in their Hearts on the morning of [the] Ever Memorable 19th of April 1775 Husbands left their wifes and Fathers their daughters Sones their Mothers Brothers their Sisters to Meet a Haughty Foe.

" On this eventful morning an Express From Concoid to Tho⁵ Plympton Esqʳ who was then a Member of the Provintial Congress [stated] that the British were on their way to Concord: In 35 Minites between 4 and 5 oclock in the Morning, the Sexton was immadelly Called on, the bell Ringing and the Discharge of Musket which was to give the alarm. By sunrise the greatest part of the inhabitants were Notified. The morning was Remarkable fine and the Inhabitants of Sudbury Never can make such an important appearance Probably again. Every Countenance appeared to Discover the importance of the event. Sudbury Companies were but a short distance From the North Bridg, when the first opposition was made to the Haughty Enemy. The Dye was Cast and the Torch Lit by which means we Have Becom an independent Nation, and may the present generation and those unborn, preserve unimparred the Libertys, sivel and Religious so long as Time Endures —

" On the 19 of April, I was Runing across a Lot where there was a bend in [the] Road in order to get a Fair Shot, at the Enemy, in company with a Scotchman who was in Braddock's Defeat 19 year Before, after we had Discharged our Guns I observed to the Sco' who appeared very Com-

THE COMMON.
Unitarian Church, Town House and Methodist Church,
Sudbury Centre.

posed I wished I felt as Calm as he appeared to be — [He said] its a Tread to be Larut,

" Before I served through one Campain I Found the Scots Remark to be a just one —

" The old soldiers Name is John Weighton He informed me he had been in seven Battles and this Eight." (Stearns Collection.)

MILITARY PREPARATIONS.

Nov. 14, 1774, " it was voted, that the town recommend to the several companies of militia to meet for the choice of officers for their respective companies, as recommended by the Provincial Congress. Also voted, that a company of militia on the East side, meet on Thursday next at twelve o'clock at the East meeting house in Sudbury, to choose their officers ; and that the companies on the West side to meet at the West meeting house at the same time and for the same purpose."

Besides looking after the militia, the town took measures to form companies of minute men. These, as the name implies, were to hold themselves in readiness to act at a minute's warning. The officers received no commissions, but held their positions by vote of the men. Two such companies were formed, one on each side of the river. There was also a troop of horse composed of men from both precincts. Besides these companies of able-bodied men, there was an alarm company composed of men exempt from military service. The names of the companies were, —

North Militia Co. West Side, Capt. Aaron Haynes 60 men
East Militia Co. East Side. Capt. Joseph Smith, 75 men
South Militia Co. (Lanham District) both Sides. Capt. Moses Stone 92 men.
Troop of Horse. Both Sides. Capt. Isaac Loker. 21 men.
Minute Co. West Side. Capt. John Nixon. 58 men
Minute Co. East Side. Capt. Nathaniel Cudworth. 40 men.

These make, besides the alarm list of Jabez Puffer, six companies — three hundred and forty-eight men — in process of preparation for the coming struggle.

The muster rolls of these companies, as present at the Concord and Lexington battle, have for the most part been preserved, and are here given as found in State and town documents. They may not, in every case, give the names of all who were on the rolls of either militia or minute men in 1774; and they may also contain names which were not properly of the companies in whose rolls they stand. But this may be explained by the fact that these rolls represent those who were in the Lexington and Concord fight, and that the alarm company and troop were mingled with other companies of the town on that memorable day.

A muster Roll of Militia Company and part of an Alarm Company that marched to Cambridge by Concord on the Alarm on the nineteenth of April last under the command of Capt, Aaron Haynes of Sudbury and returning home.

Aaron Haynes Capt,	Thomas Puffer
Daniel Bowker Lieut,	Rufus Parmenter
James Puffer Lieut,	James ——
Joshua Haynes Sergt,	Ebenezer Plympton
Samuel Dakin "	Abel Tower
Samuel Puffer "	Francis Green
Jonathan Haynes "	Jason Haynes
Benjamin Smith Corp.	Joseph Haynes
Ashael Balcom "	Israel Brigham
Hope Brown "	Abel Willis
Ithamon Rice "	Isaac Rice
Phineas Puffer, Clark	John Bemis
Aaron Haynes	Moses Noyes
Abel Maynard, Private	David Moore
Micah Maynard	Abijah Brigham
John Maynard	Israel Haynes
Jonas Haynes	Edmund Parmenter
Isaac Puffer	Henry Smith
Oliver Dakin	Dea Thomas Plympton
Silas How	Lieut Dakin

Sworn to by Capt. Aaron Haynes, Jan. 20, 1776

A muster roll of the Company under the Command of Capt. Joseph Smith, in Col. James Barret's Regiment from Sudbury on April 19th 1775, in persuit of the ministerial Troops

Capt, Joseph Smith	Isaac Damon
Lieut, Josiah Farrar	John Tilton Jr.
Lieut, Ephraim Smith	John Cutting
Ensign Timothy Underwood	Samuel Tilton Jr,
Sergeant William Bent	Amos Addaway
Sergeant Samuel Griffin	—— Travis

Sergeant Robert Cutting
Sergeant John Bruce
Corporal Samuel Tilton
Corporal Nathaniel Smith
Corporal Peter Johnson
Corporal John Merriam
Drumer Thomas Trask
Edmund Sharman
Timothy Bent
Micah Rice
Isaac Gould
John Barney
Jacob Gould
Benjaman Dudley
Zachariah Briant Jr,
Ebenezer Johnson
Jonathan Bent
Simon Belcher
Joel Stone

Roland Bennett
Isaac Stone
John Stone
Isaac Rice Jr,
William Dudley
John Peter
Francis Jones
James Sharmon
Samuel Sharmon
Joseph Goodenow
Josiah Allen
Elisha Cutting
John Dean
James Goodenow
Ephraim Bowker
Jonathan Cutting
James Davis
Jason Parmenter

Middlesex Dec 21ˢᵗ 1775, The above named Joseph Smith made solemn oath to the truth of the above roll, Before me, Moses Gill, Justice Peace.

These Certify that the mens names hereafter annex'd marched on yᵉ 19ᵗʰ of April last to Head Qʳˢ we being under Command of Lt Colᵒ How of Sudbury and Moses Stone Cap˙

Moses Stone Capᵗ
Jonᵃ Rice Lᵗ
Joseph Goodenow 2 Lt.
Joseph Moore Sergᵗ
Ephrᵐ Carter Corpˡ
David How
Benjᵃ Berry
Jonᵃ Carter
Elijah Goodnow
David How
Ezekˡ How jr.
Jonas Wheeler
Isaac Lincoln

Thoˢ Ames
Thomas Burbank
Nathˡ Bryant
Israel Maynard
Thoˢ Carr junʳ
Isaac Moore
Uriah Moore
Abner Walker
Wᵐ Walker
Abel Parmenter.
Danˡ Osburn
Thoˢ Derumple

The above named were out four days.

Peter Haynes
Lᵗ Elisha Wheeler
Aaron Goodnow
Thomas Walker
Ebenʳ Burbank

Thoˢ Derumple
Nathˡ Brown
Uriah Hayden
Israel Willis
Calven Clark

The above named were out three days.

Province of the Massachusetts D^r to Isaac Locker and the men under me by name in ye Colony for service done in defence of the Country on ye 19th day of April to ye 21st of the same when the alarm at Concord. agreable to the General Courts Order — made up this Acco^t

Isaac Locker	Tim^o Sharmon
Lt Oliver Noyes	Danl Moore J^r
Q^r Mr Ja^s Puffer	David Curtis
Čorp^l Ja^s Noyes	Zach^h Heard
Corp Jesse Gibbs	Jacob Jones
Corp^l Abel Smith	Nathl Knowlton
Da^l Woo^d Moore	Jonas Rice
Eph · Moore	Nathan Stearns
Jonas Wheeler	Micah Greaves
Jesse Mossman	Nathl Jenison
Rufus Bent	Steph^n Locker
Jason Bent	Asaph Travis
W Wyman	Jonas Locker
Jo^s Rutter	Simon Newton
Wm Noyes	David Heard

A List of a Company of Minute Men under the command of Capt. John Nixon, in Col Abijah Pierce's Regiment who entered the service April 19th 1775

David Moore Lieut	Abel Holden "
Ashael Wheeler 2^d Lieut	Hopestill Brown Corp.
Micah Goodnow Serg^t	Jesse Moore "
Elijah Willis "	Uriah Wheeler "
Jeremiah Robbins "	William Moore

PRIVATES.

Joseph Balcom	Rueben Haynes
Philemon Brown	Joshua Haynes
Samuel Brigham	Caleb Wheeler
Samuel Cutting	John Weighten
Asher Cutler	Simon Kingman
William Dun	Israel Willis
Aaron Ames	Hopestill Willis
Robert Ames	Ebenezer Wood
Eliab Moore	Jonas Holden
Uriah Moore	Elisha Wheeler
Isaac Moore	Daniel Loring
John Moore	Thadeus Moore
Josiah Richardson	William Maynard
Nathan Read	Daniel Maynard
Charles Rice	John Shirley
James Rice	Peter Smith
Ezra Smith	Abraham Thompson

Samuel Gleason	Daniel Weight
Thomas Goodenow	Nathaniel Rice
Jesse Goodenow	Daniel Putman
William Goodenow	Micah Grant

Sworn to by Lt. Asahel Wheeler, Feb. 3, 1776.

A muster Role of the Minute Company under the command of Capt. Nathaniel Cudworth in Col. Abijah Pierce's Regiment.

Nathaniel Cudworth Capt.	Samuel Pollard
Thadeus Russel, Lieut.	Daniel Rice
Nathaniel Maynard Ensign	Samuel Whitney
Nathaniel Reeves Sergent	Benjamin Adams
Jonathan Hoar "	Samuel Curtis
Caleb Moulton "	Richard Heard Jr
Thomas Rutter "	Samuel Bent
Joseph Willington Corp.	Samuel Haynes
Thadeus Bond "	Joseph Nicolls
David Clough "	William Grout
Joshua Kendall "	Samuel Merriam
John Trask. Drummer	David Underwood
Phineas Gleason Private	Naum Dudley
Ebenezer Dudley	James Phillips
John Noyes Jr	Edmund Rice Jr.
Timothy Underwood	Nathaniel Parmenter
Peter Britnell	David Damon
Zebediah Farrar	David Rice
Jonathan Parmenter Jr	Edward How
Jonathan Wesson	Timothy Sharmon

Sworn to by Nathaniel Cudworth, Feb. 21, 1776.

In 1776, the town "voted to pay each of the minute men one shilling and sixpence for training one half day in a week, 4 hours to be esteemed a half day, after they were enlisted and until called into actual service or dismissed; and the Captains 3 shilling and Lieutenants 2 shillings and six pence and the ensign 2 shillings."

The foregoing muster rolls represent about one-fifth of the entire population. The number in actual service at the Concord and Lexington fight three hundred and two. The following report shows to what extent these companies were equipt.

" Sudbury March ye 27th 1775:

" The Return of the Severall Companys of Militia and Minute in s^d Town viz.

" Capt. Moses Stone's Company — 92 men of them, 18 no guns. at Least one third part ye forelocks unfit for Sarvis others wais un a quipt.

" Capt. Aaron Hayns Company — 60 men weel provided With Arms the most of them Provided with Bayonets or hatchets a boute one quarter Part with Catrige Boxes.

" Capt. Joseph Smith's Company consisting of —— —— 75 able Bodied men forty well a quipt twenty Promis to find and a quip themselves Emedetly fifteen no guns and other wais un a quipt

" The Troop Capt. Isaac Locer (Loker) — 21 Besides what are on the minit Role well a quipt.

" Returned by Ezekiel How. Left^n Con^l " (Stearns Collection.)

It is not strange that, at the time this report was given, the troops had not been fully equipped. It was not easy to provide for so many at once, but the following record may indicate that the town had been endeavoring to supply the deficiency since the preceding fall, Oct. 3, 1774.

To Capt. Ezekiel How for 20 guns and Bayonets	27— 0— 2
600 pounds Lead	8—16— 0
300 french Flynts	[9 or] 19— —11
Chest for the arms and carting them	7— 2— 2

Probably before the 19th of April they were fairly equipped for service, as there is among the town papers a bill to one of the minute companies for ammunition that the town had supplied. Each man mentioned had, for the most part, received about a pound of powder and two pounds of balls for which a charge was made of one pound, one shilling.

In the matter of military drill, the men showed a spirit of perseverance which indicates their expectation of rough work. It was by no dress parade or review on some gala occasion when, with burnished muskets and uniforms gay and bright, they became proficient in the art of defence, but

on the cold barn floor in their homespun suits, with the mute
cattle their only spectators, that these men were fitting for
work, and zeal for their object was the tocsin that mustered
the clan. To show the regularity with which the minute
men met for drill as the crisis approached, we will present
Capt. John Nixon's minute company's call roll, which is still
preserved among the old documents of Sudbury. We find
in it but six blanks; showing an average of only one absentee
each night. We might expect that, when the call of the 19th
of April came, these men would be present and ready for
work.

A Call Roll of Capt Jn° Nixon's Company of Minut Men. They
Inlisted March ye 13th

	March ye 13th 1775	March ye 20	March ye 27	April 3	April ye 10th	Do ye 17th
Jn° Nixon Capt.	1	1	1	1	1	1
David Moor Lieut.	1	1	1	1	1	1
Asehel Wheeler Do	1	1	1		1	1
Josiah Langdon Clarke	1	1	1	1	1	1
Micah Goodenow Sergt	1	1	1	1	1	1
Augusta Moor Do	1	1	1		1	1
Elijah Willis Do	1	1	1	1	1	1
Jeremh Robbins Do	1	1	1	1	1	1
Hopel Brown Corpl	1	1	1	1	1	1
Jesse Moor Do	1	1	1	1	1	1
Uriah Wheeler Do	1	1	1	1	1	1
Willm Moor Do	1	1	1	1	1	1
Daniel Putnam Drum	1	1	1	1	1	
Caleb Brown Phiffe	1	1	1	1	1	1
Joseph Nixon Do	1	1	1	1	1	1
Joseph Balcum	1	1	1	1	1	1
Philn Brown	1	1	1	1	1	1
Saml Brigham	1	1	1	1	1	1
Hosea Brigham	1	1	1		1	
Saml Cutting	1	1	1	1	1	1
Asher Cutler	1	1	1	1	1	1
Wm Dun	1	1	1	1	1	1
Aaron Emes Jr.	1	1	1	1	1	1
Robert Emes	1	1	1	1	1	1
Danl Goodenow	1	1	1	1	1	1
Saml Gleason	1	1	1	1	1	1
Thos Goodenow	1	1	1	1	1	1
Jesse Goodenow	1	1	1	1	1	1
Wm Goodenow	1	1	1	1	1	1

	March ye 13th 1775	March ye 20	March ye 27	April 3	April ye 10th	Do ye 17th
Reuben Haynes	1	1	1	1	1	1
Joshua Haynes	1	1	1	1	1	1
Jonas Holden Jr	1	1	1	1	1	1
Abel Holden	1	1	1	1	1	1
Simeon Ingersol	1	1	1	1	1	1
Daniel Loring	1	1	1	1	1	1
Thadeus Moor	1	1	1	1	1	1
Wm Maynard	1	1	1	1	1	1
Daniel Maynard	1	1	1	1	1	1
Hezekiah Moor	1	1	1	1	1	1
Eliab Moor	1	1	1	1	1	1
Uriah Moor	1	1	1	1	1	1
Isaac Moor Jr.	1	1	1	1	1	1
John Moor	1	1	1	1	1	1
Josiah Richardson	1	1	1	1	1	1
Nathaniel Reed	1	1	1	1	1	1
Charles Rice	1	1	1	1	1	1
Oliver Rice	1	1	1	1	1	1
Jonas Rice	1	1	1	1	1	1
Asahel Reed	1	1	1	1	1	1
Ezra Smith	1	1	1	1	1	1
John Sheirley	1	1	1	1	1	1
Peter Smith	1	1	1	1	1	1
Abel Thomson	1	1	1	1	1	1
Daniel Weight	1	1	1	1	1	1
Caleb Wheeler	1	1	1	1	1	1
John Weighton	1	1	1	1		1
Elisha Wheeler	1	1	1	1	1	1
Israel Willis	1	1	1	1	1	1
Hopestil Willis	1	1	1	1	1	1
Ebenezer Wood	1	1	1	1	1	1

It was becoming more and more evident that a collision with the King's forces was close at hand. A considerable quantity of Continental supplies had been deposited at Concord; there also was a centre of strong patriotic influence; at that place, therefore, the blow was liable to fall first. March 29, a report came that the British were about to proceed to that place. The Committee of Safety for the Province met at Cambridge, and ordered the removal therefrom of stores. The order was carried out and the stores sent in several directions. To Sudbury were sent fifty barrels of beef, one hundred of flour, twenty casks of rice, fifteen hogsheads of molasses, ten hogsheads of rum, and five hundred candles, fifteen thousand canteens, fifteen thousand iron pots; the spades, pickaxes, bill-hooks, axes, hatchets, crows, wheel-barrows, and several other articles were to be divided, one-third to remain in Concord, one-third to be sent to Sudbury, one-third to Stow, and one thousand iron pots were to be sent to Worcester. (Shattuck.)

The rumor at this time proved false, yet a little later the event came about. General Gage, who was stationed in Boston as Commander-in-chief of the British troops, took measures to send a detachment to Concord for the destruction of Continental stores. For the accomplishment of this purpose he sent out spies to examine the land. Two of these secret messengers, Captain Brown and Ensign D'Bernicre, went to Worcester in February, and to Concord, March 20. They went by way of Weston and Sudbury, stopping in the former town at the Jones Tavern, which still stands on the main street of Weston, and passed through East Sudbury by way of the South bridge. Having received the report of these spies, the British prepared to advance. General Gage detached eight hundred of light infantry, grenadiers and marines from the ten regiments under his command, and, on pretence of instructing them in a new military exercise, took them from regular duty on April 15. His plan was for the troops to cross Charles River by night, and at daybreak be far on their way toward Concord and thus take the place by surprise. But there were those who were watching his wary course, and a sly, swift courier was to precede him on his way. A previous arrangement had been made by which a lantern was to be displayed in the belfry of the old North Church when the British began their march. Paul Revere, at the signal, was to start with the news and proclaim it from place to place. About that messenger, his mission, his midnight ride, it is unnecessary for us to relate. The oft-told tale is very familiar, how Paul Revere went forth and "spread the alarm through every Middlesex village and farm."

THE MUSTERING AND MARCH.

The news thus started by Paul Revere reached Sudbury between three and four o'clock in the morning. As the town is eight miles southwestward of Concord, intelligence of the approaching column was received later than at towns on the Boston and Concord highway. But, notwithstanding the distance, the sun was not yet arisen when the summons arrived in town, and then followed a scene of activity unparalleled in the annals of Sudbury. The course taken by the various companies to reach Concord was, probably, not the same, as they started from different parts of the town. Two companies from the West Side — the minute company and the North Militia — would go by the road through North Sudbury, while the East Side men would, most likely, go by way of Lincoln. Captain Nixon's company started from the West Side meeting-house. The companies of Nixon and Haynes designed to cross the Concord River by way of the old South bridge, or " Wood's bridge," on the site of the county bridge near the Fitchburg Railroad. From doing this, however, they were deterred by an order which reached them when about half a mile away, and by which they marched on to the North bridge. The appearance of this host of town's people, on an errand like that before them, must have been imposing and sad. The gathering and the start were enough of themselves to stir the idlest spectator, and move the most indifferent soul. The morning was peaceful and lovely. Nature was advanced for the season. The fields were green with the grass and grain which even waved in the April breeze, and the buds were bursting, prophetic of early spring. But, in strange contrast, the souls of the people were stirred as if swept by a tempest. The appearance of that hurrying pageant as it swept through the town was at once solemn, strange, and sublime. Their haste was too great to admit of a measured or dignified pace. They were impatient to arrive at the front. Daniel Putnam may be excused if no drum taps are heard save the " long roll " at the very start. Caleb Brown may put by his " Phiffe " until he hears from Luther Blanchard, at the old

north bridge, the strains of " The White Cockade." The
music of the morning was made by the quickened heart-
throbbing in those patriotic breasts, as in double-quick they
strode over the old north road to be on hand at the approach of the foe. Along the route, mothers and children
appeared, to catch a glimpse of the loved ones, who fast
flying were soon lost to view. A kiss lovingly cast into the
morning air, the passing benediction of word or look, and
the crowd rushed by. The loved ones were left to sad
conjecture as to what the dread issue might be. We have
heard a great-granddaughter of Captain Nixon say that she
has been told by her grandmother that a messenger came at
night to the house and said, " Up, up! the red-coats are up
as far as Concord!" that Mr. Nixon at once started off on
horseback, and that sometime during the day Mrs. Nixon
went out of the house, which was on Nobscot hillside, and
putting her ear to the ground could hear the sound of distant
guns.

The north militia and minute company, as we have stated,
designed to reach Concord village by way of the old south
bridge, but when about half a mile from it were ordered to
proceed to the north bridge by Col. James Barrett, the
commander of the minute regiment, whose son Stephen had
been sent to convey the message to the approaching companies. By obeying this order, the Sudbury companies
would join a force already assembled on the north side of
the village, and also avoid speedy contact with the British
guard that already held the south bridge.

When the British arrived at Concord by way of the
Lexington road, which leads from the easterly into the town,
Colonel Smith, the commander, made a threefold division
of his force of eight hundred men. The light infantry were
sent in two detachments to guard the bridges and destroy
the stores on the village outskirts, while the grenadiers and
marines he detained with himself and Major Pitcairn at the
centre. In the execution of this plan, Capt. Lawrence
Parsons took possession of the north bridge, Capt. Mundy
Pole did the same at the south bridge, and each sent
detachments from their force to destroy Continental stores.

The Americans, meanwhile, were powerless to prevent this occurrence. As yet, but comparatively few Continental troops had arrived. It was only about seven or eight o'clock in the morning, and but a few hours since the general alarm. They knew not positively about the work at Lexington Common, nor that the British had come with a deadly intent. They wanted to know just what was right, and waited for strength to enforce the right; while thus waiting, they withdrew over the river beyond the north bridge. To this vicinity were the Sudbury men sent. But there was, at least on the part of one of the company, a reluctance to turn from their more direct course. They were in the country's highway, and this one person, perhaps, felt like Captain Davis of Acton, who before leaving that town said, "I have a right to go to Concord on the King's highway, and I intend to go if I have to meet all the British troops in Boston." The person referred to as reluctant to turn from his course was Deacon Josiah Haynes, who was eighty years old. It is stated that he was " urgent to attack the British at the south bridge, dislodge them, and march into the village by that route." Had his opinion prevailed, the battle might have been then and there, and the old south rather than the old north bridge have been the place of note forever. But the south bridge was avoided. In accordance with Colonel Barrett's command, Captains Nixon and Haynes with Lieut. Col. Ezekiel How started, as we have stated, for the old north bridge.

When at the South bridge they were on the westerly side of Concord village, while the North bridge was a little to the north of east. Their way, therefore, was by something of a circuitous course ; and, to reach the point to which they were ordered, they were to pass the house of Colonel Barrett, a mile and a half north-west of the village, where Captain Parsons with three British companies were destroying Continental stores. When the Sudbury soldiers came within sight of Colonel Barrett's house they came to a halt. Before them were the British engaged in their mischievous work. Gun carriages had been collected and piled together to be burned, the torch already had been applied, and the residence of their Colonel had been ransacked. They halted, and Colonel How exclaimed, "If any blood has been shed not one of the rascals shall escape!" and, disguising himself, he rode on to ascertain the truth. It was, probably, not far from nine o'clock when this event took place. This indicates the celerity with which the Sudbury troops had moved. From the morning alarm, by which the minute men met at the West Side meeting-house, until the foregoing transaction but about five hours had passed, and, meanwhile, the mustering, the march, the arrival. While the Regulars were engaged in their destructive work at Colonel Barrett's, the Provincials were concentrating their forces in preparation for what was to come. Their place of gathering was at Punkatasset Hill, about a mile north of the Concord meeting-house. While here, they increased their forces by repeated arrival of troops. Says Drake, "Meanwhile," that is while the British were engaged at Colonel Barrett's, "the Provincials on Punkatasset were being constantly reinforced by the militia of Westford, Littleton, Acton, Sudbury, and other neighboring towns, until the whole body numbered about four hundred and fifty men, who betrayed feverish impatience at playing the part of idle lookers on while the town was being ransacked; but, when flames were seen issuing in different directions, they could no longer be restrained. A hurried consultation took place, at the end of which it was determined to march into the town at all hazards, and if resisted to "treat their assailants as enemies." Colonel Barrett told the troops to advance. From Punkatasset they moved to Major Buttricks, but a short distance above the North bridge, and from Major Buttricks they marched to the bridge where the Americans and English met face to face. The circumstances at the bridge are too familiar to need any narration by us. The British attempted to remove the planks, a remonstrance was made and the work ceased. The Provincials advanced with rapid steps; when a few rods away a single shot was fired by the foe, which was at once followed by a volley. The first shot wounded two of the Americans, and the volley killed two — Davis and Hosmer of Acton. The order then came for the Provincials to fire. It was obeyed, and three British soldiers were slain, besides several officers and four soldiers wounded. Then came the retreat and pursuit. Whether or not the companies of Nixon and Haynes had joined the Provincials at Punkatasset when the command to move forward came, we leave the reader to judge for himself. Drake implies that they had ; some circumstances may also favor this theory, for, after leaving Colonel Barrett's, they would likely hasten to join the main force, which was not far distant. But other things would lead us to conclude that they had not caught up with the column when it reached the bridge.

Shattuck says, " Two companies from Sudbury under How, Nixon and Haynes came to Concord, and having received orders from a person stationed at the entrance of the town, for the purpose of a guide, to proceed to the North instead of the South Bridge, arrived near Col. Barrett's just before the British soldiers retreated." The same author, after speaking of what we have just narrated of Lieutenant-Colonel How, states, " Before proceeding far, the firing began at the Bridge, and the Sudbury companies pursued the retreating British." From these statements and facts, we may infer this, — that these companies passed the British at Colonel Barrett's and pushed on to meet the force at the bridge, that before they joined it the foe made his attack and that they joined in the hot pursuit. This theory accords with the statement that we have quoted before, as made by a survivor of the fight, which is that "Sudbury Companies were but a short distance from the North Bridge when the first Opposition was made to the Haughty Enemy."

Thus, to an extent, have we traced the course of two Sudbury companies during a part of that eventful day. As to the others, it is supposed they attacked the British at different points along the line of the retreat. The men who came from East Sudbury would, as we have hitherto said, be likely to march through Lincoln to Concord. If so, they would be likely to strike the British retreat; there it is that we hear of them. Two encounters, at least, are mentioned in which East Sudbury soldiers were engaged. To rightly understand how and where these engagements took place, let us notice the movements of the British after the events that transpired at the old North bridge. Having fired on the Americans as they approached the bridge from the opposite bank, by which fire two Acton minute men fell, and having received the Provincial fire in return, by which three of the English were slain, Lieutenant Gould of the regulars withdrew his shattered guard to the village. Three signal guns having been fired by the British just before their troops fired at the bridge, all the distant detachments came in. Captain Parsons hurried his companies from Colonel Barrett's to the old North bridge; and, seeing the havoc that had been made with Gould's guard and their dead comrades upon the bank, " they were seized with a panic and ran with great speed to join the main force." Captain Pole withdrew his companies from the old South bridge, and then Colonel Smith began to retreat towards Boston. But it was not only a retreat but a rout. The battle at the bridge was but the beginning of aggressive work. The foe were followed and hard pushed from point to point. At the cross-roads they met fresh arrivals of Provincial troops. The stone walls and stumps were coverts from which they directed their fire. In addition to an almost continuous engagement, occasional encounters occurred which were exceptionally sharp and severe. In two of these severe encounters the soldiers from East Sudbury were engaged, — one at Merriam's Corner, the other at Hardy's Hill.

The action at Merriam's Corner occurred at about half-past twelve. Three circumstances concurred to bring about and make severe this conflict. First, there was a junction of roads, the one from Bedford meeting that leading to Lexington along which the English marched. By this road had come reinforcements from Reading, Chelmsford, Bedford and Billerica. To this point, also, had come some Provincials across the great fields in the direction of the old North bridge. Another circumstance that made the fight sharp was that here the British massed their forces because of the lay of the land. In their march from Concord, which was about a mile thus far, the British threw out a part of their infantry to serve as a guard to their flanks and to protect the main body as it marched on the road. These flankers moved along the dry upland on the right of the road, as it curves gently from Concord village, until they reached Merriam's Corner where they joined the troops in the road, in order to avoid the moist land by the wayside, and pass the dry causeway to the highway beyond. As this flank guard thus joined the main force it gave the Provincials, who as we have indicated were there gathered in force, an opportunity which they were not slow to make use of. They poured upon the regulars a destructive fire. " Now and here began," says Drake, " that long and terrible conflict unexampled in the Revolution for its duration and ferocity, which for fifteen miles tracked the march of the regular troops with their blood." A company from East Sudbury were in time for this second conflict. This, doubtless, was the one commanded by Joseph Smith. Rev. Mr. Foster, an historian of 1775, says of this conflict: " Before we came to Merriam's Hill we discovered the enemy's flank guard of about eighty or a hundred men, who on the retreat from Concord kept the height of the land, the main body being in the road. The British troops and the Americans at that time were equally distant from Merriam's Corner. About twenty rods short of that place the Americans made a halt. The British marched down the hill with a very slow but steady step without a word being spoken that could be heard. Silence reigned on both sides. As soon as the British gained the main road and passed a small bridge near the common, they faced about suddenly, and fired a volley of musketry upon us. They overshot and no one to my knowledge was injured by the fire. The fire was immediately returned by the Americans, and two British soldiers fell dead at a little distance from each other in the road near the brook. Several of the officers were wounded, including Ensign Lester." The other engagement in which the Sudbury soldiers are especially noticed was at Hardy's Hill, a short distance beyond. One narrator has spoken of it as a spirited affair, where one of the Sudbury companies, Captain Cudworth, came up and vigorously attacked the enemy.

It is interesting that we can thus trace our soldiers and know so much of their whereabouts and what they did on that memorable day. An incident of the fight was related to the writer by the late Mr. Josiah Haynes when eighty-five years old. He said that his grandfather, Josiah Haynes, one of the militia of Sudbury at the Concord fight, captured a gun from a British sergeant. The Briton was with a squad of soldiers a little removed from the main body, probably a part of the flank guard before mentioned. Mr. Haynes lay concealed behind a stone wall with some comrades who soon left him alone. As the squad approached, he thought they were coming directly upon him, but, as the main body followed a curve in the road, the squad turned also. With this movement, Mr. Haynes placed his gun on the wall, and on firing the sergeant fell. Mr. Haynes sprang and seized the sergeant's gun and tried to tear off his belt and cartridge box, but these last he did not secure. The squad, but a few rods away, turned and fired. The balls whistled about him, but he escaped unhurt. It would be interesting to know more of the incidents and adventures of our soldiers on that April day, but time has made havoc with tradition and the records are scant. Years ago the last survivor of the Revolution died, and years before, they were scattered, many of them into other towns and other States. But the fragments of tradition that have floated down from that far-off period are all the more valuable because they are few.

THE LOSS.

During the day Sudbury sustained the loss of two men, Deacon Josiah Haynes and Asahel Reed. Joshua Haynes was wounded. Deacon Haynes was eighty years old. He was killed by a musket bullet at Lexington. He belonged to the old Haynes family of Sudbury, where his descendants still live. He was one of the original signers of the West Precinct Church Covenant, and was made deacon May 24, 1733. He was buried in the Old Burying Ground, Sudbury Centre. The grave is marked by a simple slate stone. Mr. Asahel Reed was of Captain Nixon's minute men. His name is found on that company's call roll to which we have before referred; it is left out after the battle, probably because after his death the name was stricken from the list. He belonged to the old Reed family of Sudbury, whose progenitor, Joseph Reed, settled at Lanham about 1656. Probably he was also buried in the old ground at Sudbury Centre. Mrs. Joseph Reed, a member of the same family and grandmother of the writer, said many years ago that the body of Mr. Reed was brought to Sudbury. So, although no stone has been found which marks the grave, he doubtless rests somewhere in the old burying-ground at the centre, which was the only one at that time in the West Precinct. Joshua Haynes, who was wounded, may have been one of Captain Nixon's minute men or one of the militia of Captain Haynes. The same name is on each company's muster roll; but the one in the latter was sergeant while the one wounded is mentioned without any title. Lieut. Elisha Wheeler, whose horse was shot under him, and Thomas Plympton, Esq., who had a bullet put through the fold of his coat, were both volunteers on horseback.

After the fight the soldiers showed no undue haste to return, but some of them lingered from three days to a month to repel attack or serve their country in whatever way it might require; and, when at length they returned to their homes, it was only, in the case of some of them, to bid the loved ones good-by and then go away again to engage the foe.

CHAPTER XXI.

1775-1800.

Revolutionary War. — Sudbury Soldiers at Bunker Hill. — Muster Rolls of Captains Russell, Moore and Haynes. — Battle of Bunker Hill. — Position and Service of the Regiments of Colonels Nixon and Brewer. — Number of Casualties. — The Siege of Boston. — List of Men in Two Months Service. — List of Men in Colonel Whitney's Regiment. — Government Storehouses at Sand Hill. — Service outside the State. — List of Officers in Sudbury Companies in 1776. — List of Men in Capt. Aaron Haynes's Company. — Men in Captain Wheeler's Company at Ticonderoga; in Colonel Robinson's Regiment, in Colonel Read's Regiment. — Supplementary List. — Soldiers at Ticonderoga in 1776; in Captain Wheeler's Company, Captain Craft's Company, Cap'ain Edgell's Company, Captain Aaron Haynes's Company. — Canada Campaign. — New York Campaign. — Men Enlisted for Three Years in 1777. — Guard Roll. — Pay Roll. — List of Two Months Men in 1777. — List of Three Months Men in 1777. — Names of Sudbury Captains and Companies in the Field in 1778. — Captain Maynard's Company. — Captain Wheeler's Company. — Captain Moulton's Company. — Captain Haynes's Company. — Captain Bowker's Company. — Prices Paid for Enlistment in 1780.

> Few were the numbers she could boast;
> But every freeman was a host,
> And felt as though himself were he
> On whose sole arm hung victory.
>
> MONTGOMERY.

SUDBURY was represented by three companies at the battle of Bunker Hill. These were commanded by Sudbury captains and made up mainly of Sudbury citizens. The town also furnished three regimental officers, — Col. John Nixon, Major Nathaniel Cudworth and Adj. Abel Holden, Jr. Capt. John Nixon of the minute men was promoted to the rank of colonel, and was authorized, April 27, to receive nine sets of beating papers. Capt. Nathaniel Cudworth was made major in the regiment of Col. Jonathan Brewer, who received enlistment papers April 24, and Abel Holden, Jr., was made Colonel Nixon's adjutant. The Sudbury men who served in these companies are as follows : —

A list of Captain Russell's company in Colonel Brewer's regiment.

Thaddeus Russel Capt.
Nathan Tuckerman Lieut.
Nathan Reeves Ens.
Sergt Josiah Wellington
　"　Thomas Rutter
　"　Thad Bond

Corp. Joshua Kendall
　"　David Rice
　"　David Damon
Drumer Thomas Trask
Fifer Nathan Bent
　"　David Smith

PRIVATES.

Ephraim Allen
Longley Bartlett
Rolon Bennet
Peter Brintnall
Timothy Bent
Samuel Curtis
Edward Sorce [Vorce]
Jacob Speen
Ephram Sherman
Samuel Tilton
Asa Travis
David Underwood
Jonathan Wesson
Lemuel Whitney
Samuel Sherman
Nahum Dudley
Oliver Damon

William English
Ambros Furgison
William Grout
Elisha Harrington
Richard Heard
William Mallet
Samuel Merriam
Cuff Nimra
Benjamin Pierce
Nath^{el} Parmenter
James Phillips
Samuel Pollard
Rufus Parmenter
Edward Rice
Martin Rourke
Denis Ryan
Amos Silleway

A return of Captain Moor's company in the fifth regiment, commanded by Col. John Nixon, Sept. 30, 1775.

David Moore, Capt
Micah Goodenow 1st Lieut
Jona Hill, 2ond Lieut Framingham

SARGENTS.

Elijah Willis
Hopestill Brown
Jesse Moore

Daniel Loring
Daniel Wait
Uriah Wheeler

CORPORALS.

James Rice
Oliver Rice

Joseph Balcom
Aaron Eames Jun.

DRUMMER AND FIFER.

Ebenezer Boutwell } Framingham
Thomas Nixon

PRIVATES.

Nathaniel Bryant	Thadeus Moore
Aaron Emes	Jesse Mostman [Mossman]
Benjᵃ Bennet	Israel Maynard
Samuel Cutting	William Maynard
Micah Goodenow	Nathan Rice
Ephraim Goodenow	Israel Willis
Lemuel Goodenow	Ephraim Whitney
Asahel Gibbs	Abel Thompson
Uriah Hunt	Ezra Smith
Isaac Moore	Charles Rice
Eliab Moore	

Total in the Co. 48.   From Sudbury 33.

A list of names of the officers and soldiers in Captain Haynes's company in Colonel Brewer's regiment.

Aaron Haynes Capt	Cop Daniel Putnam
Mathias Mossman 2ond Lieut	Drummer Aaron Haynes
Sergᵗ Josiah Moore	Fifer Naham Haynes
Cop John Weighting	

PRIVATES.

John Bemis	Abel Parmenter
Nathan Cutter	Asa Putnam
Porter Cuddy	Ephraim Puffer
James Durumple	John Brewer
Joseph Dakin	Isaac Rice
Joseph Green	Aaron Mossman
Francis Green	Joshua Haynes

Prospect Hill, Oct. 6, 1775

AARON HAYNES, Capt

Total in the Co. 47.   From Sudbury 21.

The following names found in the Stearns Collection, as being in the eight months service, we give in connection with the foregoing lists.

Jonas Haynes	Jeremiah Robins
John Stone	Benj Berry [or Barry]
Caleb Wheeler	John Shirley
Hezekiah Moore	Wm Dun

Total number in these three muster rolls is one hundred and fifty-two. Of these, one hundred and four were from Sudbury, and only the latter have been here given except when designated. Lieut. Nathaniel Russell re-enlisted a part of the East Sudbury company and reported for duty April 24. Capt. Aaron Haynes went into service with his company May 3. These companies were in the regiments of Colonels Nixon and Brewer, which did valuable service in the engagement of June 17. A consideration of the plan of that battle and something of its history will show where these regiments were, what they did, and the conduct of the Sudbury soldiers.

BATTLE OF BUNKER HILL.

On the 16th of June, the Americans, under command of Colonel Prescott, to the number of about one thousand men repaired at night to what was then called Breed's Hill, to fortify the place by earthworks. Their object was to prevent the occupation of Charlestown by General Gage, who had been reinforced by about ten thousand men. Through the still hours of the night they plied the pickaxe and spade, and at daybreak General Gage, from his quarters in Boston, surveyed the newly-made works with surprise. British batteries soon opened their fire from ship and shore, yet steadily the provincials worked on. Gage summoned his officers in council, and it was determined to take the place by storm. Immediately, columns were formed and set in motion, boats were procured to carry troops to the Charlestown shore, and a scene of general activity set in. Meanwhile, the Americans were also astir forming plans to resist the assault. Reinforcements were ordered to the Charlestown peninsula, and long lines of troops filed from the neighboring encampment to join their comrades at the hill. The march was attended with hazard, for British batteries swept the way, and ranks broke into detachments and squads, rather than pass the ordeal in closely formed lines. Among those who marched over this perilous way were the regiments of Brewer and Nixon, and they arrived on the field in season to form for the fight.

When the regiments had all arrived on the Charlestown peninsula, an almost unbroken line stretched along from the Charles River on the south to the Mystic River on the north. The places of the respective regiments were as follows: Prescott held the redoubt near the summit with about one hundred and sixty-three men; a breastwork to the northerly, near this, was occupied by men of Prescott, Bridge and Frye; on the left, to the northwesterly or north, were the regiments of Brewer, Nixon, Knowlton and Stark; while on the right, to the southeasterly or south, were the regiments of Wyman and Robinson with about three hundred men. Sudbury soldiers were thus placed on the left of the line to the northerly of the Bunker Hill summit. Between the breastwork and redoubt, and the Mystic River or left flank on the northerly, there was, for a time, an unfilled space. By this way, the foe had only to advance, attack the American works in the rear, and the place was captured and retreat cut off. General Putnam discovered this gap in time, and ordered troops to man it at once. Stark, Knowlton and Reed took their stand on the north by the Mystic, Brewer and Nixon on the south of them. Thus was filled the hitherto unprotected gap, which, if neglected, had invited the foe, and caused speedy and most disastrous defeat.

The British, knowing the importance of the position thus held, brought against it a formidable force. This was led by Sir William Howe in person. Some of the troops had been recently at the Concord and Lexington fight. They were likely eager to recover their prestige or avenge the fate of their fallen friends. Furthermore, the protection of the Provincials at this point was weak; no entrenchments were there to protect them from the foe. The most favored had but a few rude improvised works, hastily constructed after they arrived on the ground, but the position of the regiment in which the Sudbury men served was the most exposed of any in that poorly protected column. A part of the line had not the slightest protection whatever. The only attempt that was made to construct a breastwork was by the gathering of some newly-mown hay that was scattered about the place. But they were prevented from the completion of even such a slight breastwork as this. The foe advanced and they were compelled to desist. But no exposure to the fire of well-disciplined, veteran troops, and no lack of breast-work protection led those brave Middlesex colonels and companies to turn from or abandon this important position. It was enough to know that there was an unguarded gap. The practised eye of Col. John Nixon, who had so often seen service in the old French wars, doubtless saw at a glance what the case required, and knowing the need took measures to meet it. Says Drake, " Brewer and Nixon immediately directed their march for the undefended opening so often referred to between the rail fence and earthwork. They also began the construction of a hay breastwork, but when they had extended it to within thirty rods of Prescott's line the enemy advanced to the assault. The greater part of these two battalions stood and fought here without cover throughout the action, both officers and men displaying the utmost coolness and intrepidity under fire." The same author also says of Gardiner, Nixon and Brewer, " Braver officers did not unsheathe a sword on this day; their battalions were weak in numbers, but under the eye and example of such leaders invincible." He states that, " with about four hundred and fifty men, they stood in the gap with Warren and Pomeroy at their head." Just before the attack, Putnam gave the order not to fire until they could see the whites of the enemy's eyes. When the foe was fairly in range the Provincials opened fire. The lines blazed with a hot discharge; whole ranks were swept down before it, men dropped on the right hand and left; no mortal could withstand that withering storm; it was an unerring, death-dealing discharge. Howe's attendants were struck down at his very side, and for a time he stood almost alone. He gave the word for retreat, and his shattered remnant withdrew from the field. He had failed to break the ranks of these left line regiments, and hence the redoubt was still safe from an attack in the rear. But these soldiers were again to be put to the test. For about an hour there was a cessation of strife, then the column advanced to a second assault. Steadily the veterans moved forward and bravely did their opponents await them. When the signal was given the engagement began. The same tactics were employed as before, and with like results: whole ranks melted away before the Provincial fire, battalions were reduced to mere companies, Howe's best officers were dying or dead, the way was mown by Provincial bullets, and again the redoubt and breastwork were safe. But the British, persisting with the tenacity that belongs to the race, reformed for still another assault, and this time they were more successful, for the ammunition of the Provincials was exhausted and there remained nothing but retreat or a hand-to-hand fight. The order was given and the Provincials withdrew, but before leaving, there was a terrible encounter. Prescott, who so bravely held the redoubt while the left line regiments held the British from an attack on the rear, now rallied his men to fight in an improvised way. With clubbed guns, and with bayonets wrenched from the foe they still fought the unequal fight, until, steadily pressed, they were compelled to give up the redoubt. This captured and the breastwork abandoned, the men in the gap were between 'two fires and the only resort was to retreat. They stood while there was any hope of success, and did not abandon the gap until General Warren, who, it is said, stood at the head of the rail fence breastwork between the regiments of Brewer and Nixon, considered it expedient. In fact, Colonel Nixon's regiment was one of the last to leave the battle-ground. Both Nixon and Brewer were wounded, the former so severely that he was borne from the field, and their brave leader, General Warren, was slain. Thus nobly was the defence maintained. The losses sustained by the regiments of Brewer and Nixon were as follows : —

Brewer's regiment: Killed 7   Wounded 11
Nixon's regiment: Killed 3   Wounded 10

Total   10   21

Of the killed, two were of Captain Haynes's company, namely: Comming Forbush, Framingham; Joshua Haynes, Sudbury. One was of Captain Russell's company, namely:

Lebbaus Jenness of Deerfield. Thus ended that day of destinies. Dismal indeed was the scene as night settled upon it. The beloved of both armies had fallen. Major Pitcairn, prominent in Concord fight, was among the English slain, while General Warren, a man of promise and much admired by the Americans, had also perished.

THE SIEGE OF BOSTON.

After the engagement at Bunker Hill the Provincials began the siege of Boston. The British bivouacked the night of the seventeenth on the battle-field, but the Americans soon environed them from Roxbury to Medford. On the 3d of July, George Washington took formal command of the Continental Army, and then commenced, under his generalship, that series of military movements which resulted in the evacuation of Boston by the British, March 17, 1776.

The soldiers of Sudbury in the battle of Bunker Hill, all or nearly all having enlisted for eight months, were engaged in this siege. During the summer, Colonel Brewer's regiment was stationed at Prospect Hill, and General Nixon had quarters at Winter Hill.

Before closing the account of Sudbury's service in the year 1775, we will insert the names of some Sudbury men who were in the two months service with Captain Wheeler in 1775, and also of a small number who were in the regiment of Colonel Whiting and did service at Hull, and after leaving there were stationed at Fort Independence.

IN THE TWO MONTHS WINTER 1775.

Capt Asahel Wheeler	Daniel Maynard
Ithamer Rice	Gideon Maynard
John Maynard Jr.	Silas Mosman
John Balcom Jr.	

COL REED'S REGIMENT.

Peter Smith	Abel Tower
Ebenezer Plympton	Joel Brigham
Jonathan Bent	James Haynes
Ruben Haynes	Daniel Frazer
Simeon Ingersol	Thomas Smith

IN COLONEL WHITING'S REGIMENT.

Micah Balcom	John Brown
Thomas Goodenow Lt.	Abel Brigham
Jas Balcom	Jacob Reed
Luther Moor	Thos. Dal [rymple]
Thad Harrington	Elijah Howe
Israel ———	Tr——— Moore

GOVERNMENT STOREHOUSES.

Besides other responsibilities the town had charge of some government storehouses containing munitions of war, which the Sudbury teamsters, from time to time, conveyed to the front. Various receipts are still preserved which were received by these teamsters. These buildings were situated on the northerly part of Sand Hill, east of the county road. There were several of them, and some were remaining within the memory of an aged citizen who conversed with the writer concerning them. One or more of them were moved to Wayland, and one was moved to the Captain Rice place where it was used as a cider mill. Recently it was moved to another spot on the same farm and made over for a stable ; the old timbers of the original structure were retained. Before its alteration the writer examined it and took measurements. It was a very low building, perhaps forty by thirty feet, with a broad sloping roof. It was without partitions, and formerly had a very wide barn-like door in front. At one time Mr. William Rice, the father of Captain William, had charge of these houses and military stores. Several squads of soldiers were employed to guard them, and at one time Captain Isaac Wood was commander of the guard. In 1777, the following soldiers did guard duty: "Corporal Robert Eames, Silas Goodenow Jr, Philemon Brown, Elisha Harrington, Jon[a] Clark." A guard of the same number was there in 1778 and 79, but all the men were not the same. The field in or near which these buildings stood was used as a training field in former years, and at one time a militia muster was held there. But now all trace even of the site has become obliterated, and for years it has been a quiet feeding place for cattle, and all is as peaceful there as if the slow pacing of the old Continental guard had never been heard at Sand Hill.

SERVICE OUTSIDE OF THE STATE.

While Sudbury was so well represented in the field during the eventful year of 1775, when the seat of war was in its own neighborhood, when its farms were liable to become the front and its very door-yards the field of battle, it was also fitly represented when the war passed to other localities. We will now present the names of some of the soldiers who served in the subsequent scenes of the war in places remote from the town. A few that have become illegible will be omitted and doubtful ones will be enclosed in brackets.

After the British left Boston the American Army went to New York, and a part of the Sudbury soldiers, including three captains, went with it. These captains were Abel Holden, Caleb Clapp and Aaron Haynes. Gen. John Nixon, it is supposed, accompanied it in the brigade of General Sullivan. On the 9th of August, John Nixon was promoted to the rank of brigadier-general, and his brother, Thomas, became colonel of his regiment. This regiment and another with a body of artillery, all under command of General Nixon, were stationed for a time at Governor's Island, New York Harbor, and after the retreat of General Washington from Brooklyn, August 27, the brigade passed up the North River with the army.

The following is a list of officers and some of the privates in the Sudbury companies in 1776, Gen. John Nixon's brigade.

COL. THOMAS NIXON'S REGIMENT.

Capt. Abel Holden	Ruben Haynes
Lieut Levi Holden	Colven Eames
Lieut Oliver Rice	Thadeus Moore
Capt Caleb Clap	Luther Eames
Lieut Joshua Clap	John Stone
Serg't Joseph Balcom	Joshua Maynard
Joseph Nixon	Roland Bennet
Luther Moore	Hezekiah Moore

The company of Capt. Aaron Haynes was in Colonel

RESIDENCE OF CHARLES P WILLIS (David Lincoln Place)
Historical Sketch of Willis Family *Page 453*

Whitcomb's regiment, having been transferred from Colonel Brewer's while stationed at Prospect Hill. The following list contains part of the names : —

Capt Aaron Haynes.	Joseph Maynard
Aaron Haynes Jr.	Jonas Haynes
John Rusk	Ephriam Goodenow

Capt. Aaron Haynes was in command of a company at Peekskill, N. Y., in the spring of 1777.

Besides the soldiers who went with the army to New York in 1776, there was quite a force that went in an expedition against Canada. A large part of the soldiers who served in these campaigns were under the command of Capt. Asahel Wheeler, and in one at least of the campaigns were in the regiment of Col. John Robinson. Of the Sudbury soldiers who served under these officers in the Canada Expedition or Ticonderoga Campaign, we give the following : —

John Merriam	Phinehas Glezen
Benj ———	David How jr.
Joseph Smith	Francis Jones
Ephraim Smith	Timothy Underwood
Zebediah Farrar	Jonathan Davis
Daniel Lawrence	Daniel Benjaman
Job Brooks.	Ithamer Rice.
Rhuben Hains.	John Peter
Roger Bigelow	Nathaniel Park
Oliver Curtis	Converse Big——
Samuel Jones	Abraham Parmenter
John Tozer	Steven Taylor
Abijah Mead	Jonas Brown
Samson Wheeler.	Andrew Green
John Lough	John Cobb
Oliver Conant	James Stedman
Jonah Gilbert	Francis Chaffin
Joseph Mason	Amos Nutting
A Buttrick	G—— Ames
John Weston	Amos Stow
Samuel Adams	William Thorney
Joel Adams	John Hives
Daniel Hosmer	Nathaniel Bemis
Phinehas Hager	Thomas Corey
Jacob Jones	John Farrar

Besides those who served in the Canada Expedition in Captain Wheeler's company, Colonel Robinson's regiment, we give the following who served in his company when in the regiment of Colonel Read. A large share of the names in this and other lists were once familiar in Sudbury. Those which were not may have been of substitutes who made up the quota.

COLONEL READ'S REGIMENT, GENERAL BRECKET'S BRIGADE, GENERAL GATES' DIVISION.

Capt. Asahel Wheeler
Sergent Uriah Wheeler
Lieut. Hopstill Willis
Corp. Daniel Osborn
Aaron Eames
Thomas Eames
Josiah Richardson
Jesse Goodnow
Uriah Hunt
Thomas Burbank
Benj. Berry,
Nathaniel Rice
Deliverance Parmenter
Isaac Moore
Daniel Noyes
John Sheperd
Wm Walker
Daniel W. Moore
Jonas Clark
Wm Dun
Nathaniel Bryant
Aaron Maynard
Jonathan Burbank
Richard Wetherbee
Phinehas Gleason
Phinehas Gleason Jr
John Barney
John Adams
John [Thonning]
Wm [Thorning]
Ebenezer Park
Edward Whitman
Thomas Emes
David Underwood
——— Rice

John Taylor
Hezekiah Hapgood
[Moris Clary]
Nathaniel Browne
Ebenezer Plympton
Gideon Maynard
Isaac Rice
Timothy Rice
Francis Green
Abel Willis
John Frazer
Jacob Kibley
Jason Haines
Samuel Merriam
Jonas [Chase]
Abel Willis
Aaron Eames Jr.
Josiah Hosmer
Benj. Tower
Solomon Taylor
Judah Wetherbee
Wm Graves
Ezekiel Smith
James Willis
Edward [Cheney]
Thomas Harrington
Jacob Stevens
Phineas Stevens
Nathan Gates
Daniel Noyes
Benj. [Hale]
Nathaniel Rice
Wm Hosmer Jr.
Amos ———
Samuel Brown

Joseph Rutter   Isaac Rice
Charles Brown   Silas Conant
John Parmenter   —— Blanchard
Francis Hemenway

Several names belonging in the above list have become illegible in the records.

The following were also in the Ticonderoga Campaign, 1776, in the company of Captain Wheeler : —

James Wright   John Hoar
Abel Tower   Ebenezer Heald
Isaac Bartlett   Christian Wagner
Mica Graves   Abel Goodenow
Thomas Bloget   [Samuel Dakin]
Ezra Parmenter   Ebenezer Heard
Abel Goodenow   Solomon Whitney
Theodore Harrington   William Thomas
Jonathan Bent   Samuel ——
Isaac Bartlett   Josiah Farrar
Abel Tower   Caleb Wheeler
Aaron Mosmon   Jason Belcher
Ebenezer Nixon   Samuel Emery
Jonas Emery   Jonas Billings
Paul Colidge   Samuel Hoar
Josiah Tomson   Samuel Osborn
Elias Bigelow   Jesse Mosmon
Joseph Abbot   Capt. David Moore
Gregory Stone   Francis Green
Nath[l] Knowlton   Joshua Haynes Lieut
Nath[el] Browne   Daniel Maynard
John Park   John Parmenter
Samuel Bond   Micah Graves
William Hosmer   Charles Rice
Peter Brintnal   Samuel Curtis
Nathan Maynard   John Adams
Aaron Maynard   Eleezer Parks
Abel Child   Jonas Bond
Jacob ——   Samuel Poland
John Carter   Abel Willis
Joseph Rutter   John Parks
Nathaniel Knowlton   Isaac Moore
Elijah ——   Micah Bowker
Jacob Jones   John Bennet
Uriah Wheeler   John Warren
W[m] Grout   John Lands
Joseph Goodenow

The following Sudbury men served in the Ticonderoga Campaign, 1776, in the company of Captain Craft, Colonel Graton's regiment: —

Peter Smith	Abel Maynard
Isaac Wise	Jesse Mosman
Aaron Mosman	Simeon Ingersol
Abel Tower	Charles Eames

The following served in the Ticonderoga Campaign, 1776, in the company of Captain Edgell, Colonel Brewer's regiment: —

Lieut. Jonathan Rice	Serg't Augustus Moore
William Maynard	Nathan Hayward.
Joel Brigham.	

Capt. Aaron Haynes had a company at Ticonderoga in 1776 in Col. Asa Whitcomb's regiment. His minute roll bears date, December, 1776, and the following names are upon it: —

Aaron Haynes Capt	Joseph Willis Ensigne
Aaron Holden 1ˢᵗ Lieut,	Aaron Haynes Drummer.

The soldiers included in the lists now given were of the armies which were endeavoring to gain Canada for the Continental cause, and force the British from the State of New York. The expedition or campaign against Canada was planned in the year 1775 by a committee of Congress which met at Cambridge in August of that year. The capture of the fortresses Ticonderoga and Crown Point on Lake Champlain in May, 1775, by Connecticut and Vermont militia, had opened the way to the St. Lawrence, and the expedition was designed to aid in getting possession of that part of Canada. Two forces were engaged in the work. One of these was composed of New York and New England troops and was placed under the command of Generals Schuyler and Montgomery and ordered to go by way of Lake Champlain to Montreal and Quebec. The other expedition left Cambridge, September, 1775, and was under the leadership of Col. Benedict Arnold. In the Canada Expedition, 1776, the following casualties occurred: Benjamin Berry lost an arm, and at Ticonderoga the same year the following persons died: —

Ensign Timothy Underwood	Phinehas Gleason
Solomon Rice	Timothy Rice

Sergeant Samuel Maynard died of small pox at Quebec with Arnold.

The service rendered by the Sudbury men who left Massachusetts with the army under Washington was largely performed in New York and vicinity. Washington arriving at New York about the middle of April, at once set about fortifying the vicinity and securing the passes of the Highlands ou the Hudson River. In the operations about this part of the country hard fighting and toilsome marches were experienced. We hear of Sudbury soldiers at Saratoga, Stillwater, Fort Edward, and other places connected with the activity of the Continental forces in New York. At Saratoga Serg. Thadeus Moore was slain and Lieut. Joshua Clapp was wounded.

Names of Sudbury men enlisted in 1777 for three years or during the war.

OFFICERS.

Gen. John Nixon	Sergeant Ruben Haynes
Capt. Abel Holden	Sergeant Aaron Haynes
Leuit. Levi Holden	Sergeant Joseph Balcom
Leuit. Oliver Rice	Sergeant Uriah Eaton
Capt. Caleb Clap	Sergent Thadeus Moore
Leuit. Joshua Clap	Sergeant Jonas Haynes,
Capt. Aaron Haynes	

PRIVATES.

Nathaniel Cutter	John Buck
Charles Gouell	Joshua Maynard
Ruben Moore Jr.	Joseph Maynard
Oliver Sanderson	Jonathan Robbinson
Uriah Moore	Zak. Robbenson
Hezekiah Moore	Oliver Robbenson
William Dun	Joseph Cutter
Joseph Nixon	Calvin Eames
Joel Puffer	Josiah Cutter
Ephraim Goodenow	Joseph Willis
Francis Green	Donal Lincoln
Luther Eames	Ruben Moore
Luther Moore	Joseph Meller
Joel Brigham	

In connection with the foregoing we give the following list of men who enlisted for the same length of time but perhaps in another year. They were from "the 4th Regiment of Foot, commanded by Col. Ezekiel How." Only five of the names given in the two lists are alike.

GUARD ROLL.

Capt. Abel Holden	3 years	Micah Grant	3 years
Benjamin Tower	"	Jesse Goodenow	"
Luther Eames	"	Thomas Burbank	"
Charles Eames		Ephraim Goodenow	"
Corneleus Wood		Jonathan Bevens	
Joel Brigham		Jonas Welch	
Joseph Nixon		Joseph Bent	
Levi Holden		Abel Thompson	"
Luther Moore		Thomas Gibbs during the war	
Uriah Moore			

PAY ROLL.

Sudbury June the 27th, 1778. We the Subscribers have received of Capt. Asahel Wheeler Nine Pounds for oure wages in full oure pay for October & Part November 1777 both for contannatel and State and mileage we say Received by ous —

Moses Stone	Samuel Knight in behalf [of]
Nathaniel Rice	Silas Knight
Abel Smith	Daniel Maynard
William Brown	Caleb Stacy
Jonathan Haynes	Timothy Emes
Wm Moore	Ephraim Moore
Timothy Moore	Asher Cutler Jr
Abel Brigham	Hopestill Willis
Mathias Mosman	Jason Haynes
Samuel Puffer	Daniel osborn
Gidon Maynard	Phineas Puffer
Silas Tower	John Parris
James Moore	Samuel Cutting
Hezekiah Johnson	Isaac Goodenow
his Silas X Parmenter mark	

Beside men who enlisted for a long term of service in 1777, we have two lists of those whose enlistment was for a very short period.

FIRST LIST.

JAN. 1777

To New York — Two months

Capt. Nathaniel Hayward's Company, Col. Thatcher's Regiment.

Cornelius Wood	Thomas Dalremple
Daniel Loring	Thomas Dalremple Jr
Ser^t Maj^r Wm Goodenow	Thomas Moore
Serg^t Uriah Wheeler	Daniel Hamynes
Wm Brown	Theodore Harrington
Abel Parmenter	

The last four of these men are spoken of as having been taken prisoners and never heard of afterwards.

SECOND LIST.

JULY 1777.

To Saratoga — Three months.

Col. Brown's Regiment.   General Gates, Commander.

Capt. Jonathan Rice	John Brown
Serg^t Abel Maynard	Ebenezer Burbank
Ezekiel How	Nathaniel Brown
Caleb Wheeler	Nathaniel Bryant
Isaac Wier	David How
Abel Willis	

As the war progressed Sudbury was still active in filling its quota. In 1778, several companies were still in the field. Four of these had three hundred and twenty-seven men and were commanded as follows: West Side men, Capt. Jonathan Rice and Capt. Asahel Wheeler; East Side men, Capt. Nathaniel Maynard and Capt. Isaac Cutting. In the Stearns Collection we have the following lists of men in two of these companies.

FOR CAP. MAYNARD'S COMPANY, SUDBURY

Lieut. Joseph Wellington, during the war.

Robert Bennet   "

Farkins Hosmer   "

Oliver Sanderson

Simon Newton

Ephraim Barker

Jonathan Barker

James Gibbs

Pathrick Flinn   during the war.
James Welch   "
Timothy Ahgen   "
John Carrol
Morris Griffin
Daniel Hickey
Samuel Whitney
Joseph Foster
Christopher Capen
Ephraim Carry   "
Ambros Fergerson   for 3 years
Timothy Bent   "
Samuel Whitney   "
Phinehas Butler
Wᵐ Cook Gleason
Thomas Jones
Abraham Parmenter
Noah Bogle
John Stover transient   "

FOR CAPT. WHEELER'S COMPANY.

Joseph Balcom	3 years	Joseph Mossman	3 years
Ruben Haynes	"	Joel Brigham	"

Capt. Jonathan Maynard had a company in the two months service in 1782 in the Seventh Regiment, Lieut. Col. John Brooks. He also had a company in the twelve months service in the same regiment.

FOR CAPT. MOULTON'S CO.

Joseph Smith	3 years	Richard Morris	3 years
John Burk	"	James Scroday	"
Joseph Maynard	"	Wᵐ Bevens	"
Joshua Maynard	"	Uriah Eaton	
Isaac Rice		Francis Green	"
Nathaniel Cutler	"	Patherick Flin	during the war
Joseph Cutler		John Carrol	"
Thadeus Moore	"	Morris Griffin	"
Oliver Sanderson	"		

Other enlistments were, —

Capt Aaron Haynes during the war	Eleazer Lawrence 3 years
Aaron Haynes Jr 3 years	James Beamis "

The following is a list of Sudbury men in Capt. Daniel

Bowker's company, together with the time when they joined Colonel Webb's regiment : —

SUDBURY.

Daniel Bowker Capt.	Steven Puffer, died Oct. 3d.
Oliver Parmenter	Silas Puffer
Ezra Mossman	John Brigham
Edward Moore	Samuel Willis
Silas Ames	Corp. Ezra Willis
Ashbel Moore	

SUDBURY EAST.

Isaac Cary	Isaac Cory Jr
Asa Holden	Ruben Graves
Oliver Travis	

The men from Sudbury joined Sept. 9th except Capt. Bowker who entered Sept. 15th. Those from East Sudbury entered Oct. 6th

Highlands, Nov 20, 1785

The following paper shows the sums paid for enlistments in 1780 : —

Sudbury June 22d 1780

We the subscribers do hereby acknowledge that we have severally received of the Committee appointed by the town of Sudbury to agree with and hire the said Town's Quota of soldiers agreeable to an act of the Gen. Court of the fifth of June instant the several sums annexed to our names —

his Benjamin X Seaver mark	£600	his Joseph X Cutter mark	£900
Joshua Hemenway	" 750	Peter ———	" 900
Jonas Haynes	" 600	Ebenezer Parmenter	" 600
Abel Brigham	" 600	his Peletiah X Parmenter mark	" 600
Abel Cutler	" 600		
Ezra Willis	" 900	Luther Moor	" 700
Naham Haynes	" 750	Luther Emes	" 900
Asa Holden	" 600		

CHAPTER XXII.

1775–1800.

Revolutionary War. — Report of a Committee Appointed by the Town to Estimate the Service of Sudbury Soldiers. — Appointment of a Committee to Make up and Bring in Muster Rolls of the Services of Each Soldier in the War. — Muster Rolls: Captain Rice's, Captain Wheeler's, Captain Maynard's, Captain Cutting's. — Whole Number of Men in the War. — Their Valiant Service. — Casualties — Sketch of Gen. John Nixon. — Town-Meetings. — Encouragements to Enlistment. — Specimen of Enlistment Papers. — Various Requisitions Made on the Town.

> Their death shot shook the feudal tower,
> And shattered slavery's chain as well;
> On the sky's dome, as on a bell,
> Its echo struck the world's great hour.
>
> WHITTIER.

HAVING now presented the names of the soldiers obtained from various other sources, we will give a list found on the Town Records, which purports to contain the names of all soldiers of the town who served in the Revolutionary War up to the fall of 1778, together with extracts from the records which led to this enrollment of names.

June 25, 1778, "The town by their vote ordered their Com. appointed to estimate the services of each particular person in Sudbury in the present war, to report at the next Town meeting."

At a town-meeting held October 19, the committee above mentioned reported as follows: — (The fractional parts of pounds we have omitted.)

That the minute men be allowed each	£3
That the Eight Months be allowed each	20
Six weeks men to Roxbury allowed each	4

Two months men to Cambridge allowed each	£6
The years men to York and the Northward allowed each	75
Six months men to the Castle allowed each	9
Five months men to Ticonderoga allowed each	50
Three months men to Dorchester with Capt Moulton allowed each	7
Two months men to York allowed each	25
Three months men to York and the Jerseys allowed each	48
Two months men to Providence allowed each	12
Three months men to Ticonderoga allowed each	52
Thirty days men to Saratoga allowed each	20
Three months men to Providence allowed each	30
Three months men to guard at Cambridge allowed each	18
Six weeks men to Rhode Island allowed each	20
Four months men to guard the troops and stores allowed each	20
Three months men to Boston allowed each	20

That those persons who have hired men to perform any of the above services at a time when there was an actual Levy for men, be allowed for Said Service as if performed in person. That those that paid fines or advanced money for the good of the service, be allowed in the same proportion as their money would procure men to perform the Services which at that time they Neglected to do in person. That no persons shall be intitled to Receive pay for any of the above Services Unless he Shall be first taxed towards the payment thereof. Also that Each person shall Receive pay only for the time he was in actual Service

Sudbury Octo^r 19th 1778

Ezekiel How
Phineas Glezen
Jon^a Rice
Asahel Wheeler } Committee
Isaac Loker
Tho Walker

The town voted to accept the above report, and appointed men to make up and bring to the town complete muster rolls of the services of each person in Sudbury in the then present war with Great Britain. This meeting was adjourned to October 26, at which date the following record was made, namely : —

Oct. 26th 1778. Capt Rice's musteroll was read, and the town voted to Grant to Each person Expressed by name in said musteroll the Sum Set to their Respective name, as may appear by said musteroll, which was as follows vizt

To Hopestill Willis	£73	Silas Parmenter	£17
Ens^n Josiah Richardson	75	Elisha Harrington	12
John Moore	53	Nathan Read	25

Uriah Moore Ju^r	£58	Lt Micah Goodenow	£116
Asher Cutler Ju^r	71	Eben^r Wood	51
Willm Goodenow	51	Jesse Moore adm^r	21
L^r Thomas Goodenow	30	Hopestill Browne ad^r	6
Israel Willis adm^r	51	Capt Saml Knight	44
Saml Cutting	41	Asher Cutler	9
Nath^{al} Rice Ju^r	35	Cor^l Saml How	46
Joseph Green	10	Aaron Johnson	77
Abel Parmenter	17	William Parmenter	9
Isaac Hunt Ju^r	62	Reuben Vorce	12
Nath^{ll} Bryant	35	Sam^{ll} Hunt	12
Uriah Hayden	95	Capt Israel Moore	102
Abel Goodenow	31	Lt Elisha Wheeler	73
David How	126	Aaron Goodenow Ju^r	52
Philemon Brown	35	Tho. Emes	26
Lt Jacob Read	76	Nath^{ll} Brown	11
James Wyse	75	Edward Bayanton	26
John Goodenow	50	John Browne	52
Lt Jon^a Carter	102	Wid^o Sarah Brigham	52
Dan^{ll} W Moore	50	Israel Parmenter	52
Wm Walker	50	Capt Moses Stone	50
Deliverance Parmenter	50	Silas Goodenow	40
Jotham Goodenow	50	Thos Carr Ju^r	48
Col. Ezekiel How	70	Uriah Gibbs	30
Dan^{ll} Osborn	70	Micah Parmenter	30
Elijah Rice	50	James Thomson	41
Peter Haynes	50	Ensⁿ Jonas Holdin	53
Jonⁿ Carter Ju^r	70	Wm Hayden	53
Nath^{ll} Rice	50	Eliab Moore	39
Capt Jonⁿ Rice	95	Jonas Wheler	18
Isaac Read	33	Tho' Dalrimple	27
Elijah Moore	10	Sam^{ll} Geason	26
Capt Cornelius Wood	9	Abel Thomson	75
Lt Rowand Bogle	63	Willm Hunt	33
Robert Emes	26	Dr Josiah Langdon	12
Eph^m Carter	25	Sam^{ll} Bent	3
John Brigham	35	Elisha Wheeler Ju	51
John Parry	45	Eph^m Goodenow Ju^r	20
Uriah Parmenter	55	David How Ju^r	3
Jos^h Parmenter	45	Moses Goodenow	3
Oliver Mors	28	John Willis	32
Eph^m Moore	45	Sam^{ll} Brown	32
Joseph Moore	35	Joseph Grout	32
Hopestill Brown	90	Capt Abel Holdin	96
Wm Brown	68	Luther Moore	29
Isaac Lincoln Ju^r	48	Aaron Emes	21

Jesse Gibbs	£48	Mr Asahel Goodenow	£12
Nahum Hayden	48	Elijah Willis Exe^r	10
Wm Parmenter	48	Aaron Goodenow	17
Reuben Willis	48	Augustus Walker	17
Thos Walker	48	Charles Emes	20
Lt Joseph Read	27	Ezekiel How Ju^r	52
Lt Joseph Goodenow	19	Ensⁿ Levi Holdin	75
Timothy Emes	27		

Capt Asahel Wheeler's Musteroll was read, and the town voted to allow to each person expressed by name therein the Sum Set to his name in said musteroll, which was as follows vizt

To Capt Asahel Wheler	£83	Phinehas Puffer	£68
Lt Joshua Haynes	78	Thos Puffer	52
Lt Abijah Brigham	41	Isaac Puffer	32
Augustus Moore	46	James Parmenter Ju^r	30
Isaac Maynard	198	Edmund Parmenter	50
Asahel Balcom	72	Thos Plympton Esqr	86
Willm Moore	71	Dan^{ll} Puffer	32
Uriah Wheler	51	Charles Rice	21
Jason Haynes	70	Wm Rice 3d	70
Peter Smith	82	Ithamor Rice	54
John Maynard Ju^r	16	Abel Smith	44
Dan^{ll} Maynard	59	John Shirly	21
Jason Bent	66	Sam^{ll} Puffer	65
Jon^a Bent	17	Lt Oliver Noyse	81
Joseph Balcom	30	Nathan Loring	32
John Balcom	49	Capt Elijah Smith	52
Jonas Balcom	52	Henry Smith	96
Sam^{ll} Brigham	18	Benjⁿ Smith	52
Hope Brown	55	Jotham Brown	26
John Clark	29	John Shepard	30
James Carter	21	Ambrose Tower	132
Joseph Dakin	38	Israel Wheler	50
Deaⁿ Sam^{ll} Dakin	25	John Weighton	34
Dan^{ll} Goodenow	32	Abel Willis	50
Moses Haynes	32	Cop^l Dan^{ll} Bowker	70
Israel Haynes	113	Lt James Puffer	52
James Haynes	129	James Puffer Ju^r	45
Jon^a Haynes	45	Dan^{ll} Loring	76
Charles Haynes	73	Jere^h Robbins	21
Capt Aaron Haynes	190	Wm Hunt Ju^r	62
Macah Haywood	49	John Mosmon	50
Moses Maynard	25	Lt Mathias Mosman	35
Nathan Maynard	35	Francis Green	20
John Maynard	150	Jesse Willis	32

Aaron Maynard	£50	Silas Tower	£4
Timo^y Moore	24	Capt David Moore Ex^r	20
Zec^h Maynard	70	Thad^s Moore Ex^r	95
Jesse Mosman	95	Simeon Ingersal Ex^r	79
Joseph Maynard Guar	75	Nath^a Cutter Ex^r	24
Dan^ll Noyse Jun	55	Jonas Rice Ex^r	20
Moses Noyse	77	Jon^a Smith	49

Then Capt Nath^ll Maynard's Musteroll was read and the town voted to allow to each person expressed by name therein the Sum Set to his name in said Musteroll which was as followeth vizt

To John Adams	£50	Lt Eben^r Staples	£18
Benjn Adams	23	Thos Trask	12
Josiah Allen	50	Isaac Woodward	7
Ephe^m Abbot	30	Lt John Noyes	73
Amos Abbot	20	Samuel Sherman	20
Wm Baldwin Esqr	50	Eph^m Allen ad^m	95
Lt Wm Barker	32	James Philips	95
Rolan Bennet	12	Lemuel Whiting	95
John Dean	45	Lt Josiah Wilinton	95
James Davis	52	John Brewer	40
Lt Josiah Farrar	13	Elijah Bent	95
Abraham Jenkinson	52	Zech^h Bent	6
Sam^ll Griffin	80	Zech^h Bryant Ju^r	70
Micah Graves	57	John Bruce	50
Phinehas Glezen	63	Maj^r Jo^s Curtis	5
Isaac Gould	4	David Curtis	32
Reuben Gould	25	Lt Sam^ll Choat	25
Jacob Gould	25	Thad^s Bond	40
Capt Josiah Hoar	5	Capt Joseph Payson	32
Lt Jon^a Hoar	40	Wm Wyman	30
Capt Nath^ll Maynard	68	Isaac Brintnal	20
Daniel Maynard	50	Peter Brintnal	20
Dan^ll Moore	34	Joshua Kendal	20
Israel Moore	12	Capt Richard Heard	132
John Noyes Esqr	50	Thos Heard	53
James Noyes	52	Richard Heard Ju^r	20
Jason Parmenter	18	Trobridge Taylor	18
Jon^r Parmenter Ju^r	15	Darius Hudson	52
Dr Eben^r Roby	50	Joseph Emerson	52
Joseph Rutter Ju^r	50	Nathl Knolton	20
Thos Rutter	20	Sam^ll Haynes	3
Jonas Sherman	25	Wid^o Ann Noyes	30
Edward Sherman	50	Isaac Moore	20
Timo^y Sherman	12	Simon Newton	70

Then Capt Cutting's Musteroll was read and the town voted to allow to each person expressed by name therein, the Sum Set to his name in said Musteroll, which was as follows, vizt

To Lt Wm Bond	£22	Lt Joseph Smith	£95
Thom^s Brintnal	5	Capt Caleb Moulton	34
Joseph Beal	32	Micah Maynard ad^r	50
Isaac Cutting	32	Amos Ordeway	4
John Cutting	50	D^n Sam^ll Parris	32
Elisha Cutting	58	Lt Isaac Rice	54
Jon^a Cutting	20	Isaac Rice	25
Sam^ll Curtis	20	Dan^ll Rice	17
Thos Damon Ju^r	57	Israel Rice Ju^r	26
Wm Damon	25	Jonas Rice	9
Isaac Damon	12	Edmund Rice	42
Benjn Dudley Ju^r	6	Lt Sam^ll Russell	32
Cor^t Joseph Dudley	50	Capt. Thad^s Russell	20
Eben^r Dudley	29	Capt Robert Cutting	55
Wm Dudley	56	Jacob Reeves	46
Eben^r Johnson	50	Lt Nath^a Reeves	20
Peter Johnson	24	Joseph Smith Capt.	76
John Loker	45	Lt Ephraim Smith	22
Jonas Loker ad^l	5	Isaac Stone	50
Capt Isaac Loker	76	David Stone	50
John Meriam	26	Joel Stone	16
Capt. Caleb Moulton	34	John Tilton	32
Capt Micah Maynard ad^r	50	John Tilton Ju^r	60
Amos Ordeway	4	Timo^y Underwood ad^r	55
Dr Sam^ll Peris	32	Timo^y Underwood	21
Lt Isaac Rice	54	Jon^a Westson	20
Isaac Rice	25	Isaac Williams	20
Dan^ll Rice	17	Lt John Whitney	88
Israel Rice Ju^r	26	Eben^r Eaton	52
Micah Rice	4	Willm Grout	35
Isaac Smith	56	Francis Jones	64
Capt Thos Damon	20	Cap^l Jesse Emes	5
John Barney	4		

The foregoing lists indicate a patriotic zeal highly commendable to the citizens of Sudbury. The town had a population of twenty-one hundred and sixty with about five hundred ratable polls; and it is supposed that, during the war, from four to five hundred men had some service either in camp or field. Of these soldiers, one was brigadier-general, three were colonels, two were majors, two were adjutants, two were surgeons, twenty-four were captains and twenty-nine were lieutenants. We hear of Sudbury men from Concord to Bunker Hill, and from there to the Highlands of the Hudson. Where Washington went they followed. They stood near Stark in that post of danger by the bank of the Mystic. They were ordered to strike the front of Burgoyne at the north, and they endured the rigors of a Canadian winter in the attempt to gain Canada for the Continental cause. It matters not where they were found, they were true to their commander and loyal to every trust. The officers were the friends of the great leaders of the American army, and the record of the achievements of the sons of Sudbury, in the old French and Indian War period, was not broken when they met in open field the discipline and experience of the veteran troops of the British throne. Wherever an English front was deployed, Sudbury soldiers, if ordered, never flinched from meeting it. They went into the field to stay, or, if they returned, to rally if again called to the conflict. The summons to town-meeting at home was but as the long roll of the civilian which called him to devise means for filling and equipping the quota of troops or to assist the families of men at the front. Ticonderoga, Saratoga, Stillwater and White Plains were familiar names in old Sudbury. The battle-fields of the Revolution were not alone heard of by the children in the little red schoolhouses on the town's common land, but they heard them talked of in the household by those who had been upon them in the measured march or counter-march, the advance, retreat, or pursuit, until they were as well known as the broad acres on their own peaceful farms. The old king's or queen's arm in the corner had its history. The bullet-pouch had been emptied time after time into the ranks of the foe, and the cocked hat that long hung by the fireside was begrimed, not by the smoke from the hearth, but by the dust and smoke of battle. That the soldiers were in places of peril is indicated by the following record of casualties, though probably but a part of them are here recorded.

CASUALTIES TO SUDBURY SOLDIERS.

KILLED.

Deacon Josiah Haynes, Aged 80, April 19th 1775

Asahel Read April 19th 1775

Joshua Haynes Jr, of Capt Aaron Haynes' Company, June th 1775, at Bunker Hill.

Sergeant Thadeus Moore, 1777, at Saratoga

Benjamin Whitney, — By accident —

WOUNDED.

Gen, John Nixon at Bunker Hill   Cornelius Wood

Nathan Maynard   :   :   Nahum Haynes

Capt, David Moore   Lieut, Joshua Clapp, wounded at

Joshua Haynes   Saratoga

Benjamin Barry, lost an arm in Canada Expedition, 1776

DIED OF SICKNESS.

Sergeant Major Jesse Moore   Sergeant Samuel Maynard, of the

Sergeant Hopestill Brown   small pox, at Quebeck with

Sergeant Elijah Willis   Arnold, 1776

AT TICONDEROGA.

Ensign Timothy Underwood   Oliver Sanderson

Daniel Underwood   James Puffer

Phinehas Gleason   Stephen Puffer, of Capt Daniel

Solomon Rice   Bowker's Co, Col Webb's Regt

Timothy Rice   died Oct 3d

Josiah Cutter

TAKEN PRISONER AND NEVER HEARD OF.

Thadeus Harrington   Thomas Dalrimple

Thomas Moore   Daniel Haynes.

LOST PRIVATEERING.

Isaac Moore   Silas Goodenow

Lemuel Goodenow   Peletiah Parmenter

PERSONS WHO MET WITH CASUALTIES THE NATURE OF WHICH IS NOT SPECIFIED.

John Brewer   James Demander

John Bemis   Timothy Mossman.

" Green be the graves where her martyrs are lying;
    Shroudless and tombless they sank to their rest;
    While o'er their ashes the starry fold flying
     Wraps the proud eagle they roused from his nest."

In closing this account of Sudbury's military service we will give some facts in the life of General Nixon.

SKETCH OF GENERAL NIXON.

Gen. John Nixon was a son of Christopher Nixon who went to Framingham about 1724, where seven children were born of whom John was the oldest. At an early age, being but a mere boy, he entered the army, and at the instigation of older persons he left unlawfully, but clemency was shown him and he was allowed to return to the ranks. His subsequent career proved him to be a true soldier.

In 1745, when he was but twenty years old, he was in the Pepperell Expedition to Louisburg, and lieutenant in Captain Newell's company at Crown Point in 1755. Later in the war he served as captain. At one time, when operating against the French forces, he was led into an ambuscade and only forced his way out with the loss of most of his men. As before noticed, at the beginning of the Revolutionary War he served as captain of a company of minute men. April 24, 1775, he received the commission of colonel. He fought and was wounded at the battle of Bunker Hill. He went with the army under Washington to New York, and was promoted, August 9, to brigadier-general. His promotion to the rank of general of brigade was on recommendation of Washington, who stated to Congress that Nixon's military talents and bravery entitled him to promotion. In his new position he had, for a time, command of two regiments and a force of artillery at Governor's Island, New York Harbor. August 27, he left there, and subsequently operated with the army in the northern campaign in New York State against Burgoyne. When it was decided to advance against the latter, General Gates ordered Nixon and two other commanders to make the attack. A cannon ball passed so near his head that the sight and hearing on one side were impaired. After the surrender of Burgoyne, General Nixon and some others were detailed to escort the prisoners to Cambridge. About that time he had a furlough of several months, in which time he married his second wife. General Nixon was on the court-martial — with Generals Clinton, Wayne and Muhlenburg, and of which Gen. Benjamin Lincoln was president — for the trial of General

Schuyler for the neglect of duty in the campaign of 1777, by which Ticonderoga was surrendered. The trial was at the request of General Schuyler, and by it he was fully acquitted with the highest honors. In 1777, General Nixon's brigade had head-quarters for a time at Peekskill, N. Y., and for a time in 1777, at Albany. On Sept. 12, 1780, he closed his military career by resigning his commission as general, and retired to private life. He married for his first wife Thankful Berry, Feb. 7, 1754; and for his second, Hannah Gleason in 1778, the widow of Capt. Micajah Gleason who was killed at the battle of White Plains, N. Y., in 1776. He had nine children, of whom five were daughters. One of them, Sarah, married Abel Cutler, the father of the late C. G. Cutler, Esq., of Sudbury.

About 1806, he went to Middlebury, Vt. At the time of the battle of Lake Champlain he was living with a daughter at Burlington; and, on hearing the sound of the cannon on the lake, he wanted a horse brought that he might go and witness the fight. General Nixon died at Middlebury, 1815, at the advanced age of ninety. When he was thirty years old he bought a tract of thirty-two acres of land of Josiah Browne on the northern side of Nobscot Hill, where he was living at the breaking out of the Revolutionary War. After he retired from the army, he lived for a time at Framingham and kept tavern at Rice's End. He afterwards returned to Sudbury, and was admitted to the church there May 22, 1803.

Although Mr. Nixon was pre-eminently a military man by nature and experience, and had known much of the hard fare and the rough companionship of the army, yet he was a man of affable address and quiet demeanor. He was of light complexion, medium size and cheerful disposition. He was a decided man and a great lover of children. One of his grandsons informed the writer that the old man used to take his grandchildren on his knee and sing war songs to them; one that he remembered was as follows: —

"Oh, why, soldiers, why, should we be melancholy, boys? whose business 'tis to die.
Through cold, hot and dry we are always bound to follow, boys, and scorn to fly."

C. G. Cutler, the grandson referred to, was about ninety years old when he repeated the verse. None of General Nixon's family, who bear the name, are now living in Sudbury. The site of his dwelling-place is still pointed out not far from the run or spring land on the northerly slope of Nobscot, but even the last faint trace of his former dwelling-place time is fast wearing away, and soon nothing but the record will tell of this illustrious citizen and soldier of Sudbury.

In considering the military service of the town in the Revolutionary War, we have only considered a part of her history. During that time important civil transactions were taking place also. There were deprivations to be endured by those at home : the country was burdened with debt, the currency was in a very uncertain state, and, because of its depreciated condition, there was more or less confusion in commercial affairs. There was as much need of sagacity on the part of the civilian in council, as of military men in the field, to direct the affairs of State and town. The town-meetings of those days were very important occasions, and, unless the people met emergencies there in a prompt and efficient manner, the fighting element in the field could accomplish but little. In this respect the people of Sudbury were not deficient. We have heard of no instance where a Tory spirit was manifest nor where a patriotic purpose was wanting. During the war, a large share of the town warrants set forth the needs of the county or town which were caused by the war; and the town-meeting that followed was about sure to result in a generous response to the demand. As the history of the war period will not be complete without presenting some of these acts we will give a few of them here.

ENCOURAGEMENTS TO ENLISTMENT.

We may well presume from the spirit manifested by the minute companies, more or less of whose members enlisted for a longer or shorter term, that patriotism was a prominent motive for entering the service. But the war was protracted, and a large share of the soldiers had families dependent upon them, and, hence, for the late enlistments extra inducements

RESIDENCE OF SAMUEL B ROGERS, So. Sudbury
Sketch of Family History. *Page 450*

were to be expected. To narrate all that was done at each successive town-meeting would be needless; we will, therefore, give only a few specimens which will serve to show the spirit of the people.

In 1777, twenty pounds were voted to each man who would enlist; also the town chose a committee to provide for soldiers' families.

In 1778, voted some three hundred and seventy pounds for clothing for the soldiers; also the town committee were instructed to hire men for the army for seventy-four pounds each "if they could if not, to give more." The same year "voted to give 50 pounds to each man who would enlist as a part of the town quota for 9 months."

The same year a committee was appointed "to hire 12 men to go to the North River for 8 months or such time as they will agree for."

The same year "14 men were hired for the service of Providence."

On May 17, 1779, voted to "hire the men to be detatched from the militia of this town to march to Tiverton, R. I., and granted 1300 pounds to hire the men with and 200 pounds to provide things for their families."

In 1779, a committee was chosen "to hire men for the public service in behalf of the town whenever there may be a call on the militia for service."

At the same date, four hundred and twenty pounds were granted "to hire five soldiers with for service of Tiverton R. I."

The same date, thirty-nine hundred pounds were granted to hire thirteen soldiers for nine months' service.

In 1781, voted that the committee should attend to "hiring the town quota for three years without loss of time and if the men cannot be obtained in town then they are to apply elsewhere," fifteen pounds in specie was granted for the purpose.

As an inducement to enlistment the town sometimes offered live stock. The following is a specimen: —

"We being a Committee appointed by the Town of Sudbury to hire the Town Quota of men for three years or

During the war agreable to a Resolve of Court Dec 2, 1780 do agree with John Ruck, Naynam Haynes, Zechrus Robison and Oliver Robison who has enlisted themselves into the Sarvis agreable to Law, Resolve to give each of them Eighteen this Spring Calves, Said Calves to be kept for and Delivered to the above Parsons when they are Regularly Discharged from the Said Sarvis, also Three Thousing Dollars old Currency to be paid Each when they are properly mustered.

"Asahel Wheeler
"Aaron Haynes } Committee."
"Jonᵃ Rice

We give below a copy of a soldier's Enlistment Paper.

We the subscribers do hereby severally inlist Ourselves into the Service of the United Colonies of America to serve until the first day of April next, if the service shall require it; and each of us do engage to furnish and carry with us into the Service a good effective Firearm and Blanket also a good Bayonet and Cartridge Pouch if possible. And we severally consent to be formed by such Persons as the General Court shall appoint into a Company of Ninety men including one Captain Two Lieutenants one Ensign four Sergeants, four Corporals one Drummer and one Fifer, to be elected by the Companies, and when formed we engage to march to Headquarters of the American Army with the utmost Expedition and to be under the command of such Field Officer or Officers as the Gen. Court shall appoint. And we farther agree during the Time aforesaid to be subject to such Generals as are or shall be appointed; and to be under such Regulations in every Respect as are provided for the Army aforesaid. Dated this Day of A. D. 1776.

Jesse Jones	Zebediah Farrar.
John Peter	Richard Heard
Sarson Belcher	Joseph Smith
Timothy Underwood	John Merriam.
Josia Farrar	Abraham Parmenter
Ephraim Smith	Benjamin Dudley
Phinehas Glezen	Israel Jones
Uriah Moore.	

Besides the furnishing of men and equipments various other services were from time to time required of the town. At one time the towns were assessed for hay for the army at

Cambridge, and Sudbury was required to furnish nine tons; only three other towns were required to furnish as much. At another time they were called on to provide men and teams to convey gunpowder to Springfield.

CHAPTER XXIII.

1775-1800.

Attention the Town Bestowed on its Home Needs during the War. — Specimen Report of a Town-Meeting. — Attitude of the Town towards the Measures of Boston Merchants relative to the Reduction of Prices. — Appointment of Delegate to a Convention Called for the Purpose of Framing a New Constitution. — Committee Appointed to Regulate Prices. — Report of Committee. — Vote on the New Constitution. — Educational Matters. — Division of the Town. — Committee on a Line of Division. — Committee Appointed to Present a Remonstrance to the Court — Instructions to the Committee. — Act of the Court Authorizing a Division. — Committee Appointed to Make a Division of the Money and Real Estate. — Report of the Committee. — Appointment of Other Committees. — Financial Report. — Official Boards for 1780 and 1781. — Miscellaneous. — Shay's Rebellion. — Erection of Meeting-House. — Miscellaneous.

> The roll of drums and the bugle's wailing
> Vex the air of our vales no more ;
> The spear is beaten to hooks of pruning,
> The share is the sword the soldiers wore.
> WHITTIER.

THE following specimen of work done at a fall town-meeting in the very midst of the war shows that home needs were not neglected while military matters were absorbing so much attention. Nov. 8, 1779, the town granted money as follows, namely : —

To pay the several town Debts   £1457 : 0 : 0
To pay the Revd Ministers their Salary   148 : 0 : 0

Gratuity to the Revd Ministers	£2000 : 0 : 0
for the Grammar School	1000 : 0 : 0
for a Reading and Writing School	2000 : 0 : 0
for the support of the Poor	2000 : 0 : 0
to pay the Assessors	200 : 0 : 0
to pay the town Treasrer	40 : 0 : 0
to the Towns Com^{ttee} for money paid to the Last Six months men to the State of New York	500 : 0 : 0
to the Selectmen the money paid to s^d men by order of the General Court	500 : 0 : 0
to pay the money that has been paid to the six months men to Rhode Island	180 : 0 : 0
to provide for the Continental families	800 : 0 : 0

At the same town meeting adjourned to Dec. 6th 1779 the town granted six hundred pounds to enable a committee chosen at said meeting to oppose a Division of the town and to carry on said affair.

JAMES THOMPSON, Town Clerk.

At a town meeting held July 12, 1779, it was

Voted that this town highly approves of the measures taken by the merchants and other the inhabitants of the town of Boston in order to reduce the exorbitant prices of the necessaries of life. Consequently to appreciate our Currency that the town will adopt such reasonable measures as may be agreed upon by the joint Committees from the several towns in this state. It also voted to send Major Joseph Curtis to represent them in the convention to meet in Cambridge for the purpose of framing a new constitution or form of government, and instructed him to cause a printed copy of the form of a constitution that might be agreed upon to be transmitted to the Select Men of the town.

Aug 9th. The town voted to appoint seven persons to state the prices of Innholders' labour, Theaming, manufactures and all other articles not taken up by the convention at Concord.

Aug. 16th. The town having met according to adjournment, the Committee appointed to state the prices of all such articles as were not taken up by the Convention at Concord reported as follows

West India Rum by the gallon	£6. 9
New England Rum by the gallon	4.15
Coffe by the pound	4.15

Sugar by the pound from 11 to 14. Chocolate by the pound 24. Bohe Tea by the pound 5 : 16. Cotton wool by the pound 37 : 6. German Steel 30 D° Salt best quality by the Bushel £10 : 10

Country Produce — Indian Corn by the Bushel 80, Rye by the Bushel, £5 : 10   Wheat by the Bushel £8 : 10   Beaf by the pound 5 Muton, Lamb and Veal by the pound 3 : 6   Foreign Beaf and Pork as sett by the convention.   Butter by the pound 11   Chese Dᵒ 6   Milk by the quart 16   English Hay qʳ hundred 30

Men's shoes 6ˡᵇˢ, women's shoes 4ˡᵇˢ, cotton cloth 4 : 6,

Labor. — teaming under 30 miles 18, carpenter work by the day 60, Mason per day 60, Maids wages per week 5 Dollars.   Oxen per day 24, Horse Hire 3 per mile.   Inn Holder a good dinner 20, common dinner 12.   Best supper and Breakfast 15, each common Do. 12, Lodgings 4.   Horse keeping 24 hours on hay 15, on grass 10, a yoke of oxen a night 15.

The grade of prices thus established was made in accordance with a resolve of a convention that met at Concord, and the list of prices made was in depreciated currency that was in ratio of about twenty shillings paper to one shilling in silver. " If any one should persist in refusing to accept these prices, their names should be published in the public News Paper and the good people of the town should withhold all trade and intercourse from them."

On May 17, 1779, a vote was taken to see how many favored the formation of a new constitution or form of government. Fifty-nine voted in the affirmative and ten in the negative. The representative was instructed to vote for calling a State convention to form the new constitution.

At a meeting held May 22, 1780, " The Constitution being read, the town voted that they think it reasonable that each town in the State should pay their own proper representatives both their travel to and attendance at the General Court, and desire that clause providing for their pay for travel out of the public treasury should be altred, 41 voting for this alteration and 8 against it. They desire that the word Protestant may be inserted in the room of, or added to the word Christian Religion, in qualifications of the Govenor and all other officers both civil and military, 30 for and 19 against it.

" They also desire that the time for revising the Constitution may not exceed seven years, 55 voting for this alteration, one against it."

EDUCATIONAL MATTERS.

Prominent among the records relating to educational matters in the early part of the period was the following: 1773. "To Daniel Bowker for building N. W. School House 18 pounds, to the same for building Lanham School House 23–6–8. To Ambrose Tower for building school house near west meeting house 17–7–4. To Wm Dudley to building the Farm end school house 26–13–4." In 1774, a vote was taken to see "if the town will order that the several school houses in said town shall be supplied with wood for the future at the charge of the town." It "passed in the negative." It may be that it had been customary for the citizens of each district to contribute wood for the school-houses and that this was an early movement made to have it supplied by the town. That the school-houses were warmed in those times is evident. The following year the town granted eight pounds for supplying the several school-houses with wood for the year, and repeatedly after this were sums granted for this purpose. That the school-houses at that time were warmed by means of a fire-place is indicated by the following record of 1782: "To Jacob Reed for mending hearth at Lanham school house." In 1778, the town voted to build a new school-house near Mr. Phineas Puffers. In 1779, it was voted to build a new school-house in the north-west corner of the town, appropriating the two old school-houses for the building of the new.

DIVISION OF THE TOWN.

A prominent event of this period was the division of the town. The proposition came before the town by petition of John Tilton and others June 25, 1778, in the East meeting-house. "The question was put whether it was the minds of the Town, that the Town of Sudbury should be divided into two towns, and it was passed in the affirmative. And appointed the following gentlemen to agree on a Division Line and Report at the Adjournment of this meeting viz Col Ezekiel How Capt Richard Heard Mr Nathan Loring Mr Phinehas Glezen Mr John Maynard and Mr John

Meriam." The committee reported that they were not agreed as to the line of division.

At a meeting held Jan. 1, 1779, the town appointed Major Joseph Curtis, Thomas Plympton, Esq., Mr. John Balcom, Capt. Richard Heard and Capt. Jonathan Rice to agree on a line of division. At the same meeting measures were taken to petition the General Court. Strong opposition at once manifested itself, and the town was warned to meet at the West meeting-house December 6,—

" 1st To choose a moderator

" 2d To see if the town will choose a Committee to act in behalf of this Town at the Great and General Court of this State to Oppose a Division of sd Town and give the Comtee So chosen Such Instruction Relating to said affair as the Town may think proper and grant a Sum of Money to Enable said Comtee to Carry on Said Business "

The meeting resulted as follows : —

" 1st Chose Asahel Wheeler moderator

" 2d Chose Col Ezekiel Howe Mr Wm Rice Jur and Thomas Plympton Esq a committee for the Purpose contained in this article and granted the sum of three hundred Pounds to Enable their Comtee to Carry on said affair then adjourned this meeting to tomorrow at three oclock at the same place.

" Tuesday Decemr 7th The Town met according to adjournment proceeded and gave their Comtee Chosen to oppose a division of this Town &c the following Instructions viz.

" To Colo Ezekiel Howe, Thos Plympton Esq and Mr Rice Jur you being chosen a Comtee by the Town of Sudbury to oppose a division of sd Town as Lately Reported by a Comtee of the Honle General Court of this State

" You are hereby authorized and Instructed to preferr a Petition or memorial to the General Court in behalf of Said Town. Praying that the Bill for Dividing Sd Town May be set a fire or altred setting forth the Great Disadvantages the Westerly part of the Town will Labour under by a Division of said Town as reported by sd Comtee viz : as said report deprives them of all the gravel and obliges them to maintain

the one half of the Great Causeways on the Easterly part
of said Town notwithstanding the necessary repairs of the
Highways on the westerly part of said Town are nearly
double to that on the East.

" Said Report also deprives them of the Pound, it also
deprives them of a Training field though Given by the Proprietors of Said Town to the Westerly side for a Training
field for Ever

" And further as there is no provision made in said report
for the Support of the Poor in Said Town which will be a
verry heavy burthen to the West side of the Town as the
report now stands. Also at said adjournment the Town
Granted the sum of three Hundred pounds, in addition to
the other Grant of three hundred Pounds to Enable their
Com^{tee} to carry on said Petition

" Then the town by their vote dissolved this meeting "

But, notwithstanding the vigorous protest made by prominent citizens, their arguments did not prevail with the
Court, and an article was passed, April 10, 1780, which
authorized a division of the town. A committee was appointed by the town to consider a plan for the division of
property and an equitable adjustment of the obligations
of the East and West parts of the town. At an adjourned
meeting, held March 14, the committee rendered the following report which was accepted and agreed upon.

" We the Subscribers being appointed a committee to Join
a Com^{tee} from East Sudbury to make a Division of the
Money and Estate belonging to the Town of Sudbury and
East Sudbury agreeable to an Act of the General Court
Passed the 10th of April 1780, for Dividing the Town of
Sudbury, proceded and agreed as followeth viz : that all the
Money Due on the Bonds and Notes being the Donation of
Mary Doan to the East Side of the River be Disposed of to
East Sudbury according to the will of the Donor. And
the money Due on Bonds and Notes given by Mr. Peter
Noyes and Capt Joshua Haynes for the Benefit of the Poor
and Schooling be Equally Divided between Each of the

S^d Towns, which Sum is 423 : 3 : 4   That all the Money Due on Bonds and Notes for the New Grant Lands, or Money Now in the Treasury or in Constables' hands be Equally Divided between Each of Said Towns which Sums are as follows viz :

" Due on New Grant Bonds and Notes   133 : 14 : 7
" Due from Constable   3110 : 10 : 7
" Due from the Town Treasurer   348 :   6 : 5

" And that all Land that belonged to the Town of Sudbury or for the benefit of the Poor shall be Divided agreeable to the Act of the General Court for Dividing Said Town.   And that the Pound and Old Bell and the Town Standard of Weights and Measures which belonged to the Town of Sudbury be Sold at publick vandue and the proceeds to be Equally divided between the towns of Sudbury and East Sudbury.

" Also that the Town Stock of Arms and Amanition be Divided as set forth in the Act of the General Court for Dividing the Town of Sudbury.   And if any thing shall be made to appear to be Estate or property that Should belong to the town of Sudbury before the Division of the above articles it Shall be Equally Divided between the Town of Sudbury and the Town of East Sudbury.   And that the Town of East Sudbury shall Support and Maintain as their Poor During their Life the Widow Vickry and Abigail Isgate, And all Such Persons as have Gained a Residence in the Town of Sudbury before the division of S^d Town and shall hereafter be brought to the Town of Sudbury or the Town of East Sudbury as their Poor Shall be Supported by that Town in which they Gained their Inhabitance.   Also that the Debts Due from Said Town of Sudbury Shall be paid the one half by the Town of Sudbury and the other half by the Town of East Sudbury which Sum is 2977 : 7 : 1

" ASHER CUTLER   ASAHEL WHEELER ⎫
" THO^s WALKER   ISAAC MAYNARD   ⎬ Committee "
" JAMES THOMSON ⎭

Other committees concerning the matter of division were appointed the same year.   The assessors were to make a

division with East Sudbury of the men required of Sudbury
and East Sudbury for three years; also to make division of
clothing, beef, etc., required of said town. A committee,
April 23, 1781, made the following financial exhibit: —

Due to Sudbury in the Constable's and Treasurer's hands £1487 . 9 . 10
That the town had to pay the sum of   1661 . 19 . 5
Sudbury's part of the Powder   142 lbs
Their part of the Lead   394 lbs
their part of the Guns on hand   4
The old Bell, Pound and Town Standard of Weights and
    Measures sold for   £1183 . 10 . 0
Sudbury's part of the above sum is   391 . 15 . 0
Received of ——— money   27 . 0 . 0
The charge of sale   20 . 8 . 0
    The remainder to be paid by the treasurer of E. Sudbury.
Money due to the town in Mʳ Cutler's hands taken out of
    the State Treasury for what was advanced by the
    Town of Sudbury for the support of Soldiers' families
    who are in the Continental Army   1206 . 2 . 0

In the division Sherman's Bridge was left partly in each
town, and the river formed about half the town's eastern
boundary. At a place on Sand Hill the town line was made
irregular in order to admit the training-field and the Caleb
Wheeler farm, which was a triangular piece of about forty-
three acres. The definition of the town boundary line and
the clause which retained the training-field and the Wheeler
farm in the town is as follows: —

" Beginning with the river between Concord and Lincoln,
thence running with the river till it comes to the mouth of a
ditch on the west side of said river between the lands of
Wᵐ Baldwin Esq, and Eliakim Rice; — thence on said ditch
to the County road leading to Stow, crossing said road;
connected (or continuing) on the South side thereof till it
comes to the line between land of Nathˡ Rice and Jona.
Carter; — thence southerly with the line between said Rice
& Carter to land of Elisha Wheelor; then running Easterly
with the line between said Carter and Wheelor to the
County roading leading to Marlboro'; — thence running up
and bounded on the Westerly side of said road till it comes

opposite to the line between the heirs of Lieut. Danl Good-
now and land in possession of Robert Emes at "Sandy
Hill"; — thence crossing said road to the corner aforesaid;
— thence running to a White Oak the head of Capt. Moses
Maynard's meadow; — thence on a straight line; — thence
on a straight line to a swamp-White-Oak on the bank of the
River — eastwardly from the dwelling house of Capt. Moses
Stone; thence up the river to Framingham line."

"And it is also enacted that the House and lands of
Caleb Wheelor — together with the Training-field adjoining
thereto, shall remain to the Town of Sudbury."

In the division provision was made for the maintenance,
by Sudbury, of the Canal Bridge and that portion of the
old causeway which extends from the bridge westerly to the
upland. As the support of the Canal Bridge came upon
Sudbury and mention is made of it in various places in the
Town Records, it may be of interest here to state something
of its history. This bridge is so named because it crossed
that portion of the river which it is supposed ran through an
artificial channel. No bridge in that immediate vicinity but
the "Town bridge" is mentioned in the earlier records, and
the stream, as before stated (see page 93), originally passed
near the eastern upland. The earliest record we have any
knowledge of, which contains reference to this bridge, is in
1768, which is a bill for the repairing of the "new bridge
near Dea. Stone's, Lanham, Sherman's, the Town bridge and
the Canal bridge." This shows its existence at that time,
but gives no intimation as to when it was made; neither is
there any record so far as we know as to when the canal was
constructed. An artificial opening might not have been
made there until years after the bridge was made. The first
water-way may have been a natural one which only required
a small crossing, and may subsequently have been enlarged
by the current. In other words, when the causeway was
built a small outlet may have been left in it at this point for
the purpose of allowing the water to pass off the meadow
more readily in time of flood. This passage way at first may
have been but an open fordway. In the process of time, as

the causeway was gradually raised and the channel or aperture naturally increased in size, a more substantial bridge may have been required. Another theory is that the making of the canal and the bridge was the result of raising the causeway at one time or another. If the town succeeded in raising the money when it tried to do so by means of a lottery in 1758, the Canal Bridge may have been built at that time. As there was opposition to raising the causeway, because it was supposed that it would set back the water, the statement being made that there was " not one foot of fall in the river for 25 or 30 miles," an aperture might have been left in the raised road or causeway or a canal cut to obviate the difficulty, and the canal would require a bridge. Still another theory is that the canal was built by private enterprise. Mr. Abel Gleason, now one of the oldest inhabitants of Wayland, states that when he was a boy, ten or twelve years old, he helped make hay on both sides of the canal for Colonel Baldwin, the owner of the land ; and that the colonel told him that " the water always made its way over the ' oxbow ' more or less ; but at one time a Mr. Goodnow and another man, whose name he could not remember, dug out a straight channel for the water to run in." A channel once dug would naturally increase until sufficiently large to allow all the water to pass through it. The short causeway from Sudbury to the Canal Bridge was laid out by the county commissioners in 1832, and the same year was made under the supervision of a committee from East Sudbury.

The following officers were chosen, just before the division, at a town-meeting held in the East and West meeting-houses, March 6, 1780 : " Selectmen — Capt. Asahel Wheeler. Wm Baldwin Esq. Mr. Thomas Walker, Capt. Caleb Moulton, Mr. Isaac Maynard. Capt. Thadeus Russel, Mr. Benjamin Smith. Town Clerk and Treasurer James Thompson. Other officers chosen were 3 Assessors, 4 Constables, A ' committee of correspondence,' consisting of five persons. 4 ' wardins.' 2 surveyors of shingles, 2 sealers of leather, 3 fence viewers. 2 deer reeves, 4 tythingmen, 4 hog reeves, 2 field drivers, 8 surveyors of highway, 2 fish reeves, and 2 clerks of the market. Total on the official board fifty-five persons."

After the division the town went on with its usual activity. At a town-meeting held March 5, 1781, the following officers were chosen: "Moderator — Capt. Jonathan Rice. Selectmen — Mr. Wm Rice, Capt. Moses Stone, Lieut. Jacob Reed, Lieut. Abijah Brigham, Capt. Samuel Knight. Clerk and Treasurer, Wm Rice." The records state that the town-meetings were frequently held at the house of Mr. Johnson. Probably this was the house of Aaron Johnson, Innholder. Some of the early town records and acts after its division are the following: Oct. 8, 1781, granted "Rev. Mr. Bigelow for salary the ensuing year seventy-four pounds in specie, also granted for a grammar school for a year, 12 pounds and ordered that said school be kept at the school house near the meeting house, also granted for support of a reading and writing school 48 pounds and ordered the same to be kept in the other four school houses in the same proportion. Also granted 60 pounds to furnish their quota of beef for the supply of the army. Also allowed 16 shillings for the taking care of the meeting house, and chose John Green to take care of the meeting house and dig graves as occasion required for the ensuing year." At the same meeting money was granted for the supply of the soldiers for the Continental army.

In the warrant of a meeting dated Jan. 15, 1781, was an article "to see if the town would choose a committee and empower them to bring an action against or proceed otherwise in a suit of law with the town of Boston for their bringing Mary Piper and her children into Sudbury, she and her children not being able to support themselves and not belonging to Sudbury." At a subsequent meeting the committee was chosen to proceed against Boston as suggested.

In 1782, it was "voted to pay Rev. Mr. Bigelow's salary in specie 111 pounds, of which Roland Bogle's part to collect as constable was £52—11^s—9^d and Mr. Joshua Haynes part as constable to collect was £58—8^s—3^d." In 1782, the town ordered their committee to build a suitable place at the school-house "near the meeting house for hanging their bell on instead of repairing the place where it now stands." In 1785, the number of selectmen chosen was reduced to three. In 1787, it was voted to rebuild the canal bridge. The same year Isaac Lincoln was chosen to take care of the meeting-house and ring the bell, for which he was to have eighteen shillings, which was the lowest price bid.

SHAY'S REBELLION.

In 1786, occurred an event called Shay's Rebellion or Insurrection. The cause of it was the unsettled condition of the country, its depreciated currency, and a lack of business prosperity in general. A small portion of the community sought to adjust matters by resorting to arms. An effort was made by some of the insurgents to prevent the holding of the county courts, and, on several occasions, the presence of troops was required to preserve the peace. Concord, being a county town, was one of the imperiled places, and there were indications that on Sept. 12, 1768, an outbreak might occur there, as on that day a company of about one hundred men assembled there under command of Job Shattuck of Groton, and Nathan and Sylvanus Smith of Shirley. Matters, however, were adjusted without any open outbreak. From the proximity of Concord to Sudbury, naturally the town would be expected to render military service at that place if it was needed, and also to furnish aid, in common with the other towns, for the suppression of the rebellion. The following papers are supposed to refer to such service.

"Sudbury 10ᵗʰ September 1786

"Sir   you will fully comply with the orders you received from me this Day, Excepting your Marching by the shotest Rout to Concord, you will instead of Marching to Concord March with your Company Imbodied to Sudbury Meeting House at Eight oclock in the Morning in order to join the Regᵗ

"Capt Benj Sawin   yours &c Jonᵃ Rice Lt. C. Comd "

" Commonwealth of Massachusetts D^r

" To the Selectmen of Sudbury for furnishing the men
that was called out to Supres the Late Rebellion agreeably
to the Militia Law to three different times to seven Days
each at four Shillings Pr Day."

Nov. 24, 1788, it was voted to hear the report of a committee who had, at a previous meeting, been appointed to
present a report of the depreciation of Mr. Bigelow's salary.
They " reported that the sum of £155—18^s—9^d was due to
Mr. Bigelow on the deficiency of his salaries for the years
1776, 1777, 1778 and half of 1779," and it was voted to pay
£120 to make up the deficiency.

In 1789, the town " empowered a committee to purchase
the land of Mr. Doane for the purpose of enlarging the
burying ground and voted that the committee provide and
build the wall around the yard." When the town were
assembled in October, 1789, and the committee reported
relative to the land for enlarging the burying-ground, it was
voted " that the inhabitants of the town now present go
out and inspect the land proposed, when the inhabitants
returned, and a vote was taken, but passed in the negative;
this question came up if they would accept of the land if
they could have it free of expense and they voted in the
affirmative."

In 1792, the town voted to sell the training field in the
southeast part of the town, and " the Committee formerly
employed to sell the Work house " were appointed to attend
to the work. The same year measures were taken for the
prevention of the small-pox. The article concerning it in
the warrant was " To see if the town would admit the Small
Pox into sd town by Inoculation." " It passed in the negative." The following year the selectmen were instructed
" to take measures to prevent the spreading of the small
pox, and to prosecute the persons who transgressed the laws
respecting the disease." Instructions were also given " to
make diligent search to see if there were any persons who
had been inoculated for small pox contrary to law."

In accordance with a vote of the General Court in 1794, a map was made of the town. This map, a copy of which is in the State Archives (Vol. II., page 7), was made by Mathias Mosmon, and bears date April 17, 1795. A copy of it is here given together with the following statement and description by the author of the map: —

" The above Plan of the Town of Sudbury in the County of Middlesex, Common Wealth of Massachusetts was taken by the Direction of a Committee Chosen by the Inhabitants of S^d Sudbury in obedience to an order of the General Court dated June 26th — 1794. on the above plan Air inserted and described Each Town line that meets or joins with Sudbury. the Rivers are also accurately surveyed and planned, the breadth of which are as followeth. the River Elsabeth is from 4 to 5 rods wide, but [there is] no public bridge over the river where it joins Sudbury, the other river called Sudbury or Concord River is from 7 to 8 or 9 rods wide, and [there is] one bridge over sd river where it joins Sudbury called Sharman's Bridge, 100 feet long, one-half belonging to Sudbury, and 25 rod of Causeway. Sudbury also [is to] build and keep in repair the Canal Bridge in East Sudbury Long causeway and 52 rods of s^d causeway. the County roads are also surveyed and planned. in Sudbury is but one house for public worship which is noted. the center of the town is about one mile northwestwardly from the meetinghouse. the distance from S^d Sudbury to Cambridge the shire-town of the county is 17 miles, and from s^d Sudbury to Boston the Metropolis of the Commonwealth of Massachusetts through Watertown and Roxbury is 22 miles, and through & over West Boston Bridge is 20 miles. in Sudbury is but 3 ponds of any considerable magnitude which has been Surveyed and planned as above. here is no falls of Water worthy of note. in S^d Sudbury is not a hill whose summit is lofty. in the Southwardly part of s^d town is part of a hill called Penobscott which will be described in the plan of Framingham. No manufactories are erected in Sudbury. in s^d [town] are three grist mills, two saw mills, and one fulling mill as above described, on a

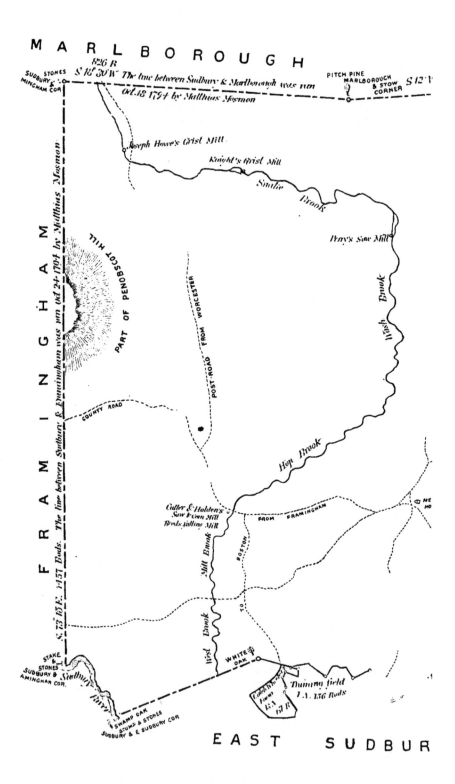

T O W

line between Sudbury & Stow
by Matthias Mosman Oct 22 1794

Pratt's Pond
36 A.

STAKE & STONES
AN ANGLE IN
SUDBURY & STOW LINE

330 rods up said river run by Jabez Brown Oct 1794
Stow River or the River Elizabeth

STAKE &
STONES
ACTON S

N 56 W
Oct 23 1794
by M.M.

STAKE & STONES
ACTON & CONCOR

FROM

MARLBOROUGH TO CONCORD

'llis's Pond
As measur

ACTON

LANCASTER

FROM

NTY ROAD FROM

THROUGH

LITTLETON

CONCORD

N 56 W 771775 R° The line between Concord & Sudbury run Oct 17 1794 by Matthias Mosman

TOWN ROAD

N 56 45 W 7177 R°

f Br°

STAKES
&
STONES

so le

LINCOLN SUDBURY, CONCORD
& E.SUDBURY CORNER

Concord

Stream known by several different names as above. the width of which where it leaves Marlborough and enters Sudbury is not much more than a yard wide and where it enters East Sudbury is about 5 yards wide. in the North-wardly part of s^d Sudbury a mine has been discovered and worked upon. the depth of the hole is about —— feet in a Ledge of rocks supposed to be a copper mine but has not been worked in since the beginning of the Revolution. here is not Iron Works or furnaces. said plan is laid down by a scale of 200 rods to an inch Surveyed by

" MATHIAS MOSMON

" Dated at Sudbury April 17 = 1795."

THE NEW MEETING-HOUSE.

In the latter part of the period the town took measures to erect a new meeting-house. In 1789, " chose a committee to look out a place suitable for a new meeting house, for drafting a plan, and receiving proposals from individuals in relation to building the same." They subsequently decided upon the shape and dimensions, but, different opinions pre-vailing relative to the location, the construction of the build-ing was deferred for some years.

Oct. 5, 1795, the town again voted " to build a new Meet-ing House, that it should be erected on the common land near to the present meeting house, and that the south and west cells of sd house should occupy the ground on which the south and west cells of the present meeting house now stand upon, and that the enlargement of the meeting house should extend North and East. Voted to accept a plan drawn by Capt Thomson which plan is 60 feet by 52 with a porch at one end with a steeple or spear on the top of sd porch. Voted that the Commitee for building the house should consist of nine persons, and that they should receive nothing for their services." In 1796, it was voted that a bell should be purchased for the meeting-house. October, 1798, the building committee presented to the town the sum-mary of receipts and expenditures which was six thousand twenty-five dollars and ninety-three cents. The town granted three hundred dollars for the purpose of grading

the ground around the new meeting-house. Those who
desired it were granted the privilege of working out their
proportionate share of the expense ; the price of labor being
nine pence per hour for a man and nine pence per hour for
a good yoke of oxen and cart. November, 1796, it was
" voted to request the Rev. Mr Bigelow to preach a sermon
at the dedication of the meeting house." At the same meeting it was " voted that the Pew Holders in the body of the
Meeting House as soon as Divine Service is over fling their
pew Doors wide open so as not to obstruct the passage of
the people in the allies — that the Speaker pass out first,
then the pew holders to pass on after as fast as Conveniently
may be out at the front Door, then those who sit in the
seats next — also voted that as soon as they are out they
move off from the door steps so as to let the people have
liberty to come out without Crowding — also voted that the
pew holders in the galleries fling their pew doors wide open
that they empty their pews, together with the fore seats
first, the 2^d and 3^d seats to follow in course — also voted
that those who come down the West pair of stairs pass out
at the West Door those who come down the East stairs pass
out at the East Door, and to move from the door steps so
as to give Liberty to empty the house as soon as conveniently may be. It was then voted to Choose a Committee
for the purpose of Regulating the Assembling of the people
at the Dedication of the Meeting House, to keep good order
on said day and prevent damage being done to said House.
Said Committee to consist of 12." At the same meeting
" voted to appropriate to the use of the Singing Society in
Said Town the front gallery and so much of the side galleries
next the front as shall be necessary for their accommodation."

May, 1799, the town-meeting adjourned to allow its committee on building stables to go out and view the land ; on
their return they reported that they had " set up a stake
and stone at the south east corner of Lt Willis stables to the
North east corner of the meeting house. Sd line being about
35 ft back of sd meeting house." " Report was accepted."

In 1796, the town-meetings were held at the house of Col.
Benjamin Sawin, innholder. This was during the building

of the new meeting-house. The same year the town appointed Col. Sawin's new barn and yard adjoining the same for a pound for a year.

October, 1797, " The Committee previously appointed to select a suitable place whereon to erect a pound reported that said pound be erected upon the East end of the Burying yard, the south side to be erected about ten feet north of Lt Reuben Rices Stone wall, the wall of sd pound to be 5$\frac{1}{2}$ ft in Height with a Hewn stick of chestnut, or white pine Timber 10 inches in Height upon the top thereof, the Burying yard wall to form one side. Sd pound to be thirty feet square within the walls." The report was accepted, and twenty dollars was granted for the purpose. The committee appointed for letting out the building of the pound were to " have the privilege of all the stones on the common round the meeting house, excepting so many as shall be necessary for horse blocks." At the same meeting forty dollars was granted for rebuilding Lanham Bridge.

April, 1797, voted " to provide a carriage for the town's use Suitable for the conveyance of Corps to the Burying yard." October, 1797, granted thirty dollars for the purpose of teaching a singing school for one month. In 1798, " Chose a Committee to let out the building of a school house in the north east district in place of the one which was burnt." Also appropriated two hundred dollars for the building. At the same meeting appropriated two hundred and fifty-five dollars for building a school-house in the centre district. Also at the same meeting, granted " for a harness for the town carriage to carry corps upon 15 : 75 " In 1799, voted " that the Committee that was appointed to build a shelter for the funeral carriage, if they think it can conveniently be done, to build a place in it for storing of the towns stock of ammunition."

CHAPTER XXIV.

Early Families Residing in Sudbury about the Beginning of the Present
Century. — Families Who Came into Sudbury during the Interval
between the Formation of the Town and about the Middle of the
Present Century. — Biographical Sketches.

> Happy he whom neither wealth nor fashion,
> Nor the march of the encroaching city,
> > Drives an exile
> From the hearth of his ancestral homestead.
> > > LONGFELLOW.

IN entering upon the history of the nineteenth century,
we may, with propriety, pause in our narrative to notice the
condition of the community at the beginning of this new
period, and compare it with the condition of things in former and distant years. We have arrived at a point when
this can be done to advantage. We have chronicled the
events of more than a century and a half, and considered
the character, customs and conduct of the earlier inhabitants,
and the town when in its formative state. We have seen
influences gather and grow from sources small and remote,
and men come in, act their part, and go out. Before proceeding to consider new facts, let us notice the results of
those already set forth and their relations to what is to come.
Let us notice to what extent early names and families were
familiar at the beginning of the nineteenth century, what
new inhabitants had come into town, and how far there had
been a transmission of customs, traits and manners of living
and doing in the home, the church and the town.

Down to about the year 1800, quite a share of the old
families remained, and, to an extent, kept their former
prestige. Such were the Goodnows, Bents, Parmenters,

Maynards and Reeds, the Hunts, Browns and Hows, also
the Haynes family, the Rices and Plymptons. In East
Sudbury there were the Rutters, Curtises and Lokers, the
Johnsons, Noyeses, Grouts and Wards. But, while so many
of the old families remained, they no longer, as at the town's
beginning, bore all the responsibility of its management, nor
were their names alone prominent upon the records. Some
of these families had begun to decline. Their ranks were
decimated, their power was on the wane. So it was with
the Hows, the Plymptons, the Maynards, the Rices, the
Reeds; and in East Sudbury with the Curtises, Noyeses and
Grouts. Indeed, the decline of some of these families,
which began before the century set in, has to such an extent
gone on that some of them have not a member in Sudbury
who bears the family name ; when it is called, no one is left
to respond. Their history is but a tradition for others to
tell, or found in fragmentary records on the town book, or
inscribed on the tombstones of Sudbury's old-time burying
grounds. But the decadence of old families is not the only
reason why, at the beginning of the present century, town
business was not wholly done by the descendants of the
early grantees. There had been, in the process of years, the
introduction of new families into Sudbury, many of which
took a prominent part in its affairs. Among those of this
class who came before or about the beginning of the
eighteenth century, there are the following names of persons ou the west side of the river : Balcom, Bogle, Bowker,
Brigham, Brintnal, Bush, Clapp, Cutler, Cutter, Dakin,
Gibbs, Hayden, Jones, Mossman, Perry, Puffer, Richardson,
Stanhope, Stevens, Taylor, Thompson, Tower, Walker,
Wedge, Wheeler, Willis; on the east side, Abbott, Allen,
Baldwin, Brewer, Bryant, Cutting, Damon, Drury, Frink,
Gleason, Graves, Heard, Jennison, Long, Paris, Reeves,
Roby, Ross, Sherman and Wellington. The following are
names of families who settled in the present territory of
Sudbury between about the years 1800 and 1850 : Adams,
Allen, Arnold, Bacon, Barton, Burr, Carr, Clark, Conant,
Dwyer, Eames, Eaton, Fairbanks, Garfield, Gerry, Harring-
ton, Horr, Hudson, Hurlbut, Lyon, O'Neil, Powers, Pratt,

Robinson, Rogers and Shaw. We will give a few facts concerning such of these families as have a member still living
in town who bears the family name, or is in some way still
identified with the place. The object of these sketches is
not to give anything like a complete genealogy, but, as in
the case of the early grantees (Chapter III.), only to give a
brief outline of family history, mainly as it has been connected with the town.

ADAMS. — At an early date the name of Adams is upon
the town records, and the indications are that one of the
name was living near the Sudbury and Concord boundary
not long after the settlement began. In 1671, James Adams
was to have liberty to feed his cattle on Sudbury bounds,
and " to take old and dry wood that shall be upon the
ground, the said Adams to prevent any trespass by Concord
herds or cattle also in our wood and timber, forthwith to
give notice to the town." (Sudbury Records.) This James
Adams is probably the one referred to in the genealogy of
Concord inhabitants (Concord History) as belonging to a
family said to have been banished from Scotland by Oliver
Cromwell, and who married Priscilla Ramsden of Concord
in 1662, and died Dec. 2, 1707. James had seven children,
— Priscilla, Elizabeth, James, Hannah, John, Nathaniel and
Dorcas. Descendants of these have lived in Acton and
Carlisle, which places were formerly in Concord. A John
Adams of Sudbury was wounded at the Swamp Fight, R. I.,
in 1675. (See period 1675–1700.) The Adams family of
Sudbury descended from the Acton branch. John Adams
was born at Acton, Sept. 27, 1746, and had six children, —
Lydia, Paul, John, Josiah H., Mercy, Mary. Josiah H. was
born Aug. 4, 1780, and lived about twenty years on the
place now occupied by the American Powder Company; he
then moved about a mile south to the present John Adams
place. He had five children, — two of them sons, Joseph B.
and John. John Adams, the present superintendent of the
Fitchburg Railroad, was born at and now owns the place
formerly occupied by his father in Sudbury.

ALLEN or ALLIN. — The Allen family was early in Sudbury. The name of John Allen is on the " Old Petition "

of 1676; on another, of 1690 are the names of John and Thomas, Jr., and Zebediah, Jr., and on a paper of 1707, subscribed to by the East Side inhabitants protesting against a parochial precinct on the West Side, are the names of John and Samuel Allen. The first Allen of the present century in Sudbury was John Plympton, who moved from Wayland to South Sudbury, where he carried on the blacksmith's trade for nearly fifty years. He married Sibel Read who was born in Sudbury in 1800. He had four children, — Francis, Franklin S., Margaret M., Abby A. Margaret M. Allen is at present a resident of South Sudbury.

ARNOLD. — The name of William Arnold is on an old petition among a list of inhabitants on the west side the river in 1707; but for an interval of years there were none by the name in town. Edwin, first Sudbury resident of the name in the present century, is grandson of Winslow and Abigail (Hagar) Arnold, who were born, married and lived in Marlboro. His father was Joel who married Ruth, daughter of Israel and Susanna (Stone) Parmenter of Sudbury, April 25, 1843. Edwin married Abby Hunt, daughter of Abel and Sally Smith of Sudbury. They have had one child, Frances A. Edwin Arnold resides at South Sudbury.

BACON. — The Sudbury ancestor of the Bacon family, which in the present century has resided in town, was Jonathan who came from Natick in 1835. His father, whose name was Jonathan, was born in Natick in 1756, married Zipporah (Goulding) Mann and had two children, Jonathan and Ebenezer. Jonathan, Jr., married Lydia Hammond of Natick, born Oct. 11, 1778, and had six children, — Zipporah, Asa, Samuel, Edward and Lydia, all born in Natick, and Adoniram born in Sudbury. He lived on the South Sudbury and Marlboro road in a house built and once occupied by Joel Jones, and at present occupied by Adoniram. Jonathan died several years ago, but his widow, Lydia Bacon, is still living at the age of one hundred and one.

BALCOM. — The Sudbury Balcoms are descended from Henry Balcom of Charlestown, Mass., a blacksmith. He married Elizabeth Haynes of Sudbury, August 12, 1666, and died April 29, 1683. Soon after his death, the family moved to Sudbury and settled in the northwesterly part in what is now Maynard, where his descendants still live. Among the children of Henry was Joseph, who was born Dec. 17, 1674, and died Sept. 17, 1745, at Sudbury. He married Tabitha Mossman. Among their children was John who was born March 13, 1713 (or 1715), and married Susanna Haynes, August 23, 1737. Among the children of John and Susanna was Asahel, born June 5, 1741, who married Jerusha Willis. Their children were Asa who married Adah Balcom, Jerusha who married Adam Howe, Rebecca who married Daniel Puffer. Asa was the father of Hollis and Asahel, two well-known citizens of the present century living in that part of Sudbury now Maynard.

BARTON. — George Barton was born in Concord, and came into town April 1, 1851. He married for his first wife Mary Susan, youngest daughter of Israel Hunt of Sudbury, and occupies the Israel Hunt farm in the Pantry district. His children are George H., born 1852; Frank P., 1857 and Alice M., 1859.

BOGLE. — Thomas was the first of the Bogle family who lived in Sudbury. He came from Scotland to Boston, and, after remaining there a short time, went to Sudbury, where he purchased the farm now occupied by Deacon Francis Walker. He had seven children, one of whom was Rowand who married Elizabeth Goodenow and occupied the old homestead. Rowand and Elizabeth had five children, — Hannah, Francis, Elizabeth, Submit and Polly. Francis married Patty Hemenway of Framingham, and had four children, — Miranda, Sarah H., Lucy and Nancy E. Miranda married Azariah Walker of Framingham, who purchased the Bogle farm in 1826, which he occupied till his death. Lucy and Nancy Bogle reside at South Sudbury.

BOWKER. — The Bowker family was in town as early as 1707; the name Widow Sarah Bowker being upon a paper of that date. A prominent member of the family was Capt. Daniel Bowker, who served in the Revolutionary War, and died early in the Nineteenth Century. He went with his wife from Hopkinton before 1756, and settled on what has since been known as the Bowker place in North Sudbury. He had ten children, two of whom were sons named Daniel and Joseph. He died Jan. 31, 1822, aged ninety-two, and his wife died June 28, 1813, aged seventy-nine. Daniel Jr., born Sept. 13, 1772, married Ruth Brown of Hubbardston and had fourteen children. He died Oct. 18, 1853, aged eighty-one, and his wife died Jan. 15, 1846, aged sixty-eight. Two sons of Daniel Jr. were Daniel and Samuel N. Daniel died May 19, 1880, leaving no children. Samuel N. was born June 16, 1799, and died Oct. 9, 1872. He married Mary Earle of Berwick, Me., and had seven children, one of whom is Frank M., born in 1850. Frank M. married for his first wife Anna Hunt of Morenci, Mich., and for his second Carrie Conley of Halifax, Nova Scotia, and has had five children. He lives on the old homestead, and his children are the fifth generation who have lived there.

BRIGHAM. — The ancestor of this family in New England was Thomas, who embarked from London for America in 1635, and settled in Watertown. He had several sons, the eldest of whom, named Thomas, lived in Marlboro, and married the granddaughter of Edmund Rice, one of Sudbury's original grantees. It is conjectured that the Sudbury Brigham's are descended from this branch of the family. The name of John Brigham is in the Indian Deed of the Two Mile Grant, and also (page 65) on the petition to Governor Dudley by the West Side people for a new precinct in 1706-7. One of the same name early settled in the territory of Maynard. The name of Samuel is found on the roll of the 2nd Foot Company in 1757. A prominent member of the family in the present century was Capt. William Brigham. His farm was that now occupied by Elisha Goodenow. Rufus, a son of William, resides at Sudbury Centre. The Brigham family have lived mostly in the north and northwest parts of the town.

BURR. — Hiram Burr, son of Daniel, came from Derby, Vt., in 1845, when a young man. His first wife was Ellen, daughter of Deacon Gardner Hunt. His second wife was Nancy J., daughter of Deacon Thomas Dakin. He owns and lives on the Gardner Hunt farm, South Sudbury. He has had four children, — Frank G., Arthur H., Clifford B., Howard C., Nellie May.

BUTTERFIELD. — Luther Butterfield was born at Antrim, N. H. He came to Sudbury in 1841, and settled in the Lanham district on the road from Sudbury to Saxonville. He has six children, — Ebenezer S., James B., George F., Sarah, Jerome, Edward C.

CARR. — The Sudbury ancestor of the Carr family now living in town was Ezra, who went to Sudbury in 1810 and resided on the old Carr homestead, then occupied by his brother John and since owned by his son Crosby. Abiathar, another son, was born in Wilmington, Vt. He married Rebecca, daughter of Israel and Rebecca (Rice) Wheeler, and had six children, four of whom are living, — Lucinda J., Charlotte M., Frederick E. and Merrick. Lucinda and Merrick are residents of Sudbury. The old homestead passed out of the family about 1850.

CONANT. — Silas Conant was born in Stow, May 31, 1747. He moved to North Sudbury in 1782, and lived until his death, Sept. 20, 1836, on the farm since owned and occupied, until his death in 1859, by Emory, his grandson. The father of Emory was Amos, who had four sons, — Emory, Dexter, Silas and Amos. John M., son of Amos, Jr., and present resident of Sudbury, is of the tenth generation from Roger, who came from England to Plymouth, New England, about 1623. John M. has served as selectman and assessor for several years. He married Lucretia A. Richards of Concord, Vt., and has had four children, — Clara J., Lillian, Edwin A. and Louisa.

CLARK. — Isaac Clark was born April 18, 1806, in Windham, N. Y., and moved to Hopkinton in 1816. He married Almira Osborn of Sudbury, Sept. 26, 1833. In April, 1837, he purchased and settled upon the Osborn place where he now resides. He has had six children, — Everett O., Eliza S., Almira A., Ellen O., Frederic P. and Franklin P.

CUTLER. — The name of Thomas Cutler is found on a petition of 1707, and that of Elisha on a muster-roll of 1755. The family have resided mostly at the south part of the town. Asher, grandfather of the late C. G. Cutler, Esq., once owned the mill at South Sudbury, which he left jointly to his sons Asher and Abel. In the early part of the century, Abel, the father of Christopher, kept a tavern near the Gravel Pit. C. G. Cutler, a well-known citizen, died at his residence in South Sudbury a few years since at the advanced age of ninety. He had four children, — Joseph, Mary, Emeline and Caroline.

CUTTER. — An early resident of this name was Nathanael, who was a soldier in Captain Nixon's Company in 1761. (See period 1750–1775.) Joseph Cutter was born in 1761, and married Prudence, daughter of James Thompson of Sudbury. He was a drum major in the Revolutionary War, and died in Sudbury in 1807. He left several children. A daughter married William Stone, who formerly kept tavern about a mile west of South Sudbury on the Boston and Worcester road (William Stone place). A son, Joseph, Jr., lived on the present Hiram Goodnow farm until his death. Joseph, Jr., married Lucy, daughter of Gideon Richardson. They had five children, — Dana, Augustus, Dexter, Caroline and Lucy Ann. Augustus married Abby A., daughter of John and Sibel (Read) Allen, and has four children, — Harry C., Howard A., Joseph, Mary Sibel. Lucy A. married Hiram Goodenough.

DAKIN. — The first Sudbury ancestor of this family was Captain Samuel who was killed in the last French and Indian War. (See period 1750–1775.) Thomas, the father of Deacon Joseph the father of Samuel, went to Concord prior to 1650. The family lived in North Sudbury near the northern boundary. Three of them have been deacons, — Samuel, June 30, 1775; Levi, March 24, 1817; and Thomas L., son of Levi, in 1838.

DWYER. — Richard Dwyer emigrated to America in 1845. He purchased the place in North Sudbury on which he still resides. He has seven children, — John, Richard, Thomas, Maria, Kate, Mary and Lizzie.

EATON. — The Eaton family descended from Jonas who was in Reading in 1642. He had eight children, among whom was Jonas, whose son John had eleven children, among whom was Jonas, born May 18, 1680. Jonas was a carpenter and bricklayer, and settled in Framingham in 1705-6, where he bought eighty acres of land and erected a house on the present John M. Harrington place, near the Sudbury and Framingham boundary. He had ten children, among whom was Noah, born July 22, 1708. Noah was known as Cornet Eaton. He had eight children, among whom was John, born July 30, 1740. John lived on the old homestead. He married Olive Conant and had twelve children, among whom were Reuben and Sally. Reuben, born May 14, 1769, married Betsy Hunt, and Sally, born Nov. 8, 1770, married Elisha Hunt of Sudbury. Reuben went to Sudbury in 1799. He lived on the Loring Eaton place (near Heard's Pond). Among his children were Loring and John. Loring lived until his death on the old homestead, and had five children. John lived on the present John Eaton place at Lanham. He had three children, — Edward, John, Sarah. The sons live on the old farm.

EAMES. — This family is descended from Thomas Eames, whose house, in what is now Framingham, was destroyed by the Indians, Feb. 1, 1675-76. He came to America by 1634, served in the Pequot war in 1637, lived for a time in Cambridge, and moved to Sudbury where he leased "the Pelham Farm" (Heard's Island, Wayland), and lived until he leased land, in 1669, at Mt. Wayte, Framingham. (See page 154.) He was twice married; the second wife, whom he married in 1662 and who was killed by the Indians, was Mary, a daughter of John Blandford of Sudbury. It is supposed he had twelve children, three of whom were born in Sudbury. John, one of the children of Thomas, born Oct. 6, 1642, built a house in Framingham, and had ten children, among whom was Henry, born April 28, 1698. Henry married Ruth Newton of Marlboro in 1722, and had eleven children, among whom was Timothy. Timothy was twice married; his first wife was Sarah Stone, who died April 25, 1763, at the age of twenty-three; his second wife, Hannah, widow of Dr. Hills, died in 1795. He lived on the Sewall Hunt place, south of Lowance Brook. He had six children, among whom was Phinehas, born May 14, 1766, who married in 1788

Jane, daughter of Col. Ezekiel How, and had eight children, among whom was Fisher, who married Laura H., daughter of Benjamin Dudley. In 1835, Fisher settled at Lanham on the place now occupied by his son, Addison E.

FAIRBANK. — This family descended from early inhabitants of Framingham, Holliston and Sherborn, who it is supposed were descendants of Jonathan Fairbank of the West Riding of Yorkshire, England, and settled in Dedham previous to 1641. The first who came to Sudbury was Jonathan, who came from Holliston or Sherborn prior to 1783. He was twice married, his first wife being Hannah Morse of Northboro, who died leaving two children, and his second wife, Bridget Parmenter, who had ten children. He settled in the south-west part of the town on what is known as the Abijah Walker place. Among Jonathan's children was Drury, who was born July 17, 1793, and married, Oct. 26, 1817, Mary Spring of Hubbardston. He lived in the west part of Sudbury on the farm now occupied by Charles Whitney, on the road from Sudbury to Hudson. He was colonel of militia, justice of the peace, and held various town offices. He had six children, — Nelson, Nancy, Winthrop, J. Parker, Hannah, Mary S., all of whom were born in Sudbury except Nelson who was born in Boston. Nelson is at present a town resident and has held various town offices. He married Susan, daughter of Aaron and Lois Hunt of Sudbury, Dec. 24, 1844, and has had four children, — Albert G., Hattie S., Sarah A. and Mary L. The latter was born Dec. 12, 1858, and married William H. Goodnow of Sudbury, Oct. 17, 1888. J. Parker married Emily, daughter of Loring Wheeler of Sudbury. His son, Winthrop H., lives on the Tilly Smith farm and has held the office of selectman.

FISHER. — The Sudbury ancestor of the Fisher family was Edward, who moved into town from Newton in the early part of the century. His wife was Mary Norcross, and they had nine children, — Emily, Mary, Edward, Fanny, Caroline, Joseph, Charles, Martha and Lyman. Six of these children were born in Newton. Charles married Harriet Brown of Sudbury, and had one child, Julia, wife of Hubbard H. Brown.

Martha married John Goodwin, an ex-speaker of the Massachusetts House of Representatives and editor of a Lowell newspaper. Lyman married Dolly Conant, and his son Fred, who resides in Sudbury, married Emma H., daughter of Everett and Mary (Dakin) Brown. Edward Fisher, Sen., was a wheelwright, and carried on business at the old shop, South Sudbury, where his son Charles also followed the same trade until his death.

GARFIELD. — A near ancestor of the Garfield families in Sudbury was Enoch. He was born in New Hampshire and his wife was from Lincoln. His sons, Francis and John, were born in Lincoln, and went to Sudbury from Concord, the former in 1860 and the latter about 1854. Francis married Sarah, daughter of Thomas B. Battles, and has four children, — Emma F., Thomas F., Henry C. and William E. John has been twice married; his first wife was Louisa Rice of Marlboro, married in 1853; and his second is Harriett M. Flagg of Lincoln, married in 1858. He has two children, Mary L. and John W. Francis is a farmer and John is in the grocery business, and both reside at Sudbury Centre.

GERRY. — According to sketches of Stoneham, by Silas Dean, Thomas Gerry came to America as boatswain on a war vessel sometime in the seventeenth century and settled at Stoneham; and, after remaining there several years, he entered the service of his country and was killed in battle. The same authority speaks of him as a man of great courage, and narrates the following incident: One day, when on his way home about dusk, he came in contact with a number of wolves. Armed with an axe, he braced himself against a tree and pitched battle with his antagonists. The next morning, on returning to the spot, he found he had killed four wolves and wounded a fifth. Elbridge Gerry, formerly governor of this State and vice-president under Mr. Madison's administration, is said to have been a member of this family. Thomas, another descendant, was born in Stoneham, March 15, 1732. He married for his first wife Jane Wilder, and for his second, Priscilla Jewett. He struck the first blow towards settling the town of Royalston by building a log-house for another party, being guided to the spot designated by marked trees. David Jewett, fourth child of

Thomas and Priscilla, was born in Stirling, Feb. 23, 1770, and came to Sudbury about the year 1817, where he died, Oct. 27, 1849, aged seventy-nine. He married Lucy Thompson of Stirling. Their children were Thomas, Eliza, and Charles. He kept the Old Pratt Tavern about five years, and subsequently engaged in roof building, then a separate trade, and bridge building. With his son Charles, he built the first span bridge across the Nashua River at Dunstable, now Nashua. Charles was born in Fitzwilliam, Feb. 3, 1802, and went to Sudbury when about fifteen years of age. He was one of the selectmen in Sudbury several years, and master builder of the Acton Powder Mills. For many years he lived on the present Farr farm. His children are Charles F., Martha A., Eliza L, Edwin A., Israel H., Laura J., Sarah A., David J., Helen F., Clara J., Henry E., Frank E., Herbert L. and two who died in infancy. Charles F. is the only son now living in Sudbury.

HARRINGTON. — The name of Daniel Harrington is on a list of nine soldiers who were impressed into the service by a requisition made on the town by the Colony in 1675. The family, however, has not been numerous in Sudbury. Edwin Harrington, born in Lexington, Feb. 21, 1821, went to Sudbury in 1843, where he married Eunice E., daughter of Reuben Moore, Nov. 27, 1845. He carried on the wheelwright's business for some years at Sudbury Centre in the shop once used by the Evangelical Union Society for religious services. (See period 1825–1850.) He built the dwelling-house adjoining, and subsequently erected the house lately moved from the site of the present residence of George E. He was town treasurer in 1861–1863. He had one child, George E., who was born in Sudbury, Oct. 27, 1846, married, June 13, 1878, Alice E. Brown of Sudbury, who died, Nov. 19, 1879, and Dec. 31, 1881, married M. Edna Newton of South Framingham. He has three children, — Beth Margaret, Ruth Elinor and Alice Erline.

HUDSON. — Martin Newton Hudson was born in Framingham Sept. 22, 1812. He went to Sudbury, and, Jan. 8, 1837, married Maria, youngest daughter of Joseph and Olive (Mossman) Read, who died Jan. 17, 1857. He lived at South Sudbury, and had three children, — John Plympton,

Alfred Sereno and Ellen R. He died at South Sudbury, Oct. 7, 1861, at the age of forty-nine. The Hudson family in Sudbury is descended from Nathaniel Hudson of Lancaster, born May 15, 1671, and whose father was probably Daniel of that town. Nathaniel married Rebekah Rugg and settled in Lancaster where his two older children were killed by the Indians. From 1709–1719 he lived in Billerica where he held town office. He afterward removed to Framingham. Nathaniel had eight children besides those killed by the Indians, — Nathaniel, Abigail, Sarah, Samuel, John, William and Johanna. William lived at Framingham, married, March 8, 1747, Dorcas Walkup, and had three children, — Nathan, Thomas and William, all of whom were baptized in Framingham. William, baptized May 11, 1755, married Tabitha Kibbey and had three children, among whom was Nathan, born Dec. 15, 1786. Nathan was twice married. His first wife was Annie, daughter of Andrew Newton, married July 3, 1808, by which marriage he had four children, among whom was Martin Newton of Sudbury.

HAYDEN. — The Hayden family was in Sudbury as early as 1701, and settled near the west boundary of the town. The name of Josiah Hayden is on the list of west side remonstrants to the division of the town into two parishes in 1707, and it is repeatedly on the muster-rolls a century and a half later. Within the last fifty years the family has gradually died out; the last one being Dana, who lived until his death on the old farm.

HORR. — The first of this family in Sudbury was Richard R., who came in 1850 from Castleton, Vt. His mother was of the old Smith family of East Sudbury (Wayland). He married for his first wife Julia N. Brown of Sudbury, in 1853, who died, 1877. His second wife is Annie Lee, a native of England. By his first marriage he had two children, — Jervis E. and Roger H., by the second he had Howard A. He has held the office of selectman three years and trustee of the Goodnow Library fifteen years.

HURLBUT. — Rev. Rufus Hurlbut was the first Sudbury ancestor of the family now living in town. He had six children, — Thomas P., Mary S., William R., Steven H.,

RESIDENCE OF RICHARD R. HORR,
So. Sudbury

John L. and James D. Thomas Prentiss married a daughter of Curtis Moore of Sudbury and had three children, — Rufus, Elisabeth and Helen. He was a prominent citizen and held various town offices. Between 1864 and 1872 he was chairman of the board of selectmen. He was a member of the Massachusetts House of Representatives in 1870 and 1873, and of the Senate in 1874. He was chairman of the town committee for the arrangement of terms at the incorporation of Maynard. For years he was deacon of the Evangelical Union Church, which position he held at the time of his death. Rufus, son of Thomas P., married Catherine, daughter of Jonas Tower of Sudbury, and has four children, — Arthur S., Marion B., Grace P. and Anza P. He was a member of the House of Representatives in 1884. He lives at South Sudbury and is one of the firm of Hurlbut & Rogers, machinists.

JONES. — An early inhabitant of this name was John, who lived at Lanham, and was a soldier in the expedition to Canada in 1690. Early in 1700 he moved to Framingham. He had two sons, both named John, one of whom died young, the other, born July 15, 1709, lived on his father's place in Framingham, was twice married, and had six children, one of whom was Samuel, born Nov. 18, 1746. Samuel settled in Framingham, and went to Dublin, N. H., about 1779, where he died in 1820. The Joneses now in Sudbury are descendants of the Jones family in Holliston, whose ancestor was, probably, Colonel John of Boston, who in 1715 removed to what is now Ashland, then Framingham. Samuel, son of Samuel of Holliston, went to Sudbury where he married Rachel Haynes, Feb. 12, 1778. He had eight children, — Joshua, Samuel, Joel, Asa, John, Lydia, Rachel and Eliza. Joshua's children were William and Cyrus. William married Sarah Bogle of Sudbury and had three children, — William, John and Marshall. John, son of William and Sarah, resides at South Sudbury. Samuel had five children, one of whom was William, who married Catherine, daughter of Israel Howe Brown, and lives at South Sudbury. Asa had three children, among whom was Smith, who lives at Sudbury Centre (Hurlbut place). John, the youngest son of

Samuel and Rachel, had seven children, among whom was Maynard and Dexter. Dexter has been twice married ; his first wife was Emily Richardson and his second Elizabeth Hurlbut, both of Sudbury. He lives on the road between South Sudbury and the Centre. He has held various town offices and was Representative to the Legislature in 1861.

LYON. — Patrick Lyon emigrated to America in 1844. He purchased a place in North Sudbury where he has resided for about thirty-five years. He has five children, — John, Frank, Thomas, Mary, and Margaret.

O'NEIL. — John O'Neil attended St. Jarlath's College, Suam, Ireland, and was a member of the government surveying party that surveyed England, Ireland and Scotland in 1845. He emigrated to America in 1849, and settled at Concord. He married Julia, daughter of Thomas McManus of Assabet. In 1863, he moved to the Samuel Puffer farm, North Sudbury, where he still resides. He has four sons, — Thomas F., John L., Charles E. and Joseph M. Thomas F. was sent as Representative to the Legislature in 1887.

OSBORN. — An early inhabitant by this name was Samuel. His father's name was Andrew, who, with his wife, came to this country from Annapolis, Ireland. Samuel was born on the water. He married Lydia Griffith of East Sudbury (Wayland), Nov. 1, 1732, and had five children, two of whom were Samuel and Daniel. Daniel married Sarah Perry of Sudbury, Nov. 16, 1769. He lived south of Hart Pond, his house being but a short distance from the County road. The Osborn place in the south part of the town was the farm since owned by Isaac Clark.

PERRY. — The Perry family is descended from Ebenezer Perry, who came from Dedham, probably not far from the beginning of the eighteenth century. He married Mercy Brigham, and lived on the farm now occupied by Obadiah and Levi Perry in the west part of the town. He died in 1731. He had a son Obadiah, whose son John was the father of Obadiah, who was the father of Obadiah and Levi E. Obadiah, the father of Obadiah and Levi E., was born March 25, 1779. He had eight children, — Betsy, Jesse, Lyman, John, Charles, Lucy, Obadiah and Levi E.

Obadiah was born Oct. 9, 1817; Levi E. was born March 18, 1820, and has two children, — Ellen Maria, born July 2, 1847, and Sylvester Dwight, born Jan. 4. 1851.

POWERS. — Abijah Powers, first of the name in Sudbury, was a native of Maine. He went from Stirling to Sudbury in 1841, and purchased a place at the Centre where he still lives and carries on the blacksmith's business. In 1838, he married Delia Maynard of North Sudbury and has had four children, — Emily R., Edwin A. (died in 1846), Clara A. and Edwin A. Edwin A. married Emma F., daughter of Francis and Sarah Garfield, in 1869, and has one son, — Willard M.

PRATT. — An early Sudbury resident of the name was Ephraim, who, with others, in 1729 signed a petition asking that the subscribers, who claimed to be owners of the New Grant lots, might hold a legal meeting "to be at the house of Jonathan Rice (North West District) in said Sudbury, Innholder." The farm occupied by Ephraim Pratt was known as the Wedge-Pratt farm, which was sold in 1743 to Jabez Puffer of Braintree, and is now included in the town of Maynard. Mr. Pratt moved to Shutesbury, where he died in 1804 at the age of one hundred and sixteen years. He was born in Sudbury in 1687. Dr. Dwight, having visited him a short time before his death, in his " Travels " gives the following facts concerning him : " He was of middle stature; firmly built; plump, but not encumbered with flesh; less withered than multitudes at seventy; possessed of considerable strength, . . . and without any marks of extreme age." But a short time before, his sight and hearing had become impaired. " His memory was still vigorous; his understanding sound and his mind sprightly and vigorous. He had been a laborious man all his life; and had mown grass one hundred and one years successively. The preceding summer he had been unable to perform this labor; but in 1802 he walked without inconvenience two miles and mowed a small quantity of grass. . . . Throughout his life he had been uniformly temperate. . . . In the vigorous periods of his life he had accustomed himself to eat flesh, but more abstemiously than most other people in this country. Milk,

which had always been a great part, was now the whole of
his diet." He was never sick but once, and then with fever
and ague. Nathan Pratt, one of the founders of the American Powder Company, was a native of Fitchburg, came to
Sudbury from Charlestown about 1833, moved to Arlington
about 1855, and left the powder business in 1865. He had
no children. Nathan, a nephew of Nathan and present resident of the town, was a son of Capt. Levi Pratt. He was
born in Fitchburg in 1829, and .came to Sudbury Jan. 1,
1849. He was for twenty-one years in the employ of the
American Powder Company, and from 1860 to 1870 superintendent of the Powder Mills. In 1870, he bought and took
possession of the property previously known as " Moore's
Mills " in the west part of the town, which consists of a saw,
grist and planing mill. Mr. Pratt is a Director in the
American Powder Company and the Hudson National Bank
and Trustee of the Hudson Savings Bank. He has also held
various town offices and was chairman of the board of selectmen for four years. In 1855, he married Harriet, daughter
of Aaron Hunt of Sudbury, and has three children, — Sarah
E., Harriet M. and Nathan R. Sarah E. has for the past
nine years been a teacher in the State Normal School, Framingham.

PUFFER. — This family first appeared in Boston in 1640,
and was granted land at Mount Wollaston, now Quincy.
George, who sometimes was called Poffer, had three children. James the oldest married at Braintree, 1656, Mary
Ludden. He had six children, — James, born 1663, and
Jabez, 1672; both removed to Sudbury in 1712. James
married Mary Ellis of Dedham in 1690, and had six children
born in Braintree; he died in 1749. Captain Jabez married
Mary Glazier in 1702 and had seven children, all but the
last two born in Braintree; he died in 1746. Jabez 2d
married Thankful Haynes in 1731, Samuel married Dorothy
Haynes in 1732. They were sons of Jabez 1st and married
sisters. Reuben, son of Jabez 2d, graduated at Harvard
College in 1778, and was settled at Berlin. He died in 1829.
He was distinguished in his profession, and received the
degree of D. D. from Harvard College in 1810. A. D.

Puffer — a great-grandson of Jabez 2d, who resides in Medford and is an extensive manufacturer of soda fountains — was born in Sudbury in 1819. Daniel, grandson of Jabez 2d, was an extensive land owner. The Puffer family have lived mostly in the north-west and north-east parts of the town. Deacon Samuel Puffer lived in the latter district in the early part of the present century. One branch of the Puffer family, in which the name Daniel has been prominent, was so noted for skill in catching wild pigeons as to give rise to the term, familiar in Sudbury, of Pigeon Catcher Puffer. Luther, a son of Samuel, Jr., graduated at Bowdoin College in 1853. Alpheus, another son, is a resident of South Sudbury. James, a son of Josiah, resides at Sudbury Centre.

RICHARDSON. — Major Josiah was the first of the Richardson family in Sudbury. He was born in Woburn Jan. 12, 1701–2, and married Experience, daughter of Benjamin Wright of Sudbury. They had four children, — Gideon, Josiah, Experience and Luther. Gideon went into the ministry and settled at Wells, Me., but soon afterwards died. The Richardsons of the present day are descendants of Josiah, Jr., who was the only son living when his father made his will in 1758. Major Josiah Richardson lived on the Israel Howe Brown place, which once included what are now the Newton and Hiram Goodenow farms, — the first of which formerly belonged to Gideon, son of Josiah, Jr., and the latter to Joseph Cutter, who married Lucy, one of Gideon's daughters. Major Richardson has already been mentioned in connection with the Sudbury militia. In 1765, Josiah was appointed coroner of Middlesex County. The family have lived mostly at South Sudbury. Abel Richardson, son of Gideon, for years owned the saw and grist mill there, and his brother Josiah was a well-known musician. Benjamin, a son of Benjamin, who was brother of Josiah and Abel, represented Sudbury in the Legislature in 1858, and is a justice of the peace. He has had eight children, — Anna M., Merrick L., Clifford W., Waldo F., Emily C., Leonard F., Ralf L., Nellie M.

ROBINSON. — A member of this family early in town lived

in a house which stood on or near the Smith Jones place (Hurlbut place). He had several children, among whom were Paul, Oliver and Silas. He went from Stow to Sudbury, where he died. Paul was born in Stow, went to Sudbury, and had several children, among whom was Dexter, who still lives at South Sudbury. Dexter had two children, Fitz A. and Martha A. Fitz married Louisa Tower of Sudbury Centre and resides in Weston. Martha married Elias King.

ROGERS. — The Rogers family has been in town more than three-quarters of a century. The first was Walter, born in Marshfield Aug. 6, 1767; he came from Braintree in 1805. His wife was Betsey Barstow of Hanover, born Aug. 1, 1772. He purchased of Mr. Waite a part of the Jonas Holden place, of which the C. G. Cutler farm is also a part, and both of which belonged to the George Pitts place in the early part of the eighteenth century. He erected a house on the farm and died in Sudbury at an advanced age. He was a person of considerable mechanical ability, having made a hand fire engine for his own use. He had nine children, — Betsey, Lydia, Lucy, Abigail, Mary, Jane, Walter, Nancy, Samuel B. Betsey, widow of Deacon Gardner Hunt, is still living at the age of about ninety. Walter married for his first wife Emily M. Hayden, Dec. 1, 1831, and for his second wife Emeline S., daughter of William Stone of Sudbury, July 10, 1855. He owns and occupies the old homestead, and has had five children, — Bradley, Edwin, Albert, Homer and Elizabeth. Samuel B. has been a prominent business man in South Sudbury. He married Eliza, daughter of Noah Parmenter, and has had four children, — Alfred S., Bradley S., Melvina A., Atherton W. Atherton resides at South Sudbury and is chairman of the present board of selectmen.

TAYLOR. — The name of Mello C. Taylor is recorded in connection with a petition to Governor Dudley by the West Side inhabitants in 1706-7; and among the inhabitants of the north-west district, early in the century, was Richard Taylor, who was one of the Proprietors of and prominently connected with the settlement of Grafton. (See page 167.)

Hezekiah and John were early settlers of what is now May-nard. The immediate ancestor of the present Taylor family in Sudbury was John, who went to Sudbury from Stow about 1800. He married for his first wife Mary Conant of Framingham, and for his second wife Elizabeth Hews of Weston. By his second marriage he had six children, — Mary, Eliza, Cyrus, Sarah, Rebecca and Susan. Sarah married Thomas B. Battles of Sudbury. Cyrus, born 1796, married Mary Barker of Sudbury and had nine children, — John, Sewall, Mary, George, Henry, Susan, Lewis, Andrew and Martha. John married Caroline, daughter of Samuel Jones of Sudbury, and has one child, Carrie, who married W. H. Bent, formerly of Sudbury. Sewall married Mrs. Susan (Moore) Moulton. George married Susan Spring of Weston, and has one son, Edward.

THOMPSON. — Tradition says that the first Thompson in Sudbury was born on the passage from England to America. While living in Sudbury, but absent from home, his house was at one time attacked by the Indians. His wife, with an infant child, escaped to the woods. In her flight she received a musket-ball in the leg from which she suffered greatly, being obliged to stay in the woods all night. A son, James, was town clerk in the latter part of the eighteenth century. Jedediah, son of James, was born and died in Sudbury. Nahum, son of Jedediah, was a prominent citizen. In the early part of his life he was town clerk, and later town treasurer. He had seven children, three of whom are sons, of whom Alfred is a Sudbury resident. The old Thompson house at South Sudbury stood just west of the track of the Massachusetts Central Railroad at its junction with the county highway. A part of it was moved to the Thadeus Moore place west of Hayden's Bridge.

WALKER. — Thomas Walker is mentioned as teacher of a free school in Sudbury in 1664. (See page 139.) He is also mentioned as an Innholder in 1672. Thomas, probably the same one, had eight children, among whom were Mary and Thomas. Mary married Rev. James Sherman ; and Thomas, born May 22, 1664, bought sixty acres of land, April 10, 1688, of Gookin and How, in the territory now Framingham,

and built a house near Rice's End. He married Martha,
daughter of Samuel How, Dec. 7, 1687, and had ten children, among whom was Samuel, born Sept. 24, 1689, who
married, Nov. 3, 1715, Hannah Jennings. Samuel and
Hannah had five children, among whom was Azariah, born
June 24, 1722, who married Abigail Seaver. The youngest
son of Azariah was Mathias, who married, in 1792, Jane
Moulton of East Sudbury, and one of whose sons, Azariah,
born Nov. 1, 1798, married Miranda Bogle and moved to
Sudbury. His son Francis married Ellen, daughter of Edward Brown of Sudbury, and lives on the old homestead.
Their children are Eugene, Prentiss, Elinor, Shirley and
Carlton. Thomas has been a common family name. It is
found on the " Old Petition " in 1676, in a list of those who
shared the town's stock of ammunition in 1688, and in the
muster-roll of the 2nd Foot Company in 1757. From
William, son of Thomas 1st, has descended the Walker
family that long lived in the west part of the town. He had
a son Thomas who was deacon of the Sudbury Church and
father of Paul, who was sent as a representative to the
Legislature. Willard Walker, son of Paul, lives on the old
farm. He has been twice married and has three children, —
Roselbie, Caroline and Georgiana.

WHEELER. — It is quite probable that this family came
from Concord, where the name appears from the settlement
of the town. It is stated (History of Concord) that the
family came from Wales, and that the descendants have been
so numerous and so many have borne the same Christian
name that their genealogy is traced with great difficulty.
The name of George Wheller is on a muster-roll of the 2nd
Foot Company in 1757 ; and the name of Caleb Wheeler is
attached to a petition to the selectmen asking that a town-
meeting be called to consider the matter of purchasing a
house for small-pox patients. A prominent member of the
family in the present century was Loring, whose father,
Abel, was born in Sudbury July 21, 1776. Loring married,
April 10, 1827, Polly Cutter of Temple, N. H., and had
seven children. He lived until his death, Oct. 15, 1855, on
the place formerly occupied by his father in the east part of

the town. He had five children, — Emily, Adaline, Loring, Henrietta and Abel. Emily married J. Parker Fairbanks; Adaline, John Goodenow; and Henrietta, James Puffer, all of Sudbury. Loring, Sen., was for years on the board of selectmen.

WILLIS. — The names of Samuel and Joseph Willis appear on a petition of 1706–7; and on a list of the 2nd Foot Company of 1757 are the names of Serg't Joseph, Jesse, Reuben and John. The family have, for the most part, lived in the westerly or north-westerly part of the town, and Willis Pond and Willis Hill are familiar landmarks. Among well-known citizens of the present century, descendants of whom still live in town, were Smith and James Prescott, brothers; Daniel Lyman and George W., brothers; and Eli. The former two were sons of Silas. Smith had two daughters, Adaliza and Iantha. James P. married Adaline R. Haynes, lived near Sudbury Centre and had five children, — James L., Albert, Adaline, Edward and Charles P. James L. married for his first wife Emily R., daughter of Abijah Powers, June 17, 1866; for his second wife, Ella S. Simpson, July 7, 1870. Charles P. married Cora E. Willard. Both are residents of Sudbury. Daniel Lyman married Sarah, daughter of Joseph Reed, and had eleven children, — Jerusha, George, Charles A., Nancy, Mary, Abi, George L., Joseph H., Samuel A., Charles A. and John F. Joseph H. married Caroline Hunt and had one child named Samuel. George W. married Adaline Haynes and had six children, — Edward, Cyrus L., Harriet E., Mary, Adaline and Ella. Eli married a daughter of Israel Haynes of Sudbury and had several children, one of whom, Eli, married Sarah Butterfield and lives at Lanham.

By this brief review of family history, we are reminded that the years have brought changes in the homesteads and among the households of Sudbury. There has been a going out and coming in of inhabitants, and not only highways, occupations, churches and schools have changed, but whole families have vanished, leaving no one to perpetuate their names.

CHAPTER XXV.

1800–1825.

> By the fireside there are old men seated
> Seeing ruined cities in the ashes,
> > Asking sadly
> Of the Past what it can ne'er restore them.
> > > LONGFELLOW.

THE interest of the community in ecclesiastical matters in the beginning of the nineteenth century was similar to that of the century that preceded it. The town was the parish and the church was still at the front. The people regarded the minister as the exponent of a system of truth that they revered and of a faith that they cherished and taxed themselves to support. Marked respect was shown him by both old and young; the former not being too busy to leave the workshop or field when he called, and the latter, not having so far outgrown that civility which is becoming to youth, as to pass unnoticed one whose calling was held in such esteem by their elders. The Sabbath was observed by a general attendance at church, and a large share of the town officials were either church members or regular church attendants. Special church occasions, such as ordinations, installations and dedications, were gala days to the community, and days of fasting and thanksgiving were religiously observed. The outward form of religion was not then divorced from the town-meeting, the school or the home.

Politically and socially, at the beginning of the present century, affairs were conducted largely as in the century preceding. Officials were elected mainly on the basis of merit. Military honors were still recognized. The same strict economy was practised and the same careful consideration of need before the smallest expenditure. If it was only to decide upon the location of a horse-shed, the town deemed the matter of sufficient importance to adjourn its town-meeting to take a look at the premises, and, if thought desirable to erect a "noon-house," it might be essential to bring the subject before the town.

The custom and manner of living had not yet undergone any radical change, and all "new fangled" things were still looked upon with suspicion. The fireplace was the same as when the family group sat about it at evening and listened to the tales of Indian warfare. The people still wore the coarse cloth their own hands spun and wove. The hired man and the housemaid might be children of some of the most well-to-do families in town. Travel was largely on horseback or on foot. The horseblock by the meeting-house was still in use. Malt was a common commodity. New England rum was considered essential in hay-time. The wooden plow was in use, and the hay-fork and other farming

tools were still made by the village smith.   As late as 1806
the following articles are mentioned in the will of Hopestill
Willis of Sudbury, which is, perhaps, a fair specimen of the
inventory of a householder about the beginning of this
century: "One calaca gown.   A small Spinning Wheel.
Wooden Ware.   Meal sieve.   Old Chist.   Pewter Ware.
Warming pan.   Flax comb.   Candle sticks and shears.
Tongs, Trowels, meat tub.   Cyder barrel."

In order to show the articles manufactured and used in
town about the beginning of the present century, the price
of work and of some common commodities, we quote a few
extracts from the account book of James Thompson of South
Sudbury.

Jeduthan Moore D^r
To making a slead	0– 4–0
to two Bushil of Malt	0 : 9 : 0
to two pecks of Ground Malt	0 : 2 : 9
to mending a Spinning Wheele	0 : 0 : 6
to a pair of temples.	0 : 1 : 0

Hezekiah Moore Dr Old Tenor   £   s   d
1770 to making a Bedstead	2– 0–0
to making a flax Breake	1– 2–6
1771. to one Days Reaping of Abel	0–15–0

Ashur Cutler Dr Old Tenor.
1772 to two days Labour at the Mill	1–16–0
1773 to Ashur's Trundle Bedstead	0–18–0
to a kneeding Trough	0– 9–0
1774 Making the Sawmill whele and work in the mill	5–10–0
Making a foot to a Little whele	0– 3–0

Credt to Mr Ashur Cutler Old Tenor
1771 by one Bushil of Rie	1– 7–0
one Bushil of Indian Corn	1– 2–6
and one Bushil of Malt	1– 5–0

Capt John Nixon Dr Old tenor
Jan ye 10th 1774 to making a Slay and finding nails	3– 0–0
May ye 26, 1774 to mending a Spinning Wheele	0– 5–0
July at the Begining to making a cart and Ladders and finding boards	3– 7–6
and making an ox yoke	0– 7–6
Jany 1775. to one Bushil of Malt	1– 5–0
April 17. 1775 to a Chist	2– 8–0

Colⁿ John Nixon D^r old Tenor

1776. to Kneeding trough	1 : 2 : 6
to four Bushils of Barley Malt	7 – 0 – 0
Dec. 27th 1776 to Coffin for his wife	3 – 0 – 0
July 1783. Rec^d of Gen^{ll} Nixon	2 : 2 : 0

1781, Isaac Hunt. Debtor in Lawful money.

to making a cart body	0 : 12 : 0
To a Coffin for his Father	0 : 10 : 0
To making a Slead	0 : 5 : 0

Jonas Holden Ju^r Debtor to James Thompson

1790 to 2 Days framing	0 : 7 : 0
and half a Day Covering the Mill	0 : 1 : 2
1791. to two Bushils of Malt	1 : 6 : 0
to four Days on the Gates	0 : 8 : 0

To Aaron Johnson Dr Old Tenour

to making two Margent window frames	1 – 7 – 0
to making three plain frames	1 – 7 – 0
to making 203 Squares of Sashes at ½	11 – 16 – 0

Confirmatory of the truth of our conjecture that, up to the time of which we write, no great changes had taken place in the customs and ways of society, we quote the following description of manners and customs by Mrs. Israel Haynes, a resident of Sudbury, written about the year 1864, at the age of eighty.

STATEMENT OF MRS. ISRAEL HAYNES.

" * * I still remember seventy-five years back more correct than what has been transacted within a week. * * I think people enjoyed their simple way of living as well as they do now. I recollect when the old meeting [house] was standing. A plain Building Ceiled with Boards and a few pews. There are several Barns now in town Finished much handsomer than that was. * * There was no bell on the house. But a small school house stood near by on the common finished of as poorly as the meeting house. there was a little entry-way where there was a little Bell Hung all that belonged to the town to ring for meetings or funerals or what not. There was Body seats below for the oldest people And seats in the gallery for other people. The most popular took the front seats and had Pegs put up to hang

their Cockt Hats on. [they] made quite a show. * * The
Deacons used to read the hymns two lines or a verse and
then they sung it. They had a pitch pipe to pitch the tune.
After awhile there was a bass viol Introduced and brought
into town and did not suit the old People, one Old Gentleman got up took his hat of the peg and march'd off, said
they had begun fidling there would be dancing next. The
children occupied the stairs when the seats were full, and I
believe they enjoyed [it]. They chose tithing men to keep
them regulated but still there was some confusion. I would
describe their dress as near as I can remember. it Consisted
of one Dress one of their Mother's old Dresses she had when
she was married or a Cheap Calico Coarser than A strainer
I ever used. I recollect the first one I had — it was thirty
three cents a yd as we recon now and I thought it as Beautiful as they think of A Nice silk. As to bonnets I dont
seem to remember as far back as I went first to meeting.
But Children went to meeting in such clothes as they had —
now if they have not such clothes as they like they stay at
home. They want a gold watch a breast pin and rings on
the finger. In my young days we did not know what such
things were. There was a minister in each adjoining town
I Believe all of one Denomination. old People called it the
old standing Order * * I have not described the men's
Attire. it Consisted of A Cotton and linen shirt a pair of
trowsers they were then called an under jacket one coat or
Frock no padding or lining * * I have heard an old lady
say she could make a coat in a day with her Baby in her lap.
It would have been thought extravigant for A young man
to have had boots before they were twenty one they wore
cowhide shoes and liggins I never saw any under clothes
they stood the cold weather better than they do now. I
must say a word about our schools. The scholars were
under as good regulations as they are now, there was no
books in school except the Bible Dillingsworth spelling Book
the primmer and Psalter and only one of a kind in A Family.
The teacher set all the Coppies made all the pens. Those
that studied Arithmetic the Master wrote down the Rules
and sums in their Books and then they had Birch Bark split

to do their sums on instead of slates. The school house was a little rough Building like a shed only it had a Door. there was A large Fire Place large enough to hold several logs and four feet wood and a stone hearth and chimney and Cross leg'd Benches for writers. The Boys wore leather aprons and breeches And for dinner they used to fetch a sausage or slice of Pork and a Crust of Bread sharpen a stick and broil it over the coals and [there were] plenty of grease spots. The girls wore short loose Gowns and skirts and thick leather shoes and woolen stockings. They wore a blanket over their heads or their Mother's old Cloak. In the summer they wore [shaped] gown and skirt and cape bonnet colour'd otter with bare feet. You might as soon look for a white Bear as to see shoes on Children in summer time. The Dwelling houses for the most part had two rooms and a fire place almost as large as they build their little Kitchens now and an oven right over the fire place and a large stone hearth. They mostly Built one room first and when they got able set up another room and if they had A son Many generally settled down at home. There was two families in almost every house that had two rooms. * * The People were farmers, most of them went on Pretty much the same way every year. Each one tried to raise enough for their family, they did not make much improvement nor speculate. They kept Oxen and Cows and hogs for their own use and raised Corn and Rye Potatoes and Beans and other vegitables, some kept A Horse, they had no Carriages except a cart and sled. They used to ride horseback to meeting have a saddle and Pilion the man ride forward the woman behind. Sometimes go to visit their friends forty Miles and carry two Children, they went to Market horseback had a wallet made of two Cloths, left open in the middle on a pair [of] paniards made of Basket stuff. The women went as often as the men, they swung the wallet over the horse's back put in their boxes each side so as to balance, then the Paniards [were] fixed on behind filled with pigeons or something else. I remember when there was but one old chaise in town and I dont remember of there being any thing that could be called A Carriage seventy years ago.

seventy years ago I dont think there was a Carpet in town
scarce a painted floor Our diet was simple not as many
luxuries as they have now. at thanksgiving we had flower
a good Chicken Pie and Mince pies and apple and Pumpkin
and Plum pudding. I think a pound answered, sometimes
a part was used in the Best mince pies ✳ ✳ if our Flower
fell short we used Rye flower we had good rye. the best
Farmers did not buy by the Barrel, 7 or 8 lbs used to answer
the purpose. we had no Factories spun and wove and made
our own Clothing ✳ ✳ I recollect when they began to go
with two and four horses tackled in a wagon it looked
as strange as these new inventions the cars or steamboats
✳ ✳ Neighbors used to visit and seemed to enjoy themselves. For supper they generally had Fresh meat or
sausage or a short rye Cake made into a toast, Pye and that
was good enough for a king. the women were Neighborly
and Industrious willing to assist each other. one would get
in a bedquilt and the others drop in and help get it out ✳ ✳
People began to improve in dress and living sixty years ago.
I earnt money enough to buy a silk Dress when I was Married and A white Bonnet, if you could see it you would say
the shape resembled a scale that store keepers use. we had
to be prudent to lay by enough to purchase a silk Dress
they was as high as they are now and wages only four
shillings a week for house work, but we did not have so
much Cloth in a dress as they do now and no needless trim-
mings. I have had Calico Dresses made out of six yards
and a half. It was customary in winter to make a party
for the middle aged, invite all the nearest neighbors and the
school master, get a meat supper and the company and table
set in the same room, for the most part there was a Bed and
trap door in the room — twas a considerable undertaking
but they enjoyed it better than to call one or two at a time."

Thus much did the beginning of the nineteenth century
partake of the spirit and ways of the past, but as the years
advanced there came a wonderful change, and before the
first period had passed, modern improvements began to creep
into society, the church and the home took on an altered

appearance ; and the second generation of the period became
as accustomed to new manners, methods and implements, as
if the former ones had belonged to some remote age.   The
change has continued to go on with accelerated speed, until
now the very architecture, compared with that of the past,
is strange ; even the products of our fields are different, and
men and women and children at church, at home and at
school do that and say that which to the fathers of 1800
would be as unfamiliar as to those of the century that went
before.   The years of the present century have taken away
the things of the olden time.

> Though we search for them long and with diligent care,
> There were joys in the past now exceedingly rare.
> The fireplace no longer burns bright as of yore
> Sending out its bright beams on the old kitchen floor,
> With its back-log all glowing as snugly it lay
> Against the huge chimney, 'mid warm ashes gray ;
> The ancient brick oven is closed from our gaze,
> Where were baked the brown loaves of the rich, golden maize,
> And the beans and " pan dowdy " and nice pumpkin pie
> That so suited our taste, and delighted our eye ;
> The " beaufet " that once so smilingly stood
> With its three-cornered shelves of unpainted wood ;
> The quaint pewter platters, substantial and bright ;
> The candle of tallow, so smooth and so white ;
> The hard, oaken floor that was scoured with such care ;
> The garret, a store-house of relics most rare ;
> The old-fashioned clock with its bell-note so clear,
> And whose pendulum-tick we could easily hear ;
> The plain, simple dress and the old-fashioned ways,
> The " raisings," the " huskings " of those early days,
> The " apple-bees," " training-days," breaking out roads,
> The turnpikes, the toll-gates, the stages, the loads
> Of rich country produce that was carried to town
> By the farmer, whose custom it was to " go down ; "
> The old-fashioned winter, the mild early spring,
> With snow-drifts and sunbeams which these used to bring ;
> The old district school with its three months a year,
> The little red school-house with benches so queer,
> Where to cipher, to read, to parse, and to write
> Were deemed wholly sufficient to educate quite ;
> The singing-school also has passed out of date,
> And the fugue-tune and fiddle have shared the same fate,

As these were made use of in country church choir,
Or on special occasions by the sitting-room fire.
Thus have the years in their flight left behind
The old-fashioned things that are now hard to find;
We may search for them long and with diligent care,
And if we find them at all, 'tis exceedingly rare.

We now pass from a consideration of general changes that
occurred about 1800, to events that took place in the first
period of the present century. First, as they are related to
highways, bridges and causeways. Early in the century an
effort was made to secure the construction of a highway
through North Sudbury. As early as 1800, complaint was
made against the town for not making a road there, and the
town appointed an agent to defend its cause.

In 1801, a committee was appointed to see about " an
alteration in the road from Rev. Mr. Bigelow's to near Mr.
Tower's by Wm Rice's Esq as far as Mr. Vose's." The
indications are that an alteration had been made in the road,
that a shorter way was proposed, and that the court had
been applied to for a discontinuance of the alteration formerly
made. In 1806, an article was in the warrant to see if the
town would take any measures " for the purpose of discharging an execution against said town it being in consequence of not complying with the requisition of the order
of the Court of Sessions for the making of the road through
the northerly part of said town." The town also appointed
an agent to oppose the acceptance of the road; but, notwithstanding the opposition, the North road was built.
About the same time the south part was interested in a
proposition to make some alteration in the South road,
known as the Boston and Worcester. In 1805, a committee
was appointed to act with one appointed by the Court of
Sessions for this purpose. The design was to straighten
portions of the road from Green Hill to the brick kilns or
Gibbs farm. In 1805, the sum of $1800 was appropriated
for highway work, and the same year $1000 was granted for
the purpose of repairing " Lancaster and Worcester Road so
called." The following year the records make mention of a

road laid out from Jonathan Fairbank's to John Perry's. In 1807, it was voted "to sell and discontinue part of the road from Ezekiel Loring's to Framingham line."

In 1801, Lieut. David How rebuilt Wash Bridge for forty-five dollars and twenty-five cents. That year, also, a committee of five was appointed " for the purpose of railing this town's proportion of the Long Causeway, and setting out a sufficient number of willow trees to answer the purpose for Guides in the time of flood." In 1804, sixty-four dollars were granted for making a wall each side of Sherman's Bridge. In 1806, the town voted to let out the rebuilding of the Canal Bridge. In 1815, the town voted twenty dollars and thirty-three cents for the Canal Bridge.

MISCELLANEOUS MATTERS.

In 1804, the town voted two hundred and twelve dollars for repairing and painting the meeting-house. In 1805, a settlement was made of a prolonged lawsuit between the town and Peter Smith "who brought forward a pauper." The suit was decided in favor of the town to the amount of ten hundred and sixty dollars and twenty-five cents. But "it remitted to Smith $544.31 out of said execution it being the balance which appeared to be due him." In 1806, the town granted thirty dollars for the purpose of enabling their selectmen to settle with Captain Barrett, the gaol keeper of Concord, " for Boarding of certain Poor persons that were confined in gaol and belonged to the town." As, formerly, the law allowed imprisonment of poor debtors, these persons probably belonged to that class. In 1816, voted that the constables see that the porch of the meeting-house, both above and below, be cleared of those people who were inclined " to occupy the avenues to the meeting house at the commencement of the exercises of each day of public worship." Also, to see that people at the close of worship went out properly. In 1817, the town engaged in lawsuits with East Sudbury, Lincoln and Stow about the support of the poor. It was successful in the first suit, but failed in the last two.

EDUCATIONAL MATTERS.

No marked changes took place during this period in educational methods. The money granted for schools was equally divided between the five districts. In the year 1800, money was granted for building three school-houses, — in the south-east district, two hundred and eighteen dollars; in the north-west, one hundred and fifty-seven dollars and fifty cents; and in the south-west, two hundred dollars. The committee that year were William Rice, Esq., centre district; Gen. Benjamin Sawin, south-east; Deacon Thomas Walker, south-west; Lieut. Hopestill Willis, north-west; and Samuel Puffer, north-east. The old building in the south-west was sold for twenty-four dollars.

The following is, in substance, part of a report of the school committee in 1802. That they had been empowered to hire all the teachers of the public schools in town for the year ensuing, and that they had been instructed, after consultation with the minister and the teachers employed, to decide what books should be used, only that the same ones should be used in all the schools of the same grade. That, if any scholar should fail to provide himself or herself with the books required, six days after notice of the deficiency had been given to the parent or guardian, the scholar should not receive instruction in the branch of study to which said book or books were assigned until supplied. Provided, nevertheless, that if any scholars were unable by reason of poverty to provide their own books they should be supplied by the committee. In 1825, leave was granted to the centre district to move its school-house to some convenient place on the Common. Besides the attention bestowed by the town on the common or day schools, encouragement was given to instruction in music.

Along the first of the present century there existed what was termed a "Singing Society," and the town, from time to time, made appropriations for its benefit. This "Society" constituted the church choir. A half century ago, the long rows of singers along the length of the gallery was quite a part of the audience; and, doubtless, it was for the purpose of benefiting the church music that the town granted aid to the " Singing Society." In 1801, a committee was appointed by the town " to get a singing master and for regulating the Singing Society." The same year liberty was given the society to occupy the several school-houses, indicating that the sessions were held in different districts. Ten dollars was granted that year to pay the master. In 1802, the town voted " to have Dr. Belknap's Psalms and Hymns introduced and made use of in the Singing Society," In 1821, twenty dollars were allowed for the society, and in 1822 thirty dollars. Early in the century quite an orchestra assisted in the old church. Mr. Josiah Richardson, familiarly known as " Uncle Siah," played the violin, Mr. Emory Hunt the clarionet, Mr. George Hunt the base viol, and Deacon Martin Brown the bassoon. At the same time, Esquire Lyman How, the last landlord of the Wayside Inn of the name of How, was among the singers. He also led the choir afterwards at the Orthodox Church.

MILITARY MATTERS.

Before the war of 1812 and 15 set in, the town of Sudbury, as did others, took action as to the state of affairs then existing between the United States and England; it also made provision by which it could supply its quota of men in case they were called for ; and passed resolutions relative to the conduct of public affairs that evinced a patriotic spirit and a steadfast purpose to stand by the government. In 1807, when the American frigate, Chesapeake, had been attacked by the English frigate, the Leopard, activity in military matters commenced in the New England towns. Sudbury voted to give to " each soldier that was called upon to stand at a minute's notice $12 per man per month including what government has made provision for, during the time they are in actual service, and six dollars to each soldier as advance pay, that shall equip himself for said service, the aforesaid six dollars to be paid previous to his marching if called upon and to be subject to deduction from his wages." In 1808, the town " voted $36 as a bounty to this town's proportion of soldiers that are called upon to hold themselves in readiness at the shortest time, being eighteen in number." Also, "directed the commanding officer of each respective company, to make out a return of the name of each soldier that held himself in readiness." A meeting was called Feb. 4, 1809, " to see if the town will express their opinion in such manner as will show to the world that we are willing to support the laws of our general government, in consequence of certain resolutions denouncing all good citizens who shall give their aid and support in the execution of the laws of said government." A committee was chosen at that meeting to draw up a preamble and resolutions to present to the town, relative to what was mentioned in the above article. The Preamble and Resolutions that were reported were passed in the affirmative and were in substance as follows: The inhabitants of Sudbury see with concern a party in the State exciting jealousies against the government and recommending resistance to its laws. Therefore, resolved,

1. That we have the highest confidence in the wisdom and integrity of the government.

2. That we believe the embargo laws are good and necessary.

3. That we have seen with regret certain resolutions denouncing all good citizens who give their support in the execution of those laws, and that such resolutions produce on our minds a determination, when called upon, to give those laws prompt and undivided support.

4. That, as the management of our foreign relations is delegated to the councils of the nation, it is inexpedient for the State legislature to interfere.

In 1812, the number of soldiers reported to be in readiness was eighteen. "Voted to give them $1.25 per day while in service and doing actual duty." The following persons from Sudbury were in service a short time during the war: Aaron Hunt, Jonas Tower, James B. Puffer, Josiah Puffer, John Carr, Cyrus Willis, George Barker, Leonard Dutton, Otis Puffer, Jesse Puffer, John Sawyer. Warren Moore was in the naval service on a privateer, was taken prisoner and spent some time in Dartmoor prison.

In the militia the officers were chosen by the men and received their commission from the Governor of the State, as in later times. In 1806, Caleb Strong gave a commission to Jesse Goodnow as captain of a company in the 4th Regiment Infantry, 2d Brigade, 3d Division Militia. To an extent, it was customary to hold the meetings for the election of militia officers at the taverns. The following is a specimen of the "Company Order" of the times.

COMPANY ORDER.

" To Reuben Gleason Corpl

" You are hereby ordered and directed to warn and notify all the men, Commissioned Officers and soldiers whose names are hereafter mentioned belonging to the company under my command, to appear at Mr. John Stone's Tavern in Sudbury, on Friday, the 18th day of March Inst. at 1 o'clock P. M., for the purpose of electing a Captain, and filling such other vacancies as may then happen.

" By Order of Ephraim Plympton Lieut. Col. Dated at Sudbury, March 14, 1814."

ECCLESIASTICAL EVENTS.

In 1814, the town settled a new pastor, Rev. Jacob Bigelow having become infirm. In 1810, Rev. Timothy Hilliard had been invited to preach as a candidate, and June 1, 1814, he became colleague pastor at a salary of six hundred and fifty dollars and five hundred dollars to begin with. The ministers, with their churches, who comprised the ordaining council were Rev. Messrs. Kellogg of Framingham, Newell of Stow, Adams of Acton, Ripley of Concord, Stearns of Lincoln, Lovering of Andover, and Dr. Kirkland of Harvard College who preached the sermon. The next year Mr. Hilliard " resigned his office as clergyman of the religious Society of Sudbury." His resignation was accepted, and he was recommended to the churches on a vote of thirty-eight to eight. A council was held for the purpose of ratifying the doings of the church and town " in dissolving the Covenant with Rev. Mr. Hilliard." He was dismissed Sept. 26,

1815.   The following is the bill allowed to Mr. Asahel Wheeler for the entertainment of the council: —

To eleven dinners and Suppers with wine	$6	'
To Horse keeping	2	''
To Liquors	2	''
	10	''

Also allowed Mr Daniel Osborn for Notifying the
    Council and for attendance $3

After leaving Sudbury, Mr. Hilliard practised medicine in his native town, Kensington, N. H., and also engaged some in teaching. He was a scholarly man and a graduate of Harvard College in 1809. He also studied divinity at Cambridge. During his short ministry forty-three united with the church, nineteen males and twenty-four females. Soon after the pastorate became vacant, the town took measures to secure another minister. May, 1816, it was " voted, at the request of Dea. Puffer, to set apart a day for fasting humiliation and prayer to the Supreme Governor of the Universe for his direction and guidance in those measures that shall be most conducive to the harmonizing us in the reestablishment of a gospel minister amongst us." The day appointed was November 3. It was voted to invite some minister to preach on that day, and also to invite the attendance of other ministers. Soon after this the town " voted to hear Mr. Hurlbut and two others on Probation." At a town-meeting Dec. 16, 1816, " it was moved to see if the town would request the church in this place to give Mr. Rufus Hurlbut a call to settle with them in the gospel ministry, and being put to vote, it passed in the affirmative by 58 for and 9 against it." The church having voted to extend the call, on December 23 the town expressed its concurrence by a vote of thirty-four for and six against. " It was then voted that Mr. Hurlbut's creed be read before the town, which was produced and read agreeable to said vote." A committee was chosen by the town to confer with the church ; and they recommended a salary of seven hundred dollars while he was in active service without the improvement of the ministerial land, " which their late minister

Rev. Mr. Bigelow had the improvement of during his life."
Mr. Hurlbut declined to accept of the sum specified, if he
was only to be allowed it while in actual service; giving as
a reason for his refusal, that, in case of inability to preach
at any time, by a reduction or withholding of his salary he
would be left without a means of support. The matter was,
therefore, reconsidered, and an offer made of six hundred
and fifty a year so long as he should continue to be their
pastor. This offer was accepted. A committee or agent
was appointed to receive a quit-claim of Mr. Hurlbut of all
the ministerial land.

Soon after the settlement of a new minister, Rev. Jacob
Bigelow passed away. He died Sept. 12, 1816, at the age
of seventy-five, having filled the Sudbury pastorate for over
forty years. He was beloved by his people, and in his last
years was granted an annuity. In 1816, two hundred and
forty-six dollars and sixty-seven cents was granted "for
Mr. Bigelow's salary." This vote, at a later meeting of the
town, was reconsidered, probably on account of his death.
The town also gave to his widow thirty dollars for the service that was rendered by the reverend clergy, as a gift to
her, by their supply of the pulpit after her husband's death.
The funeral expenses were defrayed by the town and the
following bills are on record: —

"To Mr. Jonathan Fairbanks Jr. for making the coffin for
Rev. Mr. Bigelow, $10.00.

"To Lewis Moore for digging the grave and attending the
funeral of Rev. Mr. Bigelow $2.00.

"To Capt. Jesse Moore for beef he provided at the funeral
of the Rev. Mr. Bigelow 1—13

"To Mr Ruben Moore for 7 lbs old cheese he found at the
funeral of Rev Mr Bigelow.

"To Doctor Ashbel Kidder for dining the clergy & com-
mitteee of arrangements &c at the funeral of Rev. Mr.
Bigelow $16.20

"To Mr Daniel Goodenow for spirit an sugar &c provided
at the funeral of the Rev. Mr. Bigelow, $15.40."

Mr. Bigelow was a native of Waltham. He was twice married. His first wife was a sister of Dr. Heard of Concord. By this marriage he had a daughter. He married for his second wife Mrs. Wells, and had two sons. One of these was Dr. Jacob Bigelow of Boston, a noted physician, and at one time Professor of Materia Medica in Harvard Medical School. He died at the age of ninety. An old inhabitant of Sudbury (C. G. Cutler) described Rev. Mr. Bigelow to the writer as being " a large man with a large face, very pleasant and full of jokes." He was said to be affable and social. He built the house now known as the George Goodenow place, about a quarter of a mile from Sudbury Centre, and there he lived and died. He was ordained Nov. 11, 1772. During his ministry one hundred and forty-two were added to the church, fifty-five males and eighty-seven females.

The year of Mr. Bigelow's death the following records were made relating to the enlargement of the Burying Ground: "Bought of Walter Haynes in 1816 about a half acre of land on the whole south side the grave yard for enlarging it." The price paid was one hundred dollars. Among the town debts: " To Walter Haynes for building the burying yard wall and a small gate, $19.50." There are other records relating to placing posts near the yard. The indications are that the yard, at that time, was nearly full, and, probably, the death of the minister called the town's attention to the fact. As Mr. Bigelow's grave is on the southerly side of the yard, it may have been made in the portion that was bought at that time. Besides the addition on the south, in 1800 the town bought a " piece of land for three dollars of Asher Goodenow on the east end of the burying ground." Another matter in this period, pertaining to the burial of the dead, was an order, in 1806, "for a bier for the Burying yard," and in 1818 for building a hearse.

About the time of Rev. Jacob Bigelow's death a movement was made to dispose of the land which had been set apart for the support of the ministry, for cash or notes at interest. As has been observed, a committee was appointed at the settlement of Rev. Mr. Hurlbut to obtain of him a

THE BIGELOW PARSONAGE, Sudbury Centre

quit-claim to these lands, which act was, doubtless, in antici-
patiou of the movement in 1818. In 1816, a committee was
appointed to apply to the Legislature for leave to dispose of
the ministerial land, and it was granted. The following
year there was constituted what was called "the Sudbury
Ministerial Land Corporation." In March, 1818, the trustees of this corporation reported that, in accordance with an
act of the Legislature, June 14, 1817, they had sold the land
lying near Mr. Elisha Jones', containing by plan seventeen
acres and fifty-three rods, on July 24, 1817, in two lots:
No. 1 to Capt. Silas Puffer for $67 per acre, No. 2 to the
same party for $43 per acre. The first lot contained a little
over ten acres, the other a little over six acres. The whole
amount received was $996.56. Other lots were as follows:
Ministerial river meadow near Mr. Israel Wheeler's was sold
July, 1817, in two lots. No. 1 to Lewis Moore for $146.69,
• No. 2 to Israel Wheeler for $154.40. "The ministerial land
laying near the meeting house" was sold August, 1817. It
contained about thirty-eight acres, and was disposed of in
lots as follows: No. 1 to Walter Haynes and Thadeus
Tower for $462, No. 2 to William Moore for $406.87, No 3
to Capt. William Rice for ———, No. 4 to Joshua Jones for
$372.15, No. 5 to Israel Moore for $336.81, No. 6 to Joshua
Jones for $10. "The total sum arising from the sale of the
ministerial lands in said town amounts to $3200.96. At the
close of this period, March, 1825, the following report was
rendered to the town by the Ministerial Fund Corporation : —

Capt Silas Puffer	Note the sum of				996 "	56
Mr Lewis Moore	"	"	"	"	146 "	69
Mr. Israel Wheeler	"	"	"	"	154 "	40
" Walter Haynes	"	"	"	"	200 "	31
William Moore	"	"	"	"	406 "	87
Thadeous Towers	"	"	"		200 "	31
Haman Hunt	"	"	"	"	376 "	86
Josua Jones	"	"	"	"	382 "	15
Joel Moore	"	"	"	"	336 "	81
					$3200 "	96

The interest on this amount was paid to the Rev. Rufus
Hurlbut, agreeable to the act of incorporation.

CHAPTER XXVI.

1825-1850.

History of the Sudbury Methodist Episcopal Church. — Members of a
Baptist Society in Sudbury in 1828. — Town Farm. — Town House.
— Erection of Tombs. — Ecclesiastical Disturbance. — Formation of
a New Parish. — Building of a Meeting-House. — Dedication of it. —
Death of Rev. Rufus Hurlbut. — Sketch of his Life. — Settlement of
Rev. Josiah Ballard. — The Old Parish. — Settlement of Rev. Linus
Shaw. — Sketch of his Life. — Succession of Pastors. — Miscellaneous.

> Our theme shall be of yesterday,
> Which to oblivion sweeps away
> Like days of old.
>
> LONGFELLOW.

BETWEEN 1825 and 1850, important ecclesiastical events
transpired in Sudbury. Measures that resulted in the formation of the Methodist Episcopal Church were taken in the
last part of the preceding period, but, as this church became
established or largely developed in this period, the history
of it properly comes here.

THE METHODIST CHURCH.

In 1823, a class was formed by Rev. Erastus Otis, in
connection with the "Old Brick Church" at Marlboro,
which consisted of the following members: Varnum Balcom, leader, Webster Cutting, Buckley Willis, Emerson
Brown, Abel Noyes, Samuel Dudley, Miss Abigail Dudley,
Mrs. Noah Smith, Mrs. Edwin Cutting, Mrs. A. Noyes,
Mrs. Varnum Balcom, and some others. Previous to the
formation of this class there were but two members of the
Methodist church in Sudbury. In the early stages of the enterprise, meetings were occasionally held in the school-house
of the north-west district; but, in 1835, the town voted not

to allow the school-houses to be used for religious meetings. After this, preaching services were sometimes held in a hall at the house of Mr. Walter Haynes; but not long was the little company to be without a church home. A paper was soon started by Emerson Brown, soliciting aid for the erection of a meeting-house. A part of the names are lost: the following are some of the subscribers and their gifts, — Emerson Brown, $500; Edwin Cutting, $500; Isaac Parmenter, $500; Marshall S. Rice, $200; Martin Brown, $200; Solomon Weeks, $100; Amos Hagar, $50; Noah Smith ——.

A piece of land for a meeting-house, consisting of sixty rods, was purchased of Luther Goodnow for the sum of one hundred and twenty-five dollars. It was conveyed by deed to Isaac Parmenter, yeoman, and Emerson Brown and Edwin Cutting, shoemakers; and bears date Sept. 19, 1835. The meeting-house was soon erected, and in 1836 was dedicated. Rev. Abel Stevens, LL.D., preached the dedication sermon. In 1841, a bell was purchased at a cost of three hundred and three dollars and twenty-five cents, Edwin Cutting giving one hundred dollars. The new church was in what was then called the "Needham Circuit." After the erection of the meeting-house, meetings were held five days and thirty-one evenings in succession; at which time it is supposed about fifty persons were converted. In the early years of the church, E. O. Haven afterwards Bishop Haven, then a young man, taught school in the vestry. The fact that the career of that widely-known and useful man was connected in its early beginning with this quiet spot adds to it a special interest and pleasantness. In that little meeting-house, hard by the margin of the town's common land and one of its old-time burial places, was the spot where at least two of Sudbury's college graduates now living pursued their early studies. (See College Graduates.) Here, too, at least one worshiper, who afterwards entered the ministry, took the first step that led to that service (Rev. L. P. Frost). Rev. Charles Rogers, who for several years has been Presiding Elder, was one of the later preachers, and at the same time a teacher in the Wadsworth Academy. The very surroundings of the place are suited to stir to reflection; and when nature, in spring-time, clothes with green the shrubbery about it or there rests on it the stillness of the soft summer day, then the scene accords with the associations of the meeting-house, the wayside burial place, and the memories that cluster around the village green. From the time the meeting-house was completed the new church has moved steadily on. At its quarterly meeting, February, 1837, the Presiding Elder present was D. Kilburn. The same year the Conference sent as first pastor, Rev. Elias C. Scott. He taught school for which he received eighty-four dollars, and this, with what he received from other sources, made his salary three hundred and twenty-three dollars and fifty-five cents. Succeeding Mr. Scott are the following pastors of the church with their dates of service: —

Luman Boyden	1837–8	Porter M. Vinton	1863–64
George W. Bates	1839–40	George Sutherland	1864–65
J. S. Ellis	1840–41	Philo P. Gorton	1865–66
P. R. Sawyer	1841–42	J. W. P. Jordan	1866–67
W. Tucker	1642–43	George E. Chapman	1867–69
G. W. Weeks	1843—	Miles R. Barney	1869–71
Benjamin King	1845–46	Walter Wilkins	1871–74
Luther Caldwell	1846–47	John S. Day	1874–75
W. F. Lacount	1847–48	A. M. Sherman	1875–76
Horace Moulton	1848–49	Nathaniel Bemis	1877–79
George Frost	———	J. Richardson	1879–80
L. P. Frost	———	J. A. Ames	1880–81
John W. Lee	1852–53	F. O. Holman and M. D. Sill	1881–83
J. H. Gaylord	1853–55	A. R. Archibald	1883–84
M. Leffingwell	1855–57	J. Marcy	1884–87
Wm. A. Clapp	1857–59	Geo. H. Bolster	1887–88
Charles S. Rogers	1859–61	H. E. Wilcox	1888–89
Joseph Scott	1861–63		

Nearly a half century ago the little congregation was gathered from various parts of the town; the Butterfields came from Lanham, the Parmenters and Noyeses from Peakham, the Battleses from the Gravel Pit district, the Bents and Hayneses from Pantry. Years ago, some of these early worshipers passed from this place of prayer to the temple above. In 1875, Amos Haynes the old sexton died. For thirty-two years he had faithfully stood at his post and rung the bell at the hour of prayer. The familiar form of Thomas B. Battles about the same time was missed from the choir. Then the tall, slender form of George Goodnow, who had been a tower of strength, was also called to his reward; and thus, one by one, they have passed away, till now only two remain whose names were on the church records forty years ago. Amid its many vicissitudes the church has never been closed more than one Sabbath at a time. The highest salary ever paid its minister was seven hundred dollars. The ladies have been associated in a society which has aided in all the church enterprises; and a prominent member among them has been Mrs. George Goodnow who has faithfully planned and labored for the maintenance of the church through many years of its history.

BAPTIST SOCIETY.

In 1828, the following persons were members of a Baptist society in Sudbury : —

Leander G. Wiley,	Obadiah Osborn.
Joseph G. Hunt,	Azariah Walker.
James Moore,	John W. Haynes.
Abijah Walker,	Amos Haynes.
Ruth Walker,	Wm Stone Jr.,
Cyrus W. Jones,	Thadeus Tower,
David Lincoln,	Hollis Gibbs.
Marden Moore,	Joel Dakin, Clerk.

TOWN FARM.

March 5, 1832, the town voted to purchase a Town Farm. The place selected was the property of Asa Noyes, situated in the north part of the town, and the same now used for the town's poor. In 1843, the town voted to build a house on the farm, and in 1845 it granted one thousand and seventy-six dollars and sixty-seven cents to pay for it. Some years ago the barn was burned and another was erected soon after.

TOWN HOUSE.

In 1845, the town voted to build a Town House. A committee was chosen consisting of five persons, one from

each school district, to select a spot, bring in a plan, and
estimate the cost. April 20, 1846, the town granted one
thousand dollars for the building, and appointed a committee
to confer with the First Parish about the terms on which
the town could have a spot on the common to set a building
upon. At a legal meeting of the First Parish held in April,
1846, it was "voted that sd Parish give to the town of
Sudbury liberty to set a town house on the meeting house
common, nearly or partly on that part now occupied by
the Center school house sufficient for the occupation of sd
Town House, and ten feet passage around it. Provided,
sd gift to sd town shall not be construed in any way to
injure the title of sd Parish to the remainder of sd common."
The town "voted to place the Town House where the school
house now stands, provided, said Parish adheres to their
agreement." A few years ago an iron safe was procured,
in which to keep the town records, and placed in the Town
House; and recently, a fire-proof depository of brick-work.
The west part of the Town House was formerly used as an
armory of the "Wadsworth Rifle Guards;" and rows of
rifles and military accoutrements were ranged on the side of
the long, narrow room. A part of this room is now used as
a selectmen's office.

ERECTION OF TOMBS.

A petition having been presented to the town by William
Hunt and others, for leave to erect a number of tombs on
the northerly part of the meeting-house plot, nearly opposite
the burying-ground, April 3, 1826, the town granted permission, and appointed a committee of five to locate the
ground where they should be built, and to confer with the
petitioners as to the plan, so as to have them uniform. In
November, the committee reported a place, and recommended
that leave be given the petitioners to fix upon some uniform
plan of building to suit themselves. The report was accepted.
April 3, 1830, Luther Goodnow, Asher Goodnow, Tilly Smith
and Levi Smith received permission to erect tombs on the
east side of the powder house.

ECCLESIASTICAL DISTURBANCE.

A prominent ecclesiastical event in this period was the formation of a new parish. The causes which brought this about had been at work for some years previously, and were, mainly, the same as those which wrought similar results in other New England towns about that time. In the early part of the century a controversy took place concerning certain theological questions, principal among which were the nature and mission of Christ, the measure or extent of human depravity, and man's need of regeneration by a personal Holy Spirit; or, in other words, the Divinity of Christ, the Atonement, Total Depravity, Regeneration and the Personality of the Holy Spirit. The advocates of the liberal movement — among whom were Ware, Buckminster, Norton and Channing — sought to extend the principles of Unitarianism. On the other side, prominent theologians, among whom were Prof. Moses Stuart of Andover and Rev. Lyman Beecher, stoutly set themselves to oppose it. The controversy spread through society. In this part of the country the age became one of theological discussion, and, in the course of a few years, many old churches and parishes were divided into two organizations, one of which took the name of Unitarian Church, and the other of Orthodox Congregational or Trinitarian Church. The influence of this wide-spread discussion did not produce any marked result in the Sudbury church till about 1839. There were in the town records, some years before that time, various statements which indicate that dissatisfaction prevailed respecting the minister's theological views. The desire was expressed that Mr. Hurlbut would exchange more with the neighboring clergymen, "as formerly;" and there was querying as to why he did not. Notwithstanding, however, the existence of dissatisfaction there was no outbreak until Mr. Hurlbut, whose health had become feeble, procured the services of another minister to supply the pulpit for a Sabbath. The attitude of the congregation then became clearly defined. On the Sabbath morning two new clergymen appeared on the scene, one provided by Mr. Hurlbut, the other by the parish committee. When Mr. Hurlbut and his minister arrived at the steps of the church, he found the door had been fastened, and that the minister whom the parish had provided was within. Says one, who was standing by and witnessed the affair and heard the conversation, " Mr. Hurlbut informed the committee that he would like to introduce his minister. The request being granted, they passed in, and Mr. Hurlbut, after making a few remarks to the people, left the meeting-house. A large share of the congregation left also, and, with their minister, went over and worshiped that morning with the Methodists." Soon after, they hired a hall, which stood on the site of Mr. Sewall Taylor's wheelwright's shop. It had two stories and a gallery on three sides of the audience room. It was subsequently used as a wheelwright's shop by Edwin Harrington and was destroyed by fire about thirty years ago.

FORMATION OF A NEW PARISH.

Shortly after the events just narrated a new religious society was organized. March, 1839, a warrant was issued by Christopher G. Cutler to Israel How Brown, an applicant for the same, requiring the said Brown to notify all the legal voters " who have congregated the year last past for public worship in a building owned by Wm Brigham in said Sudbury to meet at said building" March 25, at one o'clock in the afternoon, for the purpose of " organizing according to law a religious society for the public worship of God." The petitioners for the warrant were Enoch Kidder, A. B. Richardson, Israel H. Brown, Abel Dakin, Joseph Cutter, Roland Cutler and Gardner Hunt. The meeting was held pursuant to warrant, and, in the absence of C. G. Cutler, Esq., and at his request, Lyman How, Esq., presided. Samuel Puffer was chosen clerk and William Brigham moderator. Nahum Goodenow, William Brigham and I. H. Brown were chosen assessors, and William Rice collector and treasurer. The assessors were also chosen as the prudential committee, and the same persons were also appointed to report a name for the new society. It was voted at the same meeting to grant eight hundred dollars for preaching the ensuing year. The

committee presented the name of The Sudbury Evangelical
Union Society, which was accepted and adopted. The
word Sudbury was afterwards struck off, leaving the name
of the society as it stands to-day. A second meeting was
held, April 8, 1839, at which Lyman How, Esq., was chosen
moderator. The society at that meeting voted to build a
meeting-house " on the plan of the Orthodox Society of
Marlboro." A committee chosen at the previous meeting
for selecting a suitable building spot reported " that it is
expedient to set the house on the ground near the Blacksmith's shop owned by Jonas Tower." A building committee was chosen of which Mr. Gardner Hunt was chairman.
This committee was instructed to borrow money for building
the house on the credit of the society; and, after the completion of the building, to sell the pews to defray the
expense of construction. A contract was concluded May 27,
1839, between Gardner Hunt, William Brigham and Jonas
Tower, building committee, and Mr. Jeremiah Flint. Mr.
Flint, by the terms of the contract, was to have for the work
fifty-seven hundred dollars. The society was to provide the
foundation and the steps, and the work was to be completed
by the following November. At a meeting Dec. 25, 1839,
it was voted to direct the building committee to sell the
pews on the appraisal that had been reported, reserving
the right to tax to an amount not exceeding five per cent.
per annum on the appraised value. Also voted to direct the
committee to sell the pews on the day after the dedication
of the house, and give deeds of the same. In the sale of the
pews, No. 1 was to be reserved for the minister, and the
four under the gallery were to be reserved for free seats.
The valuation of the pews varied from forty dollars to one
hundred and five dollars, and the total amount was forty-
seven hundred and five dollars. At a meeting of the society,
held Feb. 10, 1840, it was voted to direct the parish and
assessors to " circulate a petition for to obtain money to
procure a bell." The money was raised and a bell was
purchased at Medway. Jan. 1, 1840, the meeting-house was
dedicated; Rev. Mr. Horsford of Saxonville preached the

sermon. April, 1840, it was voted to sell rights to build sheds on the society's lands.

While the new meeting-house was in process of completion, Rev. Rufus Hurlbut passed away. He died May 11, 1839, having been pastor of the church twenty-two years. He was a son of Steven Hurlbut, and was born in Southhampton April 21, 1787, graduated at Philips Academy in 1808, and at Harvard College 1813. He studied theology with Rev. Thomas Prentiss, D.D., of Medfield, whose daughter Mary he married Dec. 17, 1817. His wife was the granddaughter of Dr. John Scollay, who was for over forty years town clerk of Boston. Mr. Hurlbut was tall and thin, of dignified demeanor, agreeable and gentlemanly in his ways. He lived at the present Smith Jones house. He was buried in the old burying-ground where a slate stone marks his grave.

SETTLEMENT OF FIRST PASTOR.

Feb. 15, 1841, Rev. Josiah Ballard was called at a salary of six hundred dollars, and accepted the call. His installation took place March 2, 1841. The council was composed of the following ministers with their churches: Rev. Messrs. Brigham of Framingham, Harding of East Midway, Corner of Berlin, Hyde of Wayland, Horsford of Saxonville, Dyer of Stow, —— of Medfield, Woodbridge of Acton, Means of Concord, Day of Marlboro. Rev. Mr. Buckingham of Milbury preached the sermon. For a time the tax for preaching was levied upon each person on the basis of the town valuation, but later, the money was raised by subscription, and recently the envelope system has been employed.

THE OLD PARISH.

After the division took place, the old parish disclaimed any formal or legal relationship to Rev. Rufus Hurlbut. March, 1839, it declared by vote that it no longer considered him their minister as he had withdrawn from them. The records state that after " a portion of the church and congregation had withdrawn and formed a new Society called

THE HURLBUT PARSONAGE, Sudbury Centre

Orthodox the old Society enjoyed the outward services of the Gospel irregularly," and that the church was reduced to a small number. We have not ascertained from record what membership was left; but Deacon Thomas P. Hurlbut was accustomed to state that "but one member remained with the old Parish." All the property was retained by the old society; but the indications are that a portion, at least, of that which was portable was transferred to it by those who no longer worshipped at the old meeting-house, since one of the records of the Evangelical Union Church, dated February, 1839, is as follows: "To choose a committee to settle with Levi Dakin, the present Treasurer of the Church, and take the papers and money now in his hands, and keep them until claimed by the church, which may be formed in the first Parish." A few years afterwards the First Society had an increase of membership, and the church was reorganized as the records of the old parish state. (Page 38.) "In the Fall of 1844 the Church was reorganized, and a number of persons came forward and united in the Lord's Supper, with the few who were members before, and were acknowledged members of the First Church. The number then uniting was twelve."

For a time the old society had different preachers to supply the pulpit. From March 30 to September 22, according to a record book of Capt. Israel Haynes, no less than twelve different ministers preached there. In the summer of 1841, Rev. Linus Shaw was invited to preach, which he did till fall. Soon after, the meeting-house was remodelled, and in 1844, he was invited to preach there again; he did so, and the result was his settlement as pastor. He was installed June 5, 1845, and continued in the pastorate till his death.

REV. LINUS H. SHAW.

Linus H. Shaw was born in Raynham Nov. 29, 1804, where he fitted for college with Rev. Enoch Sanford, pastor of the Trinitarian Congregational Church. He entered Brown University, which he left at the close of two years in 1827, to engage in teaching. He was for a time second principal of the Bristol County Academy at Taunton, and in 1830, he entered the Divinity School, Cambridge, where he remained three years. In 1834, he was ordained at Athol. He married Louisa Alden Jones, and had five children, — Louisa, Henry, Joseph, Maria and Helen. In 1850, he built a house on Plympton Hill, a little north-east of Sudbury Centre, where he lived until his death, Jan. 5, 1866. Mr. Shaw was an estimable man, a valuable citizen, and much respected by the community. He was small in stature, dignified and gentlemanly in demeanor, quiet and unassuming in his ways. Nov. 24, 1864, he preached a sermon at a union service, held by the several churches of Sudbury, on the subject, "The Black man and the War;" which, at the people's request, was printed. Since the death of Rev. Linus Shaw, the following ministers have acted as pastors for the First Parish: Revs. Bond, Dawes, Webber, Knowles, Willard, Sherman, E. J. Young and Gilman. For several years the church has had preaching but a small portion of each year.

MISCELLANEOUS.

In 1825, "the building Lanham Bridge was let out to E. Fairbank and David How for the sum of eighty eight dollars."

In 1826, the town granted thirty dollars "to furnish dinners and powder for soldiers muster day."

In 1828, voted to exchange the old bell for a new one.

April 7, 1828, a road was accepted "from Wm Hunt's land, over land of Elisha Hunt to Lanham."

Nov. 14, 1831, "the town gave leave to have stoves placed in the porch of the meeting house, the funnel passing into the house up through the roof." Rev. Rufus Hurlbut offered to pay fifty dollars towards the expense of the stoves, provided others would raise the remaining amount. A subscription paper was started to which thirty-five names were subscribed. The sums pledged varied from fifty cents to six dollars, making in all one hundred dollars. Only three of the thirty-five are now living, — Walter Rogers, Hopestill Brown and Willard Walker.

In 1832, a road was accepted by the town "from the Berlin road to Ephraim Moore's." "Voted that the Poor be left to the Overseers of the Poor to let them out to one or more contractors for one year as they shall think best."

In 1833, the town chose a committee to petition the Postmaster-General for a post office at the Centre, and also "to have the North and South offices discontinued. At the same meeting "voted to take the map [of the town] of Mr Wood at sixty-eight dollars." Also "voted that each individual in town shall have a map of the town for twenty-eight cents." Also "voted to authorize some person to give a warranty deed of the John Green farm."

In 1835, the town gave liberty to Thomas Plympton to enclose with a fence "the graves of his father and mother and family connections now buried in the grave yard."

In 1848 and 9, much excitement was caused in Sudbury, in common with other places, by the discovery of gold in California. The discoverer was James W. Marshall, who first saw it near the saw-mill of Capt. John A. Sutter, Feb. 2, 1846. The "gold fever" became quite general, and a number of persons started out in the hope of making their fortune, among whom were Humphrey Sawyer, Hiram Burr, Haman Hunt, Nichols Brown, Samuel and Edward Bacon, Thomas Stearns, Samuel Carr, Eli H. Willis, Samuel Garfield, Elbridge Haynes and Levi Dow.

CHAPTER XXVII.

1850-1875.

> We may build more splendid habitations,
> Fill our rooms with paintings and with sculptures,
>   But we cannot
> Buy with gold the old associations.
> LONGFELLOW.

As we enter upon the history of the last half of the
present century, it may be appropriate and interesting to
pause in the narrative and notice some changes that have
taken place in the various villages and districts as these
relate to the occupants of homesteads, to industries, and the
location of dwelling-houses, stores and shops. In doing this,
it is desirable and essential to describe things as they are in
the present period, not only that by the contrast we may
better note the change which the passing years have brought,
but that a knowledge of the present may thus be imparted
to those who are to come after us, to whom the present will

be the past. Different terms have been used to designate the different parts of the town in different stages of its history. In early times, it was the " East and West Side of yᵉ great River;" later, it was the "East and West Precinct," or the "East Side" and "Rocky Plain." After a time, the West Side was divided into wards for the purpose of notification of town meetings, road repairing, and militia organizations. At one time the territorial limit of certain official duties was the old Lancaster road. This ancient highway, probably, divided the town more equally than any other landmark of that time. Still later, the town was divided into districts for school purposes. The locality gave its name to the school, and the school gave its name to the district. But soon after the middle of the century the school districts underwent a change. The Pantry school-house at the road corners was removed, and a new building was erected by the "Great Road" for the North part or North Village. Another school-house was erected about a quarter of a mile south of Pantry bridge, and two schools were established at the Centre. A year later a school-house was built at South Sudbury. These events somewhat changed the designation of different parts of the town by districts; yet, notwithstanding this, the history of the town is so associated with the five old and familiar school districts, that it is expedient to follow this division in describing different parts of the town outside the villages. Before describing the various school districts, however, we will give a description of the villages. The town has three distinct villages, — South Sudbury, Sudbury Centre and North Sudbury. These all lie in a line, north and south, about midway of the town.

SOUTH SUDBURY.

The village of South Sudbury is about a mile south of the Centre, on the Boston and Worcester highway and the Massachusetts Central and northern branch of the Old Colony Railroad. Until recently it was known as "Mill Village." It has a store, post office, machine shop, blacksmith's shop, school-house, chapel, grist-mill, a junction depot, the Good-

now Library, and about fifty dwelling-houses.   The depot is
a little westerly of the village, in the locality known to the
old inhabitants as "Dana Hunt's swamp," formerly part
wood and part pasture, which belonged to the old Thompson
estate.   The place was once resorted to by the villagers for
bilberries, and children picked young checker-bush there.
The swamp, though not large, contained a variety of shrubbery, mixed with pines, oaks and birches.   In winter it was
quite a resort for partridges, affording both feeding-ground
and shelter for them.   An old hunter informed me that he
had passed through there in the morning and shot birds, and
returning at night had taken others, which had flown in
during the day from the neighboring woods.

The oldest house in the village is the "John Allen house,"
first east of the store on the north side of the road.   It
probably dates as far back, at least, as 1700, and may have
been built by Abraham Woods, who near that time leased
the mill, or by the Noyeses who built it.   The house formerly had a long sloping roof on the back, was painted red,
and had a door on the east side.   Tradition tells of a small
house that stood near the site of the blacksmith's shop by
the mill.   It also says that, one day, the Indians appeared
on the rising ground just over Mill Brook (Leavett's Hill),
and a woman at the house made them think men were about
by calling out, "Be quick, boys, the Indians are coming!"
whereupon the Indians fled.

South Sudbury has undergone various changes.   The
Boston and Worcester highway formerly went south of
Green Hill, then followed "the old road" to the village,
and beyond the bridge it turned southerly and left the Cutler
and Walter Rogers houses on the north, and came out by the
Wheeler house near the clay-pits that were formerly on the
old Gibbs farm.   This highway in former times was much
travelled.   Loaded teams came from as far as Vermont, and
sometimes two or three stages daily passed over it.   One
day a three-horse team from Brookfield was coming up Green
Hill when a flash of lightning killed every horse.   Along this
road the village was built.   The only buildings on the south
side of it fifty years ago, between Abel Smith's at Green Hill

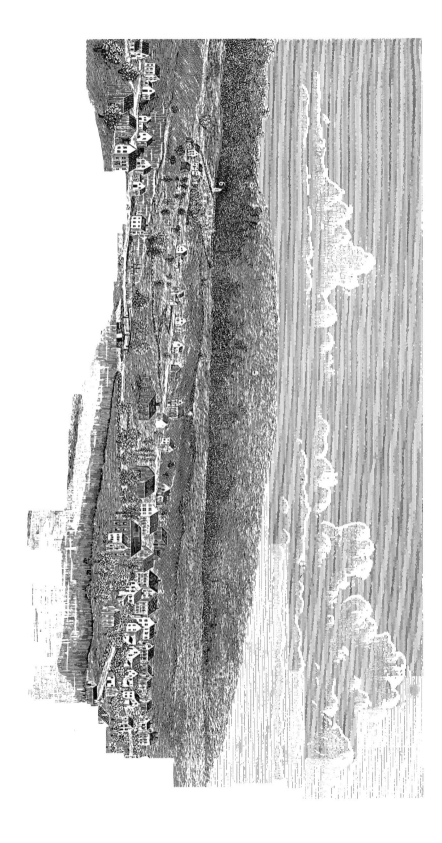

and the bridge, were Capt. Enoch Kidder's house (John B. Goodnow's), built in 1813 or 14, the mill buildings, the blacksmith's shop (J. P. Allen's), built in 1826 and lately demolished, and an old barn nearly opposite the Allen house. In this old barn, tradition says, a noted character, commonly called Tom Cook, sometimes stopped for the night. This man was a notorious tramp or itinerant thief, well known for his eccentric ways. A little later the Kidder shoe shop was built, just east of the Kidder house. On the north side of the road were about a dozen buildings between Green Hill and the bridge. The first by the brook was a blacksmith's shop, where the Browns made billhooks, cleavers, hatchets and knives; next to this was the Thompson malt house, to which the town's people brought barley for malt; beyond this was the William Brown place, a low, one-story house; and further on at the west corner of the Boston and Worcester and meeting-house roads was the "tavern stand;" beyond the tavern, on the opposite corner, was the store kept by Gardener and Luther Hunt, a small building with an L running north; next in order came a dwelling-house since burned, Fisher's wheelwright's shop, the Woods or Allen house, the Fisher house, and a few rods up the hill the house occupied by Josiah Richardson, which is still standing. Between this house and Green Hill was only the Cutter place (Hiram Goodnow's) and the Gideon Richardson place (now Newton place). Up to 1825, there was no house on the "meeting-house road" to the Israel How Brown place. Such was South Sudbury half a century ago. The changes that have come over it have been gradual; no sudden or single stroke has swept the landmarks away, but one by one they have gone. The old store was burned Feb. 14, 1841, and the one built in its place shared a like fate in 1887. A new mill was erected in 1853, which in 1886 was burned, and the same year another was built on its site. The blacksmith's shop and malt house, after years of disuse, were torn down, one about thirty, the other about forty years ago. About 1864, the tavern buildings were demolished. In 1861 and 62, the Goodnow Library was put up by John Harriman. In 1857, Wadsworth Academy was built, and in 1879 it was burned,

and the Congregational Chapel erected in its place in 1880.
Thus change has been active with its busy hand. The
history of some of these buildings that have thus passed
away is of considerable interest. The old store was the only
village grocery for scores of years, as was also its successor.
Tradition says it was established by Capt. Levi Holden, who
commanded the "south militia company." Subsequent to
Captain Holden's possession, it was owned by Asher Cutler,
and kept by Abel Cutler and Jesse Goodnow, and was purchased by Messrs. Gardener and Luther Hunt near the
beginning of the present century. Much spirituous liquor
was sold at this grocery to the people in all the country
round, till the starting of the temperance cause, when the
traffic in rum there ceased. G. and L. Hunt were succeeded
by Charles and Emory Hunt. The present proprietor is
George, son of Emory. Formerly, this store was the centre
of an extensive trade. About the year 1850, there was a
large barter in straw braid. Women and children braided
straw in their homes from the material cut green in the rye
field, then dried, whitened and split, and turned straw upon
straw in "seven strand," which brought from a half cent to
two cents a yard. Teams from the neighboring towns
brought this work, which was exchanged for a variety of
wares, and the hitching-posts of the entire store front were
sometimes all in use at one time. An old store sign was
"Furniture, Feathers & Crockery Ware Rooms," and this
included stoves, carpets, and sundry commodities not always
found in a country store. In process of time the braid trade
ceased, the old mill that "brought custom" ceased for a time
"to grind the town's corn," the old "firm" was dissolved,
and a part of the store became a private dwelling-place;
since then the other part has been an ordinary store for the
sale of English and West India goods. Besides Hunt's
store another place of some interest was the "Kidder shoe
shop." This has lately been remodelled and made into a
private residence, but for years the upper part was a shoe
shop and the lower used as a grocery. In the earlier life of
the well-known proprietor, business at this shop was very
brisk. In addition to the local patronage, marketers were

accustomed to leave orders as they came from the towns beyond. This was, perhaps, one of the last places where the old "tongue" boot was made. The Kidder shop was quite a resort for the villagers on a wet day or winter's evening. There they gathered and gossiped and smoked as the night's early hours went by. It was a quaint old place. Pictures of a patriotic and political character — "The Battle of Bunker Hill," "The Storming of a Mexican Fort," likenesses of Webster, Benton, Calhoun and Clay — were upon the walls, and near the ceiling hung two flint-lock muskets left over when the militia broke up. Captain Kidder was bent in form and looked old when those now middle-aged were young. He was a Whig and held various town offices. His wife was the village florist, and various and wonderful to our eyes were the plants and flowers that grew in Mrs. Kidder's "front yard." Besides these, there were in the side yard beds and boxes of plants. In this collection was a fig-tree which she had cultivated from the seed and which at one time bore one or two hundred figs. On the place were high cherry-trees, heavy in their season with luscious fruit, and apple-trees that were choice and in those days rare. Mrs. Kidder was a good-hearted, benevolent woman, of large hospitality, and, like her husband, was much esteemed. As the Kidders were so well and so widely known, a short sketch of the household may properly be considered a part of the historic sketch of South Sudbury.

Enoch Kidder was born in 1777 and died in 1865. He was a brother of Dr. Kidder, a physician of Sudbury. (See Chapter on Physicians.) In early life he learned the tanner's trade. On moving to Sudbury he commenced the manufacture of boots and shoes. For a time he occupied the Josiah Richardson house. After building the Kidder house, for a time he used the east part of it for a shop or a lodging-place for his apprentices. His trade was largely with the old shoe firm of Faxon and Company of Boston, and his reputation was known far and near as a manufacturer of reliable work. At one time he was captain of the militia, and was sent as representative to the Legislature. His wife, Hannah Newton of Marlboro, born in 1781, was, before her

marriage, a school teacher, and was a personage as conspicuous as was the shrubbery that adorned her home. Her
loud, cheerful voice was a familiar sound in the village, as,
on a bright morning in June, she bustled about the premises
as busy as the bees among her bright flowers. A green
turban sat on her head which broadened her genial face, and
when she went out for a neighborly call she wore a " calash "
of the same color.   Besides Mr. and Mrs. Kidder, the household consisted of a daughter Nancy, born in 1807, who was
the only child living, and Miss Almira Cutter, the housekeeper.   Nancy was the pet of the home and a general
favorite ; she was of delicate health and died in 1856.
" Mira " Cutter, as the housekeeper was familiarly called,
belonged to the Cutter family of Sudbury. She went to
Mrs. Kidder's to spend the day and remained forty years,
having the main charge of the household and outliving the
whole family. She died a few years ago and was buried in
the Kidder tomb in Wadsworth Cemetery.

Another object of interest is the mill.   At one time it was
owned by Asher Cutler. We were informed by his grandson,
the late C. G. Cutler, that he was very rigid, and would shut
down the mill at sundown Saturday night. Asher Cutler
left the mill jointly to his sons, Asher and Abel, the former
of whom lived in the " Woods house." The fact that the
house and the mill were both owned by the same parties at
different periods leads to the conjecture that the two pieces
of property, for a time at least, went together, and possibly
the " Woods House " was built by the Noyeses who put up
" the mill." Later owners have been General Sawin, a
militia officer, who also owned. the old tavern stand, Jesse
Brigham, and Mr. Knight who sold it to Abel Richardson.
This mill has not only ground the town's corn, but some also
for the region around.   For years it was a grist and saw-mill
combined : the former was run by a large breast-wheel and
had two run of stones, the latter, by a wheel of itself which
ran an upright saw. The " Mill Lane," which led from the
county road, used to be well filled with " saw logs," mostly
white pine and oak. A few years ago, the old upper dam,
which was a few rods north of the bridge, was in use.

Three gates that could be raised with an iron bar controlled the waters that for acres above, at certain seasons, set it back nearly to Hayden's bridge. The present dam by the bridge is of recent construction, and was built by Charles O. Parmenter, the present owner. The old mill was demolished about 1853, and another was put in its place, which, about 1866, was leased to Samuel Rogers and Company for manufacturing purposes. After being used for making hats and leather board it again became a grist-mill, and so continued until, a few years ago, it was destroyed by fire. A new mill has been erected on the site of the old one, and still the farmers of Sudbury bring their grists to the same old spot where their grain has been ground for about two hundred years. Another building of interest was the Wadsworth Academy. (See Period 1850–1875.) The old tavern stand was another familiar spot. (See Chapter on Taverns.)

The principal object of interest in this village is the Wadsworth Monument. From the hill slope (Green Hill), just east of the monument, is a magnificent prospect, as the country outstretches for miles to the westward without a hill to obstruct the view. On this hill-top was Wadsworth's last battle-ground. (See Period 1675–1700.) A part of South Sudbury village is situated in a quiet vale, with a spur of Green Hill on the north and Leavitt Hill on the south; the former takes its name from the evergreens that once grew upon it, and the latter from Leavitt How whose home was on the south side of it; an old cellar hole still marks the spot.

INDUSTRIES.

The industries of South Sudbury have been various. In 1794, besides the saw and grist-mill run by Cutler and Holden, there was a fulling-mill run by Mr. Reed. About three-quarters of a century ago, bricks were made at the Gibbs place and also at the Farr farm. Clay-pits at both places are yet to be seen unless recently filled. As has been noticed, malt was made at the malt house (Thompson's), people coming from all parts of the town for this product. Leather was tanned by William Wheeler at a place just beyond the bridge, near the old "upper dam." There were also tanning vats on the "Island" (land between the machine shop and the mill). On the "meeting house road" was a bakery. It was moved from the spot just east of the Willard Wheeler house, and is now owned by John Jones. About 1850, William Jones and Theodore Brown had a shoe manufactory at what is now the Bowen place. Since 1850, shoe tacks and nails were made at the mill by Calvin How, and hats and leather board by Rogers and Moore. The main business in and about South Sudbury has been farming. Of late years, early gardening has received much attention and greenhouses have been used by some. The first greenhouse in Sudbury was erected in 1879 by Hubbard H. Brown for raising cucumbers. He has since erected three more, all of which cover six thousand feet of ground. Since 1882, thirty greenhouses have been built. There is now used for raising vegetables and flowers nearly one hundred thousand square feet of land covered with glass. Fifteen farmers and gardeners are engaged in the work. It is estimated that seven hundred tons of coal are consumed yearly, and about fifty thousand dollars are invested in the business. The buildings are all heated by hot water except in one instance where steam is used. Most of these are used for raising vegetables, such as cucumbers, lettuce, rhubarb, tomatoes, etc. One house has twenty-eight thousand lettuce plants, another has twelve thousand carnation pinks. In 1881, the manufacture of machinery was begun at South Sudbury by Rufus H. Hurlbut. The business is now carried on by the firm of Hurlbut & Rogers. The machine shop is near the Parmenter mill and the Massachusetts Central Railroad.

MODERN IMPROVEMENTS.

The first carriage in town was owned by John Brown. A wagon was owned by Christopher Cutler nearly fifty or seventy-five years ago which cost eleven dollars. The first kerosene lamp was used by Miss L. R. Draper (Mrs. A. S. Hudson) at the Willard Wheeler house. The first mowing machine was owned by John Whitman Rice, and used on the Farr farm. The first sewing machine was, perhaps, the one used by Richard Horr at the Kidder shop for stitching "shoe uppers." It was operated by a crank turned by hand. Hard coal was, perhaps, first used at Hunt's store.

The former owners of most of the farms in and about South Sudbury have been given in connection with other parts of its history; we will, therefore, only mention the few that remain. The Thadeus Moore place was the Ashbel Hayden place; the main house was the Thompson house, moved from just beyond the bridge at South Sudbury village. The Nathan Haynes place, just beyond Lowance Brook or Hunt's Bridge, was the Jonas Hunt place. The small red house with gable roof, on the South Sudbury and Framingham highway, just beyond the Old Colony Railroad, was moved to its present position, many years ago, from the Bryant place just beyond the William Stone house. Walter Rogers' farm was formerly part of the Cutler place and was owned by Major Holden, and before that by Mr. Seger, a sea captain. The C. G. Cutler place was the old George Pitts place. A building formerly stood south of the present one, near which the old road passed. It was once used for a tavern, and was probably kept by George Pitts, at whose house one of the early meetings was held to consider the matter of having preaching on the West Side. (See Period 1700–1725.) The George Pitts farm once contained a large land tract which was granted to him in 1715. The record of this grant is as follows: In 1715, at a meeting of the proprietors of the common and undivided land in Sudbury, "Said Proprietors by unanimous vote without any Contradiction did give and grant to George Pitts of Sudbury and his heirs and assigns forever all the common land as the committee hath viewed it and returned and bounded it that is to say, all ye common Land Lying between the new Mills in Sudbury and so from there as the road goeth to Marlborough to the gate y^t Leads to Capt Brown's y^t is, all the Land on the South Side of the road as it is bounded and the meadows called Lowance meadows Lying east south and west of the land, all which land the Proprietors have granted to George Pitts, only the Proprietors reserve for our convenient Drift ways to the above said Lowance Meadows, and gravell to mend the Mill Dam and the highways as there shall be occasion. This vote passed into an act as attest.

"Peter Haynes Moderator

"This said land is on the west side of Sudbury river."

(Proprietor's First Book of Records, page 175.)

SUDBURY CENTRE.

The "Centre," or, as it was formerly called, the "Middle of the Town," is situated on the northern branch of the Old Colony Railroad, and nearly midway of the town. It has three churches, a school-house, town-house, blacksmith's shop, wheelwright's shop, grocery store, depot and three or four dozen dwelling-houses. The place was anciently called "Rocky Plain," afterwards "The West Precinct," and dates its beginning as a village about 1725. The oldest house in the village is, probably, the "Tower house," now owned by Frank E. Bent, and situated next south of the Orthodox Church. Its date is unknown, but it looked old in the youth of the oldest inhabitant, as did also the Lewis Moore house, the next but two further south, where Mr. Moore, the village cooper, in an L running northerly, once plied his trade. The Tower house, prior to its possession by Mr. Jonas Tower, was occupied by a man named Noyes. This house may have been the first one erected on "Rocky Plain," and the one referred to in the Town Records as "the new house." This village has undergone much change within the past seventy-five years. Early in this century there was a blacksmith's shop at what is now the corner of the railroad and highway, and northerly of the house of Horace Parmenter. The shop was kept by Josiah Haynes; nearly opposite, north of the road, was a house since demolished occupied by Asa Haynes; and a little beyond this on the bank, was the George Barker house, a low building with its four-sided roof, which stood until a few years ago. Dr. Taft, a physician, once lived there. Subsequently a store was kept at the place by Reuben Moore. Where Garfield and Parmenter's grocery stands, there was formerly a store kept by Ephraim Stone and Asahel Dakin, which was burnt about forty years ago, together with a tavern house which stood on the corner nearly north of it. Nearly opposite the grocery site the Powers house once stood, at which time it was painted red. At the Joel Moore place, since the residence of Lemuel Brown, the first house west of the Unitarian Church, a store was kept by Capt. Asahel Wheeler. This country store-keeper, we are informed by an old inhabitant, "was large, smart, and lived to be very old." For a long time he led the singing in the old church choir. Nearly opposite Captain Wheeler's store was a low, unpainted house which looked old seventy-five years ago. The school-house was near the bank by the town-house. It was a small, red structure, built towards the close of the last century. Its successor stood on the common at its south-east corner, and was moved to its present position only a few years ago. On the common, nearly front of the old parish meeting-house and under the large buttonwood-tree, was the horse-block where the people mounted and dismounted when they went on horseback to church. Near the site of the Orthodox Church once stood the blacksmith's shop of Abijah Powers. It was moved to its present location about 1839, and was an old building then. Before its possession by the present owner it was occupied by Myron Wright, and still earlier by John Wallace. A "noon house" stood near the horse-sheds; perhaps there were more than one. These buildings were erected by private parties and furnished with fireplaces for the benefit of people between services on the Sabbath. Beyond the Common to the easterly, in what was then the first house towards Boston (Loring parsonage), a tavern was kept by Walter Haynes. Beyond this, at the George Goodnow house, Parson Bigelow lived. On the road to South Sudbury, at what is now the Smith Jones place, Rev. Rufus Hurlbut lived.

The house now occupied by Luman Willis was the old Ashur Goodnow store. There a grocery was kept for years, and many a townsman still remembers the bent form of the aged proprietor as he dealt out his wares. The second building westerly of the Unitarian Church was erected by Dr. Thomas Stearns, about a half century since, and used for his residence till his decease; and after the "old Corner

Tavern " was burnt it was used for a public house by
Webster Moore.   The present store building was moved to
its present location since 1848.   The lower story was formerly the old Centre school-house.   Various traders have
sold at its counters, prominent among whom were Stone and
Dakin, Jonas Hunt and Smith Jones.   The house occupied
by Horace Parmenter was formerly owned by Capt. William
Brigham, and was moved to its present location from a spot
to the north-easterly, to give place to the railroad.   The
wheelwright's shop of Sewall Taylor is on the site of the
building once used for religious services by the Evangelical
Union Church.   It was built in 1853, and was moved from
South Sudbury, where it was originally Haynes's carpenter's
shop, and later, Jones and Brown's shoe shop.   In 1851, a
saw and grist mill was built near Wash Bridge by Asahel
Haynes.   It is now owned by the Prescott Willis heirs.   A
small saw-mill once stood southerly of the Asa Jones place,
which was built by Mr. Jones in 1842.   It was moved about
five years afterwards and demolished in 1851.   Beyond the
Willis mill is the Wash Brook bridge.   About seventy-five
years ago, the father of the late Reuben Rice of Concord was
killed crossing this bridge ; he was engaged hauling lumber
for the meeting-house when the load fell on him.   Before
leaving this part of the town, it may be of interest to mention the outlying estates as they were known to the older
inhabitants.   For the sake of brevity, we will place in two
columns the present or recent and former names of the
places, owners or occupants.

PRESENT.	FORMER.
Charles Haynes.	Curtis Moore.
The Prescott Willis heirs.	David Lincoln.
Elisha Goodnow.	Capt. William Brigham.
Widow Asahel Dakin.	Asa Jones.
Francis Haynes.	Samuel Jones, prior to him Maynard.
John Quinn.	Lyman Willis.
Elisha E. Smith.	William Maynard.
George Moore.	Newell Bent.
Calvin J. Morse.	Martin Moore.
Theodore Morse.	Jason Bent.
Asahel F. Hunt.	William Hunt.

W. H. Fairbank.

Luke McCann.

Charles Haynes.

John W. Rice (House recently burned).

Horatio Hunt.

Lucius Bent.

Isaac Clark.

Aaron Hunt.

Tilly Smith.

Henry Goodnow.

Reuben Moore.

Capt. William Rice.

Thomas Hurlbut.

Reuben Moore, Jr.

—— Osborn.

Thomas Plympton (House demol- in 1886).

Among the objects of interest about the village of Sudbury Centre is the old Burying-Ground. The Common, also, is a place of interest. Thither the minute-men repaired at the bell strokes on the morning of April 19, 1775. The train-bands of Sudbury afterwards made it their place of parade and spread their tents upon it on " old Election " or the Fourth of July. Generations of church-goers from the West Precinct's very beginning have strolled over it, or sat on its grassy covering during the intermission of Sabbath services ; and all that is mortal of many a former inhabitant has been borne over its quiet roadway to the church-yard beyond. The school children from the old red school-house made it their play-ground for many years. There the people talked politics on town-meeting day when the meeting-house was their voting-place, and about it clustered the first homesteads that made a village of Sudbury Centre.

NORTH SUDBURY.

The village of North Sudbury is in the northerly part of the old Pantry school district, which it was once a part of, and borders on Concord. It contains about thirty dwelling-houses, which is about the same number as were there both fifty and one hundred years ago. Whatever of village this locality has is mainly made up of scantily scattered farm-houses along the Boston and Fitchburg highway, which was built about 1800. It has a post office, kept by Edwin Conant. The school-house is by the " Great Road ; " it was built during the late war and cost three thousand dollars. Before its erection the pupils went to "the Pantry school."

The post office was established about 1830, on petition of Willard Maynard and others. The following postmasters served up to 1839 : Josiah Adams, Joseph Wheelock, William Hunt, 3d. For a time, the postmaster at Lincoln took charge of the North Sudbury mail ; but, on petition of three-fourths of the town voters for the removal of the South office to the Centre, the South postmaster, wishing to retain his office, suggested to the people of the north part to petition for the re-establishment of a post office there, which they did with success. The petition for an office at the Centre was refused on the ground that it was nearer the South office than the department rules would allow. The new office at the North was kept by John Sawyer. Various small industries have engaged the attention of the people of this neighborhood in the past. In 1770, a Mr. Brown had a harness and whip shop near the south side of the Tavern Plain. In 1780, Samuel Dakin and Deacon Dakin had cooper's shops, and there was another near J. H. Adams's in 1825. A shoemaker's shop was at J. Puffer's tavern in 1800, and N. Barrett had a shoe shop one-half mile east of Pratt's tavern. Daniel Bowker had a blacksmith's and axe shop between 1790 and 1820, and John Haynes had a blacksmith's shop from 1820 to 1840 and a wheelwright's shop from 1835 to 1845. Abijah Brigham had a blacksmith's shop one mile west of Pratt's tavern from 1770 to 1800. The site is now in Maynard. Thus the ring of the anvil and hammer have been heard in the past where now not a shop exists. In 1827, iron ore was taken from the edges of bog meadows and from different farms to the amount of over one hundred tons, which was carted to Concord River at Lee's Bridge and taken in boats to Chelmsford.

About 1815, a grocery store was kept a few years by Asa Puffer, one-half mile west of Pratt's Tavern, and at the same place groceries and dry goods were kept by Josiah H. Adams from 1822 to 1830. In 1820, William Hunt, 3d, and William Wheeler kept a grocery and dry goods store, a half mile east of Pratt's tavern, and at the same place from 1825 to 1851 Nahum Thompson kept a stock of the same articles. Groceries were also kept by John Sawyer, three-quarters of a mile west of Pratt's tavern, from 1830 to 1840. In this part of the town the most noted tavern was perhaps the old Pratt Tavern, burned in 1887. This was built previous to 1820 by Nathan Wheeler, adopted heir of Isaac Puffer, who many years kept a tavern in a house now owned by Mrs. McNulty. Since the first proprietorship the following persons have kept this inn: David Gerry, 1822; Earl Stratton, Willard Wiley, 1826; Lucius Dickinson, one year; Joseph Wheelock, William Hunt 3d, Lyman Haynes, Solomom E. Pratt, about ten years; Jesse Gibbs, Robert Burrington, Leonard Carter, 1863. The farm and buildings were purchased of the Burrington heirs about 1864, by Capt. Abel B. Jones, who annexed the land to his farm and discontinued the tavern. Four stages daily, Sundays excepted, stopped at this inn for passengers and a relay of horses. The stage route belonged to Chedorlaomer Marshal, commonly called Kidder Marshal, of Fitchburg, who was mail contractor.

This stage route continued after Mr. Pratt kept the tavern until the completion of the Fitchburg Railroad. Jonas Puffer, brother of Isaac, kept a tavern a half mile from his brother's during the last quarter of the last century, on the old Concord and Marlboro road, then much travelled, now almost deserted. The road through North Sudbury is called by the people of the place the "Great Road," and by those of the centre and South Sudbury the "North Road." The true name is the Boston & Fitchburg Road.

But few homesteads in North Sudbury are possessed by the posterity of original proprietors. It is supposed that the ancestors of Frank M. Bowker, Jonathan C. Dakin and Frederic Haynes were probably the first settlers on the farms that their descendants now occupy, but other places have largely changed hands. There are in the district but few old houses. Most of those built from 1700 to 1725, which had two stories in front and one in the rear, and nearly all of which faced southward, whatever direction the road, were nearly all pulled down between 1820 and 1840, and were succeeded by houses of two stories, only one room in width with a projecting kitchen called an "L." It is said this style continued about twenty years and was followed by the modern house of various shape. A saw-mill once stood near the place now owned by George Barton, which was built by Joseph Noyse about 1775. The water power was insufficient, and the mill was finally sold, taken down and carried to Maynard.

It is said that the saw, as it dragged down through the log and then went up, sounded as if saying, " Shall I go or shall I not."

CHAPTER XXVIII.

1850–1875.

> Each man's chimney is his golden mile-stone,
> Is the central point, from which he measures
> Every distance
> Through the gate-ways of the world around him.
>
> LONGFELLOW.

LANHAM DISTRICT.

THIS word has been spelled Lanham, Landham and Lannum or Lanum. (For origin, see page 70.) As a school district, it formerly extended a half mile westerly of Mill Village (South Sudbury) and southerly to just beyond Hunt's Bridge. Lanham proper extends from the South Sudbury and Wayland highway to Framingham line, and from Heard's Pond to Lowance Brook. Various changes have taken place in this district, noticeable among which is the removal of the school-house to its present location. It formerly stood on the town's common land, near the Coolidge place, between the three roads, and was removed but a few years since. Its predecessor was an old red structure built, probably, about a century ago. We remember it as a nearly or quite square building with a roof sloping four ways and a small L for an entry on the south. The windows were high, and on the rude benches and desks were the signs of misspent hours, where the idler with his jackknife had made his mark. As the customs of district school life here were, probably, the same in the other districts, we will allude briefly to some of them. There were two terms in the year, called the "winter school" and the "summer school." The former began the first Monday in December and closed about the first of March. The beginning and the ending were both great events. The first was attended by early rising and repairing to the school-house to get a "good seat." While propriety gave the back seats to the elder scholars, the principle acted on was "first come, first served." Weeks beforehand, books were put in the desks as a kind of half claim, but the day the school was opened the room was occupied long before daybreak. At nine o'clock the schoolmaster appeared, sometimes attended by the local "committee man." He at once became the object of common and curious scrutiny, his sagacity, stature and strength being then and there duly considered. The names and ages of the scholars were then taken, and the questions to each, "What have you studied?" "How far have you been?" "What studies do you expect to take?" were quickly put and answered, and the classes were formed. The order of exercises in the morning was as follows: roll-call, reading of the Scriptures, each scholar rising and read-ing a verse in turn, prayer at the option of the master, and classes in reading, arithmetic and writing, interrupted by a short recess at half-past ten. In the afternoon the order was, usually, reading, beginning with the first class, geography, grammar, history and spelling. The recess was at half-past two. The "nooning" was from twelve to one. This was usually employed by the boys, in good weather, at ball, "round ball" being the favorite. The Massachusetts Central Railroad now runs over the old ball-ground, which lay east and west of the bridge.

Such was the usual routine as the weeks passed by. Now and then some little episode would break in, as when the "committee came in" or the school had a sleigh-ride some bright winter's day, or a half holiday for some reason was given. At the close of the term was examination day, familiarly called the "last day." This was the great event of the term, when the committee, and friends, and visitors from other districts came in. The day before was always devoted to washing and trimming the school-room. The floor was scoured till it was almost white. The woods were searched for evergreens, and wreaths and festoons were made to decorate the nicely cleaned walls. When all was completed, the weary workers sat down to a feast, made up of pie and cake brought by the girls, and confectionery purchased by the boys with a collection of small change. After the recitations of examination day were over the committee "made remarks," the clergyman offered prayer, and the visitors retired. The master lingered for a time to make some parting remarks, or perhaps to present a card or book or bestow a reward for good conduct, and then "school was done." The summer school was always taught by a woman, and lasted two or three months. The older boys and girls were kept at home this term to assist in the household and on the farm.

Besides changes connected with the school, many others have occurred in Lanham in the last hundred years. A stone bridge has taken the place of the wooden one. On the site of the Nahum Goodnow house, built in 1886, the old house of John Goodnow the centenarian once stood. The latter, built by Mr. Gooodnow when a young man, is still standing a few rods to the north. At or near its present site was a small building where Mr. Goodnow lived when he first came to his Lanham estate. The lane, running westerly by Lanham meadows towards Lowance to William Goodnow's, is old. On the north side of it various dwellings once stood, a man named Gibbs living in one of them. Near where the Brooks house now stands was the old Elisha

Hunt homestead. Several generations of Hunts have lived in this house, which was probably built at least one hundred and fifty years ago. It is now moved easterly, to the north side of the road, and is used as the farmhouse of the Brooks estate. The first house on the place, tradition informs us, was built of planks, and was half frame and half log house; it stood at or near the original site of the farmhouse. By the roadside, at the corner a few rods west, was a small, low, unpainted building consisting of two rooms, once used for a school-house. At one time Isaac Moore, a Revolutionary soldier, lived there. His son, Warren, was in the privateer service of 1812, and was made prisoner and taken to Dartmoor Prison, England. In this district was the old Goodnow Garrison. (See page 199.) In this district are several clay-pits; some are near Heard's Pond, and some are mentioned in the records as being near the town line. Lanham brook is the lower part of Hop brook. Robinson brook, near Green Hill, has its name from the Robinson family, which lived south of the road on the east bank of the brook. The Massachusetts Central Railroad station in this district is called East Sudbury.

SOUTH-WEST DISTRICT.

This district has also been called Peakham. It is stated that a man by the name of Peakham once owned a little land in that part of Sudbury, and that the land was called after the name of its owner; from which circumstance the whole locality thereabouts came to be called Peakham. The area embraced in the original limits of this district is large, but it contains neither post office, village, nor even any considerable hamlet. The school-house is situated a little northerly of the South Sudbury and Marlboro road, and was built towards forty years ago. A school-house has stood on the spot at least a hundred years. Latterly, the school was called the "Wayside Inn School," but for several years it has been discontinued, and the scholars being few are carried to South Sudbury.

Formerly, children attended the Peakham school from as far south and east as the Brown farms near the Framing-

RESIDENCE OF NAHUM GOODNOW

ham line, and from as far north as the Perry and Moore places. This district lies along a large share of the town's western border, but is perhaps at no point more thickly in-habited than within a half mile of the school-house. The Massachusetts Central Railroad runs through it, and has a station called the "Wayside Inn Station." The situation of this depot is exceptionally secluded, no other building being in sight on account of the woods by which it is nearly sur-rounded. The district has several places of considerable historical interest, and has been the birthplace and home of some of Sudbury's most prominent men. Here is "Howe's Tavern" or the "Wayside Inn." (See chapter on Taverns). Here is the old Walker Garrison House, and the sites of the Parmenter and old Brown garrisons. (See Chapter XI.) Here, at Nobscot, was the house of John Nixon, and here was the small-pox hospital. For years there were three mills in this district, — Howe's, Dutton's and Moore's. The first, early in the century, was owned by Buckley Howe, and still earlier by Joseph Howe. It was for years a grist-mill only, but subsequently it was made use of by J. C. Howe as a manufactory of shoe nails. It stands on Hop Brook a short distance above the Wayside Inn, and was the most westerly mill on this stream in town.

Dutton's mill was built by Joel and Samuel Knights about 1780. They also owned and used it. About the same time they established a West India goods store on the "Dutton farm." Moore's or Pratt's mill was erected about 1740, by Daniel Woodward, its first owner, who died in 1760. In 1794, it was called Perry's saw-mill. Mr. Woodward also, about one hundred and fifty years ago, built the house occu-pied by Capt. James Moore, whose grandfather married Mr. Woodward's daughter. At first this mill was only a saw-mill, but in 1830 a shingle mill was started there, and in 1837 a grist and bolting mill were put in by Ephraim and James Moore, who divided the property in 1848. Colonel Ephraim Moore used the mill until about twenty-five years ago, since which time it has been owned by S. B. Rogers, and latterly owned and used by Nathan Pratt.

Heavy timber once grew on the Peakham district. (See

Chapter I.) These lands, though some of them sandy and light, have yet been fairly productive by the diligence and thrift of its inhabitants. In the hundred years last past, great changes have taken place in the occupants of old homesteads.

The following are some of these changes, as given by Capt. James Moore when over eighty years of age. In the left column are present or late owners or occupants, and opposite, in the right column, are the earlier owners or occupants of the same places.

Newton and Spencer Brown.	Samuel Brown.
Hubbard Brown.	John Brown.
Luther Cutting.	William Brown, brother of John.
John Dakin.	Caleb Brown, later Abel Dakin.

The above farms were probably one estate originally, and belonged to William Brown, an early grantee. (See Chapter III.)

Nahum Goodnow.	Isaac Gibbs.
George Stone.	Wm. Stone, Innholder. (See chapter on Taverns.)

Above the Stone place, on the left of the road that goes to the north, was the Jeduthan Moore farm. Two old, unpainted buildings stood there until within thirty or forty years.

Jonathan Bacon.	—— Rily, later, Joel Jones.

Near the junction of the South Sudbury and Marlboro road with the road to the school-house, was a house owned by a man named Dalyrimple.

Abel Willis.	Ezekiel Loring.

Beyond the Willis place was the Dutton house now removed. Next to the Dutton house, on the corner, and now removed, was a house formerly occupied by Peter Willard, carpenter.

Abel Parmenter.	Peletiah Parmenter.

This was an old Garrison House. (See Chapter XI.)

Addison Parmenter.	Jedediah Parmenter, brother of Peletiah.

The next building is the Wayside Inn.

Calvin Howe.　　　　　　　　　David Howe.

West of Nobscot Hill there was a house destroyed by fire which was formerly occupied by David Howe.

Otis Parmenter.　　　　Israel Parmenter (original owner).

In a lane near the Dutton place was a farm once owned by Caleb Clark, but now a part of the Dutton place.

Solomon Dutton.　　　Samuel Knight of Charlestown (original owner).
Abiathar Carr.　　　　—— Plympton (original owner).
Willard Walker.　　　　Deacon Thomas Walker (Garrison).

Above the Willard Walker place was the Abner Walker place, buildings now gone.

Madison Parmenter.　　　Micah Parmenter (original owner).
Abijah Walker.　　　　　Oliver Morse.
Hayden farm.　　　　　　William Hayden.

Back of Hayden's farm lived John Moore, grandfather of Deputy Sheriff John B. Moore of Concord. (Building now gone.)

Joseph Noyes.　　　　　Eliab Hayden.
Dudley place.　　　　　Benjamin Dudley.
Perry place.　　　　　　Ebenezer Perry (original owner).
Woodward Moore.　　　Daniel Woodward Moore.
Capt. James Moore.　　Daniel Woodward.

This house is in point of age perhaps second or third in Sudbury. Cider-mills once stood in this district at the houses of Buckley Howe, David Howe at Nobscot, Micah Parmenter, Paul Walker, Capt. James Moore, John Brown, and at the Wayside Inn. A prominent person who lives in this district, and one of the oldest citizens of the town, is Capt. James Moore. He is a descendant on his mother's side of Daniel Woodward, before mentioned as the builder of Moore's Mill. For years Captain Moore was one of the town's selectmen and moderator of its meetings.

THE NORTH-WEST DISTRICT.

This district formerly bordered on Concord and Stow, but when Maynard was set off, about two thousand acres of it became a part of that town. This locality was a school district for probably at least a hundred and fifty years. The school-house stood in about the centre of the district, by the county roadside, not far from the Balcom estate. As only a part of the original district comes within the present town limits, only a few facts about it will here be stated. The village of Assabet, now Maynard, was for years the commercial centre. A paper-mill was built there about seventy years ago, it is supposed, by William May, and a grocery store was kept by J. Sawyer. Near Jewell's mills, over the river, a saw-mill once stood, and there was also on a brook near the Daniel Puffer house another mill, which was connected with the farm. It had but little head of water, and because it ran slowly the people used to start it and then go to their work. A tavern was kept nearly ninety years ago at what has since been the Levi Smith place. But the old-time tavern best known in the district was kept by Jonathan Rice. It was an inn for about a hundred years. Says an old resident, "The last quarter of the last century on the very old Concord and Marlboro road then much travelled, now almost deserted, in the west part of Sudbury, was the noted Rice tavern, kept by the same family as early or earlier than 1750. Col. Jonathan Rice was the last proprietor, and closed it about 1815." The building stands just north of the present town bounds.·

The oldest house in the district is supposed to be the Daniel or Jabez Puffer house. It is not known when or by whom it was built, but it is surmised to have been built by a Pratt, Puffer or Wedge. Some of the earlier occupants of this district were Jonathan Rice, Jabez Puffer and Peter Smith; other early occupants were Amos, Asahel and Hezekiah Smith, Richard Taylor, Mathias Rice, Jonas Balcom, —— Wedge, Ephraim Pratt, William Rice; and still later, but yet early, Benjamin Smith, Henry Vose, Ithamer Rice,

Abijah Brigham, Joel, Micah and Asa Balcom, Loring Wheeler, Daniel and Reuben Puffer and Abel Willis.

THE NORTH-EAST OR PANTRY DISTRICT.

Another district in Sudbury is that which has been familiarly called the " Pantry School District." This is in the north-easterly part of the town, and takes in the region about the head of " Gulf Meadow " and of a small stream called "Pantry Brook." The district may have been named after the aforesaid brook, but whence the name of the brook, probably no one knows. It may be from a shortening of the term Pine-tree.

A natural feature of the district is the extensive " Gulf Meadows," which at high water are overflowed in places, nearly up to the county road. This district is sparsely peopled, if we exclude the village of North Sudbury, which is now hardly within its limits. It has neither store, shop, nor mill, but scattered about it are well-kept homesteads and farms, where live a thrifty and industrious people. A sawmill stood by the brook many years ago. The northern branch of the Old Colony Railroad passes through the locality, and has a station which is called North Sudbury. About a half mile southerly of the station is a school-house, and about an equal distance north-easterly is the North Sudbury cemetery. One of the marked changes of this district in the past quarter century is the removal of the " Old Pantry School-House," a place once dear to many an inhabitant now middle aged or already grown old. This school-house formerly stood at the road corners near the Pantry bridge, and was latterly like others of the town, a one-story, white building, with two doors towards the south. There for years the youth of the " North part " went to school. From the east and north they came, from nearly as far as the town line, and from the south and west from half to three-quarters this distance. But the children of this district go to school at that spot no more.

A few years since, the old school-house was moved and became the depot of the Old Colony Railroad, and has since

been destroyed by fire.   Its former site remains unmolested
as the town's common land ; and the place once merry with
the shouts of glad school children is now voiceless, save as
the words of the transient traveller break the silence of the
play-ground of this old-time school.   The routine of school
life here was doubtless like that of the other school districts,
and such as is described in our sketch of " Lanham."   It
may not however be inappropriate to introduce here a poetic
description by Hon. C. F. Gerry, an old pupil of " Pantry."

PANTRY SCHOOL.

I'm thinking of the school-house, Ned,
   Where, sitting side by side,
We studied Webster's spelling-book,
   And laughed o'er Gilpin's ride ;
And traded jackknives now and then,
   When not engaged in play,
And got our jackets nicely warmed,
   How often I'll not say.

I'm thinking of the roadside green,
   Of every tree and nook,
And how, in sultry hours of noon,
   We swam in Pantry Brook ;
And, when upon the casement came
   The ruler's tattoo loud,
How each of us in passing in
   Took off his hat and bowed.

I'm thinking of the benches rude,
   And desks so broad and steep,
On which we left our autographs,
   In letters wide and deep ;
And of my first new writing-book,
   Without a stain or spot,
So soon adorned, on every page,
   With many an off-hand blot.

I'm thinking of the " Old Slough," Ned,
   Whose waters dark and cool
So often laved our sunburnt feet,
   While on the way to school ;
On whose warm rim the tadpoles lay,
   In spring-time, many a score,
While golden lilies richly bloomed
   In summer, near the shore.

I'm thinking of the forest hoar
  Where fir-trees densely grew,
And tired feet in mosses sank,
  While hunting gum to chew ;
And of the pleasant meadows, where,
  On many a scattered tree,
The red-winged blackbird sang in spring,
  His love song, " Quonk-a-ree."

I'm thinking of the hour-glass, Ned,
  With sands so white and fine,
On which our teacher smiling gazed,
  As neared the hour to dine ;
But feel my sands are wasting, Ned,
  For oft the children say,
While fondling them upon my knee,
  " Papa, you're growing gray."

A short distance from the North Sudbury Depot is the old residence of the late Israel Haynes, who, it is said, cast the decisive vote that elected Charles Sumner to the United States Senate.

Mr. Haynes was an old-line Democrat, and that year represented Sudbury at the General Court. When the vote was taken for Senator there was for a time no choice ; but Mr. Haynes liked the young man Sumner, and he changed the equipoised balance by a break from the party vote. By this ballot Sumner went to the United States Senate, where he championed liberty's cause and stirred up those elements that burst forth into civil war, which made our whole land free. What an influence thus went out from this quiet place, and how changed our nation's history by this silent act! Mr. Haynes belonged to the old Haynes family of Sudbury and had a numerous progeny, some of whom still live on the old estate. On the Haynes farm, and south of the homestead, perhaps forty or fifty rods distant, once stood a block house. It was a small structure, heavily built, and demolished nearly a century ago. This doubtless was the stronghold for the neighborhood in the Indian war. (See page 200.) South-westerly of the depot a half mile or more is the Town Farm, or the " Poor Establishment," as it is sometimes called. In the southerly part of the district, on the estate of the late William Hunt, stood the old residence of Rev. Israel Loring. The building was latterly an old red structure with a long slope roof at the back, and was used for years by Mr. Hunt as a lodging place for some of the town's poor, under the system of boarding paupers at the lowest price bid. Such are some of the features of " Pantry," as it is and was, in the not far distant past. Like other districts, it is dear to many who remember the days of the old district schools, but the reminiscences that are rich about it are passing or are passed away with the generations to which they belonged.

THE GRAVEL PIT.

Another locality of interest, though not called a district, is the vicinity of the old causeway or gravel pit. The place is partly in Wayland, the town line running nearly midway of it. It takes its name from the gravelly bank by the road-side, from which the town has taken gravel for public purposes from the time of its settlement. Repeatedly on the records, as the years passed by, has the term Gravel Pit been inscribed ; and one objection of the East Side people to the division of the town was that by such an event they would lose the gravel pit. The locality had early occupation, and is often referred to, but outside the records little is left to indicate what it has been. The natural objects remain, but persons and their dwelling-places have passed away. There, was probably the west side of the ferry, before the building of the causeway. Peter Noyes's boat may have been moored to those meadow banks, when it furnished the main means of transit to the town's early grantees as they went to the West Side. Before the town was divided into two parochial precincts, an effort was made to have a meeting-house built there. (See page 289.) There was the beginning of the old Lancaster road which went to " Nashuway " (Lancaster). There the road started that went to Noyes's mill at Hop Brook ; and, from that point, a meadow path was laid out north and south over which the people hauled their hay. Several taverns have been kept there. During the Revolution a man named Wheeler kept a tavern there.

The house stood on the Thomas Battles place, which was formerly owned by John Taylor, and since, by the Wheeler Haynes heirs. It was burned down years ago. Later, a tavern was kept by Abel Cutler, and at another time by a Mr. Carter. A school-house was once located there, and a blacksmith's shop used by Mr. William Brown, and Thomas Plympton kept a store there. Near the gravel pit is a place once called " Judge's Point." There, by the hillside, Micah Goodnow, a fisherman, lived, whom they called " Judge," which circumstance probably gave a name to the place. On the upland, not far from the training-field and northerly or north-easterly of it, is a spot where, tradition says, an Indian is buried. It is said he was shot from the east side of the river as he was exploring thereabout in a time of hostility, and that the gun is now in possession of John Morse, son of Noyes Morse of Wayland. It is a long, heavy piece, a rare specimen of firearm, and has been in the Noyes family for successive generations.

The vicinity of this section is memorable in connection with the Revolutionary period. South-westerly on the hill, about a quarter of a mile away, were the government store-houses. (See period 1775–1800.) The land about the place was called Training-field Hill, the town owning about an acre there for training purposes. At one time a muster was held there. At the beginning of the present century there was an old, low building standing on or very near the spot where the George Taylor house stands; in this house some of the government guard were boarded. The town's eastern boundary, as it runs through this locality, turns abruptly towards Wayland, takes in a small space, and then goes on in its regular course. The occasion of this was as follows: when the town was divided, a remonstrance was made by the inhabitants of the West Side, because, among other reasons, they would lose their training-field. Remonstrance was also made to the division by Caleb Wheeler, who strenuously opposed having his farm of forty-three acres included within the limits of East Sudbury. It is supposed that, to compromise matters and so adjust things as to secure a division, the whole farm and the training-field were allowed to remain in Sudbury. At various times, propositions have been made for straightening the line, but all efforts to accomplish it have thus far failed. The piece of land is triangular shaped, situated on Sand Hill, and the South Sudbury and Wayland highway passes through it. It belongs to the Farr farm, and is still called the " Wheeler place."

CHAPTER XXIX.

1850–1875.

The Wadsworth Monument.—Petition to the Legislature. — Response.— Description ot the Monument. — The old Slate Stone. — Fac-simile of it. — Dedication of the Monument. — Dismission of Rev. Josiah Ballard. — Sketch of his Life. — Ordination of Rev. Charles V. Spear. — His Dismission. — Installation of Rev. Erastus Dickinson. — His Dismission. — Sketch of his Life. — Rev. Webster Patterson. — Settlement of Rev. Philander Thurston. — His Dismission. — Sketch of Rev. George A. Oviatt. — Rev. Calvin Fitts. — Rev. David Goodale. — Rev. Warren Richardson. — Deacons. — Donation of Samuel Dana Hunt. — Bequest of Miss Emily Thompson. — Gifts from Mrs. Abigail Smith and Miss Ruth Carter. — Wadsworth Academy. — Congregational Chapel. — Changes in School Districts. — In School-Houses. — Numbering the Districts. — The Goodnow Library. — The Building. — The Donor. — Incorporation of Maynard. — The Framingham and Lowell Railroad. — The Massachusetts Central Railroad. — Miscellaneous.

> Look, how they come, — a mingled crowd
>   Of bright and dark, but rapid days;
> Beneath them, like a summer cloud,
>   The wide world changes as I gaze.
>   BRYANT.

THE period between 1850 and 1875 was an eventful one to the country. In it occurred the great and calamitous Civil War; and Sudbury, in common with other towns, bore a share in the toil and the sorrow that were incident to it. Before, however, entering upon this subject we will give the annals of the town exclusive of those relating to the war. In presenting these, we shall, in some instances, make our narrative more consecutive by mentioning events that occurred outside the period.

THE WADSWORTH MONUMENT.

An important event that occurred early in the last half of the present century was the erection of the Wadsworth Monument.   February, 1852, a petition was presented to the Legislature of this Commonwealth, in which, after a brief rehearsal of the events in connection with the Wadsworth fight, the petitioners say " that a small, temporary monument was erected many years ago by the Rev. Benjamin Wadsworth, President of Harvard College, over the grave of his father, Captain Wadsworth, and his associates in arms. Said monument being in a dilapidated condition, it is desirable that it be rebuilt in a more durable form.   Wherefore, at a legal town-meeting held for that purpose, your petitioners were chosen for a committee and instructed to petition your Honorable body for aid in erecting a suitable monument to the memory of said officers and men."

Signed, " Drury Fairbank and thirteen others."

The committee on military affairs, to which was referred this petition, in closing their report say : " The petitioners further state that said monument, which still bears the names of those brave officers, is now in a dilapidated condition, and must soon go to destruction unless some immediate measures are taken to rebuild it; and that the inhabitants of Sudbury, being actuated by a strong desire to preserve it, are willing to defray a portion of the expense attending its rebuilding, if the State will aid them in so doing; although, independent of the fact of its being located within the limits of their town, they feel no greater interest in its preservation than should be felt by every patriotic citizen of the Commonwealth.   Your committee concur with the petitioners on this point.   True, the monument is intimately connected with the early history of Sudbury; but is it not also quite as intimately connected with the history of the State? And should not every son of Massachusetts venerate and hold sacred these ancient landmarks, so to speak, wherever upon her soil they are found, which serve so forcibly to remind him of the struggles, the trials, and the valor of his forefathers?... They do not ask the State to erect a new monument over the remains of those who survived a sanguinary strife, and died among their own kindred and friends after a long enjoyment of that for which they contended; nor do they ask to have such a monument erected away from the scene of that strife; but they ask that the State will aid them in the discharge of a duty which they feel belongs to every patriotic citizen of the Commonwealth, — that of endeavoring to preserve from destruction a simple and not expensive monument, built by their forefathers nearly a century and a quarter ago, over the single grave of the twenty-nine gallant men whose memory it was designed to perpetuate, and upon the very spot where their lives were sacrificed in the service of their country, and which is fast going to decay. Your committee are of the opinion that this case ... has no precedent and can establish none. And, even if it should establish a precedent, it is a good one, and one which should be followed in all similar cases, if any such should be hereafter presented, for it would be an indelible stain upon the escutcheon of Massachusetts and a source of the deepest mortification to her sons, if a single spark of patriotic feeling remained in their bosoms, if these sacred memorials of her past history were permitted to go to destruction, merely because their preservation would involve the expenditure of a few paltry dollars from the public treasury." Accompanying this report is the resolve, "That a sum, not exceeding five hundred dollars in all, be and the same is hereby appropriated towards defraying the expense of repairing or rebuilding, in a substantial manner, the monument in the town of Sudbury, erected by President Wadsworth of Harvard College, about the year 1730, to the memory of Capt. Samuel Wadsworth and a large number of other officers and soldiers and others in the service of the colony, who were slain upon the spot marked by the monument, . . . in the defence of that town against the Indians, — the said sum to be expended under the direction of His Excellency the Governor, in connection with a committee of said town of Sudbury."

Agreeable to the foregoing resolve, at a legal town-meeting held June 14, 1852, it was voted that Nahum Thompson, Drury Fairbank, Ephraim Moore, Enoch Kidder and J. R. Vose be a committee to superintend the building of the Wadsworth Monument. It was then voted to appropriate a sum of money, sufficient to complete said monument and finish about the same, out of any unappropriated money in the Treasury, said sum not to exceed five hundred dollars. His Excellency George S. Boutwell, then Governor of this Commonwealth, in connection with the committee of the town, "procured a handsome monument, consisting of three large square blocks of granite, one and one-half, two, and three feet thick, raised one above the other; from the upper one of which rises a granite shaft, tapering towards the top; the whole being twenty-one and one-half feet in height. On the front of the centre block appears the following inscription:

This monument is erected by the Commonwealth of Massachusetts and the town of Sudbury, in grateful remembrance of the services and suffering of the founders of the State, and especially in honor of

CAPT. SAMUEL WADSWORTH, OF MILTON;

CAPT. BROCKLEBANK, OF ROWLEY;

LIEUT. SHARP, OF BROOKLINE;

and twenty six others, men of their command, who fell near this spot, on the 18th of April, 1676, while defending the frontier settlements against the allied Indian forces of Philip of Pokanoket.

1852.

(The date of the fight as above given is incorrect: see page 218.)

In front of the monument is the slate stone which stood at the head of the old grave. "There is, in the rooms of a Boston Society, a broken slab, which is an exact *fac-simile* of the lower part of this stone, and is claimed by some to be the original erected by President Wadsworth over the remains of his dead father and the men who fell with him. But there are no records or traditions to identify it, and the only mode of accounting for its existence is by supposing that a slab, first made, was accidentally broken in the stone-yard in Boston, and that the broken piece found its way into the collection, while another was made and sent to Sudbury where it has ever since remained." This monument is firmly set upon a foundation of split stone, six feet thick, five feet of which are covered with earth. At the foot of the monument, in front, was an aperture through which the remains of the ancient martyrs, which had been disinterred, were deposited in the tomb, after which it was hermetically sealed. The monument is surrounded by a handsome iron railing twenty feet square, durably and strongly set. The whole cost of monument, fence, and grading was one thousand and fifty dollars. The foregoing quotations concerning the monument, and the following account of the dedication, are taken from a Report, published by the town in 1853 : —

" This new tribute to the memory of our fathers was dedicated on the 23d of November, A.D., 1852. There would, probably, have been a very full attendance had it not been for a steady, continued snow-storm through the day.

" A number of military companies had been expected, and had the day been pleasant the ceremony would have been imposing. As it was, the affair went off well.

" At a little after ten o'clock a procession was formed at the Town Hall, under the marshalship of Col. Drury Fairbank, in the following order: —

" Sudbury Brass Band, Marshall Eaton, leader; Sudbury Wadsworth Rifle Guards, in grey uniform and full numbers, commanded by Capt. Ephraim Moore; this corps marched and looked well, and the band attached performed excellently, although it has been formed scarcely a year; carriages containing His Excellency George S. Boutwell, Governor of this Commonwealth, and the invited guests; citizens on foot. The procession moved over the road to Saxonville, southward, and within a mile of the Town Hall, turned to the left, where, in the rear of a newly located burying-ground, appeared a neat granite column. It was in this vicinity that the event which the ceremonies of the day commemorated took place; the scalped and mangled bodies of Captain Wadsworth and his command having been found scattered over a small space of ground in the brushwood. After marching around the monument, the procession moved back to the Town Hall, the upper floor of which was soon thronged with many hundred guests, nearly one-half of whom were ladies. The remains of the ancient dead were then brought in, and the six boxes containing them deposited in the hall near the door. These remains are in a remarkable state of preservation, many teeth being perfect, and the skulls and other bones of several bear the marks of the Indian bullet and the Indian tomahawk, the evidence of blows that fell one hundred and seventy-four years ago.

"The medical gentlemen who have had the care of these bones since their disinterment are Dr. O. O. Johnson of Mill Village, Sudbury, and Dr. Goodnough; they find twenty-seven pairs of thigh bones and fragments of two pairs more, corresponding to the number of men that are mentioned by history as having been slain. In one skull there is a hole half an inch wide and several inches long, directly over the temple in the left side of the top of the head, answering exactly to the size of a tomahawk blade; in another, the lower jaw shows a similar aperture below the teeth where the weapon has crushed in sideways. But the most remarkable thing is the completeness of the teeth; and in the left side of the lower jaw of one skull two of the teeth are worn down, as if by the constant use of a pipe, making a semicircular cavity, the surface of which is perfectly smooth. The jaw indicated an aged man. One of the skulls was, evidently, that of a young man, the wisdom teeth not having been cut, but the majority were all of middle age, and the size of the bones of all gave evidence that, if they were not picked men, the trials of a colonist's life and the rough training of the early settlers was calculated to develop the physical nature of our ancestors in high perfection.

"As soon as the Chief Marshal had arranged the audience and obtained silence, Nahum Thompson, the President of the Day, arose and said: Fellow Citizens, — we have assembled upon this interesting occasion to recall to our minds the services and sufferings of our forefathers, those devoted men, who sacrificed their lives that they might become, as it were, stepping-stones to the attainment of those innumerable and inestimable blessings and privileges, both civil and religious, which we their descendants are permitted to enjoy, and to dedicate to their memory yonder monument, that Granite Pillar, durable as the names of Wadsworth, Brocklebank and Sharp are imperishable; in doing this, it becometh us to acknowledge Him whose superintending providence has continually been over us; I would therefore introduce to ou the Rev. Linus H. Shaw, who will address the Throne of Grace that God's mercy still rest upon us. The reverend gentleman made a very appropriate prayer; a hymn was then read by Rev. C. V. Spear and sung by all present to the tune of ' Old Hundred.'

" His Excellency George S. Boutwell was then introduced, and made an address."

The proceedings which followed the address are thus described in the published account of the exercises : —

" The company then adjourned to the lower room of the Hall, where dinner had been prepared by Mr. Wright, at which a blessing was invoked by the Rev. Mr. Spear and thanks returned by Rev. Mr. Lee. The entertainment was good, though the guests were not numerous and no speeches were made. It had been originally intended to have the dinner near the monument in Mr. Wright's tent, which had been erected; but early in the morning, after everything had been prepared for the reception of fifteen hundred guests, the irons which fastened the upper part of the canvas to the masts suddenly unbent, in consequence of the immense weight of snow which had covered the tent, and the awning, with its superincumbent weight of snow, fell upon and covered the tables. No damage will accrue, except the breaking of a small quantity of crockery and glass ware.

" The dinner being over, all present reascended to the upper hall, where the bones were exhibited to the multitude, after which the boxes were removed, and the regular toasts of

the day were read by Nahum Thompson, Esq., and responded
to by the band, so that all present were entertained with a
succession of military pieces, well played, for the space of
over an hour. At half-past four o'clock the Governor withdrew and returned to Boston. After the regular toasts had
been read and volunteer sentiments had been called for, Col.
Winthrop E. Faulkner of Acton, having stated some facts
respecting the action that resulted in the death of Captain
Wadsworth and his company, gave the following sentiment:

"'The sons of Sudbury. — May they be as marked for
martial courage, for prompt and vigorous action and true
republican principles, as were those whose remains have just
been removed to their last resting-place.'

"To this, Colonel Fairbanks, the Marshal of the day,
responded.

"The clergyman of the Orthodox Society in town, Rev.
Mr. Spear, then — having alluded to the unique character and
great interest of the occasion, as the dedication of a monument commemorating an event, the earliest in our history
thus commemorated, and having referrred to the interesting
character of Governor Boutwell's Address — gave the following: 'The Orator of the day. — He deserves our warmest
thanks for his lucid and deeply interesting sketches of the
times and the scenes passed through, the causes of alienation
which operated, and the characters developed and exhibited,
during the progress of King Philip's War.'

"Mr. S. D. Hunt of Concord then, by a well-timed classic
allusion, complimenting the band which had contributed so
much to the interest of the occasion, gave, as the closing
sentiment, the following: —

"'The Sudbury Brass Band. — May their shadow never
be less.'

"The occasion went off well, under the care of the following gentlemen : —

"Committee of Arrangements. — Asahel Balcom, Lyman
Howe, Abel B. Jones, Ephraim Stone, John P. Allen, in
addition to the Building Committee: Nahum Thompson,
Drury Fairbanks, Enoch Kidder, Ephraim Moore and Jonathan R. Vose.

" Pall Bearers. — Tilly Smith, William Brigham, Israel Haynes, David Lincoln, Charles Gerry, Asa Jones, Jonas Tower, Jonathan Fairbanks.

" After the closing sentiment, the audience, which throughout the exercises had given the most fixed attention, quietly dispersed."

" The entire lot left by the proprietors for the Wadsworth monument consists of a parallelogram ten rods by four." An old deed mentions " the monument," meaning the old mound, as being " marked out in an oblong or square just about the centre of the farm." This was the Israel How Brown farm. When the committee decided not to erect the monument on the site of the old mound, but a little to one side (see page 250), they procured a piece of land of Mr. Brown, a portion of which was taken for the enclosure that contains the monument. The avenue leading to it was opened about the same time, and was a part of the same farm. In 1855, the selectmen were instructed " to plant trees around the monument and on the avenue leading to it, the trees to be set at a distance of not more than thirty feet apart." A few years ago a large white pine-tree stood within the enclosure easterly of the monument, but it was struck by lightning and afterwards cut down. The town expended over nine hundred and fifty dollars, besides what was received from the State, in erecting the monument and enclosing it with an iron fence.

ECCLESIASTICAL EVENTS.

During the third period of the century several changes took place in the Evangelical Union Church. March 15, 1852, the society voted to concur with Mr. Ballard in calling a council for his dismission, and his pastorate in Sudbury soon after ceased. During the latter part of his ministry here he lived at the present George Parmenter place, which was then owned by several persons and leased for a parsonage. The following is a brief sketch of his life : —

REV. JOSIAH BALLARD.

Josiah Ballard was born at Peterboro, N. H., April 14, 1806. He learned the mason's trade, and worked at it for

J. Ballard

some years. He fitted for college, completing his studies at Munson Academy, and graduated at Yale in 1833. He studied theology two years with Dr. Whiton of Antrim, N.H., and was licensed to preach in 1835. The same year he married Elizabeth D., daughter of Rev. John Whiton, D.D. He was settled at Chesterfield, N. H., then at Nelson, N. H. He was installed at Sudbury, March 3, 1841, and dismissed April, 1852. He was afterwards settled at New Ipswich, N. H., and at Carlisle, Mass., at which latter place he died, Dec. 12, 1863, aged fifty-seven. He had two children, — Edward O. and Catherine E., both born at Nelson, N. H. Mr. Ballard and his wife were buried at Carlisle, but were afterwards removed, and laid, in accordance with their desire, in the New Maplewood Cemetery at South Antrim, N. H., occupying one of the five family lots joining each other. Mr. Ballard was much esteemed in Sudbury. His influence was widely felt, and the remembrance of him was fondly cherished for many years after he left town. He was a reserved, dignified man, rather grave in manner and a hard worker.

July 26, 1852, the society voted to extend a call to Rev. Charles V. Spear, at a salary of $650 ; and October 27 of the same year he was ordained and installed. The ministers who composed the council were as follows: Revs. John Todd, D.D., of Pittsfield, E. Russell of East Randolph, J. C. Bodwell of Framingham, Henry Allen of Wayland, W. C. Jackson of Lincoln, L. H. Angier of Concord, J. Ballard of New Ipswich, N. H., J. C. Woodbridge of Auburndale, and B. G. Northrup of Saxonville. The sermon was by Dr. Todd. Sept. 18, 1855, Mr. Spear was dismissed on account of ill health ; and May 14, 1856, Rev. Erastus Dickinson was called as his successor at a salary of $800. The council of installation was as follows: Revs. R. S. Storrs, D.D., of Braintree, Henry Allen of Wayland, Marcus Ames of Westminster, Levi A. Fields of Marlboro, and C. V. Spear of Pittsfield. The sermon was by Dr. Storrs. Mr. Dickinson remained in the pastorate of the church till June 30, 1868, when he was dismissed. He was born at Plainfield, Mass., and graduated at Amherst College in 1832. He studied theology at Auburn Theological Seminary, and was ordained at Canton, where he preached a year. Subsequently he was settled at Chaplin and at Colchester, Ct., and Sudbury. While at the latter place he was sent as Representative to the Legislature. On leaving Sudbury, his health being somewhat impaired, he went to Lakewood, N. J., where he was postmaster fifteen years. He died Sept. 4, 1888, at the age of eighty-two.

From the time of Mr. Dickinson's dismission the pulpit was most of the time supplied by Rev. Webster Patterson, until the settlement of Rev. Philander Thurston, Feb. 1, 1870. The salary of Mr. Thurston was $1200. The installing council was composed of the Revs. T. D. P. Stone of Assabet, M. J. Savage of Framingham, C. H. Williams of Concord, A. S. Hudson of Burlington, E. R. Drake of Wayland, G. G. Phipps of Wellesley, and H. J. Richardson of Lincoln. The sermon was by Dr. J. M. Manning of Boston. Rev. Mr. Thurston was dismissed Sept. 22, 1874. Shortly after the close of this pastorate, Rev. George A. Oviatt became acting pastor of the church, and continued to serve in that capacity for a period of eight years. As a pastor he was kind and sympathetic, and one of those men who never grow old. Jan. 1, 1883, being enfeebled by sickness, he asked to be released from his charge, and the request was reluctantly granted. He had been a preacher for half a century, and had held five pastorates, — at Belchertown and Chicopee, Somers and Talcottville, Conn., and Sudbury. He was one year Secretary of the American Sunday-School Union, and three years engaged in mission work in Boston. The Shawmut Church, Boston, was organized as the result of his labors. In the War of the Rebellion he went to Louisiana in the division of General Banks, as chaplain of the 25th Connecticut Regiment. In that service he lost his health and it was never fully regained. He died at Sudbury, June 1, 1883, aged seventy-six, and was buried at Mount Auburn.

Rev. Calvin Fitts preached for a few months after Mr. Oviatt resigned, and died at Sudbury in the fall of 1883. Rev. David W. Goodale commenced preaching in June, 1884, and remained about three years. Rev. Warren Richardson, the present acting pastor, commenced his term of service in the fall of 1887.

The following persons have served as deacons in the Congregational Church: Gardner Hunt, Thomas L. Dakin, Thomas P. Hurlbut, Emory Hunt, Benjamin H. Richardson, Francis F. Walker. The last two are in service at the present time.

Aug. 10, 1874, the society voted to accept of one thousand dollars donated by Samuel Dana Hunt, for " the preaching of the Gospel essentially in its present doctrine or belief." If the church was ever removed to South Sudbury, or a new name given it, the gift was to remain.

In 1881, the society voted to accept of a bequest by Miss Emily Thompson. A gift was also received of Mrs. Abigail Smith of Sudbury, and one hundred dollars of Miss Ruth Carter.

EDUCATIONAL MATTERS.

Considerable change occurred in educational matters during this period. One important event was the establishment of Wadsworth Academy.

WADSWORTH ACADEMY.

In 1856, measures were taken to establish an academy at South Sudbury. A corporation was formed, the object of which was to hold property, consisting of a building, land, and suitable fixtures for educational and religious purposes. The design of the projectors of the enterprise was to erect a building, the upper part of which could be used for a school, and the lower part for social and religious services. There had been no hall at " Mill Villiage," as South Sudbury was then called, except one over the " old wheelwright's shop," where sometimes a meeting was held on Sabbath evenings, and occasionally a private school was kept, where the tuition was ninepence a week. This hall was low and dilapidated, and reached by a flight of stairs on the outside, and wholly unfit for public use. Besides the need of a hall was the need of a higher school than was provided by the town. To meet these needs a corporation was formed, the capital stock of which was three thousand dollars. The parties who composed it, and the number of shares taken by each were as follows: Samuel D. Hunt, three shares; Dexter C. Jones, three; Gardner Hunt, one and one-half; Samuel Puffer, three; A. B. Richardson, three; Charles Hunt, three; Joseph Richardson, three; Walter Rogers, six; Samuel Rogers, three; Emory Hunt, three; George Parmenter, three; Levi Goodenough, three; Roland Cutler, six; Elizabeth Hunt, one and one-half; Nancy J. Moore, three; J. D. and C. A. Cutter, three; Abigail B. Brown, three; Arthur Bowen, three.

The first meeting was held March 11, 1857, and the following officers were elected: President, Dr. Levi Goodenough; Directors, Roland Cutler, Samuel Puffer; Treasurer, Samual D. Hunt. The land was purchased of Nichols B. Hunt, and the building was erected by Arthur Bowen of South Sudbury. It was two stories high, had a colonade in front and faced the west. It was named in honor of Captain Wadsworth. Among the studies pursued in the school were the higher mathematics, the classics, French, drawing and painting. The tuition varied with the studies taken. The first teacher was Erastus N. Fay, formerly teacher of the Wayland High School, and graduate of Dartmouth College. Then followed Mr. James Russell, a graduate of Amherst College, Miss Lydia R. Draper (Mrs. A. S. Hudson), a graduate of New Hampton Seminary, Miss S. Jennie Holden (Mrs. E. P. Tenney), Miss Gibbs, Mr. Charles Rogers, a graduate of Middleton University, Conn., Mr. Edwin Hunt, a graduate of Amherst College, and Miss Sarah Russell. After a time the school ceased to exist as an academy. It had done its work of affording advanced educational privileges to a class of young men and women, some of whom had entered higher institutions of learning, others had become school teachers, and others still had entered upon the practical duties of life in the household, or on the farm, or in some branch of business or trade. The need of an academy having been met, the demand for its continuance ceased, and the rooms were used

THE WADSWORTH ACADEMY,
South Sudbury
From an original sketch by A S Hudson

for one of the town's common schools. A few years later the building was destroyed by fire, and on its site was erected a Congregational chapel in 1880; but, though the old academy has passed away, there are some who trace their success and many of life's pleasant relations to their beginnings in that peaceful spot.

Important changes took place during this period in connection with the common schools. Old districts were divided, and new ones were formed; old school-houses were moved and new ones built. A large share of the territory of the north-west district was taken from Sudbury by the incorporation of Maynard; but in the districts that remained the schools and school-houses increased. The centre school-house, that had stood on the common, was moved to its present location south of the Methodist meeting-house, and after its removal was fitted up for the use of two schools, — a primary and grammar. In 1868, the Lanham school-house was moved from the road corners by the Coolidge place to its present location, north of the Boston and Worcester highway, on land that once belonged to the Goodnow farm. In 1869, eight hundred dollars was granted for repairs on the south-west school-house. In 1870, the town voted to build a new school-house in the north-east district, to be located at or near the junction of Puffer Lane and the north road. The building was erected at a cost of $2884.82. The same year measures were taken for the removal of the old Pantry school-house, and the result was that a new school-house was built in the southerly portion of the north-east district, and the Pantry school-house was moved and became the depot of the Framingham & Lowell Railroad. The new school-house was located near the house of Alfred Thompson, and cost $3825.23. About the same time the town voted to build a school-house in the west part of the town in a locality where, hitherto, there had been none. It was erected on the Boston and Berlin road, near the house of John Coughlin, at a cost of $2508.77. The building committee rendered their report to the town March 4, 1872, and at the same meeting the committee appointed to number the school districts reported that plates had been procured, lettered and numbered at a cost of $7.50, and that commencing with the centre district, which they designated as number one, the committee next proceeded to the house in the south-west district, which they numbered two. Thence, passing to the right of the centre of the town, the remaining houses were numbered in their regular order, closing with the new house near the residence of John Coughlin, which was numbered six. The town opened a new school at South Sudbury, and March 1, 1875, . " voted to allow the proprietors of Wadsworth Hall $100 for rent of said hall for school purposes."

In 1881, a school-house was built in the Wadsworth district by C. O. Parmenter, at a cost of $2560.61. It was placed on a lot containing a half acre of land, which was purchased of Walter Rogers, and situated on the south side of the Sudbury and Marlboro road, about midway between the Massachusetts Central and Old Colony Railroads.

THE GOODNOW LIBRARY.

In 1862, the town received the means of establishing a Public Library through the generosity of John Goodnow of Boston. The gift came in the form of a bequest, which was set forth in his will as follows : —

"First: I give, devise, and bequeath unto my native Town of Sudbury, in the County of Middlesex, the sum of Twenty Thousand Dollars, to be appropriated for the purpose of purchasing and keeping in order a Public Library, for the benefit of the inhabitants of that Town."

"Second: I also give, devise and bequeath to the said Town of Sudbury, three acres of land on the northerly part· of the Sudbury Tavern Estate, adjoining the land of Howe Brown, beginning at the Meeting-house road, and running with equal width with Brown's line to the brook, for the purpose of erecting thereon a suitable building for a Library ; and the further sum of Twenty-five Hundred Dollars for the erection of such building ; and whatever portion of said land shall not be needed for the purposes of said Library building, the said Town of Sudbury shall have full power and authority to apply to any other Town purposes, but without any power of alienation."

"At a legal meeting held at Sudbury, on the seventh day of April, 1862, the Town voted to accept the bequest contained in the first and second clauses of the last Will and Testament of John Goodnow, late of Boston; and Messrs. James Moore, John H. Dakin, and George Parmenter, Selectmen of the Town, were appointed and authorized to receive and receipt for the said bequests." At the same meeting it was voted to adopt the following resolution: "Resolved by the Inhabitants of Sudbury, in Town meeting assembled, That we accept with thankfulness the noble bequests given to the town by the late John Goodnow of Boston; and that, as an evidence of our gratitude, we pledge ourselves to endeavor to the utmost of our ability, Honestly and Honorably to carry out the benevolent intentions of the Donor."

July 14, the town instructed the committee to erect a building for the library given by John Goodnow, according to plan reported to them, the sum not to exceed $2500. April 4, 1864, the committee reported the cost of the building, including $32.43 for setting out shade trees, to be $2691.35. The building was enlarged several years ago by an addition on the west; and at present there is little, if any, unoccupied space. Four catalogues have been issued; the first, at the opening of the Library, when it contained less than 2300 volumes; the second in 1867; the third in 1874, when it contained nearly 5000 volumes; and the fourth in 1887, when it contained over 9700. The grounds about the Library are ample, and tastefully laid out, consisting of a level lawn adorned with shade trees. The building is reached by a circular driveway extending from the county highway. In the rear the land extends to Hop brook.

John Goodnow, the donor of this library fund, was a son of John and Persis Goodnow, who lived at Lanham. He was born at Sudbury, Sept. 6, 1791, and died in Boston, Dec. 24, 1861. His remains were placed in his tomb at Sudbury Centre.

INCORPORATION OF THE TOWN OF MAYNARD.

In 1871, an area of about 1900 acres of land was set off from Sudbury, which, with about 1300 acres taken from Stow, formed the town of Maynard. The new town was incorporated April 19, 1871, and took its name from Amory Maynard, formerly of Marlboro. The town of Sudbury opposed the separation and, Jan. 23, 1871, appointed a committee of three to nominate a committee of three to oppose any petition to the General Court to set off any part of the territory of Sudbury. Deacon Thomas Hurlbut, Charles Thompson, Esq., and James Moore, Esq., were nominated. The town accepted the nomination and authorized the committee to use all honorable means to prevent the formation of a new town, including any part of the territory of the town of Sudbury.

The committee chosen Jan. 23, 1871, to oppose the incorporation of any portion of the territory of Sudbury into a new town, reported April 1, 1872, that previous to any hearing before the committee of the Legislature on the petition of Henry Fowler and others for an act incorporating the town of Maynard, certain propositions were made by the petitioners as terms of separation and settlement between the town of Sudbury and the proposed new town. These propositions having been laid before the town of Sudbury, Feb. 20, 1871, the committee were given discretionary power, provided they accept of no terms less advantageous to the town of Sudbury than those contained in the agreement. By mutual consent a bill was agreed upon and passed by the Legislature, by which the town of Maynard was incorporated. Subsequently the committee were authorized to settle with the authorities of the town of Maynard, according to the provisions of their charter. They reported that they had attended to that duty, also that the proportion of the town debt, together with the money to be paid by the town of Maynard to the town of Sudbury, or Maynard's share of the stock in the Framingham & Lowell Railroad Corporation owned by the town of Sudbury, with interest on the same, amounted to $20,883.28 ; which sum was paid by them to the treasurer of the town of Sudbury, Oct. 6, 1871. They say they have also attended to establishing the line between the said towns, and erected a stone monument at the angle in said line near the iron-works causeway, which will also answer as a guide-board, and will be kept in repair by the town of Sudbury; that they have also erected a stone monument marked S. and M., at such places as said line crosses the highway.

May, 1871, it was "voted that the committee chosen by the town, January 23, consisting of Messrs. Thomas P. Hurlbut, Charles Thompson and James Moore, Esq., shall be a committee to act for and in behalf of the town of Sudbury with the authorities of the town of Maynard, in all matters pertaining to said town, according to the provisions of the charter incorporating said town of Maynard."

RAILROADS.

No railroad passed through the present limits of the town until about the beginning of the last period of the present century. A branch of the Fitchburg Road went through Assabet village, but, after that place became Maynard, it left Sudbury without a railroad. The only public conveyance for years was by the stage-coach which went from South Sudbury, and passed through the centre of Sudbury, Wayland and Weston, carrying for each of those places one mail daily. It started about seven o'clock, and arrived at the Stony Brook station of the Fitchburg Railroad in Weston about nine; and starting from there about five P.M. arrived at its destination about seven. It was an old-time stage drawn by four horses, with the driver on the "box," under which were kept the mails. The trunks were strapped on a rack behind. Prior to the starting of this coach, South Sudbury was accommodated by a stage that passed through the town to Marlboro. About 1870, the Framingham & Lowell Railroad was begun, and in the fall of 1871, the cars began passing through the town. A station was built at North and South Sudbury and at the centre. The one at South Sudbury was built a little northerly of the junction of

the Sudbury and Marlboro and Framingham highways, and
has since been moved.

July 22, 1870, it was voted "That the Town Treasurer be
authorized and instructed to subscribe for, take and hold
Capital Stock in the Framingham and Lowell Railroad
Company to the amount of Thirty thousand dollars.   ..
Provided said Railroad shall not be located in any place more
than half a mile from the last survey in the Town of
Sudbury."

The first station master at the South Sudbury depot was
B. H. Richardson, who served in that capacity ten years.
Since the railroad started, trains have regularly been over it,
but the indirectness of the route to Boston, and the high
passenger rates, made the road of little practical value to the
town.   The old coach continued to run its regular course,
and more or less of the business to the eastward was done by
this and private conveyance.   The road has recently been
leased to the " Old Colony " company, and is now known as
the " Northern Branch of the Old Colony Road."   In 1887,
every station of this road within the limits of Sudbury was
burned.   Recently, new and more commodious ones have
been built on or near the sites of the former ones.

MASSACHUSETTS CENTRAL RAILROAD.

In October, 1880, the first rails were laid at South Sudbury
on the track of the Massachusetts Central Railroad, beginning at its junction with the Framingham & Lowell road.
During the following winter the road was continued towards
Hudson on the west and Boston on the east; and July 22,
1881, nine car loads of rails passed over the Central road,
entering upon it at Waverly and going to Hudson.   April
20, 1881, a train of cars passed over the road from Boston to
Hudson; and October 1, the same year, regular trains began
to run.   May 16, 1883, the cars stopped running, and commenced again Sept. 28, 1885, under the management of the
Boston & Lowell Railroad.   Recently the road was leased to
the Boston & Maine Railroad corporation.   The Junction
Station is a fine one, and the town is now provided with
excellent railroad facilities.

MISCELLANEOUS.

In 1854, the committee were instructed to finish the Wadsworth monument by building a road to said monument and fencing the land. They were also instructed to print the proceedings at the dedication of the monument. The same year the town appropriated thirteen hundred dollars to build a road and bridge at Assabet village.

In 1855, it was voted to instruct the school committee to place the dictionaries presented by Mr. Plympton in the several schools, also that the school-houses be free for lyceums and singing schools for the year.

In 1857, it was voted "that the four libraries now in existence be so divided as to make five; and that these be distributed among the five school districts." The same year it was voted "to allow the town of Wayland to copy such of the records as they wished at the home of the clerk, or to employ any person in town to do the same." The same year it was voted to build a stone bridge at the canal bridge. The bridge was let out to Charles Haynes and Thomas E. Bent for five hundred dollars.

February, 1859, the selectmen were instructed "to petition the Legislature to remove or cause to be removed the Middlesex Canal Dam, erected across the Concord River at Billerica, or such part thereof as the Legislature shall deem expedient or just for reclaiming the meadow lands bordering upon Sudbury and Concord river."

In 1859, it was voted to choose a committee to let out the raising of the Causeway from Sudbury to Wayland, as ordered by the county commissioners. The same year it was voted "to establish the Town Poor house as a work house, as the law provides."

In 1861, the selectmen were instructed to procure gravel pits in the several wards where they are needed. The same year the selectmen were instructed to build a suitable wall around the new burying ground wherever needed.

Dec. 17, 1862, the town authorized "the selectmen to give a deed of a lot in the new cemetery to the executors of the will of the late John Goodnow of Boston for the purpose of building thereon a tomb." The same year the town voted to choose two agents to remonstrate against the petition of C. P. and T. Talbot for the repeal of an act in relation to a flowage of the Sudbury and Concord River meadows.

In 1864, the town granted the use of the Town Hall for a year to the " Comprehensive Temperance Society."

In 1866, the town granted the use of the Town Hall for a year to the " Musical Union " and for " Musical Instruction."

In 1867, a vote was passed to straighten the road over Meeting-house hill.

March 11, 1867, the town voted that the management of the Goodnow Library should be entrusted to a Committee of three persons, one member to be chosen each year, for the term of three years.

Nov. 3, 1868, it was " voted that the regulations of the New Burying ground should be so changed that one-third of said ground at the north end be reserved for free lots, instead of one-third part of the westerly end, and that persons taking said free lots shall have the same control of them as other persons have of lots taken in other parts of the yard."

April 5, 1869, the town voted to instruct the selectmen to build a receiving tomb. March 7, 1870, the selectmen reported the work completed at a cost of $488.86 ; they also reported that they had procured a cooler for the use of the inhabitants in preparing bodies for burial at a cost of thirty-seven dollars.

In 1871, the town granted fifty dollars to aid the Grand Army of the Republic on Decoration Day, the amount to be payable to the commander of the Post of the G. A. R., located in Assabet village. May, 1871, " The town, by a vote of fifty-seven yeas to thirty nays, voted to prohibit the sale of Ale, Porter, Strong Beer or Lager Beer, in said town."

April 2, 1875, the town voted to send to the Centennial Celebration at Concord, of the 19th April, 1775, thirty-two of the oldest citizens as delegates, and provide a carriage for them at the town's expense, also to provide a fife and drum if necessary, also to provide a marshal.

CHAPTER XXX.

1850–1875.

> The sturdy patriots went forth
> From city, village, hamlet, farm ;
> Unsparing was the sacrifice
> To shield our native land from harm.

THE CIVIL WAR.

THE events of the Civil War are so familiar to many now living, that it may be thought unnecessary to give even an outline of its cause or nature. But there is a generation who were not living while that war was in progress. To these it is a matter of history only, and the tales of it come to them as the tradition of the wars that preceded it. A few words, then, of introduction may be important. The war began in 1861. For many years previous there had been a disagreement between the North and the South on the subject of slavery. At the North there had been a growing sentiment that the system was wrong, and, as time passed on,

535

opinions grew more and more positive and outspoken. The South looked upon this growing sentiment with suspicion, and when the strength of it was made manifest by the election of Abraham Lincoln, and he had been inaugurated President of the United States, it broke out into open revolt. State after State passed the "Act of Secession," and measures were taken to defend their position by force of arms. On April 12, an attempt was made to capture Fort Sumpter, Charleston Harbor, by bombardment; on the 13th it surrendered, after bravely sustaining an attack from the rebel batteries for thirty-three hours. This attempt to capture United States property aroused the North to a condition of intense activity. The news sped from city to town, and from the town to the most remote hamlet and farm. The North was resolved to save the Union at all hazards, and men came forward and offered themselves and their money for the safety of their country. April 15, 1861, President Lincoln called for seventy-five thousand soldiers to serve for three months. At this time military activity began, which did not cease for the space of four years. From 1861 to 1865, there was the establishment of camps, the occasional filling of quotas, and war meetings were held in the towns throughout the Northern States to raise money and men to carry on the war. These meetings were sometimes held at evening. It was no remarkable occurrence in those times to see the people at the close of a hard day's work on the farm, or in the busy workshop, wending their way to the town-house to provide means to furnish their quota of troops, and to do or act as some emergency called for. Never was the free spirit of the Republic more manifest, nor its readiness to respond to what its institutions required, than in those stirring days. Sudbury was fully abreast of the average New England town in its promptness and zeal. The first war meeting was a citizens' mass meeting held in the Town Hall. The people did not wait for the slow call of a warrant. They assembled spontaneously to consult as to what was required of them, with full confidence that in a town meeting to be subsequently called their acts would be ratified and made legal. This meeting was characterized by unanimity and enthusiasm. The spirit of the heroes of '75, when they were assembled on Sudbury Common, with arms in their hands as militia and minute men, to start on their march to Concord, was evinced on this April evening nearly a century later, when the citizens of Sudbury were again met to defend their homes and native land.

The principal business of this meeting related to the fitting out of the " Wadsworth Rifle Guards." This was a company of State militia which belonged to Sudbury, and was attached to the Second Battalion of Rifles, and was commanded by Major Ephraim Moore of Sudbury until his death, which occurred some years previous. The following record of a legal town meeting held April 29, 1861, sets forth the business that was transacted at the mass meeting, and its ratification by the town.

" The town voted to furnish new uniforms for the members of the Wadsworth Rifle Guards, Company B, Second Battalion of Rifles, M. V. M., forthwith, also to furnish each member of said company with a revolver, in case said company is called into the service of the country, the revolvers to be returned to the selectmen of the town when the holders of them shall return home and be discharged from the service ; also the uniforms to be returned to the town if the members of the company are not held in service more than three months. Voted also to pay to each member of said company, in case they are called into service, a sum of money in addition to their pay received from the government, which shall make the whole amount of their pay twenty dollars per month while they are in such service, and that ten dollars of the above sum be paid to each member whenever he shall enter such service. Voted also that the families of those who may leave shall be furnished with all necessary assistance at the expense of the town, and the business of those who may leave it shall be properly cared for by the town and not allowed to suffer by their absence."

" Voted, also, that each commissioned officer of the company belonging in town be presénted with a suitable sword at the expense of the town, and that the other commissioned officers not belonging in town be furnished with the same, if they are not otherwise provided for." " Voted to grant the sum of one thousand dollars," for the purposes above mentioned.

The amount of money actually expended in fitting out this company was nine hundred and eighty-seven dollars. About the time of the holding of the first war meeting there were enlistments into the Sudbury company, with the expectation of soon being called into the service for three months, and the company for a time continued to drill. No call, however, came for this term of service. The emergency had been met, Washington for the time was safe, and it was at length discovered that the company as such would not be received into any existing regiment, for the term of three months. The next demand was for soldiers to serve for three years or the war, and the " Wadsworth Rifle Guards " were soon ordered to Fort Independence that they might enlist in the Thirteenth Regiment for this length of time. Twenty-five of them enlisted, and July 30, the regiment left the State. This was the largest number of Sudbury men who enlisted at any one time, and they have the honor of being the first Sudbury soldiers who enlisted from the town. The history of the regiment will be given further on.

From the time of the first enlistments there were repeated calls for troops. " Three hundred thousand more " became a familiar term, and at each new call the town took measures to fill its quota. July 4, 1862, the President issued a call for volunteers for three years, and July 28, the town " voted to pay a bounty of one hundred and twenty-five dollars to each volunteer who has enlisted or may enlist into the service of the U. S. * * to the number of fourteen." Also, " Voted to instruct the selectmen to look after and provide for any sick or wounded volunteer belonging to the Town of Sudbury." In August of the same year, a call came for soldiers for nine months' service ; and Aug. 19, 1862, the town " voted to pay the sum of one hundred dollars to each person who voluntarily enlists into the service of the United States for the term of nine months, on or before the first day of September next, to a number not exceeding the quota of their town."

Dec. 17, 1862, the town voted to fill up their quota by paying one hundred and forty dollars bounty. December 22, the committee reported at a town meeting held in the evening, "that they had procured sixteen men to fill up the town's quota for the military service of the U. S., that said men had been accepted and sworn into the said service, and had been properly accredited to the town of Sudbury, and that said committee paid the sum of one hundred and thirty dollars for each man."

Oct. 17, 1863, the President issued another call for three hundred thousand men, and December 7, the town "voted to authorize the selectmen to use all proper and legal measures to fill up the town's quota of volunteers, agreeable to the call of the President of the United States for three hundred thousand volunteers, dated Oct. 17, 1863."

March 14, 1864, the President issued a call for two hundred thousand men, and March 22 the town appointed a committee " to take all proper and legal measures to fill the quota of the town " under this call. June 9, the town voted to " raise money sufficient to pay one hundred and twenty-five dollars to each volunteer who shall enlist into the service of the U. S., and be duly accredited as a part of the quota of the Town of Sudbury in anticipation of a call from the President to recruit the armies now in the field, and that the selectmen be required to use all proper measures to procure said volunteers." It was voted also "that the selectmen be authorized to procure not less than seventeen men." At the same meeting " the committee appointed by the town at a meeting held March 22, 1864, to take all proper and legal measures to fill the quota of the town under the call of the President of the U. S. for two hundred thousand men, dated March 14, 1864, reported that the town's quota was ten men ; that there had been seven men accredited to the town by volunteer enlistment at an expense of nine hundred and ten dollars, and that the remaining three were drafted and accepted."

Nov. 8, 1864, it was "voted to grant the free use of the Town Hall for the Soldiers' Aid Society." This was an organization formed in the war period for the purpose of assisting the soldiers. May 29, 1865, it was " voted to refund all money contributed by individuals to fill the quotas of the town of Sudbury in the year 1864."

ENLISTMENTS OF SOLDIERS.

In meeting the requisitions made upon the town, enlistments were made at various times and in various regiments. Where there was a considerable number of enlistments in any one regiment, we will give not only the names of the soldiers, but a very brief sketch of the regiment in which they served.

THE THIRTEENTH REGIMENT.

Twenty-three men enlisted in this regiment for three years, July 16, 1861, and two others a little later.

Thomas C. Richardson, Band Leader, age 26, enlisted July 26, 1861; expiration of service, Aug. 31, 1862.

James F. Fish, age 27, enlisted July 24, 1861; dropped, Sept. 1, 1862, detailed on gunboat service.

William H. Green, age 26, expiration of service, Aug. 1, 1864.

Mortimer Johnson, age 19, expiration of service, Feb. 19, 1864, to re-enlist; transferred, July 13, 1864, to Thirty-ninth Infantry.

Corp. Almer H. Gay, age 28, expiration of service, May 20, 1862, disability.

Corp. Spencer Smith, age 20. expiration of service, Aug. 1, 1864.

Corp. George L. Willis, age 18, expiration of service, Aug. 1, 1864.

Henry S. Battles, age 24.

Francis H. Brown, age 19, expiration of service, Jan. 16, 1863, disability.

George S. Dickey, age 35, died at Williamsport, Md., March 4, 1862.

Samuel H. Garfield, age 18, expiration of service, Dec. 22, 1862, disability.

Charles E. Haynes, age 24, expiration of service, Aug. 1, 1864.

George W. Jones, age 22, expiration of service, Aug. 1, 1864.

John H. Moore, age 21, expiration of service, Aug. 1, 1864.

Proctor Pingree, wagoner, age 35, expiration of service, May 10, 1862, disability.

Cyrus E. Barker, age 23, expiration of service, Jan. 30, 1863, disability.

Edward Blake, age 33, expiration of service, Aug. 1, 1864.

Lyman W. Brown, age 18, expiration of service April 15, 1863, disability.

Albert Conant, age 22.

Charles E. Duley, age 18, expiration of service, Dec. 15, 1862, disability.

Dana F. Dutton, age 29, transferred, July 14, 1864, to Thirty-ninth Infantry.

Leander A. Haynes, age 27, expiration of service, Aug. 1, 1864.

Henry F. Moore, age 22, expiration of service, Aug. 1, 1864.

George W. Woodbury, age 18, expiration of service, Feb. 11, 1863, disability.

Eugene L. Fairbanks, age 21, expiration of service, Feb. 11, 1863, disability.

George T. Smith at the age of twenty-two re-enlisted from Sudbury in this regiment, and was transferred to the Thirty-ninth Infantry, July 19, 1864. The Thirteenth Regiment was commanded by Col. Samuel. H. Leonard of Boston, and saw hard fighting. It was in the battles of Antietam, Fredericksburg and the second Bull Run in 1862, and at Fredericksburg and Gettysburg in 1863. Jan. 1, 1864, it was in camp at Mitchell's Station, Va., near the Rapidan River, on the extreme front of the army, where it had a camp of log huts, and did important service picketing the river. In the spring following it moved south, and from May 4 to June 6 it is stated that the regiment was under fire night and day. June 16, it marched to the James River, crossed in transports and moved towards Petersburg. July 15, the regiment left City Point, Va., for Washington, and arrived at Boston July 21, 1864.

THE SIXTEENTH REGIMENT.

Five men were members of the Sixteenth Regiment, all of whom were mustered in July, 1861. Their names are: Gardner H. Darling, John Forsyth, Henry H. Parmenter, Horace Sanderson, Warren B. Witherell; John Forsyth and Horace Sanderson were killed; Warren B. Witherell was wounded in the leg and discharged for disability July 28, 1863; Gardner H. Darling was wounded and taken prisoner at the battle of Fair Oaks, and exchanged. He was mustered out July 27, 1864. Henry H. Parmenter was discharged at the expiration of his term of service, June 29, 1864.

The Sixteenth was one of the earliest regiments of three years men that was organized in Massachusetts. It was commanded by Col. Powell T. Wyman of Boston. Before its close of service one of its lieutenant-colonels was Daniel S. Lamson of Weston. The regiment left the State Aug. 17, 1861. It was in the battles of Fair Oaks, Glendale, Malvern Hill, Kettle Run, Chantilly and Fredericksburg in 1862, and at Chancellorsville, Gettysburg and Locust Grove in 1863. It was engaged in the campaign under the leadership of General Grant, which resulted in the capture of Petersburg; and during the year 1864, was engaged in some of its hardest fighting. In May it started southward, and for days it had marchings and fightings. Says one in writing the history of this regiment: "May 4th, at 11 A.M., crossed the Rapidan. At 3 P.M., encamped on the same grounds where one year previous we fought the battle of Chancellorsville. * * The bones of our fallen companions, whitened by the frosts of winter, were scattered over the field and through the woods, about which were blooming in innocent beauty the violet and other spring flowers.

"May 6th [battle of the Wilderness]. * * At 6 A.M. the entire line was advanced about one mile, the battle raging fiercely until 11 A.M., when the heavy reinforcements of the enemy were thrown in masses upon our lines. At this time the Sixteenth showed its real pluck, and held the ground until the entire line both to the right and left had fallen back. At 5 P.M. General Longstreet's corps made its famous charge upon our line. The advance line of battle fought the masses of the enemy until their ammunition was expended, when they were obliged to evacuate the works and seek shelter in our rear. While so doing the enemy occupied the advance line. In a moment, as if by magic, the Sixteenth leaped the works and charged the enemy, forcing him back, and captured a large number of prisoners. * * The flag of the Sixteenth first waved over them after the recapture. * * May 12. * * [The battle of Spottsylvania]. At 12 M., the Sixteenth was ordered along the crest of a hill where the enemy had regained a few rods of the works lost in the morning. * * Our object was that the enemy should capture no more of the works. * * The musketry fire was terrific. It was at this point a tree, some fourteen inches in diameter, was actually fallen — being cut down by bullets — it being between the fire of the contending parties. Regiment after regiment was thrown into this deadly position, and were cut down before the terrific fire like grass. Indeed, the blood flowing from so many killed and wounded, mixing with the rain then falling, gave the running water the appearance of streams of blood. The men fired upwards of three hundred rounds of ammunition, after which they were relieved to clean their pieces. In this action our loss was heavy. The Regiment arrived in Massachusetts July 22, 1864, and was mustered out the 27th."

THE EIGHTEENTH REGIMENT.

Five men enlisted for three years in this regiment, namely : —

Edwin S. Parmenter, age 20, mustered, Aug. 22, 1863, died, June 9, 1864.
Leander Haynes, age 27, mustered, July 16, 1861, expiration of service, Aug. 1, 1864.
Henry Moore, age 22, mustered, July 16, 1861, expiration of service, Aug. 1, 1864.
Eugene L. Fairbanks, age 21, mustered, July 16, 1861, expiration of service, Feb. 11, 1863, disability.
George W. Woodbury, age 18, mustered, July 16, 1861, expiration of service, Feb. 11, 1863, disability.

The Eighteenth Regiment was commanded by James Barnes of Springfield. Eight of its companies were mustered into the United States service Aug. 27, 1861, and left the State the next day. The other two companies joined the regiment in the fall of the same year. The regiment was at the battle of Gaines' Mill, Second Bull Run, Shepardston and Fredericksburg in 1862, and at Chancellorsville, Gettysburg, Rappahannock Station and Mine Creek in 1863. May 1, 1863, it crossed the Rappahannock. Shortly after, it was under command of Col. Joseph Hayes and formed a part of the Third Brigade, First Division, Fifth Corps, and until the 20th of July, when it was ordered to Washington, because near the expiration of its term of service, it was repeatedly engaged with the enemy. Lieutenant-Colonel White, in giving a report of the regiment from Dec. 3, 1863, to June 19, says: "I am pleased to say that both the officers and men of my command, during the series of operations to this date, have behaved in a manner which has entirely satisfied me. All have acted so well, there is little reason to particularize." A battalion, made up of men whose term of service would not expire with the regiment, was detached, and remained a part of the Third Brigade; it was engaged with the enemy about Petersburg, and at one time captured fifty prisoners and a battle-flag belonging to the Twenty-seventh South Carolina Regiment. After the expiration of its term of service, the battalion was consolidated with the Thirty-second Massachusetts Regiment.

THE TWENTIETH REGIMENT.

Besides the foregoing enlistments, which were largely made up of Sudbury citizens, there is among the town papers the following list of men, who in December, 1862, were furnished by the town for the three years service. All, except the first, were in the Twentieth Massachusetts Regiment and mustered in December 19.

AGE		OCCUPATION.	REGIMENT.	MUSTERED.
23	Patrick Wilson,	Laborer,	First,	Dec. 18, 1862.
22	John Stewart,	Carpenter,	Twentieth,	19, "
35	Thomas Faver,	Barber,	"	" "
22	William Johnson,	Cigar-maker,	"	"
27	John McCluskey,	Boatman,		
22	David Henry,	Seaman,		
22	James Maloney,	Cooper,		
21	Joseph Powell,	Pressman,		
21	William J. Robinson,	Steward,		
21	John White,	Seaman,		
22	John Wiley,	Stone-cutter,		
26	Charles Rogers,	Laborer,		
23	John Morgan,	Seaman,		
29	James Walsh,	"		
39	Henry Price,	"		
22	Charles Daniels,	Harness-maker,	"	

The Twentieth Regiment was commanded by Col. William Raymond Lee of Roxbury, and left Massachusetts Sept. 4, 1861. It was in the battle of Balls Bluff in 1861, and in the battles before Richmond, Antietam and Fredericksburg in 1862, and at Fredericksburg, Gettysburg, Bristow's Station and Mine Run in 1863. May 3, 1864, the regiment left winter quarters, crossed the Rapidan, and on the 5th marched to the Wilderness and there engaged the enemy. It fought bravely and suffered severely. In one engagement of three hours it had one major killed, a colonel, three captains and two lieutenants wounded. In its march southward from the Wilderness to the front of Petersburg, it had hard fighting and lost many men.

THE TWENTY-SIXTH REGIMENT.

Sixteen men were enlisted in the Twenty-sixth Regiment, namely : —

Elias E. Haynes, 2nd Lieut., age 28, mustered, Nov. 12, 1862, expiration of service, April 21, 1865, resigned.

John M. Haynes, Corp., age 18, mustered, Sept. 20, 1861, Dec. 31, 1863, re-enlisted.

John M. Haynes, Sergt., age 20, mustered, Jan. 1, 1864, expiration of service, Aug. 26, 1865.

Albert L. Weeks, Sergt., age 22, mustered, Jan. 1, 1864, expiration of service, Aug. 26, 1865.

William Barr, age 37, mustered, Jan. 1, 1864, expiration of service, Aug. 26, 1865.

James Dooner, age 20, mustered, Jan. 1, 1864, expiration of service, Aug. 26, 1865.

James W. Fisk, age 28, mustered, Jan. 1, 1864, expiration of service, Aug. 26, 1865.

William T. Sawyer, age 19, mustered, Sept. 6, 1861, expiration of service, Nov. 21, 1865.

Silas Willis, age 22, mustered, Sept. 4, 1861, expiration of service, Nov. 22, 1862, to enlist in United States Army.

Michael Dooner, Oct. 18, 1861, expiration of service, Aug. 26, 1865.

George Flood, mustered, Oct. 18, 1861, expiration of service, Aug. 26, 1865.

John A. Haynes, mustered, Oct., 1861, expiration of service, Aug. 26, 1865.

James Hefferman, mustered, Oct. 18, 1861, expiration of service, Aug. 26, 1865.

John Kelly, mustered, Oct. 18, 1861, expiration of service, Aug. 26, 1865.

John O'Donnell, mustered, Oct. 18, 1861, expiration of service, Aug. 26, 1865.

Marcus M. Puffer, mustered, Oct. 18, 1861, expiration of service, Aug. 26, 1865.

This regiment left the State Nov. 21, 1861. It was commanded by Col. Edward F. Jones of Pepperell, and was an offshoot of his old regiment, the Massachusetts Sixth, which was attacked when passing through Baltimore, April 19, 1861. The regiment previous to January, 1864, was for a time in Louisiana. July, 1864, it went to Bermuda Hundred, Va., and was for a time in the army of the Shenandoah with General Sheridan. It was in the battle of Cedar Creek and lost several men.

THE THIRTY-FIFTH REGIMENT.

Eight men were mustered into the Thirty-fifth Regiment, Aug. 16, 1862, for the term of three years, namely : —

Sergt. Rufus H. Hurlbut, age 20, expiration of service, June 9, 1865.
Corp. William F. Bowen, age 20, expiration of service, June 9, 1865.
Corp. George F. Moore, age 20, expiration of service, June 9, 1865.
William B. Bailey, age 25, expiration of service, June 9, 1865.
Francis Garfield, age 32, transferred, March 15, 1864, to V. R. C.
George H. Hall, age 22, expiration of service, June 9, 1865.
Albert H. Moore, age 26, expiration of service, June 9, 1865.
Eli H. Willis, age 21, expiration of service, June 9, 1865.

This regiment was recruited in July, 1862, and left the State the 22d of August under command of Col. Edward A. Wilde of Brookline. September 6, it started from Arlington Heights for Maryland, and began active service while the soldiers were yet but an undisciplined collection of enlisted citizens, or raw recruits having had but one battalion drill. Its first battle was at South Mountain, in which Colonel Wilde lost an arm, which obliged him to leave the regiment, and Lieut.-Col. Sumner Carruth of Chelsea was promoted colonel. The regiment was in the battles of Antietam and Fredericksburg in 1862. After this, the regiment was assigned to General Burnside's corps, and sent into Kentucky to hunt guerillas, where it continued until June 4, 1863, when it was sent to Washington to reinforce General Grant. After the surrender of Vickburg, July 4, 1863, it was sent to Jackson, Miss., in pursuit of General Johnston, where it had several days' fighting, which resulted in the retreat of Johnston. The Thirty-fifth was the first regiment to enter the city, and it secured the rebel flag from the State House. The campaign was a severe one because of the extreme heat and scarcity of water. The regiment then returned to Kentucky, and Sept. 30, 1863, started for Knoxville, Tenn., and remained there during the siege of that place. While at Knoxville the regiment endured severe hardship and deprivation. The rations were short and the clothing scant. At times during the winter, when the ground was covered with snow, some of the Sudbury soldiers had no shoes. One of them cut off the tail of his coat and sewed it on his feet. Some of them sewed on pieces of green hide with the hair left on the inside. Throughout the winter the soldiers were on half rations ; and during the siege, which lasted nineteen days, they were allowed some days only one pint of unbolted corn-meal ; one day they had only one ear of corn apiece, and other days they had nothing. During this time they were on picket duty more than half the time, and were obliged to be awake every alternate twenty-four hours, and sometimes forty-eight hours at a time. This occurred after the retreat from and battle with General Longstreet, which kept them fighting and marching without rest for three nights and two days.

In the spring of 1864, the regiment was sent back to the Army of the Potomac, and was engaged in the battles of the Wilderness, Spottsylvania, Cold Harbor, and all the hard fighting to the James River. It remained in front of Petersburg till the close of the war.

THE FORTY-FIFTH REGIMENT.

Thirteen men were mustered into the Forty-fifth Regiment, Sept. 26, 1862, for the term of nine months, namely : —

Marshall L. Eaton, 1st Sergt., age 30, expiration of service, July 7, 1863.
Homer Rogers, Sergt., age 22, expiration of service, July 7, 1863.

Arthur Dakin, Corp., age 22, expiration of service, July 7, 1863.
Bradley Hemenway, Corp., age 26, expiration of service, July 7, 1863.
Frank H. Hunt, Musician, age 18, expiration of service, July 7, 1863.
Albert B. Richardson, Musician, age 19, expiration of service, July 7, 1863.
Asa B. Bacon, age 41, expiration of service, July 7, 1863.
James B. Butterfield, age 22, expiration of service, July 7, 1863.
John H. Eaton, age 24, expiration of service, July 7, 1863.
Theodoric A. Jones, age 18, expiration of service, July 7, 1863.
Alpheus Puffer, age 22, expiration of service, July 7, 1863.
William Scott, age 19, expiration of service, July 7, 1863.
Charles C. Spaulding, age 24, expiration of service, July 7, 1863.

This regiment was organized in the summer of 1862, and the companies composing it came from different towns. It left the State, Nov. 5, 1862, and July 21, 1863, it returned to Boston and was recruited. The regiment took part in the battle of Kingston, N. C., Dec. 14, 1862, and in the battle of Goldsboro. It was also engaged in the movements about Newbern. Its losses in battle were twenty killed and seventy-one wounded, exceeding that of all the other nine months regiments taken together. The loss from sickness and disease was also very heavy. The march to Goldsboro, under a sultry sun, is spoken of as a long and weary one to men unaccustomed to such hardships, but they stood it like true soldiers, and held on their way till it was ended. One of the younger ones in his company was Theodoric Jones; though his feet were badly blistered by his coarse army shoes he never flinched nor lagged behind; and when, for once having climbed a fence by the roadside for a momentary rest, he heard it intimated that he was giving out, he instantly sprang to the ground, and with some vigorous remarks resumed his journey with apparent ease. When he arrived in camp his shoes were a curiosity, — it is said they were so completely run down that the heels were nearly bottom side up, and the owner's feet were in such a condition that, for a number of days, he was entirely disabled.

Of the Sudbury men in this regiment, perhaps William Scott did as much as any towards breaking up the monotony of the weary march and the tedious camp life. " Billy," as the boys called him, was short and stout, a good soldier and full of fun. Sometimes he would act as barber, and get his

pay in the sport he made of his patrons. On the march of
the regiment from Goldsboro to Newbern, Billy captured
a small mule about the size of a heifer; and, having loaded
the beast with such articles as had been picked up by the
way and his gun and accoutrements, he mounted it and the
journey was resumed towards camp. A lieutenant, having
his attention called to the animal, required him to give it
up, but Billy clung to the bridle without saying a word; the
officer threatened, but Billy rode on, and when at length he
arrived at Newbern he presented a comical spectacle. He
had, besides the blankets, muskets, haversacks, etc., two
geese, some hens, and a large number of canteens, so that
the little mule was well nigh covered. Billy was smiling,
as usual, and the boys smiled too. The mule was unloaded
and given up, and Billy, so far as known, received no repri-
mand but what he had at the start.

THE FIFTY-NINTH REGIMENT.

The following men enlisted in the Fifty-ninth for three
years : —

Cyrus E. Barker, age 25, mustered, Jan. 14, 1864, died April 9, 1865.

Curtis Smith, age 21, mustered, Jan. 14, 1864, died Oct. 19, 1864.

Benjamin Ryde, age 35, mustered, Feb. 9, 1864, transferred, June 1, 1865,
    to Fifty-seventh Infantry.

Alfred Moore, age 21, mustered, April 2, 1864, transferred June 7, 1865,
    to V. R. C.

This regiment was raised and commanded by Jacob P.
Gould of Stoneham, who was formerly Major of the Thirteenth. It left the State for Washington, April 26, 1864.
Ten days after, it was engaged in its first fight; and in 1864
it took part in the battles of the Wilderness, Spottsylvania,
North Anna, Coal Harbor, the battles before Petersburg, and
the battle of Weldon Railroad.

With the exception of the instances now mentioned, the
soldiers who went from Sudbury, for the most part, enlisted
in different regiments, and their names are scattered along
in the various rolls of the Massachusetts Volunteer Militia,
and bear date from the first to the last year of the war. The

following are the names of these soldiers as given in the State Adjutant General's Report or the Sudbury Soldiers' Record Book, from which we have also taken the foregoing lists.

ENLISTMENTS IN OTHER REGIMENTS OF INFANTRY.

NINE MONTHS MEN IN THE SIXTH REGIMENT.

Samuel G. Brown, Corp., age 27, mustered, Aug. 31, 1862, expiration of service, June 3, 1863.

Solomon Davis, age 36, mustered, Aug. 31, 1862, expiration of service, June 3, 1863.

Francis Dutton, age 26, mustered, Aug. 31, 1862, expiration of service, June 3, 1863.

Augustus Newton, mustered, Aug. 31, 1862, expiration of service, June 3, 1863.

Matthew Smith, age 19, mustered, Aug. 31, 1862, expiration of service, June 3, 1863.

ONE HUNDRED DAYS MEN IN THE SIXTH REGIMENT.

Rockwood Puffer, age 18, mustered, Aug 18, 1864, expiration of service, Oct. 27, 1864.

THREE YEARS MEN IN THE NINTH REGIMENT INFANTRY.

Walter Lee, age 38, mustered, March 28, 1864, transferred, June 10, 1864, to Thirty-second Infantry, expiration of service, June 29, 1864.

Michael Muller, age 29, mustered, Aug. 21, 1863.

THREE YEARS MEN IN THE NINETEENTH REGIMENT.

Cornelius Buckley, age 38, mustered, March 26, 1864, expiration of service, June 30, 1865.

Thomas Smith, age 28, mustered, March 26, 1864, died, Jan. 26, 1865.

Josiah Garfield, mustered, July 26, 1861, expiration of service, June 30, 1865.

MEN IN THE TWENTY-FOURTH REGIMENT.

Michael Malone, age 32, mustered, March 26, 1864.

THREE YEARS MEN IN TWENTY-EIGHTH REGIMENT.

Michael Fitzgerald, Corp., age 22, mustered, Jan. 26, 1865, expiration of service, June 30, 1865.

THREE YEARS MEN IN THE THIRTIETH REGIMENT.

Stillman Willis, mustered, Jan. 4, 1862, expiration of service, ——.

THREE YEARS MEN IN THE THIRTY-SECOND REGIMENT.

John Herschel Moore, mustered, July 2, 1862, discharged for disability.

THREE YEARS MEN IN THE TWENTY-SECOND REGIMENT.

John Rothe, mustered, Oct. 5, 1861, expiration of service, Oct. 20, 1864.

THREE YEARS MEN IN THE THIRTY-THIRD REGIMENT.

John Roth, age 40, mustered, Aug. 5, 1862, expiration of service, Jan. 11, 1865.

Robert Arnold, mustered, Aug. 13, 1862, regiment mustered out, ——.

THREE YEARS MEN IN THE THIRTY-EIGHTH REGIMENT.

Marcus T. Baker, age 21, mustered, Jan. 21, 1865, transferred, June 22, 1865, to Twenty-sixth Infantry.

George A. Jones, age 18, August 21, 1862, expiration of service, June 30, 1865.

MEN IN THE THIRTY-NINTH REGIMENT.

James M. Sawyer, age 19, mustered, Aug. 18, 1862, expiration of service, July 18, 1865.

NINE MONTHS MEN IN THE FORTY-SEVENTH REGIMENT.

Silas H. Blake, age 38, mustered, November, 1862, expiration of service, Sept. 1, 1863.

THREE YEARS MEN IN THE FIFTY-SIXTH REGIMENT.

William F. Coombs, age 37, mustered, Feb. 25, 1864, expiration of service, Aug. 1, 1865, order War Department.

MEN IN THE SIXTY-FIRST REGIMENT.

Edward A. Farnsworth, age 24, mustered, Jan. 10, 1865, expiration of service, July 16, 1865.

Peter McDougal, age 38, mustered, Jan. 16, 1865, expiration of service, May 27, 1865, order War Department.

SUDBURY SOLDIERS IN THE CAVALRY SERVICE.

THREE YEARS MEN IN THE FIRST CAVALRY.

Averill F. Willis, mustered, September, 1861, expiration of service, June 26, 1865.

George F. Butterfield, mustered, September, 1861, expiration of service, June 26, 1865.

This regiment was commanded by Col. Robert Williams of Virginia, and left the State by battalions; the First on the 25th, the Second on the 27th, and the Third on the 29th of December, 1861. It was stationed in the Department of the South until August 19, 1862, when eight of its companies joined the Army of the Potomac. The two men from Sudbury served in Company L, Capt. William Gibbs of

Waltham. It is stated that, while in South Carolina, " they suffered from hunger, storm, wind and heat, and were at the terrible battles of James Island, Fort Wagner, and Morris Island." After leaving South Carolina, they were in Virginia with the Tenth Army Corps, commanded by Major-General Gilmore, and served in front of Petersburg until its surrender. In 1864, a part of the battalion of cavalry, known as the Independent Battalion Massachusetts Cavalry, that served in the Department of the South and was formerly of the First Massachusetts Cavalry, constituted, with the First Battalion Veteran Cavalry, the Fourth Massachusetts Cavalry.

THREE YEARS MEN IN THE SECOND REGIMENT CAVALRY.

Hartson D. Sinclair, age 21, mustered, Feb. 14, 1865, died, May 26, 1865.

John F. Casey, age 19, mustered, Aug. 9, 1864, expiration of service, June 17, 1865.

Richard H. Graham, age 19, mustered, Aug. 9, 1864, expiration of service, June 17, 1865.

John O'Brien, age 20, mustered, Aug. 9, 1864, expiration of service, June 17, 1865.

THREE YEARS MEN IN THE FOURTH REGIMENT CAVALRY.

John Lee, 2nd Lieut., mustered, July 13, 1865, expiration of service, Nov. 14, 1865.

George F. Butterfield, Corp., age 20, mustered, Sept. 23, 1661, expiration of service, Sept. 24, 1864.

Frank E. Willis, Bugler, age 19, mustered, Sept. 23, 1861, expiration of service, Sept, 24, 1864.

THREE YEARS MEN IN THE FIFTH REGIMENT CAVALRY.

Daniel Robinson, age 21, mustered, Aug 25, 1864, expiration of service, May 23, 1865.

Lyman Taylor, age 21, mustered, Aug. 25, 1864, expiration of service, May 23, 1865.

SUDBURY SOLDIERS IN THE ARTILLERY SERVICE.

THREE YEARS MEN IN SEVENTH BATTERY OF LIGHT ARTILLERY.

John P. Hudson, age 23, mustered, May 21, 1862, died, March 7, 1864.

THREE YEARS MEN IN FIRST REGIMENT, HEAVY ARTILLERY.

Edward R. Cutler, Asst. Surg., age 22, mustered, Sept. 25, 1863, Surg. Dec. 19, 1864.

THREE YEARS MEN IN THE FIRST BATTALION, HEAVY ARTILLERY.

George A. Dean, age 18, mustered, Feb. 11, 1865, expiration of service, Oct. 20, 1865.

THREE YEARS MEN IN SECOND REGIMENT, HEAVY ARTILLERY.

Thomas Corcoran, age 21, mustered, Aug. 18, 1864, died, April 11, 1865.

ONE YEAR MEN IN THE FOURTH REGIMENT, HEAVY ARTILLERY.

Sidney Smith, age 21, mustered, Aug. 12, 1864, expiration of service, June 17, 1865.

Alexander Black, age 42, mustered, Aug. 25, 1864, expiration of service, June 17, 1865.

Joseph Clear, age 19, mustered, Aug. 23, 1864, expiration of service, June 17, 1865.

Jonathan G. Leavett, age 34, mustered, Aug. 25, 1864, expiration of service, June 17, 1865.

James F. Rundell, age 19, mustered, Aug. 17, 1864, expiration of service, June 17, 1865.

Charles R. Taylor, age 22, mustered, Aug. 23, 1864, expiration of service, June 17, 1865.

ONE YEAR MEN IN THE TWENTY-NINTH UNAT. CO., HEAVY ARTILLERY.

Cornelius Fitzpatrick, age 23, mustered, Sept. 1, 1864, expiration of service, June 16, 1865.

Matthew Heaphey, age 21, mustered, Aug. 25, 1864, expiration of service, June 16, 1865.

Michael Shea, age 21, mustered, Sept. 1, 1864, expiration of service, June 16, 1865.

UNITED STATES SANITARY COMMISSION.

Two Sudbury men, Edwin Hunt and Alfred S. Hudson, were with the army in the service of the Sanitary Commission. The first remained until obliged to return on account of ill health; the other entered the service July, 1864, and was stationed at City Point, Va., at the junction of the Appomatox and James Rivers, near Petersburg, at the time of the siege.

Notwithstanding the promptness of the town in taking means to fill its quotas by voluntary enlistments at home, and by offering bounties for enlistments from abroad, before the war closed it was subjected to a draft. July 17, 1863, the names of the town's citizens included in the First Class List were deposited at Concord, and the following names were drawn therefrom.

LIST OF CONSCRIPTS IN THE TOWN OF SUDBURY, DRAWN AT CONCORD, JULY 17, 1863.

M. W. Evans,	exempt.	William L. Stone,	exempt.
Albert T. Parmenter,	substituted.	Frank Webster	"
William Gormin,	paid.	G. H Murphy,	
Francis H. Moore,	exempt.	Edwin Rogers,	"
Francis H. Brown,	"	Hubbard H. Brown,	paid.
Michael Newell,	"	Joel F. Parmenter,	"
Jonas Goodnow,	"	Luther G. Hunt,	"
Samuel Bent,		Winsor Pratt,	substituted.
T. M. Brenn,	"	Lorenzo Parmenter,	exempt.
George H. Murphy,	enlisted,	Joseph B. Adams,	"
E. S. Butterfield,	exempt.	C. W. Floyd,	"
Luther S. Cutting,	paid.	Henry H. Cheney,	"
E. R. Chase,	"	James J. Puffer,	"
Dana W. Hayden,	exempt.	N. C. Haynes,	paid.
William E. Eager,	"	Francis F. Walker,	exempt.

In the foregoing lists are the names of some of Sudbury's most valuable citizens. Voluntarily they came forward, and offered themselves at their country's call. Young men left the farm, the store, and the work-shop, and in the best of their years and their strength engaged in the work of war. The death rate among them, according to the records, is very small. Yet the history of the regiments in which most of these soldiers served shows that they sometimes occupied positions of extreme peril. Some, who passed through the severest engagements, escaped unharmed; while others were wounded repeatedly, and recovered and again entered the ranks. Some of the strongest were the first to succumb to the power of disease; while others, slender of stature and unaccustomed to out-door toil, came back at the end of their term of service robust and strong. Such are the fortunes of war.

LIST OF CASUALTIES.

The fatal casualties that occurred to persons who were accredited to or natives of Sudbury, as we have found them recorded in the Town Book or the Adjutant General's Printed Report, are as follows: —

KILLED OR MORTALLY WOUNDED IN BATTLE.
Horace Sanderson.   John Forsyth.   Edwin S. Parmenter.

THE WADSWORTH MONUMENT
South Sudbury. *See page 555.*

DIED IN THE SERVICE OF DISEASE OR HARDSHIP INCIDENT TO
ARMY LIFE.

John P. Hudson.	Thomas Corcoran.
Curtis Smith.	Hartson D. Sinclair.
George T. Dickey.	Thomas Smith.
Abel H. Dakin.	Cyrus E. Barker.

The following is a sketch of the above-named soldiers so far as we have information concerning them.

HORACE SANDERSON.

Horace Sanderson, born at Waltham in 1837, was a member of Company K, Sixteenth Regiment, M. V. M. He enlisted for three years and was mustered in July, 1861. He was killed at the battle of Chancellorsville, May 3, 1863.

JOHN FORSYTH.

John Forsyth, son of John and Hannah Forsyth, was born in Waltham, Feb. 12, 1835. He enlisted at Newton in Company H, Sixteenth Regiment, for three years, and held the position of sergeant. He was mustered into the service in July, 1861. By trade he was a carpenter, and his former home was in the east part of the town. He was killed at the battle of Gettysburg, July 3, 1863.

EDWIN S. PARMENTER.

Edwin S. Parmenter, son of Charles and Fanny Parmenter, was born in Sudbury, August 19, 1844. He was by occupation a farmer, and lived at his father's home in the north-easterly part of the town. When the draft came, July 17, 1863, his brother, Albert T., was among the Sudbury conscripts, and Edwin went as his substitute; making the second son in the family to go in the defence of his country. He belonged to Company H, Eighteenth Massachusetts Regiment, and was mustered in August 22, 1863. He was mortally wounded at the battle of Bottom Bridge, Va., and died, June 8, 1864.

JOHN P. HUDSON.

John Plympton Hudson was mustered into the United States service, May 21, 1862, and was a member of the

Seventh Massachusetts Light Battery. He was with it in its first engagement, which was with the artillery of Gen. Roger Pryor, at the "Deserted House," near Suffolk, Va. This action was noted for the effective work of the battery. Said the "New York Tribune," in the news of Feb. 3, 1863, "The Seventh Battery achieved great honor in sustaining a furious cannonading and in more than matching it [Pryor's Battery] in this its first engagement." In describing the action, it states, "Follett's Battery [that is the Seventh Massachusetts] was then wheeled into position, and at twenty minutes to four o'clock, the action commenced in earnest. Then ensued an exhibition of artillery practice, such as has rarely been seen in this war. For three hours and eleven minutes this artillery duel continued, and the service of the guns on both sides, it is said, was not surpassable. During this time the enemy was slowly giving way before the superiority of our cannonading. Their pieces were all silenced by seven o'clock, and they had been driven two miles from the Deserted House." In his own description of the action in a letter to his brother, dated Suffolk, Va., Jan. 31, 1863, Mr. Hudson said, "I was in a battle yesterday and a desperate one too, but I am safe and uninjured. . . . I was in the hottest of the fight, all of it, and got a hole torn in my overcoat by a shell. It was a regular artillery duel for three hours. Our company had two men killed and ten wounded." In another, description of the battle, he states that the ground was plowed with the shot and shell, and that the trees above the battery looked as if seared by the frost or by a fire. In one instance his clothing was sprinkled with the earth that was thrown up by the shot. During the same year the battery was engaged at South Quay, Somerton, Providence Church Road and Holland's House. It was afterwards ordered to New York to prevent a riot in the enforcement of a draft. While there, Mr. Hudson became unfitted for duty through disease, contracted while in the service in Virginia, and entered the hospital. After rejoining the battery, while yet in an enfeebled condition, he obtained a furlough to go North. He arrived at Sudbury in November, 1863, where his illness increased until his death, which occurred at the Luther Goodnow house, near the old Haynes Garrison, March 7, 1864. John P. Hudson was born at Wayland, "Wayland and Weston Corner," Oct. 5, 1838. He was the son of Martin Newton and Maria (Reed) Hudson, and early went with his parents to Sudbury, where the most of his life was spent. He was held in high esteem by his associates, and had the confidence of the community in every position that he occupied from his early youth to the time of his going forth a young man in his country's service. As a soldier, he was true to every trust, and faithfully stood at his post until health gave way in camp life about the swamps of Suffolk, Va. In a letter sent by a comrade in the battery, Dr. William H. Ruddick of South Boston, it was said, "He had not an enemy in the company, always did his duty faithfully like a good soldier, his conduct and bearing was an example for the rest to follow, he was loved by all." He died at the age of twenty-five, and was buried at Wadsworth Cemetery in the family lot. His grave is marked by a marble stone, which is inscribed as follows:—

VOLUNTEER'S GRAVE.

JOHN P. HUDSON
A MEMBER OF
THE 7TH MASS. LIGHT BATTERY
DIED
IN THE U. S. SERVICE MARCH 7TH 1864
Aged 25.

" How sleep the brave, who sink to rest,
   With all their country's wishes blest.

 • • • • • • •

   By fairy hands their knell is rung;
   By forms unseen their dirge is sung;
   There Honor comes, a pilgrim gray,
   To bless the turf that wraps their clay;
   And Freedom shall awhile repair,
   To dwell a weeping hermit there."

CURTIS SMITH.

Curtis Smith, son of Joseph and Olive (Moore) Smith, was born at Sudbury, Dec. 22, 1842. He enlisted, January, 1864, for three years in the Fifty-ninth Regiment, and was a member of Company E. He was a farmer, and the second son of the family to enter the service of his country. May 6, ten days after leaving the State, his regiment was engaged in its first fight, and between that time and the middle of June it was in the battles of the Wilderness, Spottsylvania, North Anna and Cold Harbor. Between June 3 and 17, by which time the regiment was before Petersburg, fifteen of its men had been taken prisoners, among whom was Mr. Smith. He was taken to Andersonville June 10, and died there October 19. The town of Sudbury had one son offered as a sacrifice to her country in that terrible prison pen. The story is sufficiently told by the Town Record Book, which says, " Died, Oct. 19, 1864, of starvation in prison at Andersonville, Ga."

GEORGE T. DICKEY.

George T. Dickey was a son of Ira S. and Eliza Dickey. He was born in Weston, and afterwards lived in the westerly part of Wayland, but the proximity of his house to Sudbury and his family connection with it allied him socially to that town. He was by occupation a farmer, and, perhaps, few soldiers were better equipped physically for the endurance of army life than he ; and his cheerful disposition was well suited to brighten the rough experience of the camp and the march ; but, like some others who were exceptionally robust, he was stricken down by the hand of disease, and after but about a half year's service as a soldier, he died in the hospital at Williamsport, Md., March 4, 1862.

ABEL H. DAKIN.

Abel Henry Dakin enlisted from Natick in Company I, Thirty-ninth Regiment, M. V. M. He entered the army as a drummer, but afterwards held the position of bugler. He died of consumption near Kelly's Ford, Va., Dec. 20, 1863. In the Wadsworth Cemetery is a stone bearing the following inscription : —

ABEL H. DAKIN,
MEMBER OF CO. I, 39TH REG'T MASS. VOLS.
Aet. 31 Years.
" REST, SOLDIER, REST."

Mr. Dakin was a son of Abel and Emeline (Stone) Dakin, and was born at Sudbury, Dec. 28, 1832. His life was mostly spent in his native town at the home of his uncle, John H. Dakin, at the present Carpenter place. He was a young man of excellent character, and, while in his country's service, he faithfully performed his part. One of his company, in a letter to his sister, Mrs. Mary S. Brown, after his death, stated, that "he did his duty cheerfully, was never heard to complain," and that "they could feel that he was a true and faithful soldier." At the time of his enlistment he resided in Natick. He was married April 17, 1858, and has left one daughter, Garrie O. Dakin. He gave his life for his country, and was one of the great army of martyrs that marched to the South to be offered as a sacrifice in the sacred cause of freedom.

Thomas Corcoran, died, April 11, 1865, at Kingston, N. C.
Hartson D. Sinclair, died, May 26, 1865, at Cumberland, Md.
Thomas Smith, died, Jan. 26, 1865.
Cyrus E. Barker, died at Annapolis, Md.

> "On Fame's eternal camping ground
> Their silent tents are spread;
> While glory guards with solemn round
> The bivouac of the dead."

SKETCHES OF RESIDENT SOLDIERS.

We will now give a sketch of the Sudbury soldiers who are living in town, so far as our information of them extends. The task will be an easy one, for time has made more havoc than the bayonets or bullets of the foe. The ranks of the veterans have been thinned, year by year, through death and removal. Fewer and fewer have become the survivors, till but about a half score are left to decorate the graves of their comrades as the spring-time returns; and when a few more years have passed the last veteran will be gone. The Sudbury soldiers who are non-residents of the town are somewhat widely scattered; but, as in the case of residents, more or less of them are at the head of households, occupy honorable positions, and are useful and substantial citizens.

They laid down the weapons of war and took the implements of peaceful pursuits, glad of the repose that comes after victory.

> Welcome with shouts of joy and pride
>   Your veterans from the war-path's track;
> You gave your boys untrained, untried,
>   You bring them men and heroes back.
>   ALICE CARY.

JAMES B. BUTTERFIELD.

James B. Butterfield, son of Luther and Mary Butterfield, was born in Wayland, July 22, 1840. He was the second member of the family to serve in the war, his brother George having enlisted Aug. 18, 1861, in the First Massachusetts Cavalry. His early home was at Lanham, at which place he has recently resided.

WILLIAM B. BAILEY.

William B. Bailey, son of Mathew and Roxanna Bailey, was born at Palmer in 1837. He was a resident of Sudbury at the time of enlistment, and by occupation a shoemaker. He married Alvina Darling of Sudbury, and since his discharge from the army has lived at the place in South Sudbury formerly owned by his father-in-law, Trobridge Darling. He belonged to Company D, Thirty-fifth Regiment.

JOHN H. EATON.

John Henry Eaton, son of John and Ruth Eaton, was born in Sudbury, Nov. 17, 1838. His home was in the Lanham district and his occupation that of a farmer. He belonged to Company F, Forty-fifth Regiment. Since his discharge from the army he has lived at his former home.

JOSIAH GLEASON.

Josiah Gleason, born in Sudbury Aug. 8, 1826, was son of Reuben and Jerusha Gleason. He was by occupation a farmer, and since the war has resided in town.

FRANCIS GARFIELD.

Francis Garfield, son of Enoch and Priscilla Garfield, was born in Lincoln, October 1830. He was by occupation a shoemaker, and became a citizen of Sudbury several years before entering the army. He married Sarah, daughter of Thomas B. Battles, and resides at Sudbury Centre.

CHARLES E. HAYNES.

Charles E. Haynes, son of David and Rachel Haynes, was born at Sudbury June 12, 1837. He enlisted for three years in the 13th Reg't., M. V. M., Co. F, and was mustered into service July 16, 1861. At the time of enlistment he was a farmer by occupation and a member of the "Wadsworth Rifle Guards." After he was mustered out of the United States service, Aug. 1, 1864, he returned to Sudbury where he now resides. He married Abi, daughter of Daniel L. and Sarah Willis, and has one son, Charles Ernest. He was several times wounded. His first wound was caused by a fragment of shell which struck him on the head at the second battle of Bull Run, Aug. 30, 1862. In the same battle he was also taken prisoner, but escaped. He was wounded next at the battle of Antietam, Sept. 17, 1862, by a musket ball, which passed through both legs. The third wound was received May 8, 1864, at the battle of Spottsylvania, where he was shot through the hand and at the same time was struck by some missile in the side which knocked him down.

RUFUS H. HURLBUT.

Rufus H. Hurlbut, only son of Thomas P. and Mary (Moore) Hurlbut, was born at Sudbury, July 16, 1842. He enlisted at the age of twenty, in the Thirty-fifth Regiment, and was promoted to sergeant, May 8, 1865. While his regiment was before Petersburg, Sept. 30, 1864, he was wounded in the head. During his march through the Wilderness he was taken sick, and for a time he was in danger of being left behind; a comrade, John Morse, then of Wayland, nobly offered to remain with him. At Fredericksburg, as he went up the perilous heights, he was obliged to pass through a gap in a fence, the position of which was so exposed that he was forced to tread upon a heap of bodies which had just been slain, but he escaped unhurt. He continued with the army till the expiration of his term of service, June 9, 1865, when he returned to South Sudbury, where he still resides.

JOHN H. MOORE.

John Herschell Moore was born in the west part of Sudbury, June 30, 1841, and was the youngest son of James and Sally (Thompson) Moore. He enlisted for three years when a student, and was a member of Company G, Thirty-second Regiment. This regiment was engaged in the battles before Richmond, at Antietam and Fredericksburg in 1862, and at Chancellorsville, Spottsylvania and Rappahannock Station in 1863.

ALPHEUS PUFFER.

Alpheus Puffer was born at Sudbury in 1840. He was the son of Samuel and Laura Puffer, and his early home was in the north-east part of the town. At the time of enlistment he was a resident of South Sudbury and by occupation a carpenter. He was a member of Company F, Forty-fifth Regiment. He is at present a resident of South Sudbury, and engaged in the business of a machinist.

ELI H. WILLIS.

Eli H. Willis, son of Eli and Mary Willis, was born in Sudbury in 1841. He was by occupation a farmer. He married Sarah, only daughter of Luther and Mary Butterfield, and resides in the Lanham district. He was a member of Company E, Thirty-fifth Regiment, and was the second member of his father's family to go to the war; a brother, Averill, having enlisted August, 1861, in the First Massachusetts Cavalry.

SUMMARY OF SERVICE.

According to Schouler in his " History of Massachusetts in the Civil War," Sudbury furnished one hundred and sixty-eight men, which was eleven over and above all demands. He states that " four were commissioned officers. The whole amount of money appropriated and expended by the town on account of the war, exclusive of State aid, was seventeen thousand five hundred and seventy-five dollars. The amount of money raised and expended by the town during the war for State aid to soldiers' families, and repaid by the Commonwealth, was $6,199.18."

" The population of Sudbury in 1860 was 1,691; the valuation, $1,043.091. The population in 1865 was 1,703; the valuation, $1,052,778. The selectmen in 1861 and 1862 were James Moore, John H. Dakin, George Parmenter; in 1863, A. B. Jones, George Goodnow, H. H. Goodnough; in 1864 and 1865, Thomas P. Hurlbut, Charles Hunt, Walter Rogers. The town clerk during all the years of the war was J. S. Hunt. The town treasurer during the years 1861, 1862 and 1863 was Edwin Harrington; in 1864 and 1865, S. A. Jones."

Shortly after the war, Sudbury's rank among the towns of the county in population was the thirty-ninth. In 1776, it was the only town in Middlesex County having a population of two thousand.

It may be of interest, as well as important as a matter of history, to give the names of Sudbury citizens who were included in the first and second classes of those subject to a draft in November, 1863.

Provost Marshal's Office,
Headquarters Seventh District, Massachusetts.
Concord, November 24, 1863.

By order of the Provost Marshal General of the United States, the following list of the names of all persons enrolled in the Sub-District of Sudbury, is published for the information of whom it may concern.

Any person enrolled as below may appear before the

Board of Enrolment on Monday, December 14th, 1863, and claim to have his name stricken from the list, if he can show to the satisfaction of the Board that he is not liable to military duty on account of, 1st, Alienage; 2d, Non-Residence; 3d, Unsuitableness of Age; 4th, Manifest Permanent Physical Disability.

As all disabilities must be manifest and permanent, certificates of physicians cannot be examined or considered.

All persons who were exempted from the recent draft on account of having furnished a Substitute, or paid Commutation Money, need not appear.

FIRST CLASS.

Adams, Joseph B., 33, farmer.
Butterfield, S. Ebenezer, 21, shoemaker.
Bones, Patrick, 33, laborer.
Brown, Francis H., 21, farmer.
Bacon, Adoniram J., 24, "
Bent, William H., 24, "
Bent, Cyrus A., 23, "
Bent, Lucius P., 31, "
Bent, Samuel, Jr., 30, "
Brinn, Thomas M., 32, tailor.
Brown, Spencer W., 37, farmer.
Brown, Hubbard H., 24, "
Brown, Edward E., 33, "
Brown, Newton E., 24, "
Conant, E. Luman, 23, "
Conant, Edwin A., 33, "
Conant, John M., 24, "
Carr, Erwin S., 25, "
Carter, Leonard, 33, hotel keeper.
Cutting, George F., 27, trader.
Cutting, Luther S., 30, farmer.
Chase, Eli R., 25, clerk.
Cheney, Henry H., 21, carpenter.
Conant, Albert, 25, laborer.
Dadman, Orin, 43, farmer.
Evans, Moses W., 22, laborer.
Eaton, Edward N., 26, farmer.
Eager, William E., 31, laborer.
Floyd, Charles W., 28, laborer.
Goodnow, John B., 33, farmer.

Hunt, Samuel M., 33, farmer.
Horr, Richard R., 30, shoemaker.
Hunt, Horatio, 34, carpenter.
Haynes, Nathan C., 28, farmer.
Haynes, George F., 28, "
Jones, John C., 31, laborer.
Jones, Levi S., 38, farmer.
Linehan, John, 28, laborer.
Lamson, Frederick A., 21, laborer.
Moore, Francis U., 29, carpenter.
McCann, Owens, 31, farmer.
Maynard, Moses W., 43, farmer.
Moore, William H., 33, miller.
Moore, Benjamin, 20, miller.
Murphy, George H., 31, laborer.
Nilligan, Morris, 28 "
Newell, Michael, 24, "
Parmenter, Lorenzo, 31, farmer.
Parmenter, Alfred N., 23, "
Parmenter, Alfred T., 23, "
Parmenter, John W., 27, carpenter.
Phillips, John H., 25, laborer.
Puffer, Dexter R., 32, clerk.
Priest, Abraham, 27, farmer.
Puffer, James F., 23, farmer.
Prouty, Augustus, 34, clerk.
Puffer, James J., 34, carpenter.
Parmenter, Joel F., 33, trader.
Pratt, Nathan L., 33, powder-maker.
Pratt, Windsor, 31, cooper.
Pratt, Francis, 24, farmer.

Garfield, John W., 30, shoemaker.
Goodnow, Nahum, 20, laborer.
Gleason, Josiah, 37, laborer.
Goodnow, Elisha, 24, farmer.
Gormain, William, 30, overseer.
Gay, Almer H., 27, shoemaker.
Garfield Samuel H., 20, laborer.
Goodnow Jonas, 42, laborer.
Goodnow, John, 3d, 24, trader.
Heffiman, James, 20, paper-maker.
Hayden, Dana W., 28, farmer.
Hunt, Luther G., 27,   "
Haynes, Andrew, 25,   "
Haynes, Marshal, 22,   "
Hemenway, Adoniram J., 21, clerk.
Hudson, S. Alfred, 23, student.
Haynes, James, 25, laborer.
Haynes, Sylvester, 27, laborer.
Hunt, Edward, 34, farmer.

Pratt, Levi L., 37, farmer.
Parmenter, Tisdale W., 26, farmer.
Rogers, Edwin, 27, butcher.
Richardson, Thos. C., 28, musician.
Richardson, Lyman B., 22, miller.
Stone, William L., 21, farmer.
Stone, George W., Jr., 25, farmer.
Smith Curtis, 20,   "
Smith, Elisha E., 34,   "
Sherman, Theo. S., 30, shoemaker.
Thompson, Alfred N., 31, farmer.
Thompson, Charles, 36,   "
Tilton, John F., 35,   "
Vinton, Porter M., 29, clergyman.
Willis, James L., 25, farmer.
Walker, Francis F., 26, farmer.
Webster, Franklin, 28, machinist.
White, Calvin, 30, laborer.

SECOND CLASS.

Agnew, James, 36, spinner.
Brigham, Rufus, 44, farmer.
Burr, Hiram G., 36, trader.
Casey, Martin, 36, farmer.
Cutter, Joseph D., 42, farmer.
Cutter, Charles A., 37, butcher.
Dakin, Asahel, 41, farmer.
Doyle, Edward, 35, "
Dittling, Felix, 36, "
Dakin, John H., 43, "
Dakin, Jonathan C., 43, farmer.
Fairbank, Nelson, 43,   "
Fairbank, Jona P , 37,   "
Goodnough, Hiram H., 37, farmer.
Goodnough, John, 2d., 38,   "
Goodnow, George, 43,   "
Gough, William J., 36, carder.
Hunt, Jonas S., 36, trader.
Haynes, Reuben, 41, farmer.
Haynes, Hiram, 39   "
Harrington, Edwin, 43, "
Hunt, Aaron, Jr., 43,   "
Haynes, Warren H., 41, farmer.
Hurburt, Thomas P., 43,   "
Hunt, Nicholas B., 42,   "
Haynes, Francis, 39,   "

James, Charles A., 43, machinist.
Jones, William P., 43, shoemaker.
Jones, William F., 35, laborer.
Joice, John, 40, laborer.
Ladd, Thomas, 41, laborer.
Moore, Curtis B., 35, farmer.
Milleman, Elisha, 35, "
Moore, George, 35, "
Murphy, James, 36, laborer.
Noyes, Joseph, 38, farmer.
Puffer, Napoleon B., 42, overseer.
Parmenter, Madison, 36, farmer.
Parmenter, Samuel O., 43, "
Puffer, Otis, 38, mariner.
Parmenter, Addison, 36, farmer.
Pierce, Luke, 40, farmer.
Perry, Levi E., 42, farmer.
Rice, Isaac, 43, laborer.
Rice, John W., 41, farmer.
Rice, Oliver R., 37, farmer.
Richardson, Benj. H., 42, carpenter.
Seymore, Charles, 43, farmer.
Smith, Farwell, 39, farmer.
Sawyer, Theodore W., 44, farmer.
Taylor, Sewall B., 43, machinist.
Taylor, John, 44, carpenter.

Howe, Joseph C., 44, manufacturer. Taylor, George, 41, farmer.
Harriman, John K , 38, carpenter. Tilton, Edward F., 37, powder-maker.
Heard, Augustus, 44, farmer. Tilton, George W., 38, "
Jones, Dexter C., 42, farmer. Willis, George W., 42, carpenter."

But few events of especial prominence, not already mentioned, have transpired in Sudbury thus far during the closing period of the century ; and no record of its commonplace annals will be given. After mentioning the Bicentennial of the Wadsworth Fight, the laying out of an important highway, the George Goodnow Bequest, and the organization of societies, we shall consider in the subsequent chapters several subjects that stand related to each period of the history of Sudbury.

BICENTENNIAL.

April 18, 1876, the town celebrated what was supposed to be the two hundredth anniversary of Wadsworth's Fight at Green Hill   (For true date see page 218.)   At early dawn a salute was fired, and a procession of " Antiques and Horribles " paraded, making a trip to South Sudbury.   Later in the day a procession of the citizens, including the school children, was formed and marched to Wadsworth Monument, which was decorated with the national colors. The following sentiment was offered by Jonas S. Hunt, Esq., and was responded to by Hon. T. B. Hurlbut : " Wadsworth Monument, — The joint tribute of the State of Massachusetts and the town of Sudbury."

Services were held at the Unitarian Church, which consisted of prayer by Rev. George A. Oviatt, an oration by Prof. Edward A. Young of Harvard College, and remarks by Rev. George A. Oviatt, Luther H. Sherman, who spoke for Wayland, John H. Hillis, who spoke for Maynard, and Capt. E. D. Wadsworth of Milton, a descendant of Capt. Samuel Wadsworth.   J. P. Fairbanks was president of the day.   Jonas S. Hunt, Esq., was toast-master, and Homer Rogers chief marshal.   Music was furnished by the Sudbury Cornet Band, Alfred M. Moore of Malden, leader.   The exercises closed by the singing of America.

Nov. 7, 1882, a committee appointed to consider the laying out of a road between the Horatio Hunt place and the railroad junction, reported favorably, and the road was completed.

THE GEORGE GOODNOW BEQUEST.

In November, 1884, it was voted to " accept of a donation of Ten Thousand Dollars offered the Town of Sudbury, by George Goodnow of Boston, for the purpose of establishing a fund, the income of which he desires to be used by the selectmen of said Town for the time being, to assist such citizens of the Town who are not, at the time of receiving the assistance, paupers, but who may for any cause be in need of temporary or private assistance." By motion of Rev. George A. Oviatt, the town voted that, " we do now as a town by vote express our hearty thanks to the donor of this generous Fund, assuring him of our appreciation of his love of his native town, and equally of his noble desire to render aid to the needy therein. And may his sunset of life be bright to the last, and terminate in the day of endless light and blessedness."

Dec. 24, 1884, Goodman Council, No. 868, of the Royal Arcanum was organized.

March 5, 1885, the Sudbury Grange, No. 21, was organized.

In 1889, an unsuccessful effort was made by the Society of the Orthodox Congregational Church to hold their regular Sabbath Day services at South Sudbury. The same year the town took measures for securing a suitable spot for the erection of a High School Building at Sudbury Centre.

CHAPTER XXXI.

CEMETERIES.

First Burial Place. — Old Burying-Ground at Sudbury Centre. — Mount Wadsworth Cemetery. — Mount Pleasant Cemetery. — New Cemetery. — North Sudbury Cemetery. — Burial Customs.

> Our vales are sweet with fern and rose,
>   Our hills are maple-crowned;
> But not from them our fathers chose
>   The village burying-ground.
>
> WHITTIER.

THERE are few, if any, places in our New England towns more suggestive of the past than its ancient burial places. It is there that we find names now but rarely spoken in the places that knew them once, and the old headstones give a record of births, ages and deaths, which perhaps could be found nowhere else. Sudbury has at present five cemeteries within its limits: one at South Sudbury, one at North Sudbury, and three at the Centre; but the first burial place of the town was in East Sudbury, now Wayland.

SUDBURY'S FIRST BURYING-GROUND.

This ancient burial place is in Wayland, on the north side of the road leading to Sudbury Centre, and about a half mile from the railroad station. It has the general appearance of an old-time graveyard. The wild grass covers the toughened and irregular sod, and the uneven surface of the ground indicates that it was long, long ago broken by the sexton's spade. These indications of the existence of old graves are correct. It was the burying-ground of the settlers, and here —

> " Where heaves the turf in many a mouldering heap,
>   Each in his narrow cell forever laid,
>   The rude forefathers of the hamlet sleep."

The older part of this cemetery lies near or beside the county highway, and may be the half acre bought of John Loker for a burial place. Tradition says that prior to the selection of this spot a few interments were made just over the hill to the north, where tradition also states that there was an Indian graveyard. These traditions have perhaps some confirmation in the fact that on the northern hillside remains of human skeletons have been exhumed. An old citizen, Mr. Sumner Draper, states that in his boyhood, when men were at work in the gravel pit in what was known as the "old Indian graveyard," he saw bones which they dug up, that he thought belonged to several human skeletons, and that he had himself in later years dug up a human skull. He also stated that there were two or three flat stones on some graves, which he believed were without any inscription, and that he thought some such stones were removed from the spot long ago.

The town owned thereabouts two or three acres of land, which was generally known as the "old Indian graveyard." But if this land was reserved by the settlers for a burial place, it was not long made use of; for the southerly slope was soon set apart for this purpose, and has continued to be used for more than two centuries and a half. Additions have repeatedly been made to this latter portion, as the generations have passed away, and new graves have been opened to receive them; and thus has the slow, solemn march of that silent company been moving over that midway space, until the two portions are almost joined. Besides the age of the yard, there are other things that make it an interesting spot to the inhabitants of Sudbury. Within its enclosure stood the first meeting-house. (See page 100.) Here lie buried the bodies of those who bore the name of Goodnow, Curtis, Grout, Rutter, Parmenter, Rice, Bent, and others of the early grantees, besides still others of Sudbury's most prominent citizens before the division of the town. Because of the interest that thus attaches to the place, although it is not now within the limits of the town, we will give the inscriptions on some of the older gravestones which lie along the common highway.

MEMENTO MORI.

Here lyethe remains of Ephraim Curtis ESQ^r who departed this lyfe Novr the 17th A D 1759 in the 80th Year of his age. He was a Loving Husband and a Tender Parent a faithful Friend, as a Justice of the Peace he Hon'^d his Commission by adhering steadily to the Rules of Justice. he was Major of a Regiment, in which Office he conducted in such a manner as gave General Satisfaction. He was many years Representative in the General Court, a lover of True Piety, belov'd by all that knew him and Equally Lamented at his Death.

> " Here lea^rn
> the end of man
> Know that thy life
> is but a span."

On this gravestone is a skull and crossbones.

In memory of Capt. Joseph Smith Who died March 9th 1803, aged 87 years.

> Farewell my dear and loving wife
> Farewell my children and my friends
> Until the resurrection day.

Probably the captain of the east side militia. (See period 1775–1800.)

Here lyest ye Body of Mrs Abagail Paris wife to Mr Samuel Paris, who departed this life Feb^ry ye 15th 1759 in y 55th Year of her age.

Probably the wife of the son of Samuel Paris of Witchcraft fame. (See period 1675–1700.)

Here Lyes ye Body of Mrs Patience Browne wife to Maj^r Thomas Browne Aged 59 years. Died Aug^st ye 15, 1706.

Major Thomas Browne was a very prominent Sudbury citizen. (See page 36.)

In memory of Mr. Joseph Rutter, who died Dec. 19th 1781 in ye 78th year of his age.

> Down to the dead, all must descend,
> The saints of God must die.
> While Angels guard their souls to rest,
> In dust their Bodies lie.

Erected in memory of Mrs Mary Rutter wife of Mr. Joseph Rutter who died Sept 2^ond A E 82

Joseph Rutter was a descendant and probably grandson of John Rutter, builder of the first meeting-house, which stood just beside where the remains of Joseph Rutter now lie. (See page 43.)

MEMENTO MORI.

In memory of

Mr. Thomas Bent who died Wednesday morning July the 26th 1775.	Mrs. Mary Bent wife of Mr. Thomas Bent who died Wednesday morning July ye 26th 1775
Ætatis 69.	Ætatis 57.

Our term of time is seventy years
  An age that few survive
But if with more than common
  strength
To eighty we arrive
	Yet then our boasted strength de-
	  cays,
	  To sorrow turns and pain
	So soon the slender thread is cut
	  And we no more remain

Two notable stones are those that mark the graves of Capt. Edmund Goodnow and wife. They are in a horizontal position, and just east of the old meeting-house site. The inscription is rudely cut, and in the language of other years. It is as follows: —

HEARE – LYETH – YE – PRETIOUS – DUST –

OF – THAT – EMENANT – SARVANT –

OF –

GOD – CAP – EDMOND – GOODENOW –

WHO – DIED – YE – 77 – YEARE – OF – HIS –

AYGE – APRIL – YE – 6 – 1688.

HERE – LYETH – YE – BODY – OF – ANNE – YE –
WIFE – OF – CAP – EDMOND – GOODENOW –
WHO – DYED – YE : 9 : OF : MARCH 1676 : AGED –
67 – YEARS.

HERE – LYETH – YE – BODY – OF – JOSEPH –
GOODENOW – WHO – DYED – YE – 30 – OF – MAY :
1676 : AGED – 31 – YEARS. FEBRY – 18 – 1691.

Here lies Buried The Body of yᵉ worthy Joshua Haynes Esq Deceased March yᵉ 29 1757 in the 88 year of His Age. He was a Hearty
Promoter of the Public weal Whose . . Humanity Integrity and Laud-
able Munificence Embalm His name. He was charitable to the Poor
and at his Death gave many Gifts to Particular . . Besides 2 Thousand
Pounds Old Tenor to a Publick School and yᵉ Poor of yᵉ Town of
Sudbury.

Joshua Haynes was the donor of the fund called, in the list
of bequests to Sudbury, the " Ancient Donation Fund."

HERE – LYES – YE – BODY – OF – MR – JONATHAN –
SIMPSON – LATE – OF – BOSTON – WHO – DE-
PARTED – THIS – LIFE – NOVR – 1ˢᵗ – 1773 – IN – THE –
54ᵗʰ YEAR – OF – HIS – AGE.

> Charlestown doth claim his birth,
> Boston his habitation;
> Sudbury hath his grave,
> Where was his expiration.

THE OLD BURYING-GROUND AT SUDBURY CENTRE.

> A winding wall of mossy stone,
> Frost-flung and broken, lines
> A lonesome acre thinly grown
> With grass and wandering vines.
>
> WHITTIER.

The oldest graveyard within the present limits of Sudbury
is at the Centre. It is situated in the north-easterly part of
the village, along the Concord road east of the Methodist
Church. An early record of this burying-place is found in
the proprietor's book, and bears date Feb. 26, 1716–17.
(See pages 121 and 122.) Another record referring to it is
dated June 12, 1725. (See page 292.)

In this old graveyard, for a century and a half or upwards,
what was mortal of many of the west side inhabitants was laid.
The names of Haynes, Hunt, Parmenter, Goodnow, Brown,
Moore and Howe, Bent, Rice, Richardson, Willis, Wheeler,
Jones, Puffer, Hayden, Walker, and a host of others, long
familiar in Sudbury, are to be found on the stones. Unlike the older part of the first yard, at what was East Sudbury, the gravestones are here quite numerous; but, though

many, they do not mark all the graves, which nearly cover the entire space of that "thickly peopled ground." The enclosure is encompassed by a substantial stone wall, which within a few years has been well repaired. The place has but little shrubbery and few trees. Just beyond the road was the pound, near by or on the site of which the hearse house now stands. Within the past few years this yard has been but little used. Now and then the ground has been broken as the fragment of some ancient family has found its resting place among a group of old graves; but these instances are fewer and farther between as time passes by, and it will probably soon cease to be used for new burials, but remain with unbroken turf until the morning of the resurrection. It is a place of sacred association, and as such has been regarded by the town's people; especially was it much visited by them during the intermission between the Sabbath services, when two sermons were preached in one day. Then they visited this quiet spot, read epitaphs, talked of the past, and derived, it may be, such lessons from the suggestive scenes as were a moral and spiritual help. Along the northerly side of the yard is the Sudbury and Concord highway; and ranged beside this are family tombs. One of these is that of Mr. John Goodnow, the donor of the Goodnow Library. Upon others are names of old Sudbury families. Within the yard is only one tomb and that is underground and about westerly of the Plympton monument, and surmounted with a small brick work upon which lies a slate stone, with these words: —

HOPESTILL BROWN, ESQ., TOMBE.

1731.

This tomb contains the remains of descendants of Dea. William Brown, an early grantee, who once resided near Nobscot. The tomb was years ago nearly full, the last burial being about 1852. This burying-ground contains several marble monuments of some considerable size. The first one was erected in 1835, and is commemorative of the Plympton family. The graves of two, at least, of Sudbury's old ministers are there, — Reverends Bigelow and Hurlbut; the inscriptions on the headstones are as follows : —

Sacred to the memory of Rev. Rufus Hurlbut late minister of the church and society in Sudbury. He was born in Southampton, April 21, 1787, and died May 11, 1839. Aged 52.

" Precious in the sight of the Lord is the death of His saints " Jesus said " I am the resurrection and the life, he that believeth in me though he were dead yet shall he live "

In memory of Rev. Jacob Bigelow, Pastor of the Church and Congregation at Sudbury. Born Mar. 2, 1743. Graduated at Harvard College 1766. Ordained in the Gospel Ministry 1772. After a happy and harmonious connexion with the People of his charge 44 years he died Sept 12, 1818. Æt 75 years. Habitual in piety and exemplary in his life & conduct, Cheerful and active in health, patient and resigned in sickness : beloved and respected while living, he was followed to the tomb with grateful remambrance by his relatives and the flock of his charge.

This yard is the burial place of more or less of those who participated in the Concord fight, and subsequent battles and scenes of the Revolutionary period. Notable among these is the grave of Deacon Haynes, upon whose gravestone is this epitaph : —

In memory of Deacon Josiah Haynes who died in Freedom's Cause yᵉ 19th of April 1775 : in the 79th year of his Age.

Come listen all unto this call
Which God doth make to day
For you must die as well as I
And pass from hence away.

(For more concerning Deacon Haynes see Chapter XX.) Other stones at the graves of prominent men of those times are inscribed as follows : —

In memory of Capt. Asahel Wheeler an officer in the Revolution, Died Oct. 28 1822 aged 81 years.

In the northerly part is the grave of Capt. Jabes Puffer, marked with a slate stone slab.

Sacred to the memory of Col. Ezekial How who died Oct. 15, 1796. Ætatis 77.

Sacred in memory of Wm Rice. Esq. who died Dec. 5, 1819. Æt. 82. Whose true character will be better known at the resurrection.

Erected in memory of Mr. John Goodnow who died Oct. 13, 1863. Æt. 101 yrs. 8 mos. 14 ds " The Lord is my Shepherd."

The grave of a servant of Rev. Israel Loring has a stone there thus inscribed : —

Here Lies ye Body of Simeon ye Once Faithful & Beloved Servant of ye Rv^d M Isra^ll Loring, who Died May ye 10, 1755. In ye 22 Year of His Age.

On the stone of Capt. David Haynes, who died 1775, in his eighty-fifth year, is this inscription : —

> Reader
> Death is a debt to Nature Due
> As I have paid it so must You.

On that of Mrs. Mary Willis the inscription is as follows : —

Sacred to the memory of Mrs. Mary Willis who died Oct. 9, 1805. Aged 84 years.

> Sickness sore long time I bore
> Physicians was in vain
> Till GOD did please to give me ease
> And free me from my pain.

Some of the oldest have the following inscriptions : —

Here lyes ye Body of Mr Joseph Brintnal Died June ye 28 : 1731 in ye 49th year of his age.

Here lies Buried ye Body of Deac^n James Haynes who Departed this life Octob^r ye 15th A. D. 1732 In ye 72^d year of his age.

Here lies buried ye body of Mr Abraham Woods J^unr who departed this life July ye 11th A. D. 1742. Age 58 years, 2 M. & 25 D.

The oldest graves are near the centre of the yard. Probably for the first few years after the lot was laid out, burials were less numerous than a little later, as the associations connected with the more ancient churchyard in the east part of the town would naturally lead to its somewhat continued use by the west side inhabitants.

MOUNT WADSWORTH CEMETERY.

It lies upon a sunlit slope,
  Where, lingering late, the sunset rays
Aslant their golden radiance cast,
  And lovingly day longest stays.

This cemetery is at South Sudbury, and formerly belonged
to the Israel Howe Browne estate. It was originally quite
small, having been enlarged several times. Formerly the
last lot to the eastward was that of Asahel Haynes, and the
northern boundary was just north of the tombs or about midway of the present width of the cemetery. The entrance
was formerly south of Dr. Levi Goodenough's house and
joined his grounds, but it was changed about the time the
Wadsworth monument was erected, and now leads from the
avenue that goes to the monument. In presenting the various changes that have been made in this cemetery, we quote
from a paper prepared by A. J. Goodenough in 1881, and read
before an audience in Sudbury Town Hall: " The cemetery
was first enlarged in 1842. Miss Jerusha Howe, who died
Feb. 21, 1842, had provided in her will a sum of money for a
monument, which at that time seemed an extravagant outlay.
Her brother, Lyman Howe, Esq., wishing to obtain a suitable site for so costly a structure, and no satisfactory place
within the old grounds being found, he selected the eminence north of the grounds — then a stony pasture — as
being more sightly and appropriate. Mr. Browne was unwilling at first to have him occupy this place, as it involved
the enlargement of the grounds, and among other difficulties
did not wish to see land further north [used] for burial purposes without the consent of Dr. Goodenough, as it might
injure his well of water. After considerable consultation on
the subject, Mr. Browne yielded, Dr. Goodenough giving his
consent, *provided* no lots should be sold any nearer his land
than Miss Howe's. This increased the size of the cemetery
to about double the original extent. But many years did
not pass before the new ground was almost wholly occupied;
Miss Howe's monument attracting much attention, and being
probably the principal cause of many selecting their lots

here. By some means, however, four lots were sold between Miss Howe's and Dr. Goodenough's land, and three of them were occupied. This proved a difficulty, as they not only interfered with the entrance to Miss Howe's lot, but Dr. Goodenough became anxious lest the water in his well should be injured by this encroachment. Accordingly he bought the three lots that had been occupied, paying the owners for new lots, as well as the expense of removing the remains, and Esquire Howe buying out the unoccupied lot. Thus they hoped to secure for the future open grounds, which might be either a grassy lawn, or be beautified with flowers, and thus render those living near free from danger in their wells of water, Mr. Brown assuring the doctor that the ground should not be used for burial purposes during his lifetime. One of these lots came so close to Miss Howe's that access could scarcely be had to it, no space being left for a walk between. This probably was the reason why Mr. Howe united in purchasing the lots. It is presumable that this was the occasion of a general agreement between the owners of lots, to make walks between their lots, for no provision was made for walks when the cemetery was first laid out."

Since the paper from which we have quoted was written, the cemetery has been still further enlarged until it now extends nearly back to the hill. A few years ago, there was a small growth of trees along the avenues and about more or less of the lots, but they were recently removed lest they should deface the stones. The arch at present over the east entrance to the cemetery was erected in 1879, by Mr. Israel H. Browne over the west entrance. It was completed July, 1879. There are those who remember the old man as he stood and surveyed it, leaning on his staff, his eyes filled with tears. "This will stand," he said, "when I am gone. The rest will live to see it, but I shall not be here long." He died within a few weeks.

The following is from a newspaper notice of his death: "Mr. I. H. Browne, who recently caused the arch to be erected over the entrance to Mt. Wadsworth, was suddenly stricken with paralysis Aug. 10 [1879]. He rallied for a

few days, then swiftly sank away, and in two weeks passed
from earth, dying Aug. 25, proving his own words prophetic,
that he might be the first from town borne beneath the arch
for burial." The erection of this arch permanently affixed the
name Mount Wadsworth to the grounds. After the cemetery came under the control of the cemetery corporation the
arch was removed to its present position.

The first monument erected in this yard was that of
Jerusha Howe, and placed in the first enlargement of the
grounds. The next was a plain marble shaft put up by Dr.
Goodenough, which was the first in the old ground. According to an estimate made about the year 1881, the
number buried in the old part of the cemetery was about
one hundred and thirty-three, and in the new parts one hundred and thirty-nine. This estimate does not include those in
the tombs, nor several graves nearly or quite levelled down.
The plan of making this a common burial place, it is supposed, was first conceived of by Mrs. Lucy Hinckly, a
daughter of Mr. I. H. Browne, whose brother had recently
died and been interred in the family tomb at the Centre.
About that time there also died at South Sudbury Mrs.
John Browne, Sen., and Mr. Gideon Richardson and wife,
who were likewise buried at Sudbury Centre. The desire to
have the bodies of these friends nearer by, the fact that the
old burial-ground was so full, and that the spot was suitable,
and made appropriate by the grave of Captain Wadsworth
and his men, all contributed to the setting apart of this
ground as a cemetery. The first interments were of remains
removed from the old burying yard, and were made June 20,
1835. It is supposed the bodies then removed were those
of Elbridge, Melissa, and John Calvin Richardson and Edwin
H. Browne; that the latter was one of them is indicated by
the following from a letter of Mrs. L. Fairbanks, daughter of
I. H. Browne: "I have just been to the new cemetery, where
dear little Edwin now rests. He was removed with some
others some time ago from the old brick tomb where our
ancestors were all buried, and now they are only a little distance from our home. Lucy was the first to suggest to have
Father plan this new burial place."

Mr. John Browne, Sr., the brothers Gardner, Luther, and Sewall Hunt formed a plan to build jointly three tombs. Mr. Luther Hunt, dying April 17, 1836, did not see the work completed which he had helped to plan. The tomb of Mr. John Browne, Sr., has inscribed on it J. and E. Browne. These tombs were erected in 1836. The stone was quarried at the foot of Nobscot hill, on the north-east side, and cut, hewn and fitted at the cemetery by Messrs. Damon and Penniman, who were the principal workmen. The granite, it is supposed, was from a hugh boulder, rather than from a ledge native to the hill. The next tomb was erected by C. G. Cutler, in 1839, and later, followed those of Roland Cutler and A. and E. Kidder; the latter of which has been somewhat altered within the last few years. In this tomb were deposited for a little time the remains of Captain Wadsworth's men, after they were taken up for removal to the present enclosure.

ORGANIZATION OF THE MOUNT WADSWORTH CEMETERY CORPORATION.

COMMONWEALTH OF MASSCHUSETTS.

MIDDLESEX SS.   SUDBURY, Jan. 12, 1887.

To the proprietors of "Mount Wadsworth Cemetery" in Sudbury, in said County.

A majority in interest of the proprietors of Mount Wadsworth Cemetery, having petitioned to Jonas S. Hunt, a justice of the peace in said county, that they desire to organize a corporation under the public statutes, the said justice of the peace has issued his warrant directed to the undersigned, and the substance of said warrant is: That a meeting of said proprietors will be held at the chapel in South Sudbury on Monday, the 31st day of January, A. D. 1887, at 2 o'clock P. M., for the purpose of organizing a corporation of the proprietors of Mount Wadsworth Cemetery, to elect all necessary officers of such Corporation and to transact such other business as may properly come before the meeting.   HUBBARD H. BROWN,

One of said Proprietors.

CERTIFICATE OF ORGANIZATION.

We, Rufus H. Hurlbut, President, Hubbard H. Brown, Treasurer, and Joseph C. Howe, John B. Goodnow and Nahum Goodnow, being a majority of the Board of Directors of the Mount Wadsworth Cemetery Association, in compliance with the requirements of the Public Statutes, do hereby certify that the following is a true copy of the agreement of association to constitute said corporation, with the names of the subscribers thereto :

"We whose names are hereto subscribed do, by this agreement, associate ourselves with the intention to constitute a corporation according to the provisions of the eighty-second chapter of the Public Statutes of the Commonwealth of Massachusetts and the acts in amendment thereof and in addition thereto.

"The name by which this corporation shall be known is 'Mount Wadsworth Cemetery.'

"The purpose for which the corporation is constituted is to hold land and tombs for a place of sepulture, and such buildings as may be necessary for such purpose, with the right to sell burial lots, erect tombs, and with all privileges such corporations are entitled to under the Statutes of Massachusetts.

"The place within which the corporation is established or located is the town of Sudbury, within said Commonwealth.

"In witness whereof, we have hereunto set our hands this twelfth day of January, in the year eighteen hundred and eighty-seven."

SAMUEL B. ROGERS,	JONAS S. HUNT,
JOHN B. GOODNOW,	EDWARD E. BROWN,
NAHUM GOODNOW,	HIRAM G. BURR,
HUBBARD H. BROWN,	JAMES P. CARPENTER,
RUFUS H. HURLBUT,	WILLIAM L. STONE,
ATHERTON W. ROGERS,	EDWARD N. EATON,
LUTHER S. CUTTING,	W. A. AMES,
JOSEPH C. HOWE,	STEPHEN MOORE,
WALTER ROGERS,	HOMER ROGERS,
CHARLES L. GOODNOW,	GEO. A. OVIATT,
FRED. C. FISHER,	MRS. JOHN A. GOODWIN,
GEORGE W. HUNT,	MRS. J. D. GOODENOUGH.

"That the first meeting of the subscribers to said agreement was held on the thirty-first day of January, in the year eighteen hundred and eighty-seven, and by adjournment on the fourteenth day of February, in said year.

"In witness whereof, we have hereunto signed our names this fourteenth day of February, in the year eighteen hundred and eighty-seven."

RUFUS H. HURLBUT,
HUBBARD H. BROWN,
JOHN B. GOODNOW,
JOSEPH C. HOWE,
NAHUM GOODNOW.

COMMONWEALTH OF MASSACHUSETTS.

MIDDLESEX SS.   Feb. 14, 1887.

Then personally appeared the above-named Rufus H. Hurlbut, Hub-

bard H. Brown, John B. Goodnow, Joseph C. Howe and Nahum Goodnow, and severally made oath that the foregoing certificate, by them
subscribed, is true to the best of their knowledge and belief.

Before me,

JONAS S. HUNT,
Justice of the Peace.

TOWN CLERK'S OFFICE, SUDBURY, March 1, 1887.

The above certificate received and recorded with " Sudbury Records
of Organization of Corporations."

ATTEST :

JONAS S. HUNT,
Town Clerk.

PROCEEDINGS OF FIRST MEETING.

Jan. 31, 1887.

Pursuant to a warrant issued by Jonas S. Hunt, justice of the peace,
dated Jan. 12, 1887, on petition of Samuel B. Rogers and others interested in the Mount Wadsworth Cemetery, so called, a meeting was held
in the chapel at South Sudbury, for the purpose of organizing a corporation under the Public Statutes of Massachusetts.

Said meeting was called to order and the warrant read by Hubbard
H. Brown, to whom said warrant was directed, and the several articles
were acted upon as follows :

ARTICLE 1.   Chose Rufus H. Hurlbut moderator.

ART. 2.   Chose Jonas S. Hunt clerk.

ART. 3.   Voted to proceed to organize a corporation to be called the
Mount Wadsworth Cemetery.

ART. 4.   Voted to choose necessary officers for said corporation by
ballot ; said officers to consist of the following, viz. : a President, Clerk,
Treasurer, three Trustees and five Directors, and the following were
chosen : Rufus H. Hurlbut, President ; Jonas S. Hunt, Clerk ; Hubbard
H. Brown, Treasurer ; John B. Goodnow, Nahum Goodnow and Joseph
C. Howe, Trustees ; Rufus H. Hurlbut, John B. Goodnow, Nahum
Goodnow, Joseph C. Howe and Hiram G. Burr, Directors.

Soon after the death of Mr. Israel H. Browne, the former
owner of the cemetery grounds, his heirs sold their interest
in the property to five persons, who conveyed it to the
Mount Wadsworth Corporation soon after its organization.
On the southerly side of the cemetery is the grave of Hon.
John Goodwin, once Speaker of the House of Representatives.   In the north-easterly corner, as it was about 1850,
was the original Wadsworth grave.   Because of the former
existence of that grave and the present Wadsworth monument, this cemetery is of more than ordinary importance,

and will long be visited by those interested in the history of
Captain Wadsworth and his men.

MOUNT PLEASANT CEMETERY.

" In that village on the hill
   Never is sound of smithy or mill;
   The houses are thatched with grass and flowers,
   Never a clock to tell the hours;

.   .   .   .

All the village lie asleep;
   Never again to sow or reap;
   Never in dreams to moan or sigh,
   Silent and idle and low they lie."

The third cemetery laid out in Sudbury is at the Centre
and is called Mount Pleasant.   As its name suggests, it is
pleasantly situated on a hill and is just north of the common.
The original name was " Pine Hill," and later, it took the
name of "Pendleton Hill."   In the second book of Town
Records is the following, referring to land near it, "laid out
to the right of Briant Pendleton sixteen acres and one hundred and forty rods on and adjoining to the Pine Hill near
to and north-westerly of the meeting house on Rocky Plane
(Sudbury Centre) in the West Precinct in said Sudbury."
(See page 292.)   This cemetery contains about four acres,
which were bought of Mrs. Reuben Rice, afterwards Mrs.
Thomas Bent, by a company of proprietors, the original
members of which were Aaron Hunt, Cyrus Hunt, Charles
Gerry, William Maynard, Abel B. Jones, Thomas Stearns,
Samuel Jones, Asa Jones.   The land cost one hundred
dollars, and the proprietors paid twelve dollars and a half
apiece.   After the original purchase, a small three-cornered
strip was bought of William Maynard for a passage-way to
the town graveyard.   It was set apart for burial purposes
soon after 1840.   The first proprietor's meeting was held
May 24, 1845, and the following officers were elected: Abel
B. Jones, Moderator; Charles Stearns, Clerk; Aaron Hunt,
Treasurer; Aaron Hunt, Abel B. Jones, Charles Stearns,
Directors.   The first body buried there was that of Capt.
Samuel Jones, and about the same time that of Dr. Thomas

Stearns. There is a fine view from the hill to the northward, and, though the place is so near a much travelled
highway, it is so situated as to be quite secluded.

THE NEW CEMETERY.

Near Mount Pleasant is a new cemetery that is owned by
the town. It was purchased a few years ago, and has an
entrance on the south to the county road, near the tomb of
John Goodnow.

NORTH SUDBURY CEMETERY.

It knew the glow of eventide,
  The sunrise and the noon,
And glorified and sanctified
  It slept beneath the moon.
                    WHITTIER.

The North Sudbury Cemetery is situated upon a sunny
knoll and consists of one and six-tenths acres of land, formerly owned by Reuben Haynes, and purchased by a company for a cemetery in 1843. It is about one-eighth of a
mile from North Sudbury village on the county road leading from Framingham to Concord. It is quite regularly
laid out in paths, with a carriage-way extending about it.
The lots are in area twenty-four by thirty feet; there are
about two hundred and eleven persons buried in the yard
and tombs. The first person buried there was Sumner
Haynes, son of Josiah, Jr., and Mary Haynes, who died
Aug. 6, 1843.

Soon after, the bodies of the following persons were removed from the old cemetery at Sudbury Centre and interred
here.

LYDIA,
WIFE OF JOSIAH HAYNES,
Died Mar. 3, 1843.
Aged 66.
Gone from earth to bloom in heaven.

HARRIET AMELIA,
DAUGHTER OF LEANDER AND HARRIET HAYNES,
Died Nov. 28, 1839.

SUSAN HUNT,

DAUGHTER OF ISRAEL AND RUTH HUNT.

Died Jan. 2, 1817.

In this yard lie buried Capt. Israel Haynes, Nahum Thompson, Esq., and Deacon Levi Dakin. Among the aged people are John Hunt, born Aug. 16, 1777, died April 1, 1873; Willard Maynard, died June 29, 1879, aged ninety-two, and Josiah Haynes, died Sept. 6, 1857, aged eighty-nine years, five months. Two soldiers who died during the Civil War are buried here.

OLIVER M. RICHARDS,

MEMBER OF CO. G.

47TH REG'T MASS. VOLS.

Died Sept. 5, 1863.

Aet. 36 yrs. 5 m.

The grave has claimed our cherished one.
Father, teach us to say, " Thy will be done."
On those bright plains, that ever blessed shore,
We hope to meet thee there, to part no more.

HENRY L. HAYNES,

KILLED AT THE BATTLE OF

BERRYVILLE VA.

Sept. 19, 1864.   Aet. 36 yrs.

A MEMBER OF COMPANY C, 14 REG. N. H. VOLS.

Here are two tombs, severally inscribed : —

ISRAEL HUNT'S TOMB

1845.

ELISHA MOORE

1861.

BURIAL CUSTOMS.

For thus our fathers testified —
That he might read who ran
The emptiness of human pride,
The nothingness of man.

WHITTIER.

The piety of our ancestors left little room for customs that were senseless or uninstructive. If they were severely solemn, they were devoutly so; and, if they employed some curious devices, it was for the promotion of good. The position of their gravestones shows that the dead were laid with the feet toward the east, or, as it was termed, "facing the east." Whence and why this custom, we know not. It might have had reference to the star of the east that announced the birthplace of Christ; but, whatever the cause, it doubtless was suggested by some religious idea. To us it is a strong reminder of the words of John Bunyan: "The pilgrim they laid in a large upper chamber whose window opened towards the sun rising, the name of the chamber was Peace, where he slept till break of day, and then he awoke and sang."

The character of the gravestones was another peculiarity of those primitive times. It would seem the object was to impart to these mementos of the departed the most sombre aspect imaginable. As no flowers but those that were strewn by God's pitying hand were ever suffered to intrude their gay, sweet presence within the solemn enclosure, so the nearest approach to anything like sympathetic embellishment on those dark slabs was the weeping willow, which drooped its long branches over a funeral urn. But the more common ornament was the "skull and cross-bones," under which were uncouth markings and strange inscriptions. Sometimes the stones were placed in groups, sometimes in irregular rows. Some were placed upright and others horizontal on the ground; but, as the latter are few and of very early date, we infer that this mode was exceptional or that it soon passed out of use. Perhaps it was a wise precaution in those far-off times to protect the grave from the wild beasts which were

prowling about through the adjacent forests in search of prey.
Another peculiarity is the fewness of the stones in our old
graveyards. A casual glance might lead one to think they
were full of slate-stone slabs, but actual count gives only a
few hundred for all who died in the first century and a half.
Indeed, in the older portion of the East Sudbury grave
yard there are only two or three scores of stones, yet the
yard contains the remains of a large portion of the town's
early inhabitants. Indeed, a new grave can hardly be dug
without intruding upon an old one. This seems to show
that the practice of marking graves in old times was the
exception and not the rule. Still another characteristic
feature of these ancient grounds was their barren and neglected aspect. The graves were gradually levelled by the
touch of time, the ground became uneven and rough and
covered over with briars and wild grass. Yet we may believe these spots were not in reality neglected nor forsaken,
for, though the floral and decorative offering was a thing
unknown, many an irregular, beaten path testified that the
place of their dead was an oft frequented spot.

In early times the dead were carried to the place of burial
by the hands of friends. No hearse was used till about
1800, when one was purchased at a cost of fifty dollars. In
process of time a bier was used, and, as late as the beginning
of this century, the body was carried on the shoulders of the
bearers. In 1715, the town granted " three pounds for providing a burying cloth for ye town's use." In 1792, it voted
to provide two burying cloths; these were to throw over the
remains in their transit to the grave. This is indicated by
the following record : —

" Lieut. Thomas Rutter is chosen to dig graves, to carry
the bier and the cloth to the place where the deceased person
hath need of the use thereof, and shall be paid two shillings
and six pence in money for every individual person."

In early times, gloves were provided for funeral occasions.
We are informed of this repeatedly by the records of the
town. About 1773, " To James Brown, for 6 pairs of gloves
for Isaac Allen's child's funeral — 11 — "

" To Col. Noyes for 7 pairs gloves for Isaac Allen's burial
— 13 — "

" To Cornelius Wood for 3 pairs gloves for John Goodenow's funeral." This was about 1673.

Almost down to the present time the good old custom prevailed of ringing the bell on the occasion of a death. How
it used to break into the monotony of our daily toil to have
the silence suddenly broken by the slow tolling bell, that
said plainer than words that another soul had dropped into
eternity. Now a pause — listen! three times three — a man,
or, three times two — a woman. Another pause, and then
strokes corresponding in number to the years of the deceased.
On the morning of the funeral the bell tolled again, and also
when the procession moved to the grave.

As late as 1860, it was common to have a note read, " put
up " the phrase was, in church on the Sabbath following
a death, in which the nearest relatives asked " the prayers
of the church that the death be sanctified to them for their
spiritual good."

The grounds early used for burial were owned by the town
and set apart for its common use. No private parties
possessed " God's acre " then. Proprietary lots were unknown in Sudbury one hundred years ago. Every citizen
had a right to a spot for burial wherever in the town's burying-ground the friends might choose to take it. The rich
and poor were alike borne to this common spot ; caste was
laid aside, and nothing save the slab at the grave's head
might indicate the former position of the silent occupant
of the old-time burial place. The graves of households
were often in groups, reminding one of our present family
lots, but this was by common consent, and not by any titled
right to the spot.

The expense of funerals in those early days was much less
than at present. The coffin was made by the village carpenter of common pine boards, and was usually colored red.
The following are bills for coffins about a hundred years ago :

" Aug. 21st, 1781, Isaac Hunt D^r to James Thompson ' to
a coffin for his Father, 0 : 10 : 0.' "

" 1800, ' For making a coffin for a woman, 1.67.' "

"1806, 'To Peter Willard for a coffin for Elizabeth Good-now, 1.30.'"

"The coffin of Rev. Jacob Bryelow cost $10.00, and dig-ging the grave and attending his funeral was $2.00."

CHAPTER XXXII.

TAVERNS.

Early Names. — Character and Importance. — First Tavern. — Others on the East Side. — Taverns in the South Part of the Town. — De-scription of the South Sudbury Tavern. — "Howe's Tavern," or the "Wayside Inn." — Mr. Longfellow's Connection with it. — Location and Early History. — Description. — The Last Landlord. — Tradi-tions Concerning it. — Taverns on the Central Road of the Town. — Taverns at North Sudbury.

> Whoe'er has travelled life's dull round,
> Where'er his stages may have been,
> May sigh to think that he has found
> His warmest welcome at an inn.
>
> SHENSTONE.

THE Public House was from an early date considered in Sudbury an important place. In 1653 or 1654 we find it on record that "John Parmenter, senior, shall keep a house of common entertainment, and that the court shall be moved on his behalf to grant a license to him." (Town Records, page 115.) From this early period for the space of more than two centuries public houses were kept here and there. At first they were called "Ordinaries," at other times Public Houses, but generally the term Tavern was used. In one prominent instance has the term Inn been applied, and that in connection with Howe's Tavern, which Mr. Longfellow called the "Wayside Inn."

The business of these places was to provide travelers with lodging and food, or to furnish "entertainment for man and beast." They were to an extent under the control of the town, as is indicated in a record of Oct. 4, 1684, when it was ordered that upon the "uncomfortable representations and reports concerning the miscarriage of things at the Ordinary : : : : : : : : : three or four of the selectmen, in the name of the rest, do particularly inquire into all matters relating thereto." In all of these taverns strong drink was probably sold. Licenses were granted by the Provincial or Colonial Court, and the landlords were usually men of some prominence. Taverns were considered useful places in the early times, and laws existed relating to the rights of both landlord and guest. In the period of the Revolutionary War, when a price-list was determined at Sudbury for various common commodities, the following was established for taverns : —

> 1779 — Mugg West India Phlip 15
> New England Do 12
> Toddy in proportion
> A Good Dinner 20
> Common Do 12
> Best Supper & Breakfast 15 Each.
> Common Do 12, Lodging 4.

The "Parmenter Tavern" was the first one kept in town, and was in what is now Wayland, on the late Dana Parmenter estate, a little westerly of the present Parmenter house. The building was standing about eighty years since, and was looking old then. It was a large square house, and in the bar-room was a high bar. There the council was entertained which the court appointed to settle the famous "cow common controversy." Subsequently, taverns at East Sudbury were kept as follows: one a little easterly of William Baldwin's, one at the Centre, now called the "Pequod House," one west of Reeves' hill, at the Reeves' place, one at the Corner, and one at the end of the old causeway, near the gravel pit. The tavern at the East Sudbury Centre was kept nearly a hundred years ago by John Stone, father of William who afterwards kept one at Sudbury.

The taverns that were on the west side the river, or within the present town limits, were on the three principal highways that passed easterly and westerly through the town. At the south part they were on the Boston and Worcester road. The first beyond that by the gravel pit, was on the John Taylor place, and kept by Mr. Wheeler at the time of the Revolutionary War. The next was that at South Sudbury. This house was of medium size, had two stories and a small porch in front. It stood at the corner of the Sudbury Centre and Boston and Worcester roads, and at a point south or south-east of the Goodnow Library. To the right and left of it were large barns and driveways, with numerous stalls, and between them and the house was a line of sheds, one of which had feeding troughs for horses. It could probably put up from twenty-five to fifty horses, and in the old days of staging and teaming it was a lively place. At the beginning of this century the tavern looked old, and was at about that time occupied by a Mr. Sawin. Subsequently, it had several landlords. One of the last whose sign swung there was S. G. Fessenden, who occupied the place about forty years ago. There was formerly a bowling alley and ball-room attached to the place. A stable was kept there, and it was the terminus of the stage route from Stony Brook to Sudbury. This place was formerly a landmark in the village of South Sudbury, and when removed made a great change in the old-time look of the place. It was in appearance a typical tavern. Facing southward, it looked smilingly upon the approaching traveler, with its little roofed porch around which the clustering woodbine clung, while just in front and beyond the short circular drive which gently curved from the country road, was the "sign post" and "martin box" to which the martins annually came. Besides these, was the old ash-tree that still stands, and all taken together made pleasant surroundings that were quite appropriate to a country inn. A tavern was kept for a while at the Stone place, about a mile west of Mill Village. Mr. William Stone was its only proprietor, and it years ago ceased to be used as a public house. Beyond the bridge a tavern was early kept on the George Pitts place. (See page 493.)

THE WAYSIDE INN.

The scroll reads by the name of Howe.
LONGFELLOW.

The fifth tavern on the Boston road through Sudbury, or the last toward Marlboro, is the old "Howe Tavern," or the famous "Wayside Inn" of Longfellow. This well-known hostelry scarcely needs any description by us. Pictures of it by pencil and pen have been many times made, and have variously portrayed its quaint characteristics. But a few facts here will be proper; and, first, as to the poet Longfellow's connection with it. It is supposed that he never visited the spot more than twice, and that then his visits were short. Once, in his youth, it is believed that he stopped there while on his way to New York, to take passage for Europe, and once, years later, at which time the writer saw him at South Sudbury with his friend J. T. Fields, as they stopped at the house of a relative of the Howe family to inquire about the Howe coat-of-arms. Thus limited was Mr. Longfellow's personal knowledge of the place, and even when on the premises it is said that he received legends and traditions from a source somewhat questionable. The truth is, the place was early brought into notoriety by summer boarders, who came from the suburban towns, prominent among whom were Dr. Parsons and Prof. Treadwell of Cambridge. The former of these first mentioned "Howe's Tavern" in verse, and from his writings, and from information obtained from others, Mr. Longfellow doubtless derived much of his material; and about these facts he arranged such a setting of romance and legendary lore as his ready mind knew how to employ.

But stripped of every feature of romance which may properly have been given it by the great poet's pen, the Wayside Inn is a grand old landmark. It was built about the beginning of the eighteenth century by David Howe, who in 1702 received of his father, Samuel Howe, a son of John one of the town's early grantees, a tract of one hundred and thirty acres of land in the "New Grant" territory. (See Chapter X.) The land upon which this ancient ordinary was built is situated in what was called the fourth squadron of the New Grants, and was probably either lot No. 48, which was assigned in the land apportionment in 1651 to Mr. William Pelham, or lot No. 49, which was just south of Mr. Pelham's, and was assigned at the same time to Mr. John Parmenter, Jr. Beyond these two lots, southerly, was that assigned to Thomas King, and adjacent to this, on the south, was the "Cowpen Land," which, like the others, was a one hundred and thirty acre lot, and joined the then "wilderness lands," or the territory of what is now Framingham. These lots abutted easterly, on the thirty-rod highway which ran north and south through the town, and westerly, on what is now Marlboro. The lot of land upon which the tavern was built was not the lot formerly assigned to John Howe, the grandfather of David, in the apportionment of 1651. That tract was lot No. 16, and situated in the second squadron, which was the north-easterly one of the "New Grants." But Mr. John Howe may have exchanged that lot for another, or, if it passed by inheritance to Samuel, his son, it might by him have been exchanged or sold, and No. 48 of the fourth squadron bought, or it may be that David, the grandson, made the change. As the "New Grant," though allowed in 1649, and laid out and apportioned by lot in 1651, was not purchased of the Indians until 1684, great changes doubtless took place in the ownership. But, however the change in this case came about, David selected this spot for his home, and at about the time of the gift began to build. During the process of constructing the house, tradition says, the workmen resorted for safety at night to the Parmenter garrison, a place about a half-mile away. (See Chapter XI.) The safety sought was probably from the raids of Indians, who, long after Philip's War closed, made occasional incursions upon the borders of the frontier towns. At or about the time of its erection, it was opened as a public house, and, in 1746, Col. Ezekiel Howe, of Revolutionary fame, put up the sign of the "Red Horse," which gave it the name that it went by for years, namely, the "Red Horse Tavern." In 1796, Col. Ezekiel Howe died, and his son Adam took the place and kept the tavern for forty years. At the death

THE WAYSIDE INN.

of Adam it went into the hands of Lyman, who continued it as an inn until near 1866, about which time it passed out of the hands of an owner by the name of Howe. Thus, for more than a century and a half, and by representatives of four generations of the Howe family, was this place kept as an inn. In the earlier times this house was of considerable consequence to travelers. It was quite capacious for either the colonial or the provincial period, and was within about an easy day's journey to Massachusetts Bay. The road by it was a grand thoroughfare westward. Sudbury, in those years, was one of the foremost towns of Middlesex County in population, influence and wealth, while the Howe family took rank among the first families of the country about. The seclusion of this quiet spot to-day is not indicative of what it was in the days of the old stage period, and when places since made prominent by the passage of a railroad through them were almost wholly or quite unknown. In the times of the wars against the Indians and French it was a common halting place for troops, as they marched to the front or returned to their homes in the Bay towns. It was largely patronized by the up-country marketers, who, by their frequent coming and going, with their large canvas-topped wagons, made the highway past this ordinary look like the outlet of a busy mart. Stages also enlivened the scene. The sound of the post-horn, as it announced the near approach of the coach, was the signal for the hostler and housemaid to prepare refreshment for man and beast. In short, few country taverns were better situated than this to gain patronage in the days when few towns of the province were better known than old Sudbury. This place, noted, capacious and thickly mantled with years, is thus fitly described by Mr. Longfellow: —

As ancient is this hostelry
As any in the land may be,
Built in the old Colonial day,
When men lived in a grander way
With ampler hospitality;
A kind of old Hobgoblin Hall,
Now somewhat fallen to decay,

With weather-stains upon the wall,
And stairways worn, and crazy doors,
And creaking and uneven floors,
And chimneys huge and tiled and tall.

The region about this old ordinary corresponds to the
building itself, reminding one of the Sleepy Hollow among
the highlands of the Hudson described by Washington Irv-
ing.   It is on the edge of the plain lands of the Peakham
district, just at the foot of the northernmost spur of Nobscot
Hill.   To the westward, a few rods, is the upper branch of
Hop Brook, with its faint fringe of meadow lands, over
which the county road gently curves.   In the near neighborhood are patches of old forest growth, whose tall trees
tower upward like sentinels in the view of passers along the
county road.   Indeed, so aptly does Mr. Longfellow describe
the place where the house is situated that we quote further
from his beautiful verse.

A region of repose it seems,
A place of slumber and of dreams,
Remote among the wooded hills!
For there no noisy railroad speeds
Its torch-race, scattering smoke and gleeds.

Along the highway to the eastward in the direction of
South Sudbury, which from this place is about two miles
distant, are still standing several ancient oaks.   These trees
were, doubtless, standing and had considerable growth when
lot number forty-eight was of the town's common land, and
owned by Tantamous and others who signed the Indian
deed in 1684, by which the new grant lands were conveyed.
Beneath them Washington and his retinue passed, and perhaps Wadsworth and Brocklebank when they sped in their
haste to save Sudbury from Philip, and a long procession
of travelers, since the opening of the way to Marlboro from
the Hop Brook mill, has passed under their venerable shade.
Soldiers to Ticonderoga and Crown Point, and the various
expeditions to the west and north in the Revolutionary and
French and Indian Wars have halted in their march as they
approached this picket line of ancient oaks that were deployed at the approach to the Inn.

Ancient Druid never worshipped
  Beneath grander oaks than these;
Never shadows richer, deeper,
  Than have cast these giant trees.

.   .   .   .

Monuments of earthly grandeur —
  Shrines at which the people bow,
Yielding homage as to nobles
  Of the honored name of Howe.

.   .   .   .

Like an old baronial castle
  This weird structure holds its place,
Through whose portals has departed
  Every remnant of the race.

LUCINDA (BROWN) FAIRBANKS.

There is now about the place an aspect of vacancy, as if something mighty were gone, and very appropriate are still further words of the poet Longfellow.

Round this old-fashioned, quaint abode
Deep silence reigned, save when a gust
Went rushing down the country road,
And skeletons of leaves and dust,
A moment quickened by its breath,
Shuddered, and danced their dance of death,
And, through the ancient oaks o'erhead,
Mysterious voices moaned and fled.

We will now briefly state something concerning the house, and the family in later years. The structure of the building is quaint. It has a gable roof which rests on low-posted walls, while L's extend from the main body toward the east and west. It stands by the roadside, facing the south, while here and there, not far from it, are the huge trunks of decaying trees, with branches growing more and more scant as the years pass by. It is said that in the house are eighty-one windows. There is upon one of the window panes, cut with a diamond, this sentence : —

What do you think
Here is good drink
Perhaps you may not know it,
If not in haste, do stop and taste
You merry folks will show it.

William Molineux, Jr., Boston, June 24, 1776.

The house was furnished with a hall, the typical kitchen
of a country inn, the bar-room with its high counter, while
outside and beyond the road and nearly in front was swung
the red-horse sign.

Squire Lyman Howe, the last landlord of the inn and the
one of Mr. Longfellow's poem, was a man rather imposing
in appearance, somewhat dignified and grave. He was at
one time a prominent singer in the Congregational choir, a
school committee man, and justice of the peace. Years ago,
he was a familiar object to the villagers of South Sudbury,
riding in his chaise with the top tipped back, as he went to
the post-office or to visit the district schools; and he fitly
represented, in his younger and more prosperous years, the
family of Howe. He lived a bachelor and was the last link
of an illustrious lineage. As a tavern-keeper, he did less
and less business as his years increased, and finally the
landlord died at the inn, the last of the name of Howe who
lived at that famous house. Since his death, the place has
been a resort for pleasure-seekers and people of antiquarian
tastes. It has been visited from far and near, and so it will
continue to be as time passes by. Traditions concerning it
may gather and grow, and treasures of colonial art may be
traced to it, till, like the alleged articles of the "Mayflow-
er's" illustrious cargo, the original place of deposit could
not have contained them all. Indeed, marvellous stories
have already been told of the auction that followed the death
of Squire Lyman Howe, but these stories are extravagant.
A few articles that were rare and relic-like may have been
sold, but, for the most part, it was only a commonplace sale
at the inn when the landlord died. Probably the house was
largely depleted of what it once contained; the family never
was one of great wealth, and the circumstances attending
the life of the last landlord would naturally scatter many
of the furnishings of the old-time inn. The piano that was
sold was the first one ever brought into the town. Strange
stories have also been told as to occasional guests at this
ancient "ordinary." It has been said that Captain Wadsworth here rested and refreshed his men on his way to the
Wadsworth fight; that here Washington stopped and Lafay-

ette lodged. That some of the traditions are true is probable, that some are not true is also probable; as to its connection with Captain Wadsworth and his company, it is sufficient to refer to the date of the house and the date of the fight. That General Washington stopped there is quite probable, since he went from Marlboro to Boston and dined at Weston with Colonel Lamson who commanded the Fifth Middlesex Regiment in the Revolutionary War. As the Howe Tavern would be on his direct route it would be natural for him to stop there and, at least, take a lunch with Mr. Howe, another of the colonels of the Revolution. But, though a part of the traditions of the place are improbable, there yet remains enough of reality to make this a favorite place, and it needs no embellishment of fancy to give to it a sufficient charm or make it rich in rare reminiscences. The old stage road that winds its way by it; the double eaves of its gable roof; the old oaks hollowed by the hand of time; the name and history of the family of Howe, — these, with the notoriety of Mr. Longfellow's poem, all conspire to give the place a fame akin to that of the village of Grand Pré of Evangeline. What though the tales of the Wayside Inn were never uttered at Howe's Tavern at all under such circumstance, as the poet describes; other tales as touching, as thrilling, and grand, may often have been uttered within it. Groups, characteristic of colonial and provincial times, often sat by its fireside; the inhabitants of Nobscot and Peakham gathered there from hamlet and farm, to sit and talk of a long fall night; the stage-driver and his passengers stopped there for lodging or lunch, the marketer halted as he was " going down " with his load, the teamster with his ox-wagon and yokes of slow steers, the transient traveler also, and the occasional errandless tramp. Such at times were guests at this house, and found refreshment and shelter within its time-worn walls. Surely, many scenes of a quaint character transpired there in the years of the town's early history, and though they have all passed by, the old house is suggestive of them, and stands a souvenir of other and busier days on an old stage road of the town. It recalls to mind an old family of Sudbury and familiar events in connection with it, and is a memorial of the typical tavern in those old-time days.

The taverns on the central road of the town were on the present Berlin and Boston highway, and from the "Gravel Pit" to the middle of the town. The first, passing westerly, was on the Captain Rice place, about half a mile from the Centre. Here, at an early date, was an inn which was kept during the Revolutionary period by William Rice. The house was a square, two-story building of medium size, with a large chimney in the middle. It stood a few rods north of the road and faced the south. It is many years since it was used as an inn. For a long time it was the homestead of Capt. William Rice, and was last occupied by his descendants. A short time ago it was burnt. Tradition says that formerly the road ran through the door-yard, and came out by Daniel Smith's at Water Row.

The next tavern west was the Wheeler-Haynes House, formerly the parsonage of Rev. Israel Loring. Walter Haynes kept a public house there in the early part of this century, but it has long since ceased to be used for that purpose. The third tavern was at the Centre, at the road-corner just north of the store, or at the angle made by the Berlin and Boston highway, with that leading from South Sudbury to Concord on the left side going north. This tavern was kept years ago by a Mr. Rice, who was killed at Wash bridge. Subsequently, in the early part of this century, it was kept by Dr. Kidder. About fifty years ago, it was kept by Joel Jones, and later, by Miranda Page, at which time it was burnt. A fourth tavern was at the Dr. Stearns place, the second house west of the Unitarian Church. It was not built for an inn, but was the residence of Thomas Stearns, a physician. After Dr. Stearns' death it was occupied by Webster Moore, who kept a public house there for some years. A tavern was kept at North Sudbury, well known as the "Pratt Tavern." Another was the "Puffer Tavern;" and one quite old was kept at the north-west part by Jonathan Rice, a prominent man in town.

Such are some of Sudbury's old-time taverns. They had their day and disappeared, because the means of their maintenance failed. One means, on which all these ancient hostelries depended perhaps to a greater or less degree, was the sale of intoxicating drinks. Some received patronage from the old stage routes, and all of them from the passing traveler and his team. But now the great growth of the temperance movement, and the introduction of new modes of conveyance, have so changed the condition of things that the old tavern is needed no more.

CHAPTER XXXIII.

PHYSICIANS.

Early Mention of Physicians. — Biographical Sketch of Dr. Ebenezer Roby. — Ebenezer Roby, 2d. — Ebenezer Roby, 3d. — Josiah Langdon. — Moses Taft. — Moses Mossman. — Ashbel Kidder. — Thomas Stearns. — Levi Goodenough. — Otis O. Johnson. — George A. Oviatt.

> . . . Doubtless, after us, some purer scheme
> Will be shaped out by wiser men than we,
> Made wiser by the steady growth of truth.
> LOWELL.

AN early mention of a doctor in Sudbury is on page 155 of the first book of Town Records, where it is stated that " Alrake, Physician, was to have five bushels of wheat in consideration of his care of the Widdow Hunt." Another record on page 185 of the same book states that, at a selectmen's meeting, " it was agreed with Dr. Chattock and payed him for his paynes and phisick hee gave to Debrah Wedge and agreed with him for a month to keep her for 2 shillings a week which month was out Sept the 5th 1702." We conclude there was no surgeon in town up to the year 1673, as it was then ordered that "Mr. Peter Noyes do procure and bring Surgeon Avery from Dedham to the Widdow Hunt of this town to inspect her condition and to advise and direct and administer to her relief and cure of her distemper."

EBENEZER ROBY, M. D.

One of the most noted physicians of Sudbury was Dr. Ebenezer Roby who lived on the East Side. He was born in Boston in 1701, and graduated at Harvard College in 1719. He settled in Sudbury about 1725, and in 1730, married Sarah, daughter of Rev. John Swift of Framingham. He lived in the old Roby house which was recently destroyed by fire. He was prominently connected with town matters in Sudbury, where he lived and practiced his profession till his death. He was buried in the old graveyard at East Sudbury, and the following is his epitaph : —

In memory of Ebenezer Roby Esq, a Native of Boston New England.

He fixed his residence in Sudbury in the character of a Physician where he was long distinguished for his ability and success in the healing art.

Born Sept 20th 1701
Died Sept 4th 1772   aged 71.

For a specimen of the charges of Dr. Roby see page 350. His son, Dr. Ebenezer Roby, Jr., born in 1732, also practiced medicine in Sudbury, and died July 16, 1786, aged fifty-four. Dr. Joseph Roby, son of Ebenezer, Jr., was a practicing physician in East Sudbury till 1801.

JOSIAH LANGDON, M. D.

The name of Josiah Langdon is in the town records of Revolutionary soldiers with the title of doctor attached, which indicates that he was a practicing physician in town at that time. As he died soon after the making of the record, at the early age of thirty-two, his professional career was very brief. His death occurred in 1779, and he was buried in the Old Burying Ground, which indicates that his home was in the West Precinct. The following inscription is on the stone that marks his grave : —

In memory of Doctor Josiah Langdon who died Feb. yͤ 24ᵗʰ 1779
Æt 32
Mortuus Vivit.

MOSES TAFT, M. D.

Dr. Moses Taft practiced medicine in Sudbury towards the close of the last century. He lived at the " Centre," in what has been known subsequently as the " Barker house," and where a grocery store was once kept. (See period 1850-75.) He was buried in the western part of the Old Burying Ground. His grave is marked by a slate stone, inscribed, —

Doct. Moses Taft, Died July 22ⁿᵈ 1799
Aged 45.
" Let living friends his virtues trace
Then theyˡˡ in glory see his face."

MOSES MOSSMAN, M. D.

Dr. Moses Mossman was one of the old-time physicians of Sudbury. He practiced medicine there towards the close of the last and the early part of the present century. His professional work extended over quite a portion of the neighboring country, reaching to Stow, Acton, Concord and Marlboro. The following is a specimen of his bills, which shows the expense of medical calls and medicine in those times : —

" To Doctor Mossman for doctoring Asahel Knight in his late sickness, 3 visits and medicine 2.75."

His home was in the northerly part of Sudbury at the Mossman place; and it is said that, about the locality of his garden plot, the herbs still grow which the doctor used to cultivate. He was much beloved and respected as a citizen, and it was said that he was very religious. In one of his journals he states that on one occasion, as he was riding in a very dark night, while in communion with God, a light shone about the team to guide him. He died, Aug. 15, 1817, aged seventy-five, and was buried in the western part of the Old Burying Ground. At the grave is a slate stone with this inscription : —

In memory of Doctor Moses Mossman and Mrs. Mary Mossman his wife.
Doctor Moses Mossman died Aug. 15, 1817,
Æt 75.
Mrs. Mary Mossman died Aug. 17, 1817,
Æt 66.
They lived mutually active, and highly respected, and died much lamented.

" Our lives are closed and o'er,
Our Saviour's praises now we sing,
He saves us by redeeming power
And takes us to our Heavenly King."

ASHBEL KIDDER, M. D.

Dr. Ashbel Kidder practiced medicine in Sudbury for about twenty-five years in the early part of the present century. He was born at Sutton in 1770, and studied medicine at Harvard College. Before and after the commencement of his medical studies he taught school. He married a daughter of Ezra Taylor of Southboro. He was lame and his health was not robust. He was a Free Mason and Master of Middlesex Lodge in Framingham. He was also justice of the peace, as is indicated by a record in his note-book of marriage ceremonies performed by him from 1815 to 1819. His practice extended over a considerable district and he was well known in the neighboring towns. As indicative of medical charges at that time we give the following found among his bills : —

" To Ashbel Kidder for doctoring Ephraim How of Acworth, while sick at Sudbury in 1812, to 30 visits 2 miles and medicine left each time 30.25."

He lived at Sudbury Centre in a house at the corner of the roads, which was used for many years as a tavern and was burned near half a century ago. (See chapter on Taverns.) He died in 1823, and left four children, — Almira, Francis, Dana, Caroline, and Ezra Taylor. A daughter of Francis D.

is Mrs. Frances (Kidder) Adams, wife of Dr. Z. B. Adams of Framingham. Dr. Kidder and wife were buried in the Old Burying Ground, and afterwards removed to the Kidder tomb, Wadsworth Cemetery.

THOMAS STEARNS, M. D.

Dr. Thomas Stearns practiced medicine in Sudbury for some years previous to 1840, about which time he died. He lived at the Centre, in the second house west of the Unitarian meeting-house, on the north side of the road, and since used as a tavern. He was an active citizen, of a positive nature, and energetic in the prosecution of his plans. He was interested in what pertained to the history of Sudbury, and gathered quite a collection of old documents, which, since his death, have been purchased by the town and are known as the "Stearns' Collection." He was buried in Mount Pleasant Cemetery.

LEVI GOODENOUGH, M. D.

Dr. Levi Goodenough was born in Derby, Vt., Oct. 30, 1803. He received his diploma from the Medical School of the University of Vermont, Sept. 16, 1828, and settled in Sudbury Feb. 12, 1830, where he remained till his death. He was a typical country physician. Having had the advantage of studying with a physician who kept a drug store, he acquired some skill in compounding medicines, and was accustomed largely to prepare and furnish the medicines he prescribed. In extracting teeth he made use of the "turnkey," which he never failed to adjust with due deliberation and care. As a citizen, Dr. Goodenough was public spirited, and a stanch advocate of reform; in temperance, his name stands among the pioneers. He was a professing Christian from early youth. On going to Sudbury, there being no church in it of his persuasion, he joined the Baptist Church in Weston, where he occasionally joined in worship. He also aided in the support of the Methodist Church, Sudbury, but he identified his interests with the Congregational Church of that place, all the meetings of which he took delight in attending whenever circumstances would permit. His interest in missions was very great and he gave freely in their behalf. He had two children by his first marriage, and named them Ann Haseltine and Adoniram Judson, after the well-known missionary to Burmah and his wife, Dr. and Mrs. Judson. His early educational advantages were limited, but he was a lover of learning, and in after years became somewhat proficient in Latin and the sciences, while he practiced the most rigid economy that he might give a liberal education to his own children and lend a helping hand to others who were striving to the same end. In his declining years he became deeply interested in geology and mineralogy, and was enthusiastic in the collection of specimens and in calling attention to their marvellous structure. At about the age of fifteen he was thrown from a horse, thereby incurring injuries which rendered his after life one long struggle with disease and weakness; yet he practiced medicine for over fifty-six years in Sudbury. He died, April 3, 1886, at the age of eighty-two, and was buried in Mount Wadsworth Cemetery. He married for his first wife Cynthia Rice of East Sudbury (Wayland), Feb. 11, 1830, and for his second wife Jerusha Dakin of Sudbury, Nov. 8, 1837. He adopted two children, Carrie and Grace; the former died young.

OTIS O. JOHNSON, M. D.

Dr. Otis O. Johnson practiced medicine in Sudbury for some years about the middle of the present century. He was son of John and Polly (Hemenway) Johnson, and born at Southboro, April 17, 1817. He studied medicine with Dr. John B. Kittridge of Framingham, and went from that place to Sudbury where he practiced homœopathy. He lived at the Centre and South Sudbury. He afterwards returned to Framingham where he died, Jan. 8, 1882. He married Mary, daughter of Dexter Stone of Framingham, and had two children.

GEORGE A. OVIATT, M. D.

Dr. George A. Oviatt was born in Boston, March 30, 1849. He was the son of Rev. George A. and Isabella G. Oviatt. His paternal ancestor came from Wales and settled in Mil-

RESIDENCE OF NICHOLS B HUNT,
South Sudbury

ford, Conn. His great-grandmother on his mother's side was Polly, daughter of Captain Minot of Concord. She was present at the Concord fight, and was sent with the small children of the town, who were entrusted to her care, to a place of safety till the danger was past. Dr. Oviatt fitted for College at Hartford Latin School, and graduated at Yale in 1872. He received his medical diploma at the College of Physicians and Surgeons, New York, March, 1875. April of the same year he commenced the practice of medicine in Sudbury, where he still resides. Jan. 20, 1878, he married Ella A., daughter of Nichols B. and Angeline (Brown) Hunt of Sudbury, and has one child, George Parker.

CHAPTER XXXIV.

TEMPERANCE.

Early Customs. — Effects of Cider Drinking in North Sudbury. — Connection of Taverns with the Liquor Traffic. — Drinking Customs in South Sudbury. — Common Use of Malt. — Extract from James Thompson's Account Book. — Dawn of Better Times. — Pioneers in the Temperance Cause. — Reformatory Measures. — Temperance Reform.

An honest tale speeds best, being plainly told.
SHAKESPEARE.

THIS town, now prohibitory as it relates to the liquor traffic, was formerly, we judge, very much like the average towns in the State in this matter. There is evidence that intemperance has, from an early period, made havoc and had its victims here. The following record is found upon the town book: "Upon the uncomfortable representations and reports concerning the [condition] of things at the Ordinary

of this town, it is ordered this 4th of October 1684, that three
or four of the selectmen in the name of the rest do particularly enquire into all matters relating thereto, and if upon
examination they find matters there as they are reported
that they advise with Mr. Walker and his wife, and labor by
persuasion with them with all conveniant speed to take down
their sign, and to lay down and relinquish their selling of
any drink."

In 1807, a vote was passed " that the town would use its
endeavor to assist the selectmen in carrying into effect the
law respecting Retailers and Taverns in said town [as they
were related to certain persons] viz : those persons who mis-
spend, waste and lessen their estates whereby they are likely
to become chargeable to said town."

It was the habit of the people for two centuries to use
spirituous liquors and special occasions had their special
quantities. The farmer wanted his extra cider for his
hoeing or threshing and his extra rum for haying; and in
the latter work he hardly thought it possible to get along
without it. The carpenter wanted a good allowance for
" raising," and on afflictive, and social, and gala occasions it
was thought liquor was indispensable. In 1729, there is a
record of payment " To David Baldwin for frame of Bridge
37 pounds; to twelve men to raise said bridge who went into
y[e] water 3 pounds, for drink &c 5s — 1d " In 1759, there
is a record of payment " To Caleb Moulton for material for
new bridge and 5 quarts Rum 2 — 11 — 3." In 1747, Jonathan Rice rebuilt Lanham Bridge, and the next year there
was a record in the town book of payment " To Mathew
Gibbs for rum and for raising Lanham bridge 12 shillings."
As late as 1816, on the occasion of Rev. Jacob Bigelow's
funeral, we find the following in the record of the town's
indebtedness for articles furnished : " To Daniel Goodenow
for spirit and sugar &c $15.40."

In 1779, prices were established for the common commodities, and among them for spirituous liquors as follows :
" West India Phlip 15 New England Do 12 Toddy in proportion." Malted liquor was also early made use of. Malt
was one of the articles granted the town after Philip's **War**

from the so-called "Irish Charity Fund," and valued at
18*d.* per ball. Malt liquors were extensively used, and malt
was long considered quite a useful commodity. About 1688,
when Deacon John Haines made a contract for building a new
meeting-house, he was to receive for the work in "country
pay at country price, merchantable Indian corn, Peas, Beef,
Pork and Malt." There was an old malt house at South
Sudbury owned by James Thompson. When it was demolished, which was about the middle of the century, it was
much dilapidated, as if it had not been used for many years.
This indicates the disuse of malt liquor in Sudbury from
early in the century. But a drink largely made use of, because cheap and easily manufactured, was cider. The cider
mills were in various parts of the town. The effect of cider
drinking in North Sudbury has been so forcibly set forth by
Mr. John Maynard that we quote his words: —

"In 1830, in that half of the town north of the road from
Wayland to Hudson, there were 12 cider mills owned by
farmers who ground their own apples and allowed their
neighbors the use of the mills for 8 cents per barrel of 32
galls. The amount of cider made there was much less than
50 years previously. Old orchards had decayed and new
ones bore grafted fruit for the market. The price was very
low because the use of cider as a daily drink had been super-
seded largely by that of cheap New England rum — a change
for the better somewhat, as temperate people limited themselves to 3 glasses or less per day instead of the unlimited
use of cider . . . Within the territory above named are now
only two mills making together only about 100 barrels yearly
and that for vinegar. Orchards now produce grafted fruit,
and the windfall, bruised and refuse apples are sold to large
mills at Sherborn, Maynard and S. Acton, for about 25 cents
per barrel of 2½ bushels. The product is not so strong as
that made formerly from sound ripe natural fruit. New
England families, one hundred years ago, larger than at
present, would use both in city and country 200, 400, and
sometimes more gallons of cider yearly. The mug was invariably on the table at meal times, always on the sideboard,

and too often those who went to the cellar for a supply 'drank at the tap.' Old people of intelligence who lived to see the dawn of total abstinence have expressed the opinion that much of the rheumatism, inveterate sores, and other complaints of former days was chargeable to the cider mug. Every one who called, from the minister to the tramp, was offered the common drink with the apology if it was very sour as it sometimes was in the spring 'it is pretty hard,' to which custom required the response, 'it is harder where there is none,' an assertion that often had more of politeness than truth. Many men and some women kept more or less 'boozy' week after week, and it is a question whether the larger percentage of stupid and stammering children born then, compared with those of the present time was not due to the excessive use of cider by parents."

That the custom of drinking any kind of spirituous liquor was exceedingly pernicious, notwithstanding what some have said of the quality of it in those days, is very evident. The testimony is that the tavern bars were a nuisance. Says the writer just quoted concerning them, —

"One of the incidental benefits of railroads has been the discontinuance of the old country and village taverns. They were a public necessity, were licensed for the 'public good,' kept by respectable people, afforded good accommodations for man and beast at moderate rates, but the profits came from the sale of liquors at the bar which was open seven days in the week day and night, and few landlords were willing to admit that a man unless he was furiously or beastly drunk had taken too much, until he had no money to pay for more. The taverns were nuisances to the neighborhoods where they were located, and like the modern saloons, nurseries of drunkenness and pauperism. The taverns of Sudbury were as good as the average elsewhere and probably no better."

Such is the strong language of one of Sudbury's prominent citizens, with regard to the former use of both fermented and spirituous liquors. The estimate as here given we believe facts will generally confirm. There were drunkards in those days, and sad havoc was made in the town, in the church, and in many families by intemperance. Not only was the practice of moderate drinking well nigh universal, but it was considered respectable. What everybody did was supposed to be right, and that almost everybody used intoxicants is indicated by a statement made to the writer by an inhabitant of Sudbury nearly seventy years old. He said that when he was a boy he did not know of a person in the place (South Sudbury) but what used it; and that there were three places in that small village where they could get it. He said it was not considered a disgrace to drink, but it was considered a great disgrace to get drunk, and that any one who got so was held up as a warning to others. He also said it was considered no disgrace on a holiday to get a little lively. That it was not considered disgraceful to use liquor as a beverage is evident from the open and commonplace manner of the sales. It was not by any means confined to the taverns, but was a commodity that passed over the counter of the grocery as well. On a Saturday night the staid villager would go to the store to get the supply of new rum as naturally as of molasses or salt. As indicating the commonplace way in which malt was bought and sold, we give the following from a credit page in an account book of James Thomson, a carpenter and wheelwright, who kept the malt house in South Sudbury: —

Credit to Jonas Holden Ju^r

by one pint of Rum	0 – 0 – 4.
Septr 12th 1789 by one Mugg of Flip	0 – 0 – 8.
Septr 1789 to two half Muggs of Flip	0 – 0 – 8.
Octr to one half Mugg of Flip to Flag	0 – 0 – 4.
Novr to one Pint of West India Rum	0 – 0 – 7.
June. 8. 1780 by one quart W: Rum	0 – 0 – 7
Octr 5. 1790 by 71[£] of Beef at 2^d	0 – 11 – 10.
Novr 1790 by half pound of Butter	0 – 0 – 5.
Jany 1791 by 17^{lb} of Cheese at 12	0 – 2 – 10.
Jany 13th 1791 by one Bushil of Indian corn	0 – 2 – 8.
July 1791 by fustian for the foreparts of a Jacket	
Dec. 8 to his house to Concord	0 – 1 – 4

Not only did each householder provide liquor for himself and family, but custom required that callers, not excepting the doctor and the minister even, be furnished with flip, and the more distinguished the guest, the more indispensable the article. Traders, under certain circumstances, were expected to extend the same courtesy.

Captain Kidder told the writer the story that a customer once came to his shop, and he mixed a mug of flip, supposing he had prepared enough for them both, and passed it to him ; he took it, and, placing it to his lips, drank the entire contents without stopping. When the captain took the mug from his hand and saw it was empty, he said, " Won't you have a little more ? " " Oh, no," said the man, " I never drink to excess."

But better times at length dawned on the town. With the early agitation of the subject of temperance in the land, Sudbury began to make progress. Here and there, an enterprising person thought work could be done without the use of intoxicants. One of the first to believe this in the early part of the present century was Deacon Levi Dakin, who had a barn raised without furnishing rum on the occasion. Another early advocate of the temperance reform was Dr. Levi Goodenough, who would not provide any intoxicating liquor to those whom he employed. Other pioneer advocates were Deacon Martin Brown, Nahum Thompson, Esq., Edward and Howe Brown, Abel and Joseph Richardson and Deacon Gardner Hunt. Rev. Rufus Hurlbut was one of the early reformers in his profession, and Charles Gerry was the first selectman in Sudbury to refuse a liquor license. Before the reform set in it was the custom at " Kidder's shop," at a given time each day, for an apprentice to go to the grocery opposite and get some rum for " black strap," — a concoction of New England rum and molasses. One of the apprentices, Ira B. Draper of Wayland, then quite young, concluded that it was a poor practice for him to indulge in ; he therefore refused to go for the liquor. The example was followed by others, and soon a large share of his fellow workmen found they could get along without their daily potation of " black strap."

About 1835–40, when there was an agitation of this subject in the country, temperance meetings were held at

the centre of the town on Sunday evenings, probably in
the porch of the Old Parish Meeting-house, where evening
meetings were sometimes held. Besides these meetings, an
occasional lecture was given on the subject. Soon temperance societies began to be formed ; one of which was the
"Cold Water Army," an organization for the children
formed about 1841. This society adopted a pledge, and at
times formed processions and marched with banners. Very
soon liquor ceased to be sold at the South Sudbury grocery
store, and it was left for the old tavern stand to be the sole
place for the retail of the stronger stimulants for that part of
the town. With the lessening of places for the sale, and the
growth of a better sentiment, the community became more
abstemious, the example of one person was followed by
another, until by about the middle of the present century
the entire drinking customs of society thereabouts were
changed. But even after that time liquor was sold at the
taverns. At South Sudbury the bar-room was still open to
the traveler and the occasional call of a villager; but one
by one the taverns were closed, and drunkenness grew less
and less, until at the present time this may be considered a
strong prohibitory town.

CHAPTER XXXV.

COLLEGE GRADUATES AND PROFESSIONAL MEN.

List of Graduates before 1800. — Biographical Sketches of College Graduates and Professional Men since 1800.

> " Not many lives, but only one have we ;
>   One, only one.
> How sacred should that one life ever be, —
> Day after day filled up with blessèd toil,
> Hour after hour still bringing in new spoil."

THE following is a list of college graduates prior to 1800. The names of those who graduated before 1776, are taken from a sketch of Sudbury supposed to have been written by Dr. Israel Loring.

HARVARD COLLEGE GRADUATES BEFORE 1800.

Samuel Jennison	1720	Gideon Richardson	1749
Noyes Parris	1721	Samuel Baldwin	1752
William Brintnall	1721	Jude Damon	1776
Thomas Frink	1722	Aaron Smith	1777
John Loring	1729	Ephraim Smith	1777
Jonathan Loring	1738	Reuben Puffer	1778
William Cooke	1748	Jacob Bigelow	
William Baldwin	1748		

The following are biographical sketches of college graduates and professional men since 1800, so far as we have information.

GEORGE H. BARTON.

George H. Barton, son of George W. and Mary S. (Hunt) Barton, was born at Sudbury, July 8, 1852. At the age of seventeen he attended the academy at Chester, Vt., afterwards, S. P. Frost's private school, Maynard, and the high school of the same town. After a somewhat rough experience carpentering, blacksmithing, etc., he entered the Warren Scientific Academy in Woburn, and, at the age of twenty-four, entered the Massachusetts Institute of Technology, and graduated with the class of '80· In 1881, he taught in the Drawing Department of the Institute. He was offered and declined a position on Charnay's Expedition to Yucatan and Central America. He soon after accepted an offer from the Hawaiian Government survey, and left Boston for Honolulu Aug. 9, 1881. After remaining in this survey about two years, he received an appointment in the Geological Department of the Massachusetts Institute of Technology, which he accepted and still retains.

FRANCIS F. BROWN, M. D.

Francis Frederick Brown, son of Edward and Abigail (Rogers) Brown, was born in Sudbury, Aug. 12, 1834. He studied at Warren Academy, Woburn, and in 1851 entered Amherst College, where he graduated in 1855. He studied medicine at the Harvard and Berkshire Medical Schools, graduating at the latter in 1862. Subsequently he served as assistant surgeon of the Forty-eighth Regiment M. V. M., until it was mustered out Sept. 3, 1863. He settled in Reading in 1864, where he still resides and follows his profession. June 7, 1865, he married Emma Mary Clapp of Dorchester, and has had six children.

E. R. CUTLER, M. D.

Edward Roland Cutler, son of Roland Cutler, was born in Boston Jan. 15, 1841. In his early life his parents removed to Sudbury. He attended Wadsworth Academy at South Sudbury and entered Williams College in 1858. He graduated at the Harvard Medical School in 1863, having spent a year at Rainsford Island Hospital, Boston Harbor. He entered the United States service as assistant surgeon of the First Heavy Artillery, formerly the Fourteenth Infantry. In 1864, he became surgeon of the regiment, and served in that capacity till the close of the war. He practiced medicine for a time at Hartford, Conn.; spent three years in medical study abroad, mostly in Vienna; and, Jan. 1, 1870, settled in Waltham, where he now resides. He married Melvina A., daughter of Samuel B. Rogers of Sudbury, and has had seven children.

JOSEPH CUTLER, ESQ.

Joseph Cutler, son of Christopher G. Cutler and great-grandson of Gen. John Nixon, was born at South Sudbury, Dec. 9, 1815. He entered Amherst College at the age of nineteen, from which he graduated in 1840. He studied at the Harvard Law School and began the practice of his profession in Boston. As a lawyer, he was especially able in matters of real estate. He acted for many years as counsel for the Cambridge Savings Bank. He was the author of the celebrated compendium entitled, "The Insolvent Laws of Massachusetts," three editions of which were published prior to the United States Bankrupt Law, and the fourth edition of which was revised and enlarged by him after its repeal. Said the "Boston Advertiser," "his memory will be fondly cherished as of an excellent lawyer and an honest man, as approximating closely to the highest standard in every department of life and duty, and as, if not one of the world's most famous, one of its worthiest and best."

HON. CHARLES F. GERRY.

Charles Frederick Gerry, son of Charles and Orisa Gerry, was born at Sudbury, June 3, 1823. He graduated at the Wesleyan University, Middletown, Conn., and soon after became a teacher in the Boston Mercantile Academy, and later, in the Fort Hill School, Boston. Subsequently, he engaged in the insurance business, and for a time lived at Hyde Park, being its first representative to the Legislature in 1877, and for some years President of its Savings Bank. In the midst of a busy life, he has been a frequent contributor to periodical literature, and some of his productions have been selected for school text-books, and some set to music of distinguished composers. In 1888, Lee & Shepard published his book of poems, entitled "Meadow Melodies." From

RESIDENCE OF HON. C. F. GERRY,
Sudbury Centre

Hyde Park he removed to Sudbury, from which place he went to the Legislature, serving one term in the House and two terms in the Senate, being chairman during the second term of the joint committees on Education, the State Library and Parishes and Religious Societies. He married Martha A. Clough of Canterbury, N. H., who was a literary lady of wide reputation and for some years had charge of the editorial columns of the "Boston Olive Branch." Mr. Gerry has four children, — Charles C., Eleanor M., Frank F. and Gilbert H.

ADONIRAM J. GOODENOUGH.

Adoniram Judson Goodenough, son of Dr. Levi and Cynthia (Rice) Goodenough, was born at Sudbury Aug. 6, 1833. He finished his academic studies at Warren Academy, Woburn. He entered Amherst College where he graduated in 1854. He began the study of medicine, but weakness of the eyes compelled him to abandon it. He spent several years in the South engaged in business, and returned North in 1863. His later life has been spent at Providence, R. I., where he still resides.

GEORGE M. HOWE, M. D.

George M. Howe, son of Buckley and Sally Howe, was born in Sudbury, July 2, 1824. After attending the Framingham, Leicester and East Hampton Academies, he entered Union College, but was prevented by ill health from completing his collegiate course. He pursued his professional studies at the Harvard Medical School, and settled as a physician in the town of Harvard where he practiced about ten years; he then went to Framingham, where he continued in his profession till his death which occurred Sept. 16, 1882. He was married at Harvard, Jan. 17, 1855, to Harriet M., daughter of Rev. James Howe of Pepperell, and had five children. Dr. Howe was a skillful physician, courteous and gentle in disposition and much esteemed by the community. In the words of an obituary notice of him, " he was laid away for his final rest on a bright, warm, autumnal day amid the smiles of nature and the tears of his friends.

ALFRED S. HUDSON.

Alfred Sereno Hudson, son of Martin N. and Maria (Read) Hudson, was born at South Sudbury, Nov. 20, 1839. He studied at Wadsworth Academy, and entered Williams College in 1860, at which institution he graduated in 1864. The same year he entered the service of the United States Sanitary Commission, and was stationed for a time near Petersburg, Va., during its siege. Upon his return he entered the Theological Seminary at Andover, at which he graduated with the class of '67· Sept. 26, 1867, he married Miss L. R. Draper of Wayland. He was ordained and installed pastor of the Congregational Church, Burlington, Dec. 19, 1867, where he remained six years. Subsequently he was acting pastor of the Congregational Church at Easton. In 1876 he went to Malden where he remained six years ; there he had charge of the Congregational Churches in Maplewood and Linden, both of which erected meeting-houses during his pastorate. Nov. 1, 1883, he became acting pastor of the First Congregational Church at Ayer, which position he still occupies.

EDWARD B. HUNT.

Edward Brown Hunt, son of Emory and Alice How (Brown) Hunt, was born in South Sudbury, Feb. 19, 1855. He fitted for college at the Boston Latin School, entered Harvard College in 1874 and graduated in 1878. He taught school at Newburyport three years, and has been in the Boston Public Library since 1883.

EDWIN HUNT.

Edwin Hunt, son of Sewall and Sophia (Puffer) Hunt, was born at Sudbury in 1837. At the age of fifteen he entered the High School, Concord, where he fitted for college. Two years later he entered Amherst College and graduated in 1858. He chose teaching as his profession, and taught a select school in Enfield, Haydenville, and Sherborn, and Wadsworth Academy. He served in the United States Sanitary Commission until obliged to leave on account of ill health. Resuming his profession, he became assistant preceptor at North Bridgewater, after which he accepted the position of instructor of natural science in the Free Academy at Utica, N. Y. He was especially interested in the department of botany, the study of which he had pursued through a large part of his professional life. He was a successful collector of specimens and possessed an extensive herbarium. For researches in natural science he received the degree of Ph.D. He was re-elected to his position in the Academy till failing health obliged him to withdraw. He died May 24, 1880, beloved by his pupils, trusted in his profession, and respected by all. He married Mary A., daughter of Edward Brown of Sudbury, and left several children.

OTIS E. HUNT, M. D.

Otis Eugene Hunt, son of Joseph Goodnow Hunt and Lucy Howe Hunt, was born in South Sudbury, July 7, 1822. He fitted for college at the Holliston Academy, Wayland High School and Wilbraham Academy. He entered the Wesleyan University, Middletown, Conn., in 1844, but ill health compelled him to leave at the expiration of nine months. He afterwards studied medicine with Dr. Levi Goodenough of Sudbury, and in the Boylston Medical School, Boston, and graduated at the Berkshire Medical College in 1848. He began the practice of medicine and surgery in Weston, where he remained sixteen years. He then moved to Waltham and afterwards to Newtonville, where he now resides. He has been one of the leading physicians in Middlesex County, and was the first to administer sulphuric ether as an anesthetic in the towns of Sudbury, Wayland and Weston. He married Aroline E., daughter of Nahum and Abigail Thompson of Sudbury, Oct. 9, 1849, and has two children, Nina Maria and William O.

SERENO D. HUNT.

Sereno D. Hunt, son of Sewall and Sophia (Puffer) Hunt, is a native of Sudbury. He early attended a select school at Sudbury Centre, taught by Dr. E. O. Haven. He afterwards attended the academies at Framingham and Derry, N. H. He was the first principal of the high school in Concord, Mass., and for ten years taught a select school at North Bridgewater. In 1865, he became the preceptor of the Norfolk County Academy, Milton, Mass., and subsequently principal of the high school in the same town, which position he held till 1877.

HERBERT S. JONES, M. D.

Herbert Samuel Jones, son of William P. and Catherine A. (Brown) Jones, was born at South Sudbury, Nov. 5, 1851. He entered Williston Seminary, Easthampton, 1873, and Yale College in 1875. In 1885, he entered the New York Homœopathic Medical College, and graduated in 1888. The same year he entered upon the practice of medicine in Elizabethport, N. J., where he now lives. He married Evelyn Wilson of Roselle, N. J., in 1887.

JOHN L. O'NEIL, ESQ.

John L. O'Neil is son of John and Julia O'Neil, who went to Sudbury in 1863. He studied law for a time in the office of Hon. William F. Courtney of Lowell, after which he graduated at the Harvard Law School, and was admitted to the bar in 1882. In 1884, he began the practice of his profession in Chelsea, where he still resides.

HARRIET M. PRATT.

Harriet M. Pratt, a daughter of Nathan L. and Harriet Hunt Pratt, was born in Sudbury. After a course of study at the Framingham High School, she entered Smith College, Northampton, from which she graduated in 1881.

LUTHER PUFFER.

Luther Puffer, son of Samuel, was born in North Sudbury, Sept. 11, 1833. In 1850, at the age of seventeen, he entered the sophomore class at Bowdoin College, and graduated in 1853, delivering the salutatory oration. He began the study of law in Andover, N. H., and died Oct. 27, 1854. He was a person of fine ability and excellent character, and his early death ended a career which gave promise of great usefulness.

HOMER ROGERS.

Homer Rogers, son of Walter and Emily Rogers, was born at South Sudbury, Oct. 11, 1840. He studied at Wadsworth Academy, entered Williams College in 1858, and graduated in 1862. Soon after leaving college he enlisted in Company F, Forty-fifth Regiment, M. V. M. At the expiration of his term of service he taught school one year in Douse Academy, Sherborn, and from 1864-6 in Natick High School, since which time he has been engaged in business. Jan. 15, 1868, he married Ellen E. Perry of South Natick, and has seven children. His present residence is Boston. In 1888 and 1889 he was elected alderman and is at present chairman of the Board.

HENRY SHAW, M. D.

Henry Shaw, son of Rev. Linus H. and Louisa A. Shaw, was born at Raynham, Sept. 12, 1829. In 1851, he began the study of medicine and graduated at Harvard Medical School in 1854. For a time he practiced his profession in Upton and Leominster, and in 1861-2 he went from the former town as a representative to the Legislature. He was subsequently sent by Governor Andrew to Newbern, N. C., on a service connected with the care of the Massachusetts troops in that vicinity. July, 1862, he received a commission as acting assistant surgeon in the navy, and served in all the blockading squadrons from Mobile to Wilmington. In 1865, he was promoted to the next higher rank in the medical corps. Leaving the United States service in 1866, he practiced medicine for a time in Bedford. In 1872, he became a visitor in connection with the State Board of Charities. He married, in Sudbury, Jane M. Taft of Upton, October, 1855, and has five children. He resides in Charlestown.

JOSEPH A. SHAW.

Joseph Alden Shaw, son of Rev. Linus Hall and Louisa Alden (Jones) Shaw, was born in Athol, Jan. 4, 1836. He went to Sudbury in 1845, and in 1853 attended Phillips Academy at Exeter, N. H., and graduated July, 1855, in the advanced class. The same year he entered the sophomore class at Harvard College and graduated in 1858. While at college he received a Dexter prize from the Hopkins fund, "for remarkable diligence in his studies." In 1858, he became principal of the New Salem Academy, which position he held six years. For sixteen years he has been a teacher in the Highland Military Academy, Worcester, Mass., of which he is at present the head master. He is a member of the American Philological Association, and a contributor to the periodicals of the day on the subject of philology. In 1863, he married Eliza Antoinette Thompson of New Salem. He has two children.

CHARLES THOMPSON, ESQ.

Charles Thompson, born at North Sudbury, March 6, 1827, is the eldest son of Nahum Thompson. He fitted for college at Concord, and the Pinkerton Academy at Derry, N. H. In 1845, he entered Yale College, but was soon obliged to abandon his studies on account of a severe sickness, which left his eyes in a weak condition. After some years he studied law, and was admitted to the bar Jan. 20, 1864. Jan. 15, 1864, he married Emily A., daughter of George M. Barrett of Concord. In 1872, he removed to Concord, where he now resides and follows his profession. He has been special justice of the District Court of Central Middlesex since its establishment, and from 1876 to 1885 was chairman of the Concord Board of Selectmen.

CHAPTER XXXVI.

NATURAL FEATURES.

Hills. — Forests. — The Flora. — Ponds. — Brooks.— Sudbury River. — Its Rise and Course. — Its Fish. — Poetical Description of Pickerel Fishing. — Birds about the River. — Poetical Description of Duck Hunting. — Fur Bearing Animals about the River. — Slow Current of the River.

> And sweet homes nestle in these dales,
> And perch along these wooded swells;
> And, blest beyond Arcadian vales,
> They hear the sound of Sabbath bells.
> WHITTIER.

In its natural features the town of Sudbury is highly favored. There is a good variety of hills, valleys, and plains, and these, together with the villages, hamlets, thrifty farms and smiling homesteads, give a pleasant variety to the landscape.

HILLS.

> Those hills my native village that embay
> In waves of dreamier purple roll away.
> LOWELL.

There are several hills in Sudbury of considerable prominence for a town so near the sea.

NOBSCOT HILL. — The most notable of the Sudbury hills is Nobscot. This is partly in Sudbury and partly in Framingham, the larger part being in the latter town. It is about five hundred and twenty-five feet above the sea level. The summit and sides in great part are covered with woods, but the northerly slope has long been an open pasture, greatly resorted to for the whortleberries that abound there. This slope has generally been known as the " old Nixon pasture,"

because it contains the site of Gen. John Nixon's house and
was a part of his farm. The name of this hill is of Indian
origin, and may be a contraction of the word Penobscot,
which is found in the earlier records of Sudbury. In 1674,
" Surveyors were appointed of all the field fences on the
west side of the great ·river of the town and Landham,
Penobscot new mill." Temple says, in the history of Framingham, that the meaning of this word is " at the fall of the
rocks." On the summit are heaps of stones, which perhaps
were taken there by the Indians for the purpose of building
a " look out" from which to survey the surrounding country.
The view on a clear day is charming, reaching from the State
House on the east to the far-off hills of New Hampshire.

GOODMAN'S HILL. — This is another considerable hill, and
perhaps next in prominence to Nobscot. It is a little south-
east of Sudbury Centre, and about a half mile from it. The
westerly side is mostly covered with forests, consisting
largely of chestnut and oak. This hill was the home of
Karto or Goodman, from whom it derived its name. (See
Chapter II.)

GREEN HILL. — This is a spur of Goodman's Hill, extending south-westerly, and is made historic by Wadsworth's
fight with King Philip. On its western slope, for hours the
English held the Indians at bay, and from its summit they
were driven at night-fall by the forest fires set by their
savage foes. (See chapter on Philip's War.) The slope of
Green Hill or a spur of it extends to Hop Brook meadows.
Along its western side, on a small plateau, is Mount Wadsworth Cemetery. (See chapter on Cemeteries.) The hill
takes its name from the growth of evergreen trees with
which it was formerly covered.

SAND HILL. — This hill is in the easterly part of the town
adjoining Wayland. In the Revolutionary War, government
store-houses were built there, and, subsequently, a portion
of it was used for a training-field and owned by the town.

ROUND HILL. — This is a conspicuous, well-defined hill in
the town's easterly part, and cultivated to its top. It lies
not far from the river meadows, in the vicinity of Sherman's
Bridge. Near Round Hill, and just by the junction of Gulf

brook and Sudbury River, is Weir Hill, so called from its proximity to the place of a fishing weir used by the Indians. (See Chapter II.)

WILLIS HILL. — This is in the north-westerly part of Sudbury, and takes its name from the Willis family long living in that vicinity. It is quite a prominent landmark. A hill at the north part, on which a flag-staff was erected during the Civil War, has been called for a half century Jones' Hill, but in old deeds was called Cedar Swamp Hill.

FORESTS.

The soil of Sudbury has, from its settlement, been abundantly productive in its timber lands, of which it has always possessed many acres. The principal trees are the oak, pine, chestnut, walnut, maple, white birch and spruce with here and there a poplar, elm and hemlock. The first three are the most abundant, and, until recently, many acres were covered with them. It was so in the west part of the town on the farm of the late Paul Walker, near the line of the Massachusetts Central Railroad, and on the farm of the late Curtis Moore on the line of the Old Colony Railroad, and these are but specimens of what was on many farms in the town within the last half century. Large quantities of cordwood, mostly pine, were, about forty years ago, carried by ox-team to the railroad and factories at Saxonville, and the lanes and yards of the Sudbury saw-mills were piled with hundreds of large logs to be sawn into boards. Since the more general use of coal, less wood has been cut, and probably more land is being abandoned to forest now than thirty years ago. To our personal knowledge, tracts of country that were formerly used for tillage and pasturage are now growing up to wood. In some places the growth is rapid, about twenty years only being required to obtain a fair growth. Chestnut-trees have been abundant on and about Goodman's Hill, Nobscot, and some parts of Peakham Plain and lands in the central parts of the town. Walnut-trees grow abundantly about Nobscot, and to an extent in other localities. Black birch is found and other kinds of wood besides these now mentioned, but in far less quantities. With wild berries the town is well supplied. Besides growing in the open pasture, very frequently when the land is cleared of forests the whortleberry and blueberry-bush spring up. More or less of the swamps abound with high blueberries or bilberries, notable among which are Hayden's swamp and the one about Willis Pond. Blackberries grow on the plain lands, and the barberry on the rough, stony soil of the hills. Strawberries are scattered here and there. A place years ago where they were especially plentiful was east of the old Lancaster road, between Goodman's Hill and Green Hill.

THE FLORA.

The following are some of the flowers found in Sudbury. The small cow-lily (*Nuphar kalmianum*), *Vitus riparia*, trumpet weed (*Eupatorium rotundifolium*), mountain rice (*Oryzopsis canadensis*), mountain laurel (*Kalmia latifolia*), trailing arbutus (*Epigœra repens*), the pitcher plant (*Sarracenia purpurea*), meadow beauty (*Rhexia virginica*), buckbean (*Menyanthes trifoliata*), the two orchids, the *Pogonia ophioglossoides* and the *Arethusa bulbosa*, and *Clintonia borealis*. In some of Sudbury's meadows are found the fringed gentian of Bryant (*Gentiana crinita*) and the painted cup (*Castilleja coccinea*). It is also stated on good authority that the flowering dogwood (*Cornus florida*) grows within the town limits.

PONDS.

The ponds of Sudbury are small.

WILLIS POND. — This is the largest and lies at the northwest part of the town. It is nearly surrounded by forests, and is a little lake in the woods. It has an outlet to Hop Brook called Run Brook.

BLANDFORD'S POND. — This is another which is surrounded by forests. It is situated just west of Hop Brook, about midway between South Sudbury and the Willis mill. It has an artificial outlet at high water to Hop Brook.

BOTTOMLESS POND. — This is a small pond near the

Marlboro line and has no outlet. (For area of ponds see map of 1794.)

BROOKS.

MILL BROOK. — This stream is next in importance and size to the river. It rises in Marlboro, and enters the town at its south-westerly part a very small stream, and by a very circuitous course empties into the river near Bridle Point Bridge (Wayland). Upon its banks are the mills of Howe, Pratt, Willis and Parmenter. It is crossed by at least eight highway bridges within the town limits, the first being near the Wayside Inn. It was early known as Hop Brook, upon which stood the Noyes mills, the second built in Sudbury. Later, it has had several names, being called at its lower end West Brook; farther up, Lanham Brook; at South Sudbury, Mill Brook; about the Willis mill, Wash Brook; also Piners' Brook and Piners' Wash. The lower meadows upon this brook were formerly of considerable value, but below Lanham Bridge they have, of late, largely been in a condition similar to that of the river meadows. The current of this stream is naturally rapid away from the various mill-dams, and perhaps for this reason it received its early name "Hop Brook," as, when clear of obstructions, it may have skipped over the stones, especially along the locality of South Sudbury where the fall was considerable. This is the only brook in town that affords mill privileges, and in this respect it has proved very valuable, having furnished power for both saw and grist mills.

PANTRY BROOK. — This stream is in the north part of Sudbury, and its name may have been a contraction of the word pine-tree. It rises in the north-west part of the town and empties into the river near Weir Hill. Near its mouth it receives as a tributary a small stream called Cold Brook. Along this stream are the Gulf meadows, which, before they in part shared the fate of the river meadows, produced considerable hay. Other and smaller brooks are Dudley or Trull Brook, which, running from the west part of the town, empties into Hop Brook near Blandford's Pond; and Lowance Brook, whose name is probably a contraction of "Al-

lowance," and which, running from the southerly part of
the town, empties into Mill Brook between South Sudbury
and Lanham Bridge.   Both of these brooks have been more
or less fished in for trout.   The latter has some considerable
meadow land, and is crossed by Hunt's Bridge.   All these
streams and ponds abound in fish, mostly of the kind found
in the river.   Besides those mentioned further along are the
shiner (*Stilbe chrysolencas*), cheven (*Leuciscus chephalus*),
black sucker (*Catostomus*) and the chub sucker, a fish of like
genus, and also a few trout (*Salmo fontinalis*).   We have
seen a specimen of the latter that was taken in Mill Brook a
short distance below South Sudbury mills that weighed nearly
five pounds.   This fish was caught by Mr. Nichols Brown,
once a famous fisherman and hunter in Sudbury.   This is
the only trout we ever knew of, large or small, taken in Mill
Brook.

SUDBURY RIVER.

All round upon the river's slippery edge,
Witching to deeper calm the drowsy tide,
Whispers and leans the breeze-entangling sedge ;
Through emerald glooms the lingering waters slide.

LOWELL.

The Indian name of this stream was "Musketahquid,"
meaning grassy meadows or grassy brook.   It was also called
the "Great River."   It takes its rise in Hopkinton and
Westboro, the branch from the latter town having its source
in a large cedar swamp.   Passing through Framingham, it
enters Sudbury on the south-east, and forms the boundary
line between it and Wayland.   After leaving the town, it
runs through Concord and borders on Lincoln, Carlisle and
Bedford and empties into the Merrimac River at Lowell.   It
is made use of for mill purposes at Framingham and Billerica.
This river receives but two tributaries of any account from
the town.   One of these is West Brook that empties in at
Bridle Point Bridge, the other Pantry Brook that flows
through the Gulf meadows.

In former times boats passed from Boston through the
Middlesex Canal to the Concord River, and so to Sudbury.

(Shattuck's History of Concord.)   Within the present century iron ore dug in town was laden in boats at the Old Town
Bridge and taken to Chelmsford.   Near the bridge on the
east bank, until recently, pieces of the ore could be found.

The width of this river where it enters Sudbury is about
fifty feet, where it leaves the town it is about two hundred
feet ; at the latter place it is one hundred and fourteen feet
above low water mark at Boston.   (History of Concord.)
Its course is very crooked, seldom running far in one direction, but having many sharp curves.   The banks are quite
bare of shrubbery, except the occasional bunches of water
brush that here and there assist in tracing its course.   Fish
abound in this river, of which the more useful and commonly sought are the pickerel (*Esox reticulatus*), perch
(*Perca flavescens*), bream or sunfish (*Pomotis vulgaris*),
horned pout (*Pime loduscatus*), and common eel (*Anguilla
tenuirostris*).   The kind most sought for the sport in taking
is the pickerel.   Indeed Sudbury River has become somewhat noted for the pastime it affords in pickerel fishing.
Specimens weighing a half dozen pounds are sometimes
caught.   A good description of this sport has been given in
verse by one of Sudbury's poets, Hon. C. F. Gerry, in a
poem entitled, " A day on the Sudbury Meadows."

> The clouds drift slowly o'er the sky,
> But dense and black to westward lie,
> Assuring with the east wind's chill,
> A splendid day for pickerel.
>
> .   .   .   .
>
> The river gained, we launch our boat
> And slowly down its current float,
>
> .   .   .   .   .   .
>
> Till, roused, we fish on either shore,
> Still moving with a silent oar,—
> Now trolling with the greatest heed
> Through lily pads and pickerel weed,
> Until a whirlpool near is seen
> Beside a floating mass of green ;
> The bait moves off with race-horse speed,
> And, down beside a quivering reed,
> Is swallowed with a gourmand's greed.
> A twitch sends through my frame a thrill,—

The hook is fast in the red-fringed gill
Of a steel and gold-hued pickerel,
And drawn aboard with hearty will.
And, as we view him o'er and o'er,
About his weight we speculate,
And set him at a pound or more,
And vainly try to catch his mate !

"MEADOW MELODIES."

The horned-pout may be caught almost at the rate of a
peck in an evening, when the water and season are right.
The fisherman simply ties his boat to a stake in a suitable
place, perhaps some quiet, snug nook where the waters are
still, and on a warm night in late spring or summer, between
the mosquitoes and pouts, his time will be fully occupied.

In early times the river abounded in fish now unknown in
its waters. Of these were the alewives, salmon and shad.
The obstructions caused by the dam at Billerica long ago
prevented these valuable fishes from ascending the stream,
and petitions were early presented to the General Court to
have the obstruction removed, on account of the fisheries.
Shattuck informs us that at certain seasons fish officers of
Concord went to the dam at Billerica, to see that the sluice-
ways were properly opened to permit the fish to pass, and he
states that the exclusive right to the fisheries was often sold
by the town; the purchasing party having a right by his
purchase to erect what was called a weir across the river, to
assist in fish-taking.   Probably not far from " Weir Hill," in
the north-easterly part of Sudbury, near the mouth of Gulf
Brook, the Indians caught the fish in this way.

In the time of migration, various kinds of ducks visit the
place, and often tarry till the cold weather sends them southward.   The first to come are the blue and green winged
teal (*Anas discors* and *Anas carolinensis*.)   These come about
the middle of May and September.   A little later the dusky
or black duck (*Anas obscura*) arrives.   This latter bird is the
most numerous of the ducks that stop about the river in the
migratory season, and sometimes comes in flocks of one or
two scores.   Besides the kinds mentioned there are others,
such as commonly inhabit the river courses of New England

in the spring and fall.   Notable among these are the dipper
(*Bucephala albeola*), and the sheldrake (*Mergus americanus*).
The dipper is generally seen by itself, or in pairs or in flocks
of but three or four; but the sheldrake comes in large
flocks.   In the spring, when the floods are high, flocks of
these birds may sometimes be seen floating majestically at a
safe distance from the shore, their white plumage flashing in
the sunlight.   Besides the ducks that come in the migratory
season, there are some that breed on and about the meadows.
These are mostly the black duck and wood duck (*Anas
sponsa*).   The latter birds make their nest in some tree in
the woods and bring their young in their beaks to the water.
They are seldom found in flocks of more than three or four.
A few years ago duck hunting was quite a sport on and
along the Sudbury River.   The wet meadows afforded here
and there a pool or lagoon, where the turf had been torn up
by the ice and borne away from the spot.   To follow a flock
to these meadow pools, or to watch for their coming from a
bow house previously made near the place, was a matter of
pleasurable excitement.   The birds are usually more active
at night-fall or just before an approaching storm.

The following description of duck hunting on these
meadows is given by the author in " Fireside Hymns," published in 1888.

DUCK HUNTING ON SUDBURY MEADOWS.

When the broad meadows soft, reposing lie
Beneath the haze of Autumn's mellow sky,
And the crisp frost of chill, October morn,
Sparkles in crystals on the ripening corn,
Then the wild water fowl begin to come
To streams and ponds, from far-off northern home.
Along the river that through Sudbury town
Ranges its course through meadows broad and brown,
They sometimes tarry for awhile to feed,
Ere on their southern journey they proceed.
By day, in flocks, they wing their dusky flight
High in the air, but at approach of night
They seek some shallow pool or sheltered bay,
Where they may rest secure till break of day.

But not unnoticed do they always pass
To snug retreat, amid the meadow grass.
Traced is their course sometimes by sportman's eye,
Who knows the reedy cove to which they fly.
His trusty gun he takes from off the hook,
And starts at once for the secluded nook.
His boat is launched from off the shelving shore,
And glides along with quiet, dipping oar.
Close to the margin of the stream he clings,
Where, mid the water brush, the blackbird sings.
Now the shy muskrat starts with sudden bound
From off the bank, with harsh and splashing sound,
That makes the anxious sportsman start with fear,
Lest upward start the ducks ere he draws near.
He rows more gently, as he now detects
Through the tall grass-tops, slowly gliding specks,
That tell him there the dusky squadron lie,
All snugly sheltered in the pool hard by.
And as he listens, lo! the Quack, Quack, Quack,
A noise so welcome to his ear, comes back.
In river bend his little craft he steers,
As place abreast the pool he slowly nears.
Then with one long and calculating peep
Upon the flock, he takes his gun to creep
A little closer, but ere this he do,
His fowling-piece he takes to prime anew.
When all is ready, and the distance right
To make the shot effective, then keen sight
He takes along both barrels.   Lo, a flash!
And fast the deadly missiles hurrying dash.
At once the startled flock, with sudden fright,
Rise from the pool to make a hasty flight.
But stop! behold again another flash!
And yet once more the deadly missiles dash
Amid the flock, and lo! the feathers fly,
And round about the dead and wounded lie.
Quickly the sportsman springs to seize his prize,
That flutters there before his eager eyes.
The wounded first are seized, then all secured,
He quickly goes to where his boat is moored.
This he draws up beside the reedy bank,
Where it is left concealed mid grasses rank.

Then he goes back and waits for further flight
Of birds, to come there ere he leaves it quite.
Round him the twilight deepens into gray,
And fast fade out the beams of ebbing day.
The wet dews, foggy, heavy, damp and chill,
The night with moisture now begin to fill.
But soon he starts! a sound comes through the air.
'Tis whistle of the wood-duck's wing that's there.
Quick to his eye his fowling piece is raised,
The trigger pulled, once more the piece has blazed.
And still again, from off the meadow land,
The fluttering bird is seized with eager hand.
Reloading, he again with listening ear,
Is all intent, still other birds to hear.
But hark! that rushing, whistling, nearing sound
Shows that a large sized flock flies near the ground.
Low lies the hunter, nearer comes the flock,
Upward he springs, and click, click goes the lock.
Whang! Bang! the charges of both barrels go,
As swoop the flock in circle small and low.
The feathers fly, and scattered here and there
A dusky form is falling through the air,
While quick with sudden start and wheel and curve,
The unhurt fowls to other quarters move.
With loaded hand, but step and heart that's light,
The sportsman does not wait for further flight,
But starts at once to launch his waiting boat,
And soon again he finds himself afloat.
Stoutly he plies the bending, splashing oar,
That swiftly bears him towards the sought-for shore.
Around the curve of river bend he speeds,
Now dark with bush or overhanging reeds.
Afar he sees the gleam of distant lamp
Beyond the meadow's mist, so dark and damp,
And on the still air now and then is heard
The whistling wing or night-call of a bird.
Soon nearer comes the sounds he gladly hears,
That show him that the causeway road he nears, —
A sound of travel and of rattling team,
Which rolls along the bridge that spans the stream.
Soon he has nearly reached the wished-for shore,
And slacks his speed and lays aside his oar,

Takes carefully his game and gun in either hand,
Safe moors his boat, and nimbly springs to land.
With brisk walk, quickly to his home he goes
To tell his story, as the game he shows.

Beside the *natatores* or swimmers there also are found the *gralatores* or waders. Among these the great blue heron or crane (*Ardea herodias*) is quite common, and the green heron or " Fly up the Creek " (*Butorides virescens*) is also seen. But the most abundant is the night heron or " Qua Bird " (*Ardea nycticorax*). A few years ago a colony of these inhabited the woods just south of West Brook, and not far from Heard's Pond. They built their nests on trees of a young growth, and would leave them at night-fall to visit the neighboring ponds. In the early evening it was quite common to hear the peculiar note, " qua," " qua," " qua," from the birds far out of sight overhead, and in the early morning they would return to their nesting places, where they would generally remain through the day. After a time the colony removed a mile or two westward and located in the vicinity of the Lowance Meadows.

Of the bitterns, the stake driver (*Ardea minor*) is the most numerous. The note of this bird so resembles the words " plum pudding " that it is called by that name. The least bittern (*Ardetta exilis*) is found sometimes, a fine specimen of which we possess, which was shot on the meadow.

There are also found in their season the snipe, yellow legs, plover, sandpiper, rail, and various smaller birds such as frequent similar localities in this section of the State. Wild geese sometimes stop for a brief period, but are seldom taken.

The fur-bearing animals about the river are, mainly, the muskrat or musquash (*Mus zibethicus*) and an occasional otter. The muskrats are quite plentiful; as many as a dozen or more are sometimes taken in a day, when the high water drives them from their cone-shaped houses to the causeway. Not an otter has been taken on the river for years, although they have sometimes been seen. And no beaver has been seen in the memory of the oldest inhabitant, although formerly they probably lived there to a considerable extent.

A chief characteristic of this river is its slow moving current, which in places is scarcely perceptible at a casual glance. This slow current is supposed to be occasioned by various causes, any one of which may perhaps be sufficient, but all of which at present doubtless contribute something to it. The chief reason is its very small fall, which may be occasioned by both natural and artificial causes. It is said to have but two inches to the mile for twenty-two miles. This slow current tends to keep the river from straightening its course, and to increase the water weeds that grow in the channel. To speak of the river in its general historic connection is here unnecessary, as in the course of this work mention has frequently been made of historic objects and events that have existed or transpired in its vicinity.

CHAPTER XXXVII.

THE RIVER MEADOWS.

Width of the Meadows. — Former Productiveness. — Litigation and Legislation. — Change in Productiveness. — Causes of it. — Natural Features at the Present Time. — Grass.

> Where merry mowers, hale and strong,
> Swept scythe on scythe, their swaths along.
>   WHITTIER.

THESE meadows have been notable from an early period. They extend, with varying width, the entire length of the river course. In some places they may narrow to only a few rods, while in others they extend from half a mile to a mile, where they are commonly called the Broad Meadows. They

are widest below the long causeway and Sherman's Bridge.
Comparatively little shrubbery is seen on these meadows, but
they stretch out as grassy plains, uninterrupted for acres by
scarcely a bush. At an early date these meadows yielded
large crops of grass (see Chapter I.), and subsequent years
did not diminish the quantity or quality, until a comparatively modern date. From testimony given in 1859 before
a Legislative Committee, it appeared that, until within about
twenty-five years of that time, the meadows produced from
a ton to a ton and a half of good hay to the acre, a fine
crop of cranberries, admitted of "fall feeding," and were
sometimes worth about one hundred dollars per acre. The
hay was seldom "poled" to the upland, but made on the
meadows, from which it was drawn by oxen or horses. Testimony on these matters was given before a joint committee
of the Legislature, March 1, 1861, by prominent citizens of
Sudbury, Wayland, Concord and Bedford. Their opinions
were concurrent with regard to the condition of things both
past and present. The following are testimonies by some of
the witnesses from Sudbury.

John Hunt, eighty-two years (p. 105 Printed Report). —
"I have owned meadows on the Gulf Brook, one or two
hundred rods from the river. I had care of the "Ministerial
Lot" on the river; and the nine years I was out of town, I
had care of twenty lots below for some years, from 1803 to
1807. I sold the grass on the former for $10 an acre, stand-
ing. A great change has since taken place; I suppose it
would scarcely pay taxes for some years past. They have
mortgaged the 'Ministerial Lot' to pay for it, not getting
enough to pay taxes. . . . Loring's 'bank meadow,' which,
when I was a boy, was worth $100 an acre, is not now worth
$10. A horse could then be taken to the river shore, you
could not now get near the river for the water. Where I
have in the low meadows fished standing dry, it is now over
my head. There are fifteen or twenty acres in this meadow.
When I was fifteen, it produced the best of meadow grass —
a kind of red-top, resembling, though not the same as the
upland red-top — there is none of that, and not much except
coarse grass, and poor — some of what we call sedge. There

was not much poling then; then they took the horses to the river. They now pole it as far as I know. . . . The other lands in the same neighborhood suffer; cattle were turned in there for fall feed, as long ago as I can remember. It was quite an item to farms adjoining; nobody now sends them for fall feed. Cattle could then go on the shore; for years these floods have entirely destroyed the cranberries. My land on the Gulf Brook, has been torn up by freezing and breaking up."

William Stone, seventy-two years (p. 108). — "I bought, forty-three years ago, a meadow on the Sudbury River, close to the meadow mentioned by Mr. Hunt. When I bought it I used to get the hay almost every year. There were two acres of shore, and the rest, where the water came on, was such a meadow as I never saw, producing pipe and lute grass. I used to get a ton and a half per acre. I used to drive across the meadow to water my team. I mowed it about twenty years; I began then to find the water came over. I built a causeway across, but the water seemed to stay. I tried to pole the hay out, but it cost too much. I sold it for $110 for eleven acres. At first it was worth to me $80 per acre. The water seemed to go away only by evaporation. . . . I have seen cattle getting fall feed on the meadows; not even a man could now go there without miring."

William Rice, seventy-seven years (p. 109). — "I have always lived in sight of the meadows — I had seven acres, and the same in another place, separated by the road. I inherited the land. Blue grass and pipes grew there — there were other kinds of hay, good for meadow hay. We considered the river meadow hay, the best meadow hay — the quality is now affected. Sedge and water grass, of little value, now grows, which is used for cattle bedding. The lots have grown softer; we could go on with a team generally. I have known times when we did not pole a cock of hay. I have rode a horse over the meadow. I don't know when they could go on without rackets of late years. Rackets were not in fashion in the olden times. They used to drive the cattle on for fall feed, but have not for twenty or thirty years. They have not been fed there much for forty years. I do not own the meadow now, I gave it away two or three years ago. The meadows have been growing softer, as a general thing, for thirty years."

J. P. Fairbanks, thirty-three years (p. 131). — "I own meadow land; none runs clear to the river, but is on the 'Gulf' and 'Broad Meadows'... The 'Broad Meadows' are entirely worthless since I have owned them. From 1500 to 2000 acres in the 'Broad Meadow' are of about the same level. Not much, if any, of the grass on the 'Broad Meadows' has been cut of late years. The best of my cranberry vines are on the 'Broad Meadow;' but for the water, a bushel of cranberries to the rod could be obtained;... if the water should be off we could get good crops; they are now worth $11 or $12 a barrel. ... In high flood we get 6 or 7 feet of water all over the 'Broad Meadows.' The water is on them most of the year."

From such evidence it appears that a great and gradual change in the condition of the meadows came after the year 1825. The main cause alleged for this changed condition was the raising of the dam at Billerica. This dam, it is said, was built in 1711 by one Christopher Osgood, under a grant for the town of Billerica, and made to him on condition that he should maintain a corn-mill, and defend the town from any trouble that might come from damages done by the mill-dam to the land of the towns above. In 1793 the charter was granted to the Middlesex Canal, and in 1794 the canal company bought the Osgood mill privilege of one Richardson, and in 1798 built a new dam, which remained till the stone dam was built in 1828. As indicating that the dam has from time to time been raised, we give the testimony quoted from the argument of Hon. Henry F. French, before the Legislative Committee, March 1, 1861.

Jonathan Manning. — "In 1798 I helped build the dam. There was a dam previously there, — what some call a zig-zag dam, — leaky and not very high. The dam I helped build was *higher than the former one.* They made rafts to bring timber from the Merrimac, and there was not water enough to fill the canal" (p. 77). "I should think, from the difference in the height of the water, that after we made the new dam, the dam must have been raised from nine to twelve inches. I think it made the water about a foot higher in the canal " (p. 80).

Herman Bay. — " New flash-boards were on the dam in 1817 " (p. 168).

Theophilus Manning. — " After the dam of 1798 was built, they were obliged to put something upon it to fill the canal. A foot and a half was put on. They call it a figure four. In 1800 the flash-boards were on " (p. 169).

Daniel Wilson. — " In 1820 or 1821 they put timber and flash-boards on the dam of 1798, *thirty inches high* " (p. 266).

It would be difficult and take too much space to give a full and extensive account of the litigation and legislation that has taken place in the past near two centuries and a half, in relation to this subject. It began at Concord as early as Sept. 8, 1636, when a petition was presented to the court, which was followed by this act: " Whereas the inhabitants of Concord are purposed to abate the Falls in the river upon which their towne standeth, whereby such townes as shall hereafter be planted above them upon the said River shall receive benefit by reason of their charge and labor. It is therefore ordered that such towns or farms as shall be planted above them shall contribute to the inhabitants of Concord, proportional both to their charge and advantage." (Shattuck's History of Concord, page 15.) In 1644, Nov. 13, the following persons were appointed commissioners: Herbet Pelham, Esq., of Cambridge, Mr. Thomas Flint and Lieut. Simon Willard of Concord, and Mr. Peter Noyes of Sudbury. These commissioners were appointed " to set some order which may conduce to the better surveying, improving and draining of the meadows, and saving and preserving of the hay there gotten, either by draining the same, or otherwise, and to proportion the charges layed out about it as equably and justly, only upon them that own land, as they in their wisdom shall see meete." From this early date along at intervals in the history of both Concord and Sudbury, the question of meadow betterment was agitated. At one time it was proposed to cut a canal across to Watertown and Cambridge, which it was thought could be done "at a hundred pounds charge." Says Johnson, "The rocky falls causeth their meadows to be much covered with water, the which these people, together with their neighbor towne (Sudbury) have several times essayed to cut through but cannot, yet it may be turned another way with an hundred pound charge." In 1645, a commission was appointed by the colonial authorities (Col. Rec. Vol. II. page 99) "for ye btt r and imp'ving of ye meadowe ground upon ye ryvr running by Concord and Sudbury." In 1671, a levy of four pence an acre was to be made upon all the meadow upon the great river, "for reclaiming of the river that is from the Concord line to the south side, and to Ensign Grout's spring." Later, a petition was sent by the people of Sudbury, headed by Rev. Israel Loring, for an act in behalf of the meadow owners. But legislation and litigation perhaps reached its height about 1859, when most of the towns along the river petitioned for relief from the flowage. The petition of Sudbury was headed by Henry Vose and signed by one hundred and seventy-six others; and that of Wayland by Richard Heard and one hundred and sixteen others. On April 6, 1859, a joint commission was appointed, to whom the petition was referred. The committee met, and ordered publication of notice for the hearing in five different newspapers in Boston and Lowell. As data of evidence in the case, a careful survey was made of the premises along the river, the water gauge accurately taken by competent engineers, and a complete report rendered thereon.

After thirty days devoted by the committee to investigation, on the 27th of January, 1860, the report of five hundred pages was submitted to a second joint committee appointed by the Legislature of 1860. This committee reported that the findings of the committee of the year before are sustained by the evidence, and that it appears that the dam at Billerica "is an efficient cause of the flowage of nearly 10,000 acres of the most valuable meadow land in the eastern section of the State," and that "this immense injury to those lands has been gradually accomplished by the canal corporation under their charter, without the payment of a single cent of damages to any land owner for the injury." (See Ho. Doc. No. 221, argument of Mr. French.)

A bill was reported for the removal of the dam, and passed by the Legislature. It was entitled " An Act in Relation to the Flowage of the Meadows on Concord and Sudbury Rivers." It provided that the governor, with the advice of the council, might appoint three commissioners with authority to remove thirty-three inches of the dam across the Concord River, at North Billerica, at any time after the first day of September 1860, and that when the same was so removed it should not be again rebuilt.

Time was considered necessary for the mill owners to put in steam, and the act was changed so as to leave six feet, two inches of their dam. An injunction was obtained from the Supreme Court, but the Legislative enactment was sustained. An effort was made in 1861 to have the act repealed. Thus strenuous have been the efforts to have the dam at Billerica lowered. In the contest able counsel has been employed on both sides, among whom are Judge Abbott and Benjamin F. Butler, Esq.; skillful engineer service has also been made use of.

For any one to attempt with great positiveness to clear up a subject which has perplexed legislators and lawyers, might be considered presumptuous. It is safe, however, to say that while there is evidence showing that the meadows were sometimes wet in the summer at an early period, they were not generally so; it was the exception and not the rule. It was a sufficient cause of complaint if the settlers had their fertile lands damaged even at distant intervals, since they so largely depended upon them; but the fact that they did depend on them, and even took cattle from abroad to winter, indicates that the meadows were generally to be relied upon. Certain it is that, were they formerly as they have been for nearly the last half century, they would have been almost worthless. Since the testimony taken in the case before cited, these lands have been even worse, it may be, than before. To our personal knowledge, parts of them have been like a stagnant pool, over which we have pushed a boat, and where a scythe has not been swung for years. Dry seasons

have occasionally come in which things were different.
Such occurred in 1883, when almost all the meadows were
mown, and even a machine could in places cut the grass.
But this was such an exception that it was thought quite remarkable. For the past quarter century people have placed
little reliance upon the meadows; and if any hay was obtained it was almost unexpected. This condition of things
in the near past, so unlike that in times remote, together
with the fact of some complaint by the setlers, and an occasional resort by them to the General Court for relief, indicates that formerly freshets sometimes came, but cleared
away without permanent damage to the meadows. At times
the water may have risen even as high as at present. It is
supposed that at an early period the rainfall was greater than
now, and that because of extensive forests the evaporation
was less. The little stream that may now appear too small
to afford adequate power to move saw and grist-mill machinery, may once have been amply sufficient to grind the
corn for a town. But the flood probably fell rapidly, and the
strong current that the pressure produced might have left
the channel more free from obstructions than before the flood
came. Now, when the meadow lands are once flooded they
remain so, till a large share of the water passes off by the
slow process of evaporation. The indications are that something has of late years obstructed its course. As to whether
the dam is the main and primal cause of the obstruction, the
reader may judge for himself. Before closing this subject,
we give other quotations from the argument of Mr. French.

AVERY'S SOUNDINGS ON BARS IN CONCORD RIVER.

	Depth of Water on Bars.	Depth of Bar below Bolt & Dam.
On line "A. B." near dam,	3.92 feet	3.11 feet.
On line "C. D." Fordway, one mile from dam,	3.26 "	2.29 "
At Barrett's Bar, one half mile below Concord N. Bridge, eleven miles from dam,	1.91 "	1.22 "
At Junction of Assabet and Concord,	2.65 "	1.56 "
Bar below Sherman's Bridge, fifteen miles from dam,	2.45 "	1.00 "
Bar at Canal Bridge, Wayland, twenty-one miles from dam,	———	.39 "

Commenting upon the data of the report, the counsel goes on to state as follows : " Add to these depths of the bars below the bolt, which is the top of the dam, the depth of water on the dam, and you have the least possible depth on these bars, when the dam is full. But we must in fact add much more to those depths, because water requires some fall to give it motion. The more crooked the stream the more obstructed by weeds and bushes and logs, and the more rough the channel the greater is the fall required to move the water. Mr. Avery's surveys show how the water deepens as he goes up the river, till he finds a fall in all of forty-five inches in the distance. *The dam prevents any improvement.* Being higher than anything else in the river for twenty-one miles, if every bar was cut out, and the channel made into a canal, the water must remain higher than any of the bars. The land owners expect and desire to improve the channel, which is rapidly filling up with weeds and deposits of sand and mud. Formerly they could do this to some extent. Of late years the greater height of water has prevented, and unless the dam is reduced their case will grow worse and worse. With the great increase of water and the obstructed channel, and this dam higher than any other object in the whole river, their condition is hopeless. Reduce the dam thirty-three inches, the water will fall proportionably on all these bars, which may be then cut out, and the river may be brought and kept within its banks in the growing season. * * * * *
I will only add that if any man is bold enough to assert that the bars in this river prevent the water from flowing off the meadows, and that the dam, which is by actual level higher than any of these bars, has no such effect, he is welcome to all the votes he can obtain from sane legislators for the repeal of this act."

We will now turn our attention to a few things regarding the natural features that the later condition of the meadows have brought about. It is said to be an ill wind that blows nobody any good, and it may be that some new attractions have been afforded these lands that were not possessed of old. Sometimes when the flood is up, the large expanse of water with its irregular margin flashing in the sunlight, adds great beauty to the landscape. The meadow at certain seasons, when in this condition, furnishes excellent fishing ground for such as take fish with the spear in the night-time. On mild spring nights the fish resort to the warm, shoal waters near the uplands, where, all unsuspicious, they are found by the wary fisherman, as with light dipping oar his boat glides over the flood. The outfit for such fishing is a small boat capable of carrying two persons, with an iron frame-work or "jack" set on an upright rod at the bows to hold the fuel or torch which is usually made of old pine stumps, and a six-pronged spear with an eight-foot handle. With this apparatus on a still night the fisherman sets out. The margin of the upland is followed, and at one time the boat glides by open fields or pasture lands, at another darts beneath the deep shades of an overhanging wood. Every now and then, at a signal from the spearsman at the bows, the boat is "slowed up," the spear poised in the air for an instant, then a dash, and up comes the fish. The frequent flowage of the meadows, it is supposed, has caused the "punk holes," so called, to which wild water fowl resort, while the clogged channel with its sluggish stream may have made the place a favorite haunt for the pickerel. Thus beauty and utility in some ways have resulted from the present condition of the meadows.

GRASS.

Various kinds of grass grow on the meadows, which are known among the farmers by the following names: "pipes," "lute-grass," "blue-joint," "sedge," "water-grass," and a kind of meadow "red-top." Within a few years wild rice has in places crept along the river banks, having been brought here perhaps by the water fowl, which may have plucked it on the margin of the distant lakes.

CHAPTER XXXVIII.

ZOÖLOGY AND GEOLOGY.

To him who in the love of Nature holds
Communion with her visible forms, she speaks
A various language.

BRYANT.

FUR-BEARING ANIMALS.

CHIEF among these, except those mentioned in connection
with the river meadows, are the fox, rabbit, squirrel, wood-
chuck, skunk and weasel.

RARE BIRDS.

Besides the smaller birds most common in the vicinity,
and those mentioned in connection with the meadows, are
the rose-breasted grosbeak (*Guiraca ludoviciana*), indigo bird
(*Cyanospiza cyanea*), scarlet tanager (*Pyranga rubra*) and
red start (*Setophaga ruticilla*). Of late, the purple finch
(*Carpodacus purpureus*) has become quite common. A few
years ago, in a hard winter, a flock of pine grosbeaks (*Pini-
cola canadensis*) visited the town. Sparrows, vireos, flycatch-
ers, thrushes and warblers abound. Of the larger kinds, not
considered game-birds though considerably hunted, are found
the grackles (*Quiscalinae*), pigeon woodpecker (*Calaptes
auratus*) and meadow-lark (*Sturnella magna*); hawks, crows
and jays are frequent, and the latter have been so destructive that, at different times, a bounty has been paid for them
by the town.

GAME-BIRDS.

The most common of these and the most sought after is
the partridge or ruffed grouse (*Bonasa umbellus*), the quail
(*Ortyx virginianus*) and the woodcock (*Philohela minor*).

The grouse and quail vary in numbers with the nature of the season ; the former being favorably affected by a dry summer and the latter by a warm winter. Quail a quarter of a century ago were quite scarce, but of late years they have been more numerous. To shoot a half dozen partridges in the best of the season is now considered but a fair day's work for a good hunter, and so it has been for the past fifty years, such being about the average day's work of Sudbury's old hunter, the late Nichols Brown. Woodcock have become quite scarce, very few being found except in the migratory season. Formerly they nested in town, but this is now unfrequently done. Fifty years ago the wild pigeon (*Ectopistes migratoria*) was abundant in Sudbury, a favorite locality being Peakham Plain. Considerable numbers were caught in nets; grain was scattered upon a small space of ground, over which, when the birds had alighted to feed, a net was sprung by a sapling which was artfully adjusted for the purpose. Dozens were taken in this way, but the bird is now scarcely seen in the town. (For fish, see chapter on Natural Features.)

GEOLOGY OF SUDBURY.

BY GEORGE H. BARTON, S.B.

In the history of a town as well as of a country, it is fitting that a few words at least should be devoted to its geology. For geology is in itself a series of records enabling us to trace the history of our globe back into the past far beyond any human records. So far, indeed, does it carry our knowledge backward, that the very earliest traces of human history are only as the deeds of yesterday as compared with the ages that elapsed before man made his appearance on the earth.

In order to understand the geology of an isolated political division of the country, such as forms a town, it is necessary to have a general understanding of the geology of the country of which it forms a part. The United States is a fair representative of the world, furnishing within its area a more or less complete record from the earliest known ages to the present time. Here, in geological development, as it is in

RESIDENCE OF GEO. E. HARRINGTON.

human, time is naturally divided into certain grand divisions or eras, each marked by its own peculiar characteristics. The natural divisions coincide with the development of life from the lowest and most humble forms in the beginning to the high and varied ones of to-day which have finally culminated in man. Thus, as in human history, we have the Ancient, Mediæval, and Modern Periods, in geology we have the Eözoic, Palæozoic, Mesozoic, and Cenozoic eras.

In the records belonging to the first of these, the Eözoic, which means the dawn of life, we catch faint, glimmering traces of the condition of the world at that time. We see, indistinctly, a globe covered with an almost universal ocean, with here and there occasional islands rising above the general waste of waters grouped in such a way as to foreshadow the continent which was to take their place. As time went on during this era land continually arose from below the surface of the waters till before its close the embryo continent was formed.

As the name implies, the first beginnings of life are here found, but they are nothing definite, they are only strong indications. With our present knowledge we know of no method by which large beds of iron ore, or large beds of graphite, can be formed except by the agencies of organic life. As such beds are abundant in the Eözoic they furnish grounds for the belief that life existed then in some little abundance.

Then limestones, which are largely made up of the accumulations of the remains of animal life, are abundant in this series of rocks. In connection with these latter rocks occurs a peculiar structure which has been thought by some high authorities to be the remains of a low order of animal life and to which the name of Eozoon, or dawn animal, has been applied.

However the question of life in the Eözoic era may finally be settled, we find the next era, the Palæozoic, a term meaning ancient life, beginning with an abundance of the lower forms of life in the waters, though we find no evidence of its existence upon the land. Some of these forms were quite highly organized, one being about the same as the horse-shoe crab of to-day, and this would cause us to believe that life must have existed for ages before to have arrived at this stage of development.

From the beginning of Palæozoic time to the present there is estimated to have elapsed about thirty-five millions of years. The Eözoic is supposed to have comprised at least as many years.

The Palæozoic has three main sub-divisions, which may be known as the Age of Invertebrates, during which life consisted entirely of marine forms of animals and plants of the lower orders, except toward its close when fishes and a few land plants appeared; the Age of Fishes, when these first vertebrates predominated and sharks ruled the seas, when the continents first became covered with forests such as we find in the tropics to-day, and insects appeared as the first land-animals; and finally the great Coal Age, when the continent was covered with the dense growths of tropical forests which after ages of accumulations have given the coal beds of to-day, which have furnished such an important factor in the progress of our national life.

During all this time the continent had been steadily growing in a westerly and southerly direction, till the shore line, which at the beginning did not extend in either direction further than the limits of the State of New York, had reached on the south into Mississippi and west into Missouri and Kansas, with large islands in the area now occupied by the Rocky Mountains.

In the third of the grand divisions of time, the Mesozoic, middle life, there is found a great change from the preceding ages. Huge reptiles of unwieldy form and bulk predominated over the life both in the sea and on land. Birds intermediate in form between the reptiles and birds of the present day also appeared, and toward its close the first faint foreshadowings of the trees of our present forests. The climate, which at the beginning of this era had been tropical throughout the world, had at its close become much like our present climate, being only a few degrees warmer.

From the beginning of the Mesozoic to the present time from fourteen to seventeen millions of years have elapsed, and of these eight or nine millions at least were comprised in the Mesozoic.

In the Cenozoic, recent life, which began at the close of the Mesozoic and still continues, we have mammals the predominating form of life, and somewhere in very recent geological time the introduction of the human race.

Then Cenozoic has two main sub-divisions, the Tertiary and the Quaternary. The latter is again divided into three divisions: the Glacial, Champlain and Terrace. These three it is necessary to notice somewhat more fully. The Glacial Epoch is due to certain conditions that caused the entire northern portion of our continent to be covered with a sheet of ice which over New England reached a thickness of more than six thousand feet, sufficient to cover our highest peak, Mt. Washington. It reached so far south as to entirely cover New England, and its southern termination can be marked by an irregular line drawn through New Jersey, Pennsylvania, Ohio, Indiana, etc.

This ice sheet had a constant tendency to move southward, and in doing so transported with it all the loose material which had previously covered the surface of the country in the shape of decomposed rock, soil, boulders, etc. At the same time it ground down, smoothed and polished the surface of the rocks over which it passed, leaving it in many cases with a high polish, but almost invariably accompanied by scratches or grooves on the polished surface which are nearly always parallel to each other and have a nearly constant direction of S-30-E.

A large portion of the loose material, the earth or drift as it is usually termed, was eventually deposited below the ice, which passed over it and thus compacted and hardened it till it became nearly as hard and as tough as the rocks themselves. This consists largely of tough, tenacious blue clay, somewhat filled with more or less rounded boulders, bearing upon their smoothed sides the same striations we find upon the smoothed ledges. This portion is known as the lower drift.

The remaining portion of the loose material was borne upon the surface of the ice or incorporated in its mass, and when the ice sheet melted and disappeared was left as a thin covering over the surface of the lower drift and is known as the upper drift. The boulders found in connection with this are angular and show little or no signs of wear.

A prominent feature of the lower drift are the hills known as drumlins which are very numerous in some sections, very rare in others. They are round, oval, or lenticular in shape, are largely made of blue clay, and contain no ledges, except in some cases just at their bases. The upper drift covers them with a thin mantle similar to the other surface.

The melting of the ice sheet gave rise to a large amount of water, which caused large rivers, lakes, and floods, both upon the surface of the ice and the country. This worked over the materials of the upper and lower drift, exerted a sorting action upon them and deposited them anew in the three separate forms of gravel, sand and clay. The old river channels were filled with floods, and large masses of the gravel and sand accumulated in them, while the clays were carried away by the rushing water. Upon the surface of the ice rivers wore channels in which accumulated pebbles usually from an inch to a foot in diameter. As the ice melted these were left upon the surface of the country as long and very narrow ridges, often known locally as Indian ridges, to which the term Kame has been applied.

As the waters of the Champlain Epoch subsided the streams cut down into the beds of gravel and sand they had previously deposited in their broad valleys, and thenceforth ran in narrower channels leaving marked terraces on one or both banks, hence giving the name of the Terrace Epoch, which still continues to the present day.

Before considering the special geology of our town it will be well to speak briefly of that of our State as a whole, that we may better understand the general relations of our town. Nearly the whole of Massachusetts is composed of rocks formed during the Eözoic era, but not belonging to its oldest divisions. Nearly the oldest of the Palæozoic, in the Age of Invertebrates, is represented by the area known as the Boston Basin, extending from Medford, Malden, etc., on the north, to Braintree, Quincy, etc., on the south, and from the

ocean on the east to Waltham on the west. The Age of
Fishes is not represented. The Coal Age is represented by
an area extending into the State from Rhode Island, in Attle-
boro, Mansfield, etc. The Mesozoic era is represented by
the red sandstones of the Connecticut Valley, in which have
been found numerous evidences of the reptilian life of that
time, and by the trap ridges which form Mts. Tom, Holy-
oke, etc.

Then in the Cenozoic we have the entire State covered
with its mantle of drift, in some places very thin, in others
reaching a thickness of three to four hundred feet, as in the
southeastern portion of the State.

Now in regard to the special geology of our town. The
formation which underlies it is made up of a series of crystalline rocks, approaching a dark granite in general appearance,
which are included in two divisions, diorite and diabase,
but so intimately are these mixed that it is not convenient
to separate them, and with these are a series of quartzites
and baked slates. The crystalline rocks are of volcanic
origin, and in those early ages were probably erupted
through and between the layers of quartzite and slate which
had been formed by deposition under the waters of the sea.
These rocks all belong to a period somewhere near the middle of the Eozoic, and from that time to the glacial epoch we
have no records to tell us of the history of the town. We
know that long before the latter time the Sudbury River had
hollowed its channel out of these hard rocks and was flowing nearly in its present position on the eastward of the
town. That Nobscot and Green Hills were prominent objects in the topography, but that Plympton's Hill, the hill at
the Centre, Cutting's Hill, and those near Alfred Thompson's, Parker Fairbank's, and Andrew Haynes' had no existence, as we shall see later.

As a whole, Sudbury is a somewhat sandy town, but there
are certain areas that are quite rocky. In the north of the
town Captain Jones' small hill, and the high lands north of
Cold Brook and west of the railroad are composed of outcrops of the crystalline rocks previously mentioned. The hill
between Patrick Lyons' and Calvin Morse's is also largely

of rock. In the area bounded generally by the road, from Plympton Hill to the river on the north, the river meadows on the east, the Central Massachusetts Railroad on the south, and the road from South Sudbury to the Centre on the west, is the largest series of continuous outcrops in the town. In the extreme south, Nobscot rises a solid mass of rock to its summit. There are many other places where small ledges outcrop, but not of sufficient importance to mention in this short paper.

Much of the rock shows stratification, which in some cases is due to its formation in layers under water, in others to successive sheets of lava flowing over each other. Wherever this is shown the prevailing direction is about north-east, south-west.

The rocks at Newbury, containing the ores mined there some years ago, have the same general trend, and belong to the same series. This has caused some search for ores, but nothing of importance has been found, though just over the line in Concord digging was carried on to some depth, show-iug the presence of some lead and silver, but not enough to be of any economic value.

A small amount of limestone is found just to the east of the so-called county road on the north bank of Cold Brook. At some time in the past it has been burned for lime, traces of the burned fragments still being found, but beyond the memory of any one now living. In this I have found slight traces of the structure, eozoon.

So far as my knowledge extends there is no rock in Sudbury that will ever admit of extensive quarrying for building purposes.

In turning our attention to the drift we find that to it are due many of the features of our landscape. Over many portions of the town the lower, upper and modified drift forms a considerable thickness, but there are no means of measuring its depth.

Those interesting features of the lower drift, the drumlins, are well represented. Perhaps the two more typical ones are the ones known as Cutting's Hill in the northwest portion of the town, and the one a half mile west of Sherman's bridge on the Sudbury River known as Fairbank's or Round Hill. The former represents the typical lenticular hill, its longer axis running a little north of west, the latter is nearly circular in outline. On the line between Sudbury and Concord is a somewhat large one, on the top of which is the residence of Andrew Haynes. On the old county road, about a mile and a half north of the centre of the town, is a complex mass made up of two or three drumlins united together. Upon the crest of the lowest is situated the residence of the late Aaron Hunt, while the larger ones rise directly back of A. N. Thompson's. Plympton's Hill and the hill directly back of the Unitarian Church and Town Hall are also well-marked examples. There are also many other small elevations in the town belonging to this type but not worthy of special notice. The southern portion of the town seems to be quite free from them, though I am not familiar with the extreme southwest corner.

The upper drift does not need particular mention, though some portions of the better soil of the town are furnished by it. Boulders of sufficient size to attract attention are rare, a single prominent one being situated on the road leading from the Town Farm to the Centre on land belonging to the town. There are a few others scattered in the woods away from the roads.

The modified drift is an important factor, furnishing the sand-plains which are the most objectionable feature from an economical standpoint. Of these Peakham Plain is the largest, and this is but a portion of the large plain continued west into Marlboro, Hudson and Stow. To this belongs all the area south of the Maynard line, and stretching to the foot of Nobscot, while on the east it is bounded by an irregular line, in some cases reaching nearly to the Old Colony Railroad. Other smaller but well-marked areas occur scattered over the remainder of the town, one extending along the north road from the Pratt Tavern to the Old Colony Railroad and about a mile southward, another to the eastward of the residence of the late Andrew Hunt, and a third northward from George Taylor's along the river meadows. In the Peakham area are several small sheets of water such as

Willis Pond, Bottomless Pond, etc., which probably owe their origin to large masses of ice having been left there, around which the sand was deposited by the currents, and later as these masses of ice melted they left the hollows which now hold the ponds.

Kames are not well represented in our town, though there is one very typical example crossing the road directly in front of the house of Elbrit Goding, and continuing northward immediately to the east of the road till reaching the northern boundary of the town. This same gravel ridge extends northward nearly through the town of Acton. Southward it does not cross the north road so as to be plainly seen, though there are traces of it nearly as far south as the Wayside Inn.

In the southern part of the town another kame begins just south of Lanham Brook, and east of Sewell Hunt's, and runs generally parallel to the road toward Framingham till it crosses the boundary of the latter town.

Now in conclusion, taking a hasty review, we see that our town is situated in that part of America that appeared above the waters of the ocean in the earliest ages, and thus ranks in age with not only nearly the oldest parts of America but also of the world; that from that time to the present it has remained above the sea, forming a part of the dry land of the continent, and hence, though there are no records of all those vast ages preserved, it has witnessed all the grand panorama of the development of life; that during the ice age, which was only about ten thousand years ago, its topography was very much changed and nearly all its hills, which till then had no existence, were formed, and that it was at the close of this latter age that so much of its territory was buried beneath the sand that causes several large areas to be scarcely worthy of cultivation. Immediately at the close of the ice age, if not before, primitive man began roving over the country, and then geological is united with human history.

CHAPTER XXXIX.

Public Bequests. — Action of the Town relative to the Publication of the History of Sudbury. — Preparations for the Observance of the Two Hundred and Fiftieth Anniversary of the Incorporation of the Town.

> Till at last in books recorded,
> They like hoarded
> Household words, no more depart.
>
> LONGFELLOW.

BEQUESTS.

THE "Goodnow Library Fund," $20,000, donated by John Goodnow. The "Samuel D. Hunt Fund, $1,000; the income of this fund is to be distributed among the poor, sick, and needy, who are not inmates of the almshouse or otherwise assisted by the town. Accepted, Nov. 3, 1874. The "Elisha Goodnow Fund," $4000; the income of three-quarters of this is to be distributed in substantially the same manner as the "S. D. Hunt Fund;" and the income of the other fourth is to be used in the purchase of books for poor children attending the public schools. The "Jerusha Howe Fund," $1000; the income to be expended in fuel for the industrious poor. The "Ancient Donation Fund," $453.78; given to the town by Joshua Haynes, two-thirds of the income to be used for the poor, and one-third for schools. A considerable portion of the original fund last named has been lost by bad investment. The "George Goodnow Fund," $10,000; the income to be used for the industrious poor not otherwise assisted by the town. Accepted, November, 1884. The "Henry Plympton Fund," $250. The "George Goodnow Fund," $400. The "Lois Hunt Fund," $500. The income of the last three are to be used for cemetery purposes or improvements.

Total amount of bequests, $37,603.78.

ACTS RELATIVE TO THE PUBLICATION OF THE HISTORY OF
SUDBURY.

The subject of publishing a History of Sudbury was first
brought before the town at a meeting held Nov. 4, 1862,
under the following article : —

"To see if the town will take any measures to have a history of the town written."

The result was that a committee, consisting of **Dr.** Levi
Goodenough, Rev. Limus H. Shaw and Charles Thompson,
Esq., was appointed "to consider the matter and report at
some future meeting what action, if any, may be advisable
for the town to take in reference to said subject." This
committee made a verbal report April 6, 1863, and were authorized to make arrangements with Mr. Andrew Ward of
Newton to prepare a history of the town. Mr. Ward commenced the work, but soon afterwards died. The subject
was again brought forward, March 6, 1876. A committee
composed of Steven Moore, Jonas S. Hunt, and Richard R.
Horr was appointed to consider the matter and report at a
subsequent meeting. Their report was submitted to the
town and accepted April 3, 1876. The following is a part of
this report : —

"Your committee believe that when this ancient Town
has its history compiled it should not be done hastily, but
with care and skill, and with such research as may be necessary to such a history as will not only be a matter of satisfaction but of pride to the town. As the history of Sudbury
is also a history of Wayland to a comparatively recent date,
it seems proper that she should be consulted as to the propriety of uniting with us in the preparation of the joint history of the two towns, at least to the time of their separation.
It is therefore recommended that the town choose a committee whose duty it shall be to ascertain if Wayland will
unite with Sudbury in having a joint history of the two
towns prepared; to collect such material as they may be able,
and report their doings at November meeting, with estimates
of the probable cost of the completed work." This report
was accepted by the town, and the committee making it were

continued in office and authorized to take such action as they thought proper to carry forward the recommendations contained in their report. The chairman of the committee soon after left town and no further action was taken in the matter. March, 1885, a committee consisting of Capt. James Moore, Jonas S. Hunt, Esq., and Horatio Hunt was appointed "to confer with Rev. A. S. Hudson in regard to a publication of the History of Sudbury." April 6, of the same year, the committee reported to the town the result of their interview. This was in part that the work be devoted to the annals of the town, but not any part of it to genealogy as it is usually inserted in books of this kind.

April 2, 1888, the town "voted to publish not less than 750 copies of the History as written and compiled by Rev. A. S. Hudson, and to pay him $1500 for his services in writing and superintending the publication of the work; and that the Trustees of the Goodnow Library be a committee associated with him to have charge of the publication of the work." The town also voted at the same meeting $1500 for the publication. The names of the library Trustees are as follows: Hubbard H. Brown, Atherton W. Rogers and Edwin A. Powers.

ARRANGEMENTS FOR THE 250TH ANNIVERSARY CELEBRATION.

At a meeting held November 1888, the town voted to petition the Legislature for permission to grant money to be expended in the observance of the 250th Anniversary of the Incorporation of Sudbury. Permission having been obtained, at a subsequent meeting the sum of three hundred dollars was appropriated, and a committee was appointed to make and carry out such arrangements as would be appropriate to the proposed celebration. The committee consisted of Jonas S. Hunt, Rufus H. Hurlbut and Edwin A. Powers, who were to coöperate with a committee from Wayland, and the joint committee were to act for the two towns.

The joint committee met at Sudbury and organized with J. S. Hunt for chairman, and R. T. Lombard, Esq., of Wayland for secretary. The following outline of a plan was proposed, and left open subject to change if deemed expedient before the day arrived.

1. A gathering of the children of the two towns at Wayland on the morning of Sept. 4, when entertainment and a collation would be furnished.

2. A return by railroad at noon to South Sudbury, when a procession will form and march to Sudbury Centre.

3. Dinner in the Town Hall.

4. Speaking from a platform on the Common, if the day is fair, and, if not, in the Unitarian Church.

5. Fireworks and music in both towns, with ringing of bells morning and night.

It was voted to extend an invitation to Hon. Homer Rogers of Boston, to act as president of the day ; to Richard T. Lombard, Esq., of Wayland, to serve as chief-marshal ; and to Rev. Alfred S. Hudson of Ayer, to deliver the oration.

Ample opportunity was to be provided for addresses by speakers from abroad, who are expected to be present and assist at the celebration.

CHAPTER XL.

CONCLUSION.

IN concluding a work of such magnitude and importance, we naturally pause and reflect over the long, long story of the past, before we leave its pages and close the history. Many notable events have been considered, and many prominent persons have been brought to view, who long since passed away. Successive periods have been presented in order, from the beginning of our existence as a town, until we come to a generation amid which we live and of which we are an actual part. It may be difficult to comprehend the changes that the years have wrought, but a passing glance at the chief of them indicates that the town has had a varied experience. First, we behold a small number of settlers making their homes amid the woodlands of a new country. They clear fields, erect homesteads, and let in the light of civilized life; but the scene is soon changed; shadows darken the prospect, the town is invaded by Indians, and all its resources are brought into requisition to preserve its existence. The conflict passes, and there are years of peace. Again the settlement is disturbed by war, and again peace follows. The town makes progress in the succeeding years, and then again, comes a season of strife. Thus alternate sunshine and shadow have played on the scene as the years have advanced, giving to the town a history of mingled prosperity and adversity. But through all these changes it has maintained a steady growth and developed a more substantial character by these rockings by the storm. As we look back over the scenes of its history there is much for which to be grateful. 1. That our ancestors were of such sterling worth. Few, if any, New England towns perhaps are more favored

in this respect. The record of their actions is evidence that
they did not emigrate to this country as mere aimless or
reckless adventurers, but as men with worthy purposes.
They evinced a perseverance in subduing the soil and a
fortitude in meeting the privations of pioneer life that is
commendable in a large degree. Their faith, zeal and stead-
fastness in the service of God, and their reverence for things
sacred is prominently noticeable in the records; and uprightness in their dealings is indicative of like theory and practice. 2. That the town has had such a wholesome and far-
reaching influence. Town after town received from Sudbury
some of its early settlers, and in this process of colonization,
a formative influence was carried forth by her citizens, which
has strengthened and widened as the years have rolled by.
3. That the town has never shrunk from bearing its part in
the burdens of the country at large. In peace and in war, it
has stood ready to meet all the demands that have been made
upon it. Even when its own borders were imperiled it did
not refuse to furnish aid to others if needed; and the long
muster-rolls and the enactments of town meeting are evidence of its patriotism. 4. That to so large an extent the
traits of the fathers have been transmitted to their posterity.
This may be due to the comparative stability of its population. Generation after generation occupied old homesteads,
and, with the lands, the characteristics became as heirlooms
in old families. While we have these things for which to be
grateful, it is also gratifying to contemplate the historic
character of the town. Although, hitherto, it has been considered historic, yet as we have noticed consecutively and in
detail its prominent events, we are more and more convinced
of the importance of its history. The story of the past is
associated with its hills and valleys and plains and streams.
Its fields have been fields of battle, its soil contains the bones
of the fallen. King Philip once strode over its territory, and
there he was stayed in his devastating march towards the
sea. The highways of the town were trodden by the militia
and minute men on their way to oppose the British at Concord. The town's common land was their place of parade,
and from its belfry sounded the call to arms.

Thus the God of our fathers has blest us by giving such founders of our town, by bringing us safely forth from the vicissitudes and exposures and perils of two hundred and fifty years, and by the benign influences of the institutions that our ancestors established and maintained. From the faith of our fathers that was God-given, and that clung so closely to his Son, our Saviour, Jesus Christ, has come the prosperity, the integrity, the worth of our town, and the wholesomeness of its far-reaching influence. "Praise God from whom all blessings flow," should be our general acclaim; and together with this devout ascription should be the cultivation of a cherished purpose to maintain and perpetuate what of good the past has bequeathed. To do this requires the use of the same means which our ancestors employed in procuring this good, namely, a reliance on God and His word, a reverence for the Sabbath and love for His church. The Bible to our fathers in the wilderness was literally "the man of their counsel." By it they were led in their daily duties, comforted in the time of calamity, and strengthened in the hope of "a better country, that is, an heavenly." Next to the Author of all good we should bear in grateful remembrance the privations and hardships endured by our ancestors. Our sunny hillsides and fields were cleared by their toil: let these be objects that quicken to gratitude. Let the places that are designated as historic be suggestive of their deprivations. As from the far-reaching and silent past survive the signs of its many changes, may we take knowledge that these are indicative of changes yet to be. It is a law of human destiny that one generation passeth away and another cometh. The old burial places were once new; and the town's inhabitants when they set them apart provided as they believed for a far-distant future. That future has come and gone, and they who looked forward to it have joined the silent procession in their march to the city of the dead; and among the moss-covered stones and monuments, strangers scan the inscriptions for their names and fragmentary scraps of family history. The new cemeteries will one day be as the old, the resting-place of the generation that set them apart; and in the years that are yet to be, and which to some it may be are in a distant cloud-land, the stranger will look for and read other epitaphs, even those which tell of our history.

The paths we travel may be closed and new ones opened, which stranger feet will tread. New dwellings, new manners, and new men will be here, and *we* shall be "only remembered by what we have done." May we then so live that our lives will be associated with as much of good, our memories with as much affection, as those which we have been considering. It is the desire of the author that the record of the past, which is contained in this history, be helpful in this respect to ourselves, to our families, and to those who shall come after us.

ERRATA.

On page 15, read Edmund for Edward.

On page 22, line 20, read Massachusetts for Narragansetts.

On page 34, line 30, read Goodnow for Haynes.

Pages 35 and 36. The farm of William Browne at Nobscot was not the two hundred acres allowed him by special grant of the General Court and referred to on page 62, that land being situated at the north-west corner of the town.

On page 58, line 9, read south for north.

On page 70, line 17, read (W. by S.).

On page 116, line 16, read twenty-five for twenty.

.On page 167, lines 2 and 3, read and an ancestor of Dr. Moore formerly president, etc.

On page 212, line 17, read Watertown for Weston.

On page 274, line 29, read Stow for Stowe.

On page 355, line 23, date wrong.

On page 389, line 37, read Fairbanks for Forbush.

On page 399, Haynes for Hamynes.

On page 409, line 5, read June 17th.

On page 487, line 38, read 1855 for 1857.

On page 494, line 28, read north-easterly for northerly; line 31, read Noyes for Haynes.

On page 609, line 38, read horse for house.

On page 634, line 1, read between for below.

List of Illustrations, No. 6, read Brigham for Haynes.

Lightning Source UK Ltd.
Milton Keynes UK
UKHW011224061118
331795UK00010B/1411/P